Mixed Jurisdictions Compared

EDINBURGH STUDIES IN LAW

Series Editor
Elspeth Reid (University of Edinburgh)

Editorial Board
David L Carey Miller (University of Aberdeen)
George L Gretton (University of Edinburgh)
Hector L MacQueen (University of Edinburgh)
Kenneth G C Reid (University of Edinburgh)
Reinhard Zimmermann (Max-Planck-Institute of Comparative and
International Private Law, Hamburg)

EDINBURGH STUDIES IN LAW
VOLUME 6

Mixed Jurisdictions Compared
Private Law in Louisiana and Scotland

Edited by Vernon Valentine Palmer
and Elspeth Christie Reid

EDINBURGH UNIVERSITY PRESS

© The Edinburgh Law Review Trust and the Contributors, 2009

Edinburgh University Press Ltd
22 George Square, Edinburgh

www.euppublishing.com

Typeset in New Caledonia by
Koinonia, Manchester, and
printed and bound in Great Britain by
CPI Antony Rowe, Chippenham and Eastbourne

A CIP record for this book is available from the British Library

ISBN 978 0 7486 3886 4 (hardback)

Contents

Preface   vii
List of Contributors   xii
List of Abbreviations   xiii
Table of Cases   xviii

1 Praedial Servitudes   1
    Kenneth G C Reid

2 Title Conditions in Restraint of Trade   30
    John A Lovett

3 Servitudes: Extinction by Non-Use   67
    Roderick R M Paisley

4 Inheritance and the Surviving Spouse   104
    Ronald J Scalise Jr

5 Ownership of Trust Property in Scotland and Louisiana   132
    James Chalmers

6 The Legal Regulation of Adult Domestic Relationships   146
    Kenneth McK Norrie

7 Impediments to Marriage in Scotland and Louisiana:
    An Historical-Comparative Investigation   173
    J-R Trahan

8 Contracts of Intellectual Gratification – A Louisiana-Scotland
    Creation   208
    Vernon Valentine Palmer

9 The Effect of Unexpected Circumstances on Contracts in Scots
    and Louisiana Law   244
    Laura J Macgregor

10 Hunting Promissory Estoppel   281
    David V Snyder

11 Unjustified Enrichment, Subsidiarity and Contract   322
    Hector L MacQueen

12 Causation as an Element of Delict/Tort in Scots and Louisiana Law   355
     Martin A Hogg

13 Personality Rights: A Study in Difference   387
     Elspeth Christie Reid

     Index   411

Preface

Scotland and Louisiana are mixed jurisdictions. They are built upon the dual foundations of Common Law and Civil Law and belong to a legal family that includes South Africa, Quebec, Puerto Rico, Sri Lanka, Israel and others around the world.[1] The idea of classifying legal systems in this way can be traced back more than 100 years, but it was only in the second half of the twentieth century that the Scottish scholar Sir Thomas Broun Smith urged the mixed jurisdictions to engage in cross-comparative studies as a means of overcoming the perils of isolation and steady assimilation by the Common Law.[2] Smith's work is generally credited with a revitalisation of the Scottish system, but it also raised the consciousness of colleagues in many countries, including in Louisiana. Smith, who held a chair at the University of Aberdeen and subsequently at Edinburgh, occupied a visiting post at Tulane Law School in 1957-1958 and Louisiana State University in 1972, and was made an Honorary Member of Council of the Louisiana State Law Institute in 1960. In his inaugural lecture at the University of Edinburgh Smith commended to his Scots audience the example of the "flourishing legal literature and journals" of Louisiana.[3] And respect was reciprocated. When, in turn, Professor Leonard Oppenheim of Tulane Law School was invited to give a course of lectures at the University of Edinburgh in 1960, he began by looking forward to a "succession of visits" between the two jurisdictions. This would allow scholars to "broaden their views by mutual contacts and expand

---

1 For a detailed treatment of mixed jurisdictions more generally see V V Palmer (ed), *Mixed Jurisdictions Worldwide: The Third Legal Family* (2001).

2 For further detail on the scholarly exchanges stimulated by Smith see K Reid, "The idea of mixed legal systems" (2003) 78 Tulane LR 5 at 11-16. For a full assessment of Smith's contribution by fifteen authors, see E C Reid and D L Carey Miller (eds), *A Mixed Legal System in Transition: TB Smith and the Progress of Scots Law* (2005).

3 "Strange Gods: The crisis of Scots law as a Civilian system" 1959 JR 119 at 140, reprinted in *Studies Critical and Comparative* (1962) 72 at 88.

their interests" and also "assist in maintaining our civilian systems".[4] Over the
next three or four decades contacts between Scotland and Louisiana became
less frequent, but in the early years of the twenty-first century interest in the
mixed jurisdictions has been revitalised,[5] and a call for cross-comparative
studies has been answered by an outpouring of scholarly articles and books
on the mixed jurisdictions.

Bilateral comparisons of mixed jurisdictions have hitherto been rare, but
the potential value of such work was recently illustrated by a comparative
study of the private law of Scotland and South Africa, published in 2004,
*Mixed Legal Systems in Comparative Perspective: Property and Obligations
in Scotland and South Africa*, edited by Reinhard Zimmermann, Daniel
Visser and Kenneth Reid. That project inspired colleagues in Scotland
and Louisiana to reopen the possibilities of academic exchange that half a
century ago held such promise for Professor Oppenheim. This volume is
an early result of that cooperation, following on from conferences held in
Scotland in June 2007 and in Louisiana in April 2008. In many respects *Mixed
Legal Systems in Comparative Perspective* served as a model for the work
presented here. But there are important differences. This volume covers
only selected topics in the private law of the two jurisdictions. Our book is
therefore on a smaller scale, favouring microcomparisons and detailed treatment of relatively narrow areas. The number of chapters here is thirteen, as
compared to twenty-seven in the previous work. We have followed a rather
different methodology as well. Here each contributor was responsible for
mastering the comparative exposé of the two laws without the assistance of
a co-author from the other system, although each was assigned a "mentor"
to assist with problems of research and understanding the approach of the
less familiar system. Perhaps the most significant difference between the two
ventures was the relative novelty of comparing Louisiana and Scotland at all.
Scotland and South Africa have received greater attention and are better
known to have many comparable aspects in their respective private law
systems, due to a deeply-connected legal history, the uncodified structure of

4   "The Civil Law", in Lectures 1-3, *Reception of the Civil Law in the American continents* (1960),
     unpublished, quoted in Reid, "The idea of mixed legal systems" (n 2) at 14.
5   For the collected papers of the First Worldwide Congress on Mixed Jurisdictions held at Tulane
     Law School in November 2002, see (2003) 78(1&2) Tulane LR (special issue). The papers of the
     Second Worldwide Congress on Mixed Jurisdictions held at Edinburgh University in June 2007
     are dispersed in three journals: (2008) Tul Eur & Civ L F; 2007(3) and 2008(2) Stell LR and
     2008(3) J Comp L. The entire set is found online in (2008) 12(1) *Electronic Journal of Compara-
     tive Law*, available at *http://www.ejcl.org/121/issue121.html*. For the papers of the conference
     on "Mixed legal systems: Patterns of development" held at the University of Edinburgh in
     December 2000 see 2002(1) JR.

their laws, the role of authoritative writers in both systems and their mutual reliance upon precedent as a source of law. But Scotland and Louisiana are not so closely associated and there have been no previous comparative studies linking them. The premise for comparative treatment was therefore untried and untested.

Indeed the potential for detailed bilateral comparison initially seemed doubtful, since the elements which make up the mix of the two legal systems are in many ways dissimilar. One is in America, the other in Europe. One is codified and the other is not. The Civilian element in Louisiana is French and Spanish, whereas in Scotland it is also Dutch and German.[6] The Common Law element in Louisiana is American whereas in Scotland it is English. Moreover, one legal system had its beginnings only in the nineteenth century, whereas the other has a legal literature extending over many hundreds of years. As an historical matter there has not been extensive contact between Scotland and Louisiana. Although our contributors have remarked in several instances that the basic terms and grammar of Scots and Louisiana law are surprisingly similar, clearly this has not come about as a result of direct cross-influence but instead because in both cases the law is drawn from the same European source. Opportunities for borrowing legal ideas and learning from each other's experience have been scant.[7] This statement may be qualified in one respect, for in the period immediately following Louisiana's codification in 1825 Scottish writers were for a time included in the authorities cited by the Louisiana courts. At that time Louisiana had almost no legal literature or university of its own, and it faced many cases of first impression under its newly-minted code. It was then the practice of judges and counsel to cite authors from all parts of Europe, including Voet, Grotius, Huber and Scottish institutional writers such as Erskine and Bell. This outreach, however, was never extensive, nor reciprocated, and vanished later in the century.

Yet if such differences put the comparability question to the test, our present study, we believe, convincingly puts that question to rest. The presence of a civil code in one of the two jurisdictions under comparison was generally not as significant a barrier to comparison as it is sometimes portrayed. A civil code plainly plays a substantial role in entrenching the Civil Law within the system and slowing the mixing process. However, in this

---

6 Although on the influence of Pothier and Toullier on Scots law see F P Walton, "The relation of the law of France to the law of Scotland" (1902) 14 JR 17.

7 Although Smith's favourable impression of the Louisiana State Law Institute seems to have inspired him to establish in 1960, on a more modest scale, the Scottish Universities Law Institute.

project the Louisiana Civil Code certainly did not interject an intellectual obstacle or restrict the flow of information and insights by the Scottish side, any more than Scotland's institutional literature or case-based system posed a problem for the Louisiana scholars. In this respect it is probably important to note that Louisiana has a French-derived code with an open and transparent texture, far friendlier to the uninitiated than, say, the German Civil Code. Furthermore the free exchange is enhanced by the compatible form of Louisiana's jurisprudence and Scotland's jurisprudence, although the former is admittedly very much more plentiful on a year-by-year basis than the latter. Like Scotland's case law, Louisiana decisions are fully argued, factually developed, and decidedly un-French. The cases restate the code articles as well as the prior decisions, thus offering a second (and somewhat wider) gateway to the codified law.

Moreover, prevailing similarities within the two jurisdictions facilitate communication and comparison and produce fruitful insights. Louisiana and Scotland have many historical and institutional points in common.[8] In each case a Civil Law was initially implanted that was shaped by the reception of Roman and Canon law; a tide of Common-Law influence later ensued; and a neo-Civilian reaction to that influence occurred in the twentieth century. The timing as well as the content of the Civil Law implantation was of course somewhat different in each case.[9] Due to their Roman and Canon law foundation the systems have a rationally organised taxonomy. The legal discourse of one system is thus readily intelligible to the other. Each recognises the ordering scheme of Gaius and the grammar of Roman categories, and these produce conceptual markers even in areas where considerable Common Law assimilation has taken place.[10] Furthermore, the mixing process within their respective private laws has certain tendencies and patterns, the Common Law penetrating more easily the most porous points of entry, such as delict, while

8 See Palmer, *Mixed Jurisdictions Worldwide* (n 1) 76-80; V V Palmer, "Two rival theories of mixed legal systems" (2008) 3 JCompL 7 at 19.

9 In Scotland the Civil Law reception dates from late medieval times, whereas Louisiana received French, then Spanish law at different times in the eighteenth century. A point in common, however, is that the influence of French legal thought revived in Scotland in the early nineteenth century, largely due to Pothier, while in more or less the same period Louisiana adopted the French-inspired Civil Code of 1825. See Walton, "The relationship of the law of France to the law of Scotland" (n 6); V V Palmer, "The French connection and the Spanish perception", in *The Lousiana Civilian Experience* (2005) ch 2.

10 As Peter Birks once noted, the "true difference" between English and Scots law is not in regard to the content of particular rules, but in regard to structure. The latter retains a "commitment to the institutional scheme or, in other words, to a more systematic approach" ("More logic and less experience", in D L Carey Miller and R Zimmermann (eds), *The Civilian Tradition in Scots Law* (1997) 167 at 174).

leaving resistant institutions like property law relatively less affected. As for judicial institutions, the office of the judge and the form of the judgment are built along the same Common Law lines, and court decisions are accorded strong precedential value. No division between law and equity, however, has ever been recognised. Civil procedure is adversarial and bears the imprint of Anglo-American influence. Finally, in each case the commercial law has yielded to the economic forces of the national market. Anglo-American commercial statutes have replaced the old law merchant.

Against this background the chapters in this volume offer detailed analysis of similarities and differences. While close attention has been given to primary sources, the contributors explore the reasons for the rules, as well as the rules themselves, considering legal history, social and cultural factors and the operation of rules in practice. In this way the material which follows here contributes to the insights provided by existing literature on the development of the law in mixed legal systems and patterns for future development.

We owe a deep debt of gratitude to Professor Kenneth Reid for helping to plan this volume from its early stages and also for organising the first conference between the Louisiana and Scottish contributors held in Edinburgh in June 2007. We would also like to express our appreciation to the Eason Weinmann Center of Comparative Law and its Director Professor A N Yiannopoulos for partially funding the preliminary conference in Edinburgh as well as the second conference of the participants in New Orleans in March 2008. In addition thanks are due to the Edinburgh Legal Education Trust which gave support to the Edinburgh event.

Vernon Palmer
Elspeth Reid
New Orleans and Edinburgh
March 2009

List of Contributors

JAMES CHALMERS is Senior Lecturer in the School of Law, University of Edinburgh.

MARTIN HOGG is Senior Lecturer in the School of Law, University of Edinburgh.

JOHN A LOVETT is Professor of Law, Loyola University New Orleans.

LAURA J MACGREGOR is Senior Lecturer, and Director, Edinburgh Centre for Commercial Law, School of Law, University of Edinburgh.

HECTOR L MACQUEEN is Professor of Private Law, University of Edinburgh.

KENNETH McK NORRIE is Professor of Law, University of Strathclyde.

RODERICK R M PAISLEY is Professor of Commercial Property Law, University of Aberdeen.

VERNON VALENTINE PALMER is Thomas Pickles Professor of Law and Co-Director, Eason-Weinmann Center of Comparative Law, Tulane University.

ELSPETH CHRISTIE REID is Senior Lecturer in the School of Law, University of Edinburgh.

KENNETH G C REID is Professor of Scots Law, University of Edinburgh.

DAVID V SNYDER is Professor of Law, Washington College of Law, American University, Washington, DC.

RONALD J SCALISE JR is A D Freeman Associate Professor of Civil Law, Tulane University.

JOHN RANDALL TRAHAN is James Carville Alumni Professor of Law, Louisiana State University.

List of Abbreviations

BOOKS

Bankton, *Inst*

Andrew McDouall, Lord Bankton, *An Institute of the Laws of Scotland in Civil Rights* (1751-1753), reprinted by the Stair Society, vols 41-43 (1993-1995)

Bell, *Comm*

George Joseph Bell, *Commentaries on the Law of Scotland and the Principles of Mercantile Jurisprudence*, 7th edn, by J McLaren (1870; reprinted 1990)

Bell, *Prin*

George Joseph Bell, *Principles of the Law of Scotland*, 10th edn, by W Guthrie (1899, reprinted 1989)

Craig, *Jus Feudale*

Thomas Craig of Riccarton, *Jus Feudale*, 3rd edn, by J Baillie (1732); transl Lord Clyde (1934)

Erskine, *Inst*

John Erskine of Carnock, *An Institute of the Law of Scotland*, 8th edn, by J B Nicholson (1871, reprinted 1989)

Grotius

Hugo de Groot, *Inleidinge tot de Hollandsche Rechts-geleerdheid* (eds F Dovring, H F W D Fischer, E M Meijers), 2nd edn (1965)

Hume, *Lectures*

Baron David Hume, *Lectures 1786–1822* (ed G C H Paton), Stair Society vols 5, 13, 15-19 (1939-1958)

Mackenzie, *Institutions*

Sir George Mackenzie, *The Institutions of the Law of Scotland* (1684)

McLaren, *Wills & Succession*

J McLaren, *The Law of Wills and Succession as administered in Scotland*, 3rd edn (1894), with a supplementary volume by D Oswald Dykes (1934)

Reid & Zimmermann, *History*

K Reid and R Zimmermann (eds), *A History of Private Law in Scotland* vols 1 (Introduction and Property) and 2 (Obligations) (2000)

SME

Sir Thomas Smith et al (eds), *The Laws of Scotland: Stair Memorial Encyclopaedia* (25 vols, 1987-1996) with cumulative supplements and reissues

Stair

James Dalrymple, 1st Viscount Stair, *Institutions of the Law of Scotland*, 6th edn, by D M Walker (1981)

Voet

Johannes Voet, *Commentarius ad Pandectas* (Hagae-Comitum, 1707)

Zimmermann, Visser & Reid, *Mixed Legal Systems*

R Zimmermann, D Visser and K Reid (eds), *Mixed Legal Systems in Comparative Perspective: Property and Obligations in Scotland and South Africa* (2004)

OTHER ABBREVIATIONS

A	Atlantic Reporter
AC	UK Law Reports, Appeal Cases
Add	Addams' Reports (England and Wales)
Ad & El	Adolphus & Ellis's Reports, King's Bench and Queen's Bench (England and Wales)
AJCL	American Journal of Comparative Law
All ER	All England Reports
App Cas	UK Law Reports, Appeal Cases, House of Lords
APS	Act(s) of the Parliament of Scotland (until 1707)
ASP	Act of the Scottish Parliament (from 1999)
Bell App	S S Bell's Scotch Appeals, House of Lords
BGB	Bürgerliches Gesetzbuch (German Civil Code)
BS	Brown's Supplement, Court of Session reports
c(c)	chapter(s) (legislation)
C	*Codex Iustiniani*
CA	Court of Appeal
Ch	English Law Reports, Chancery Division
Ch D	English Law Reports, Chancery Division

CJ	Chief Justice
CLJ	*Cambridge Law Journal*
CLR	Commonwealth Law Reports (Australia)
CSIH	Court of Session Inner House
CSOH	Court of Session Outer House
D	Justinian's Digest
D	Dunlop's Session Cases (Scotland)
D (HL)	House of Lords Cases in Dunlop's Session Cases
DP	Discussion Paper
EdinLR	*Edinburgh Law Review*
EHRR	European Human Rights Reports
EJCL	*Electronic Journal of Comparative Law*
ER	English Reports
EWCA	Court of Appeal, Civil Division (England and Wales)
EWHC	High Court (England and Wales)
Ex	English Law Reports, Exchequer
Ex D	English Law Reports, Exchequer Division
F	Fraser's Session Cases (Scotland)
F (HL)	House of Lords Cases in Fraser's Session Cases
FC	Faculty Collection, Court of Session
Gai Inst	Gaius's *Institutes*
GWD	Green's Weekly Digest (Scotland)
Harvard LR	*Harvard Law Review*
HC	House of Commons
HL	House of Lords
HLC	Clark's House of Lords Cases
Hume	Hume's Decisions, Court of Session
ICLQ	*International and Comparative Law Quarterly*
IH	Inner House of the Court of Session (Scotland)
JLSS	*Journal of the Law Society of Scotland*
JR	*Juridical Review*
J Inst	Justinian's *Institutes*
KB	English Law Reports, King's Bench Division
La	Louisiana Reports
La App	Louisiana Court of Appeals Reports
La Civ Code	Louisiana Civil Code
La LR	*Louisiana Law Review*
Law Com	Law Commission (England and Wales)
LC	Lord Chancellor

LCJ	Lord Chief Justice
LJ	Lord Justice
LJC	Lord Justice Clerk
LJCP	Law Journal Reports, New Series, Common Pleas (England and Wales)
LJEx	Law Journal Reports, Exchequer (England and Wales)
Loy L Rev	*Loyola Law Review*
LQR	*Law Quarterly Review*
LR CP	English Law Reports, Common Pleas
LR QB	English Law Reports, Queen's Bench
LT	Law Times Reports
M	Macpherson's Session Cases (Scotland)
Macq	Macqueen's House of Lords Reports (Scotland)
MichLRev	*Michigan Law Review*
MLR	*Modern Law Review*
Mor	Morison's Dictionary of Decisions, Court of Session
MR	Master of the Rolls
NZLR	New Zealand Law Reports
OH	Outer House, Court of Session
OJ	Official Journal of the European Communities
Pat	Paton's House of Lords Appeal Cases (Scotland)
pr	*principium*
QBD	Queen's Bench Division
R	Rettie's Session Cases (Scotland)
R (HL)	House of Lords cases in Rettie's Session Cases
RLR	*Restitution Law Review*
Rob	Robinson's Scotch Appeal Cases
S	Shaw's Session Cases (NE indicates New Edition) (Scotland)
SC	Session Cases (Scotland)
SC (HL)	House of Lords cases in Session Cases
SCLR	Scottish Civil Law Reports
Scot Law Com	Scottish Law Commission
Sh Ct Rep	Sheriff Court Reports
SI	Statutory Instrument
SLPQ	*Scottish Law & Practice Quarterly*
SLR	Scottish Law Reporter
SLT	Scots Law Times
SLT (News)	News Section in Scots Law Times

SLT (Notes)	Notes of Recent Decisions in Scots Law Times
SLT (Sh Ct)	Sheriff Court Reports in Scots Law Times
So	Southern Reporter
SSI	Scottish Statutory Instrument
Stell LR	*Stellenbosch Law Review*
SW	South Western Reporter
Tulane LR	*Tulane Law Review*
Tul Civ LF	*Tulane European and Civil Law Forum*
UKHL	United Kingdom, House of Lords
US	United States Supreme Court Reports
Ves	Vesey's Reports (England and Wales)
Ves Jun	Vesey Junior's Reports (England and Wales
W& S	Wilson and Shaw's House of Lords Cases (Scotland)
WLR	Weekly Law Reports
Yale LJ	*Yale Law Journal*

Table of Cases

A & G Paterson v Highland Railway 1927 SC (HL) 32 .... 301, 308

Abadie v Metropolitan Life Insurance Co 784 So 2d 46 (La App
5th Cir 2001) 384

Abbot of Halyruidhous v the Laird of Inverleith, 20 January 1549, Balfour,
Practicks 146 cviii 250

Aberdeen Varieties Ltd v James F Donald (Aberdeen Cinemas) Ltd
1940 SLT 58, revd 1940 SC (HL) 52 .... 46–8, 50

Aberfoyle Plantations Ltd v Khaw Bian Cheng [1960] AC 115 (PC) 87

Adam v Shrewsbury [2005] EWCA Civ 1006; [2006] 1 P & CR 27.................. 88

Adams v Asbestos Corporation Ltd 914 So 2d 1177 (La App 2005) 377

Adams v Guardian Newspapers 2003 SC 425 .... 407, 409

Adams v Howerton 673 F 2d 1036 (9th Cir 1982)..................................... 160

Adams v Owens-Corning Fiberglas Corp 923 So 2d 118 (La App 1st Cir 2005) 381

Adamson v Martin 1916 SC 319 402

Addis v Gramophone Co Ltd [1909] AC 488 .... 212, 219–20, 221, 222, 226

Administrator, Natal v Edouard 1990 (3) SA 581 213

Advice Centre for Mortgages v McNicoll [2006] CSOH 58; 2006
SLT 591 .... 312, 314, 318

Aguado v de Bearn et Consorts, Cour de Paris, 1 May 1875, (1875) 2 D 204   263

Airco Refrigeration Service Inc v Fink 134 So 2d 880 (1961) 335

Ajayi v R T Briscoe (Nigeria) Ltd [1964] 1 WLR 1326 (PC) 286

Alvis v Harrison 1991 SLT 64 84

Amalgamated Investment & Property Co Ltd (In Liquidation) v Texas
Commerce International Bank Ltd [1982] QB 84 286

Anderson v Anderson 1961 SC 59.. 311

Anderson v Grant (1899) 1 F 484 122

Anderson v Handley (1881) 2 Guthrie's Select Sheriff Court Cases 532........... 26

Andry v Murphy Oil 935 So 2d 239 (La App 4 2006) ... 364, 365, 366, 367, 375–6

Anent Trusts and Back-Bonds (1677) 3 BS 185 78

Anns v Merton London Borough Council [1978] AC 278 358

Argyllshire Commissioners of Supploy v Campbell (1885) 12 R 1255 101

Ark Entertainment, LLC v C J Gayfer & Co 2000 US Dist LEXIS
3867 (D La 2000) 306, 307, 315

Asbestos Plaintiffs v Bordelon Inc, In re 726 So 2d 926 (La App ....
4th Cir 1998) 383–4

Associated Acquisitions v Carbone Properties of Audubon 962 So 2d 1102
(2007) 258
Atkins v Johnson 535 So 2d 1063 (La App 2d Cir 1988) 73
Atkinson v Celotex Corp 633 So 2d 383 (La App 1994) 377
Attorney General v Blake [2001] 1 AC 268 349
Aubert v Talon, Cour d'Aix 7 July 1856 D 1856.1.285, S 1857.1.755 69
Axis West Developments v Chartwell Land Investments 1999 SLT 1416 95

Baehr v Lewin 852 P 2d 44 (Haw 1993) 160
Bailey v Porter-Wadley Lumber Co 28 F Supp 25 (DC La 1939),
affd 110 F 2d 74 (5th Cir 1940), cert denied 311 US 680, 61 S Ct 48,
85 L Ed 438 (1940) 69
Baird v Fortune (1859) 21 D 848 22
Baker v Chevron Oil Co 260 La 1143, 258 So 2d 531 (La 1972) 76
Baker v LSU Health Scis Ctr, Inst of Professional Education 889 So 2d 1178
(La Ct App 2004) 305
Baker v Maclay Properties Co 648 So 2d 888 (La 1995) 332, 335
Baker v Nelson 191 NW 2d 185 (Supreme Ct of Minnesota 1971) 160
Ballast plc v Laurieston Properties Ltd [2005] CSOH 16, unreported,
25 January 2005 .... 312, 313
B & B Cut Stone Co, Inc v Resneck 465 So 2d 851 (La App 2nd Cir 1985) 210, 241
Bank of East Asia v Scottish Enterprise 1997 SLT 1213 (HL) 276
Bank of Scotland v 3i plc 1990 SC 215 294
Bannerman v Bishop 688 SO 2d 570 (La App 2 Cir 1996) 357
Barker v Corus (UK) plc [2006] UKHL 20; [2006]
2 AC 572 .... 367, 368, 369, 376, 378
Barker v Lewis 2007 SLT (Sh Ct) 48, affd 2008 SLT (Sh Ct) 17 .... 40, 52
Bathgate v Rosie 1976 SLT (Sh Ct) 16 .... 311, 313, 314
Baugh v Redmond 565 So 2d 953 (La App 2nd Cir 1990) 401
Becket v Bisset 1921 SLT 33 45
Becnel v Whirley Indus 2003 US Dist LEXIS 21575 (D La 2003) 305
Bell v Lothiansure Ltd 1993 SLT 421 374
Bell v Scottish Special Housing Association 1987 SLT 320 375
Ben Cleuch Estates Ltd v Scottish Enterprise 2008 SC 252 .... 312, 314
Bennett v Carse 1990 SLT 454 .... 341, 351
Bernos v Canepa 114 La 517; 38 So 438 (La 1905) 16
Birmingham & District Land Co v London & NW Railway Co (1889)
LR 40 Ch D 268 (CA) 286
Black v Carrollton RR Co,10 La Ann 33 (La 1855) 213, 230
Blacklock & Macarthur v Kirk 1919 SC 57 259
Blacks v Cadell, 9 February 1804 FC; (1804) Mor 13905; (1812)
5 Pat App 567 218
Blair, Sir Adam v Creditors of William Rigg of Carberry, Jan 1686,
Marcase 243, case no 851; (1686) M 14505 100
Bliss v SE Thames Health Authority [1985] IRLR 308 223

Bonnette v Conoco Inc 837 So 2d 1219 (La 2003) 381
Boomer v Muir 24 P 2d 570 (1933) 335, 348
Borel v Fibreboard Paper Prods Corp 493 F 2d 1076 (5th Cir 1973) 378
Boudier *see* Julien Patureau-Miran v Boudier
Bourgeois v A P Green Industries Inc 716 So 2d 355 (La 1998) 381
Bourhill v Young 1942 SC (HL) 78 400
Bowers v Kennedy 2000 SC 555; 2000 SLT 1006............................. 69, 71, 79
Boyle v Glasgow Corporation 1949 SC 254 373
Boyte v Wooten 2006 US Dist LEXIS 45098 (D La 2006) 309, 320
Bridges v Lord Saltoun (1873) 11 M 588 81
British Movietonenews LD v London District Cinemas LD [1952]
    AC 166 .... 260, 275
Brookshire Bros Holding, Inc v Total Containment, Inc 2006 US Dist
    LEXIS 46061 (D La 2006) 315
Broomfield v Louisiana Power & Light 623 So 2d 1376 (La App
    2d Cir 1993) 74, 75, 101
Brown v Board of Education of Topeka 347 US 483; 74 S Ct 686 206
Brown v Burns (1823) 2 S 298 42
Brown v Nielson (1825) 4 S 271 91
Brown and Children v Macgregor, 26 February 1813 FC 218
Brown & Nielson (1825) 4 S 271 347
Bruce v John Toole & Son (Cable Contractors) Ltd 1969 SLT (Notes) 61 373
Bryant v Sholars 104 La 786, 29 So 350 (1901) 80
Buchan v North Lanarkshire Council 2000 Hous LR 98.......................... 224
Builders Supply of Ruston Inc v Qualls 750 So 2d 427 (2000) 329
Bulstrode v Lambert [1953] 2 All ER 728; [1953] 1 WLR 1064 75
Buntein v Boyd (1682) M 10872 78
Burnett v Great North of Scotland Railway Co (1885) 12 R (HL) 25,
    reversing (1883) 11 R 375... 61, 62
Burton v Pinkerton (1867) LR 2 Exch 340 223
Butler v Sudderth 784 So 2d 125 (La Ct App 2001)............................... 314

Cadell v Allan (1905) 13 SLT 10 79
Cadell and Davies v Stewart (1804) Mor App Literary Property No 4 401
Caird v Syme (1887) 14 R (HL) 37 401
Cameron's Trs v Cameron 1907 SC 407 134
Campbell v Dunn (1823) 2 S 341 (First Div) 42, 61
Campbell v Dunn (1828) 6 S 679 .... 42, 61
Campbell v Harley (1825) 1 W & S 690 (HL) 42, 61
Campbell v Mirror Group Newspapers [2004] 2 AC 457 403
Candleberry Limited v West End Homeowners Association [2006]
    CSIH 28; 2006 SC 638; 2007 SCLR 128 95
Cantiere San Rocco SA v Clyde Shipbuilding & Engineering Co
    1923 SC (HL) 105.. 253, 274, 348
Caparo v Dickman [1990] 2 AC 605 359

Capdeboscq v Francis 2004 WL 1418392.. 404

Carlill v Carbolic Smoke Ball Co [1892] 2 QB 484, affd [183] QB 256 300

Carmadelle v Johns-Manville Sales Corp 459 So 2d 621 (La App 1984)......... 377

Carpenter v Williams 428 So 2d 1314 (La App 3d Cir 1983) 265, 269–70, 271

Carriere v Bank of Louisiana 702 So 2d 648 (1996), reconsideration
  denied 709 So 2d 692 (1998) 330, 331–2

Caudle v Betts 512 So 2d 389, 391 (La 1987) 397, 401

Cenac v Hart 741 So 2d 690 (La Ct App 1999) 307

Central London Property Trust Ltd v High Trees House Ltd [1947]
  KB 130 .... 286, 308

Century Ready Mix Corp v Boyte 968 So 2d 893 (La App 2 Cir 2007) 331

Chaffe v Kinsley (2000) 79 P & CR 404; (1999) 77 P & CR 281; 1999
  WL 852817 87

Chaisson v Avondale Industries 947 So 2d 171 (La App 2006) 377

Chandler v Webster [1904] 1 KB 493 266

Chapman v Aberdeen Construction Group plc 1993 SLT 1205 311

Charles Smith and others (Trustees of Dundee Joint Stock Company)
  v David Stewart (1884) 11 R 921; (1884) 21 SLR 623........................ 85, 93

Chatenay et Blanchet v Durand, Cour d'Orléans, 16 February 1865,
  D 1865.2.60; Req November 12 1934, S 1935.1.62............................... 73

Chiasson v Duplechain 56 So 2d 615 (La App 1st Cir 1952) 80

Chisholm v Alexander (1882) 19 SLR 835 347

Choppin v Labranche 20 So 681 (La 1896) 289

Church of Scotland General Trustees v Clow (1994) Paisley and Cusine
  Unreported Property Cases 429 82

Citizens Against Rent Control v Berkeley 454 US 290 (1981)..................... 166

City of Glasgow District Council v Morrison McChlery & Co 1985 SC 52 ... 340

City of New Orleans v Fireman's Charitable Association 9 So 2d 486 (1891)... 336

Civil Service Co-op Society v General Steam Navigation [1903] 2 KB 756 ... 266

CLB Enterprises v Kittok, 575 So 2d 834 (La App 5th Cir 1991)................. 210

Cliffplant Ltd v Kinnaird 1981 SC 9 340

Coastal Environmental Specialists Inc v Chem-Lig International Inc
  818 So 2d 12 La 2001) 330, 332

Cochran v Fairholm (1759) Mor 14518 39

Cochrane v Ewart (1869) 22 D 358 .... 21, 22–3, 24, 26

Coleman v Bossier City 305 So 2d 444 (1974) 333

Colston v Marshall 1993 SLT (Sh Ct) 40; 1993 SCLR 43 .... 224, 226

Com de Girmont v Her Legegue de Bayecourt, Ch civ 11 March 1846,
  S 1846.2.472 85

Combe v Combe [1951] 2 KB 215 (CA) 286

Commissioners of Northern Lighthouses v Edmonston (1908)
  16 SLT 439... 313, 339, 340, 344

Comprehensive Addiction Programs v Mendoza 50 F Supp 2d 581
  (D La 1999) 306

Condrey v Sun Trust Bank of Ga 429 F 3d 556, 565-566 (5th Cir 2005) ... 306, 307

Co-operative Wholesale Society v Ushers Brewery 1975 SLT (Lands Tr) 9   50, 51
Corley v Craft 501 So 2d 1049 (La App 2d Cir 1987), writ denied 503
    So 2d 18 (La 1987) 76
Corporation of Tailors of Aberdeen v Coutts (1840) 1 Rob 296 ... 31, 42, 43, 44, 61
Costello v Hardy 864 So 2d 129 (La 2004) 407
Countess of Cawdor v Earl of Cawdor 2007 SC 285 ...... 298, 313, 315, 316, 319
Couprie v Lacoste, Ch Req 28 June 1865, D 1866.1.153, S 1865.1.339 85
Crawford v Field (1874) 2 R 20 101
Creditors and Donatar of the Estate of Dunfermline v Laird of Innes
    (1707) M 10913 78
Crosby v Stinson 766 So 2d 615 (La Ct App 2000) 307
Cruikshanks v Forsyth (1747) Mor 4034 395
Crumley v Lawson (1892) 8 Sh Ct Rep 307 85
Cumbernauld Development Corporation v County Properties &
    Development Ltd 1996 SLT 1106 62
Currier v Currier 599 So 2d 456 (La App 2 Cir 1992) 154
Curtis Publishing Co v Butts 388 US 130 (1967) 408
Cuthbertson v Lowes (1870) 8 M 1073 346

Dahl v Nelson (1880–81) LR 6 App Cas 38 275
Dallas Cooperage & Woodenware Co v Creston Hoop Co 161 La 1077,
    109 So 844 (La 1926) 259
Dalton v Angus (1881) 6 App Cas 740 26
Daly v Benthuysen 3 La Ann 69 (La 1848) 215
Dame Masselin v Decaens, Cass civ 29 April 1971; Gaz Pal 1971.2.554;
    D 1971 Somm 197; JCP 1971.IV.145 326
Dan Rhodes Enters v City of Lake Charles 857 So 2d 1256 (La Ct App 2003)   305
Danish Dairy Co v Gillespie 1922 SC 656 296
Daquin v Coiron 3 La 404 (La 1832) 3
Da Silva Mouta v Portugal (2001) 31 EHRR 47 161
Daugherty v Canal Bank and Trust Co 180 La 1003 (1935) 135–6
Dautreuil v Degeyter 436 So 2d 614 (La App 3rd Cir 1983) 82
Davidson v Macpherson (1889) 30 SLR 2 .... 257, 259
Davidson Bros, Inc v D Katz & Sons, Inc 579 A 2d 288 (NJ 1990) 60
Davis Contractors Ltd v Fareham Urban District Council
    [1956] AC 696 .... 251, 260, 275, 278
Davis v Bray 191 So 2d 744 (La Ct App 2d Cir 1966) 288
Dawson International plc v Coats Patons plc 1988 SLT 854, affd 1989
    SLT 655 293–4
Dear v Wilkinson (1960) 2 West Indian Reports 309 (Supreme Ct of Barbados) 89
De La Croix v Nolan 1 Rob 321 (La 1842) 73, 95
De Lathouwer v Anderson 2007 SLT 437 313
Del Cryer v M & M Manufacturing Company 273 So 2d 818 (1973) 262
Denis v Leclerc 1 Mart 297 (La 1811) 401
De Santo v Barnsley 476 A 2d 952 (Pa Super 1984) 160

Deshotels v Fruge 364 So 2d 258, 261 (La 3 Cir 1978) 40
Deuchar v Brown (1672) Mor 12386 261
Diesen v Samson 1971 SLT 49 (Sh Ct) 210, 220, 221, 224, 226
Digby Brown & Co v Lyall 1995 SLT 932 311
Dirnmeyer v O'Hern 39 La Ann 961 (La 1887) 213
Dixie Drive It Yourself v American Beverage 242 La 471; 37 So 2d
    298 (La 1962); 128 So 2d 841 (La App 1961) 361, 364, 368, 370–1, 372
Dollar Land (Cumbernauld) Ltd v CIN Properties Ltd
    1998 SC (HL) 90 .... 342, 345
Donoghue v Stevenson 1932 SC (HL) 31 .... 358, 400
Dorian v Les Ecclésiastiques du Séminaire de St Sulpice de Montréal
    (1880) LR 5 App Cas 362 75
Dorsey v N Life Insurance Co 2005 US Dist LEXIS 17742 D La 2005) 315
Double Diamond Properties, LLC v Amoco Oil Co 487 F Supp 2d 737
    (E D Va 2007) 60
Douglas Shelf Seven Ltd v Co-operative Wholesale Society Ltd [2007]
    CSOH 53 375
Douglas v Hello [2006] QB 125 .... 402, 405
Dow v Brown and Co (1844) 6 D 534 218
Dow v Tayside University Hospitals NHS Trust 2006 SLT (Sh Ct) 141 316
Dowden, In re 207 B R (Bankruptcy Reporter) 514 (1997) 334
Dowling & Rutter v Abacus Frozen Foods Ltd 2002 SLT 491 347
Drennan v Star Paviing Co 333 P 2d 757 (Cal 1958) 285, 305
Drs Bethea, Moustoukas and Weaver LLC v St Paul Guardian Insurance
    Co 376 F 3d 399 (5th Cir 2004) 306, 307
Ducote v Oden 59 So 2d 130 (La 1952) 289, 290, 303
Dugas v Guillory 719 So 2d 719 (La Ct App 1998) 307
Duke of Richmond v Milne 17 La 312 (La 1841) 3
Dumfries and Maxwelltown Water Works Commissioners v McCulloch
    (1874) 1 R 975 101
Duncan v Arbroath (1668) Mor 10075 253
Dunham v Dunham 174 So 2d 898 (La App 1st Cir 1968) 138
Dunn v Blackdown Properties Ltd [1961] Ch 433 88
Dura Pharmaceuticals Inc v Broudo 544 US 336, 342 (2005) 370
Dyce v Hay (1849) 11 D 1266, affd (1852) 15 D (HL) 14 39
Dynamic Exploration Inc v Sugar Bowl Gas Corp 367 So 2d 18 (1978) 333

Earl of Aberdeen v Baird (1694) 4 BS 126 78
Earl of Zetland v Hislop (1882) 9 R (HL) 40; (1881) 8 R 675 .... 43–5, 47, 61
East Anglian Electronics Ltd v OIS plc 1996 SLT 808 312
Edinburgh and District Tramways Co Ltd v Courtenay 1909 SC 99 338
Edmondston v Edmondston (1861) 23 D 995 292
Edmonston v A-Second Mortgage Co 289 So 2d 31 (La 1971) 327
Edwards v Conforto 636 So 2d 901 (La 1994) 331
Eerie R Co v Tompkins 304 US 64 (1938) 258

Efner v Ketteringham 41 So 2d 130 (La 1949) 19, 24
Egan v Kaiser Aluminium & Chemical Corp 677 So 2d 1027
    (La App 1996) 379–80
Eisten v North British Railway Co (1870) 8 M 980 219
E P Dobson Inc v Perritt 566 So 2d 657, 659 (La App 2 Cir 1990)................. 32
Estève v Dubois et Lacoste, Trib Toulouse, 1 June 1916, (1916)
    2 D 1128 263
Eugster & Co v Joseph West & Co 35 La Ann 119 (1883) 1 .... 254, 256
Ewart v Cochrane (1860) 22 D 358; (1861) 4 Maqu 117 .... 22, 26, 86
Ewing v Earl of Mar (1851) 14 D 314 395
Experience Hendrix LLC v PPX Enterprises Inc [2003] EMLR 25 349
Exxon Corp v Columbia Gas Transmission Corp 624 F Supp 610
    (W D La 1985) 259

Fairchild v Glenhaven Funeral Services [2003] 1 AC 32 .... 377, 380
Farley v Skinner [2002] 2 AC 732; [2000] PNLR 441 ...... 209, 210, 212, 219, 225
Farnsworth v Sewerage & Water Board of New Orleans
    173 La 1105, 139 So 638 (1932) 252, 256
Female Orphan Society v Young Men's Christian Association
    44 So 15 (La 1907) 53, 56, 57
Ferguson v McIntyre 1993 SLT 1269 69
Fèvre-Hannel v Maillefer, Ch Req 23 July 1860, S 1861.1.526 69
First National Bank plc v Thompson [1996] Ch 231 286
Fitzgerald v Cavin 110 Mass 153 (Mass 1872) 400
Fitzpatrick v Sterling Housing Association [1999] 4 All ER 705 161
Florida Ice Machinery Corp v Branton Insulation Inc 290 So 2d 415 (1974)... 335
Flynn v Nesbitt 771 F Supp 766 (E D La 1991) 317
Ford v Revlon Inc 153 Ariz 38; 734 P 2d 580 (1987) 395
Forum for Equality v McKeithen 893 So 2d 715 (La 2005) 159, 165
Fourie v Minister for Home Affairs 2006 (1) SA 524 162
Francisco v Joan of Arc Inc 692 So 2d 598 (La App 1997) 363
Fraser v DM Hall & Son 1997 SLT 808 223
Freeman Decorating Co v Encuentro Las Americas Trade Corp
    2005 US Dist LEXIS 18313 (D La 2005) 305, 315
Fricke v Owens-Corning Fiberglas Corp 571 So 2d 130 (La 1990).............. 401
Frog's Creditors v His Children (1735) Mor 4262 140

Gajovski v Gajovski 610 NE 2d 431 (1991) 167
Gangi Seafood, Inc v ADT Security Services 2005 US App LEXIS 4
    (5th Cir 2005) 305
Gardner v Ferguson (1795) unreported, Hume, Session Papers vol 87 no 97   218
Garner v Holley 968 So 2d 234 (La 2007).. 10, 11
Garther v Tipery Studios Inc 334 So 2d 758 (La App 4th Cir 1976)......... 210, 237
Gaz de Bordeaux, Conseil d'État, 30 March 1916, DP 1916.3.25 249
Gellatly vArrol (1863) 1 M 592 79

George Wimpey East Scotland Ltd v Fleming 2006 SLT
 (Lands Tr) 2, 59 .... 9, 49, 98
Gertz v Robert Welch Inc 418 US 323 (1974) 408
Gibb v Bruce (1837) 16 S 169 84
Gibbal v Bory, Ch civ 14 Dec 1864, D 1864.1.126 73
Giblin v Murdoch 1979 SLT (Sh Ct) 5 50
Gibson v McAndrew Wormald 1998 SLT 562 382
Gilfoil v Greenspan 216 So 2d 829 (La App 2d Cir 1968) 74, 75
Gisclair v Matmoor, Inc 537 So 2d 876 (La App 5th Cir 1989)................... 265
Givens v Chandler 143 So 79 (La 1932) 15
Glass v Wiltz 551 So 2d 32, 33 (4th C 1989) 235
Glover v Abney 106 So 2d 735 (La 1925) 288
Goodloe v Rodgers 10 La Ann (La 1855) 215
Goodridge v Department of Public Health 798 NE 2d 941 (Mass 2003)   116, 162
Goodyear Tire & Rubber Co v Ruiz 367 So 2d 79 (La Ct App 4th Cir 1979) ... 288
Gordon v East Kilbridge Development Corp 1995 SLT 62......................... 290
Gottschalk v De Santos 1857 WL 4688 (La 1857) 19
Govan New Bowling Green Club v Geddes (1898) 25 R 485 140
Gow's Trs v Mealls (1875) 2 R 729 24
Graeme and Skene v Cunningham (1765) Mor 13923............................... 219
Graham v Kennedy (1860) 22 D 560 157
Graham v Ladeside of Kilbirnie Bowling Club 1994 SLT 1295 224
Graham v Parker 2007 GWD 30-524 .... 9, 98
Graham v Western Union Tel Co 109 La 1070 (La 1903) 210, 236
Grant v Sun Shipping Co Ltd 1948 SC (HL) 73 373–4
Gray v Johnston 1928 SC 659 .... 292, 293, 294
Gray v MacLeod 1979 SLT (Sh Ct) 17 76
Greco v Frigerio 3 La App 649, 651 (Orl 1926) 40
Greenhorn v Addie (1855) 17 D 860.. 218
Gregg v Scott [2005] UKHL 2; [2005] 2 AC 176 381
Greiner v Greiner 293 P 759 (Kan 1930) 296
Grieves v F T Everard & Sons Ltd [2007] UKHL 39; [2008] 1 AC 281 ... 382, 386
Griswold v Connecticut 381 US 479 (1965) 159

Hadley v Baxendale (1854) 156 Eng Rep 145 226–7
Haigues v Halyburton (1704) M 10727... 80
Haldane v Watson 1972 SLT (Sh Ct) 8 311
Hall v Dixon 401 So 2d 473 (La App 2d Cir 1981) 76
Halpern v Attorney General of Canada (2003) 225 DLR (4th) 529 162
Hamilton v Lochrane (1899) 1 F 478 301
Hanks v Gulf States Utilities Co 253 La 946, 221 So 249 (1969).............. 75
Hanover Petroleum Corp v Tenneco 521 So 2d 1234
 (La App 3rd Cir 1988) 257, 258, 265
Hanszen v Cooke 246 So 2d 200 (La App 1st Cir 1971) 76
Hardey v Russel and Aitken 2003 GWD 2-50 399

Haring v Stinson 756 So 2d 1201 (La Ct App 2000)................................. 305
Harper v Flaws 1940 SLT 150 45
Harper v Home Indem Co 140 So 2d 653 (La App 2d Cir 1962) 256
Hart's Trs v Arrol (1903) 6 F 36.. 268, 270
Harvela Investments v Royal Trust Co of Canada [1984] 2 All ER 65,
    rev'd [1985] Ch 103, subsequently rev'd [1986] AC 207........................ 301
Harvey v Lindsay (1853) 15 D 768 39
Harvey v The Singer Manufacturing Co Ltd 1960 SC 155 373
Hatfield v Max Rouse & Sons Northwest 606 P 2d 944 (1980) 212
Hay's Trs v Hay (1890) 17 R 961 140
Hayns v Secretary of State for the Environment (1978) 36 P & CR 317 101
Head v Adams 275 So 2d 476 (1973) 334
Heirs of Cole v Cole's Executors 7 Mart (ns) 414 (La 1830) 288
Henderson v Chief Constable, Fife Police 1988 SLT 361 398
Henson v Gonzales 326 So 2d 396 (1976)... 335
Herbert v Dupaty 7 So 2d 580 (La 1890) 52
Heritable Reversionary Co Ltd v Millar (1892)
    19 R (HL) 43 .... 133, 134, 135, 141, 143–4
Hermann v NO and C Ry 11 La Ann, 5 (La 1856) 3
Herne Bay Steam Boat v Hutton [1903] 2 KB 638 266
Heywood v Wellers [1976] QB 446 222
Hibernia National Bank v Antonini 862 So 2d 331 (La Ct App 2003)........... 305
Hill v Lundin & Associates Inc 260 La 542; 256 So 2d 620 (1972) 363, 371–2
Hobbs v London and South Western Railway Co (1875) LR 10 QB 111 223
Hoerner v ANCO Insulations Inc 812 So 2d 45 (La 2002) 376, 383
Hogg v Gow 27 May 1812 FC 654 .... 213, 235
Holt v Bethany Land Co 843 So 2d 606 (La Ct App 2003) 305
Home Services v Marvin 37 So 2d 413 (1948) 336
Hong Kong and Whampoa Co Ltd v Netherton Shipping Co 1909 SC 34...... 259
Horn, In re 827 So 2d 1241 (La Ct App 2002) 306
Housley v Cerise 579 So 2d 973 (La 1991) 366
Howard v Johns-Manville Sales Corp 420 So 2d 1190 (La App 1982) 377
Huber Oil Co of Louisiana v Save-Time 442 So 2d 597 (La App Cir 1982) 63
Hubgh v New Orleans & CR Co 6 La Ann 495; 1851 WL 3649 (La 1851) ... 399
Hughes v Metropolitan Railway Co [1877] 2 AC 439 (HL)........................ 286
Hunter v Bradford Property Trust 1970 SLT 173..................................... 314
Hunter v General Accident etc Corp 1909 SC 344, affd 1909 SC (HL) 30 ... 300
Hunter v Hunter (1904) 7 F 136 300
Hunter v Robert Baird & Sons 1962 SLT 166 373
Hutson v Edinburgh Corporation 1948 SC 668 373

Incorporation of Tailors of Aberdeen v Coutts (1840) 1 Rob App 296 97
Industrias Magromer Cueros y Pieles SA v Louisiana Bayou Furs
    293 F 3d 912 (5th Cir 2002) 306
Inland Revenue v Clarke's Trs 1939 SC 11 141

Innes v Magistrates of Edinburgh (1798) Mor 13189, 13967 218
Investors Compensation Scheme Ltd v West Bromwich Building Society
    [1981] 1 All ER 98... 271
Irland v Barron 230 So 2d 880 (La 1970)... 11
Irvine v Talksport [2002] EMLR 32 405
Itzkovitch v Whitaker 115 La 479; 39 So 499 (1905) 402, 404

Jackson (Edinburgh) Ltd v Constructors John Brown Ltd 1965 SLT 37 253
Jackson v Horizon Holidays [1975] 1 WLR 1468; [1975] 3 All ER 92 ... 210, 222
Jackson v Lare 779 So 2d 808 (La Ct App 2000) 314
Jameel v Wall Street Journal Europe [2007] 1 AC 359 409
James B Fraser & Co v Denny, Mott & Dickson 1944
    SC (HL) 35 .... 251, 253, 255, 268
James Baird Co v Gimbel Bros 64 F 2d 344 (2d Cir 1933) 285
Jamieson v Watt's Trustee 1950 SC 265 346
Jarvis v Swan's Tours Ltd [1973] 1 QB 233 .... 210, 221–2, 226
Jaubert v Crowley Post-Signal Inc 375 So 2d 1386 (La 1979) 404
JB and C Group Management Ltd v Haren, unreported, OH,
    4 December 1992 90
Jesco Construction Corp v Nationsbank Corp 830 So 2d 989
    (La 2002) 305, 307
Jobe v ATR Marketing, Inc 1998 US Dist LEXIS 18171 (D La 1998) 305
John White & Sons v J & M White (1906) 8 F 1166; (1905) 12 SLT 662;
    revd [1906] AC 72.. 81
Johnson v Bergeron 966 So 2d 1059 (La App 5th Cir 2007) 391
Johnson v Gore Wood & Co [2002] 2 AC 1 212
Johnson v Hospital Affiliates Intern Inc 416 So 2d 207 (1982) 333
Johnston v NEI International Combustion Ltd; Grieves v F T Everard &
    Sons Ltd [2007] UKHL 39; [2008] 1 AC 281 .... 382, 386
Johnston v Paley 15 December 1770 FC 188 235
Jones v Hallahan 501 SW 2d 588 (Kentucky App Ct 1973) 160
Jones v Pritchard [1908] 1 Ch 630... 11
Joseph Constantine SS Line Ltd v Imperial Smelting Corporation Ltd
    [1942] AC 154 266
Judice v Southern Pacific Co 47 La Ann 255 (La 1895) 237
Julien Patureau-Miran v Boudier, Cass req 15 June 1892,
    S 1893.1.281 .... 325, 326, 327, 338
J W Soils (Suppliers) Ltd v Corbett 1991 GWD 32-1891; 1991
    CLYB 4533 .... 311, 313
J Weingarten Inc v Northgate Mall 404 So 2d 896 (La 1981) 211

Kavanagh v Bowers 826 So 2d 1165 (La App 5th Cir 2002) 71
Kavanaugh v Frost-Johnston Lumber Co 149 La 972 90 So 275 (La 1921) 94
Keenan v Rolls-Royce Ltd 1969 SC 322 373
Keeney v Keeney 30 So 2d 549 La 1947) 155

Keewattin Power Co Ltd v Lake of the Woods Milling Co Ltd [1930]
AC 640 (PC); (1929) 63 OLR 667; (1928) 61 OLR 363 81
Kennedy V Sheriff of East Baton Rouge 935 So 2d 669 (La 2006) 407, 408
Kenny v Oak Builders Inc 256 La 85, 235 So 2d 386 (1970) 259
Keppel v Bailey (1834) 2 Myl & K 517; 39 ER 1042 .... 33, 45, 53
Kerr, Petr 1968 SLT (Sh Ct) 61 126
Kerrigan v Commissioner of Public Health (2008) WL 4530885
(Sup Ct Conn 2008) 117, 162, 165
Kethley v Draughon Business College, Inc 535 So 2d 502 (La Ct
App 2d Cir 1988) 306
Kincaid v Dickson (1673) Mor 12143; 2 Stair 181 298
Kincaid v Stirling (1750) Mor 8403, 12417 21
Kingdom of Spain v Christie, Manson & Woods Ltd [1986] 1 WLR 1120 389
Knott v Bolton (1885) 11 Const LJ 375.. 225
Kosmala v Paul and the Baton Rouge Symphony 644 So 2d 856 (1st C 1994) 232
Kramer v Johns-Manville Sales Corp 459 So 2d 642 (La App 1984) 377
Krell v Henry [1903] 2 KB 740 266
Kroon v Netherlands (1995) 19 EHRR 263 156
Krupp Uhde GmbH v Weir Westgarth Ltd unreported, OH,
31 May 2002 .... 309–10, 312, 320

Ladele v London Borough of Islington (case no 2203694/2007, 8 July 2008)... 162
Laird of Grant v McIntosh (1678) M 10773 72
Laird of Knockdolian v Tenants of Parthick (1583) Mor 14,540 7
Lakeland Anesthesia, Inc v United Healthcare of Louisiana 871 So 2d 380
(La Ct App 2004) 314
Lambert v Dow Chemical Co 215 So 2d 673 (La App 1st Cir 1968) 404
Landry v Bellanger 851 So 2d 943 (La 2003) 391, 396
Langlois v Allied Chemical Corporation 258 La 1067; 249 2D 133 (1971)...... 392
Larrinaga & Co Ltd v Société Franco-Americaine des Phosphates de
Médulla (1923) TLR 316 266
Lauder v Millars (1859) 21 D 1353 295
Law v City of Eunice 626 So 2d 575 (La Ct App 3d Cir 1993) 313
Law v Newnes (1894) 21 R 1027 300
Lawrence Building Co v Lanark County Council 1978 SC 30.................... 340
Lawrence v Texas 539 US 558 (2003) 159, 168, 206
Lawson v Donahue 313 So 2d 263 (1975)... 335
LeBlanc v Thibodeux 615 So 2d 295 (La 1993) 71
Leeds Permanent Building Society v Walker Fraser & Steele 1995 SLT
(Sh Ct) 72 373
Leiter Minerals, Inc v California Co 241 La 915, 132 So 2d 845 (La 1961) 69
LeMarie v Lone Star Life Insurance Co 2000 US Dist LEXIS 16595
(D La 2000) 315
Lewis v D H Holmes 34 So 66 (La 1903) 210, 236
Lewis v Harris 908 A 2d 196 (Su Ct NJ 2006) 162

Lieber v Hamel 446 So 2d 1240 (La App 2d Cir 1983), writ denied 448
  So 2d 107 (La 1984) 97
Linden v Ministry of Supply 1949 SLT (Notes) 5.................................. 373
Lindley v Rutter [1981] 1 QB 128... 398
Lockhart v Cunninghame (1870) 8 SLR 151 219
Logan v A & J Stephen Ltd unreported, Cupar Sh Ct, case ref A239/91 85
London and Edinburgh Shipping Co v The Admiralty 1920 SC 309 255
Lord Advocate v City of Glasgow DC 1990 SLT 721 313
Lord Advocate v Scotsman Publications Ltd 1989 SC (HL) 122.................. 399
Losecco v Gregory 108 La 648, 32 So 985 (1901) 255
Louisiana & Arkansas Railway Co v Winn Parish Lumber Co
  59 So 403 (La 1912) 53–6, 57, 63
Louviere v Meteye 260 So 2d 377 (La App 4ᵗʰ Cir 1972).......................... 265
Love-Lee v Cameron 1991 SCLR 61 82
Loving v Virginia 388 US 1 (1967); 87 S Ct 1817 (1967) 164, 166, 194, 206

Macadam v Grandison [2008] CSOH 53 343
McAndrews v Roy 131 So 2d 256 (La App 1961)................................... 404
Maccallan v Mags of Ayr (1693) 4 BS 84 78
McCall's Entertainments (Ayr) Ltd v South Ayrshire Council 1998 SLT 1403   311
McCarthy v Magliola 331 So 2d 89 (La Ct App 1ˢᵗ Cir 1976) 288
McCosh v Crow (1903) 5 F 670... 399, 402, 405
McDermott International v Indus Risk Insurers 2003 US Dist
  LEXIS 22286 (D La 2003) 306
McDonald v Barker Auto Sales Inc 810 So 2d 1242 (2002)....................... 334
McDonald v New Orleans Private Patrol 569 So 2d 106 (La App 1990) 377
MacDonald v North of Scotland Bank Limited 1942 SLT 196 78
Macdougal (Thomas) v Mrs Barbara Macdougal and her Husband,
  10 July 1739 FC, case no 126, 206; M 10947 80
McEleveen v McQuillan's Executrix 1997 SLT (Sh Ct) 46 .... 292, 318
McElroy v Dynasty Transport Inc 907 So 2d 69 (La App 1 Cir 3/24/05) 252
McEwan's Executors v Arnot, unreported, Perth Sh Ct, 7 September 2004 28
Macfarlane v Johnston (1864) 2 M 1210 315–16
McFarlane v Tayside Health Board 1997 SLT 211, revd 1998 SC 38,
  revd in part 2000 SC (HL) 1... 373, 374
McGhee v National Coal Board 1973 SC (HL) 37;
  1973 SLT 14 .... 356, 367, 368, 376
McGuire v Central Louisiana Electric Company Inc 337 So 2d 1070
  (La 1976) 10
McJamerson v Grambling State University 769 So 2d 168 (La Ct App 2000)   315
Mackay v McCankie (1883) 10 R 537 407
McKennitt v Ash [2008] QB 73.. 403
McKie v Chief Constable of Strathclyde 2002 Rep LR 137, affd 2003 SC 317   395
McKie v Macrae 2006 SLT 43 373
McKinney v Chief Constable Strathclyde Police 1998 SLT (Sh Ct) 80 394

McLaren v City of Glasgow Union (1875) 5 R 1042 24
McMaster & Co v Cox, McEuen & Co 1921 SC (HL) 24 .... 268, 269
McMillan v Ghaly, unreported, Dundee Sh Ct, 9 September 2002 294
MacPherson and Williams [2008] CSOH 25 93
McPhail v Cunninghame District Council 1983 SC 246; 1985 SLT 149............ 91
M'William & Sons v Fletcher (1905) 13 SLT 455................................... 223
Mack v Glasgow City Council 2006 SC 543 224
Mackeson v Boyd 1942 SC 56 .... 267, 268, 269
Madison v Bolton 234 La 997; 102 So 2d 433 (La 1958) 407
Magic Moments Pizza, Inc v Louisiana Restaurant Association
    819 So 2d 1146 (La Ct App 2002) 305
Malone v Cannon 41 So 2d 837 (La 1949) 124, 153
Marcello v Bussiere 282 So2d 892 (La 1973) 264, 270, 271
Marckx v Belgium (1979) 2 EHRR 330 156
Maritime National Fish Ltd v Ocean Trawlers Ltd [1935] AC 524 266
Marlo Dabog v John Deris 625 So 2d 492 (La 1993) 366
Marriage Cases, In re 183 P 3d 384 (Sup Ct Cal 2008) 117, 162, 164, 165
Marriage of Washburn, In re 677 P 2d 152 (Wash 1984).......................... 155
Marrioneaux v Smith 163 So 206 (La App 1935) 257, 259
Marshall v First Bank & Trust 848 So 2d 660 (La Ct App 2003)................. 314
Martel v A Veeder Co 199 La 423, 6 So 2d 335 (La 1942) 76
Martin v Bigner 665 So 2d 709 (La App 2 Cir 12/06/95) 395
Martin v McGuiness 2003 SLT 1424... 402, 403
Martin v Ziheri 607 SE 2d 367 (2005) 159
Martinez 805 So 2d 242 (La App 3 Cir 2001) 64
Maruko v Versorgunganstalt der Deutschen Buhnen [2008] 2 CMLR 32 161
Marvin v Marvin 557 P2d 106 (1976) 159
Mashburn v Collin 355 So 2d 879 (La 1977) 401
Mason v A & R Robertson & Black 1993 SLT 733 311
May v Harris Management Corp 928 So 2d 140 (La Ct App 2005) 315
Meador v Toyota of Jefferson Inc 332 So 2d 433 (La 1976)..................... 238–40
Meadowcrest Center v Tenet Health System Hospitals, Inc 902 So
    2d 512 (La Ct App 5 Cir 2005) 59
Meijer v International Minerals & Chemical Corp 741 F Supp 1238
    (MD La 1990), affd 929 F 2d 697 (Table) (C A 5 1991) 69, 75
Menzies v Commissioners of the Caledonia Canal (1900) 2 F 953 45
Michelle Detraz v Victor Lee D/B/A Virgin Nails 950 So 2d 557 (La 2007) ... 366
Micosta SA v Shetland Islands Council 1986 SLT 193........................... 394
Millar v Tremamondo (1771) Mor 12395 292
Miller v Holstein, 16 La 389 (La 1840).. 230
Miller v Loyola University of New Orleans 829 So 2d 1057
    (La Ct App 2002) 307, 312, 315
Miller v Miller 817 So 2d 1166 (La Ct App 2002) 314
Miller Homes Ltd v Frame 2001 SLT 459 311
Mills v Findlay 1994 SCLR 397.. 223, 227

Miln v Stirton 1982 SLT (Sh Ct) 11 150
Milne v Gaulds Trs (1841) 3 D 345 406
Minyard v Curtis Products Inc 251 La 624, 205 So 2d 422 (1967) ... 327, 328, 329
Mire v Hawkins 249 La 278, 186 So 2d 591 (La 1966)................................. 76
Mitchell v Brown (1888) 5 Sh Ct Rep 9 .... 78, 85
Mitchell v Shreveport Laundries Inc 61 So 2d 539 (La App
    2nd Cir 1952) 210, 237
Moncrief v Succn of Armstrong 939 So 2d 714 (La Ct App 2006) 307
Moncrieff v Jamieson [2007] UKHL 42; 2008 SC (HL) 1; 2007
    SLT 989 (HL); 2005 1 SC 281 (IH) 8,10, 11, 12, 14, 16, 22, 23, 24, 74, 95
Morest v Burleigh 127 So 624 (La 1930) 288
Morgan Guaranty Co of New York v Lothian Regional Council
    1995 SC 151 .... 342, 346, 353
Morgan v Yarborough 5 La Ann 316 (La 1850) 234
Moroux v Toce 943 So 2d 1263 (La Ct App 2006) 314
Morris v Friedman 663 So 2d 19 (La 1995) 307
Morris v Morris 685 So 2d 673 (La App 3 Cir 1996) 151
Morrison v Kirkintilloch Burgh School Board 1911 SC 1127 45
Morrison v Leckie 2005 GWD 40-734 310
Morrison or Sutherland v Maclennan (1908) 25 Sh Ct Rep 93 79
Morton & Co v Muir Brothers & Co 1907 SC 1211................................. 399
Morton's Trustees v Aged Christian Friend Society (1899) 2 F 82 300–1
Moss Bros Group plc v Scottish Mutual Assurance plc 2001 SLT 641 73
Muckle Flugga case, *see* Commissioners of Northern Lighthouses v
    Edmonston
Munro v MacKenzie (1760) Mor 14533 82
Murray v Express Newspapers plc [2008] EMLR 12 403

Nardone v Birch, unreported, Lands Tribunal for Scotland (1999),
    case ref LTS/L0/1998/26 98
National Carriers Ltd v Panalpina (Northern) Limited [1981] AC 675 278
Neel v O'Quinn 313 So 2d 286 (1975), writ denied 319 So 2d 440 335
New Orleans Public Service Inc v Vanzant 580 So 2d 533 (1991),
    writ denied 584 So 2d 1168 333
Newlands v Newlands' Creditors (1794) Mor 4289 140
New York Times Co v Sullivan 376 US 254 (1964) 408, 409
Nicol v Scottish Power plc 1998 SLT 822... 382
Norsworthy v Succession of Norsworthy (1997) 704 So 2d 953 123
NV Devos Gebroeder v Sutherland Sportswear Ltd 1990 SC 291 341

O & M Const Inc v State, Div of Admin 576 So 2d 1030 (La App 1st Cir
    1991), writ denied 581 So 2d 691 (La 1991) 272
Ocean Trump Tankers Corporation v V/O Overact (The Eugenia) [1964]
    2 QB 226 260
O'Donnell v Murdoch McKenzie & Co Ltd 1967 SC (HL) 63 373

Omnitech International v Clorox Co 11 F 3d 1316 (5th Cir 1994) 306
O'Neal v Cascio 324 So 2d 539 (La App 2nd Cir 1975) 265
Optical Express (Gayle) Ltd v Marks & Spencer PLC 2000 SLT 644 32
Orrock v Bennet (1762) Mor 15009 42
Ostrowe v Darensbourg 377 So 2d 1201 (La 1979) 240

Palace Properties LLC v Sizeler Hammond Square Limited Partnership
    839 So 2d 82 (La App 1 Cir 2002) 13, 74
Palgrave v Gros 829 So 2d 579 (La App 5th Cir 2002) 74, 75, 76
Palmer v Beck 1993 SLT 485 224
Paradine v Jane (1647) Aleyn 26 250
Park Lane Developments (Glasgow Harbour) Ltd v Jesner, unreported,
    Glasgow Sh Ct, 3 May 2006 312
Patout v Lewis 51 La Ann 210; 25 So 134 (La 1899) 15
Patrick v Napier (1867) 5 M 683 39
Paul v Jeffrey (1835) 1 Sh & Macl 767 134
Payne v Hurwitz 978 So 2d 1000 (La App 1 Cir 2008) 258
Peart v Legge [2007] CSIH 70; 2008 SC 93;
    2007 SLT 982 .... 74, 77, 85, 86, 87, 88, 93, 95, 96
Penny v Spencer Business College 85 So 2d 365 (1956) 334
Peoples State Bank v GE Capital Corp 2007 US App LEXIS 6055
    (5th Cir 2007) 314
Perez v Sharp 32 Cal 2d 711 (1948) 164
Perkins v Entergy Corp 782 So 2d 606 (La 2001) 359, 364, 365
Petition of James Earl of Abercorn, 13 January 1761, Bodlien Library Oxford ... 88
Philadelphia Newspapers v Hepps 475 US 767 (1986) 408
Phillips v Lavery 1962 SLT (Sh Ct) 57 50
Pierre v Allstate Insurance 257 La 471; 242 So 2d 821 (La 1971) 371
Pollard v Photographic Co (1889) LR 40 Ch D 345 .... 399, 402
Pope v Curl (1741) 2 Atk 342 401
Porteous' Trs v Porteous 1991 SLT 129 295
Presbytery of Perth v The Magistrates of Perth (1728) M 10723 72
Preston's Trs v Preston (1844) 22 D 366; (1844) 16 SJ 433 .... 20, 21, 22, 23
Progressive Bank & Trust Co v Vernon A Guidry Contractors Inc
    504 So 2d 997 (1987) 333
Property Selection & Investment Trust Ltd v United Friendly Insurance
    plc 1999 SLT 975 340
Prudhomme v Proctor and Gamble, 800 F Supp 390 (E D La 1992) 404
Prudie v Dryburgh 2000 SC 497 224
Pullar v Gauldie, unreported, Arbroath Sh Ct, 25 August 2004,
    case ref A184/03 74
Pwllbach Colliery Company Ltd v Woodman [1915] AC 634 11
Pyer v Carter (1857) 1 H & N 916 .... 22, 26

Queensborough Land Co v Cazeaux 67 So 641 (La 1915) 37, 55–6, 57, 58

Quick v Murphy Oil Co 643 So 2d 1291 (La App 1994) 378–9, 380

R (on the application of A) v East Sussex County [2003] EWHC 167
(Admin) 406
R v Immigration Officer at Prague Airport, ex parte European Roma
Rights Centre [2004] UKHL 55; [2005] 2 AC 1 247
R & K Bluebonnet, Inc v Patout's of Baton Rouge, Inc 521 So 2d 634
(La Ct App 1 Cir 1988) 58, 59
Ramsay v Brand (1898) 25 R 1212 349
Ramsay v Maclay and Co (1890) 18 R 130 407
Rance v Elvin (1985) 50 P & CR 9 97
Regional Urology, LLC v Price 966 So 2d 1087 (La App 2 Cir 2007) 32
Reid v Mitchell (1885) 12 R 1129 400
Renfrewshire Council v McGinlay 2001 SLT (Sh Ct) 79 .... 344, 349
Republic of India v India S S Co [1998] AC 878 286
Response Handling Ltd v BBC 2008 SLT 51 403
Reynolds v Reynolds 365 So 2d 530 (La App 3d Cir 1978);
388 So 2d 1135 (La 1979) 137–9, 141
Reynolds v Times Newspapers Ltd [2001] 2 AC 127 408–9
Rezulin Products Liability Litigation, In re 361 F Supp 2d 268 (SDNY 2005)   383
Rhoads v Quicksilver Brokers Ltd 801 So 2d 1284 (La Ct App 2001)............ 307
Richard v Gary Matte Builders Inc 944 So 2d 725 (2006) 335
Ricketts v Scothorn 77 NW 365 (Neb 1898)....................................... 296
Robb v Dundee City Council 2002 SC 301 373
Roberts v Benoit 605 So 2d 1032 (La 1991) 361, 362, 364, 367, 371, 375, 376
Robertson Group (Construction) Ltd v Amey-Miller (Edinburgh)
Joint Venture 2005 SCLR 854, affd 2006 SCLR 772 311
Robertson v Anderson 2003 SLT 235 319
Robertson v Keith 1936 SC 29 402
Robinson v Healthworks International 837 So 2d 714 (La Ct App 2003) 315
Rochester Poster Services Ltd v A G Barr plc 1994 SLT (Sh Ct) 2.............. 346
Rockhold v Keaty 256 La 629, 237 So 2d 633 (La 1970) 71
Rogers v Brooks 122 Fed Appx 729 (5th Cir 2004) 305
Romano v Standard Commercial Property Securities Ltd [2008]
CSOH 105; 2008 SLT 859 8
Romer v Evans 517 US 620 (1996) 161, 166
Rosenbloom v Metromedia Inc 403 US 29 (1971) 408
Ross v Bryce 1972 SLT (Sh Ct) 76 396–7
Roxco Ltd v Harris Specialty Chems 85 Fed Appx 375 (5th Cir 2004) 315
RRC Properties v Wenstar Properties 930 So 2d 1233 (La App 2 Cir 2006)   58, 59
Rutherford v Chief Constable for Strathclyde Police 1981 SLT
(Notes) 119 .... 395, 396
Ruxley Electronics Ltd v Forsyth [1996] AC 344........................... 210, 224–5
Ryan v Money 666 So 2d 711 (La 1995) 12

Sabri-Tabrizi v Lothian Health Board 1998 SC 373 374
St Charles Land Trust v Amant 253 La 243 (1968) 139
St Charles Ventures LLC v Albertsons Inc 265 F Supp
    2d 682 (2003) 262, 263, 264, 265
St Martins Property Corp Ltd v Sir Robert McAlpine & Son Ltd
    [1994] 1 AC 85 225
Sanders v Zeagler 686 So 2d 819 (La 1997) 240
Schenk v Capri Construction Co 194 So 2d 378 (1967) 258
Schulman v Whitaker 115 LA 628; 39 So 737 (1905) 404
Schwegmann v Schwegmann 441 So 2d 316 (La App 5th Cir 1983) 159
Scott v Howard (1881) 8R (HL) 59 48
Scott v Morrison 1979 SLT (Notes) 65 301
Scott & Sons v Del Sel 1923 SC (HL) 37 273
Secretary of State for Work and Pensions v M [2006] 2 FLR 56 166
Serv Steel & Pipe v Guinn's Trailer Sales, Inc 850 So 2d 902
    (La Ct App 2003) 315
Sharp v Thomson 1995 SC 455 135
Shearer v Peddie (1899) 1F 1201 .... 22, 24, 26
Shelly v Kraemer 334 US 1 (1948) 57
Shetland Islands Council v BP Petroleum Development Ltd 1990 SLT 82 ... 345
Shilliday v Smith 1998 SC 725 342
Showboat Star Partnership v Slaughter 789 So 2d 554 (La 2001) 314
Shreveport Plaza, LLC v Dollar Tree Stores, Inc 196 Fed Appx 320
    (5th Cir 2006) 307, 308, 315
Sichi v Biagi 1946 SN 66 .... 301, 311
Sickinger v Board of Directors of Public Schools for Parish of Orleans
    147 La 479, 85 So 212 (1920) 253, 256
Simon v Arnold 727 So 2d 699 (La 1999) 332, 334
Simons v Stewart 303 So 2d 236 (La App 2d Cir 1974) 71
Sinclair v Magistrates of Dysart (1779) Mor 14,519, affd (1780) 2 Pat 554 8
Singer v Hara 522 P 2d 1187 (Court of Appeals of Washington 1974) 160
Skarpass v Skarpass 1993 SLT 343 151
Slocum v Sears Rowbuck and Co 542 So 2d 777 (La App 3d Cir 1989) 404
Smith v Bank of Scotland 1997 SC (HL) 111 247
Smith v Oliver 1911 SC 103 .... 292, 313
Smith v Riddell (1886) 14 R 95 267–8
Smith v Stuart 2004 SLT (Sh Ct) 2 311
Smith v Watson 1982 SLT 359 150
Smiths Gore v Reilly 2003 SLT (Sh Ct) 15 347
Soileau v ABC Insurance Co 844 So 2d 108 (2002), writ denied
    855 So 2d 313 (2003) 329
Spear v Rowlett (1924) 43 NZLR 801 97
Stachlinv Destrehan 2 La Ann 1019; 1847 WL 3298 (La 1847) 399
Starco Meats, Inc v Bryan Foods, Inc 2003 US Dist LEXIS 4452 (D La 2003) 305
State v Golden 26 So 2d 837 (1946) 193

State in Interest of Goodwin In re 39 So 2d 731 (La 1949) 193
Stelly v Montgomery 347 So 2d 1145 (Sup Ct La 1977) 154
Stephenson v Smith 337 So 2d 570 (1976) 335
Stevens v Yorkhill [2006] CSOH 143 396
Sticker v Southern Bell Telephone & Telegraph Co 101 So 2d 476 (La 1958) ... 15
Stokes v Georgia-Pacific Corp 894 F 2d 764 (5th Cir 1990) 317
Stone v MacDonald 1979 SC 363; 1979 SLT 288............................. 301, 311
Stovin v Wise [1996] AC 923 389
Strathclyde Joint Police Board v The Elderslie Estates Ltd 2001 SLT
    (Lands Tr) 2 49
Strathclyde Regional Council v Persimmon Homes (Scotland) Ltd
    1996 SLT 176... 295
Succession Adams (2002) 816 So 2d 988 123
Succession of Bacot 502 So 2d 1118 (La App 4th Cir 1987) 167
Succession of Caraway (1994) 639 So 2d 415 123
Succession of Franklin 7 La Ann 395, 413-414 (1852)............................ 53
Succession of Mullin v Mullin (1994) 631 So 2d 647 123
Suffield v Brown (1864) 4 De GJ & Sm 185.. 26
Suire v Lafayette City-Parish Consol Govt 907 So 2d 37 (La 2005) 305
Summers v Vermilion Parish Police Jury 784 So 2d 15 (La 2001) 16
Superior Oil Company v Transco Energy Company 616 F Supp 98
    (1985).. 257, 259
Swan v Muirkirk Iron Co (1850) 12 D 622; 22 Sc Jur 205 81
Swan v Sinclair [1925] AC 227 .... 87, 89

Tailors of Aberdeen see Corporation of Tailors of Aberdeen
Tassin v State Farm Insurance Co 692 So 2d 604 (La App 1997) 363
Tay Salmon Fisheries Co Ltd v Speedie 1929 SC 593 .... 266–7, 269
Taylor v Caldwell (1863) 3 B & S 826 .... 250, 266, 279
T Boland and Co Ltd v Dundas's Trs 1975 SLT (Notes) 80 87
Teacher v Calder (1899) 1 F (HL) 39 349
Tennant v Napier Smith's Trs (1888) 25 R 671 82
Texas General Petroleum Corp v Brown 408 So 2d 288 (1981) 334
The Chaptour of Glasgow v the Laird of Cesfurde, 29 July 1563, Balfour,
    Practicks 146 cvii 250
Theobald v Ry Passengers Assurance Co (1854) 15 Jur 583 216
Thibodeaux v Stonebridge LLC 873 So 2d 755 (La 2004) 364
Thomas v Desire Community Housing Corp 773 So 2d 755 (La App
    4th Cir 2000) 210, 241
Tilley v Lowery 511 So 2d 1245 (La App 2d Cir 1987) 73, 95
Tippecanoe Associates II v Kimco Lafayette 671, Inc 811 N E 2d 438
    (Ind Ct App 2004)... 60
Toepfor v Thionville 299 So 2d 415 (1974) 336
Tom Super Printing Supplies Ltd v South Lanarkshire Council
    1999 GWD 31-1496 314

Torrejon v Mobil Oil Co 876 So 2d 877 (La App 4 Cir) 381
Toston v Pardon 874 So 2d 791 (La 2004) 364, 368–9
Touchet v Hampton 950 So 2d 895 (La App 3rd Cir 2/7/07) 391
Trade Development Bank Ltd v Warriner and Mason (Scotland) Ltd
    1980 SC 74... 340
Trans Barwil Agencies UK Ltd v John S Braid & Co Ltd 1989 SLT 73 340
Transco plc v Glasgow City Council 2005 SLT 958 344
Travelers Insurance Co v Badine Land Limited Inc 1994 WL 577482
    (La 1994) 20
Trevalion v Blanche 1919 SC 617 266
Trigg v Pennington Oil Co 835 So 2d 845 (La Ct App 2002) 315
Tsakiroglou & Co v Noble Thorl [1962] AC 93 260

Underwood v Gulf Refining Co of Louisiana 128 La 968 (1911) 213
Union Totaliser Co Ltd v Scott 1951 SLT (Notes) 5.............................. 250
Uniroyal Ltd v Miller & Co Ltd 1985 SLT 101 311
United States v Burglass 172 F 2d 960 (5th Cir 1949) 138
United States v Craft 535 US 274 (2002) 36
US Bancorp Equipment Finance Inc v Loews Express LLC (E D La,
    9 January 2008) 257, 258
U-Serve Petroleum and Investments, Inc v Cambre 486 So 2d 821
    (La App 1 Cir 1986) 63

Varney v Burgh of Lanark 1974 SC 245 .... 340, 341, 344
Veazey v Elmwood Plantation Associates Ltd 650 So 2d 712 (La 11/30/94) ... 391
Villa v Derouen 614 So 2d 714 (La App 3rd Cir 1993) 401
Vines v Orchard Hills Inc 181 Conn 501, 435 A 2d 1022 (1980)................. 269
Vinson v Graves 16 La Ann 162 (1861).. 252
Viterbo v Friedlander 120 US 707 7 S Ct 962, 30 L Ed 776 (1887) 252, 263
Vodanovich v A P Green Industries Inc 869 So 2d 930 (La App 4th Cir 2004)   381

Wagner v Alford 741 So 2d 884, 888 (La App 3 Cir 1999) 64, 65
Wainwright v Home Office [2004] 2 AC 406 .... 389, 403
Wainwright v UK (2007) 44 EHRR 40 403
Walker v Milne (1823) 2 S 379 .... 292, 293
Walker v Scottish & Newcastle Breweries Ltd 1970 SLT (Sh Ct) 21 373
Waltons Stores (Interstate) Ltd v Maher (1988) 164 CLR 387 286
Ward v Scotrail 1991 SC 255 395–6
Wardlaw v Bonnington Castings 1956 SC (HL) 26;
    [1956] AC 613 .... 356, 364, 366, 367, 377, 379
Water Craft Management LLC v Mercury Marine 361 F Supp ....
    2d 518 (D La 2004) 306
Watkins v Secretary of State for the Home Department [2006] 2 AC 395 398
Watson v Shankland (1871) 10 M 142 273
Watson v Swift & Co's Judicial Factor 1986 SLT 217 224

Watts v Morrow [1991] 1 WLR 1421 .... 223, 225, 226
Wayling v Jones [1995] 2 FLR 1029 287
"We the People" Paralegal Services v Watley 766 So 2d 744 (2000) 333, 335
Webster & Co v Cramond Iron Co (1875) 2 R 752) 223
Weigand v Asplundh Tree Experts 577 So 2d 125 (La 1991) 16
Weymss v Bayne, Moyes and Bayne (1773) M 2999 73
Wheeldon v Burrows (1879) 12 Ch D 31 .... 26, 27
White v Durrwachter 431 So 2d 65 (La 1983) 24
White v Johns-Manville Sales Corp 416 So 2d 327 (La App 1982) 377
White v Wemyss (1700) Mor 10881 21
Whitinsville Plaza, Inc v Kotseas 390 N E 2d 243 (Mass 1979) 60
Wick Harbour Trs v The Admiralty 1921 2 SLT 109 301
Wilkie v Scott (1688) M 11189; Wilky v Scot, 28 June 1688,
      Harcase 220 case no 780 .... 78, 83
Wilkinson v Downton [1897] 2 QB 57 398
Williams v Wiggins 641 So 2d 1068 (La 1994) 24
Williams, In re: Williams v Williams [1897] 2 Ch 12 132
Williamson and Anderson v Lows (1693) 4 BS 66 78
Willis v Ventrella 674 So 2d 991 (La 1996); noted [1997] 5 RLR 219 328
Woodard v Felts 573 So 2d 1312 (La Ct App 2d Cir 1991) 306
Woolwich Building Society v Inland Revenue Commissioners [1993] AC 70... 354
Wright v Stoddard International plc [2007] CSOH 173; 2008 Rep LR 37 382
WWF World Wide Fund for Nature v World Wrestling Federation
      Entertainment Inc (No 2) [2007] EWCA Civ 286; [2008] 1 WLR 445;
      [2008] 1 All ER 74 349

X v BBC 2005 SLT 796 .... 402, 405

Yeaman v Crawford (1770) Mor 14537 .... 42, 61
Young v Ford Motor Co Inc 595 So 2d 1123 (La 1992) 229, 240–1

Zablocki v Redhail 434 US 374 (1978) 166

1 Praedial Servitudes

*Kenneth G C Reid**

A. PATTERNS OF SIMILARITY AND DIFFERENCE
(1) Introduction
(2) Bell's *Principles* and the Louisiana Civil Code
(3) Similarities
(4) A French connection?
(5) Differences
(6) Approaching the micro-topics
B. ACCESSORY RIGHTS
(1) Two cases about parking
(2) Doctrinal basis
(3) The consequences of doctrinal choice
C. SERVITUDES CREATED BY PRIOR USE
(1) Introduction
(2) Louisiana: a reception from France
(3) Scotland: a false start and a reception from England
(4) Comparison
(5) *Destination*: rejection and reinvention
D. SOME COMPARATIVE CONCLUSIONS

A. PATTERNS OF SIMILARITY AND DIFFERENCE

(1) Introduction

There is much that is similar or the same in the law of praedial[1] servitudes in Scotland and Louisiana, but there are also significant points of difference. These rather general matters are the subject of part A of this chapter, which seeks to give an overview of the law and to set that law in some kind of historical context. To be properly useful, however, a comparison must also

---

* I am grateful to Professor John Lovett for his insightful comments and for saving me from error in relation to the law of Louisiana.

1 The normal spelling in Scotland is "praedial", reflecting its derivation from the Latin word, *praedium*, and that spelling is adopted in this chapter. The Scottish Institutional writer, Erskine, however, gives the word as "predial", the spelling which is used in Louisiana: see Erskine, *Inst* 2.9.5.

descend to the particular; and while there are many aspects of servitudes where a micro-comparison between the laws of Scotland and Louisiana would yield interesting results, there seems a special value in exploring areas where the two systems have produced different solutions to similar problems. Elsewhere in this work Roderick Paisley contributes a study of the extinction of servitudes by prescription. In the present chapter my micro-topic is gap-filling. How is the law to provide where parties have failed to provide for themselves? Even this subject is quite a large one and it will only be possible to cover two specific aspects. One is the extent to which a servitude carries with it rights not mentioned in the juridical act which brought the servitude into being. The other is the circumstances under which the law will take the radical step of creating a servitude which the parties themselves have done nothing to bring about. These topics are explored in parts B and C respectively. Finally, in part D an attempt is made to draw comparative conclusions of a more general nature.

(2) Bell's *Principles* and the Louisiana Civil Code

There is no Scottish civil code, of course. But in 1830, in the wake of the *Code Napoléon* and its imitations in Louisiana and elsewhere, George Joseph Bell (1770-1843) attempted to reduce the law of Scotland to some 2,435 numbered articles. The result, published as the *Principles of the Law of Scotland*, was originally intended as a text for students at Edinburgh University, where Bell had held the chair of Scots Law since 1822.[2] In its layout, however, and in its dogmatic and generally non-discursive style, it can often appear as a kind of proto-code – as an early version of the civil code which Scotland never had.[3] Indeed so successful was Bell's attempt at systematisation and exposition that, in the course of time, the student text was admitted to the small canon of writings which are considered in Scotland to have the status of "Institutional".[4]

Bell was evidently known in Louisiana. The *Principles of the Law of*

---

2 This was the 2nd edition. A previous edition, published in 1829, was little more than a draft, running to only 896 articles. Bell produced a further two editions, the last (4th) appearing in 1839. It is this edition which is used in this chapter. The book had a long afterlife in the hands of editors who sought to keep the text up-to-date. The final (10th) edition, by William Guthrie, appeared as late as 1899. In the 1st edition, the title is given as *Principles of the Law of Scotland, for the use of students in the University of Edinburgh*, but the reference to university students was dropped in the second and subsequent editions.

3 F H Lawson comments that Bell's *Principles* "made a code unnecessary": see *A Common Lawyer looks at the Civil Law* (1953) 50 n 20.

4 On Institutional writers, see, e.g., J W G Blackie, "Stair's later reputation as a jurist", in D M Walker (ed), *Stair Tercentenary Studies* (Stair Society vol 33, 1981) 207.

Scotland was cited by Louisiana courts in 1841 and again in 1856, while another of Bell's works, the *Commentaries on the Law of Scotland and on the Principles of Mercantile Jurisprudence*, was cited on nine occasions during the nineteenth century, the first as early as 1832.[5] References to Bell also appeared in American treatises, most notably those by James Kent and Joseph Story,[6] although in the latter case at least this was no doubt partly because, on 12 December 1838, Bell sent Storey a copy of two of his books, including the third edition of the *Principles*.[7] It would not be surprising if it was through treatises like these that Louisiana practitioners were first introduced to Bell.

Bell's *Principles* and Louisiana's Civil Code provide a convenient starting point for a general comparison of the law of praedial servitudes.[8] Both comprise short, aphoristic statements of the law; each has its intellectual origins in the first quarter of the nineteenth century; and both show the influence of French law and French legal thinking. Pleasingly, they are cited together in the brief treatment of easements given in Chancellor Kent's *Commentaries on American Law* as part of a rather short list which also includes two texts from the *Digest* of Justinian, Pothier, and the contemporary Dutch jurist, Johannes van der Linden (1756-1835).[9] In Louisiana the first Code – the modestly-named "Digest of the Civil Laws now in force in the Territory of Orleans" – was promulgated in 1808, some twenty years before Bell's *Principles*, and was soon replaced by the Civil Code of 1825. The current Civil Code dates from

5 *Daquin v Coiron* 3 La 404 (La 1832); *Duke of Richmond v Milne* 17 La 312 (La 1841); *Hermann v NO and C Ry* 11 La Ann 5 (La 1856). In addition, both of Bell's works were cited frequently by the US Supreme Court in the course of the century: see R H Helmholz, "Scots law in the New World", in H L MacQueen (ed), *Miscellany Five* (Stair Society vol 52, 2006) 169 at 175-176.

6 K H Nadelmann, "Joseph Story and George Joseph Bell" 1959 JR 31. Alan Watson has concluded that Kent's, sometimes copious, citation of foreign law was usually decorative: see "Chancellor Kent's use of foreign law", in M Reimann (ed), *The Reception of Continental Ideas in the Common Law World 1820-1920* (1993) 45.

7 In the covering letter Bell explained, perhaps rather too modestly, that "You will, of course, receive them as they were intended, not for the perusal of the masters in jurisprudence, but for the initiation of students". See W W Story (ed), *Life and Letters of Joseph Story* vol 2 (1851) 302. Story's reply, which is reprinted in Nadelmann (n 6) at 38, explains that, as he has previously made extensive use of Bell's *Commentaries*, "though I have not a personal acquaintance with you, yet I feel that you are among my most familiar friends".

8 Bell, *Prin* §§ 979-1015; La Civ Code arts 646-774. For a comparison between praedial servitudes in Scotland and in another mixed jurisdiction, South Africa, see W M Gordon and M J de Waal, "Servitudes and real burdens", in Zimmermann, Visser and Reid, *Mixed Legal Systems* (2004) 735.

9 6th edn (1848) vol 3 436 note b. The reference to the Louisiana Civil Code (arts 734-738) is of course to the Code of 1825. The *Commentaries* were first published in 1826-1830. I used the 6th edition of 1848 in the hope that this would pick up the final (4th) edition of Bell's *Principles* (1839), but the page numbers used indicates a reference to the 3rd edition (1833). As we know that Bell sent the 3rd edition to Joseph Story in 1838 (see n 7 above), it may be conjectured that he sent a copy to Kent at the same time.

1870 but was substantially amended in respect of servitudes in 1977. This is the text which is used for the comparison which follows.

(3) Similarities

The similarities disclosed by a comparison of Bell's work with the Louisiana Civil Code of 1870 (as amended) are striking. The treatment in the Louisiana Code opens with a definition:[10] "A predial servitude is a charge on a servient estate for the benefit of a dominant estate". Likewise, Bell's definition begins: "Servitude is a burden on land or houses, imposed by agreement – express or implied – in favour of the owners of other tenements".[11] Praedial servitudes in both jurisdictions are classified as natural, legal or conventional.[12] Conventional servitudes are created by juridical act (including, in Louisiana, by destination) or by acquisitive prescription.[13] Once created they transmit with the dominant tenement or estate without further mention.[14] A servitude must confer benefit on the dominant tenement, and not merely on the person who happens to own or occupy for the time being.[15] The obligation imposed on the burdened owner is passive in nature – an obligation merely "to abstain from doing something on his estate or to permit something to be done on it".[16] Servitudes are extinguished by confusion,[17] by renunciation,[18] and by non-use for the years of extinctive prescription.[19]

Similarity of thought is sometimes accompanied by similarity of language. For example, the first sentence of article 748 of the Louisiana Civil Code is:

> The owner of the servient estate may do nothing to diminish or make more inconvenient the use of the servitude.

10 La Civ Code art 646.
11 Bell, *Prin* § 979.
12 La Civ Code art 654; Bell, *Prin* § 979.
13 La Civ Code art 654; Bell, *Prin* § 991. For servitudes by destination, see C.(2) below.
14 La Civ Code art 650; Bell, *Prin* § 979. In Louisiana "estate" is used instead of "tenement". For Scotland, the Title Conditions (Scotland) Act 2003 uses "benefited property" for dominant tenement, and "burdened property" for servient tenement, and in practice the two sets of terms are used interchangeably.
15 La Civ Code art 647; Bell, *Prin* § 986.
16 La Civ Code art 651. Bell's formulation is similar (*Prin* § 979): the servient owner "must submit to certain uses to be exercised by the owner of the other or dominant tenement; or must suffer restraint in his own use and occupation of their property". See also § 984 ("they are passive merely, not active").
17 La Civ Code art 765; Bell, *Prin* § 997.
18 La Civ Code art 771; Bell, *Prin* § 998.
19 La Civ Code art 753; Bell, *Prin* § 999. The period is ten years in Louisiana, but twenty in Scotland: see Prescription and Limitation (Scotland) Act 1973 s 8. A further, if modern, parallel is that each jurisdiction is served by an excellent full-length monograph: A N Yiannopolous, *Predial Servitudes*, 3rd edn (2004) (Louisiana); D J Cusine and R R M Paisley, *Servitudes and Rights of Way* (1998) (Scotland).

In § 988 of the *Principles* Bell renders the same idea in almost the same words:

> The owner of the servient tenement can do nothing to diminish the use or convenience of the servitude to the owner of the dominant.[20]

The language is so close as to argue for a common source. So far as Louisiana is concerned, the wording of the article is largely unchanged from the Digest of 1808.[21] And both the Digest and the 1825 Code also give the article in French:

> Le propriétaire du fonds débiteur de la servitude, ne peut rien faire qui tende à en diminuer l'usage, ou à la rendre plus incommode.

As is usually the case with servitudes, this is a direct transcription from the French *Code civil*.[22] So far as I am aware, it has not previously been suggested that, in writing his *Principles*, Bell borrowed from the French Code. Yet the closeness of the language used in this and some other articles[23] suggests that the topic is at least worthy of further investigation.[24]

(4) A French connection?

Although the respective French and Spanish contributions to the Louisiana Civil Code remain contested even today,[25] in the area of praedial servitudes the influence of French law, in substance as well as in language, is both obvious and inescapable. That influence, already abundantly present in the 1808 Digest and the Civil Code of 1825, has survived both the remaking of the Code in 1870, and even the major changes to the articles on servitudes which were introduced by amendment in 1977.

To some extent there are Scottish parallels. If Bell was influenced by the *Code civil*, as suggested above, he was also influenced by the writings of

---

20 This is how the passage appears in both the 3rd and 4th editions. It is slightly different in the earlier editions. For example the equivalent provision in the 1st edition (§ 249) reads: "The owner of the servient tenement can do nothing to diminish the use or convenience of the owner of the dominant".

21 La Digest 1808 art 64 at 140: "The proprietor of the estate which owes the service, can do nothing tending to diminish its use, or to make it more inconvenient". For later versions, see: Civ Code 1825 art 773; Civ Code 1870 (as originally enacted) art 777.

22 *Code civil* art 701.

23 E.g. compare the opening sentence of Bell, *Prin* § 965 with *Code civil* art 697 and La Civ Code art 744.

24 In theory it is possible that Bell borrowed from the Louisiana Civil Code rather than, directly, from the *Code civil*. But that would be surprising.

25 See most recently V V Palmer, "The French connection and the Spanish perception: historical debates and contemporary evaluation of French influence on Louisiana civil law" (2003) 63 La LR 1067 (= V V Palmer, *The Louisiana Civilian Experience* (2005) 51).

French jurists, both from amongst his contemporaries – such as Jean-Marie Pardessus, the author of the influential *Traité des servitudes*, first published in 1806 and running to numerous subsequent editions – and also from before the Revolution.[26] When Charles Sumner visited Edinburgh in 1838, Bell claimed to have been the first person to import a copy of Pothier to Scotland.[27] Indeed on at least one occasion, Bell's enthusiasm for matters French seems to have got the better of him. In a passage which first appeared in the third edition of the *Principles*, in 1833, he wrote that:[28]

> Another distinction has been made between servitudes, of CONTINUOUS or INTERRUPTED use; and again between servitudes MANIFEST or NOT MANIFEST: And both those distinctions may be of importance in the question of the constitution or extinction of servitudes.

These, of course, are the distinctions made in the *Code civil* between servitudes which are continuous and discontinuous, and those which are apparent and non-apparent.[29] Both were adopted by the Louisiana Civil Code, although the former was dropped as part of the 1977 revision.[30] In French law they affect the constitution of servitudes. In particular, a servitude can be constituted by prescription only if it is both continuous and apparent.[31] Until 1977 the law in Louisiana was the same, although today it is no longer required that the servitude be continuous.[32] For Scotland, Bell offers the perplexing thought that "those distinctions *may* be of importance in the question of the constitution or extinction of servitudes" but offers no evidence for this view in the rest of his treatment of servitudes. The truth is that the distinctions in question formed no part of Scots law before Bell was writing, and formed almost no part thereafter.[33] The importation from French law was stillborn.

Naturally, it should not be supposed that Bell used French sources in the same way as Moreau Lislet, a few years earlier, in his preparation of the Digest of 1808 and the Civil Code of 1825. The oldest reported case on

---

26 G Gorla, "Bell, one of the founding fathers of the 'common and comparative law of Europe' during the nineteenth century" 1982 JR 121. Bell also read Italian: see Gorla n 21.

27 Letter from Sumner to Joseph Story dated 7 October 1838, quoted in Nadelmann (n 6) at 37. If the claim is correct, it is surprising.

28 Bell, *Prin* § 983. The quotation is from the 4th edition, which differs in some trivial respects from the same passage in the 3rd edition.

29 *Code civil* arts 688, 689.

30 LA Digest 1808 arts 51 ("perpetual" and "interrupted"), 52; Civ Code 1825 arts 723, 724; Civ Code 1870 (as enacted) arts 727, 728; Civ Code 1870 (as revised) art 707.

31 *Code civil* art 690.

32 La Civ Code art 742.

33 When the distinctions reappeared, fleetingly, later in the century, they did so in the context of implied servitudes. See C.(4) below.

servitudes in Scotland dates from 1583,[34] and the essentials of the law had been settled long before the time when Bell was writing. If there is much in Bell's treatment of servitudes which is similar to the law of France, and hence of Louisiana, this owes more to development from shared Civil Law sources than to direct importation from French law. No doubt in places where the law in France was the same or similar to the law in Scotland, the elegant and succinct articles of the *Code civil* could be raided for the apt phrase and for state-of-the-art legal thinking. A proto-code could borrow from a real one. But where the law was different, it was usually left alone. For example, unlike Moreau Lislet, or indeed Gale in the case of England, Bell made no attempt to adopt the doctrine of *destination du père de famille*. We return to this topic later in the chapter.[35]

(5) Differences

If there is much that is similar in the law of praedial servitudes in Scotland and Louisiana, there are also important differences. On the whole these arise because Scotland developed peculiarities which have no counterpart in other Civilian systems. Three in particular seem worthy of mention.[36]

The first concerns contractual freedom. Servitudes everywhere, of course, are restricted as to content, and in both Scotland and Louisiana these restrictions run along generally familiar lines: a servitude must not impose a positive obligation (i.e. be *in faciendo*), or prohibit the alienation of land, or act as an unlawful restraint on commerce, or generally be contrary to public policy.[37] But Scotland goes much further. The law allows a bare dozen or so "known" servitudes, and in practice is unwilling to add to this list even if the right in question conforms in all respects to the standard requirements of a servitude. As Bell notes, while "[m]any servitudes are enumerated at great length in the books of the civilians", "[o]ur servitudes are few and well known".[38]

---

34 *Laird of Knockdolian v Tenants of Parthick* (1583) Mor 14,540.
35 At C. below.
36 Another difference which is worth mentioning is that La Civ Code arts 659-696 have an expansive view of legal servitudes which has no parallel in the law of Scotland. Bell, *Prin* § 979 observed that legal servitudes "are more properly police regulations for public safety in cities". They are virtually absent from Scots law. In cases where Louisiana uses the concept, Scotland would have recourse to doctrines such as nuisance, trespass, encroachment, common interest, and (in the case of forced passage) on rights intrinsic to ownership.
37 Yiannopoulos, *Predial Servitudes* (n 19) §§ 105-111; Cusine & Paisley, *Servitudes and Rights of Way* (n 19) para 2.01. For an insightful comparison, see J A Lovett, "Creating and controlling private land use restrictions in Scotland and Louisiana: a comparative mixed jurisdiction analysis" 2008 Stellenbosch L Rev 231.
38 Bell, *Prin* § 1000.

In Scotland, servitudes are "limited to such uses or restraints as are well established and defined, leaving others as mere personal agreements".[39] The reason is the publicity principle. Because real rights affect third parties, their constitution is thought to require publicity, and, in the case of land, publicity tends to mean registration. Although land registration in Scotland has a long history, dating back to 1617, its original purpose was to publicise sasine – hence the name of the register, the Register of Sasines. Servitudes, being non-feudal in character, were constituted without sasine. As a result, they escaped any requirement of registration until as recently as 2004 (although they were often registered in practice).[40] In the absence of adequate publicity, third parties were protected by restricting the types of servitudes which were available. As Bell notes:[41]

> What shall be deemed servitudes of a regular and definite kind is a secondary question, as to which the only description that can be given seems to be, that it shall be such a use or restraint as by law or custom is known to be likely and incident to the property in question, and to which the attention of a prudent purchaser will, in the circumstances, naturally be called.

The protection of the "prudent purchaser" is taken seriously.[42] When the House of Lords decided in 2007 that Scotland had a servitude of parking,[43] this was the first new servitude to be allowed for more than 200 years.[44] Since then the Court of Session has rejected as a servitude a right to place a sign on a neighbour's wall, and reaffirmed the principle that only "known" servitudes will be allowed.[45] That principle was disapplied by statute for servitudes created by registration after 28 November 2004,[46] but otherwise remains very much in place.

The modest pace of legal development in Scotland was, however, only partly due to a desire to protect innocent acquirers. Another important factor was that law and practice tended to by-pass servitudes altogether by devel-

---

39 Bell, *Prin* § 979. The passages quoted from §§ 979 and 1000 do not appear until the 3rd edition, prompting the question of how much the idea of a fixed list of servitudes was an invention of Bell.
40 By s 75 of the Title Conditions (Scotland) Act 2003 all servitudes other than pipeline servitudes require to be registered in the Land Register or Register of Sasines.
41 Bell, *Prin* § 979 (note).
42 For a list of the "known" servitudes in Scots law, see Cusine & Paisley, *Servitudes and Rights of Way* (n 19) ch 3.
43 *Moncrieff v Jamieson* [2007] UKHL 42, 2008 SC (HL) 1.
44 The most recent previous servitude was the servitude of bleaching, recognised in *Sinclair v Magistrates of Dysart* (1779) Mor 14,519, affd (1780) 2 Pat 554.
45 *Romano v Standard Commercial Property Securities Ltd* [2008] CSOH 105, 2008 SLT 859. For a commentary, see W M Gordon, "The struggle for recognition of new servitudes" (2009) 13 EdinLR 139. See also *Compugraphics International Ltd v Nikolic* [2009] CSOH 54.
46 Title Conditions (Scotland) Act 2003 s 76.

oping a dynamic new device which could not only do the work of negative servitudes – and do it better – but which also allowed what servitudes did not allow, the imposition of a positive obligation (such as an obligation of maintenance). An account of some aspects of this new device, the real burden, will be found in another chapter of this book.[47] Here it seems only necessary to say that it has much in common with the building restriction of Louisiana law,[48] and that, because it is constituted by registration, it is not confined to a narrow range of known types. So successful was the real burden that negative servitudes fell into decline and were used with relative infrequency. The Title Conditions (Scotland) Act 2003 completed the process by converting all existing negative servitudes into real burdens, and by abolishing the category of negative servitudes altogether.[49] Thus while servitudes remain the only means of giving an owner the right to do something on the land of a neighbour, in Scotland such positive (or affirmative) servitudes are no longer accompanied by negative servitudes.[50] That is a second major respect in which the law of Scotland is different from the law of Louisiana. The difference, however, is more of form than of substance: through real burdens, it has been possible to produce a flexible vehicle for tasks which are performed in Louisiana (as previously in Scotland) by negative servitudes.

The final difference is also a modern change. In 1970 Scotland, borrowing an idea from England from earlier in the century, passed legislation to allow real burdens to be varied or discharged by a special court known as the Lands Tribunal for Scotland;[51] and, unlike in England, the Scottish legislation extended to servitudes. As a result, it is possible for the owner of the servient tenement to apply to have a servitude discharged outright or, more commonly, varied in some respect. In reaching a decision the Tribunal is to have regard to a number of statutory grounds.[52] The typical application is for variation of the route of a servitude of way, and experience shows that it is usually granted, even where the new route is less convenient for the servitude holder.[53] Although

---

47 See ch 2 infra. For the history of the development of the real burden, see K G C Reid, *The Law of Property in Scotland* (1996) paras 376-385.

48 Now codified as La Civ Code arts 775-783. For a comparison, see Lovett (n 37) at 236-242.

49 Title Conditions (Scotland) Act 2003 ss 79, 80.

50 For the terminology of "affirmative" and "negative" servitudes, see La Civ Code art 706. In Scotland the usual terminology is "positive" and "negative".

51 The original legislation was the Conveyancing and Feudal Reform (Scotland) Act 1970 ss 1, 2. It has now been replaced by the Title Conditions (Scotland) Act 2003 ss 90-104. For an account of the origins of the legislation, see W M Gordon, *Roman Law, Scots Law and Legal History: Selected Essays* (Edinburgh Studies in Law vol 4, 2007) ch 18.

52 Title Conditions (Scotland) Act 2003 ss 98, 100.

53 For recent examples, see *George Wimpey East Scotland Ltd v Fleming* 2006 SLT (Lands Tr) 27 and 59; *Graham v Parker* 2007 GWD 30-524.

the legislation makes provision for compensation,[54] in practice it is rarely awarded. The significance of this "radical experiment with complete and unfettered judicial intervention" has been the subject of insightful comment from John Lovett, writing from the perspective of Louisiana.[55]

(6) Approaching the micro-topics

I now pass from the general to the specific. The rest of this chapter is an exploration of the micro-topics mentioned earlier: implied accessory rights and implied servitudes. In developing a comparison my initial concern is with questions of technique. Taking as a given – as both jurisdictions seem to have done – that there is a gap which needs to be filled, how, in each case, has the law gone about filling it? And what consequences flow from the techniques employed? Behind these questions of doctrine lie larger questions: about roots which are sometimes shared and sometimes not, about the differences between a system which is codified (Louisiana) and a system where new law is developed largely by the courts (Scotland), and about the significance, or lack of significance, of the fact that both systems are mixed jurisdictions.

B. ACCESSORY RIGHTS

(1) Two cases about parking

Sometimes a servitude is awarded accessory rights which were not provided for in the juridical act by which the servitude was created.[56] The difficulty is to know when and why.

On 3 October 2007 the Louisiana Court of Appeal decided, in *Garner v Holley*,[57] that a servitude of passage did not carry with it a right to park vehicles. Exactly a fortnight later, on 17 October 2007, the House of Lords reached the opposite decision in the Scottish case of *Moncrieff v Jamieson*.[58] The reasoning in the two cases is intriguingly different. For the Louisiana court, the result was beyond argument:[59]

---

54 Title Conditions (Scotland) Act s 90(6), (7).

55 J A Lovett, "A new way: servitude relocation in Scotland and Louisiana" (2005) 9 EdinLR 352 at 389-392.

56 This supposes that the servitude is simply silent on the point. Where it makes specific and contrary provision, there can of course be no question of implying accessory rights. See *McGuire v Central Louisiana Electric Company Inc* 337 So 2d 1070 (La 1976).

57 968 So 2d 234 (La 2007).

58 [2007] UKHL 42, 2008 SC (HL) 1.

59 At 239 per Brown CJ. One might have expected a reference to La Civ Code art 743 (discussed below) and not just to art 750.

> A servitude of passage is for the benefit of a dominant estate whereby persons or vehicles are *permitted to pass through* a servient estate. LA CC art 750 (emphasis added). This statute is unambiguous and we find no reason to expand it to allow vehicles to park on, and not just pass through, a servient estate.

In similar vein, an earlier case from Louisiana dismissed the suggestion that a right of passage might include a right to "park" boats by the side of a lake.[60] The court in *Moncrieff v Jamieson* was more accommodating. In principle, the House of Lords thought, a servitude can include ancillary rights not provided for by the parties, and in the circumstances of the present case such rights must extend to a right of parking.

If the contrast is fascinating, it is also misleading. In *Moncrieff* the land fell so steeply that it was impossible to take a vehicle from the road, over which the servitude was exercisable, on to the dominant land and to the house on that land. Unless parking was allowed on the road, it would be necessary, after depositing luggage and passengers near the house, to turn round and park some distance away at the top of a steep hill. In these unusual circumstances, the House of Lords concluded, not without hesitation, that in the absence of a right to park "the proprietor's right of vehicular access would effectively be defeated".[61] By contrast, the vehicles in *Garner* could be parked elsewhere. It should not be supposed, therefore, that accessory rights are more easily established in Scotland than in Louisiana. On the contrary, the doctrinal basis identified for such rights in Louisiana seems less limiting and more flexible than its counterpart in Scotland.

(2) Doctrinal basis

Until the decision in *Moncrieff v Jamieson* there could not be said to be any settled doctrinal basis for accessory rights in Scots law, although the existence of such rights was accepted in principle.[62] In *Moncrieff* the vacuum was filled by the simple expedient of adopting the law of England, which rested on two decisions from the early years of the twentieth century.[63] Not everyone will regard the justification by Lord Neuberger, one of the three English members of the court of five judges, as adequate:[64]

---

60 *Irland v Barron* 230 So 2d 880 (La 1970).

61 2008 SC (HL) 1 at para 34 per Lord Hope.

62 J Rankine, *The Law of Landownership in Scotland*, 4th edn (1909) 425; Cusine & Paisley, *Servitudes and Rights of Way* (n 19) paras 12.124-12.127; W M Gordon, *Scottish Law Land*, 2nd edn (1999) para 24-60.

63 *Jones v Pritchard* [1908] 1 Ch 630; *Pwllbach Colliery Company Ltd v Woodman* [1915] AC 634.

64 Para 111.

It would be surprising if that were not the law in Scotland. It accords with good sense, and it is a point on which one would not expect Scots and English law to differ. While some aspects of the juridical nature, origin and incidents of servitudes in Scotland are different from those of easements in England and Wales, there are many aspects of similarity, as can be appreciated even from a quick perusal both of Cusine and Paisley and of Gale on *Easements* (17th ed, 2002). Servitudes and easements are inherently very similar, and there is very little difference between lifestyles and standards north and south of the Cheviots. Further, courts in both jurisdictions have expressly and beneficially relied on each other's analyses and developments in this area of law.

The English – and now Scottish – rule for the acquisition of accessory rights is in two parts: the right in question must be reasonably necessary for the exercise and enjoyment of the servitude;[65] and it must have been within the contemplation of the parties – or at least of the person granting the servitude – at the time of the act by which the servitude was created. As this second requirement suggests, the basis of the doctrine is an implied term.[66] In the same way as there will be implied into a contract such terms as are necessary for its efficient operation – and hence to give effect to what the parties are supposed to have intended but forgot to say – so, equally, there must be implied into a servitude such additional rights as are needed for its proper exercise and enjoyment.[67] And, as with contracts, the focus is on the presumed intention of the parties in the light of the surrounding circumstances. The question, as Lord Scott expressed it in *Moncrieff,* is "what the parties must, if they had thought about it, have had in mind".[68]

Louisiana, of course, took its rules on accessory rights from the Civil Law and not from the Common Law, and the original Code provisions were a faithful copy from the *Code civil.* The most important, which became article 771 of the 1870 Civil Code, reads (as far as relevant):

> When a servitude is established, everything which is necessary to use such servitude is supposed to be granted at the same time with the servitude.
> Thus the servitude of drawing water out of a spring carries necessarily with it the right of passage.[69]

---

65 As opposed to for the enjoyment of the dominant tenement (which is the rule for implied servitudes, considered at C.(3) below.) The rule in Louisiana is the same: see *Ryan v Monet* 666 So 2d 711 (La 1995).

66 Naturally, this is a term implied in the circumstances of a particular contract rather than a term implied as a matter of general law. See W W McBryde, *The Law of Contract in Scotland,* 3rd edn (2007) para 9-07.

67 The connection is made explicitly by Lord Neuberger at para 113.

68 Para 52.

69 This is a direct translation of *Code civil* art 696: "Quand on établit une servitude, on est censé accorder tout ce qui est nécessaire pour en user. Ainsi la servitude de puiser l'eau à la fontaine d'autri emporte nécessairement le droit de passage."

The second sentence is simply an illustration of the general rule given in the first. No doubt the same idea could have been expressed in the form of an independent and freestanding rule, as indeed was done in the immediately following article of the Code (article 772) on a closely related topic:

> He to whom a servitude is due, has a right to make all the works necessary to use and preserve the same.

Instead, however, article 771 is tied to the idea of a "grant"; its heading is "What Grant of Implies". The parallel with the rule in Scotland (and England) is obvious.

When the articles came to be revised in 1977, the idea of an implied grant was dropped. The replacement provision, article 743, states simply that:

> Rights that are necessary for the use of a servitude are acquired at the time the servitude is established.

What was previously an adjunct of something else – in this case, the juridical act which created the servitude – thus emerged as a rule in its own right. This is a tendency which will be encountered again.

Two other articles added in 1977 are also of relevance. Article 744 re-enacts with minor changes the former article 772 (quoted above), which was already expressed as a freestanding rule.[70] It comes as a surprise, therefore, to find that another related provision, article 749, remains faithful to the idea of implied terms:[71]

> If the title is silent as to the extent and manner of use of the servitude, the intention of the parties is to be determined in the light of its purpose.

The existence of three separate articles (743, 744 and 749) for what seems to be much the same topic is a curiosity. Indeed, since the making of "works" is the very accessory right which most servitude-holders are likely to want to exercise, it can be argued that article 744 in particular does not leave much content to the general rule set out in article 743. In Scotland too, however, the extent of a servitude is treated as a separate question, with separate rules, from the question of what accessory rights a servitude might contain.[72]

(3) The consequences of doctrinal choice

Certain consequences follow, or may follow, from the doctrinal choices made in respect of accessory rights by Scotland and Louisiana. As we have seen,

---

70 For an example of its application, see *Palace Properties LLC v Sizeler Hammond Square Limited Partnership* 839 So 2d 82 (La 2002).

71 The same was true of its predecessor, art 780 of the 1870 Code.

72 K G C Reid and G L Gretton, *Conveyancing 2007* (2008) 114-115.

such rights can be characterised either as an implied term or as a freestanding rule. The former is part of the juridical act which brings a servitude to life, the latter a consequence of that act; the former is, at least notionally, a creation of the parties, the latter a rule arising by operation of law and which applies to all servitudes and all parties. Even the latter, however, is susceptible to parties' intentions, at least in a negative sense, because it is no more than a default rule, which the parties can choose to modify or even to discard.

Following the decision in *Moncrieff v Jamieson*, Scotland must be taken as favouring an analysis based on implied terms. Its central feature, as befits an idea which derives from the law of contract, is the intention of the parties.[73] But as applied to real rights, this convenient idea immediately leads into difficulty. In the first place, servitudes, unlike contracts, bind third parties and affect successors. In the case of a servitude created, say, in 1820, who is to say what circumstances surrounded its creation or what the parties might or might not have intended? And as matter of legal policy, why should it matter? Even where it is not pointless, an *ex post* inquiry of this nature is likely to be time-consuming and expensive.[74] Secondly, a complicating factor, not present in contracts, is the principle (discussed below)[75] that a granter is not to derogate from his grant. Arguably, its effect is to block accessory rights in respect of servitudes created by reservation in a deed of conveyance; for non-derogation means that there can be no "intention" to withhold anything from the grantee other than expressly. Thirdly, parties can only "intend" something that they can foresee.[76] If accessory rights are tied to the intention of the original parties – of the parties of 1820 – they cannot readily encompass changes in society and in technology or in the land and its general neighbourhood. The same point might, however, be made of article 743 of the Louisiana Civil Code which, although no longer tied to intention, is confined to accessory rights "acquired at the time the servitude is established". Finally, a theory built on the intention of the parties can only apply

---

73 An undiscussed difficulty is whether the intention of both parties is relevant, or only that of the person who is conceding the servitude.

74 For an economic analysis of different types of default rules, see I Ayres and R Gertner, "Filling gaps in incomplete contracts: an economic theory of default rules" (1989-1990) 99 Yale LJ 87. The costs of inquiry in respect of "tailored default" are discussed at 117-118.

75 At C.(4).

76 Thus Lord Hope in *Moncrieff v Jamieson* 2008 SC (HL) 1 at para 30: "[W]hile the express grant must be construed in the light of the circumstances that existed in 1973, it is not necessary for it to be shown that all the rights that are later claimed as necessary for the comfortable use and enjoyment of the servitude were actually in use at that date. It is sufficient that they may be considered to have been in contemplation at the time of the grant, having regard to what the dominant proprietor might reasonably be expected to do in the exercise of his right to convenient and comfortable use of the property."

to servitudes created by juridical act. The question of accessory rights for prescriptive servitudes remains unexplained and unexplored.

In Louisiana, too, the original wording of the article on accessory rights (article 771 of the 1870 Code) invited consideration of the intention of the parties. A straightforward illustration is *Givens v Chandler*,[77] decided by the Court of Appeal in 1932. A lot was sold subject to the reservation of "an undivided one-half interest in and to the artesian well, and the right to secure water therefrom, situated on the ground herein sold, for the use and benefit of the adjoining property". In the light of the second sentence of article 771, it could not be disputed that the servitude included, by implication, a right of passage to the well, and hence a right to carry off the water in buckets. Unsurprisingly, however, the servitude holders wished to transport the water by pipe. It was held that they could do so:[78]

> The wording of the servitude to which we have referred, the establishment of the servitude according to the custom of the place, the acquiescence of defendant [the servient proprietor] in its establishment by means of a pipe connected with the well, show very clearly that defendant granted a servitude with the understanding that the water in the artesian well would be applied and drawn to the plaintiffs' adjoining property by means of a connecting pipe. The pipe was therefore necessary for the "use" of the servitude, and the right to connect it with the well must be "supposed", under the provisions of article 771, Civil Code, referred to by the defendant, to have been granted at the same time with the servitude.

There is no suggestion that the matter was affected one way or another by the fact that the servitude was reserved rather than granted.

The replacement of article 771 with the new article 743 in 1977 might have been expected to mark a move away from a consideration of the parties' intentions. But even under the former law the intention of the parties was not always the paramount concern, if indeed it was a concern at all, while under the new law an interest in the parties' intentions, as disclosed by the surrounding circumstances, has not entirely been lost. As an example of the first, in *Sticker v Southern Bell Telephone & Telegraph Co*,[79] a decision of 1958, the Court of Appeal found the existence of accessory rights on the basis of what was "usual and customary" in cases of this kind. Significantly, *Sticker* concerns a servitude created without juridical act, making it difficult to see how rights could be "supposed to be granted" within article 771. Yet that article was expressly employed by the court. Article 771 has also been

---

77 143 So 79 (La 1932). See also *Patout v Lewis* 51 La Ann 210, 25 So 134 (La 1899).
78 At 80 per Mouton J.
79 101 So 2d 476 (La 1958).

applied to servitudes created by destination.[80] Conversely, there are signs that cases under the current provision, article 743, will continue to have regard to the parties' intentions, at least in the sense of considering the (historical) circumstances surrounding the grant. *Summers v Vermilion Parish Police Jury*[81] considered the question of whether a servitude of drainage included a right to install a "pump-off system" on the servient estate. In deciding that it did, the Court of Appeal observed that:[82]

> It is obvious that when this servitude was created, a pump-off system was expected to be installed at some point when the funds were available. We also find that the pump-off system was necessary to fully accomplish the purpose of this drainage servitude, draining neighboring lands … Therefore, we find that there are no genuine issues of material fact that the conventional servitude established by the act of dedication contemplated that the servitude included the placement of a pump-off system.[83]

It seems, therefore, that the change from article 771 to article 743 is less pronounced than the words used might suggest. The ambiguity is nicely captured by Professor Yiannopolous' view, expressed in different places, that article 743 both "does not change the law" and yet that it provides for the creation of accessory rights "by operation of law".[84] Perhaps the surprising truth is that Code provisions can be interpreted more flexibly than seems likely with the new judicial test propounded for Scotland in *Moncrieff v Jamieson*.

C. SERVITUDES CREATED BY PRIOR USE

(1) Introduction

My second micro-topic is quite different from the first, although, as we will see, there are some common features. Where land is divided and comes into separate ownership, one part of the former whole may turn out to be dependent on the other for some right or service – for access, for example, or for pipes or other service media. If the dependency is to continue, the right must be constituted as a praedial servitude. But what if this is overlooked

---

80 That at least appears to have been the working assumption in *Bernos v Canepa* 114 La 517, 38 So 438 (La 1905).

81 784 So 2d 15 (La 2001).

82 At 19 per Yelverton J.

83 In *Weigand v Asplundh Tree Experts* 577 So 2d 125 (La 1991), however, the Court of Appeal thought (at 127) that the test must "revolve around what is reasonable and necessary from the point of view of both parties". The servitude in this case was not created by juridical act.

84 Respectively in his annotations to art 743 in his own edition of the Civil Code, and in *Predial Servitudes* (n 19) § 150.

at the time of severance? Can the law do what the parties failed to do for themselves? Can the fact of prior use, either by itself or in combination with other factors, bring the necessary servitude into existence? There are cogent reasons why the answer should be no. As a real right, a servitude should only be created by public act; and as an encumbrance on land, it should only be created with the consent – by the juridical act – of the owner of that land. For it is one thing to imply terms into a servitude once created (the subject of the previous part); it is quite another to imply the creation of the servitude itself. It comes as no surprise, therefore, that many countries reject altogether the possibility of a servitude by prior use.[85] At one time that was also the position adopted in Scotland. According to Viscount Stair, "servitudes are odious, and are not to be extended beyond what is expressly granted or accustomed",[86] while Erskine's view was that "As all servitudes are restraints upon property, they are *stricti juris*, and so are not to be inferred by implication."[87] But by the time these words were written, the idea of a servitude by prior use was already entrenched in the law of England and, through the doctrine of *destination du père de famille*, in some of the *coutumes* of northern France.[88] It would not be long before this would affect the development of the law in Scotland and in Louisiana.

(2) Louisiana: a reception from France

The doctrine of *destination du père de famille* was carried from *le droit coutumier* into the *Code civil*, and from the *Code civil* into the law of Louisiana. As the provisions in the Civil Codes of 1825 and 1870 (in its original version) are largely identical, I will refer only to the latter. The starting point is the statement in article 765 that "Continuous and apparent servitudes may be acquired by title, or by a possession of ten years". To this, article 767 adds that "the destination made by the owner is equivalent to title with respect to continuous apparent servitudes". As the French text of the equivalent article in the 1825 Code makes clear,[89] "destination" in this context means *destination du père de famille*.

---

85 Indeed, one country (the Netherlands) has actually moved from allowing such servitudes to disallowing them. The first Dutch Civil Code was based on the *Code civil* and so recognised servitudes by *destination du père de famille*. But the doctrine was dropped from the new Civil Code in 1992, under explicit reference to the law of Germany, Switzerland and Greece. I am grateful to Lars van Vliet for drawing this to my attention.

86 Stair, *Inst* 2.7.6.

87 Erskine, *Inst* 2.9.33. And see also 2.9.3.

88 See, e.g., *Coutume de Paris* art 216.

89 Article 763 ("La destination du père de famille vaut titre à l'égard des servitudes continues et apparentes").

The provisions on destination – articles 767-769 of the 1870 Code – are taken directly from the *Code civil* [90] except for the second paragraph of article 767, which offers the following definition:

> By destination is meant the relation established between two immovables by the owner of both, which would constitute a servitude if the two immovables belonged to two different owners.

As the servitude in question must be "apparent", the required "relation" can only be established by works which indicate that a servitude might exist. Thus, like the Scottish doctrine of servitudes *rebus ipsis et factis*, discussed below,[91] the hypothesis underlying article 767 seems to be that, if the two properties had in fact been in separate ownership, the making of the works would of itself result in the creation of a servitude. As it is, the servitude must remain in suspension until, as article 769 puts it, the owner "sell one of these estates, and … the deed of sale be silent respecting the servitude". Creation is thus a two-stage process: the owner carries out the works, and the property is later divided by a deed in which the servitude is not mentioned.

In an influential passage in his *Traité des servitudes*, commenting on the equivalent articles of the *Code civil*, Pardessus offered a legal analysis of this factual sequence:[92]

> On appelle *destination du père de famille*, la disposition ou l'arrangement que le propriétaire de plusieurs fonds a fait, et souvent même, lorsque les choses sont fort anciennes, a laissé subsister pour leur usage respectif. Cet arrangement, d'après ce que nous venons de dire, doit être le résultat de signes permanens; sans cela on ne pourroit en induire une volonté de créer un véritable assujétissement d'un fonds envers un autre …
>
> Si, par la suite, ces fonds viennent à appartenir à différens maîtres, soit par l'aliénation, soit par la disposition qu'en feroit le propriétaire, soit par un partage entre ses héritiers, le service que l'un tiroit de l'autre qui étoit simple destination du père de famille lorsqu'ils appartenoient au même, devient servitude, une fois que les objets passent dans les mains de propriétaires différens. C'est une présomption que la loi déduit de l'intention probable des parties; mais comme toutes les présomptions de ce genre, elle n'a lieu qu'a défaut d'une volonté exprimée dans les titres, volonté qui, d'après l'article 694,[93] pourroit être différente de ce que la loi présume.[94]

---

90 *Code civil* arts 690, 692-694.

91 C.(3).

92 J-M Pardessus, *Traité des servitudes*, 8th edn (1838) vol 2 § 288. Part of this passage was to be quoted, in translation, in C J Gale and T D Whatley, *A Treatise on the Law of Easements* (1839) 49-50. See C.(5) below.

93 The equivalent article in La Civ Code 1870 is 769.

94 [By *destination du père de famille* is understood the disposition or arrangement which the proprietor of several plots of land has made for their respective use. This arrangement, following what has just been said, must be the result of permanent indications; without this one cannot infer from

Pardessus identifies two separate acts of the will, or juridical acts, corresponding to each of the stages of creation. In the first place, the owner must intend that one plot serve the other; in the second place, the parties to the deed of severance must intend that such service should continue in the future. But through the device of a presumption,[95] the presence of the first juridical act allows the second to be taken for granted. This means that, on severance, there is no need for the parties to intend anything at all, so long as they do not positively intend that the existing arrangements should be discontinued. Of the two acts of will, therefore, the important one – the one which, under article 767 of the 1870 Code, is declared to be "equivalent to title" – is the first. As the Supreme Court of Louisiana emphasised in a case decided in 1857:[96]

> [T]he rule is that he who claims the property of another, must show a title, so he who claims a servitude of the character now under consideration, must show a title to the same; that is, he must establish clearly that, not only was it once the intention of the proprietor of several contiguous lots to establish a servitude for their respective use, but that he actually executed his purpose by making such changes in his property, that this servitude could be beneficial to all the lots.

So it is the owner's intention, as evidenced by his acts, which achieves the launch of the servitude, leaving to the parties on severance only the possibility of aborting the flight. As we will see, this modest role for intention at severance is an important distinguishing feature from the Common Law doctrine of implied servitudes, with important consequences for the content of the law in both systems.

In 1977, as already mentioned, the articles on servitudes in the Louisiana Civil Code were subject to major revision. So far as destination is concerned, the provisions were combined into a single article (741), the exclusion of non-continuous servitudes was dropped, and even non-apparent servitudes were allowed if the owner took the trouble to register a formal declaration. There was also what may possibly be a move away from a requirement of

---

it the will to create a true subjugation of one plot with regard to the other ...

If afterwards these plots should become the property of different owners, whether by alienation or division amongst his heirs, the service which the one derived from the other, which was simple *destination du père de famille* as long as the plots belonged to the same owner, becomes a servitude as soon as they pass into the hands of different owners. It is a presumption which the law deduces of the probable intention of the parties; but like all presumptions of this type, it only takes effect when their will is not made express in the titles, a will which, following article 694, might be different from that which the law presumes.]

95 Pardessus returns to the idea of a presumption at § 291 ("une véritable présomption").
96 *Gottschalk v De Santos* 1857 WL 4688 (La 1857) per Cole J. See also, from a much later period, *Efner v Ketteringham* 41 So 2d 130 (La 1949).

intention. Thus no room was found for an equivalent to article 768 (which mentioned intention), while article 767 was rendered in a way which omitted any reference to an act *of the owner*:

> Destination of the owner is a relationship established between two estates owned by the same owner that would be a predial servitude if the estates belonged to different owners.

Further, destination was no longer stated to be "equivalent to title"; instead, apparent servitudes are now established "by title, by destination of the owner, or by acquisitive prescription".[97] No doubt it would be wrong to place too much weight on individual changes in wording. At least one case decided since 1977 suggests a continuing role for intention.[98] Yet, just as in article 743 of the 1997 revision, discussed above,[99] it seems possible to detect a shift in the direction of an independent – and perhaps one day even a mechanical – rule.

(3) Scotland: a false start and a reception from England

In *Preston's Trs v Preston*,[100] Sir Robert Preston, the owner of two neighbouring estates (A and B), constructed a system of pipes and cisterns to take water from A to B. When, on Sir Robert's death, the estates came into separate ownership, the owners of A sought to prevent the owners of B from continuing to take water. It was held that the owners of B had a servitude right to take the water. At first sight this looks like an example of *destination du père de famille*. As water flowed into a "large cistern", the system of pipes and cisterns was presumably visible and "apparent". The supply of water was "continuous". And in his opinion the Lord President (McNeill) attributed the constitution of the servitude to the physical acts of the common owner:[101]

> [A]re the trustees [owners of A] entitled to disconnect the pipe at the march of the estate? Considering the expensive nature of the operations, and that Sir Robert himself communicated the privilege in the way he did to Valleyfield [B], I think not. I think Sir Robert has communicated that privilege by a most effectual act, although by no written deed ... I think, *rebus et factis*, he gave communication of the privilege so far as he could give it.

But there are doubts. French law is not referred to. There is no evidence of a reception of *destination du père de famille* before this case.[102] And an

---

97 La Civ Code art 740. In the similar list given in art 654, "title" becomes "juridical act".
98 *Travelers Insurance Co v Badine Land Limited Inc* 1994 WL 577482 (La 1994).
99 B.(2), (3).
100 (1844) 22 D 366, (1844) 16 SJ 433. See further, Cusine & Paisley, *Servitudes and Rights of Way* (n 19) paras 11.09-11.17.
101 At 370.
102 It is not included in Bell's *Principles*. A possible influence, however, was Gale on *Easements*: see C.(5) below.

alternative explanation appears in two of the other judgments.[103] As it happens, B was entailed and so held by Sir Robert only as an heir of entail in possession. As the two properties were thus, in a sense, in "separate" ownership, this meant that the servitude could already be created at the time of the laying of the pipes and not, as in the doctrine of destination, only on the severance of the two estates. Lord Mackenzie analysed the position in this way:[104]

> True, *res sui nemini servit*. But this was an entailed estate. He could constitute a servitude in favour of the heirs of entail. No doubt he could have done it by grant. I think the same thing is done *rebus ipsis et factis*. It is quite competent so to constitute a servitude between buyer and seller, or with a neighbour, by allowing them to lay down and join pipes after commencing, without writing. There is no manner of doubt that this would have been a servitude; and I think the same holds here.

This analysis comes close to the doctrine of acquiescence,[105] but at any rate it is of little assistance where, at the time of the works, both properties are owned by the same person and in the same capacity.

It is the later case of *Cochrane v Ewart* which is the key decision in the development of the law. At a time when two properties (A and B) were owned by the same person, a drainage system was installed to take surface water from B to a cesspool in A. After the properties came into separate ownership, the drainage system continued to be used for many years, and substantial improvements were carried out. Eventually, the owners of A destroyed the system, and the question became whether the owners of B had a servitude right of drainage. The opinion of the First Division was given by Lord Deas, who had been the victorious counsel in *Preston's Trs*. Lord Deas was willing to entertain the idea that a servitude might have been constituted *rebus ipsis et factis*, but only in respect of the *post*-severance history – an approach which is incompatible with *destination du père de famille*.[106] In the event, however, he decided that a servitude had been granted by implication in the conveyance which separated B from A. This was a novel approach, although it can already be glimpsed in undeveloped form in a decision of 1700 which was not cited by the court and was probably unknown to it.[107] The only authority

---

103 By Lords Mackenzie and Jeffrey.
104 At 371.
105 As, apparently, in the only earlier case to refer to *rebus ipsis et factis*, *Kincaid v Stirling* (1750) Mor 8403, 12417.
106 (1860) 22 D 358 at 365.
107 *White v Wemyss* (1700) Mor 10881. I am grateful to Professor Roderick Paisley for bringing this case to my attention. When property was divided, the owner of one part continued to use the other for access to church and the local town. The court found that a servitude existed on the basis that, without one, "how many pleas this might awaken where heritors had sold off some of their baronies, and though they had not reserved their ways and passages in their dispositions,

given by Lord Deas was hardly in point.[108] If English law was the real source, as seems likely, it was not mentioned.

On appeal, the House of Lords simply applied English law.[109] The governing principle was set out by Lord Campbell, the Lord Chancellor, in what has become a famous passage:[110]

> My Lords, I consider the law of Scotland as well as the law of England to be, that when two properties are possessed by the same owner, and there has been a severance made of part from the other, anything which was used, and was necessary for the comfortable enjoyment of that part of the property which is granted, shall be considered to follow from the grant, if there are the usual words in the conveyance[111] … In the case of *Pyer v Carter*,[112] that is laid down as the law of England … And we have quotations from the Scotch authorities shewing that the law is the same in both parts of the island.

The parallels with the decision in *Moncrieff v Jamieson*,[113] 150 years later, are intriguing. In both cases the House of Lords imports a more developed rule from the law of England under explanation that the law in the two jurisdictions is the same, and in both cases that rule operates by implying a term into a deed (the conveyance separating two properties). As compared to the decision in the Court of Session, the House of Lords in *Cochrane* added the requirement that the servitude be necessary for the comfortable enjoyment of the property. That alone marks an important difference between the law in Scotland and in Louisiana.

Finally, it seems worth adding something about the later history of servitudes *rebus ipsis et factis*. They do not reappear in the law reports until the judgments of the Inner House in *Moncrieff v Jamieson*, where Lord Marnoch quoted with approval the statement in Bell's *Principles* § 992 that: "A servitude cannot be constituted *rebus ipsis et factis*", a statement vouched for by the decision of the House of Lords in *Cochrane v Ewart* which is said to "overrule" *Preston's Trs*.[114] But this passage was written not by Bell (who

---

yet these servitudes being *innoxiae utilitatis*, it must be presumed, if they had been mentioned at the time of the sale, they would have been presently granted and yielded to."

108 *Baird v Fortune* (1859) 21 D 848.

109 According to the report in Macqueen ((1861) 4 Macq 117 at 125-126), counsel for the respondents cited *Code civil* art 690 and C-B-M Toullier, *Le droit civil français*. These highly unusual citations are presumably explained by the shortlived interest in French law brought about by Gale on *Easements*: see C.(5) below.

110 (1861) 4 Macq 117 at 122. It is for example quoted in E Washburn, *A Treatise on the American Law of Easements and Servitudes*, 2nd edn (1867) 58 (1.3.25). It does not appear in the 1st edition of 1863.

111 By "the usual words" seems to be meant words such as "as presently possessed". In practice this requirement is disregarded: see *Shearer v Peddie* (1899) 1 F 1201 at 1209 per Lord Kinnear.

112 (1857) 1 H & N 916.

113 2008 SC (HL) 1, discussed at B. above.

114 2005 1 SC 281 at para 29.

died in 1843) but by Bell's editor, William Guthrie; and the House of Lords in *Cochrane* did not overrule *Preston's Trs* as such but merely declined to apply the doctrine of *rebus ipsis et factis* to the facts in front of it.[115] It seems premature to conclude that it is no longer part of Scots law.

(4) Comparison

There are obvious similarities between implied servitudes in Scotland and servitudes by destination in Louisiana. Both doctrines accept that, where one part of a property makes use of another part, there may be merit in allowing that use to continue even after the parts are severed from each other. At the same time both accept that the interest of the putative dominant part in acquiring a servitude must be balanced against the need to protect the owners, present and future, of the putative servient part. The control factors which are used are, however, different. In an acknowledgement of the importance of publicity, Louisiana requires that the servitude be apparent, although it has now abandoned the need for it to be continuous. In Scotland, the requirement of apparency was only weakly received and is not now part of the law.[116] Instead, the right in question must be among the "known" servitudes, and it must be reasonably necessary for the comfortable enjoyment of the part which is claiming it.

Similarities in practical effect mask fundamental differences in doctrine. Like the accessory rights discussed earlier, implied servitudes are founded on the idea of implied terms. The orientation is the law of contract and not the law of property. The link is made explicit by Lord Neuberger in *Moncrieff v Jamieson*:[117]

> [I]t appears to me that these two types of case[118] are no more than examples of the application of a general and well established principle which applies to contracts, whether relating to grants or land or other arrangements. That principle is that the law will imply a term into a contract, where, in the light of the terms of the contract and the facts known to the parties at the time of the contract, such a term would have been regarded as reasonably necessary or obvious to the parties.

Intention is important in Louisiana too, but it is primarily intention at the time that the physical arrangements are made – the actual making of which amounts virtually to a juridical act of its own. If intention is also relevant at

---

115 In *Moncrieff* at para 82 Lord Hamilton goes too far when he says that the court in *Cochrane* "roundly rejected that as a competent mode of constitution".

116 Compare Rankine, *Landownership* (n 62) 435 with Cusine & Paisley, *Servitudes and Rights of Way* (n 19) para 8.09.

117 2008 SC (HL) 1 at para 113.

118 I.e. implied servitudes and accessory rights.

the time of severance it is only in the negative sense that the owner can, as it were, change his mind by indicating, expressly or by implication, that, after all, no servitude is to be created.[119] In Louisiana the servitude is not born as a result of an implied term of the deed of transfer.

These doctrinal differences have practical consequences. Although the role of intention may possibly have weakened in Louisiana, it remains sufficiently strong to insist that the physical arrangements are put in place by the owner (the *père* of the *destination*) and not merely by, for example, a lessee.[120] In Scotland, the recourse to a theory of implied terms has had a decisive effect on the scope of the rule. Occasionally, it may serve to admit a servitude even where the physical arrangements occur after severance and not before, on the basis that the parties' intentions can be derived from future acts as well as from those which have already taken place.[121] Much more commonly, it has the effect of preventing a servitude from coming into existence at all. One reason for this is that, in ascertaining the intention of the parties, the courts have regard to the principle that a granter is taken not to derogate from his grant, with the result that a servitude is rarely found in favour of land retained by the granter.[122] If the logic is impeccable, the result is absurd, for whether a servitude is or is not implied will depend on the chance of which part of the former whole was first to be sold.[123]

The effect of these differences is to make the rule much wider in Louisiana than in Scotland. In Louisiana indeed it often seems to operate automatically: if the necessary physical arrangements are made, and if the properties are then severed, a servitude is the almost inevitable result. In Scotland the physical arrangements are only a beginning. Unless in addition the servitude is among the "known" types, unless it is reasonably necessary for the comfortable enjoyment of the dominant tenement, unless, above all, the right would be in favour of the property being conveyed and not of the property being retained, there is unlikely to be a servitude. On the whole the courts have been rather eager to say no.[124]

---

119 For an example where the servitude was prevented by implication, see *White v Durrwachter* 431 So 2d 65 (La 1983).

120 *Williams v Wiggins* 641 So 2d 1068 (La 1994).

121 Or so it may be argued. See *Cochrane v Ewart* (1869) 22 D 358 at 365 per Lord Deas; *Moncrieff v Jamieson* 2008 SC (HL) 1 at para 30 per Lord Hope, para 128 per Lord Neuberger; Cusine & Paisley, *Servitudes and Rights of Way* (n 19) para 8.18.

122 D 8.4.10. And see C.(5) below.

123 Sensibly, Louisiana has avoided this problem: see *Efner v Ketteringham* 41 So 2d 130 (La 1949).

124 See, e.g., *Gow's Trs v Mealls* (1875) 2 R 729; *McLaren v City of Glasgow Union* (1878) 5 R 1042; *Shearer v Peddie* (1899) 1 F 1201.

(5) *Destination:* rejection and reinvention

As adopted in Louisiana, *destination du père de famille* seems much closer to the reasonable expectations of the parties involved in the division of land than the unduly rigid and technical rule of the Common Law which has come to be used in Scotland. A further advantage is its tendency to promote the efficient use of resources by avoiding the costs of re-establishing previous entitlements or, failing that, in duplicating facilities.[125] It is perhaps unsurprising, therefore, that destination has sometimes tempted even the fastidious practitioners of the Common Law.

When Charles James Gale wrote his ground-breaking work on *Easements* (1839),[126] he drew, like George Joseph Bell before him, on the *Code civil* and on Pardessus.[127] In particular, Gale saw in *destination du père de famille* a solution to a vexing problem in the English law of implied easements.[128] Traditionally that law had been analysed as an application of the principle that no man can derogate from his grant, allowing easements to the grantee of the deed bringing about severance but denying them to the granter. This, said Gale, was a misperception. In this area English law had drawn from French law or at least was not inconsistent with it. Hence the proper explanation of implied servitudes was destination or, as Gale rendered it, "disposition of the owner of two tenements". Implicit in Gale's analysis was the view that implied easements were created, not or not mainly by the deed of severance itself – which would inevitably bring with it the non-derogation principle – but earlier, when the necessary physical arrangements were made by the owner. The key event was thus the owner's "express volition evidenced by his acts".[129]

At first this re-writing of history met with some success. It was adopted, at least in substance, by *Pyer v Carter*,[130] where an easement was allowed

---

125 See the remarks of the American Law Institute in *Restatement of the Law Third, Property: Servitudes* (2000) vol 1, 160, in commenting on § 2.12 (discussed below).

126 C J Gale and T D Whatley, *A Treatise on the Law of Easements* (1839). The 2nd edition (1849) is by Gale alone.

127 C Seebo, *Servitus und Easement: Die Rezeption des römischen Servitutenrechts in England* (2005) 103 ff.

128 Gale & Whatley, *Easements* 49 ff. See generally A W B Simpson, "The rule in *Wheeldon v Burrows* and the *Code civile*" (1967) 83 LQR 240. In the 2nd edition of his *A History of the Land Law* (1986) 262 n 78, Simpson describes this article as "embarrassingly marred by an error as to gender" (i.e. the extraneous "e" at the end of "*civile*"). Curiously, precisely the same mistake is made by Gale.

129 Gale & Watley, *Easements* 51. In support of his view, Gale quotes at length from § 288 of Pardessus' treatise on servitudes (see 49-50) but stops the quotation just before the sentence (given at the end of the quote at n 94 above) which, by referring to the probable intention of the parties at severance, is capable of being read as contrary to that view.

130 (1857) 1 H & N 916.

in favour of the granter of the deed of severance, and it was exported to
Scotland, along with the rest of the Common Law of implied servitudes, in
Cochrane v Ewart where, in a passage already quoted, *Pyer v Carter* was
cited with approval by the House of Lords.[131] But this triumph was short-
lived, for only three years later, in 1864, Lord Westbury castigated as "a mere
fanciful analogy" the attempt by Gale, "that learned and ingenious author",
to re-cast implied servitudes as destination,[132] and in 1879 the doctrine of
non-derogation was emphatically and conclusively reasserted by the Court
of Appeal in *Wheeldon v Burrows*.[133] Within two years the same position had
been taken up in Scotland.[134] Of this brief dalliance with the *Code civil*, all
that has survived is the requirement that an implied servitude be continuous
and apparent[135] – a survival which, in the modern law, has become attenuated
or even meaningless. For unlike in Louisiana, where "continuous" retained its
French meaning of something which is exercisable without the act of man,[136]
English law renders it as nothing more demanding than that the servitude
be permanent, as most servitudes are.[137] Furthermore, the requirement of
continuous and apparent has become intertwined with the requirement of
reasonable necessity so that it is unclear whether the two are alternative or
cumulative.[138] In Scotland, as already mentioned, the requirement of continuous and apparent disappeared as stealthily as it was once introduced.[139]

In the Common Law jurisdictions of the United States the reception of
destination initially followed much the same pattern. The way was paved
by the assertion, in the preface to the first edition of Emory Washburn's *A
Treatise on the American Law of Easements and Servitudes* in 1863 – the
first American work on the subject – that "No lawyer need be told that many
of the principles of the common law of Easements are derived directly from
the Civil law, and may be found in the Scotch and Continental systems of

---

131 *Ewart v Cochrane* (1861) 4 Macq 117 at 122 per Lord Campbell LC, quoted at C.(3) above.
132 *Suffield v Brown* (1864) 4 De GJ & Sm 185 at 193, 195.
133 (1879) 12 Ch D 31.
134 *Anderson v Handley* (1881) 2 *Guthrie's Select Sheriff Court Cases* 532; *Shearer v Peddie* (1899)
     1 F 1201.
135 For its link to Gale and the *Code civil*, see *Dalton v Angus* (1881) 6 App Cas 740 at 821 per Lord
     Blackburn.
136 LA Civ Code 1870 art 727. This article did not survive the 1977 revision. For discussion, see
     Yiannopoulos, *Predial Servitudes* (n 19) § 16; V L Knight, "Article 727 and the act-of-man-test"
     (1977) 51 Tulane LR 389.
137 As Simpson (n 128) points out, at 241, this reading stems from "a loose passage" in Gale &
     Watley, *Easements* (n 126) 53. The position in American law is the same: see, e.g., R R Powell
     and P J Rohan, *Powell on Real Property* (looseleaf) para 34.08[2][c].
138 K Gray and S F Gray, *Elements of Land Law*, 5th edn (2009) para 5.2.38.
139 See C.(4) above.

jurisprudence";[140] but it was not until the second edition, of 1867, that the subject of destination was introduced, under explanation that, in the Common Law, "the same principle has been adopted, by analogy, to a great or less extent, by different courts, as a basis of construing grants".[141] By that time, however, the doctrine was already under pressure in England, as Washburn acknowledged,[142] and before the end of the century it had been displaced in America too in favour of the line taken in *Wheeldon v Burrows*.[143]

At this point, however, American and English law began to go their separate ways. Already in 1863 Washburn had justified the writing of his book by explaining that hardly any American cases were cited in Gale on *Easements*,[144] and in the tenth edition of Gale, which appeared in 1925, the editor loftily announced that:[145]

> [T]he few references to decisions of the Courts of the United States of North America which appeared in former editions have been deleted. Since Mr Gale wrote nearly a century ago the practice of citing such decisions in our Courts has gradually been abandoned, and any reference to them is now out of place in an English text-book.

In Scotland, too, references to American case law on servitudes largely died out after the last edition of Sir John Rankine's *Landownership* in 1909.[146] Uncoupled from England, American law began to reconsider its espousal of *Wheeldon v Burrows*.[147] The change can be caught at mid-point in the first Restatement of Property where the commentary on the relevant provision (§476) offers the measured view that "circumstances which may be sufficient to imply the creation of an easement in favor of a conveyee *may* not be sufficient to imply the creation of one in favor of the conveyor".[148] In the most recent Restatement, the distinction between grant and reservation has all

---

140 At vii-viii. In relation to Scotland, Washburn makes use of Erskine's *Institutes* (see, e.g., at 5), a work which by then was already more than 100 years old.

141 At 56-57 (1.3.25).

142 At 62-71 (1.3.25a).

143 See, e.g., L A Jones, *A Treatise on the Law of Easements* (1898) para 136. For early and trenchant criticism, see the unsigned article on "Easements by implied grant" published at (1869) 4 Am L Rev 40. The writer concludes with the thought (at 61) that: "All rules of conveyance, and of evidence will be undermined, and infinite confusion follow attempts to remedy by principles borrowed from foreign codes, inconveniences arising from omissions and blunders of parties to conveyances."

144 E Washburn, *A Treatise on the American Law of Easements and Servitudes* (1863) v-vi.

145 W J Byrne (ed), *Gale on Easements*, 10th edn (1925) v.

146 Scattered references are found in that edition, and by no means only in the context of servitudes. Washburn is cited at 437 n 6 and 439 n 18.

147 Powell & Rohan, *Powell on Real Property* (n 137) para 34.08[3].

148 American Law Institute, *Restatement of the Law of Property* vol v (1944) 2979 (my emphasis).

but disappeared, the provision on servitudes implied from prior use (§ 2.12) beginning:[149]

> Unless a contrary intent is expressed or implied, the circumstance that prior to a conveyance severing the ownership of land into two or more parts, a use was made of one part for the benefit of another, implies that a servitude was created to continue the prior use if, at the time of severance, the parties had reasonable grounds to expect that the conveyance would not terminate the right to continue the prior use.

Although, in adopting these words, the American Law Institute does not seem to have been influenced by Louisiana, still less by the *Code civil*, § 2.12 is close to the doctrine of destination wisely borrowed and then unwisely discarded 100 years earlier. Scotland, languishing as before in the English law camp, would do well to exhibit a similar independence of thought.[150] For this a good starting point would be the Civil Code of Louisiana.

D. SOME COMPARATIVE CONCLUSIONS

It is possible to suggest some comparative conclusions. In the first place, the law of servitudes in Scotland and Louisiana is broadly similar in terms both of concepts and of content. But this does not take us very far, because much the same could be said in a comparison with the law in Common Law jurisdictions such as England and the other states of the USA, and for the same reason, namely the dominant role of Roman law as the source of the modern-day rules.

Secondly, although both jurisdictions are "mixed", the mixture presents itself in different ways. In Louisiana the law of servitudes is entirely Civilian and largely French. In Scotland, as so often, the mixture is complex and eclectic. Unlike in Louisiana, the influence of French law has been relatively slight, often ephemeral and, in the case of *destination du père de famille*, mediated through England. English law contributed the rules on implied servitudes but little else. Elsewhere the law in Scotland derives from Roman law, the *ius commune*, and from the deliberations over hundreds of years of local judges and jurists.

Thirdly, while it is not necessary to have a civil code to be Civilian, it undoubtedly helps. In Louisiana, the Civil Code has acted as a barrier against the Common Law. In uncodified Scotland the law has tended to wander,

---

149 American Law Institute, *Restatement of the Law Third, Property: Servitudes* vol 1 (2000) 159.

150 For a recent attempt to escape, see *McEwan's Exrs v Arnot* 7 September 2004, Perth Sheriff Court, unreported, discussed in K G C Reid and G L Gretton, *Conveyancing 2005* (2006) 89-92.

leading in this, as in other, areas of private law to rules which are more obviously mixed – a result which can be presented, according to taste, as either enriching or incoherent.

Fourthly, a code, or its absence, is important in other respects as well. In Scotland the law of servitudes developed slowly and incrementally, taking unexpected turns along the way, so that even today there are gaps and uncertainties which surprise.[151] Further, there was a tendency for new law to emerge under cover of existing law, sometimes artificially extended, rather than as independent rules in their own right. The result has been for predominantly Civil Law rules to be developed by a predominantly Common Law methodology. In Louisiana, by contrast, the law arrived ready-made from the *Code civil*, itself the product of prolonged legal development and thought, and has been subject to little in the way of fundamental change since other than through the alterations to the Code made in 1977. The difference in experience can be seen in the difference in the case law. Although there are many more servitudes cases in Louisiana, those in Scotland, in the tradition of judge-made law, contain opinions which are often lengthy and sometimes intellectually accomplished.

Finally, and in relation to the micro-topics chosen for examination, accessory rights and servitudes by prior use, Scotland favours an analysis based on implied terms whereas Louisiana, which has never taken the role of intention so seriously, shows signs of moving in the direction of freestanding rules. On these topics, therefore, the two jurisdictions are surprisingly far apart. And, importantly, the differences are the result, not of policy choice – a matter which seems never to be mentioned in Louisiana and only rarely in Scotland – but of the working out of doctrinal positions adopted for quite other reasons.

---

151 We have seen, for example, that the rules on accessory rights remained unclear until as recently as 2007. See B.(2) above.

2 Title Conditions in Restraint of Trade

John A Lovett[*]

A. INTRODUCTION
(1) Two primary sub-categories of commercial title conditions
(2) The search for a satisfactory account of the *numerus clausus*
(3) Native assessments of the *numerus clausus*
(4) Similarities in content limitations on servitudes – the fundamental but ambiguous concept of *utilitas*
B. TITLE CONDITIONS IN RESTRAINT OF TRADE
(1) Scotland
(a) From ambiguity to apparent standardisation: 1760-1840
(b) The importance of value and amenity and the prohibition on affirmative commercial obligations: 1880-1920
(c) From *Aberdeen Varieties* to the Title Conditions (Scotland) Act 2003: commoditisation anxiety and the return of praedial servitudes
(2) Louisiana
(a) The Provosty Triumvirate (Of Real Obligations): 1907-1915
(b) Modern period: 1988-2006
C. TYING STIPULATIONS AND AFFIRMATIVE BUSINESS OBLIGATIONS
(1) Scotland
(2) Louisiana
D. COMPARATIVE CONCLUSIONS

A. INTRODUCTION

Title conditions in legal instruments conveying interests in land can do many things in Scotland and Louisiana. They can allow a benefited property owner[1]

---

[*] The author expresses his deep appreciation to K G C Reid, R R M Paisley, and all the participants in this project whose comments helped improve this chapter. All errors remain those of the author alone.

[1] I use the terms "benefited property" and "burdened property" respectively to refer to what Scottish and Louisiana lawyers mean by "dominant tenement" or "dominant estate" and "servient tenement" or "servient estate."

to gain access to or do something on a burdened property.[2] They can impose restrictions on the size, location and nature of improvements that may be constructed on a burdened property.[3] They can restrict burdened property from being used for certain specific activities – a commercial or industrial enterprise for instance[4] – when the restriction is designed to protect some obvious "amenity" interest linked to the benefited owner's actual enjoyment of his property.[5] They can even, in certain circumstances, impose affirmative obligations on the owner of the burdened property – to build a house of a certain size or quality, or to pay annual fees to support the maintenance of common areas or facilities.[6]

Almost any title condition, of course, can be said to have some commercial component, at least to the extent that a dismemberment of ownership, a restriction on use, or an advantage given to another person inevitably diminishes the market value of the burdened property. But this chapter is concerned with a narrower and often more problematic category of title conditions – those nakedly aimed to benefit the business interests of the person who at the moment happens to own the benefited property. Thus this chapter enquires whether title conditions can prohibit a burdened property owner from operating a theatre, a seafood restaurant, a public house, an optician's shop, or even an outpatient surgical and diagnostic centre, that competes with a similar business operated on a benefited property? Can they require a burdened owner to engage in some kind of trade with a benefited proprietor or to construct some facility that will benefit the business interests of the person who owns the benefited property?

Many legal systems permit these kinds of arrangements as a matter of contract law – as long as the specific agreement in question is not broad enough to violate some external principal of public anti-competition law.[7]

2 La Civ Code arts 699, 705 (1977) (servitudes for drawing water, aqueduct, pasturage and passage). In Scotland, these tasks are accomplished primarily through "rural servitudes", K G C Reid et al, *The Law of Property in Scotland* (1996) paras 487-490, and less commonly through "real burdens" (Title Conditions (Scotland) Act 2003 s 2(3)).

3 La Civ Code arts 700, 701, 703 and 775 (1977) (providing for servitudes of support, view, prohibition of view, and of light, and for the practically limitless kind of construction limitations under a building restrictions scheme). In Scotland, servitudes of support and servitudes protecting light and prospect are "urban servitudes" (Reid, *Property* (n 2) paras 484 and 486). Other limitations on constructions and improvements are accomplished through "negative real burdens" (Reid, *Property* (n 2) paras 375-438; 2003 Act s 2(1)(b) and 2(2)(b)).

4 La Civ Code art 706(2) (1977). 2003 Act s 2(1)(b) and 2(2)(b).

5 See discussion at section B.(1)(b).

6 La Civ Code art 778 (1977). 2003 Act s 2(1)(a) and 2(2)(a); *Corporation of Tailors of Aberdeen v Coutts* (1840) 1 Rob 296.

7 See, e.g., M R Friedman and P A Randolph, Jr, *Friedman on Leases*, vol 3, 5ᵗʰ edn (2004), s 28.1-28.2, s 28.8 (trade restraints in leases generally permitted); *Restatement (Third) of Property:*

But the more difficult question – and the one that simmers at the centre of this chapter – is whether such an agreement can "run with the land" and be enforced by and against singular or particular successors of the original parties. In other words, can a title condition that imposes a restraint of trade on the burdened property for the sole purpose of conferring a commercial advantage on the benefited proprietor be treated as property? If the answer to this question is affirmative, then a powerful and perhaps new kind of property interest has emerged in Scottish and Louisiana law, one that tells us something significant about the nature of property law itself in these two mixed jurisdictions.

(1) Two primary sub-categories of commercial title conditions

This chapter examines two primary sub-categories of commercial title conditions. First, it considers conditions arising out of sales or feudal grants that seek to restrict the commercial activities that can be undertaken on the burdened property when the primary objective is to enhance the profitability of a commercial activity undertaken on the benefited property. I call these agreements simply *title conditions in restraint of trade*.

Second, the chapter briefly addresses title conditions imposed in sales or feudal grants that purport to require the burdened proprietor to perform some affirmative act for the benefited proprietor – to trade with or buy some product from the benefited proprietor, to perform some service for the benefited proprietor, or to construct some building or operation that will inure to the advantage of the benefited proprietor. I call these agreements *tying stipulations or affirmative business obligations*.

Another common type of commercial title condition is a *lease exclusive*, an agreement between a landlord and tenant that one of the parties may not use or lease any other property he owns in a defined area for certain commercial activities that compete with those of the other party. Although *lease exclusives* raise many of the same policy and doctrinal problems,[8] this chapter generally must leave them aside.

Servitudes (2000) s 3.6, comments (a)-(b) (trade restraints in deed covenants generally found not to create monopolies); P J Sutherland, "Contractual restrictive covenants", in Reid and Zimmermann, *History*, vol 2, 283-304 (discussing limits of contractual trade restraints in Scotland); J D Heydon, "The frontiers of the restraint of trade" (1969) 85 LQR 229 (discussing limitations at English common law). Louisiana allows non-compete clauses in employment contracts if limited in duration and in geographic scope (La Rev Stat § 23:921(A)-(C); *Regional Urology, LLC v Price* 966 So 2d 1087 (La App 2 Cir 2007)).

8 Compare *Optical Express (Gayle) Ltd v Marks & Spencer PLC* 2000 SLT 644, with *E P Dobson, Inc v Perritt* 566 So 2d 657, 659 (La App 2 Cir 1990).

In neither jurisdiction has the legal doctrine developed autonomously in either of the two sub-categories that are the focus of this chapter. Rather, decisions in each have often influenced development in the other. Consequently, the discussion often blurs, rather than clearly delineates, boundaries. The rules concerning both brands of title conditions relating to trade have also at times been affected by decisions implicating essentially non-commercial title conditions. These, too, must be considered.

(2) The search for a satisfactory account of the *numerus clausus*

In a famous 1987 essay,[9] Bernard Rudden asked a simple question: why do all non-feudal legal systems establish a restrictive list of legal entitlements that count as real rights? Why, he wondered, do these legal systems distinguish between, on one hand, certain standardised and hence permitted property interests and, on the other hand, legal arrangements that are too idiosyncratic or, borrowing a phrase from Lord Brougham's famous speech in *Keppell v Bailey*,[10] too "fancy" to be considered as property. In short, Rudden asked: why is there a *numerus clausus*, a closed list of property forms?

Rudden was puzzled for a number of reasons. First, the development of functioning land registration systems should obviate concerns about future owners' inability to obtain notice of the existence of fancy property rights and should minimise concerns about excessive transaction costs.[11] Second, property owners can usually accomplish by contract – albeit expensively and somewhat awkwardly through long leases and security devices – the same ends that are sought by the fancier but prohibited property rights.[12] Finally, drawing on the insights of Richard Epstein and others, he reasoned that if permitting fancies to become property rights might increase future transaction or information costs with respect to an affected property object or might limit its future marketability or land utilisation potential, these negative consequences – "externalities" to use the language of law and economics mavens – should be capitalised or discounted into the object's price. Parties desiring to create a fancy or purchase an object subject to one should thus internalise any negative externalities, and the market should limit any economic inefficiency that too much contractual freedom might portend.[13] And yet despite these

9   B Rudden, "Economic theory v property law: The *numerus clausus* problem", in J Eekelaar and J Bell (eds), *Oxford Essays in Jurisprudence* (1987) 239.
10 (1834) 2 My & K 517, 535.
11 Rudden at 246, 262.
12 Rudden at 247-248, 255, 260.
13 Rudden at 246, 252-257, 263. See R Epstein, "Notice and freedom of contract in the law of servitudes" (1982) 55 So Cal Law Rev 1360.

objections, Rudden acknowledged, the *numerus clausus* of property forms remains; its content evolving slowly, if at all;[14] the source of its persistence ultimately a mystery.[15]

Civil Law scholars, of course, have long been aware of and have also sought to explain the *numerus clausus* principle since it is an express feature of many Civil Law systems.[16] These scholars have taught us to distinguish between a *numerus clausus* of property *types* (what the Germans call *Typenzwang*) and a *numerus clausus* as to the *content* of real rights (*Typenfixierung*).[17] In explaining the principle's existence, they have pointed to the need to preserve certainty and predictability in property arrangements, especially for third parties, and noted that content flexibility often provides sufficient elasticity for parties in practice despite rigidity as to the menu of forms.[18] This chapter is primarily concerned with limitations on the *content* of real rights (*Typenfixierung*), though at times it discusses how both Louisiana and Scotland have expanded the list of property *types* available to land owners and their transferees (*Typenzwang*).

As important as Civil Law scholarship is in this area, this chapter is particularly influenced by the rich response to Rudden's seminal essay in the Common Law world. In 2000 Thomas Merrill and Henry Smith responded to Rudden's puzzle in a groundbreaking article.[19] At the heart of their account of the *numerus clausus* of property forms is a keen appreciation of the effect of information costs. Merrill and Smith claim that all persons who interact with the objects of a certain class of property right (whether in land, movables or some intangible creation) encounter some kind of information processing or measurement cost in detecting whether the property right exists and in assessing its implications. Standardisation of property forms and real right content reduces the information processing or measuring costs faced by three classes of persons: (1) the *originating parties* who create the property right; (2) the *potential successors in interest* to the asset subjected to the property right; and (3) all *other market participants,* people who deal with

---

14 For Rudden, the most significant content change is the gradual acceptance of affirmative land obligations, particularly in Israel, the American Common Law states, *Scotland*, and in a narrow grudging accommodation, *Louisiana* (at 242, 257-258, 261).

15 Rudden also acknowledged that adherence to the *numerus clausus* might be explained by (a) Hegelian and Kantian linkages of freedom of will and personality with the free alienability of property, or (b) Hohfeldian formalism (at 249-252).

16 See, e.g., the collection of essays in S Bartels and M Milo (eds), *Contents of Real Rights* (2004). See also A N Yiannopoulos, *Property*, 4th edn (2001) §§ 219-226.

17 S Bartels and M Milo, "Introduction", in Bartels and Milo, *Contents of Real Rights* at 16-22.

18 Bartels and Milo, "Introduction", at 17.

19 T W Merrill and H E Smith, "Optimal standardization in the law of property: The *numerus clausus* principle" (2000) 110 Yale L J 1.

or buy or sell the universe of objects potentially affected by a novel property right and all those who must avoid violating property rights in this universe of objects.[20]

In essence, Merrill and Smith claim that a *numerus clausus* is especially helpful to persons *outside* the "zone of privity" between the original creators of the property right and their potential successors. When these *other market participants* wish to buy an asset potentially subject to a novel property right, or take a security interest in such an asset, or simply make sure they are not violating other persons' property rights, they must expend more time and resources ascertaining whether a fancy property right exists and, if so, evaluating its implications for their own plans. In other words, allowing the creation of idiosyncratic property rights creates extra risks and uncertainties for these other market participants. Merrill and Smith also argue that as neither the originating parties nor their potential successors take these effects on other market participants into account, these additional information and measurement costs become never-internalised externalities. A limited menu of the types of property rights available for a particular class of objects or of the internal content permitted within such rights limits these externalities because novel rights and novel content will not be enforced.[21]

Standardisation, as Merrill and Smith acknowledge though, imposes its own costs. It can frustrate the originating parties' intentions and any unique value they might otherwise achieve by customising their rights with respect to an asset.[22] The optimal level of standardisation is thus reached when a legal regime determines the appropriate trade-off between the measurement and error costs produced by allowing customisation of property rights on one hand and the frustration costs that result from limiting the menu of options on the other hand. The optimal level of standardisation will shift over time as information processing costs and frustration costs increase or decrease.[23]

Merrill and Smith, of course, do not have the last word on the *numerus clausus*. Henry Hansmann and Reiner Kraakman have criticised their information cost account as too focused on the general right to exclude all non-owners and not enough on the narrower question of enforceability

---

20 Merrill and Smith at 27-28.
21 Merrill and Smith at 29-33.
22 Merrill and Smith at 35.
23 Merrill and Smith at 38-40. The rise of well-functioning registries for property rights, which tend to *lower* the cost of notice and thus information gathering, may well lead to a loosening of the *numerus clausus* if all other factors remain the same. Conversely, if customisation is perceived to add significantly more value to certain property transactions, rigid standardisation may yield higher frustration costs leading in turn to pressure to relax the *numerus clausus*. Merrill and Smith, at 40-42.

of property rights against subsequent transferees.[24] For Hansmann and Kraakman, the *numerus clausus* is simply the law's way of regulating the quality and quantity of effort required to verify or determine when a claim of rights with respect to a particular type of asset is enforceable as a property right – when it will run with the asset and be enforceable against subsequent transferees.[25] Sounding one of Rudden's themes, Hansmann and Kraakman claim that because two parties can use contract rights to achieve practically the same results as property rights through the use of "contractually structured running rights",[26] the *numerus clausus* merely tells us how expensive it will be to verify the existence of property rights. If only a single form of property right is mandated for a given type of claim in an asset, verification will be simple and cheap. If much greater choice is permitted, more costly verification rules and procedures are required, especially for those who must maintain the verification mechanisms and those who must use them.[27] The *numerus clausus* is thus a technique for achieving a rough balance among the user costs, nonuser costs and system costs associated with any property rights regime.

Economic efficiency is not the only current justification for the standardisation of property forms. Daphna Lewinson-Zamir has argued that the *numerus clausus* is best explained as a device that protects some underlying core of property rights – in particular the notion that property rights must enhance individuals' "objective well being".[28] In the case of servitudes, she argues that the *numerus clausus* thus requires that their burden should have some bearing on the utilisation of land and must not interfere significantly with the liberty and autonomy of numerous distant parties.[29]

Building on a recent United States Supreme Court decision[30] and the scholarship of Joseph Singer,[31] Hanoch Dagan similarly argues that property institutions are not "free-floating logical forms that can be addressed by means

24 H Hansmann and R Kraakman, "Property, contract and verification: the *numerus clausus* problem and the divisibility of rights" (2002) 31 J Legal St S373.
25 Hansmann and Kraakman at S398-399.
26 Hansmann and Kraakman at S389.
27 Hansmann and Kraakman at S399. Mandating use of a land registry is a strategy that offers a high degree of flexibility in the structure of rights, highly reliable verification, and a low cost of establishing rights", but imposes relatively high costs "in establishing and maintaining the registry" and on those who must search the registry. Hansmann and Kraakman at S395.
28 D Lewinsohn-Zamir, "The objectivity of well-being and the objectives of property law" (2003) 78 N Y U L Rev 1669, 1730-1739.
29 Lewinsohn-Zamir at 1736.
30 *United States v Craft* 535 US 274 (2002) (federal tax liens can attach to a husband's interest in a tenancy by the entirety).
31 J W Singer, "The reliance interest in property" (1988) 40 Stan L Rev 614, at 652-655.

of deductive reasoning or counting incidents" and are not an assemblage of independent and interchangeable "sticks".[32] Instead, the individual forms in the *numerus clausus* consolidate expectations about and express basic normative ideals for different kinds of human relationships.[33] For Dagan, the list of existing forms is "never frozen", but rather subject to "ongoing normative (and properly contextual) reevaluation and possible reconfiguration".[34] As we consider developments in Scotland and Louisiana, we should remember that the existence of and changes to the *numerus clausus* can reveal conscious or unconscious social values rather than merely an inexorable trend toward economic efficiency.

(3) Native assessments of the *numerus clausus*

Scholars in Scotland and Louisiana have not been silent about the structure and content of the *numerous clausus* of property rights either. In Louisiana, Professor Yiannopoulos offers the standard account.[35] He claims that Louisiana has evolved from a position of doctrinal rigidity to a more open textured embrace of contractual freedom.

For Yiannopoulos, the decisive step was the rejection of a narrow interpretation of article 487 of the 1870 Civil Code, which, following article 543 of the French Civil Code, listed only three different kinds of real rights: (1) full ownership; (2) a right to mere use and enjoyment (i.e. usufruct); and (3) praedial servitudes affecting immovable estates.[36] Other significant real rights – mortgage, pledge and other accessory real rights – were not enumerated by article 487, suggesting its inherent limitations.[37] Following enlightened French jurisprudence,[38] Louisiana courts eventually concluded that "parties to a contract may create real rights 'apart and beyond' those regulated in the Civil Code, subject to close judicial scrutiny in the public interest."[39] Current article 476 codifies this understanding by declaring that "[o]ne may have various rights in things: (1) Ownership; (2) Personal and predial servitudes; and (3) *Such other real rights as the law allows*."[40]

This contractual freedom, Yiannopoulos claims, is not unlimited. Several

---

32 H Dagan, "The *craft* of property" (2003) 91 Cal L Rev 1517, 1562.

33 Dagan at 1558-1563.

34 Dagan 1558.

35 Yiannopoulos, *Property* (n 16) s 217.

36 La Civ Code art 487 (1870).

37 Yiannopoulos, *Property* (n 16) s 217, at 414.

38 Yiannopoulos, *Property* (n 16) s 218.

39 Yiannopoulos, *Property* (n 16) s 217, at 415 (quoting *Queensborough Land Co v Cazeaux* 67 So 641, 645 (La 1915)).

40 La Civ Code art 476 (1978).

important content limitations on the nature of permissible real rights remain.[41] In particular, Yiannopoulos advises that Louisiana law should not allow title conditions in restraint of trade to become real because in part "existing economic needs may be amply satisfied by means of personal obligations".[42] He also asserts that little use, in fact, has been made of this contractual freedom to dismember real rights granted by the Louisiana Civil Code.[43]

In Scotland, Professor Paisley has recently defined the scope and content of the *numerus clausus* of real rights.[44] After providing a careful enumeration of the recognised real rights in Scotland today,[45] and after assuring that Scots law indeed "has a *numerus clausus* of real rights relating to land", Paisley admits that "there is no absolute certainty" that his enumeration "comprises the whole content of that list".[46] Yet this uncertainty is also a virtue, Paisley contends, because it provides for "a degree of flexibility" that courts and the legislature alike can use both to supplement and sometimes shorten the list.[47] Citing Merrill and Smith, Paisley lauds the recent abolition of the feudal system of landholding precisely because of its potential to simplify and un-clutter property interests in land, which makes it more likely to lead to an optimal standardisation of property rights.[48]

The primary difference between these two accounts, apart from the more recent vintage of Paisley's, is the latter's willingness to embrace uncertainty as an advantage, indeed as a sign of Scottish property law's inherent flexibility. Professor Yiannopoulos' account on the other hand seems determined to justify, maybe even calcify, an understanding of Louisiana's experience with the *numerus clausus* as of the late 1970s when the revision of much of Book II of the Civil Code was completed and had codified the major jurisprudential additions to the list of recognised real rights.[49]

---

41 Yiannopoulos, *Property* s 217 (n 16) at 416 (mentioning prohibitions on perpetual restraints on alienation and on the imposition of affirmative obligations through personal or praedial servitudes).

42 Yiannopoulos, *Property* s 227(n 16) at 444. See also A N Yiannopoulos, *Predial Servitudes*, 3rd edn (2004) § 108.

43 Yiannopoulos, *Property* s 217 (n 16) at 415.

44 R R M Paisley, "Real rights: practical problems and dogmatic rigidity" (2005) 9 EdinLR 267.

45 Paisley, "Real rights" at 268-269; R R M Paisley, *Land Law* (2000) paras 2.4-2.9. Paisley's list is similar to that of Professor Reid (Reid, *Property* (n 2) para 5).

46 Paisley, "Real rights" at 269.

47 Paisley, "Real rights" at 269-270, 276-277, 282-283.

48 Paisley, "Real rights" at 281-283.

49 Those were the codification of building restrictions, La Civ Code arts 775-785 (1977), and of limited personal servitudes (rights of use), La Civ Code arts 639-645 (1976), in Book II of the Civil Code, and of mineral rights in the Louisiana Mineral Code (1974).

(4) Similarities in content limitations on servitudes – The fundamental but ambiguous concept of *utilitas*

Finally, before embarking on this chapter's primary exploration, we should note several fundamental harmonies between the two systems' content limitations on praedial servitudes. These content restrictions provide a common framework for jurists in both systems when they approach the problem of title conditions in restraint of trade.

In both systems, praedial servitudes must, above all else, satisfy the classic (and originally Roman) *utilitas* requirement. In other words, a praedial servitude must be of direct utility to the dominant tenement. Although the Romans originally conceived of a rural servitude serving the natural character and condition of the dominant estate, usually in terms of its propensity for agricultural production, by the time of the Scottish institutional writers the concept had broadened to include other economic, industrial or commercial purposes associated with the dominant estate.[50] In the words of Erskine, praedial servitudes must have "some tendency to promote the advantage of the dominant tenement".[51]

Over the course of the eighteenth and nineteenth centuries (and occasionally even into the twentieth), Scottish courts generally read this requirement strictly in two sets of circumstances: (1) in rejecting purported servitudes aimed to provide mere recreation or entertainment for the owner of the dominant tenement;[52] and (2) in limiting the scope of servitudes that had a more obvious economic potential, such as servitudes of pasturage and for the taking of raw materials.[53] The recent codification of private land use regulation in the Title Conditions (Scotland) Act 2003 preserves this fundamental *utilitas* requirement in two ways. First, it incorporates *utilitas* into the *ex ante* requirements for the creation of a real burden by providing that "[i]n a case in which there is a benefited property, a real burden must, unless it is a community burden, be for the *benefit* of that property".[54] Second, *utilitas* reappears in the *ex post* requirement for enforcement of a real burden

---

50 See generally M J de Waal, "Servitudes" in Reid and Zimmermann, *History* 321-325.

51 Erskine, *Inst* 2.9.33. Stair was broader still in his statement of the principle: praedial or rural servitudes must be "for the profit or pleasure" of the dominant tenement. Stair, *Inst* 2.7.9.

52 *Cochran v Fairholm* (1759) Mor 14518 (no golfing and roaming rights); *Dyce v Hay* (1849) 11 D 1266, affd (1852) 15 D (HL) 14 (no servitude for recreating, walking or "taking air"); *Harvey v Lindsay* (1853) 15 D 768 (no right of skating or curling on a frozen lake); *Patrick v Napier* (1867) 5 M 683 (no right of angling or rod-fishing).

53 In both instances, the Scottish courts held that the number of animals that could be permitted to graze on the servient estate or the amount of seaware, slate or peat or other materials that could be taken had to be proportionate to the needs of the dominant tenement itself and not for general purposes of commercial exploitation. See generally De Waal, "Servitudes" (n 50) at 324-325.

54 Title Conditions (Scotland) Act 2003 s 3(3).

where the 2003 Act requires that the benefited party must have "an interest to enforce" in the sense that an inability to make the burdened proprietor comply will result in some "material detriment to the value or enjoyment of the [benefited] person's ownership of, or right in, the benefited property".[55] The first reported decision interpreting this "interest to enforce" require- ment, however, imposes a very strict, almost nuisance- based, interpretation of the concept, suggesting real burdens may be difficult to enforce except where they serve the most obvious amenity preservation purposes.[56]

In Louisiana, the same core *utilitas* requirement is currently expressed not only in the definition of a praedial servitude as "a charge on a servient estate for *the benefit* of a dominant estate",[57] but more particularly in Civil Code article 647 which notes that the benefit need not exist at the time the servitude is created but might simply be one contemplated to provide a "possible convenience or a future advantage".[58] All the same, the charge must be "reasonably expected to benefit the dominant estate".[59] Article 647's revision comments (and the cases to which they refer) indicate some potential for elasticity within the *utilitas* requirement, specifying that while praedial servitudes cannot stand if they merely serve "unreasonable whims of parties", the "socially useful purposes" can include "merely aesthetic" as well as "economic" benefits.[60]

Other core constitutive limitations on the content of praedial servitudes are also similar as they all tend to flow from the *utilitas* requirement. In both systems, for instance, praedial servitudes need not be contiguous with each other but only in close enough *proximity* that the servitude provides some obvious benefit to the dominant estate.[61] And in both systems praedial servitudes cannot impose affirmative obligations on the owner of the burdened

---

55 2003 Act s 8(1) and (3)(a).
56 *Barker v Lewis* 2007 SLT (Sh Ct) 48, affd 2008 SLT (Sh Ct) 17, discussed in J A Lovett, "Creating and controlling private land use restrictions in Scotland and Louisiana: A comparative mixed jurisdiction analysis" 2008 Stell L Rev 231 at 249-250.
57 La Civ Code art 646 (1977).
58 La Civ Code art 647 (1977).
59 La Civ Code art 647 (1977).
60 La Civ Code art 647 (1977), cmt b. Compare *Greco v Frigerio* 3 La App 649, 651 (Orl 1926) (holding that a servitude requiring the owner of the servient estate to maintain a bathroom for the benefit of the dominant estate was *praedial* because, even though the uniquely personal benefits were undeniable, they flowed to any owner of the dominant estate) with *Deshotels v Fruge* 364 So 2d 258, 261 (La 3 Cir 1978) (holding that a setback requirement in a deed was merely a personal obligation, not a praedial servitude, because the vendor admitted one reason he inserted the requirement was to avoid having to see the side of his neighbour's house).
61 Compare Erskine, *Inst* 2.9.33; De Waal, "Servitudes" (n 50) at 318-321; Paisley, *Land Law* (n 45) at 226, with La Civ Code art 648 (1977). Even in Roman law, *vicinitas* "merely became one of the criteria on the basis of which it could be determined whether or not the more fundamental requirement of *utilitas* (utility) was satisfied" (De Waal, at 319).

property; they can only impose passive obligations to allow something to be done or to refrain from some undertaking some activity on the burdened property.[62]

These content limitations do not answer our fundamental question for two reasons, though. First, as we shall see, both systems created new types of title conditions to do more of the necessary work of modern private land use regulation (real burdens in Scotland and building restrictions in Louisiana) than classically defined praedial servitudes would allow. Second, even if the *utilitas* requirement applies to these new institutions, asking whether a real burden, a building restriction, or a negative praedial servitude (in Louisiana) serves to provide a direct benefit to the dominant estate only begs the underlying policy question – whether the benefit provided by such an arrangement can have as its sole purpose the commercial advantage of the person who happens to own the benefited property in operating a trade or business on that tenement or estate.

B. TITLE CONDITIONS IN RESTRAINT OF TRADE

The development of the fundamental rules on the enforceability of title conditions imposing nakedly commercial restraints either in feudal grants or other dispositions in Scotland or in sales and donations in Louisiana follows different patterns in each jurisdiction. The outcomes are different as well.

One overriding similarity between the two systems should be mentioned at the outset, though: the relative paucity of reported decisions in both jurisdictions, and especially in Scotland in the last half-century. Consequently, we must be careful not to overstate conclusions, as this relatively small sample of judicial decisions may not always be representative of broader trends in conveyancing practice and may not always accurately predict the outcome of future cases.

(1) Scotland

(a) From ambiguity to apparent standardisation: 1760-1840

The earliest reported decisions of Scottish courts confronting title conditions in restraint of trade imposed in feudal grants are difficult to classify. Two

---

62 Compare De Waal, "Servitudes" (n 50) at 326-329; Paisley, *Land Law* (n 45) at 227, with La Civ Code art 651 (1977). In both jurisdictions, one exception to the passivity limitation is the same – a servitude of support which requires the owner of the building or wall providing the support to maintain it. Compare De Waal, at 327-328, with La Civ Code art 700 (1977). Scotland has one other classic, yet now obsolete and prohibited exception – thirlage (De Waal, at 328).

early decisions, dating from the second half of the eighteenth century,[63] have been interpreted by some as invalidating any title condition that attempts to confer a trade monopoly.[64] But both decisions also imply that a trade restraint originating in a feudal grant is capable of being characterised as property, as an indestructible right enforceable against successors, if the burdened feuars received some notice of the trade restraint at the time they or their predecessors acquired their interest in land.[65]

In the 1820s the Court of Session continued to send equivocal signals. In one 1823 case, it refused to enforce a broad title condition prohibiting a host of commercial uses, but primarily because the feudal superior acquiesced to the commercialisation of many other properties affected by the condition.[66] In another case (actually involving a tying stipulation), the Court of Session eventually upheld a condition requiring feuars to have their property disposition documents prepared by the feudal superior's agent, even though several judges along the way questioned not only the wisdom of the condition[67] but also its morality and legality.[68] In short, there was still no clear consensus as to whether a title condition in restraint of trade or a tying stipulation could be enforceable as a property right under Scottish common law.

With the decision in *Corporation of Tailors of Aberdeen v Coutts*, in 1840,[69] and particularly Lord Corehouse's crucial opinion in the Court of Session, however, the contours of a more definitive Scottish *numerus clausus* of title conditions implicating trade restraints began to take shape. At the outset, Lord Corehouse established three simple, relatively clear requirements for a real burden to be enforceable against singular successors: (1) there must be a clear expression of the original parties' intent to make the condition run with the land; (2) the condition must be recorded in a public registry, and (3) there

---

63 *Orrock v Bennet* (1762) Mor 15009 (barring a baron from restricting his *existing* feu and tack holders from erecting breweries on their properties because such action has the taint of "oppressive" monopolies); *Yeaman v Crawford* (1770) Mor 14537 (terminating suit by feudal superior seeking to require vassals to have their iron work performed by the superior's blacksmith).

64 R Rennie, *Land Tenure in Scotland* (2004) 68.

65 *Orrock* at 15010 (indicating a baron might impose brewery restrictions on newcomers who chose to reside on the baron's lands with notice); *Yeaman* at 14538 (noting that tenants and possessors had for many years observed a blacksmith-tying condition and that subsequent transfers made since "the servitude first obtained could not dissolve the obligation unless it had been lost by immemorial use, or by express liberation given up").

66 *Brown v Burns* (1823) 2 S 298.

67 See *Campbell v Dunn* (1823) 2 S 341, 342-343 (First Div); *Campbell v Harley* (1825) 1 W&S 690 (HL); *Campbell v Dunn* (1828) 6 S 679.

68 Eventually this sceptical view prevailed as the result of statutory intervention. Conveyancing (Scotland) Act 1874 s 22.

69 (1840) 1 Rob 296.

must be "an interest to enforce it"[70] – a guarantee that changed circumstances will not render the condition's enforcement practically pointless.

In addition, Corehouse also added a number of negative limitations. A real burden, he declared, must *not* be: (1) "contrary to law, or inconsistent with the nature of this species of property"; (2) "useless or vexatious"; or (3) "contrary to public policy, for example by tending to impede the commerce of land or create a monopoly".[71] These negative content restrictions for real burdens were crucial, it seems, because they would guard against any tendency for real burdens to diminish the marketability and value of the burdened properties and prevent the erection of counter-productive monopolies.[72] Though the rationalisations are not fully developed, *Tailors of Aberdeen* represents a decisive initial step in the direction of standardisation of title conditions. It recognises the general utility of real burdens as a new real right enabling owners to assure some uniformity in burgeoning residential development. But it also entails an attempt to limit parties' contractual freedom to customise land use rights in the name of promoting wider circulation of property and more commerce. Because the actual title conditions at issue in *Tailors of Aberdeen* were not designed to eliminate commercial competition,[73] however, the decision did not decisively establish the outer limits of title conditions in restraint of trade.

(b) The importance of value and amenity and prohibition on affirmative commercial obligations: 1880-1920

After *Tailors of Aberdeen*, new decisions both relaxed the apparent prohibition on title conditions in restraint of trade and introduced other considerations into the mix. The pivotal development here is *Earl of Zetland v Hislop*,[74] a case in which the House of Lords, overruling the Court of Session,[75] enforced real burdens that restricted feuars from selling or retailing "any kind of malt or spirituous liquor", or from maintaining "victualling or eating houses".[76]

---

70 *Tailors of Aberdeen v Coutts* (1840) 1 Rob 296, 307. The last, strictly speaking, is *ex post*, rather than *ex ante*.
71 At 307.
72 At 317-319. Admittedly, Corehouse's discussion of the authorities here is difficult to parse, but the overall message is one of discomfort with trade restraints because of their potential for monopoly.
73 The conditions at issue imposed building obligations and restrictions, maintenance obligations, and prohibited the burdened proprietors from carrying on certain trades – tanning leather, candle-making, slaughtering cattle – that might constitute a nuisance in the respectable residential neighbourhood of Bon Accord Square in Aberdeen. *Tailors of Aberdeen* at 322-325.
74 (1882) 9 R (HL) 40.
75 (1881) 8 R 675.
76 At 41.

Although in the Court of Session Lord Young had grounded his opinion invalidating the conditions in the *numerus clausus* of known servitudes,[77] in the House of Lords Lord Selborne disregarded broad concerns about standardisation, holding that the title conditions, which might have the incidental effect of restricting trade for monopolistic purposes,[78] were nevertheless enforceable because they "affect the value and amenity of dwelling houses or property suitable for the erection of dwelling houses, and the comfort of the persons residing in them".[79]

Like the notoriously vague "touch and concern" rule in the Anglo-American law of equitable servitudes and real covenants, this focus on a title condition's effect on the "value and amenity" of the benefited property blurs the bright line rule that seemed to emerge in *Tailors of Aberdeen*. Not only must market participants dealing with heritable property now determine whether a title condition in restraint of trade affects the benefited property, they must also assess whether it passes this value and amenity test. In Merrill and Smith's terms, information-processing costs could well be higher for other market participants. On the other hand, the frustration costs stemming from a complete prohibition on all title conditions in restraint of trade would have been higher, too, especially as Scottish land owners increasingly diversified their economic interests to include commercial ventures along with traditional agricultural rent gathering.[80]

At the same time that we witness this loosening of the content limits on the *numerus clausus* of commercial title conditions, Lord Selborne's judgment in *Earl of Zetland* still draws one clear line across which property owners cannot venture. They cannot impose a personal (i.e. affirmative) trade obligation on the feuar or burdened property owner.[81] Lord Selborne's primary concern was not the limited land development obligations permitted in *Tailors of Aberdeen* and its progeny (to pay feuduty, to build houses in a certain style or to pay fees for the maintenance of common facilities), but rather affirmative obligations imposed on burdened proprietors to carry on trade with a benefited proprietor.

---

77 (1881) 8 R 675 at 681.

78 Rather than reflecting any anti-competitive designs, these trade restrictions may have simply been motivated by the powerful nineteenth-century Scottish temperance movement (T M Devine, *The Scottish Nation: 1700-2007* (2006) 353-356).

79 *Earl of Zetland v Hislop* (1882) 9 R (HL) 40 at 42. Lord Watson similarly rejected the notion that the content of real burdens is limited to restrictions on the structural character of buildings (at 50).

80 As Devine notes, this transformation was much more prevalent in the interwar period of the 1920s, but probably got underway in the 1880s as crop prices and land rents sagged. (Devine, *Scottish Nation* at 453-458).

81 *Earl of Zetland v Hislop* (1882) 9 R (HL) 40 at 43.

We can guess this because the key source cited by Lord Selborne here is Lord Brougham's judgment in the Court of Chancery in *Keppell v Bailey*,[82] which famously held that a covenant purporting to bind the owners and successors of an iron works to procure all their limestone from a particular quarry and to transport it on a railroad constructed and owned by the benefited proprietors could *not* "run with the land" as a real covenant.[83] Brougham was concerned that novel and idiosyncratic *tying stipulations* like this were not among the "certain known incidents to property and its enjoyment". Allowing them to run with the land "at the fancy or caprice of any owner", he feared, would significantly increase information processing costs for all market participants.[84] In sum, even though *Earl of Zetland* might be read to open the door somewhat wider to title conditions in restraint of trade, it also inserts a door jamb of sorts limiting the breach by open reference to English law.

In the early twentieth century, Scottish decisions regarding title conditions in restraint of trade remained somewhat schizophrenic. In one notable case, the Court of Session upheld a real burden restricting a feuar and his successors from erecting a public house or inn that would sell liquor because such activities might injure the superior's patrimonial interest in retained land housing workmen for a nearby canal and lock establishment, and because the liquor sales might pose a threat to public health and safety.[85] However, other decisions involving real burdens restricting the use of school buildings for kirk purposes,[86] and restricting hunting and fishing rights,[87] demonstrated a general reluctance to allow for any expansion of the *numerus clausus* of real burdens.

82 (1834) 2 Myl & K 517, 39 ER 1042.

83 *Keppell* at 1048.

84 *Keppell* at 1049 ("[e]very close, every messuage, might thus be held in a several fashion; and it would hardly be possible to know what rights the acquisition of any parcel conferred or what obligations it imposed"). Lord Brougham also grounded his holding in the rules that Anglo-American lawyers will recognise as the "touch and concern" doctrine (id at 1049, 1050-1053).

85 *Menzies v Commissioners of the Caledonia Canal* (1900) 2 F 953 at 962. Although broadly consistent with the value and amenity test articulated in *Earl of Zetland*, this decision also focused on the burdened successor's notice of the condition and the relatively limited age of the condition (just under thirty years) in rejecting an argument that a change of circumstances had undermined the superior's interest to enforce the condition (at 960-61).

86 *Morrison v Kirkintilloch Burgh School Board* 1911 SC 1127 at 1131-1133 (condition purporting to reserve right to use rooms in a school for kirk purposes when not being used for educational purposes held not to be a real burden).

87 *Becket v Bisset* 1921 SLT 33, 34-35 (exclusive right to shoot game on the land of another proprietor could not be a perpetual real burden, but noting that a temporary lease of exclusive hunting and shooting rights was certainly permissible). But see *Harper v Flaws* 1940 SLT 150 at 153-154 (appearing to recognise possibility that an exclusive right to fish – specifically a right to go rod fishing for trout – might constitute a real burden, but holding that the condition was unenforceable because of a conveyancing blunder).

(c) From Aberdeen Varieties to the Title Conditions (Scotland) Act 2003: commoditisation anxiety and the return of praedial servitudes

In the past seventy years a handful of major decisions and legislative interventions may have created a slightly wider opening for title conditions in restraint of trade and thus signalled a potential relaxation of the *numerus clausus* of real rights. The starting point here is the 1940 decision in *Aberdeen Varieties Ltd v James F Donald (Aberdeen Cinemas) Ltd*,[88] concerning a real burden (originating in a non-feudal disposition) that purportedly gave the owners of a new theatre in Aberdeen the right to prevent an older, nearby theatre from being used for theatrical performances and stage plays. The Court of Session held that the real burden was unenforceable between singular successors, reasoning in part that the condition did not benefit the owners of the dominant tenement in their praedial capacity, but only in a commercial capacity as businessmen.[89] If this restatement of the praedial requirement from the traditional Scottish law of servitudes[90] is all the decision stands for, this chapter would be much shorter. But the decision also reveals a curious ambiguity in the Scots attitude toward title conditions in restraint of trade in particular and real burdens more generally.

Two factors, frequently noted by Scots property law scholars, were undoubtedly important. One was the potentially unlimited duration of the real burden. As noted in several of the judgments, the real burden at issue sought to establish a *perpetual* restraint on trade.[91] This concern seems overwrought, though. It is not clear why a *perpetual* real burden restraining trade is any more problematic than a traditional praedial servitude, which is also theoretically perpetual, except that visual detection through inspection *might* be somewhat less likely to occur.[92] And if a perpetual restraint is too long, how short must the duration be? More importantly, as the real burden was initially recorded in the Register of Sasines,[93] and was thus detectable by anyone contemplating transactions relating to the burdened property,

---

88 1940 SLT 58, revd 1940 SC (HL) 52. The House of Lords found that the benefited proprietors' appeal was improper because there was too much ambiguity as to whether they had patrimonial interests in the benefited estate (at 54-56).

89 *Aberdeen Varieties* 1940 SLT at 62-66.

90 Reid, *Property* (n 2) para 444.

91 *Aberdeen Varieties* at 62 per Lord Wark, at 66 per Lord Jamieson. Indeed, the dispute that prompted the litigation arose almost thirty years after the real burden was confected (see special case set out at 58-59).

92 Of course, in the case of a negative urban servitude, such as a servitude of light or prospect, visual detection is no less obvious.

93 *Aberdeen Varieties* at 58.

information processing costs were not necessarily any higher because of its unlimited duration.

Another factor frequently remarked upon was the impression that the properties were not in close enough *proximity* to each other to merit treating the condition as a real right.[94] (Recall this is one of the common characteristics of praedial servitudes derived from *utilitas*.) In fact, the distance between the two theatres in *Aberdeen Varieties* was approximately half a mile. The theatres were also apparently in different districts of Aberdeen, "with properties of all kinds intervening".[95] But why does this matter? Is proximity such a useful guidepost? Even at a distance of half a mile the theatres may have been actual competitors such that the real burden would have added to the "value", if not "the amenity" of the benefited theatre within the meaning of *Earl of Zetland v Hislop*.[96] Conversely, even if the real burden produced little or no direct competitive advantage to the benefited proprietor because there was a large supply of theatres in the area,[97] what business is it of the law? Further, if half a mile is too far away, how close a physical relationship is required? A quarter of a mile? An eighth? Is a mile close enough in a rural or suburban area with fewer intervening properties and where customers typically travel by car? One also wonders whether proximity really reduces information processing costs. It is conceivable that some one buying a theatre might logically inquire about the existence of any restrictive trade conditions if another competing theatre is located next door or within plain view on the same street. But given the registration requirement,[98] the relative ease of locating the real burden in the public land registries, and the tendency for an interested party to investigate the public records in search of other kinds

---

94 Reid, *Property* (n 2) para 407; Paisley, *Land Law* (n 45) para 9.10, at 260. But see Rennie, Land Tenure (note 64 above) 69, suggesting the "short distance between the two properties was [only] a factor".

95 *Aberdeen Varieties* at 58, 61.

96 (1882) 9 R (HL) 40. Lord Justice Clerk Aitchison, at 64, acknowledged this possibility, but discounted its significance due to a lack of clear authority and by stressing that in decisions like *Earl of Zetland* real burdens prevented activities that were "nauseous, troublesome or dangerous to the neighbourhood". Lord Jamieson, at 66, also discounted the potential for value enhancement because it flowed to the business, not the heritable property itself.

97 There were most likely many theatres in Aberdeen at the time, as Scotland experienced the birth of mass entertainment options from the 1870s onward. But traditional variety theatres like those in *Aberdeen Varieties* came under intense competition from lower-priced motion picture entertainment in the 1910s through the 1930s (Devine, *Scottish Nation* (n 78) 360-361).

98 If a real right can be created without being recorded, however, potential purchasers must inspect the property more carefully and interrogate the original parties more thoroughly. Property rules like the "touch and concern" requirement or the praedial requirement can reduce these verification costs (Hansmann and Kraackman (n 24) S401-402).

of encumbering property rights,[99] the proximity between a burdened and benefited property does not by itself seem to make much of a difference.[100]

All this is to say that the judgments in *Aberdeen Varieties* did not provide compelling information processing justifications for either the durational or the proximity limitations on the enforceability of title conditions in restraint of trade. Moreover, they did not define those limits within predictable parameters. But perhaps that is expecting too much and such a critique is surely subject to the objection of presentism. The decision's resort to traditional praedial servitude principles is understandable enough on doctrinal grounds since the feudal, contract-based foundation of real burdens gave way as neighbour burdens increasingly replaced feudal burdens.[101] Nevertheless, my point is that this decision cannot easily be explained by contemporary law and economics accounts of the *numerus clausus*.

The decision in *Aberdeen Varieties* went on to dress up its return to classic praedial servitude concepts instead by adopting the notion of the "law of neighbourhood" derived from a late nineteenth-century treatise, Rankine's *The Law of Land Ownership in Scotland*.[102] For all of the judges, in fact, Rankine was a useful source. He confirmed their insistence that real burdens are only enforceable to the extent (1) there is sufficient "proximity" (though not necessarily "contiguity") between the benefited and burdened tenements; and (2) the benefited proprietor has some "patrimonial interest" or "demonstrable interest" to enforce, by which they seemed to mean some kind of interest in protecting "the amenity or comfortable enjoyment" of the benefited property.[103] Rankine was helpful, I contend, not because his notion of "neighbourhood" was analytically rigorous or captured any intuitive concerns about information costs, but because it gave their Lordships a way to express a latent anxiety.

If all a title condition in restraint of trade does is enhance the market

---

99 This tendency, it has been argued, undermines Merrill and Smith's optimal standardisation account of the *numerus clausus*. Hansmann and Kraakman (n 24) at S401; Lewinsohn-Zamir (n 28) at 1733.

100 There can also be significant measurement costs in determining the precise scope and nature of an idiosyncratic title condition. A good example is *Scott v Howard* (1881) 8R (HL) 59, where a real burden purported to provide certain persons or their successors or assignees with free admission to a theatre and to restrict the theatre's proprietors from converting it to any other use without the consent of the benefited parties or their successors. After successive fires, the issue was whether the free admission right continued to apply to a replacement building. The House of Lords, reversing the Court of Session, held that the admission right was extinguished.

101 See Reid, *Property* (n 2) para 393.

102 The first edition of Rankine's treatise was published in 1879, but it is the 4th edition, published in 1909, that is cited in *Aberdeen Varieties*.

103 *Aberdeen Varieties* at 61-64.

value of a benefited property and give its owner a potential veto over the burdened property's use for a competitive business, then the property right in the trade restriction is nothing more than a commodity. By preventing title conditions from rising into a different sphere – the sphere of "real rights" to quote Rankine[104] – unless they (a) promote neighbourly relations or (b) limit disagreeable activities or constructions that diminish the physical use and enjoyment of the benefited property, the Lords were also suggesting that the existence of a property right cannot be justified solely by its market based value as a commodity. This aversion to commoditisation is consistent with other modern developments in the Scottish law of real burdens, particularly with recent decisions of the Lands Tribunal of Scotland that have rejected benefited proprietors' claims for compensation for loss of the ransom value of a real burden or servitude after a variation or discharge application has been granted by the Lands Tribunal of Scotland.[105] It is also in line with the Scottish Law Commission and Scottish Parliament's recent insistence and codification of the principle that a land use restriction can be permitted to be perpetual (with limited exceptions for conservation and maritime burdens) only if it serves to benefit some other parcel of land.[106]

This anxiety about property commoditisation is perhaps attributable to a wide ranging transformation in Scottish conceptions of land owner-ship in many other areas. All throughout the nineteenth century, as Tom Devine points out, landownership in Scotland increasingly came to be seen as a market-based source of wealth, not as a source of social cohesion. In this period, the nation witnessed widespread agricultural "improvement", dramatic clearances of peasant occupants by large landowners in both the Scottish lowlands and highlands, the replacement of multiple tenancies with single tenancies, the movement from "bailes" and "ferm touns" to a "crofting society", the spread of carefully drafted and rigorously enforced agricultural leases, and finally the massive expansion of export-driven industrialisation in the late nineteenth century.[107] In the twentieth century, this trend only intensified. "Land [in Scotland today] is simply a commodity",[108] one contem-porary critic writes.

104 J Rankine, *The Law of Land Ownership in Scotland,* 4th edn (1909) 369.
105 *Strathclyde Joint Police Board v The Elderslie Estates Ltd* 2001 SLT (Lands Tr) 2; *George Wimpey East Scotland Ltd v Fleming* 2006 SLT (Lands Tr) 2 and 59. The first case is discussed at length in J A Lovett, "Meditations on *Strathclyde*: controlling private land use restrictions at the crossroads of legal systems" (2008) 36 Syr J Int'l L Comm 1.
106 Report on Real Burdens (Scot Law Com No 181, 2000) paras 9.8-9.9; Title Conditions (Scotland) Act 2003 s 3(3).
107 Devine, *Scottish Nation* (n 78) *passim*.
108 A Wightman, *Who Owns Scotland* (1996) 191.

If this is true, perhaps the judges in a case like *Aberdeen Varieties*, with their professed adherence to Rankine's notion of the "law of neighbourhood", are not only falling back on the familiar pillars of the traditional law of praedial servitudes, but are also protesting against the thoroughly commoditised understanding of land ownership that had actually taken hold in most of Scottish society by 1940. The limits on what can constitute a real right in *Aberdeen Varieties* thus tells us something important, as Hanoch Dagan would suggest, about Scottish judges' normative vision of human relations. The judges may be trying to preserve an enclave for a more traditional, communitarian understanding of what property is for in the midst of an otherwise relentlessly commoditising property law system.

After *Aberdeen Varieties*, there was another period of stasis. Two unsatisfying sheriff court decisions, one involving competing butchers and grocers,[109] and the other competing hairdressers,[110] applied the principles of *Aberdeen Varieties* without much useful elaboration.

But then in an important 1975 decision, *Co-operative Wholesale Society v Ushers Brewery*,[111] the Lands Tribunal of Scotland signalled that title conditions in restraint of trade might well be enforceable against successors as real rights. In this case, the facts and procedural setting were, it must be admitted, tailor-made to produce a different result. To begin with, there was much greater *proximity* between the burdened and benefited properties, a supermarket and public house, originally established as part of an economic development scheme in a small crofting community at the head of Loch Linnhe.[112] In addition, the trade restriction, which prohibited the supermarket from selling excisable liquor "for any purpose whatsoever which may … injuriously affect the *amenity* of the neighbourhood property"[113] was more easily linked to the goal of supporting community sustainability and was, moreover, just one of a series of "other amenity restrictions" which were made enforceable by the original superiors (the council) and by the proprietors of the affected properties *inter se*. The Lands Tribunal could thus easily find that the interlocking trade restrictions served a legitimate neighbourhood interest

---

109　*Phillips v Lavery* 1962 SLT (Sh Ct) 57. In *Phillips*, the original parties were still before the court, thus making it easier for the court to find the condition not enforceable by and against successors.

110　*Giblin v Murdoch* 1979 SLT (Sh Ct) 5. In *Giblin*, the court largely treated the matter as a contractual restraint of trade, not a potential property right, and thus delved into the murky English case law on contractual restraints of trade.

111　1975 SLT (Lands Tr) 9.

112　In fact, the properties were practically adjacent as they both surrounded a common parking area.

113　At 10 (emphasis added).

by guaranteeing the sustainability of a "small neighbourhood or precinct" and by inducing the original proprietors to commit to the community building project.[114] In this sense, the facts of *Co-operative Wholesale* gave the Lands Tribunal an opportunity to demonstrate just exactly what a Rankinesque vision of neighbourliness might mean.

Finally, the dispute itself in *Co-operative Wholesale* arose before the Lands Tribunal of Scotland after the passage of the Feudal Conveyancing and Reform (Scotland) Act 1970. Thus, rather than face an all-or-nothing choice between enforcement and non-enforcement, the Lands Tribunal could now, thanks to legislative intervention: (a) recognise that the title condition might well provide the owners of the dominant tenement with a "patrimonial interest sufficient in law to entitle them to enforce the restriction and that the latter is capable of elevation into a real burden";[115] but (b) still discharge the condition on the ground that circumstances had changed enough since its creation that enforcement would be unreasonable;[116] and (c) award compensation (here £4,600) to the benefited proprietor for the loss of its legal right to enforce.[117] In short, the Lands Tribunal could adopt a *liability rule*, as opposed to a *property rule*, approach to the problem of whether a title condition in restraint of trade creates a property entitlement.[118] The lesson here may simply be that if it is easier to modify or terminate obsolete, unreasonable or inefficient title conditions, then courts can be more relaxed about recognising particularly novel conditions in the first place, even if they initially impose potentially long-lasting trade restrictions.

With this last development, we can also comment on the role of institutional choice in the development of Scottish law on title conditions in restraint of trade.[119] For more than 200 years, the courts were the active force, gradually refining doctrine, consolidating new ground, and then imposing limits

---

114 At 11.

115 At 13.

116 Here the new circumstances justifying the limited discharge were said to be new drinking and shopping habits (at 13-14).

117 At 13-14. As the tribunal's detailed accounting analysis demonstrates, quantifying the exact monetary value of a commercial trade restriction will never be particularly easy.

118 See G Calabresi and D Melamed, "Property rules, liability rules, and inalienability: One view of the cathedral" (1972) 85 Harvard LR 1089. For more on the significance of the Lands Tribunal's statutory discharge power, see Lovett, "Creating and controlling" (n 56) at 250-251, and Lovett, "Meditations" (n 105) at 19–22.

119 Merrill and Smith claim that the institution primarily in charge of the *numerus clausus* is the legislature because of its ability to disseminate information about changes most cost effectively and with the greatest potential clarity (at 56-68). See also N Davidson, "Standardization and pluralism in property law" (2008) 61 Vanderbilt L Rev 1597 (arguing that the *numerus clausus* is fundamentally a regulatory mechanism through which legal systems define and control the public or social aspects of private property; i.e., it serves "the political function of property").

on their creations. But in the past forty years, the legislature has taken the decisive role, first by establishing a new *ex post* approach to the problem of obsolescent title conditions in 1970,[120] and then more recently in the Title Conditions Act (Scotland) 2003, which strengthened the powerful title condition modification and termination power of the Lands Tribunal of Scotland,[121] and at the same time took the traditional *utilitas* requirement from the law of servitudes and enshrined it in the modern law of real burdens.

But even here there is a note of continued uncertainty. The decision of the Scottish Law Commission and Scottish Parliament to leave courts (and especially the Lands Tribunal) with primary responsibility to determine what kind of title conditions imposing restraints of trade will be "reasonable"[122] may signal a return to the somewhat blurred, muddled rules that we observed in Scots law at the end of the eighteenth century. While there might be some room for proprietors to customise title conditions in restraint of trade to accomplish their particular – and sometimes even idiosyncratic – commercial objectives, they will also have to weigh not only the possibility that a court might fail to find an interest to enforce,[123] but also the likelihood of modification and discharge before the Lands Tribunal. Information processing and verification costs, it seems, will still be high. Scotland's law on title conditions in restraint of trade thus remains in a state of flux, perhaps nearing a point of optimisation or perhaps about to return to a much more conservative, narrow approach, more reminiscent of the late eighteenth century.

(2) Louisiana

(a) The Provosty Triumvirate (Of Real Obligations): 1907-1915

The law addressing the enforceability of title conditions in restraint of trade was much slower to develop in Louisiana than in Scotland. The earliest decision directly concerning a covenant in restraint of trade did not arise until 1890 and only then in a lease setting.[124] Despite this late start, during a crucial

---

120 Feudal Conveyancing and Reform (Scotland) Act 1970 s 1.
121 Title Conditions (Scotland) Act 2003 ss 90-104.
122 2003 Act s 3(6) ("A real burden must not be contrary to public policy as for example an *unreasonable* restraint of trade and must not be repugnant with ownership …"); Report on Real Burdens (n 106) para 2.27 (reporting consultees' consensus that "questions of reasonableness [of restraints on trade] seem best left to the courts to develop in the light of changing social and economic circumstances"). See also Heydon, "Frontiers" (n 7) at 245-251 (endorsing wide application of English common law doctrine of restraint of trade with its use of a flexible "rule of reason" approach to controlling trade restrictions).
123 See *Barker v Lewis* 2007 SLT (Sh Ct) 48, affd 2008 SLT (Sh Ct) 17.
124 *Herbert v Dupaty* 7 So 580, 581 (La 1890) (holding that a trade restriction covenant in favour of a lessee did not run with the land because the lessor only obligated himself personally).

eight-year period in the early twentieth century, the Louisiana Supreme Court addressed the extent to which novel title conditions with significant commercial effects would be enforceable as real rights under Louisiana law in three foundational decisions, all featuring opinions by Justice Oliver Provosty.

In the first, *Female Orphan Society v Young Men's Christian Association*,[125] the court held that a title condition imposing a *perpetual* restraint on alienation, even if made as part of a donation to an incorporated charitable institution, is void as a matter of public policy.[126] The decision's primary significance lies in Provosty's justifications for the well-established principle. First, Provosty explicitly invokes the Civilian *numerus clausus* of property forms – in particular the limited number of permissible ways to dismember ownership set forth in the 1870 Louisiana Civil Code.[127] He also cites an excerpt from an 1852 Louisiana decision quoting at length from Lord Brougham's speech in *Keppell v Bailey*,[128] and in particular Brougham's information-processing cost concern with allowing a landowner to impress on his lands "a peculiar character, which should follow them into all hands, however remote". In the end, Provosty returns to French law (specifically Laurent) to emphasise that "inalienability is in opposition to the fundamental law of political economy – the law which requires the free circulation of property".[129] In sum, the decision mixes Common Law concerns about the costs of idiosyncratic property right customisation with Civilian positivism and the Civilian preference for the unlimited alienability of land to establish a crystalline rule that completely prohibits one kind of novel title condition.

Five years later in *Louisiana & Arkansas Railway Co v Winn Parish Lumber Co*,[130] Justice Provosty once again argued powerfully in favour of another bright line rule limiting the nature of permissible property rights. This time it was the traditional *in faciendo* principle – the notion that a servitude running with the land should generally only impose negative restrictions or duties of abstention, not affirmative obligations, on the burdened proprietor. The case concerned a condition imposed in a 1902 sale of 18,000 acres of timberland

125   44 So 15 (La 1907).
126   The party seeking to invalidate the condition here was the grantee from the original owner who, in this instance, sought to enforce a contract of sale to a third party (the YMCA) (*Female Orphan Society* at 16).
127   "These affirmative provisions" of the Civil Code, Provosty writes, "are pregnant with the negative, that other modes are disallowed. Parties are not left free to invent and create such tenures as they please, but are required to hold their property in the modes thus prescribed. All other modes are impliedly forbidden." (*Female Orphan Society* at 16.)
128   *Female Orphan Society* at 17 (quoting *Succession of Franklin* 7 La Ann 395, 413-414 (1852) (quoting *Keppell v Bailey* (1834) 2 Myl & K 517, 39 ER 1042)).
129   *Female Orphan Society* at 19 (quoting Laurent t 11, No 460).
130   59 So 403 (La 1912).

in North Louisiana that purported to require the purchasers, their assigns and successors to transport all timber or logs cut from their land over the tracks of a railroad company in which the seller-covenantee had a significant financial stake. The primary issue was whether the condition was enforceable against the covenantor's successors as a servitude running with the land.

Although the Louisiana Supreme Court ultimately avoided reaching the main issue,[131] Provosty wrote a separate concurrence expressing his fear that granting a condition like this the status of a real right would risk re-establishing feudalism on Louisiana soil.[132] Indeed, Provosty predicted that if Justice Monroe's original majority decision holding that the stipulation was an enforceable servitude came to be the law,[133] it would open the door to a whole host of feudal services that sound – ironically – just like Scottish feudal conditions. For Provosty, this would not only violate a central tenet of the law of servitudes in Louisiana,[134] but unwind the progress of the Civil Law itself, which starting in an idealised state of Roman purity, passed through the corruption of continental feudalism, only to be gloriously restored by the French revolution.[135]

Provosty's concurrence also specifically rejected Justice Monroe's suggestion that the tonnage stipulation could be enforced as a "real obligation", an explicitly hybrid category of right-duty that the drafters of the 1825 Louisiana Civil Code had borrowed directly from Toullier.[136] Although it might look like a classic servitude in that one person is authorised to draw utility from the property of another, such a condition should be prohibited, Provosty argued,

---

131   The court determined, *inter alia*, that the covenantor's successors had expressly assumed the obligation (at 410-411).

132   According to Provosty, "schemes" were presently afoot to "divide large sugar plantations and sell them with the obligation attached to sell the cane grown on them to a particular mill, and schemes to lay off immense tracts of land as rice fields and sell them with the obligation that all rice grown on them shall be milled at a particular mill" (*La & Ark Ry* at 425). Other justices on the court apparently shared this concern that certain, unnamed "promoters in our midst" were seeking to establish "a system of serfdom similar to that which took a revolution in France to uproot and destroy" (*La & Ark Ry* at 411, per Justice Somerville on rehearing).

133   *La & Ark Ry* at 411.

134   Provosty's key sources of the *in faciendo* principle in the Civil Code were La Civ Code arts 655 and 709 (1870).

135   *La & Ark Ry* at 414-419. The culminating moment in Provosty's teleology of servitude law is the adoption of art 686 of the French Civil Code, which abolished all personal servitudes except usufruct, use and habitation and was transplanted whole cloth into Louisiana and blossomed into arts 644 and 709 of the 1870 Civil Code. These articles, according to Provosty, impliedly prohibited the creation of, in his famous phrase, "whatever unregulated brood of personal servitudes owners of estates may chose to create" (*La & Ark Ry* at 419).

136   La Civ Code arts 1992, 2005-2014 (1825); La Civ Code arts 1997, 2010-2019 (1870). For a discussion of Toullier's doctrine, see Yiannopoulos, *Property* (n 16) § 209. For an even more contemporary critique, see K G C Reid, "Real rights and real obligations", in Bartels and Milo, *Contents of Real Rights* (n 16) 25.

because it is no different than the example Marcade gave of a prohibited feudal service – "the obligation to have all the wheat grown on one estate ground at the mill of an adjacent estate",[137] or what Scots would simply call "thirlage".[138] Although a property owner burdened with such a real obligation could theoretically escape it by abandoning the servient estate to the owner of the dominant estate,[139] this exit strategy was nothing less than a lie ("ce mensonage"), Provosty claimed, quoting Marcade, for the servient estate owner would thereby condemn himself to penury.[140]

Even if Provosty's fulminations against the affirmative real obligation in *Louisiana & Arkansas Railway* signify a desire to combat the subjugation inherent in feudalism,[141] it is important to recognise that not all of the justices were in accord. In his dissenting opinion on rehearing, Justice Monroe dismissed Provosty's objections as "wholly chimerical" and suggested that any concerns about "a downtrodden or oppressed peasant" could be handled appropriately by criminal statutes on peonage.[142] To Monroe, the key point was that the original parties were sophisticated business persons for whom the tonnage stipulation was, if anything, most analogous to an ordinary – and perfectly legal – contract for the purchase of a crop of growing sugarcane or ripening oranges.[143]

Monroe's view that once firm limits on the nature of property can melt away under the pressure of sophisticated private ordering turned out to be prescient. Just three years later in *Queensborough Land Co v Cazeaux*,[144] Justice Provosty and a nearly unanimous Louisiana Supreme Court held that a covenant prohibiting the sale or lease of immovable property to a negro for twenty-five years could run with the land and bind successors.[145] Further, in

137 *La & Ark Ry* at 425.
138 Reid, *Property* (n 2) para 492 (explaining debate over whether to classify thirlage as a servitude or a feudal service).
139 *La & Ark Ry* at 407.
140 *La & Ark Ry* at 425.
141 Dagan would see in this a classic normative justification for a strict *numerus clausus* limit, grounded in an ideal conception of human relations based on notions of human liberty and dignity (Dagan, *"Craft"* (n 32) at 1558-1563).
142 *La & Ark Ry* at 431 and 432.
143 *La & Ark Ry* at 432. Monroe's reference to oranges was, of course, a not so subtle reminder to Provosty of his deference to private ordering and risk assumption in another famous case, *Losseco v Gregory* 32 So 985, 992-996 (1901) (on second rehearing), in which Provosty J held that the purchaser was obliged to pay full price for the sale of "[a]ll oranges that my trees may produce" for a period of two years, despite destruction of the trees before the first crop was due.
144 67 So 641 (La 1915).
145 The case arose when defendant, Cazeaux, the owner of the burdened lot, sold his property to an unnamed negro, and the plaintiff development company, the original vendor and benefited proprietor, sued to have the sale rescinded, relying on the stipulation in the original deed to Cazeaux (at 642).

startling contradiction to his concurrence in *Louisiana & Arkansas Railway*, Provosty found that a racially restrictive covenant (RRC) like this could be a "real obligation" or a "real right". In effect, Provosty recognised a new kind of property interest in Louisiana law – a remarkable innovation in *Typenzwang*, if not in *Typenfixierung* as well.

To reach this result Provosty made three key moves. First, he concluded that the RRC did not violate the policy against perpetual restraints on alienation set forth in *Female Orphan Society* because here the restraint's duration was only twenty-five years.[146] Second, Provosty distinguished his ringing endorsements of a rigid *numerus clausus* in both *Female Orphan Society* and *Louisiana & Arkansas Railway* by emphasising that the RRC did not violate the *in faciendo* principle.[147] It only imposed a negative restriction, a duty of abstention, on the purchaser and his successors. In effect, Provosty seems to limit the *numerus clausus* of property dismemberment to the narrow proposition that servitudes cannot impose affirmative obligations. As always, he finds authority in French commentators (principally Toullier and Laurent) who he says clarify that French law has essentially dispensed with the *numerus clausus* principle when it comes to dismembering ownership, so long as the dismemberment does not violate "good morals or public order".[148]

Finally, to illustrate the wide scope for property dismemberment, Provosty equates the RRC to a simple use condition in which one branch of use is severed by the seller and withheld from the buyer and his successors. Here the original owner/developer has merely retained the right to sell or lease the property to a black person and perhaps transferred that right to the other white occupants in the subdivision as a kind of *"stipulation pour autrui"*.[149] Most ironically of all, Provosty relies heavily on the malleable notion of "real obligations" and quotes directly from article 2013 of the 1870 Civil Code,[150] the very same provision he had cabined and distinguished in *Louisiana &*

---

146 Although he did not specify how long such a restriction could last, one senses that the court would have countenanced a fairly long-lasting RRC, provided it avoided the perpetual label, since Louisiana law favours the "fullest liberty of contract" and the "widest latitude possible in the right to dispose of one's property" (*Queensborough Land* at 642, citing La Civ Code arts 1764 and 491 (1870) respectively).

147 *Queensborough Land* at 644.

148 *Queensborough Land* at 645. According to Provosty, the restraint here was *not* "contrary to good morals, public morals or express law, but was founded on substantial reason, rather than caprice" as the landowner was only seeking to dispose of his property "advantageously to himself and beneficially to the city wherein it lies" (*Queensborough Land* at 642).

149 *Queensborough Land* at 646.

150 *Queensborough Land* at 644 (quoting La Civ Code art 2013 (1870)), at 646 (concluding that the stipulation creates a "real obligation").

Arkansas Railway.[151]

From an information-processing and marketability perspective, the implications are clear. By sanctioning this unusual customisation of property rights (a dismemberment of the right to sell property to different racial groups), the court was surely raising information-processing costs for all market participants who thereafter would deal with immovable property in Louisiana, even though RRCs like this would be detectable in the public records. The court was also not only limiting the ability of black Louisiana residents to acquire property, but also surely limiting the universe of potential buyers for the burdened property. Of course, the court probably did not even worry about these increased information-processing costs and marketability limitations, or fret over whether they would be compensated by a perceived decrease in frustration costs. Instead, the court probably just took it for granted that this particular form of customisation would add more value to the burdened property, and all the similarly burdened properties in the neighbourhood, by appealing to the powerful white desire for racial segregation. Sadly, these customisation gains, real as they might be for the white homeowners and developers, would be achieved solely at the expense of decades of diminished market opportunities for would-be black homeowners and increased information-processing costs for society at large.[152]

Over the course of these three seminal cases then, the Louisiana Supreme Court in effect created a new default regime for real right customisation in Louisiana – one that relied primarily on public registries to do the limited job of protecting public interests. Moving from an immutable prohibition on perpetual restraints on alienation in *Female Orphan Society* to a hotly-contested debate over the importance of the *in faciendo* prohibition on affirmative obligations in *Louisiana & Arkansas Railway*, the court in *Queensborough Land* finally cabined the traditional policies disfavouring restraints on alienation and idiosyncratic customisation of property rights as easily bypassed default rules. As long as originating parties provide potential transferees and market participants with notice through recording of

151 *La & Ark Ry* at 423 and 427.
152 Racially restrictive covenants were not declared unconstitutional by the US Supreme Court until 1948 in *Shelly v Kraemer* 334 US 1 (1948). By then, the US government's official requirement of the use of RRCs as a condition for borrowers to obtain low-interest government-insured mortgages in the 1930s helped set in motion a catastrophic cycle of investment in all white suburbs and disinvestment in black inner-city neighbourhoods that has plagued the US to this day. See C Rose, "Property stories, *Shelley v Kraemer*", in G Korngold and A P Morris (eds), *Property Stories* (2004) 169 at 186. Provosty's decision in *Queensborough Land*, the first state supreme court decision in the US to validate RRCs, thus played a decisive role in this sad tale (Rose at 176-179).

RRCs and, by implication, many other novel trade restrictions, the door to wide-ranging real right innovation had been thrown wide open. Indeed, the *Queensborough Land* decision effectively launched the rapid judicial invention and later legislative codification of Louisiana's *sui generis* building restrictions regime.[153]

(b) Modern period: 1988-2006

In several decisions spanning the past two decades, Louisiana's intermediate appellate courts have opened the door even wider to the use of title conditions in restraint of trade, but with little examination of the underlying policies at stake. In the first decision, *R & K Bluebonnet, Inc v Patout's of Baton Rouge, Inc*,[154] the court held that a covenant prohibiting a burdened property from being used as a "seafood restaurant" for five years was enforceable against successors as a negative praedial servitude, merely because "two estates were involved" and the restriction facially benefited immediately adjacent property retained by the vendors of the burdened lot.[155] The court did not address the traditional objection voiced by Yiannopoulos that a praedial servitude should somehow serve the dominant estate itself, not the purely commercial interests of the dominant estate owner.[156] Instead, relying on article 731 of the revised Civil Code,[157] the court simply intuited that some benefit had been created, without identifying exactly what that benefit entailed. The court was much more concerned with protecting the original benefited proprietors' reliance interests, not Louisiana's traditional limits on private ordering in the dismemberment of ownership.[158]

In a 2006 decision, *RRC Properties v Wenstar Properties*,[159] the court recognised the enforceability of a more sophisticated anti-compete covenant

---

153   Lovett, "Creating and controlling" (note 56 above) at 242, 253-255.

154   521 So 2d 634 (La Ct App 1 Cir 1988).

155   In this case, the original proprietors owned ten acres of land, sold off six to Diez who covenanted not to use this land for a seafood restaurant for five years, while the vendors operated a well-known seafood establishment, Ralph and Kaccoo's Restaurant, on the retained four acres. The dispute arose after Diez filed bankruptcy and a successor opened "Patout's Restaurant" which offered a variety of seafood items (*R and K* at 635).

156   Yiannopoulos, *Predial Servitudes* (n 42) s 108; Yiannopoulos, *Property* (n 16) s 227.

157   La Civ Code art 731 (1977) ("a charge established on an estate for the benefit of another estate is a predial servitude although it is not so designated"); *R & K* at 635.

158   The court explained that "[t]he plaintiffs [the vendors] knew that a restaurant would be built on the subject property. They intended to prevent the restaurant from operating in direct competition with their business, a seafood restaurant" (*R & K* at 636).

159   930 So 2d 1233 (La App 2 Cir 2006). The suit was filed by the original owner of the servient estate who sought a declaratory judgment that the praedial servitude was invalid so it could sell the property to a prospective purchaser planning to build a Kentucky Fried Chicken restaurant.

against successors, once again characterising it as a "negative, nonapparent servitude" capable of running with the land in circumstances similar to those in *R & K Bluebonnet*. The only material differences here were that the covenant's duration was longer (twenty years or until the dominant estate was no longer used for a Wendy's restaurant) and that a covenant violation was measured by a complex formula involving sales percentages of certain fast food products.[160] Although aware of the information-measurement costs the covenant entailed,[161] this court was also oblivious to Professor Yiannopoulos' position that trade restrictions of this sort should not be countenanced as a praedial servitude.[162]

In *Meadowcrest Center v Tenet Health System Hospitals, Inc*,[163] another appellate court recently held that a condition which prohibited a purchaser or its successors from using the subject land and a planned office building as an outpatient surgical or diagnostic centre without the written consent of the vendor hospital was enforceable as a real right. Even though the condition did not contain *any* temporal limitation and, at the time of the dispute, was already sixteen years old, the court was completely unmoved by the arguments of the successor owner of the servient estate that enforcement as a praedial servitude would effectively take the property out of commerce. For one thing, the court noted, the parties here were "two independent corporations on equal footing" who entered into an "arms-length agreement for sale of real estate".[164] In addition, the court observed that the clause did not "effectively" remove the property from commerce because (1) uses other than as diagnostic and or surgical centres were permitted, and (2) the dominant owner had in the past sometimes even granted permission for such uses.[165] Finally, the court also saw the successor's arguments as a threat to the validity of article 706 of the Civil Code which expressly allows for negative servitudes prohibiting commercial or industrial uses.[166]

In all these cases, the proximity test imposed by Scottish courts would clearly have been met, but in none of the decisions do the judges wrestle with either traditional policy concerns about monopoly promotion or with

160 *RRC Properties* at 1234-1237.
161 Although it held that the servitude was facially valid, the court noted that the servitude did not prevent a KFC restaurant from being built as long as the anti-compete formula was not violated. Determining whether such violations occur, the court observed, would not be easy (*RRC Properties* at 1237).
162 Yiannopoulos, *Predial Servitudes* (n 42) s 108.
163 902 So 2d 512 (La Ct App 5 Cir 2005).
164 *Meadowcrest Center* at 515.
165 *Meadowcrest Center* at 515.
166 *Meadowcrest Center* at 515.

traditional doctrinal requirements that servitudes should enhance the utility of an immovable itself – not the purely personal interests of the person who happens to be the owner at one moment in time. Instead, the courts defer to the customisation choices and reliance interests of property owners and their vendees, as long as the original parties have provided notice of their choices by recording their agreements regarding trade restrictions in the public records. These decisions can be understood on one hand as simply evidence of the uncritical drift of Louisiana jurisprudence toward American Common Law norms which have grown increasingly receptive to treating "reasonable" covenants in restraint of trade as property interests.[167] It may also mark the inevitable by-product of the decisive embrace of unlimited dismemberment of ownership by the Louisiana Supreme Court in *Queensborough Land*.

In any event, unlike in Scotland, we see no effort to cabin the scope of title conditions in restraint of trade to serve any kind of neighbourhood or amenity protection values. Louisiana courts seem willing to give the originating parties and subsequent transferees almost free rein to impose information-processing externalities on other market participants. As long as verification is made relatively easy and cost-effective by requiring recordation in the conveyance registries of Louisiana parishes, the once venerable *numerus clausus* of Louisiana property forms seems not much of a limitation at all.

C. TYING STIPULATIONS AND AFFIRMATIVE BUSINESS OBLIGATIONS

We have already noted a few examples of our second sub-category of title conditions – those that require the burdened property owner to engage in trade with a business operated on the benefited property or to perform some other act for the benefited proprietor. Although both jurisdictions have long stressed that the *in faciendo* principle is at the core of their traditional servitude doctrines, both have created legal institutions – the real burden in Scotland and building restrictions in Louisiana – designed in part to evade

---

167 *Restatement (Third) of Property: Servitudes* (2000) s 3.6. The leading US authorities are *Whitinsville Plaza, Inc v Kotseas*, 390 N E 2d 243 (Mass 1979); *Davidson Bros, Inc v D Katz & Sons, Inc*, 579 A 2d 288 (NJ 1990). Recent examples of this trend of enforcing "reasonable" trade restraints as real covenants include: *Tippecanoe Associates II v Kimco Lafayette 671, Inc* 811 N E 2d 438 (Ind Ct App 2004) (restrictive covenant in commercial lease held enforceable); *Double Diamond Properties, LLC v Amoco Oil Co* 487 F Supp 2d 737 (E D Va 2007) (restrictive covenant prohibiting sale of any petroleum products not originally supplied by an oil company held enforceable).

this traditional prohibition. Beyond those special realms, both systems still claim to adhere to this basic content limitation, but there are some tentative signs in each jurisdiction that the commitment may be weakening.

(1) Scotland

In 1840 with *Tailors of Aberdeen v Coutts*,[168] the Court of Session and the House of Lords made it clear that a new kind of real right, the real burden, would be enforceable against singular successors. One of the great advantages of the real burden was that it allowed feudal superiors and other parties disposing of property rights in heritable property to impose on feuars and other purchasers affirmative obligations relating to land development.[169] For example, a feuar or purchaser of a lot could be obligated to construct a building in a certain architectural style, to install railings and pavements, and to pay fees for the maintenance of common areas and facilities.[170] But could a feuar or purchaser of heritable property be required affirmatively to engage in certain kinds of trades with the benefited proprietor?

As we have already seen, in the 1760s and 1820s the Scottish judges were deeply divided on this question in cases concerning obligations to bring ironwork to a superior's blacksmith,[171] or legal documents to a superior's agent.[172] Forty years later in *Earl of Zetland v Hislop*,[173] at least one judge (Lord Selborne in the House of Lords), still clung to the prohibition on imposing "personal" (read: affirmative) obligations on a burdened feuar.

A few years later, the cleavages over the propriety of affirmative obligations persisted. In *Burnett v Great North of Scotland Railway Co*,[174] land was feued to a railway company subject to a real burden obliging the feuar to construct a railway station "at which all passenger trains shall regularly stop". The Court of Session was not sympathetic. Lord Young compared the pursuer's action enforcing the obligation to Shylock's pursuit of a "pound of flesh".[175] The House of Lords reversed, holding that a feudal superior's successor could enforce the obligation to stop passenger trains at the subsequently constructed station, with the Lord Chancellor noting that the whole

168 (1840) 1 Rob 296.
169 K Reid, "Modernising land burdens: the new law of Scotland", in S van Erp and B Akkermans, *Towards a Unified System of Land Burdens* (2006) 63 at 65.
170 *Tailors of Aberdeen* at 322-324.
171 *Yeaman v Crawford* (1770) Mor 14537.
172 See *Campbell v Dunn* (1823) 2 S 341 (First Div); *Campbell v Harley* (1825) 1 W&S 690 (HL); *Campbell v Dunn* (1828) 6 S 679.
173 (1882) 9 R (HL) 40 at 43.
174 (1885) 12 R (HL) 25, reversing (1883) 11 R 375.
175 (1883) 11 R 375 at 386.

arrangement was "perfectly voluntary" and remarking on "good consideration given".[176]

More than 100 years later, judicial anxiety about affirmative trade obligations has not necessarily vanished, but with the emergence of the Lands Tribunal of Scotland and its remarkable power to vary or discharge title conditions, its intensity may be diminished. In *Cumbernauld Development Corporation v County Properties & Development Ltd*,[177] a local development corporation feued land subject to a detailed real burden obligating the feuar to erect, maintain and operate an especially elaborate ice-rink.[178] As a result, the property's price was reduced to well below its unburdened retail development value. The originating parties also confected an escape clause permitting the burdened feuars to change the property's use by paying a specified sum. After the ice-rink was constructed and proved to be unprofitable, the property was acquired by a successor that sought permission from the superior to create a "new age bingo hall" on the premises. When the superior rejected this request, the new proprietor sought and obtained a variation of the real burden from the Lands Tribunal, a decision upheld on appeal to the Court of Session.

What is striking here is that nobody, at any point, seems to have questioned that the affirmative obligation to construct and operate an icerink on the burdened property was, in the first instance, an impermissible real burden. Instead, the only question was whether a variation was merited on the basis that it was unduly burdensome[179] and how much compensation, if any, was owed to the benefited proprietor.[180]

Admittedly, this is just a single decision, and one arising from a feudal, as opposed to a neighbour burden, at that. Nevertheless, there does appear to be some judicial comfort with the obligation. Perhaps it is explained by

---

176 (1885) 12 R (HL) 25 at 26. As Reid notes, the logic of the House of Lord's conclusion is doubtful given that a future successor of the feuar, the burdened proprietor, might not even be in the railway business any more (Reid, *Property* (n 2) para 391).

177 1996 SLT 1106.

178 The pertinent terms of the feu disposition were as follows: "[The Feuars shall be bound] to commence as expeditiously as possible … the erection of, and to erect with all due diligence, and … thereafter maintain in good order and repair, and when necessary re-erect on the Feu, substantial buildings and relative offices for an ice rink which … shall be of international standard and quality" (at 1107).

179 The answer, at 1111, was yes, the restriction "impedes some reasonable use of the land", despite the existence of the escape clause.

180 The answer, at 1112, was that compensation was owed, but only one-third of the amount stipulated in the escape clause, apparently because the escape clause allowed for a change to any retail use, but the variation granted by the Lands Tribunal limited the use of the property to a bingo hall.

the feudal nature of this particular burden. Perhaps it is awareness that the original parties could have achieved the same functional end by crafting a negative restriction prohibiting all uses of the property *except as an ice-rink*. If sophisticated parties can accomplish through other legal means outcomes nominally banned by a strict *numerus clausus*, then a *numerus clausus* might not be worth the candle. Or perhaps there is simply a sense that it is unremarkable to impose affirmative commercial obligations on parties who, with ample notice, have factored these obligations into their bargains, especially if the Lands Tribunal can take care of any inefficiency arising from an unexpected change in circumstances. If these latter explanations are accurate, one of the major vestiges of Scotland's *numerus clausus* of real burdens might be slipping away.

(2) Louisiana

Louisiana, in contrast, still clings to the classic *in faciendo* prohibition and generally has cabined affirmative obligations in the special category of building restrictions where they clearly serve traditional land use development goals such as paying for maintenance of common areas and facilities. In two cases decided in the 1980s, intermediate appellate courts held that gas supply agreements benefiting gasoline distributors did not create "real obligations" running with the land.[181] Neither decision, however, cited article 651 of the revised Civil Code, which still provides that praedial servitudes, and by extension limited personal servitudes (rights of use), cannot impose affirmative obligations on a servient estate owner.[182] Instead, the courts held in conclusionary terms that the contracts merely created personal obligations,[183] and in one decision noted that the agreement benefited a person rather than a dominant estate.[184]

---

181 *Huber Oil Co of Louisiana v Save-Time* 442 So 2d 597 (La App 3 Cir 1982); *U-Serve Petroleum and Investments, Inc v Cambre* 486 So 2d 821 (La App 1 Cir 1986). These cases resemble the "solus agreement" cases that troubled the English courts in the 1960s (Heydon, "Frontiers" (n 7) at 229-251).

182 La Civ Code arts 651 (1977) (prohibiting affirmative obligations in praedial servitudes) and 640 (1976) (providing that a right of use can only "confer an *advantage* that may be established by a predial servitude") (emphasis added).

183 *Huber* at 601; *U-Serve* at 824. In *U-Serve*, the parties clearly tried to create a real right, specifying in their original contract that it was to "run with the land" and that a sale or lease of the burdened property would not negate it, and by recording the contract in the public records.

184 Ironically, the court did end up enforcing the gas supply obligation on the successor, but, in an echo of *Louisiana & Arkansas Railway*, reasoned that the successor explicitly assumed the obligation. There were also hints, though, that the obligation might be real after all for the court noted that the contract had been properly recorded and was therefore effective against successors (*U-Serve* at 824-825).

In 2001, another Louisiana intermediate appellate court had an opportunity to resolve whether a purported right of use could run with the land if it imposed an affirmative trade obligation to pay a small charge on each gallon of gasoline sold on the burdened property.[185] But once again the court dodged the main issue by finding that the original agreement did not clearly express an intent to bind the successors of the servient estate.[186] One dissenting judge, however, asserted that this intent was sufficiently expressed and was prepared to enforce the obligation despite the prohibition on affirmative obligations in Article 651.[187]

In perhaps the most well-developed decision addressing the outer limits of personal and praedial servitudes in Louisiana law in recent years, the Louisiana Third Circuit Court of Appeal held that an unusual "service agreement" confected between the owners of a condominium unit in a planned resort and the proprietors of the resort was not enforceable as a "right of use" against a successor owner of the resort.[188] Here, the original proprietors of the resort had agreed to provide a bundle of services – garbage pickup, sewerage and water, cable TV, telephone, property maintenance and upkeep – to the unit owners and had also agreed to provide them with a variety of use rights (lifetime gold club membership, use of golf carts, tennis courts, pools and recreational facilities). All this was in exchange for a monthly service fee of $75. The original agreement further specified the "services to be binding on all future owners of [the resort] property" and was recorded by the unit owners in the public records. Even though the successor had constructive and actual notice of the agreement, the court nevertheless refused to enforce the agreement as a real right.

A majority of the court held that the portions of the agreement requiring the provision of services violated article 651's prohibition on requiring a servient estate owner to do something. The agreement's remaining provisions, which the majority acknowledged were "closer to the traditional rights of use", were nevertheless held to be unenforceable because they were created in a document labelling them as "services" and because they were conditional on payment of a monthly fee. These facts, the majority observed, gave them a "peculiar nature" which disqualified them from constituting real rights. Here, in a clear echo of Merrill and Smith's information-processing account of the numerus clausus, the court specifically noted that future parties might have

---

185   *Martinez v Trans Ossun Corp Inc* 805 So 2d 424 (La App 3 Cir 2001).
186   *Martinez* at 426.
187   *Martinez* at 427 (Saunders J dissenting).
188   *Wagner v Alford* 741 So 2d 884, 888 (La App 3 Cir 1999).

difficulty interpreting the agreement's terms.[189] Yet once again at least one dissenting judge was fully prepared to expand the list of permissible rights of use in this case and suggested that courts should show flexibility in recognising the undertakings of parties, especially in a case like this where, in her view, the nature of those undertakings perfectly clear.[190] In the end, then, it seems that Louisiana's adherence to the *in faciendo* principle endures, though it is obviously under some pressure to yield to well-informed private ordering.

D. COMPARATIVE CONCLUSIONS

This study of Scottish and Louisiana law on title conditions reveals significant differences, even though both mixed jurisdictions have sometimes framed key questions in similar ways. With respect to our core sub-category, title conditions nakedly restricting commercial activities to benefit the commercial interests of benefited proprietors, we find significant divergence. Scottish law is marked most of all by subtlety, by Scottish courts and lawmakers' resistance to taking a definitive position, and by confidence in the ability of judges to make fine-tuned, contextually-informed decisions about the costs and benefits of title conditions in restraint of trade and the extent to which such conditions are consistent with important social norms and values. There is a sense that property rights must not merely represent raw market power, but must serve real social needs, whether those needs are expressed by the traditional *utilitas* principle or through recent legislative requirements of an "interest to enforce" or the presence of some palpable "benefit" to some actual parcel of land. Property owners may lose the benefit of certainty in transactional planning, and may often have to turn to "contractually structured running rights" to accomplish their ends, but that seems to be a price the Scottish property law system is willing to pay as the outer limits of its *numerus clausus* of real rights remain blurred.

In Louisiana, the development is more condensed yet evidences a more dramatic transformation in the system's attitudes. Courts overcome an initial hostility to treating title conditions in restraint of trade as real rights just as they overcame fears about the re-establishment of feudal services. This embrace of contractual freedom to dismember ownership – albeit in the name of achieving racial housing segregation – eventually led the way not only to the establishment of building restrictions as a new regime of complex and highly malleable real rights but eventually also to an uncritical alignment

189 *Wagner* at 888.
190 *Wagner* at 890-891 (Cook J dissenting).

of Louisiana law with American Common Law jurisdictions that increasingly treat title conditions in restraint of trade as real covenants capable of running with the land. Perhaps this shows what happens when a mixed jurisdiction like Louisiana lacks Civil Code provisions expressly defining the limits of the *numerus clausus* of real rights. Sophisticated parties entering commercial real estate transactions expect their Louisiana lawyers to provide them with the same legal products they can obtain in other American jurisdictions. And now Louisiana courts seem quick to oblige, afraid perhaps that Louisiana might be seen as offering a less than perfectly friendly investment environment compared to its sister states.

With respect to tying stipulations and affirmative business obligations, both Louisiana and Scotland continue to profess traditional Civilian principles – namely facial adherence to the *in faciendo* principle in the realm of praedial servitudes. There are some tentative signs that Scots attitudes may be growing more relaxed because of the presence of the Lands Tribunal's variation and discharge power, but in the face of the recent abolition of feudal tenure and the complete demise of feudal conveyancing, traditional servitude principles may well reassert themselves with renewed vigour. In Louisiana, beyond the domain of building restrictions, most courts seem reluctant to erode this last traditional limit on contractual freedom to create real rights, even though the pressure of future commercial development needs might yet tear this limit down one day.

At a global level, this comparative study does not prove which account of the *numerus clausus* has the most explanatory power in this frequently contested corner of property law. It does show, though, that concerns about minimising information-processing costs, assuring more reliable verification of property rights, protecting carefully negotiated reliance interests, and promoting certain core social values and certain kinds of neighbourly relations have all, at various times, motivated change (and resistance to change) in the content of Scotland and Louisiana's *numerus clausus* of real rights.

3 Servitudes: Extinction by Non-Use

Roderick R M Paisley

A. INTRODUCTION
B. POLICY OF EXTINCTION
C. THE COMMERCIAL CONTEXT
(1) Landlocked Property
(2) Future Development Sites
D. LEGAL RELIEF AFFORDED
E. EXTINCTION OF SERVITUDES: GENERAL POSITION
F. OBSTACLES TO EXERCISE
G. EXCEPTIONAL CASES: CLEAR AND JUSTIFIED?
H. *RES MERAE FACULTATIS*
(1) Property Right
(2) Servitude
(a) First aspect
(b) Second aspect
(c) Third aspect
(d) Fourth aspect
(e) Fifth aspect
(3) Length of initial period
(4) Assistance from the Common Law?
(5) Assistance from the Civil Law?
(6) Suspensively conditional servitudes
(7) Drafting suspensive servitudes
(8) Conclusions on *res merae facultatis*
I. MANNER OF EXERCISE OF THE SERVITUDE
(1) Positive and negative aspects
(2) Acquisition: prescription
(3) Extinction: prescription
(4) Coincidence of positive and negative
J. CONCLUSION

A. INTRODUCTION

This chapter examines servitudes and their extinction by non-use. The type of right investigated is limited to "praedial" or "predial" servitudes benefiting a plot of land, known in Scotland as "the dominant tenement"[1] and in Louisiana as "the dominant estate".[2] Although it will touch upon "legal" servitudes the coverage will exclude "natural"[3] servitudes that are implied by law from a certain state of affairs without reference to the will of the owners of the dominant and servient tenements. As "negative" servitudes[4] have been abolished in Scotland[5] but not in Louisiana, this chapter concentrates on the common element: servitudes which afford the dominant proprietor the right to carry out certain activities on the servient tenement. These are known in Scotland as "positive" servitudes and in Louisiana as "affirmative" servitudes.[6] The doctrine at the heart of the analysis is known in Louisiana as extinction by "prescription of non-use",[7] and in Scotland as "negative prescription", or more anciently as "prescription of liberty".[8]

B. POLICY OF EXTINCTION

Prescription by non-use in Louisiana[9] and negative prescription in Scotland, albeit existing in statutory form, are ultimately both generated by public policy. They ensure the marketability of land by freeing it from useless and unused restrictions. Grounded as they are in the general public interest, the doctrines are intended to override the will of individuals in specific cases. Consequently, in Louisiana parties may not by agreement renounce a prescription before it has occurred.[10] So too in Scotland any provision in any agreement that purports to provide that any right or obligation is free from the effect of extinction by negative prescription shall be null.[11] The parties to

---

1 A recent innovation is "benefited property": Title Conditions (Scotland) Act 2003 s 75; R R M Paisley, "Servitudes – the new Scottish regime", in R Rennie (ed), *The Promised Land: Property Law Reform* (2008) 91 at para 4-03.

2 La Civ Code art 646.

3 These are not extinguished by non-use in Louisiana: La Civ Code art 758. The Scottish position is obscure.

4 Consisting only of restraints on the servient tenement.

5 Title Conditions (Scotland) Act 2003 ss 79 and 80. The "appointed day" was 28 November 2004.

6 La Civ Code art 706.

7 La Civ Code art 3448.

8 Stair, *Inst* 2.7.4.

9 A N Yiannopoulos, *Predial Servitudes, Louisiana Civil Law Treatise*, vol 4, 3rd edn (2004) 447 § 163 n 7.

10 La Civ Code art 3449. See also Louisiana Mineral Code LSA-RS 31:74: if a period of prescription greater than ten years is stipulated the period is reduced to ten years.

11 Prescription and Limitation (Scotland) Act 1973 s13.

a servitude cannot contract out of the effect of the doctrines in advance by purporting to extend the period during which a right of servitude will remain extant despite non-exercise. They remain free to provide that a servitude will be extinguished by non-exercise within a shorter period.[12]

After the accrual of prescription by non-use in Louisiana the extinguished servitude cannot be revived by further use.[13] So too in Scotland is a servitude extinguished by negative prescription when the relevant period of non-exercise has elapsed, and further actings on the part of the dominant proprietor purporting to exercise it will not revive the right. However, in both jurisdictions the parties to an extinguished servitude may reconstitute it *de novo* after extinction. This may be done in Louisiana by the dominant proprietor's renouncing the prescription that has accrued in favour of his estate.[14] In Scotland the method of reconstitution is to obtain a new grant or to allow exercise for the period of positive prescription. Both jurisdictions also facilitate neighbourly co-operation and foresight. Where the unexercised servitude right is still extant but the period for extinction is soon to expire, the parties in both Louisiana and Scotland may create a new identical right, thus effectively putting off the evil day for the entire length of the period allowed by law.

C. THE COMMERCIAL CONTEXT

There will always be commercial pressures to circumvent the extinction of servitudes by non-use. The shorter the period required for extinction the greater the pressures. These may be illustrated in relation to two different types of cases: (a) "landlocked"[15] property and (b) future development sites.

(1) Landlocked Property

There is no rule in Scotland[16] or Louisiana excluding from extinction by non-exercise the sole servitude of access to any plot of land. Land may become "landlocked" if all servitudes of access thereto are extinguished

---

12 *Ferguson v McIntyre* 1993 SLT 1269; *Meijer v International Minerals & Chemical Corp* 741 F Supp 1238 (MD La 1990), affd 929 F 2d 697 (Table) (C A 5 1991); *Leiter Minerals, Inc v California Co* 241 La 915, 132 So 2d 845 (La 1961) at 940 and 854 per Justice Hawthorne.

13 Yiannopoulos, *Servitudes* (n 9) 450 § 164.

14 Yiannopoulos, *Servitudes* (n 9) 450 § 164. See *Bailey v Porter-Wadley Lumber Co* 28 F Supp 25 (DC La 1939) affd 110 F 2d 974 (5th Cir 1940) cert denied 311 US 680, 61 S Ct 48, 85 L Ed 438 (1940). Similar French cases: *Aubert v Talon* Cour d'Aix 7 July 1856, D 1856.1.285, S 1857.1.775; *Fèvre-Hannel v Maillefer* Ch Req 23 July 1860, S 1861.1.526. See J Dainow, "Prescription" (1953) 14 La LR 129 at 130-131.

15 Otherwise known as "enclaved" or "enclosed" land.

16 *Bowers v Kennedy* 2000 SC 555; 2000 SLT 1006.

by non-use.[17] This could become a problem for individuals who buy land simply as an investment and never visit the land. The possibility became real in Scotland when (now withdrawn) tax advantages in the latter part of the twentieth century encouraged investment in forestry plantations by people who had no interest in trees. The operations involved planting and waiting for extraction.[18] The life-span of the trees was longer than the period of negative prescription applicable to the attendant servitude of access. As the trees grew the servitude access right waned and eventually died leaving the fiscally efficient but un-visited plantations landlocked. A similar problem may be replicating itself with regard to airspace in some Scottish cities in a commercial fashion imported from North America. With a view to long-term development, airspace is conveyed separately from the underlying land and buildings although it is acquired together with servitudes of access across the underlying properties. As the developers patiently await the moment to build their castle in the sky, the rights to construct the manmade stairways to heaven are not exercised.

(2) Future Development Sites

The pressures arising from extinction of rights by virtue of non-exercise are particularly acute in modern societies where developers seek to steal a march on their competitors by purchasing land that is not yet zoned for development. These early bird developers will wish to acquire the land with all required servitudes, hoping to develop it at some relatively distant time in the future. In Scotland this phenomenon is known as "land-banking". Even when land is presently zoned for development or will be so in the relatively near future there may still be a significant waiting period whilst various regulatory consents are obtained prior to work starting on the ground. All this is coupled with the phenomenon of developers who have no intention of building anything themselves but who wish to put together a comprehensive set of rights that they can sell on to someone who will carry out the construction works. In the jargon of Scottish developers this is known as "putting a package together" or "turning" the land. Clearly the package of land and attendant rights must be complete and capable of sale before the construction has even started and any of the servitude rights have ever been exercised. The attendant rights invariably include servitudes of access

---

17 A similar problem can also arise in relation to servitudes for provision of service media, but for simplicity the text will largely refer only to access. The solution for the former in both jurisdictions is achieved largely by affording rights to the service provider and not to the landowner.

18 See the comments about several suspensive servitudes of access linked to different stages of the trees' development: text after n 161 below.

and servitudes of drainage and water supply. Such an "in-and-out" developer runs the risk that he may timeously acquire servitude rights necessary for a future development but that these rights may be extinguished just at the time the development looks likely. Of course it will be possible to reconstitute the servitude *de novo* but as the actual development comes closer to realisation the neighbouring proprietors are likely to increase their price as they seek to cash in on the opportunity.

D. LEGAL RELIEF AFFORDED

Although one might have little sympathy for individuals who take such little interest in their own land that they never access it, both jurisdictions have provisions with the potential to assist them. The underlying policy is not benevolence to the individual but the public interest in retaining the market-ability of land.[19] In Louisiana there is a well- developed set of provisions permitting a right of forced passage to landlocked land from the public road.[20] There is an express exception to the effect that if an estate becomes enclosed as a result of the voluntary act or omission of its owner, the neighbours are not bound to furnish a passage to him or his successors.[21] Whether this served to deny the right to a forced passage when a servitude of access was lost by prescription of non-use remained an open question until it was judicially declared by the Supreme Court of Louisiana that it did not.[22] As the purpose of the right of forced passage is to secure the "full utility"[23] of the enclosed estate, article 690 of the Civil Code declares that the right shall be suitable for the kind of traffic that is reasonably necessary for the use of the enclosed estate. This is sufficiently expansive to afford a vehicular access for commercial use[24] and probably also for a proposed development not yet started, albeit in such a case the compensation payable to the servient proprietor would be higher than that payable if only the existing use of the enclosed estate were to be continued.[25] In contrast to this detailed provision, the right of access to the public road from landlocked land in Scotland has only recently been confirmed at common law[26] and remains obscure in many respects. It is clear, however, that the access right to landlocked land is regarded in

19 *Rockholt v Keaty* 256 La 629, 237 So 2d 633 (La 1970).
20 La Civ Code arts 689-696.
21 La Civ Code art 693.
22 *LeBlanc v Thibodeux* 615 So 2d 295 (La 1993).
23 *Rockholt* (n 19) at 641 and 668 per Justice Barham.
24 E.g. *Kavanagh v Bowers* 826 So 2d 1165 (La App 5th Cir 2002).
25 *Simons v Stewart* 303 So 2d 236 (La App 2d Cir 1974) at 237 per Judge Ayres.
26 *Bowers* (n 16).

Scotland as a property right that is not subject to negative prescription.[27] So too in Louisiana a right of ownership cannot be extinguished by non-use.[28] However, the right to forced passage in that jurisdiction is not justified as a property right. Instead it is regarded as a "legal" servitude[29] that cannot be extinguished by non-use.[30] The taxonomy of the law of Louisiana is arguably more acceptable, in that the activity of access taken to landlocked land is non-exclusive, being geographically co-existent with the property right in the surrounding burdened land held by another party, and the access right is inseparable from the benefited landlocked plot of land.

E. EXTINCTION OF SERVITUDES: GENERAL POSITION

In Louisiana the Civil Code provides that: "a predial servitude is extinguished by non-use for ten years".[31] In Scotland there is no provision applicable to servitudes alone, but, insofar as they do not fall within the class of mysterious imprescriptible rights exercisable as a *res merae facultatis*,[32] they are affected by the Prescription and Limitation (Scotland) Act 1973 s 8.[33] This provides as follows:

> (1) If, after the date when any right to which this section applies has become exercisable or enforceable, the right has subsisted for a continuous period of twenty years unexercised or unenforced, and without any relevant claim in respect of it having been made, then as from the expiration of that period the right shall be extinguished.
> (2) This section applies to any right relating to property, whether heritable or moveable, not being a right specified in Schedule 3 to this Act as an imprescriptible right …

There is clearly a general similarity in the structure of these provisions. In Louisiana the period of time required to extinguish positive servitudes by non-use begins to run "from the date of their last use".[34] For example, this is

---

27 Prescription and Limitation (Scotland) Act 1973 s 8 and Sch 3 item (a). For the common law position see *Presbytery of Perth v The Magistrates of Perth* (1728) M 10723; *Leck v Chalmers* (1859) 21 D 408.
28 La Civ Code art 481.
29 Yiannopoulos, *Servitudes* (n 9) 260 § 92.
30 Yiannopoulos, *Servitudes* (n 9) 79 § 24 and 447 § 163. Cf the right to indemnity against the owner of the enclosed estate which may be lost by prescription although this has no effect on the right of passage: La Civ Code art 696.
31 La Civ Code art 753.
32 Prescription and Limitation (Scotland) Act 1973 s 8(2) and Sch 3 item (c). See text at n 73.
33 D J Cusine, "Discharge of servitudes by prescription" (1995) JR 82. Apart from shortening the period, the 1973 Act largely re-states the common law: M Napier, *Commentaries on the Law of Prescription in Scotland* (1854) 586; *Laird of Grant v McIntosh* (1678) M 10773 per counsel.
34 La Civ Code art 754. For minerals see La Mineral Code LSA-RS 31 arts 28 and 30.

when passage was last taken over a servitude of way.[35] In Scotland the rule is likely to be the same, at least where the servitude may be continuously exercised by the dominant proprietor.[36] If, however, it may be used only at stated times and intervals it is arguable that the period begins to run only from the point of time when the servitude could have been used but was not. Such servitudes are commonly encountered and include, for example, a servitude of access to be exercised "only on Saturdays", "only in July", "only in emergency"[37] or "only for funerals",[38] or a right of water supply to be used "in case of scarcity"[39] or "only in drought"[40] or the leading of seaware which is done only at certain times of the year.[41] The effect of this wording is to impose a servitude condition in terms of which, except at the stated times, the servient proprietor may prevent exercise of the positive activity permitted by the servitude.[42] It is when the interval between the times of permitted use is longest that the interaction with negative prescription is potentially most difficult. However, a servitude of water supply "only in case of drought" should not be extinguished just because there has been no drought in the past twenty years, because use at any other time is dis-conform to the terms of the servitude and will not serve to protect it from negative prescription.[43] This leads one to enquire whether a servitude of access for fire escape "in emergencies only" would be rendered more vulnerable to negative prescription if the grant also permitted use "for practice fire drills" given that the latter could be carried out whenever the dominant proprietor wished.

In Louisiana if a positive servitude has never been used the period of time begins to run "from the date the servitude is created and its exercise is possible".[44] In broad outline this also corresponds to Scots law and the rule

---

35 *Atkins v Johnson* 535 So 2d 1063 (La App 2d Cir 1988).

36 Bell, *Prin* § 999; *Bowers* (n 16).

37 *Moss Bros Group plc v Scottish Mutual Assurance plc* 2001 SLT 641.

38 See Voet *Pandects* 8 6 11, citing D 8.6.4 (Paul).

39 E.g., the reservation "in case of scarcity" of water rights to a mill and coal works: *Wemyss v Bayne, Moyes and Bayne* (1773) M 2999.

40 E.g., the grant in Disposition by the Trustees of the late John Grant in favour of David Grant dated 20 Oct 1958 and recorded GRS (Angus) (Book 2764: Folio 238) on 13 Nov 1958.

41 Sir James Steuart of Goodtrees, *Dirleton's Doubts and Questions in the Law of Scotland, Resolved and Answered*, 2ⁿᵈ edn (1762) 383 and 384.

42 In this respect it differs from the fifth variant of *res merae facultatis*: see text at n 116. See also K G C Reid and G L Gretton *Conveyancing 2007* (2008) 121.

43 D 8.6.18pr (Paul). See also the revisals inserted by the editor in Erskine, *Principles of the Law of Scotland*, 21ˢᵗ edn by J Rankine (1911) 2.9.21.

44 Yiannopoulos, *Servitudes* (n 9) 446 § 164 text at n 12 citing *Tilley v Lowery* 511 So 2d 1245 (La App 2d Cir 1987); *De La Croix v Nolan* 1 Rob 321 (La 1842). This is supported by French jurisprudence: *Gibbal v Bory*, Ch civ 14 Dec 1864, D 1864.1.126 (the right does not begin to prescribe when the building on the dominant tenement is completed); *Chatenay et Blanchet v Durand*, Cour d'Orléans, 16 February 1865, D 1865.2.60; Req November 12 1934, S 1935.1.62.

usually admits of easy application. However, the Louisiana qualification to the effect that the period will begin to run only if "exercise is possible" is potentially problematic. This does not appear to have been the subject of much litigation in Louisiana but it may be illustrated from the corresponding position in Scotland. The present rule in Scotland is probably to the effect that the period of negative prescription begins to run from the date of creation of the servitude as a real right even if at that time some engineering works are necessary to make the servitude capable of exercise.[45]

The entitlement to carry out these engineering works to make the servient tenement fit for the right of passage is a right ancillary or accessory to the primary servitude in both Scotland[46] and Louisiana.[47] It is created by legal implication at the same time as the underlying servitude unless excluded by the terms of the deed creating the right.[48] Subject to the exception of a servitude right exercisable as *res merae facultatis*,[49] Scots law seems to regard the primary servitude as being open to exercise when the dominant proprietor may exercise his ancillary rights to carry out these preparatory engineering works. For example, the period of negative prescription may start on the creation of a servitude where a road has to be constructed to make the route capable of use or where a wall at the boundary of the dominant tenement has to be demolished to enable access to be taken from the dominant to the servient.[50] So too, it would seem, as regards a servitude of drain, the period of negative prescription may start even though the servient ground must be trenched and a pipe laid before the water can start to flow. The position in Louisiana appears to be the same[51] except, of course, that Louisiana does not recognise the particular variant of *res merae facultatis* which may be relevant in Scotland.

This position does not fit entirely comfortably with how both legal systems regard the exercise of accessory rights in the context of halting the period of negative prescription or non-use after it has started to run. In both Scotland[52] and Louisiana the use of an accessory right is probably imprescriptible

---

45 See text at n 50.

46 *Moncrieff v Jamieson* [2007] UKHL 42; 2008 SC (HL) 1; 2007 SLT 989; *Pullar v Gauldie*, unreported, 25 August 2004, Arbroath Sheriff Court, case ref A184/03, Sheriff Ian G Inglis.

47 La Civ Code arts 743-745; *Palace Properties, LLC v Sizeler Hammond Square Ltd Partnership* 839 So 2d 82, 2001-2812 (La App 1 Cir 2002).

48 La Civ Code art 743.

49 See text at nn 69 ff.

50 *Peart v Legge* [2007] CSIH 70; 2008 SC 93; 2007 SLT 982 at para 27 per Lord Macfadyen.

51 *Palgrave v Gros* 829 So 2d 579 (La App 5th Cir 2002); *Broomfield v Louisiana Power & Light* 623 So 2d 1376 (La App 2d Cir 1993); *Gilfoil v Greenspon* 216 So 2d 829 (La App 2d Cir 1968).

52 It would be regarded as *res merae facultatis*. See text at n 94.

whilst the underlying servitude right subsists, unless the titles provide to the contrary. For example, the holder of a servitude of access may repair the underlying road albeit he has never done so before and even if a period of time in excess of the period of negative prescription or non-use has elapsed since the creation of the servitude.[53] However, in Louisiana the use of an accessory right alone is not regarded as a use of the principal servitude and it does not stop the prescription of non-use running against that servitude.[54] In this respect Louisiana remains true to the position indicated in the *Digest*.[55] Given that servitudes are probably the aspect of Scottish property law most strongly influenced by Civilian principles, the position is probably the same in Scotland albeit there appears to be no reported case on the matter.[56] Consequently, in both jurisdictions, the holder of a servitude over a road, who has never used it to take access to the dominant tenement, cannot keep the servitude alive simply by taking access for the purposes of surveying or repairing the road. Again this can have implications for the servicing of development sites as much of the "off-site" infrastructure, such as roads or drains, is installed on adjacent servient properties long before the dominant site is actually used.

Practitioners have responded by drafting deeds in which the ancillary rights are styled as part of the primary servitude. Aficionados of modern deeds of servitude will be familiar with wording such as:[57]

> a right of way and servitude to lay, construct, operate, inspect, maintain, repair, renew, substitute and remove one pipeline … for the transportation of liquids, gases, or mixtures or any or all thereof.

Here the ancillary activities are grafted into the narrative of a servitude almost as if they were the primary activities in that right. Clearly the courts should not allow widespread use of such drafting to override and obliterate doctrinal classification of primary and ancillary rights. However, there are cases in which a wide specification of the servitude will assist in bringing within the ambit of the primary servitude activities which otherwise could be regarded

---

53 *Hanks v Gulf States Utilities Co* 253 La 946, 221 So 249 (1969); M A Meyer, "Servitudes – prescription for partial non-use" (1970) 44 Tulane LR 625; V R Mayhall Jr, "Prescription of a mode of use of a servitude" (1969) 30 La LR 354; Yiannopoulos, *Servitudes* (n 9) 457 § 167.
54 La Civ Code art 761; *Meijer* (n 12); *Palgrave* (n 51); *Broomfield v Louisiana Power & Light* 623 So 2d 1376 (La App 2d Cir 1993); *Gilfoil v Greenspon* 216 So 2d 829 (La App 2d Cir 1968); Yiannopoulos, *Servitudes* (n 9) 422 § 150 and 454 § 166.
55 D 8 6 17 (Pomponius) referring to Labeo.
56 *Viz* England: *Bulstrode v Lambert* [1953] 2 All ER 728; [1953] 1 WLR 1064. See also Quebec: *Dorion v Les Ecclésiastiques du Séminaire de St Sulpice de Montréal* (1880) LR 5 App Cas 362.
57 See the deed considered in *Meijer* (n 12).

as ancillary. For example, some pipelines for the transport of materials such as carbon dioxide, when not being used for this, are injected with nitrogen gas for the purpose of preventing corrosion of the pipe. It would appear arguable that the passage of nitrogen along the pipe is purely ancillary to the transport of carbon dioxide. However, where the wording quoted above was used in a deed of servitude it was held by the District Court in Louisiana that the primary servitude involved the transport of *any* gas and the transport of nitrogen was not accessory to the transport of carbon dioxide. The decision appears questionable.

F. OBSTACLES TO EXERCISE

The relative shortness of the period for extinction of servitudes by non-use in Louisiana is counteracted to some extent by a further provision in the Civil Code.[58] Prescription of non-use is suspended for a period of up to ten years if the owner of the dominant testate is prevented from using the servitude by an obstacle that he can neither prevent nor remove.[59] There is no similar statutory provision in Scots law though there remains the tantalising albeit faint potential of developing a functional equivalent from some intriguingly incomplete judicial pronouncements,[60] Institutional writings,[61] and isolated statutory provisions of local application,[62] all of which refer to "suspension" of a servitude whilst its exercise is impossible. Unfortunately, the law of negative prescription is barely considered in the vast majority of the sources from which this development may come.

In Louisiana servitudes permitting minerals extraction[63] are not subject to the limitation period of ten years for the period of suspension.[64] This has the potential of making a mineral extraction servitude imprescriptible without

58 La Civ Code art 755.
59 *Palgrave* (n 51); *Baker v Chevron Oil Co* 260 La 1143, 258 So 2d 531 (La 1972); *Mire v Hawkins* 249 La 278, 186 So 2d 591 (La 1966); *Martel v A Veeder Co* 199 La 423, 6 So 2d 335 (La 1942); *Hanszen v Cocke* 246 So 2d 200 (La App 1st Cir 1971).
60 *Gray v MacLeod* 1979 SLT (Sh Ct) 17; D J Cusine and R R M Paisley, *Servitudes and Rights of Way* (1998) paras 2.98, 17.11 (at n 97 the possibility is mooted that such a right may be *res merae facultatis*) 17.15 and 17.18.
61 Erskine, *Inst* 2.9.37; Erskine, *Principles* 2.9.21.
62 E.g., British Railways Order Confirmation Act 1994 c.i Sch 1 para 27(2); Edinburgh Airport Rail Link Act 2007 asp 16 s 27(2); Cusine & Paisley, *Servitudes* (n 60) para 12.04.
63 Effectively a form of personal servitude; Yiannopoulos, *Servitudes* (n 9) 13 § 4.
64 Louisiana Mineral Code LSA-RS 31:59; *Corley v Craft* 501 So 2d 1049 (La App 2d Cir 1987) writ denied 503 So 2d 18 (La 1987); *Hall v Dixon* 401 So 2d 473 (La App 2d Cir 1981). See E A Nabors, "Louisiana mineral servitude and royalty doctrines, fiduciary problems and the obstacle theory" (1951) 25 Tulane LR 485; Note by E L L, "Mineral rights – obstacle to exercise of servitude" (1942) 5 La LR 153.

limit of time. One may compare the position in Scots law where a minerals extraction servitude is not specially exempted from negative prescription.[65] However, Scots law permits those seeking to extract minerals to acquire a property right in the minerals themselves or a tenant's right in a recorded long lease of the minerals.[66] Both of these rights are specifically exempted from extinction by non-exercise for the prescriptive period.[67] This is one of a number of advantages enabling these two rights effectively to elbow out servitudes as a commercial means of minerals extraction in Scotland.[68] By making special provision for negative prescription in the context of minerals extraction, albeit in different ways, both Scots law and the law of Louisiana deal with the commercial reality that minerals can lie un-worked for decades due to difficult ground conditions before the market improves to make their extraction economically viable.

G. EXCEPTIONAL CASES: CLEAR AND JUSTIFIED?

Exceptions to negative prescription should be clear in both their extent and justification. Unfortunately this is not so in Scotland. From the application of negative prescription one finds an express statutory exclusion of "any right exercisable as a *res merae facultatis*".[69] It is a rare example of the use of Latin in a modern Scottish statute. Normally lawyers have recourse to that language for its precision – and its use in connection with servitudes in both Louisiana and Scotland is frequent[70] – but the reason is otherwise in this case. Here the Latin phrase was adopted in the statute to preserve the common law[71] probably for no reason other than no-one was certain what it entailed. The general notion may have been copied by Scots common law from *ius commune* sources.[72] In a rather backhanded judicial acknowledgement of this origin it has been observed that "it may be thought that the doctrine

---

65 Albeit there is protection from variation or discharge in the Lands Tribunal: Title Conditions (Scotland) Act 2003 s 90(3) and Sch 11 para 1. *Quaere* if drafting to indicate the servitude was intended to be used only at some indefinite future time could convert it into a *res merae facultatis*.

66 A lease for a period exceeding twenty years: Registration of Leases (Scotland) Act 1857 s 1 as amended.

67 Prescription and Limitation (Scotland) Act 1973 s 8 and Sch 3 items (a) and (b).

68 Napier, *Commentaries on the Law of Prescription* (n 33) at 591.

69 Prescription and Limitation (Scotland) Act 1973 s 8 and Sch 3 item (c).

70 E.g., those familiar words *non aedificandi, tantum praescriptum quantum possessum, civiliter* and *in re aliena*.

71 *Peart* (n 50) at para 24 per Lord Macfadyen.

72 E.g. Voet, *Pandects* 8.4.5. Occasionally regard has been taken of these sources: Bell, *Prin* § 2017, 10th edn W Guthrie (1899) fn (p); D Johnston, *Prescription and Limitation* (1999) paras 3.07-3.18 and 15.17.

has been borrowed from some Civilians without sufficient consideration or definition".[73] The same could be said for the use of the term in the modern statute. It was simply a case of keeping the antique in the attic because it might be worth something in the future.

H. *RES MERAE FACULTATIS*

Res merae facultatis may be translated as "a mere facility" or, more loosely, a power which the holder may exercise or not at his pleasure.[74] Another Latin phrase, commonly used in older Scottish cases, with an identical meaning is *actus merae facultatis*.[75] Rarer, but again of identical meaning, is *res merae voluntatis*.[76] A fuller version of the rule, stated by Sir George Mackenzie to be "a general rule in all servitudes", was: *ea quae sunt merae facultatis non praescribuntur*[77] and Erskine largely adapted this variant in his formulation *in iis quae sunt merae facultatis non praescribitur*.[78] Even more emphatic is the quoted formulation adopted by counsel in argument in one Scottish case: *in eis quae sunt merae facultatis nunquam praescribitur*.[79]

However, there has been considerable difficulty in Scotland in determining what these phrases entail in the context of servitudes. The present position, only recently further developed by the Scottish courts, is not entirely plain or beyond criticism. Some clarity may be provided by a comprehensive examination. The concept of *res merae facultatis* can be examined by reference to property rights (where it has potential application to both dominant and servient tenements) and to the right of servitude itself. In the course of the examination it will become clear that although the phrase *res merae facultatis* or any of its variants is not used in Louisiana much of its import is recognised in the law of Louisiana. In addition, to the extent that it is not recognised in Louisiana, Scots law is thereby challenged as to why it should be accepted at all. Is it really necessary?

---

73 *Mitchell v Brown* (1888) 5 Sh Ct Rep 9 at 13 per Sheriff-Substitute W Guthrie.

74 Erskine, *Inst* 3.7.10.

75 *Anent Trusts and Back-Bonds* (1677) 3 BS 185; *Buntein v Boyd* (1682) M 10872; *Wilkie v Scott* (1688) M 11189 at 11190; *Williamson and Anderson v Lows* (1693) 4 BS 66; *Maccallan v Mags of Ayr* (1693) 4 BS 84; *Earl of Aberdeen v Baird* (1694) 4 BS 126; *The Creditors and Donatar of the Estate of Dunfermline v Laird of Innes* (1707) M 10913.

76 See Answers for *William Vint, Thomas Whitson, Thomas Bird, and others, Brewers in Dalkeith, Defenders to the Petition of His Grace the Duke of Buccleugh, and the Tacksmen of His Grace's Mills at Dalkeith, Pursuers*, 4 October 1765, page 17, available in the British Library and on the ECCO database Gale Document Number CW3323649521.

77 Mackenzie, *Institutions* 175.

78 Erskine, *Principles of the Law of Scotland* 2.9.17.

79 *MacDonald v North of Scotland Bank Limited* 1942 SLT 196 at 201.

(1) Property Right

In Scotland a specific statutory exception exempts a right of property from extinction by negative prescription.[80] Similarly in Louisiana a right of ownership cannot be extinguished by non-use.[81] Both jurisdictions admit that ownership may be lost when a right of exclusive property in the same subject is acquired by another person, as when, in Louisiana, acquisitive prescription accrues in favour of an adverse possessor[82] and, in Scotland, a right of property is acquired by a third party by means of positive prescription.[83] However in neither jurisdiction does the creation of a servitude cause this: both remain faithful to the basic Civilian rule expressed by Ulpian in the *Digest*:[84]

"Loci corpus non est dominii ipsius, cui seruitus debetur, sed ius eundi habet."	"The actual substance of a tract of land is not the property of the man who has a servitude over it; what belongs to him is a right of way across it."[85]

In both jurisdictions the property right in the servient tenement or estate is not extinguished or transferred to the dominant proprietor: rather that right of property and servitude co-exist in the same thing. Only when the servitude results in the extraction of material such as water or stone will the property in that substance be transferred.

In Scotland all legitimate methods of exercise of a property right are regarded as *res merae facultatis* for so long as the property right itself endures. Consequently, a proprietor's entitlement to use his own land in ways such as exercising an implied right of ish and entry and of access,[86] installing drains,[87] digging minerals,[88] removing parts of walls,[89] or by building[90] is *res merae facultatis*. Merely by refraining from these activities for any length of

---

80 Prescription and Limitation (Scotland) Act 1973 s 8 and Sch 3 item (a). That had also been the position at common law: Napier, *Commentaries on the Law of Prescription* (n 33) at 86.

81 La Civ Code art 481.

82 La Civ Code art 481.

83 K G C Reid, *The Law of Property* (1996) para 674.

84 D 8.5.4pr.

85 Mommsen, Krueger, Watson, *The Digest of Justinian*, vol 1, 267 provides the translation.

86 *Bowers* (n 16) respectively at 561 and 1010 para 16 per the opinion of the Court delivered by Lord Rodger.

87 *Morrison or Sutherland v Maclennan* (1908) 25 Sh Ct Rep 93 at 95 per Sheriff MacWatt.

88 Erskine, *Inst* 3.7.10; *Cadell v Allan* (1905) 7 F 606; (1905) 13 SLT 10 respectively at 627 and 21 per Lord Kinnear; *Crawford v Bethune* (1821) 1 S 111.

89 *Gellatly v Arrol* (1863) 1 M 592.

90 Viz: Voet, *Pandects* 8.4.5 where the wording is "*res mere facultatis*". C A Hesse, *Die Rechtsverhältnisse zwischen Grundstücksnachbarn* 2nd edn (1880) 620, s 129.

time a proprietor does not thereby subject himself to a negative real restraint prohibiting their being carried out in future.[91] Scots law shares this approach with Louisiana[92] where one finds that the incidents of ownership incapable of prescription include the right to demand relocation of a servitude.[93] In both jurisdictions the servient proprietor is restrained from acting in a manner that would cause a material interference with an extant positive servitude.[94] For example, he cannot build a wall across a servitude road. However, when the servitude is extinguished the restraint flies off and, by virtue of his underlying property right, the servient proprietor can carry out the very activity which was previously restrained. He does not have to re-acquire the right to carry out this activity.[95] It has always remained his – un-extinguished by negative prescription or prescription by non-use – even though it had remained unexercised whilst the servitude subsisted.

(2) Servitude

There is some indication in Scotland of the existence of a view that *res merae facultatis* was confined to property rights and did not extend to servitudes. Witness the argument of counsel for the pursuer in one early eighteenth-century case:[96]

> The *res merae facultatis*, which cannot prescribe, are the powers a man has in virtue of his own dominion or property; but a right that gives him a power over the estate of another may be lost by prescription, altho' it was optional for him, so long as the right subsisted, whether he should use it or not; which is the case, for example, of all the rural servitudes.

This, however, was not the approach finally adopted by Scots law and the notion of *res merae facultatis*, for better or worse, has been refined and admitted to aspects of praedial servitudes as well as to property rights. The position now is that as long as a positive servitude exists its lawful exercise by the dominant proprietor is *res merae facultatis*. There are five aspects of this principle that will be examined in turn. The first four are well established and the fifth is controversial.

91 Such restraints were formerly known as negative servitudes: Erskine, *Inst* 3.7.10; Bankton, *Inst* 2.12.22; *Haigues v Halyburton* (1704) M 10727 and now converted into negative real burdens: Title Conditions (Scotland) Act 2003 s 2.
92 *Bryant v Sholars* 104 La 786, 29 So 350 (1901).
93 Yiannopoulos, *Servitudes* (n 9) 440 § 159.
94 Cusine & Paisley, *Servitudes* (n 60) paras 12.94-12.107; Yiannopoulos, *Servitudes* (n 9) 435-438 § 158.
95 *Chiasson v Duplechain* 56 So 2d 615 (La App 1st Cir 1952); Yiannopoulos, *Servitudes* (n 9) 442 § 161.
96 *Thomas Macdougal v Mrs Barbara Macdougal and her Husband*, 10 July 1739 FC, case no 126, 206 at 209; M 10947 at 10951.

(a) First aspect

First, for so long as the servitude endures the dominant proprietor has the facility of retaining the right. Alternatively, he can unilaterally relinquish the servitude in full or in part as and when he pleases.[97] This also applies to ancillary or accessory rights.[98] The dominant proprietor may retain the servitude and expressly discharge these rights in whole or in part.[99] He cannot, however, discharge the primary servitude and retain the ancillary rights. This also appears to be the law of Louisiana.[100]

(b) Second aspect

Second, if he retains it, the dominant proprietor can also decide to exercise the servitude or not as he wishes. This also applies to the ancillary or accessory rights. In consequence the unused "excess" of an expressly granted servitude right is not lost by partial use for the prescriptive period.[101] This is also the rule in Louisiana.[102] In Scotland the dominant proprietor can also restrain the servient proprietor from causing material obstruction to the servitude or he can decide not to bother.[103] The general principle has been judicially recognised in Scotland:[104]

> A servitude is a burden on the servient tenement, and a right *merae facultatis* in the dominant. There is no instance in any of the known servitudes, whether of way, of aqueduct, of water, of light,[105] or of support, of compelling the dominant tenement to exercise a right which it wishes to relinquish.

---

97 Cusine & Paisley, *Servitudes* (n 60) para 12.141.
98 *Swan v Muirkirk Iron Co* (1850) 12 D 622; 22 Sc Jur 205.
99 Cf D 8.3.34pr (Papinian) which initially suggests the converse but is best applied only to discharge of a servitude *quoad* a *pro indiviso* (i.e. undivided) share in the dominant or servient tenement. This is how the passage is applied by the law of Scotland and Louisiana.
100 The rule in Québec is identical: "L'accessoire s'éteint évidemment avec le principal" (D-C Lamontagne, *Biens et propriété*, 5th edn (2005) 401 para 617).
101 Erskine, *Inst* 2.9.4; *John White & Sons and Others v J & M White and others* (1906) 8 F 1166; (1905) 12 SLT 662 reversed on consideration that the underlying grant was incompetent in [1906] AC 72; (1906) 8 F (HL) 41; (1905) 13 SLT 655. See also the Canadian case *Keewattin Power Co Ltd v Lake of the Woods Milling Co Ltd* [1930] AC 640 at 657 per Viscount Dunedin (PC) with earlier proceedings at (1928) 61 OLR 363; (1929) 63 OLR 667.
102 La Civ Code art 759.
103 However, if he does not bother and the obstruction remains, the servitude can be restricted by abandonment. Similarly, if the material obstruction endures for the entire period of negative prescription and precludes any exercise of the servitude for that entire period, it may negatively prescribe.
104 *Bridges v Lord Saltoun* (1873) 11 M 588 at 594 per Lord (Ordinary) Gifford.
105 This type of negative servitude is now converted into a real burden and may be created only as a real burden: Title Conditions (Scotland) Act 2003 ss 2, 79 and 80.

A more specific application of this was given by Erskine:[106]

> A servitude is not lost or even impaired, *non utendo*, though he to whom it is due forbear at certain seasons the full exercise of his right, provided that such forbearance can admit of an interpretation consistent with an *animus* of preserving the right entire.[107] Thus, a right of pasturage constituted upon an adjacent common, suffers not the least diminution, though the owner of the servitude should regularly, for the summer months, have carried his cattle from the servient to a field of his own; because such act is *merae facultatis*, and is presumed to be done, not with any view of relinquishing his right, but of feeding his cattle upon grounds which he thinks are the most proper for them, that they may give a higher price in the market.

This broad approach is also accepted in the law of Louisiana where it has been judicially observed:[108]

> A servient estate cannot force a dominant estate to use a right-of-way which exists in favour of the dominant estate ... The servient estate cannot compel the owners of the dominant tenement to exercise their right of passage.

In Scotland and Louisiana the position may be varied by conditions expressly attached to the servitude and stated to be enforceable by the servient proprietor. Counter-intuitive though it may seem at first, it may be in the interest of the servient proprietor to require a consistent exercise of the servitude and to preclude discharge of the right. For example, if the servitude is one of minerals extraction the servient proprietor may benefit from an expressly reserved payment for every ton of material extracted. If the servitude relates to oil transport through a pipe, the servient proprietor may similarly receive a regular payment corresponding to the volume of liquid transported. If the right involves access over a shared road there may be a correlative servitude condition that the holder will contribute to the road's upkeep. This would be lost if the servitude could be renounced.[109] In all of these cases the commercial viability of the overall scheme is dependent upon a specific provision dis-applying the default rule that the retention and exercise of a servitude by the dominant proprietor is *res merae facultatis*.[110]

---

106 Erskine, *Inst* 2.9.37, citing *Munro v MacKenzie* (1760) Mor 14533. See also *Church of Scotland General Trustees v Clow* (1994) *Paisley and Cusine Unreported Property Cases* 429 at 439 per Sheriff Principal D Risk QC.

107 The qualification here would be consistent with the doctrine of abandonment.

108 *Dautreuil v Degeyter* 436 So 2d 614 (La App 3rd Cir 1983) at 618 paras 7 and 8 per Judge Cutrer.

109 *Tennant v Napier Smith's Trs* (1888) 25 R 671. This consequence can be avoided in Scotland if the obligation to maintain the road is created as a real burden affecting the dominant tenement in the servitude: *Love-Lee v Cameron* 1991 SCLR 61.

110 Cusine & Paisley, *Servitudes* (n 60) para 14.62.

(c) Third aspect

The third aspect deals with negative servitudes. This may at first seem out of place in an analysis of the characteristics of a positive servitude. However, as will be examined later,[111] a positive servitude has a negative aspect, that is, the right to stop the servient proprietors and others from obstructing the positive activity justified by the servitude. Consequently, this third aspect of *res merae facultatis* has potential relevance to positive servitudes particularly those where the negative and positive aspects are dislocated geographically or temporally. In one early Scottish case[112] the Court of Session considered a negative servitude *altius non tollendi* created in a deed of 1607. The dominant proprietor had first sought to enforce it when the servient proprietor attempted to heighten his building over eighty years after the deed was originally granted. This length of time was twice the length of the then applicable period of negative prescription. Counsel for the dominant proprietor argued the negative servitude was still enforceable. His argument is recorded as follows:[113] "In negative servitudes (such as this of *altius non tollendi*) there is no prescription, being *actus merae facultatis*, until there can be an attempt or contravention." This argument succeeded and the court held that the servient property was still liable to the servitude. This formed the basis of the rule that a negative servitude did not prescribe from the date of its creation but from the time the party acted contrary to the servitude, by building, or obtaining a declarator of immunity from servitude.[114] The period does not begin to run at all if the dominant proprietor successfully obtains interdict against a breach of the servitude. This continued to be accepted as the position of Scots law after the enactment of the Prescription and Limitation (Scotland) Act 1973 reformulating the law of negative prescription.[115] It also remained the rule until the abolition of negative servitudes.[116] The position of the law of Louisiana is identical in that the prescription on non-use commences to run for negative servitudes from the date of the occurrence of an event contrary to the servitude.[117] The upshot of this is that negative servitudes are potentially permanent and are not doomed to be limited to period of time equivalent to

---

111 See text at n 173.
112 *Wilkie v Scott* (1688) M 11189. See *Wilky v Scot* 28 June 1688 *Harcase* 220 case no 780.
113 At 11190.
114 Erskine, *Inst* 2.9.37; Bankton, *Inst* 2.7.61; Bell, *Prin* § 999. Stair, *Inst* 2.7.4 is silent as to negative servitudes. Erskine and Bankton both refer to D 6.2.6 (Gaius).
115 Prescription and Limitation (Scotland) Act 1973 s 8(2) expressly excluding *res merae facultatis*. See Reid, *Property* (n 83) para 471; W Gordon, *Scottish Land Law*, 2nd edn (1999) para 24-102.
116 Title Conditions (Scotland) Act 2003 ss 79 and 80. It remains the rule for the negative prescription of negative real burdens albeit the prior is reduced to five years: 2003 Act s 18.
117 La Civ Code art 754.

the period of negative prescription in Scotland and the period of prescriptive non-use in Louisiana.

(d) Fourth aspect

Fourth, where the servitude was originally constituted to benefit a class of permitted activities on the dominant tenement Scots law adopts the position that at any time the dominant proprietor can use the servitude for some or all of the permitted purposes. Use for any single permitted purpose will retain the possibility of using the servitude for all of the remaining permitted purposes, as long as the burden on the servient tenement is not unwarrantably increased. The matter may be otherwise stated: a dominant proprietor using a servitude for the sole purpose of benefiting a single type of permitted activity on the dominant tenement will not for that reason alone lose the right to continue to enjoy the same servitude when he wishes to develop the dominant tenement and change its use to another permitted use. This arose for consideration in an early nineteenth-century Scottish case where the servitude was originally reserved in an agreement of 1833 "for the benefit of the house of Easter Castleton". The dominant proprietor wished to construct new offices to the house on her land and use the servitude to transport building material for that purpose. In rejecting an attempt to interdict use of the servitude for this purpose it was judicially observed (with the entire First Division concurring):[118]

> Whether possession of the road, under the agreement of 1833, had ever been had for this precise purpose or not, it is clearly one of the purposes for which the use of the road was reserved by the written agreement of the parties. And it was *res merae facultatis* on the part of the proprietor of the [dominant proprietrix] to use it for this purpose whenever she pleased.

The facts of that case show that the dispute arose within a period of time after the original grant shorter than the then applicable period of negative prescription. However, it is submitted that the same judicial observation would remain valid even if the dispute had arisen at any time during the existence of the servitude after this initial period had elapsed. Similarly in Louisiana the dominant proprietor retains the right to alter the use of his dominant tenement and to continue to use the servitude for that new purpose provided always the changed purpose is within the class of purposes for which the servitude originally could have been used and the change does not aggravate

118 *Gibb v Bruce* (1837) 16 S 169 at 171 per Lord Gillies, referred to with approval in *Alvis v Harrison* 1991 SLT 64 at 67 per Lord Jauncey. (The quotation does not appear in the report at (1837) 10 Sc Jur 111.)

the condition of the servient estate.[119] The commercial point arising is this. Where a business on the dominant tenement fails, the person acquiring the site is likely to want to do something else and will not want to continue the same loss-making activity. It would tend to frustrate economic regeneration if the servitude of access benefiting that site had been extinguished by negative prescription to the extent that it permitted only the continuation of activity that was now demonstrated to be a business failure. Of course one can vary the default position by suitably-worded servitude conditions but this would tend to make the title unattractive to a bank and potentially unmarketable.

(e) Fifth aspect

Fifth, the Inner House of the Court of Session has recently re-interpreted opaque and unsatisfactory Scottish case law[120] arriving at what is arguably an even more impenetrable and peculiar result. Faced with the difficult task of distinguishing earlier authority which it did not wish to apply, the court in *Peart v Legge* developed the fifth category of *res merae facultatis*: a servitude right of access may be regarded as a *res merae facultatis* if [121]

> the terms of the instrument constituting the right, properly construed, indicate that the right was not to be exercised at once, but was to subsist until exercised at an indefinite future date to be chosen by the proprietor of the dominant tenement.

There is no reason to assume that this approach is limited to servitudes of access.[122] The quotation also indicates that even if he expects there to be no exercise for an initial period, the servient proprietor has no right to exclude exercise during that time. There is nothing to preclude the dominant proprietor from changing his mind and commencing use of the servitude much earlier or later than he originally envisaged. He does not have to justify his decision on the basis of changed circumstances. He appears to be able to

---

119 Yiannopoulos, *Servitudes* (n 9) 432 § 156. This is supported by French cases: *Couprie v Lacoste* Ch Req 28 June 1865, D 1866.1.153, S 1865.1.339; *Com de Girmont c Her Lebegue de Bayecourt* Ch civ 11 March 1846, S 1846.2.472.

120 *Charles Smith and others (Trustees of Dundee Joint Stock Company) v David Stewart* (1884) 11 R 921; (1884) 21 SLR 623 (relevant papers are to be found in National Archives under reference: CS 246 2 McNeill S 13/6 and in the Advocates' Library in (1884) *General Collection of Session Papers* vol 704 case no 165). See also *Mitchell* (n 73); *Crumley v Lawson* (1892) 8 Sh Ct Rep 307; D J Cusine (ed), *The Conveyancing Opinions of Professor J M Halliday* (1992), Opinion 143, 613; C Waelde (ed), *Professor McDonald's Conveyancing Opinions* (1998), Opinion 54, 238.

121 *Peart v Legge* [2007] CSIH 70; 2008 SC 93; 2007 SLT 982 at para 28 per Lord Macfadyen. See D L Carey Miller, *Res merae facultatis: Mysterious or misunderstood?* (2008) 12 EdinLR 451. For comment on the earlier proceedings: R R M Paisley, "Right to make roads and *res merae facultatis*" (2007) 11 EdinLR 95.

122 See D 8.6.19 (Pomponius); *Logan v A & J Stephen Ltd*, unreported, Cupar Sheriff Court, case ref A239/91 Sheriff J McInnes QC and Sheriff Principal John J Maguire (the matter was left open).

do so on a whim. There is no absolute requirement that he should have to give notice of his wish to initiate use, although this may be implied from the obligation to exercise the right *civiliter* (i.e. reasonably), in particular, given that the underlying right is a servitude, where the initial exercise involves works of construction or engineering operations.[123] The fact that the dominant proprietor may bring forward the use into the period when it was originally thought that positive activity would not occur distinguishes this variant of *res merae facultatis* from the device of a servitude condition restricting the time of exercise of a servitude. In the latter case the servient proprietor has an absolute right to prevent such activity by the dominant proprietor.

This immediately appears to be a dream ticket for developers who wish to constitute rights over adjacent servient land where development on their own dominant site is still a long way off. However, the same type of right has the potential to cause problems if the adjacent servient land is also to be developed.[124] The terms of the judgment in *Peart v Legge*, admittedly not beyond controversy, appear to indicate that the right will cease to be *res merae facultatis* and will then be susceptible to negative prescription as soon as it begins to be exercised.[125] Though not expressly ruled out, it does not appear likely that the Court would have wished to indicate that the right was forever exempted from prescription whether exercised or not, or that the right could periodically revert to a state of suspended animation during repeat periods of non-use. As the court observed, certain indications that the right was not to be exercised at once were to be gleaned from inferences from the wording of the deed. Contrary to what some had previously thought, it was not sufficient merely to demonstrate that an obstacle such as a wall had to be removed before the right could be exercised:[126]

> We are not prepared to hold that every servitude which, in order to be exercised, requires work to be done to open a gap in a wall or other boundary structure, or otherwise to render the servient tenement fit for the exercise of the right, is on that account to be regarded as indicating that the right is intended to subsist whether exercised or not until such indefinite future time as the dominant proprietor may chose to carry out the works.

One may query why such inferences of intention from the deed itself can

123 *Ewart v Cochrane* (1860) 22 D 358 at 365 per Lord Deas. Presumably it would not detract from the categorisation as *res merae facultatis* if such notice were required by means of servitude condition. *Quaere* if this would make certain that the right was converted into a suspensively conditional servitude.
124 A Watt, "Future access rights: *Res merae facultatis*" (2008) *Greens Property Law Bulletin* 1.
125 Reid and Gretton, *Conveyancing 2007* (n 42) 121 text at n 5, referring to the use of the word "until" in *Peart* (n 121) para 28 by Lord Macfadyen.
126 *Peart* (n 121) at para 28 per Lord Macfadyen.

lead to such a relief from the ravages of negative prescription when an express statement purporting to exclude negative prescription in relation to a servitude would apparently be excluded by statute.[127] Perhaps it is now the case that an express statement in a deed, deliberately modelled on *Peart*, to the effect that the right is not to be exercised at once, but is to subsist until exercised at an indefinite future date chosen by the proprietor of the dominant tenement, will not be regarded as contracting out of the statutory rules of negative prescription but instead, as claiming the specific exception of *res merae facultatis*. Who knows? However, if this is indeed the case, it is truly "a shift towards party autonomy in an area of law where such autonomy would not be expected".[128] The public policy underpinning negative prescription has been undermined.

(3) Length of initial period

One might query the length of the initial period during which a right may remain as *res merae facultatis*? On the observations made in *Peart* that it was right in principle to construe the exception to the general principle of negative prescription "narrowly"[129] one commentator has commented:[130]

> It is expected that this assertion will be warmly welcomed by conveyancers as this should hopefully prevent long forgotten and unused access rights from rearing their heads after unreasonably lengthy periods of time.

This is optimistic, perhaps unduly so. Unlike the approach found in some English cases[131] there is no direct authority in Scotland confirming that if no period for exercise is specified it should be exercised within a "reasonable" time, although there remains the potential to develop this from the law on suspensive conditions in contracts.[132] That said, given that servitudes are normally perpetual rights and contracts generally relate to comparatively ephemeral matters, what is regarded as a reasonable period of time in relation to a servitude could be quite long. Furthermore this limitation of a "reasonable" period is a default position that could be excluded even by an illustrative, albeit not binding, statement of what the period is anticipated to be. Unlike

---

127 Prescription and Limitation (Scotland) Act 1973 s 13. See text at n 11.
128 Reid and Gretton, *Conveyancing 2007* (n 42) 121.
129 *Peart* (n 121) per Lord Macfadyen para 28.
130 Watt, "Future access rights" (n 124) at 2.
131 *Chaffe v Kinsley* (2000) 79 P & CR 404; (1999) 77 P & CR 281; 1999 WL 852817; *Swan v Sinclair* [1925] AC 227.
132 *T Boland and Co, Ltd v Dundas's Trs* 1975 SLT (Notes) 80, following *Aberfoyle Plantations Ltd v Khaw Bian Cheng* [1960] AC 115 (PC) on appeal from Court of Appeal of the Federation of Malaya.

some Common Law jurisdictions[133] Scots law has no limitation based in the law of perpetuities to invalidate servitudes (indeed in the pleadings of an eighteenth-century Scottish case such a right was referred to by the colourful title of "a Perpetuity of a Servitude").[134] If they are somehow excluded from negative prescription, they could remain extant and unexercised forever. In some Common Law jurisdictions easements are subject to the rule of perpetuities, and, if the existence of a future easement depends on a contingency that may occur outside the perpetuity period, it is regarded as a contingent interest in property. If the possibility exists that the easement may arise after the expiration of the relevant perpetuity period, the grant will be rendered void.[135] This rule can operate to frustrate commercially desirable easements such as easements over roads and drains yet to be constructed although, in some jurisdictions, what has become known as the "wait and see" rule would appear to save a grant not expressly confined within the perpetuity period.[136] This abolishes the requirement that every estate or interest must necessarily vest within the perpetuity period. An estate or interest created after the legislated date does not infringe the rule where it is capable of vesting outside the period. In Scotland there is no semblance of this "tiresome and incomprehensible"[137] rule as regards servitudes.[138] Consequently, servitude rights falling within the classification *res merae facultatis* may confer on the benefited proprietor what is in effect a perpetual option to exercise a servitude any time in the future as decided by him. Unless there is suitable drafting in the deed of constitution, the burdened proprietor is powerless to draw the period to a close by any means, even if he himself attempts to force the pace by laying the drain or making the relevant road over which the servitude is to be exercised. The functional distinction between this form of right and a simple option to take access at some time in the future is not easy to make. However, the formulation of the right set out by the court in *Peart* tends to

133   *Dunn v Blackdown Properties Ltd* [1961] Ch 433; J Gaunt and P Morgan (eds), *Gale on Easements*, 17th edn (2002) paras 1-99-1-106; C Sara, *Boundaries and Easements*, 3rd edn (2002) 235-236; G Battersby, "Easements and the rule against perpetuities" (1961) 25 Conv (NS) 415; The Law Reform Commission (Ireland), *Report on the Rule against Perpetuities and Cognate Rules* (LRC 62-2000) ch 3 paras 3.01-3.07; R A Rehbock, "Customary and expansible easements: applicability of the rule against perpetuities" (1977) 56 Oregon L Rev 518.

134   *Petition of James Earl of Abercorn* 13 January 1761 Bodleian Library Oxford, available on ECCO Database Gale Document Number CW3324967485, page 13.

135   E.g., *Adam v Shrewsbury* [2005] EWCA Civ 1006; [2006] 1 P & CR 27.

136   E.g. Alberta Perpetuities Act, RSA 2000, c P-5, ss 3-5; British Columbia Perpetuity Act RSBC 1996, c 358 s. 22; Ontario Perpetuities Act RSO 1990, c P 9, ss 3-4.

137   Report by the Law Commission, *The Rules against Perpetuities and Excessive Accumulations* (Law Com No 251, 1998) 80 para 7.8.

138   Scots law does not disclose the same hostility to perpetuities as found in Common law jurisdictions: R Burgess, *Perpetuities in Scots Law* (Stair Society vol 31, 1979).

make the option into a real right from the date of its creation and not when the right is exercised.

(4) Assistance from the Common Law?

A developer, as proprietor of dominant subjects, may wish not only to take access over a road on adjacent servient land but impose an obligation on the servient proprietor to build it. When these works are complete the servitude of access will be available for exercise. What is the nature of this servitude until the works are completed? Is it *res merae facultatis* on the basis that one might reasonably foresee that the required works will take a certain time to complete and the servitude of access may not physically be exercised until then? Parties wishing to avoid the risk that the right of access would fail to be a *res merae facultatis*, in the past, have sought to bring the servitude into existence only when the works are complete. The logic is that negative prescription cannot extinguish a right yet to be born. There is some support for this approach in the reported case law. Over eighty years ago a Scottish judge, Lord Shaw of Dunfermline, had occasion to consider the nature of a *res merae facultatis*, sitting in the House of Lords in an English appeal where the issue for consideration related to the existence of an easement of access.[139] The title deeds to the servient property contained a reservation in favour of a neighbour of a right to take access over a road when it was formed by the servient proprietors who had first to knock down a wall so it could be built. The right to require the servient proprietors to make the road was never exercised and the issue arose as to whether the easement had been lost by abandonment. In holding that no such easement ever existed Lord Shaw distinguished *res merae facultatis* on the one hand and the grant of a right *sub conditione* and *sub obligatione* on the other. In circumstances of this case the access easement had never come into existence as the contingency of its existence was the performance of an obligation that had never occurred. Lord Shaw opined:[140]

> The case is not one … of the exercise of a right, the physical conditions of which are in existence so as to enable the right to be exercised.[141] All the arguments as to non-use of a subject which is *res merae facultatis* can find no place in the present case. For there was no *res*, no right, and the physical basis of the right, including

139 *Swan v Sinclair* [1925] AC 240.
140 At 243.
141 On this point *Swan* was distinguished in *Dear v Wilkinson* (1960) 2 *West Indian Reports* 309 (Supreme Court of Barbados) where no pathway was in existence as at the date of the grant of the easement but no works were required to make it passable as at that date. Subsequent acts led to the abandonment of the right.

the very construction of the road over which the right of way was to run, has never yet been in existence.

If this reasoning were to be applied in a corresponding Scottish case, it would simply appear to shift the issue from one recognised type of *res merae facultatis* to another. No longer are we dealing with a servitude but with an aspect of property. In Scotland, where it is constituted in the form of a real burden (broadly similar to the Common Law "restrictive covenant"), a benefited proprietor's option to require a burdened proprietor to construct a road would itself be an aspect of the property right in the dominant tenement, albeit it requires to be specifically provided for. Consequently, if it permitted the dominant proprietor to call for a road to be made "on demand" or at some indefinite time, it too would be regarded as *res merae facultatis* and not subject to negative prescription just because it has not been exercised for decades.[142] However, once the servient proprietor is called upon to make the road and thereafter fails to do so for the prescriptive period, the remedies for this breach will prescribe.[143]

(5) Assistance from the Civil Law?

The view of the Roman jurist Pomponius was recorded in the *Digest* in the following terms:[144]

"Si partem fundi uendendo lege cauerim, uti per eam partem in reliquum fundum meum aquam ducerem, et statutum tempus intercesserit, antequam riuum facerem, nihil iuris amitto, quia nullum iter aquae fuerit, sed manet mihi ius intergrum: quod si fecissem iter neque usus essem, amittam".	"Suppose I sell part of my estate and make it a term of the contract that I am to have the right to channel water across that part to the rest of my estate, and suppose that the prescribed period elapses without my constructing a water course. I do not lose any right, as there is no channel for water to flow through; in fact, my right remains unimpaired. However, if I had made a water course and not used it, I would lose my right".[145]

---

142   See *JB and C Group Management Ltd v Haren*, 4 December 1992, unreported OH, Lord Cullen (available on LEXIS). The obligation to make a road was imposed in feudal deeds dating from 1937 and 1938.

143   Title Conditions (Scotland) Act 2003 s 18.

144   D 8.6.19 (Pomponius). See also Voet, *Pandects* 8.6.11.

145   Mommsen, Krueger, Watson, *The Digest of Justinian*, vol 1, 275 provides the translation.

Over the centuries various ways have been suggested as to how this enigmatic passage is to be interpreted.[146] The view held by many writers in the tradition of the European *ius commune* is that the passage describes a situation in which there is never any servitude but simply a mere obligation to create a servitude.[147] This is also the view of the leading Louisiana commentator on servitudes.[148] The difficulty of finding a basis to disapply the law of negative prescription is elided in that negative prescription cannot begin to extinguish a real right before its creation. This is virtually the mirror image of the solution suggested in the Common Law by Lord Shaw of Dunfermline.

However venerable the authors who have taken this view, or those who have translated it, the fact remains that it is a gloss on what the original passage actually says. It remains the case that the passage could describe exactly the arrangement that is regarded as *res merae facultatis* in Scots law.

(6) Suspensively conditional servitudes

The passage quoted above from the writings of Pomponius could also describe a suspensively conditional servitude. Perhaps *res merae facultatis* as recognised in Scotland in relation to servitudes is a species of that legal genus.

Although suspensively conditional servitudes are acknowledged by commentators in both Scots law[149] and the law of Louisiana[150] there appears to be little authority directly on point. Consequently, the law in both jurisdictions is relatively undeveloped and the nature of the rights is rather obscure. The analysis that follows is therefore exploratory. Some assistance may be drawn from the law of contract where it is clear that negative prescription does not start to run whilst a right is suspensively conditional and not capable of exercise.[151] Again following the general pattern of contract law[152] there appear to be at least two distinct types of suspensively conditional servitudes.

146 See some variants summarised in R Elvers, *Die Römische Servitutenlehre* (1856) 772-773 § 73(1) note c.

147 E.g. Pothier, *Pandectes de Justinien*, vol 4, (1820) 8.6.20 372-373; Voet, *Pandects* 8.6.11; Elvers, *Die Römische Servitutenlehre* (n 146) 772-773 § 73(1) note c; C F Mühlenbruch, *Doctrina Pandectarum*, 4th edn (1839), vol 2, 156 text at n 21.

148 Yiannopoulos, *Servitudes* (n 9) 449-450 § 164 text at n 13.

149 Cusine & Paisley, *Servitudes* (n 60) paras 2.42-2.43, 2.98, 7.05 and 17.14. They must be distinguished from suspensively conditional contracts to create servitudes: *Brown v Nielson* (1825) 4 S 271 (new edn 276) noted in W W McBryde, *The Law of Contract in Scotland*, 3rd edn (2007) 118 para 5-38 n 198.

150 Yiannopoulos, *Servitudes* (n 9) 35 § 10 text at fn 6.

151 *McPhail v Cunninghame District Council* 1983 SC 246; 1985 SLT 149.

152 W W McBryde, *The Law of Contract in Scotland*, 3rd edn (2007) 117-118, paras 5-35-5-37. The similarity is arguably not complete and the first type of suspensive condition may be excluded because of the principle excluding postponed vesting of real rights noticed in *PMP Plus Ltd v Keeper of the Registers of Scotland* 2009 SLT (Lands Tr) 2 at para 56.

In the first type the entire right is suspensively conditional on the happening of a certain event and there is no servitude at all until the contingency occurs. Neither the positive aspect (the right to carry out positive activity) nor the negative aspect of the servitude (to restrain impediments to that positive activity) can be enforced whilst the servitude is suspensive in this way. Such would be the case where the contingency was the acquisition by the grantee of the dominant tenement. As a servitude must benefit a dominant tenement, there clearly could be no servitude until this is owned by the grantee of the servitude.[153]

Second, there may be a servitude where the right exists immediately but its exercise, in the sense of the right of the dominant proprietor to carry out positive activity on the servient tenement, is suspensively conditional upon the occurrence of some event.[154] However, this differs from the first type of suspensive condition in that negative aspect of the servitude will remain enforceable even though the entitlement to exercise the positive aspect is suspended. For example, the holder of such a servitude of water extraction from a well which is suspended until the occurrence of a contingent event – such as a drought – can interdict the servient owner if he proposes to fill in the well. A further aspect of this will be examined below in the context of partial exercise of a servitude.[155]

As regards both types of these suspensive conditions the contingency can relate to the occurrence of various things including the following:

(a) Something in the power of the servient proprietor. This could be, for example, the installation of a road on the servient property over which the servitude of access would pass or the construction of a building into which a beam may be inserted.[156] It may also be the installation of sewers through which a servitude of drainage would flow. It could even be the case that the event is merely the serving of a notice by the servient proprietor indicating his intention to allow the dominant proprietor to pass over a part of the servient tenement. Clearly, however, this is not the sort of suspensive condition consonant with the type of *res merae facultatis* envisaged in the Scottish cases; rather that is a right which can be exercised, or not exercised, at some time in the future as the dominant proprietor chooses.

---

153 Cusine & Paisley, *Servitudes* (n 60) paras 2.42-2.43.
154 Voet, *Pandects* 8.6.11 citing D 8.6.4 (Paul) identifies an instance of this in the right of foot passage to a tomb, as the occasion for exercise does not arise until a loss of life, which is uncertain.
155 See text at n 209.
156 D 8.6.18(2) (Paul).

(b) Something in the power of the dominant proprietor. This could be, for example, the building of a house on the dominant tenement[157] or, alternatively, demolishing a structure on the dominant tenement.[158] It could even be the case that the event is merely the serving of a notice by the dominant proprietor indicating his intention to pass over a part of the servient tenement. Perhaps the fifth variant of *res merae facultatis* is essentially this, albeit the contingent event is simply the dominant proprietor deciding to exercise the right rather than confirming by notice that he is now minded to exercise the right. This, however, would be a very wide definition of the notion of suspensive condition as contracts and other rights are not normally considered suspensively contingent until the entitled party decides to enforce them, even if he has previously indicated he may not seek enforcement for some time.

(c) Something beyond the power of both dominant and servient proprietor but within the gift of a third party. This might be, for example, the zoning of the dominant tenement for a particular type of use. In some cases this event may occur upon application of either the dominant or servient proprietor. This could be the obtaining of a statutory consent.[159] In such a case the deed may impose obligations on the dominant or servient proprietor to make the relevant application. As this is a positive obligation, if it is intended to fall on the servient proprietor it must be established in Scotland by means of a real burden.[160] Where it is intended to fall on the dominant proprietor it may be imposed either by real burden or servitude condition.

(d) Something like an act of God or *damnum fatale*. An instance might be a servitude over a substitute access granted on the suspensive condition that it may be exercised if a flood blocks another servitude over an existing access. In appropriate cases this could perhaps be otherwise styled as a power on the part of the dominant proprietor to re-route the existing servitude around the flood.[161] Another possibility is the growth

157 D 8.2.23(1) (Pomponius); Voet, *Pandects* 8.1.2.
158 This is how *Charles Smith and others (Trustees of Dundee Joint Stock Company)* (n 120) is best interpreted and this approach has not been rejected if the suspensive condition is expressly linked to the demolition of the wall. The decision in *Peart* merely rejected the implication of a suspensive condition arising from the fact that the wall existed and required to be demolished.
159 See *MacPherson and Williams* [2008] CSOH 25 for an example of a vehicular servitude of access suspensive on the grant of planning permission for development for the erection of a dwelling house on the dominant tenement. Until such planning permission was obtained the servitude was restricted to pedestrian access only.
160 Title Conditions (Scotland) Act 2003 Act s 2.
161 Bankton, *Inst* 2.7.28.

of trees. No-one can force them to grow: instead, all must wait until the trees are ready for felling and extraction. In this context the Supreme Court of Louisiana has held that where parties to a timber deed agreed to create a servitude of passage for the removal of trees they did not intend that the servitude would come into existence immediately and be open to extinction by non-use while the trees grew.[162] Instead, by the link of the servitude to the purpose of extraction, it was clear from the facts surrounding the deed that the servitude was intended not to be exercisable until the trees were ready for extraction. In resorting to inferences from facts to clarify the meaning of an unclear deed the approach taken by the Louisiana Supreme Court is remarkably like the approach taken by the Scottish court in *Peart*. The reasoning of the Supreme Court is recorded as follows:[163]

> The right granted in the deed to enter upon the land and to construct a tramroad for the purpose of removing the timber in question, and for the purpose of removing timber from other lands in the vicinity, not belonging to plaintiff, is a servitude. In so far as respects the timber in question, the servitude is a mere accessory to that right, and it was contemplated that it should not come into existence until needed to remove the timber. In so far as respects the second phase of the question, the existence of the servitude for the removal of timber from other lands in the vicinity, it is fair to conclude that the parties did not contemplate that the servitude would be used, or begin to run, for that purpose, until the time came to remove the timber from plaintiff's land. The removal of timber is expensive, and is usually systematically done. All belonging to a company, in the vicinity of a particular tract, therefore, is removed generally about the same time. This the parties evidently had in contemplation when the grant was made; and it should be interpreted in relation to that fact, in order to ascertain their intention. This being so, as defendant had reached the timber in its logging operations only shortly before the institution of this suit, the prescription of 10 years has not yet run.

This leads one to query whether when drafting a servitude of access for a forestry plantation it would be prudent to acquire a multiplicity of separate servitudes, each linked to a different stage in the growth of trees. As regards a general servitude of access for the purpose of forestry the period of negative prescription or prescription by non-use arguably would begin to run on day one. By contrast, four different periods for extinction may begin to run at different points of time for several separate servitudes of access each linked to a different aspect of forestry such as planting, surveying, thinning and extraction.

---

162 *Kavanaugh v Frost-Johnston Lumber Co* 149 La 972 90 So 275 (La 1921).
163 At 976 per Overton J.

(7) Drafting suspensive servitudes

Clearly a suspensively conditional servitude is not the norm. It can be created only by a deed and not by prescriptive exercise. Even within the class of servitudes created by a deed, it is rare. With this in mind the courts in both Scotland and Louisiana require a grant or reservation to be clearly expressed before they will interpret a servitude as suspensive in any of the ways noted above. In Louisiana it has been confirmed that simply because the deed creating it does not specify the exact route of the servitude no suspensive condition will be implied to delay its creation until this is done.[164] The result is likely to be the same in both jurisdictions since Scots law,[165] like Louisiana law,[166] contains mechanisms whereby the exact route may be determined after the servitude is created. A similarly restrictive approach may be observed in a recent Inner House case in Scotland[167] where the court considered a provision in a deed that the party who would benefit from a servitude of access was "the owner for the time being of any dwellinghouse". The court rejected an argument that a housebuilder who was intending to build a house on a vacant plot was unable to avail himself of the servitude for the purposes of construction.[168] In the view of the court the wording used also included a plot upon which a house was yet to be constructed. They effectively declined to interpret the wording in a manner that would render the servitude suspensive upon a house being built on the dominant tenement. Clearly there is a reluctance in Scotland to recognise a suspensive condition in a servitude unless there is clear wording. This makes the approach to the fifth variant of *res merae facultatis* all the more odd as the court in *Peart* scoured the deed for inferences to suggest that the immediate exercise of the right was not intended.

(8) Conclusions on *res merae facultatis*

For present purposes it is sufficient to conclude briefly as follows. Faced with the impenetrable morass of obscurity that has endured centuries of analysis, one tends to become less critical of the recent Scottish decision in *Peart v Legge* but no less frustrated that there is still no clear way through the

---

164 *Tilley v Lowery* 511 So 2d 1245 (La App 2 Cir 1987); *De La Croix v Nolan* 1 Rob 321 (La 1842).

165 Bankton, *Inst* 2.7.18; *Axis West Developments v Chartwell Land Investments* 1999 SLT 1416 (HL); *Moncrieff* (n 46) at para 12 per Lord Hope; Cusine & Paisley, *Servitudes* (n 60) para 12.131.

166 La Civ Code art 750.

167 *Candleberry Limited v West End Homeowners Association* [2006] CSIH 28; 2006 SC 638; 2007 SCLR 128.

168 At para 18 per Lord Nimmo Smith.

obstacles. Two points, however, can be made. First, it is likely that this form of *res merae facultatis* is a form of suspensively conditional servitude. Thus the integrity of the law of negative prescription is preserved. Secondly, the previous interpretation of the fifth aspect of *res merae facultatis* was that an intention to delay exercise of a servitude could be inferred where a wall had to be demolished to enable the servitude to be exercised at all. The existence of such a thing can be objectively determined and the development of this form of *res merae facultatis* exception could thus be kept in check.[169] The court in *Peart v Legge* did not say that the existence of such a physical obstacle is completely irrelevant to the determination of *res merae facultatis* but that, by itself, it is insufficient and, in addition, something more within the deed is needed to demonstrate the intention of the dominant proprietor to delay exercise. Where such a physical obstacle is present very little in addition may be required, but where the physical obstacle is not present quite definite signs of intention may be needed before the court concludes that there is a *res merae facultatis*.

I. MANNER OF EXERCISE OF THE SERVITUDE

In both Scotland and Louisiana the doctrine of extinction by non-use or negative prescription must recognise that positive servitudes have both positive and negative aspects. Initially this notion appears a little confusing and requires unpacking.

(1) Positive and negative aspects

In a leading nineteenth-century treatise on the Scots law of prescription it was observed that "servitudes, like prescription, have been arranged by lawyers under the threadbare distinction of positive and negative".[170] Despite this criticism, Scots law maintained the traditional Civilian distinction[171] between positive and negative servitudes until 28 November 2004.[172] The same broad distinction is still found in the law of Louisiana where servitudes of the former type are known as "affirmative" servitudes.[173] Given this impressive pedigree one might expect there to have been a neat distinction between positive and

---

169 Reid and Gretton, *Conveyancing 2007* (n 42) 120.
170 Napier, *Commentaries on the Law of Prescription* (n 33) 585.
171 The distinction is not express in the *Digest* but is found in writers of the Civilian tradition, e.g. Heinneccius, *Elementa Iuris Civilis Secundum Ordinem Pandectarum* (1731) 235 8.1.1.40.
172 The "appointed day" in terms of Title Conditions (Scotland) Act 2003. Negative servitudes are now abolished in Scotland and re-categorised as real burdens – broadly akin to Common Law "restrictive covenants" (ss 79 and 80).
173 La Civ Code art 706; Yiannopoulos, *Servitudes* (n 9) 43-44 § 14.

negative servitudes. For the most part there was and there still is. However, there are some complexities.[174] One of these, the negative aspect of positive servitudes, will be outlined here, followed by an examination of how this impacts upon negative prescription.

Let us start with the obvious. For the burdened proprietor in both Louisiana and Scotland all servitudes are *in patiendo* only to the extent that this passivity, in the words of a Scottish judge, may be regarded as "the criterion of that species of right".[175] Consonant with the Roman rule[176] *servitus in faciendo consistere non potest* servitudes involve passivity and cannot generally oblige the burdened proprietor to do anything. Despite some mistaken observations,[177] it was not this passivity that marked the distinction between positive and negative servitudes: positive servitudes do not normally impose positive obligations on the burdened proprietor.[178] There cannot even be an imposition of a positive obligation by the "back door", such as an implied warranty of fitness for purpose by the granter of a right of access obliging him to render the servient tenement suitable by cutting back undergrowth and levelling ravines.[179] As regards positive servitudes, the owner of the burdened property can be obliged only to suffer certain activity on his land, such as the taking of passage. As regards negative servitudes, until their abolition in Scotland and still in Louisiana,[180] the burdened proprietor could be obliged to refrain from certain activity, such as building. Clearly in both Louisiana and Scotland a positive servitude necessarily imposes certain negative restraints. So, the aspect of negative restraint was a *leit motif* in both positive and negative servitudes. This was noticed by Stair:[181]

174 Difficulty remained with the classification of support but the balance of authority is that the right is a positive servitude: see the discussion of authorities in Discussion Paper on Real Burdens (Scot Law Com No 106, 1998) 35-36 para 2.51; Cusine & Paisley, *Servitudes* (n 60) para 3.73. Cf the classification of the servitude of levee in Louisiana as a negative servitude: *Lieber v Hamel* 446 So 2d 1240 (La App 2d Cir 1983) writ denied 448 So 2d 107 (La 1984).

175 *Incorporation of Tailors of Aberdeen v Coutts* (1840) 1 Rob App 296 at 310 per Lord Corehouse. See also La Civ Code art 651.

176 D 8.1.15(1) (Pomponius). This is consistent in the Civilian tradition e.g. Heinneccius (n 175) 221 7.1. 100.

177 E.g. the categorisation of a right to receive water through pipes as being a negative easement because the servient proprietor could not be obliged to supply water: *Halsbury's Law of Australia*, vol 22, "Real Property" Service 0 1998 para [355-12010] referring at n 4 to *Rance v Elvin* (1985) 49 P & CR 9 (this citation is incorrect – it should be (1985) 50 P & CR 9).

178 Yiannopoulos, *Servitudes* (n 9) 15-18 §5; A J M Steven, "Reform of real burdens" (2001) EdinLR 235 at 238 n 37.

179 See the observations to this effect in *Spear v Rowlett* (1924) 43 NZLR 801 at 804 per Salmond J.

180 La Civ Code art 706; Yiannopoulos, *Servitudes* (n 9) 43-44 §14.

181 Stair, *Inst* 2.7.5. See also Discussion Paper on Real Burdens (Scot Law Com No 106, 1998) 35-36 para 2.51.

A positive servitude is that whereby the servient tenement is not only restrained of its liberty, but is constrained to suffer some things to be done to the behoof of the dominant tenement, contrary to its liberty. Negative servitude is that whereby the freedom of the servient tenement is only restrained.

Recently this dual aspect of a positive servitude has been considered by the Lands Tribunal in a manner indicating the subsidiarity of the negative aspect to the positive. In a case concerning the diversion of a servitude of way, it confirmed that:[182]

> The purpose of a servitude of access is to confer a benefit on the dominant tenement and not to create a restriction on use of the servient tenement. The obligation may have the effect of restricting the use of the servient tenement but that is not its purpose.

In Louisiana it is more difficult to locate similar succinct express recognition of the negative aspect of positive servitudes. The definitions provided appear *prima facie* to indicate that the restraint imposed by servitudes is confined to negative servitudes. For example, article 706 of the Louisiana *Civil Code* states:

> Affirmative servitudes are those that give the right to the owner of the dominant estate to do a certain thing on the servient estate. Such are the servitudes of right of way, drain, and support.

> Negative servitudes are those that impose on the owner of the servient estate the duty to abstain from doing something on his estate. Such are the servitudes of prohibition of building and of the use of an estate as a commercial or industrial establishment.

Similar formulations are used by both French[183] and Louisiana[184] commentators.

It is fanciful to suggest that both Stair and the Lands Tribunal in Scotland are sketching out an otherwise unknown development of basic principles that are foreign to a sister legal mixed system such as Louisiana. Rather, the passages quoted above have expressed something so obvious that it has rarely needed expression. One does find aspects of it in the *Digest*[185] and *Las Siete Partidas*.[186] In addition, in the part of the Louisiana Civil Code dealing

---

182 *Nardone v Birch*, unreported, Lands Tribunal for Scotland (1999), case ref LTS/LO/1998/26; see also *George Wimpey East Scotland Ltd v Fleming* 2006 SLT (Lands Tr) 2 and 59; *Graham v Parker* 2007 GWD 30-524.

183 E.g. M Planiol and G Ripert, *Traité pratique de droit civil français*, 2nd edn ed Picard (1952), vol 3, 875 para 895.

184 A Yiannopoulos, "Predial servitudes; general principles" (1968) 29 La LR 1, 6-8 and 30-31.

185 D 8.2.20(3) (Paul) and D 8.5.9pr (Paul).

186 *Las Siete Partidas* 3.31.6 (*Las Siete Partidas*, tr by S P Scott, ed by R I Burns, (2001) vol 3, "Medieval law: Lawyers and their work" 857).

with general principles of predial servitudes[187] one finds article 651 which provides that "The owner of the servient estate is not required to do anything. His obligation is to abstain from doing something on his estate or to permit something to be done on it." Although the word "or" is still used, it appears this is not a disjunctive suggesting two alternatives. Instead, it is overwhelmingly clear that the sources of both Scots law and Louisiana law have consistently recognised the phenomenon of the negative and positive aspects of positive servitudes. In both jurisdictions there is an acceptance that the burdened proprietor must refrain from activities that will obstruct the proper exercise of the positive servitude.[188] That is the very essence of the negative aspect of the positive servitude. The negative aspect of a positive servitude is inherent in the positive right. Indeed if the dominant proprietor were to seek to discharge the negative aspect of a positive servitude the correlative positive aspect of the servitude would be treated as similarly discharged.[189]

(2) Acquisition: prescription

The negative aspect of the positive servitude does not convert all or part of the positive servitude into a negative one, or enable the negative aspect to be severed from the servitude and transformed into a self-standing negative servitude.[190] This has an impact on creation and extinction in both jurisdictions. Apart from a few highly specialised exceptions, negative servitudes probably could never be created by exercise for the period of acquisitive or positive prescription[191] and certainly did not arise just because the allegedly burdened proprietor voluntarily refrained from carrying out the relevant activity precluded by such a servitude. As has already been noticed such activity is *res merae facultatis* on the part of the proprietor of the land.[192] However, the negative aspect of a positive servitude will automatically arise when the positive servitude has been created by acquisitive prescription or positive prescription.[193]

187 Title 4 ch 1.
188 Erskine, *Inst* 2.9.33; Cusine & Paisley, *Servitudes* (n 60) paras 12.93-12.107; Yiannopoulos, *Servitudes* (n 9) 435-438 § 158.
189 D 8.4.17 (Papinian); D 8.6.8pr (Paul).
190 Still less is it the case that the negative aspect of existing positive servitudes was converted into a negative real burden in terms of Title Conditions (Scotland) Act 2003 s 80(1).
191 See the authorities discussed in Cusine & Paisley, *Servitudes* (n 60) paras 10.02-10.03; Yiannopoulos, *Servitudes* (n 9) 390-395 § 135 noting the exception for a servitude of light on a common wall.
192 See text at n 87.
193 La Civ Code arts 740 and 742 on apparent servitudes; Prescription and Limitation (Scotland) Act 1973 s 3(2).

(3) Extinction: prescription

The converse situation with negative prescription is less clear at least in Scotland. Let us consider the case where the benefited proprietor merely asserts his positive servitude of access by interdicting building over the route but, for twenty years, actually takes no access over the burdened property. One could argue that it is unclear whether the servitude would be regarded as "unexercised or unenforced" in terms of the relevant statutory provision.[194] The argument would run that the word "or" is disjunctive and that "exercise" relates to the positive aspect whilst "enforcement" could relate to the negative aspect. Certainly the statutory provision is unhappily phrased as regards servitudes in particular because it is intended to apply to many rights and obligations, although the matter has never been litigated.[195] If, however, one adopts what is probably the more conventional view to the effect that such a positive servitude is regarded as both "unexercised" and "unenforced" where there is an absence of positive activity for twenty years, then both the servitude of passage (and the inherent right to object to obstructions) would both negatively prescribe. This indeed appears to be the approach espoused by Erskine:[196]

> Servitudes are lost *non utendo*, or by negative prescription; that is, if the owner of the dominant tenement neglect to use his right for forty years together, or if the owner of the servitude[197] do acts repugnant to the servitude, without interruption by him who claims it. Where the owner of the servient tenement is bound ... to suffer something to be done, on his property, as in the servitude of ... roads, etc. it is sufficient if ... the owner of the dominant tenement shall have neglected to use his right, for a full course of prescription.

It appears unlikely that the Prescription and Limitation (Scotland) Act 1973 would have altered this, except for the period of time required. Whatever the position, it is not the case that the positive aspect would negatively prescribe and the negative aspect would survive as a residual negative servitude or negative real burden. It is *a fortiori* the case that the benefited proprietor cannot voluntarily discharge either the positive or negative aspect of the positive servitude and attempt to retain the other aspect.[198] And what of

---

194 Prescription and Limitation (Scotland) Act 1973 s 8(2) quoted above in text at n 33.

195 Cf *Sir Adam Blair v Creditors of William Rigg of Carberry*, Jan 1686, Harcase 243, case no 851; (1686) M 14505: inhibition on a bond of servitude to make levels on servient tenement sufficient to create the right real albeit there had been no actual use.

196 Erskine, *Inst* 2.9.37. See also Erskine, *Principles of the Law of Scotland* 2.9.21.

197 By "owner of the servitude" Erskine appears to mean "owner of the servient tenement".

198 D 8.4.17 (Papinian); D 8.6.8 (Paul). This is subject to the qualification that where a positive servitude comprises an ancillary right that is wholly negative in character, the ancillary right may be discharged without affecting the primary servitude.

Louisiana? The provisions of the Civil Code relevant to the extinction of servitudes refer to "non-use".[199] This most easily is applied to positive activity and there appears to be no reported case in which it has been held that a positive servitude may be kept alive simply by interdicting the servient proprietor or third parties from obstructing its route.

(4) Coincidence of positive and negative

Normally the positive and negative aspects of positive servitudes coincide in their extent. The dominant proprietor may interdict obstructions where and when the positive activity is exercisable: likewise the servient proprietor is usually restrained in time and space according to the extent of the positive right afforded to the dominant proprietor. However, this exact coincidence is not always required. In some instances there is a dislocation between the positive and negative aspects. In some cases the negative aspect of a positive servitude places restraints on the servient proprietor over a geographic area larger than the area over which the positive activity may be conducted.[200] On occasion this arises by implication of law.[201] More often the matter is a result of deliberate drafting. For example, on either side of a pipeline the servitude may expressly provide for "non-build" strips. There are similar rights in electricity cabling servitudes.[202] In servitudes of access the deed may provide for a view or a sight line over adjacent land. Servitudes of water supply may provide for limitations on the chemicals that are sprayed on adjacent land.

In other cases the dislocation of positive and negative aspects of positive servitudes relates to the factor of time. This has been recognised since Roman times where servitude conditions imposed restrictions on the days and times during which a positive servitude could be exercised.[203] Moreover, the period of time during which positive exercise was excluded might in some cases occur right at the start and this could endure until a set time or the occurrence of some event.[204] This is recognised in Louisiana.[205] Even

---

199 La Civ Code arts 753 and 754.
200 It does appear to be impossible for the servitude to permit the positive aspect to be more extensive in time or geographic extent than the negative. See D 8.6.8 (Paul).
201 *Crawford v Field* (1874) 2 R 20 at 25 per Lord Deas; *Argyllshire Commissioners of Supply v Campbell* (1885) 12 R 1255 at 1263 per Lord Shand; *Dumfries and Maxwelltown Water Works Commissioners v McCulloch* (1874) 1 R 975; Cusine & Paisley, *Servitudes* (n 60) para 14.14. Cf the English authority: *Hayns v Secretary of State for the Environment* (1978) 36 P & CR 317.
202 E.g., *Broomfield v Louisiana Power & Light* 623 So 2d 1376 (La App 2d Cir 1993).
203 D 8.4.14 (Julian); D 8.6.7 and 10 (Paul); D 8.1.5(1)(Gaius)); D 8.3.2(1) and (2) (Neratius); D 8.6.16 (Proculus) and D 8.6.11 (Marcellus); see also Heinneccius (n 168) 242 8.4.159.
204 D 8.1.4 (Papinian); D 8.4.7(1)(Paul). See Voet, *Pandects* 8.1.2 and 8.4.18.
205 La Civ Code art 652.

whilst exercise of the positive aspect of the servitude is excluded it appears obvious that negative aspect is present and may be enforced by the dominant proprietor. For example, in a servitude of access exercisable only on Mondays the dominant could interdict the servient proprietor from building a house on the road on any other day because this construction has the potential to obstruct positive exercise the following Monday and every Monday after that. This is suggested by the Roman jurist Gaius who is recorded as follows:[206]

Item si tigni immissi aedes tuae servitutem debent et ego exemero tignum, ita demum amitto ius meum, si tu foramen, unde exemptum est tignum, obturaveris et per constitutum tempus ita habueris: alioquin si nihil novi feceris, integrum ius suum permanet.	Moreover, if your house is subject to the insertion of a beam, and I remove the beam, I lose my right only if you fill up the hole from which the beam was taken, and retain things in this state during the time prescribed by law; but if you make no change my right remains unimpaired.[207]

The clear inference is that the blocking up of the hole may be precluded and any blockage removed if the blockage has not remained *in situ* for the prescriptive period. In this regard it is appropriate to speak of the indivisibility of servitudes.[208] A servitude exercisable only on certain days of the week is an entire servitude and not a part of a right.[209] This becomes all the more clear when one realises that the limited times of permitted positive exercise are linked by the fact that the negative aspect of the same servitude has no such limitation. The negative aspect exists as a continuum during and between the periods of the positive exercise and, where appropriate, before and after such periods of positive exercise.

It is possible that a similar dislocation in time may provide part of the explanation for the new and difficult variation of *res merae facultatis* found in Scots law, in respect of which positive exercise is envisaged as occurring only at some indefinite future date.[210] During the initial period the negative aspect of the servitude is enforceable and the dominant proprietor may preclude the servient from building on the area in question. However, until this initial period is complete the positive aspect of the servitude is not exercised. It is

---

206 D 8.2.6 (Gaius).

207 Whether Scots law and the law of Louisiana would go this far is questionable. Both jurisdictions appear to regard support or *tigni inmittendi* as a positive servitude (n 177) whereas the Romans regarded it as wholly negative.

208 Yiannopoulos, *Servitudes* (n 9) 38 § 11.

209 La Civ Code art 652.

210 See text at n 120.

perhaps going a little too far to say that during this period it is not exercisable because the fact that positive use is not immediately envisaged at the date of creation of the right does not appear to impose an obligation to refrain from such use – to exercise the right immediately all the dominant proprietor has to do is to change his mind. That said, it appears likely that negative prescription would begin to run from the first day of positive activity.[211] An unanswered question is whether it would begin to run from the first day of enforcement of the negative aspect? If it were so, it would work to the advantage of the servient proprietor to threaten to build on the servient area and be interdicted, as the negative prescription would then begin to run. However, such an interpretation seems unlikely because it would tend to promote litigation and reward breach. In addition, the case law from Scotland on the third aspect of *res merae facultatis* indicates that a successful enforcement of a negative servitude does not start a period of negative prescription.[212] It appears likely that this will be applied to the negative aspect of a positive servitude, at least where it is dislocated geographically or temporally from the positive aspect.

J. CONCLUSION

Extinction by non-use is an issue that has arisen in relation to servitudes from the earliest of times. Despite this not all issues have yet been resolved and difficult issues continue to arise in the law of Louisiana and Scotland. Each jurisdiction may learn from each other. The law in each jurisdiction continues to evolve to respond to the stresses that accompany modern commerce in the context of land development. Although the rules of extinction by prescription are designed to limit the freedom of parties in the creation and exercise of servitudes there remains a high degree of flexibility. In both Scotland and Louisiana this will enable the law of servitudes to respond to modern commercial needs whilst retaining a sufficient degree of rigour and clarity.

211 See text at n 125.
212 See text at n 111.

4 Inheritance and the Surviving Spouse

Ronald J Scalise Jr[*]

A. INTRODUCTION
B. A FIRST GLANCE: A FACIAL SIMILARITY
(1) Surviving spouse and no children
(2) Surviving spouse and children
C. A FURTHER LOOK INTO THE HISTORICAL DEVELOPMENT
    OF THE INHERITANCE RIGHTS OF THE SURVIVING SPOUSE
(1) Louisiana law
(2) Scots law
D. ARE THEY REALLY SIMILAR AFTER ALL? EVALUATING
    PREFERENCE VERSUS PROTECTION
(1) Preference
(a) Who is the surviving spouse?
(b) Prior rights
(c) Community property
(2) Protection
(a) Community property
(b) Legal rights
(c) Various other protective rights
E. WHAT CAN BE LEARNED?
F. CONCLUSION

A. INTRODUCTION

Inheritance laws affect everyone.[1] That reason alone is sufficient for their

[*] The author wishes to express his appreciation to Vernon Palmer for inviting him to participate in this project, to Kenneth Norrie, Kenneth Reid, David Nichols, and James Chalmers for helpful comments on an earlier draft, and to Laura Mary for editorial assistance.

1 In fact, most individuals die intestate. This is true in Scottish law. See Report on Succession (Scot Law Com No 215, 2009) para 2.1 (stating "[m]ost Scots do not have a will"); D R Macdonald, *Succession,* 3rd edn (2001) para 4.01 (estimating that "perhaps two thirds of Scots people die intestate"); but see Report on Succession (Scot Law Com No 124, 1990) para 2.1 (estimating that only a third of estates overall were intestate, but almost half of small estates were intestate). It is also true in American law: J C Dobris, S E Sterk, and M B Leslie, *Estates and Trusts: Cases and Materials,* 2nd edn (2003) 62 ("Most Americans die without wills."); A Dunham, "The method, process and

study. By virtue of their broad application, the laws on inheritance contain significance that few rules of law can duplicate. Even aside from their scope of application, inheritance laws are equally significant in substance, as they "embody broad principles as to how a society considers property should be disposed of on death".[2] Although some have characterised the topic of intestacy as "unimportant" because "it is a mass of detail",[3] it is precisely some of that detail which must be examined to discern what value judgments are made by society, either for a decedent or in spite of him. From a comparative perspective, this is important because the laws of inheritance have the potential to reveal not only differences or similarities in black letter rules but also differences and similarities in the societal principles, mores, and values that underlie those rules.

Despite the broad application of these rules, scholars are not entirely in agreement on their purpose.[4] In fact, inheritance laws serve many purposes. Some goals of inheritance law include "avoid[ing] complicating property titles and excessive subdivision of property", "promot[ing] and encourag[ing] the nuclear family", "encourag[ing] the accumulation of property by individuals", and "produc[ing] a pattern of distribution that recipients believe is fair and thus does not produce disharmony".[5] Most commonly, however, the

---

frequency of wealth transmission at death" (1963) 30 UChiLRev 241 at 248; M L Fellows, R J Simon, and W Rau, "Public attitudes about property distribution at death and intestate succession laws in the United States" (1978) *American Bar Foundation Research Journal* 324 at 337 (finding only about 45% of the sample population had wills); M L Fellows, R J Simon, T E Snapp, and W D Snapp, "Empirical study of the Illinois Statutory Estate Plan" (1976) *University of Illinois Law Forum* 717 at 718 n 3; M K Johnson and J Robbennolt, "Using social science to inform the law of intestacy: The case of unmarried committed partners" (1998) 22 *Law & Human Behavior* 479 (finding only 40% of respondents with opposite-sex partners had wills, but finding a majority of those with same-sex partners had wills); E H Ward and J H Beuscher, "The inheritance process in Wisconsin" (1950) 1950 WisLRev 393 at 396. But see M B Sussman, J N Cates, and D T Smith, *The Family and Inheritance* (1970) 64 (finding approximately 58% of the sample population had wills); L W Waggoner, G S Alexander, M L Fellows, and T P Gallanis, *Family Property Law: Cases and Materials on Wills, Trusts, and Future Estates* (2002) 35 (suggesting that the conventional wisdom may be incorrect, and that perhaps "it's more accurate to suggest that most people who die prematurely die intestate"); J R Price, "The transmission of wealth at death in a community property jurisdiction" (1975) 50 WashLRev 277 at 295 (finding that 59% of the respondents in the Washington study were testate).

2 Macdonald, *Succession* (n 1) at para 4.01.

3 W W Buckland, *A Text-Book of Roman Law From Augustus to Justinian*, 3rd edn rev by P Stein (1963) 365.

4 A J Hirsch, "Default rules in inheritance law: A problem in search of its context" (2004) 73 FordhamLRev 1031 at 1036-1037.

5 Waggoner et al, *Family Law Property* (n 1) at 2-5. Although all of these goals begin with a background assumption that inheritance is the goal of a succession law (see, e.g., G Tullock, "Inheritance justified" (1971) 14 J L & Econ 465, and G Tullock, "Inheritance rejustified" (1973) 16 J L & Econ 425), not all societies share this background assumption. See, e.g., V Gsovski, "Family and inheritance in Soviet law" (1947) 7 Russian Rev 71 at 71-87.

purpose of inheritance laws is to effectuate the intention or *preference* of the decedent (either actual or presumed) and to *protect* financially dependent members of the family.[6] Certainly the goal of testate succession is to implement a decedent's preference, as is the goal of the rules of intestacy, which are modeled on the "presumed will" of the deceased.[7] On the other hand, family protective devices, such as forced heirship and shared marital property regimes in some systems, emphasise financial protection of close familial relations. The give-and-take between these two – sometimes competing – policy goals of preference and protection are aptly demonstrated in a comparative examination of inheritance law of two mixed jurisdictions,[8] Scotland and Louisiana.

Although both systems do share a mix of Common and Civil Law, Scotland, arguably the oldest mixed jurisdiction, and Louisiana, one of the youngest, do not immediately appear to be obvious candidates for comparison.[9] Scottish inheritance law is unique, not obviously English[10] and apparently a product of Roman law.[11] Louisiana inheritance law, although foundationally French, has been much influenced in recent times by American values and mores. Thus, the comparative exercise involving Louisiana and Scotland is a difficult but nonetheless valuable one. Mixed jurisdictions, by virtue of their Civil and Common Law influences, are uniquely positioned to choose the institutions from each tradition that best suit their needs and best accomplish their goals. For those reasons, then, it is important to examine how Louisiana and Scotland have implemented inheritance laws. The vast array of intestate rules, however, is too broad a topic for the confines of this paper. Rather, this paper will consider only one significant aspect of intestacy, the position of the surviving spouse, and how each system achieves the dual goals of preference and protection.

6 D P S Collins, "Intestate Succession", in SME, vol 25 (1989) para 675. ("The rules for a division of an intestate estate are based on the assumed intentions of the owner of the estate if he had decided to make a testamentary writing.") Uniform Probate Code art II, pt 1 gen cmt (1969) (The laws of intestacy are an attempt "to reflect the normal desire of the owner of the wealth as to the disposition of his property at death.")

7 Stair states that "[w]here there is a custom of succession, the defunct's will is presumed to be according to that custom; which being a law by the common authority where the defunct lived, importeth his will or consent, at least by submission" (*Inst* 3.4.2).

8 V Palmer, *Mixed Jurisdictions Worldwide: The Third Legal Family* (2001) 228.

9 Palmer, *Mixed Jurisdictions* at 5.

10 Palmer, *Mixed Jurisdictions* (n 8) at 228.

11 W D H Sellar, "Succession Law in Scotland – a historical perspective", in K G C Reid, M J de Waal and R Zimmermann (eds), *Exploring the Law of Succession: Studies National, Historical and Comparative* (2007) 49. But see W M Gordon, "The conditiones si sine liberis decesserit" 1969 JR 108.

B. A FIRST GLANCE: A FACIAL SIMILARITY

At first glance, the order of succession in both Scotland and Louisiana appears remarkably similar. In Scotland, the free estate of an intestate devolves in the following order: (1) children; (2) parents and siblings; (3) siblings in the absence of parents; (4) parents in the absence of siblings; (5) surviving spouse; (6) uncles and aunts; (7) grandparents; (8) siblings of grandparents, and so on.[12] In Louisiana, the order of succession of separate property is (1) children; (2) parents and siblings; (3) siblings in the absence of parents; (4) parents in the absence of siblings; (5) surviving spouse; (6) other ascendants; and (7) other collaterals.[13] With the exception of the very last classes, i.e., other collaterals (aunts, uncles, and so on) and other ascendants (grandparents), the order of succession is nearly identical in the two systems. The surviving spouse in both systems figures fourth or fifth in line, after children, parents, and siblings. As an initial observation, this is a remarkably low position in the inheritance scheme.

While the intestate order of succession is interesting in the abstract, a careful evaluation of the applicability of the rules is necessary to ascertain the policy judgments implicit in the law. For example, by listing a surviving spouse ahead of (or behind) other relatives in the order of succession, society communicates an assessment of the value of those relationships. Consequently, under the inheritance law of both Louisiana and Scotland, the spousal relationship is deemed by both systems more valuable than, for instance, the relationship of cousins but less important than the parental or sibling relationship. To appreciate fully the significance of each jurisdiction's spousal inheritance laws, two common scenarios are presented below.

(1) Surviving spouse and no children

Assume A and B are married and maintain a house purchased during the marriage, which is valued at 250,000 units of the relevant jurisdiction's currency (hereinafter, "units"). The house contains modest furnishings, valued at 20,000 units, and A acquires various other items of movable or personal property, valued at 175,000 units. The marriage of A and B does not produce children, and neither A nor B comes to the marriage with any children. A's mother and a sibling are alive. If A dies without a will, the question is to whom will A's property be distributed under the laws of intestacy.

Under Scottish law, the surviving spouse, B, would receive the house

---

12 Succession (Scotland) Act 1964 s 2.
13 La Civ Code arts 891-896.

and the furnishings. A's £175,000 of personal property would be distributed £125,000 to B and £50,000 to A's mother and sibling to be split between them.[14] Under Louisiana law, resolution of the scenario depends upon how the property is classified. If, as is the typical case, the spouses have chosen the community regime and acquired the property during marriage, then B, would receive the house, the furnishings, and the movable property.[15] In short, despite the initial lowly ranking of the surviving spouse under both jurisdictions' intestacy laws, the surviving spouse in both systems receives all or almost all of the deceased spouse's property in the above scenario.

(2) Surviving spouse and children

Assume the same scenario, except that the marriage of A and B does produce children, namely C and D. In Scotland, B again will receive the house and the furnishings. Now, however, B will receive only £42,000 of the personal property and one-third of the residual £133,000, with C and D splitting the remaining two-thirds.[16] Under Louisiana law, again assuming a community property regime,[17] the entirety of the estate will go to B in usufruct,[18] with C and D maintaining only the residual right of naked ownership over A's former property.[19]

Thus, although the orders of succession are not identical in Louisiana and in Scotland (in fact it would be surprising if they were), the ultimate

---

14 The Scots rules of intestacy as applied to a surviving spouse are outlined at part C.(2) below.

15 The application of the Louisiana rules of intestacy in relation to community property is discussed further below at part D.(1)(c). If, instead, the property was separate, A's mother would receive all A's property in usufruct with A's sibling being a naked owner.

16 In this scenario, C and D take one third as legal rights and the other third as residual rights under section 2 of the Succession (Scotland) Act 1964.

17 If separate property, however, exists, the children, C and D, will receive the property and the spouse will receive nothing.

18 Usufruct is defined as a "real right of limited duration on the property of another" (La Civ Code art 535). If the usufruct is over consumable things, the usufructuary "becomes owner of them" and "may consume, alienate, or encumber them as he sees fit" with the obligation to pay to the naked owner at termination of the usufruct "either the value the things had at the commencement of the usufruct or deliver to him things of the same quantity and quality" (La Civ Code art 538). If, on the other hand, the usufruct is over nonconsumable things, then the usufructuary "has the right to possess them and to derive the utility, profits, and advantages that they may produce, under the obligation of preserving their substance" and to act as a "prudent administrator and to deliver them to the naked owner at the termination of the usufruct" (La Civ Code art 539). For elaboration of the difference between consumable and nonconsumable things, see La Civ Code arts 536 and 537.

19 A naked owner "enjoys prerogatives of ownership to the extent that they do not interfere with the enjoyment of the usufructuary. Accordingly, during the existence of the usufruct, the rights of the naked owner begin where the rights of the usufructuary end." See A N Yiannopoulos, *Personal Servitudes, 3 Louisiana Civil Law Treatise*, 4th edn (2000) §150.

distribution patterns in both jurisdictions are very similar, even when one spouse dies and is survived by children. In fact, in that scenario, the surviving spouse continues to receive the majority of rights in the estate with children receiving lesser distributions either of personal property, as in Scotland, or in naked ownership, as in Louisiana.[20]

C. A FURTHER LOOK INTO THE HISTORICAL DEVELOPMENT OF THE INHERITANCE RIGHTS OF THE SURVIVING SPOUSE

Although the intestate order of succession in both systems disfavours the surviving spouse, in practical terms and through a variety of mechanisms, both Louisiana and Scotland elevate the position of the surviving spouse. A historical overview of the rules of intestacy is helpful for a full understanding of the inheritance systems in place in both jurisdictions.

(1) Louisiana law

There can be no conclusion but that the laws governing inheritance in the earliest of Roman and English times were significantly different. To begin with, Roman law, unlike English law, made no distinction for purposes of intestacy between that of heritable and personal property.[21] The underlying principle was that succession occurred by virtue of a blood relationship and then within relatives to the nearest in degree. For example, in Roman law, the distribution was to children in equal shares, first;[22] then, to relatives (*agnates*) nearest in degree who were related to the deceased through a male line (at least through those males not emancipated);[23] then, (at least in Praetorian

---

20 Interestingly, neither Scots law nor Louisiana law makes a distinction as to whether *C* and *D* were children of the marriage or children of *A's* union with a prior spouse. In other words, the law makes no distinction when the remaining spouse is not the parent of the child. See part E. below.

21 As common as intestacy is today in both Louisiana and Scotland, it was certainly not that way in Roman times and arguably not so either in earlier English times. Buckland, *Textbook* (n 3) 365 (stating that "[l]ong before classical times intestacy had become unusual"). This observation, however, has been the subject of great dispute and controversy. See D Daube, "The preponderance of intestacy at Rome" (1964) 39 Tulane LR 253 (stating that "[i]t is safe to sum up that, from beginning to end, intestacy was the rule and testacy the exception, and both very much so"); D Johnston, *Roman Law in Context* (1999) 51 ("It is a vexed question how common it was to make no will"). Despite the controversy, Johnston concluded that "[t]hose who had nothing are likely to have left no will. But the evidence seems to suggest that men were significantly more likely to make wills than women." Johnston, *Roman Law* at 51.

22 Gai *Inst* 3.2 (S P Scott trans 1932). Although the provisions of the *ius civile* allowed only children under the father's power to inherit, see Gai *Inst* 3.2, the praetor extended this right to emancipated children as well. See Ulpian 28.8 (S P Scott trans 1932). Strictly speaking, however, the Praetor granted individuals only *bonorum possessio*; he had "no power to make heirs." Ulpian 3.32.

23 Gai *Inst* 3.10.

times) to the extended family succeeding through lines of *cognati* (or those descended from a common ancestor), which included both males and females;[24] and finally, to the surviving spouse, who inherited last in line, only before the state.[25] This lowly position was actually a Praetorian improvement from classical law under which the spouse had no claim, as he or she was not a blood relative of the deceased.[26] Even at the time of Justinian's Novels, the inheritance rights of the surviving spouse remained last in line.[27]

The surviving spouse's prospects remained the same even in medieval France, at least in the areas of the written law.[28] In the regions of the customary law, the surviving spouse had few rights until the sixteenth century, at which point the law granted to the surviving spouse the right to succeed to the property of the decedent in full ownership, but only in the absence of other relations.[29] This concept was recognised by the Parlement of Paris and eventually adopted in article 767 of the Code Napoléon, which provided that "[w]hen the deceased leaves neither relatives of a degree capable of succeeding, nor natural children, the property of his succession belongs to his surviving spouse."[30] The surviving spouse inherited only before the Republic itself.[31]

Originally, Louisiana's law of intestate succession with regard to the surviving spouse was very similar to early French law. The surviving spouse had almost no claim to a decedent's separate property. At death, one's separate property passed to his descendants, parents, siblings, other ascendants, and other collaterals, with preferred classes excluding lower ones. No role existed for the surviving spouse, and any collateral relation – no matter how far removed – would receive property before a surviving spouse would. From

---

24 D 38.8.1 (Ulpian, On the Edict, Bk XLVI) (S P Scott trans 1932). The Praetorian scheme of succession by cognates replaced the older scheme of the *ius civile*, which next granted intestate succession rights to *gentiles*. See Gai *Inst* 3.17.

25 D 48.11. Johnston, *Roman Law* (n 21) at 51; W W Buckland, *Roman Law and Common Law: A Comparison in Outline*, 2ⁿᵈ edn (1952) 180; XII Tables, Table V (S P Scott trans 1932).

26 Although a wife who was *in manu* could inherit from a decedent, as she occupied the position of his daughter, Ulpian 3.3, "in classical law this is practically obsolete and is utterly gone centuries before Justinian." See Buckland, *Roman Law and Common Law* (n 25) at 184.

27 J Novels 118 and 127 (S P Scott trans 1932). See also Buckland, *Textbook* (n 3) 375; D H Van Zyl, *History and Principles of Roman Private Law* (1983) 209; Buckland, *Roman Law and Common Law* (n 25) at 185 (noting a minor improvement of the granting of rights in the decedent's succession where there was no *dos*, and citing J Novels 53.6, and 117.5).

28 M Planiol, *Traité élémentaire de droit civil* (La State Law Institute trans 1959) para 1862.

29 Planiol, *Droit civil* para 1862 (citing Customs of Berry, Title XIX, art 8 (1539); Customs of Poitou, art 299 (1559)).

30 *Code civil* art 767 (1804).

31 *Code civil* art 768 (1804) ("In default of a surviving spouse, the succession is acquired by the Republic").

the 1808 Code through the 1870 Code and until 1981, the law provided an inheritance to the surviving spouse only in the absence of descendants, ascendants, and collaterals.[32] In 1981, the law was amended to advance the position of the surviving spouse from last in line for separate property to fourth or fifth in line behind descendants, parents, and siblings and their descendants.[33] For the past twenty-seven years, the law has remained unchanged.

Even with regard to community property, the surviving spouse's position has historically been a tenuous one. Until 1844, the surviving spouse had no rights to the decedent's half of the community property. Only with the passage of Act 152 of 1844 did the surviving spouse become entitled to a usufruct over the decedent's half of the community, either for life if no descendants or ascendants existed or until remarriage if descendants were present.[34] In 1910, the law was amended to provide full ownership to the surviving spouse if no descendants or ascendants existed.[35] Again in 1916, the law was changed to advance the role of the surviving spouse by providing that the existence of parents would no longer preclude the surviving spouse from receiving property.[36] Instead, the decedent's share of the community would be split, half to the surviving spouse and half to the parents.[37] Further substantial advancements took place in 1981,[38] whereby the surviving spouse was granted full ownership of the decedent's share of the community property in the absence of descendants, and in 1990, when the law granted a surviving spouse usufruct if descendants existed.[39]

(2) Scots law

In contrast to early Roman law, the early English law and early Scots law of descent and distribution attached great significance to the distinction between personal property and heritable property.[40] That is, property was distributed at death in accordance with rules of the common law, with heritable property being distributed to descendants, collaterals, and then ascendants

---

32 La Code art 43 (1808); La Code art 911 (1825); La Code art 917 (1870).
33 Acts 1981, No 919.
34 Acts 1844, No 152.
35 Acts 1910, No 57.
36 Acts 1916, No 80.
37 Acts 1916, No 80.
38 Acts 1981, No 919. A correction was made in 1920 whereby the term "ascendants" was changed to "father" and "mother". Acts 1920, No 160. Also, in 1938, the law was amended to designate a surviving spouse as a "legal heir" rather than an "irregular successor". Acts 1938, No 408.
39 Acts 1990, No 1075.
40 Buckland, *Roman Law and Common Law* (n 25) at 180. This is true at least until 1925 when the Administration of Estates Act was passed. For an excellent overview of the history of Scottish succession law, see Sellar, "Succession law in Scotland" (n 11).

with a preference at every stage for male heirs.[41] As to personal property, the preference for male heirs did not exist.[42] And although variation occurred, the distribution scheme was again generally to descendants, collaterals, and then ascendants.[43] What is obvious, of course, is the complete absence of the surviving spouse in the order of succession.

Scottish law, however, recognised certain claims or charges against the estate of the decedent and in favour of the surviving spouse that preceded the rights of heirs. This legal right, known as terce, in favour of a widow, gave her a liferent interest to one-third of her husband's heritable property and existed if the marriage lasted for a year and a day or a child was produced from the union.[44] A corresponding right, known as courtesy, existed in favour of the husband by which he had a liferent in his spouse's heritable property, provided their marriage produced a child. With regard to personal property, spouses also had rights. The widow's right, *jus relictae*, granted the wife one-third of the husband's personal property if children existed, or one-half if no children existed. The widower had a *jus relicti*, which provided him the same corresponding share.[45]

In 1911 and 1919, Scotland made statutory provision for surviving spouses under the Intestate Husband's Estate (Scotland) Acts by which a widow was given a right to £500 of her husband's estate if he died wholly intestate and without issue. In 1940 and 1959, this right was broadened to include widowers, to raise the amount of the claim to £5,000, and to include instances of partial intestacy. These rights took precedence over legal rights such as terce and courtesy, but not over the claims of creditors.[46]

In 1964, Scots succession law was overhauled and modernised. The goal in part was to reflect more accurately the desires and preferences that an individual would choose had he made a will.[47] No longer was the surviving spouse excluded from the intestate scheme. In the 1964 Act, the surviving spouse was placed fourth in line, behind descendants, parents, and siblings.[48]

---

41 D M Walker, *Principles of Scottish Private Law*, 4th edn (1989) vol 4 at 134.

42 Walker, *Scottish Private Law* at 134.

43 Walker, *Scottish Private Law* at 134.

44 Walker, *Scottish Private Law* at 134.

45 Walker, *Scottish Private Law* at 119-123. Although many of these rights "appear to be of ancient customary origin, predating the Norman Conquest, and to owe nothing to Roman law", the widower's jus reliciti originated in the Married Women's Property (Scotland) Act 1881. See Sellar, "Succession law in Scotland" (n 11) at 60.

46 Walker, *Scottish Private Law* at 118.

47 M C Meston, *The Succession (Scotland) Act 1964*, 5th edn (2002) 15 (citing the Report of the Departmental Committee on The Law of Succession in Scotland (chairman, the Hon Lord Mackintosh) (Cmd 8144: 1950).

48 1964 Act s 2.

Although the existence of any such "prior" relation completely excluded the spouse, the surviving spouse came before grandparents, aunts, uncles, and any ascendants other than parents.

In addition to the advancement of the surviving spouse's position in the order of succession, the 1964 Act also granted the surviving spouse additional rights, "prior rights", which are reminiscent of terce and courtesy. Prior rights confer upon a surviving spouse in intestacy the rights to the dwelling house (or £300,000 if the deceased's share in the house is worth more than that figure), furniture and plenishings (unless the value exceeds £24,000, in which case the surviving spouse gets to choose furnishings up to that value), and a right to £75,000 of cash if no issue exists (or £42,000 if there is issue).[49]

Besides creating prior rights, the 1964 Act preserved the concept of legal rights, which entitle a spouse to a percentage or fraction of the deceased's movable estate. If a decedent is survived by a child or remoter issue, the surviving spouse has a legal right to one-third of the deceased's personal estate (i.e., one-third goes to the child; one-third, to the spouse; and one-third, as the free estate). In all other cases, one-half of the personal estate goes to the surviving spouse, with the other half constituting the free estate or the "dead's part". Legal rights exist in the nature of secondary debts and apply only after claims of creditors and payment of prior rights. Although some have argued that legal rights in Scotland can be traced back to Roman institutions, that conclusion has been debated.[50]

D. ARE THEY REALLY SIMILAR AFTER ALL? EVALUATING PREFERENCE VERSUS PROTECTION

Although the surviving spouse's role in intestacy appears similar in Scotland and in Louisiana, and has advanced over time in both jurisdictions, the mechanism by which each system arrives at a similar result is different indeed. The differences at first appear to be ones of history, but recent revisions indicate that the differences are also produced by the competing policy choices made in each system as to whether to favour the individual "preference" of the decedent or the societal "protection" of heirs.

---

49 1964 Act ss 8(1)(a) and (b), 8(3)(a) and (b), 9(1)(a) and (b), as amended by the Prior Rights of Surviving Spouse (Scotland) Order 2005, SSI 2005/252. This prior right to a financial provision is paid ratably out of heritable and movable property. 1964 Act s 9(3).

50 J C Gardner, *The Origin and Nature of the Legal Rights of Spouses and Children in the Scottish Law of Succession* (1928); H Hiram, "Reforming succession law: Legal rights" (2008) 12 EdinLR 81.

(1) Preference

In terms of achieving a decedent's preference, each system maintains a number of obvious institutions designed to implement that objective.

(a) Who is the surviving spouse?

Fundamental (and prior) to the question of what preferential-based rights are accorded to spouses is the underlying issue of who is a surviving spouse. While some jurisdictions, such as Scotland, respond to popular preference in deciding this basic question, others, like Louisiana, take a different approach. Evaluation of this inquiry extends beyond substantive succession law and into family law, which is intimately connected with intestate distribution schemes.

In both Scotland and Louisiana, a surviving spouse is one who outlives the deceased and who, prior to the death of the deceased, was legally married to the decedent under an official government prescribed standard. Both Louisiana and Scotland limit marriage to those of a certain age and of opposite genders who have contracted themselves into the institution of marriage. Cohabitants, either of the opposite or the same sex, are not recognised as spouses under laws of intestacy in either jurisdiction. Even though there is strong support for more equal treatment of cohabitants and spouses in Scotland,[51] such parity is not yet generally reflected in current law, although recent enactments in Scotland have granted cohabitants some rights and the Scottish Law Commission has proposed granting them testate as well as intestate succession rights.[52]

---

51 See Scottish Social Attitudes Survey 2004 Family Module Report (Scottish Executive Social Research, 2005) 17 (available at *http://www.scotland.gov.uk/Publications/2005/08/02131208/ 12092*, reporting that 87% of respondents agreed that cohabitants should have the same rights to an occupational pension upon the death of the other as spouses do).

52 Report on Succession (n 1) paras 4.1-4.32. The Family Law (Scotland) Act 2006 s 29 provides limited rights at death to same or opposite sex couples who were cohabiting and living together as either husband and wife or as civil partners: namely, if one cohabitant dies intestate, the surviving cohabitant may apply to a court for a discretionary award of a capital sum or even specific heritable or personal property. Despite popular misconceptions, neither system maintains a "common law" marriage doctrine, which would accord rights of cohabitants to rights of a married couple. Scottish Social Attitudes Survey 2004 (n 51) at 41 (reporting that 51% of respondents believed the idea of a "common law" marriage existed in Scotland). However, until 2006 Scots law allowed for "marriage by cohabitation with habit and repute", an institution abolished by the Family Law (Scotland) Act of 2006 s 3. Louisiana maintains a doctrine of putative marriage, which in some cases allows spouses who have contracted a marriage in violation of a requirement, or in the face of an impediment, to enjoy the legal benefits of marriage. See generally La Civ Code art 96. The concept of putative marriage, however, does not apply to those who contract marriage with a member of the same sex. See La Civ Code art 96 ("A purported marriage between parties of the same sex does not produce any civil effects").

Although Scots and Louisiana law seem at first to be in accord, the differences between the two systems are significant. First, even though Scots family law (and thus Scots succession law) does not recognise same-sex partners as spouses, Scots law extends almost the same inheritance rights to a civil partner.[53] In 2004, the Civil Partnership Act was passed granting civil partners of the same sex virtually identical rights in the successions context to those of a surviving spouse. Under the Civil Partnership Act, two people of the same sex not within a prohibited degree of relation and not otherwise married or involved in another civil partnership may sign a schedule in the presence of each other, two witnesses, and a registrar – the legal effect of which is to grant each other many of the same rights as a surviving spouse would have.[54] "In Scotland, the first civil partnership was registered on 20 December 2005 and by the end of the year a total of 84 had been registered – 53 male couples and 31 female couples."[55] By the end of 2006, Scotland had 1,131 registered civil partnerships.[56]

The recognition of civil partner rights in Scottish law accords with the majoritarian preference in Scotland. In a recent survey, 81% of respondents agreed that partners of either the opposite or same sex who have no children and who have cohabited together should have a guaranteed right or claim against the estate of the other.[57] Moreover, most respondents endorsed a fixed share rather than a discretionary award by a court.[58] This preference among Scots seems to be a manifestation of a liberal and permissive attitude toward homosexual relations. In Scotland, 43% of respondents view sexual relations between adults of the same sex as "rarely wrong" or "not wrong at all", while only 41% view such arrangements as "always wrong" or "mostly wrong".[59]

In Louisiana, a constitutional amendment precludes recognition of the rights of marriage, such as intestate inheritance, to same-sex couples.[60] It

---

53 Discussion Paper on Succession (Scot Law Com No 136, 2007) para 1.3 (stating that "[s]urviving civil partners have the same succession rights as surviving spouses"). But see para 3.53 (stating that "[i]t would appear that a surviving civil partner does not have the right" of aliment from a deceased's estate).

54 Civil Partnership Act 2004 part III.

55 *Scotland's Population 2006*: The Registrar General's Annual Review of Demographic Trends 152nd Edition (General Register Office for Scotland 2007) 47 (available at *http://www.gro-scotland.gov. uk/statistics/publications-and-data/annual-report-publications/rgs-annual-review-2006/index. html*).

56 *Scotland's Population 2006* at 47.

57 *Attitudes Towards Succession Law*: Finding of a Scottish Omnibus Survey, (Scottish Executive 2005) 16-17 (available at *http://www.scotland.gov.uk/Publications/2005/07/18151328/13297*).

58 Scottish Social Attitudes Survey 2004 (n 51) at 17.

59 Scottish Social Attitudes Survey 2004 (n 51) at 41.

60 La Constitution art 12 § 15. See also La Civ Code art 96.

provides that "[m]arriage in the state of Louisiana shall consist only of the union of one man and one woman".[61] Although a minority of other states in the United States has allowed arrangements such as same-sex marriages, domestic partnerships, civil unions, and reciprocal beneficiary registration,[62] Louisiana has not. Louisiana's opposition to same-sex marriage is a strong one. In fact, Louisiana's constitutional prohibition on marriage further prohibits recognition of "[a] legal status identical or substantially similar to that of marriage for unmarried individuals".[63] Louisiana has even adopted an express prohibition to the recognition of same-sex marriages contracted elsewhere. Although marriages contracted in other states are ordinarily "treated as a valid marriage" in Louisiana,[64] such recognition will not be granted if doing so "would violate a strong public policy of the state".[65] In 1999, Louisiana adopted an amendment to Civil Code article 3520 to make it clear that "a purported marriage between persons of the same sex violates a strong public policy of the state of Louisiana ... and shall not be recognised in this state for any purpose".[66]

The difference between Louisiana and Scotland is striking in this regard. As more and more countries in Western Europe, such as Scotland, allow same-sex marriage or the functional equivalents,[67] more and more states within the United States, such as Louisiana, seem to be moving in the opposite

---

61 La Civ Code art 96.

62 For a thorough discussion of these varying approaches, see T P Gallanis, "Inheritance rights for domestic partners" (2004) 79 Tulane LR 55; R J Scalise Jr, "New developments in United States succession law" (supp 2006) 54 AJCL 103.

63 La Constitution art 12 § 15.

64 "Full Faith and Credit shall be given in each State to the public Acts, Records, and judicial Proceedings of every other State. And the Congress may by general Laws prescribe the Manner in which such Acts, Records and Proceedings shall be proved, and the Effect thereof": US Constitution art 4 § 1.

65 La Civ Code art 3520. Federal Defense of Marriage Act ("DOMA"), 28 USC 1738C (2000) ("No State, territory, or possession of the United States, or Indian tribe, shall be required to give effect to any public act, record, or judicial proceeding of any other State, territory, possession, or tribe respecting a relationship between persons of the same sex that is treated as a marriage under the laws of such other State, territory, possession, or tribe, or a right or claim arising from such relationship"). See also L D Wardle, "Non-recognition of same-sex marriage judgments under DOMA and the Constitution", (2005) 38 CreightonLRev 365, 372 ("As to public acts and records (choice of law, essentially) DOMA merely restates the long-established choice of law rule and Full Faith and Credit clause principle that interested states may refuse to apply or enforce laws, rules and doctrines of sister states that are contrary to the strong public policy of the forum").

66 La Civ Code art 3520 para 2.

67 France (Loi no 99-944 du 15 nov 1999 relative au pacte civil de solidarité), Germany (Lebenspartnerschaftsgesetz – LpartG, 16.2.2001), Spain (BOE núm 157 2005, 11364), the Netherlands (Act of 21 December 2000 amending Book 1 of the Civil Code, concerning the opening up of marriage for persons of the same sex (Act on the Opening up of Marriage) Stb nr 9), Switzerland (Registered Partnership, 2004), the UK (Civil Partnership Act (2004)), and others have all adopted same-sex marriage or the equivalents thereof.

direction.[68] Some have argued that the reason for this difference is the greater influence of the Christian right in America than elsewhere,[69] but it is not the purpose of this article to enter into that debate. Irrespective of the reasons for prohibiting same-sex marriage, there seems clearly to be an overwhelming preference in America to prohibit such an arrangement. At the same time, however, empirical evidence suggests that Americans feel strongly that such a prohibition should not apply in succession law. A study conducted in 1998 regarding the preference of individuals toward domestic partners in intestacy revealed that "[a] substantial majority of respondents … preferred the partner to take a share of the decedent's estate".[70] The study further demonstrated that respondents "consistently preferred same-sex and opposite-sex committed couples to be treated the same".[71]

Maintaining both a preference against same-sex marriage and one for same-sex inheritance rights is not inconsistent. One can believe that marriage should be limited to opposite-sex partners, but at the same time recognise that intestacy law functions differently and attempts to track the personal preferences of decedents. Discussions of same-sex marriage are often occupied with concern about the expressive theory of law and societal endorsement of same-sex marriage by laws that permit such an arrangement.[72] Inheritance law, however, is a particularly bad vehicle for societal expression and is more properly designed to reflect a decedent's preferences.[73] If a decedent were

68 Until recently, only Massachusetts allowed same-sex marriage, *Goodridge v Department of Public Health* (2003) 798 NE 2d 941. Although the California Supreme Court has recently struck down as unconstitutional a state ban on same-sex marriage, *In re Marriage Cases* (2008) 183 P3d 384, as subsequent amendment to the Californian constitution to restrict marriage to between men and women was declared permissible in *Strauss v Horton* 2009 WL 1444594. The Connecticut and Iowa Supreme Courts have struck down state prohibitions as unconstitutional, *Kerrigan v Commissioner of Public Health* (2008) 2008 WL 4530885; *Varnum v Brien* (2009) 763 NW 2d 862. Legislation in Vermont and Maine has recently legalised same-sex marriage in these states, 2009 Vermont Laws No 3 (S 115); 2009 Me Legis Serv ch 82 (SP 384). The governor of New York has directed state agencies to recognise same-sex marriages performed elsewhere, J W Peters, "New York to back same-sex unions from elsewhere", NYTimes, 29 May 2008. The District of Columbia Council has done likewise, N Stewart and T Craig, "DC Council votes to recognize gay nuptials elsewhere", *Washington Post*, 8 Apr 2009. A small minority of states allow civil unions or domestic partnerships. See n 128 below.

69 C Cox, "To have and to hold – or not: The influence of the Christian Right on gay marriage laws in the Netherlands, Canada, and the United States" (2005) 14 *Law & Sexuality* 1.

70 M L Fellows et al, "Committed partners and inheritance: An empirical study" (Winter 1998) 16 *Law & Inequality* 1 at 89.

71 Fellows et al, "Committed partners" at 89.

72 See, e.g., G W Dent, Jr, "Traditional marriage: Still worth defending" (2004) 18 BYU Journal of Public Law 419.

73 See R J Scalise Jr, "Honor thy father and mother?: How intestacy law goes too far in protecting parents" (2006) 37 SetonHallLRev 171 at 206, arguing that "any system that seeks to enforce moral or social duties through the laws of intestacy or that attempts to express society's view that

allowed to leave a same-sex partner a legacy in a will (something allowed in every American jurisdiction), there is no reason to impose an absolute preclusion in intestacy law, which after all only attempts to distribute one's property in the way one would have done if one had made a will. Thus, on this basic issue of who is considered a "surviving spouse", Scottish law clearly endorses preference; Louisiana law does not.

(b) Prior rights

The Scottish idea of prior rights, although sometimes classified as arbitrary, is clearly an example of the law manifesting the preference of the decedent. These rights are an invention of the 1964 Act, not a result of Scottish history.[74] The Scottish system of prior rights grants to the surviving spouse rights in the house, furnishings, and cash that precede or are "prior" to the operation of the order of succession and thus grant to the spouse a preference over these essential items. In other words, prior rights, in a sense, allow the spouse to come first in line in the order of succession for certain important items, despite an otherwise lowly ranking in the general distribution scheme.

Some view prior rights as a protective device for the surviving spouse, entitling him to the essentials for a successful life. In the Scottish Grand Committee during the enactment of the 1964 Act, "[c]oncern was ... expressed ... about the position of a surviving spouse, particularly a widow",[75] because, under the previous law, it was not uncommon for a house to be titled in the name of the decedent alone and thus pass on his death to a collateral to the exclusion of the widow, who then could "find herself without a roof over her head if the heir at law decided to sell the house".[76] Prior rights were seen by some as a way to remedy this inequity.

Be that as it may, prior rights do not "function as family protection devices", as prior rights are exigible only from the intestate estate, and a decedent can frustrate such rights by writing a will leaving the house and other items to another.[77] The surviving spouse would then have no recourse or relief under the doctrine of prior rights. Prior rights are best explained as manifesting the majoritarian preference that a surviving spouse should receive the house,

---

some relations or statuses are favored and others disfavored is inherently flawed. It is flawed by virtue of its disparate impact and disproportional imposition on the poorer, lower educated, underemployed part of the populace, while leaving its message or its mores not only unheard by but also unvoiced to the more affluent, well-educated, and professional class."

74 Legislation in 1911 and 1919, however, introduced a limited form of prior right. See section C.(2) above.

75 M C Meston, *The Succession (Scotland) Act 1964*, 5th edn (2002) 38.

76 Meston, *Act 1964* at 38.

77 Meston, *Act 1964* at 37.

furnishings, and money. In fact, this priority in the law appears to accord well with the preferences of individuals. A recent omnibus survey conducted at the behest of the Scottish Law Commission helped discover the preferences or attitudes of the Scottish populace as to how property should be distributed at death.[78] On being asked for their preference of intestate distribution when a man is survived by his wife, mother, and brother, 88% of respondents either "agree" or "strongly agree" that the whole estate should go to his wife.[79] Similarly, when asked to whom property should be distributed when a woman is survived by a husband and their two children, responses were almost equally split among those who wanted to prefer the husband to the exclusion of the children and those who wanted the children to share in the estate with the husband.[80] When provided with more nuanced alternatives, 67% of respondents either agreed or strongly agreed that the "husband should have a right to a fixed amount", with anything left over divided equally between the husband and the children as a group.[81]

In short, "[t]he great social significance of these rights lies in the fact that in the large majority of intestacies, prior rights will exhaust the estate and ensure that the surviving spouse is the sole beneficiary, even though others my have nominal rights of succession".[82] Thus, in the two hypotheticals above, it is the Scottish concept of prior rights to the house, furnishings, and cash that allows *B* to receive priority to those items over *A*'s parents and siblings, as well as the children, *C* and *D*. This result in practice accords well with the theoretical presumed preference of the decedent. Once again, Scottish law enacts this concept in furtherance of preference.

(c) Community property

Similarly, the Louisiana conception of marital property is another device that helps advance a decedent's preference. Unquestionably, the conception of community property in Louisiana has multiple purposes. At base, a regime of community property is "a system of principles and rules governing the ownership and management of property of married persons" whereby "[e]ach spouse owns a present undivided one-half interest" in the "property acquired during the existence of [marriage] through the effort, skill, or industry of

---

78 *Attitudes Towards Succession Law* (n 57).
79 *Attitudes Towards Succession Law*.
80 *Attitudes Towards Succession Law* at 5-6.
81 *Attitudes Towards Succession Law* at 6.
82 Meston, *Act 1964* (n 75) at 37; Report on Succession (n 1) para 2.14, estimating the average confirmed estate in Scotland in 2007 at £147,822.

either spouse".[83] A regime of community property in Louisiana is the default regime, meaning that spouses at marriage enter into a community regime unless they affirmatively elect out of the regime via a matrimonial agreement or a judgment decreeing separation of property.[84]

Most married couples in Louisiana live under a community regime.[85] This regime, in addition to creating special rights and obligations outside the context of this paper, alters the general order of intestacy in which the spouse comes fourth in line behind the children, parents, and siblings of the decedent. In fact, the alteration is dramatic. First, under the intestate regime affecting community property, the surviving spouse receives the entire estate if no children exist, and receives a usufruct (i.e., a right to use and derive the fruits) over the decedent's half of the community property if there are children. This right applies to movables and immovables alike, as well as to consumables and nonconsumables.

This marital property arrangement is certainly a "preferential" mechanism that can, like prior rights, be thwarted by a will and thus offers little protection for the surviving spouse. Here too, though, the legal rules match individual preferences quite well. Although no specific survey data exists for Louisiana, data from the United States prove insightful. When an individual is survived by a spouse and parent, a majority of individuals surveyed prefer to leave their entire estate to the surviving spouse, regardless of family size and wealth.[86] In fact, the preference for the surviving spouse is greater in the United States than in Scotland. Even in the case where a spouse and minor children survive a decedent, a majority of respondents prefer distributing the estate exclusively to the surviving spouse.[87] Thus, in the above hypotheticals, B, the surviving spouse, receives the entirety of A's property when no children exist, and usufruct when C and D exist, not by virtue of general intestacy laws or any especially elevated treatment of the surviving spouse, but only because of those special rules constructed for the acquisition of community martial property in Louisiana.

---

83 La Civ Code arts 2325, 2336, and 2338.
84 La Civ Code art 2370.
85 C A Samuel, W M Shaw, Jr, and K S Spaht, "Successions and donations" (1984) 45 La LR 575 at 581 (stating that most spouses in Louisiana live under a community property regime).
86 Fellows et al, "Public attitudes" (n 1) at 354.
87 Fellows et al, "Public attitudes" (n 1) at 359. Although Louisiana is somewhat unique in being a Southern state that is a mixed jurisdiction with community property laws, other Southern community property states with Civilian heritage manifest the same preference for the surviving spouse. See, e.g., W W Gibson, Jr, "Inheritance of community property in Texas – A need for reform" (1969) 47 TexLRev 359 at 364 ("[M]ost testators prefer that their spouses receive all their property to the exclusion of others, including their own children").

(2) Protection

Although the above discussion centred on mechanisms of succession law that further or advance the preferences of decedents, inheritance law also serves to protect heirs of the deceased.

(a) Community property

In addition to the preference-advancing role of community property in Louisiana, the community regime also has protective elements. The protective elements, however, are not in the character of intestate rights, but instead are a direct result of how property is owned during the marriage. As discussed above, the community regime creates an arrangement by which each spouse has an undivided one-half interest in the property acquired during the marriage. The death of one spouse terminates the community and results in its bifurcation whereby each spouse's "undivided one-half interest" is segregated into a one-half divided interest in various assets. Thus, at the death of A under a community regime, the community is split, with B separately owning half the marital assets and A's half being distributed according to his will or the laws of intestacy.

The community property concept implements an idea based on the preference of the parties that marriage is a "partnership", whereby "husbands and wives pool their fortunes on an equal basis, share and share alike".[88] But "another theoretical basis for [community property] is that the spouses' mutual duties of support during their joint lifetimes should be continued in some form after death in favor of the survivor".[89] This support undoubtedly protects the indigent spouse after the death of a wealthier one, and *this* protective function cannot be thwarted by will. Although A can distribute her half of the community property to the exclusion of B under a will, B has a guaranteed right to his own half of the community property, even if all assets are titled in A's name. Thus, the protective function of community property is obvious. At A's death, the community is bifurcated with B receiving his half and the other half being distributed by the laws of successions.

(b) Legal rights

Legal rights in Scottish law also further the protective function, although the interaction between prior rights and legal rights is a complex one. While

88 M Glendon, *The Transformation of Family Law* (1989) 131.
89 Uniform Probate Code, pt 2, general comment (describing the "elective share" right). See R C Brashier, "Disinheritance and the modern family" (1994) 45 CaseWesternLRev 83 at 98 (stating that the community property regime makes the forced or elective share right unnecessary).

both prior rights and legal rights operate in favour of a surviving spouse, prior rights can be defeated by will, but legal rights cannot.[90] In fact, "Scots tend to be proud of the way in which legal rights operate as a bar to capricious disinheritance by a testator".[91]

Legal rights (*jus relictae* or *jus relicti*) grant to the surviving spouse one-half of the decedent's movable property (if no children) or one-third (if children exist). Thus, in the hypotheticals above, while *B* received rights in the house, furnishings, and a fixed share of *A*'s movable property by virtue of defeasible prior rights, *B*'s interest in the remainder of *A*'s movable property is a product of legal rights. The significance of legal rights, while great, should not be overstated because legal rights are subordinated to the payment of prior rights.[92] Thus, as protective a function as legal rights serve in theory, "the practical result of the postponement to prior rights may be that legal rights are of no significance."[93]

(c) Various other protective rights

Although Scottish legal rights and Louisiana's community property regime comprise the vast majority of protective devices for the surviving spouse, both systems, Louisiana and Scotland, contain other less significant protective rights. In Scotland, for instance, the surviving spouse maintains a right of aliment, which can be either temporary or permanent. Temporary aliment is designed to provide temporary support for an individual immediately after the death of a husband or father.[94] Aliment may also be more permanent if the surviving spouse is left unprovided for by the decedent.[95] In cases in which the spouse receives nothing from the decedent's succession, some courts have granted aliment for as long as needed.[96] The claim to aliment has existed since

90 Lifetime transfers or transfer of property into heritable property, however, will defeat legal rights.
91 Meston, *Act 1964* (n 75) at 53.
92 "Legal rights are traditionally regarded not as a right of property but a debt" ("Legal rights as a debt", in SME vol 25 (1989) para 792.
93 Meston, *Act 1964* (n 75) at 53.
94 Report on Succession (Scot Law Com No 124, 1990) para 9.6, explaining that historically, when a widow's claim against her spouse's estate consisted of a liferent, temporary aliment continued until the liferent began on the next legal term; see also E M Clive, *The Law of Husband and Wife in Scotland*, 4th edn (1997) at 601-606. Now, however, a widow's liferent claim is just as likely to run from the date of death as from the next legal term. Clive, *Husband and Wife* at 603. Cases from the beginning of the twentieth century concerning temporary aliment have awarded it for six months following a husband's death. Clive, *Husband and Wife* at 604.
95 Clive, *Husband and Wife* at 601-606.
96 The right of aliment functions as a debt of similar standing with general creditors. Clive, *Husband and Wife* at 601-606. See also *Anderson v Grant* (1899) 1 F 484.

the common law but was statutorily recognised by the Family Law (Scotland) Act of 1985.[97] Legal rights, however, make successful claims for continuing aliment unlikely.[98] Both the rights to temporary and continuing aliment have been characterised as "obsolete" and "completely unjustifiable", and thus the Scottish Law Commission has recommended abolition of both.[99]

More pertinent in today's society is Louisiana's protective device of the "marital portion" or "marital fourth".[100] The marital portion, which comes from Roman law through Spanish law,[101] grants to the surviving spouse one-fourth of the decedent's property if there were no children; one-fourth in usufruct if there were three or fewer children; and a child's share in usufruct to the extent there were more than three children.[102] Although it has been debated whether this right is one of inheritance or a charge,[103] modern legislation considers it a "charge on the succession of the deceased spouse".[104]

While the marital portion is not insignificant, recent cases are somewhat uncommon.[105] For the martial portion to be applicable, the deceased spouse must be "comparatively rich" to the surviving spouse, a term modern jurisprudence defines as having assets valued at five times the assets of the surviving spouse.[106] In a jurisdiction where community property is the default rule and both spouses share equally in assets acquired during the marriage, a five to one disparity between the spouses is somewhat unlikely. Most commonly, these cases arrive when spouses elect out of the community property regime and choose one of separate property (in which each spouse owns only those

---

97   "Law relating to intestate and testate succession", in SME vol 25 (1989) para 711. See also Family Law (Scotland) Act 1985. Moreover, in Scotland the surviving wife has a right to mournings, described by Lord Stair as a debt of the husband (*Inst* 1.4.10). This right is a privileged one that is paid even ahead of creditors. Clive, *Husband and Wife* (n 94) at 601. The right, however, has never been recognised in favour of a husband and is seldom enforced given the "decline in the wearing of mourning clothes" ("Law relating to intestate and testate succession" para 712). It has been described as "a rather unrealistic rule" and recommended for repeal by the Scottish Law Commission. Clive, *Husband and Wife* (n 94) at 601; 1990 Report on Succession (n 94).

98   Clive, *Husband and Wife* (n 94) at 601-606.

99   Clive, *Husband and Wife* (n 94) at 601-606. See also Report on Succession (n 1) paras 7.34-7.39.

100 La Civ Code art 2432. For an overview of the martial portion in Louisiana, see A N Yiannopoulos, "From Justinian to Louisiana with love: The legend of the marital portion", in O Moréteau et al eds, *Essays in Honor of Saúl Litvinoff* (2008) 373.

101 See *The Laws of Las Siete Partidas*, tr L M Lislet and H Carleton, vol 2, partidas 6, title 13, law 7.

102 La Civ Code arts 2432 and 2434.

103 K A Cross, *A Treatise, Analytical, Critical and Historical on Successions* (1891) 391.

104 La Civ Code art 2433.

105 See, e.g., *Succession of Mullin v Mullin* (1994) 631 So 2d 647; *Norsworthy v Succession of Norsworthy* (1997) 704 So 2d 953; *Succession of Adams* (2002) 816 So 2d 988 (finding the marital portion inapplicable); and *Succession of Caraway* (1994) 639 So 2d 415 (finding the marital portion inapplicable).

106 La Civ Code art 2432 cmt (c).

assets acquired in his own name), or in instances where one spouse comes to a community marriage with a large amount of separate property.[107]

E. WHAT CAN BE LEARNED?

Despite the initial similarities of both systems, the differences that emerge are stark. The question that then presents itself is what, if anything, can be learned from the study? Four insights or lessons can be gleaned from the above analysis. First, René David was wrong, at least insofar as he stated that "[l]egal families do not exist like human families".[108] Legal families *do* exist like human families – not in a biological sense, but in the sense that some (perhaps all) are dysfunctional. Legal families may be dysfunctional, not in a pejorative way, but merely because they do not operate or function in the normal way. If, in fact, the idea of "legal families" is, as David states, "only for didactic ends"[109] and "[exists] for taxonomic purposes" in the hope that "one or two legal systems prove representative of ... large groups",[110] then the above discussion has demonstrated that within the mixed legal family, substantial variation in approach, and sometimes in results, exists from two different family members. In fact, it is a clear example of one member, or perhaps both members, not functioning in the normal or usual way.

Second, this study also provides a lesson for comparative law in general – namely, to eschew, or at least be wary of, facial similarities. Recall that at the beginning of this paper, Louisiana and Scottish inheritance law seemed similar in that the general intestate order of succession both placed the surviving spouse fourth in line after children, siblings, and parents. Behind that initial similarity, however, were lurking stark differences that a superficial

---

107 Louisiana also has old and somewhat insignificant protective devices still in its law. Since 1852, Louisiana law has attempted to offset the lowly role of the surviving spouse in intestacy by granting to him or her certain rights or claims against the estate. Article 3252 created the "widow's homestead", which granted to a widow a right to $1,000 of property of the decedent if no children existed or $1,000 in usufruct if children did exist. La Civ Code art 3252. This right was granted to the extent she was in "necessitous circumstances" and has been characterised as "welfare legislation ... granted in the interest of society, to prevent the surviving spouse and the minor children 'from becoming wards of the state'". A N Yiannopoulos, *Predial Servitudes*, 3 *Louisiana Civil Law Treatise*, 4ᵗʰ edn (2000) s 219 (quoting *Malone v Cannon* (1949) 41 So 2d 837 at 844); Cross, *Treatise* (n 103) at 387. This right was prior to all creditors' rights except a vendor's privilege and expenses of selling property. La Civ Code art 3254. The privilege is of almost no significance today.

108 R David and C Jauffret-Spinosi, *Les grands systèmes de droit contemporains*, 9ᵗʰ edn (1988) at 22. Here, I borrow the translation offered by Vernon Palmer in *Mixed Jurisdictions* (n 8) at 14. The exact quote from David is that "[l]a notion de 'famille de droits' ne correspond pas à une réalité biologique".

109 David, *Les grands systèmes* at 22.

110 K Zweigert and H Kötz, *Introduction to Comparative Law*, 3ʳᵈ edn (1998), trans T Weir, at 64.

study might have overlooked. It is ironic that although both systems start with a low role for the surviving spouse in intestacy, both augment or correct that role by various complex mechanisms, resulting in a similarity at the end that is the very opposite of the one with which this paper began. It is popular in comparative law to say that systems generally get to the same result but differ in approach. Here, perhaps, Louisiana and Scotland demonstrate that idea.

Third, aside from the above, this comparative exercise is a useful one because, in the words of Lord Bingham, in studying foreign law, a "lawyer gains valuable insights into his own law".[111] What is it, then, that Scots can learn about Scottish law and Louisianans about Louisiana law? Here, there are lessons for each jurisdiction in terms of both preference and protection. Although both systems seek to implement legislation that will further preference and establish protection, neither system does so particularly well. As far as protection goes, the protective devices in each system are somewhat illusory, as both can be easily evaded. Scottish legal rights are only exigible from movable or personal property and thus are defeasible by transferring one's property into immovable property or heritage. Since prior rights in heritage can be frustrated by a will, a spouse can easily be left unprotected. Louisiana's protection of granting each spouse one-half of the community is also a weak protection since the community regime is only a default one that can be altered by matrimonial agreement. Although other ancillary protective devices exist in both systems, their significance is minimal since Scottish aliment is almost obsolete, and Louisiana's marital portion applies only in extreme cases of economic disparity.

On the preference side, both systems have inadequate orders of succession with respect to the surviving spouse. Scholars have noted that a global tendency in inheritance law is the "strengthening of the rights of the surviving spouse".[112] Although both systems make progress toward that goal, neither ultimately achieves it. Louisiana augments the surviving spouse's role through its conception of community property, but studies in America demonstrate that individuals prefer the surviving spouse to inherit all of the decedent's property, ahead of all relations, including children. Louisiana, however, only grants usufruct when a child exists.[113] In the context of separate property,

111 Zweigert and Kötz, *Comparative Law* at 64.

112 S van Erp, "New developments in succession law" (2007) 11 *Electronic Journal of Comparative Law*, available at *http://www.ejcl.org/113/article113-5.pdf*.

113 Furthermore, some believe this fragmentation of ownership into usufruct and naked ownership on the death of one spouse has created inequities and difficulties in the redevelopment of many parts of New Orleans after Hurricane Katrina. See, e.g., Louisiana House Concurrent Resolution No 28 (2006) ("WHEREAS the law governing the rights and duties of usufructs and naked owners was very complicated prior to the recent hurricanes, and the property issues

Louisiana's preferential scheme is wholly inadequate, with the spouse coming fourth in line after children, parents, and siblings.

Scotland also tries to correct the order of distribution by manifesting majoritarian preference both in its definition of a surviving spouse and its concept of prior rights. While both instances are beneficial additions to Scottish law, prior rights are not sufficient. Scottish prior rights extend only to a fixed monetary value in the deceased's house, furnishings, and cash. In cases of large estates or instances in which a deceased lived in rented accommodation rather than owning a house, a deceased's siblings and parents may receive a larger share than the deceased's surviving spouse.[114] Given the "asset-specific nature of ... prior rights" it is possible that a surviving spouse may receive only a small fraction of a deceased's estate.[115]

Moreover, the Scottish corrective measures, such as prior rights, are so complex that they can even encourage perverse behaviour by individuals in order to achieve desired results. For example, in *Kerr, Petitioner*, a widow who had been left by her husband his "whole means and estate, heritable and moveable" renounced the will and elected to receive her "prior rights" in his estate in order to thwart a claim for the legitim to be brought by the testator's only child. Because the legitim is paid in preference to the disposition in a will, but not in preference to prior rights, only by renouncing a legacy of the entire estate and claiming prior rights under the laws of intestacy could the widow achieve her husband's desired distribution that she receive all his property.[116]

Furthermore, neither system specifically addresses the important issue of second families or step-parents, such as when *A* dies survived by two children *C* and *D* and a spouse *B* who is not the parent of *C* or *D*. This situation is increasingly common. In 1991, in the United States, four of every ten marriages involved a remarriage.[117] Similarly, in Scotland, 25% of marriages are remarriages and one in eight children lives in a family with a step-parent.[118]

---

caused by the destruction of property will cause even more inequities and hardships for usufructuaries and naked owners ...").

114 See, e.g., Discussion Paper on Succession (Scot Law Com DP No 136, 2007) para 2.17. Leases, however, are also generally heritable. See Housing (Scotland) Act 2001 s 22. Moreover, a spouse who leaves home due to domestic violence ceases to be ordinarily resident there for the purposes of prior rights, Report on Succession (n 1) para 2.2.

115 2007 Discussion Paper, para 2.17.

116 *Kerr, Petitioner* 1968 SLT (Sh Ct) 61.

117 A J Norton and L F Miller, "Marriage, divorce, and remarriage in the 1990's" (Bureau of the Census 1992) 5 (available at *http://www.census.gov/population/socdemo/marr-div/p23-180/p23-180.pdf*).

118 *For Scotland's Children Report* (2000) 8 (available at *http://www.scotland.gov.uk/library3/education/fcsr-00.asp*); *Family Formation and Dissolution: Trends and Attitudes Among the Scottish Population* (Scottish Executive Social Research, no 43 (2004) available at *http://www.scotland.gov.uk/Publications/2004/03/19144/35015*) 3.

Current Scottish law makes no distinction between the inheritance rights of surviving spouses who are parents of the surviving children and those who are not; Louisiana makes a very subtle, and perhaps irrelevant, one.[119] In both jurisdictions, however, the preference of most individuals is that the two cases are not to be treated the same. While most Scots want a parent of children to receive all on the death of a spouse, only 19% thought such an outcome was appropriate when the surviving spouse was a step-parent of the children.[120] Similarly, in the United States a significantly smaller portion of the population was willing to award the entire estate to a spouse who is not the parent of the surviving children.[121]

This is an area clearly in need of reform in both jurisdictions. Scotland has unfortunately missed an opportunity to solve this difficult but important problem. The Scottish Law Commission in its 2009 Report on Succession expressed an inclination that no distinction should be made between the various classes of surviving spouse or civil partner because "the range of possible situations is too great and it is not clear that any new rule would produce more satisfactory results than the existing one".[122] This solution has already been soundly criticised in Scotland as a "sterile" one born of preference for "simplicity".[123] Difficulty and complexity should not be reasons for avoiding reform.[124] Clearly the problem here is one of channelling. If the surviving spouse is not the parent of some or all of the surviving children, the concern is that at the death of the surviving spouse the property will not be channelled to the decedent's children. Although no definitive solution is proposed here, such a problem can be addressed by the granting of a partial monetary award or inheritance directly to the surviving children, thus avoiding the channelling problem.[125] Thus, by studying other systems, jurists

119   If a deceased has community property and is survived by children and a surviving spouse who is not the parent of the children, security may be requested by the naked owner from the usufructuary. See La Civ Code art 573B ("Security is dispensed with by operation of law when a surviving spouse has a legal usufruct under Civil Code Article 890 unless the naked owner is not a child of the usufructuary ... ").

120   2007 Discussion Paper para 2.66.

121   Fellows et al, "Public attitudes" (n 1) at 366.

122   2007 Discussion Paper para 2.70. Report on Succession (n 1) para 2.30.

123   K Norrie, "Reforming succession law: Intestate succession" (2007) 12 EdinLR 77.

124   The complications are many as preferences may differ depending upon the age of the children involved, whether the children lived with the step-parent, and whether the decedent's first marriage was terminated by death or divorce. Fellows et al, "Public attitudes" (n 1) at 365-366. A further complication noted by the Scottish Law Commission is that different treatment between spouses who are parents of surviving children and those who are not will "draw a sharp distinction between spouses and civil partners in that the latter are far less likely to be the legal parents of their partner's children". 2007 Discussion Paper para 2.70.

125   See, e.g., Uniform Probate Code § 2-102. The Scottish Law Commission correctly points out that the situation involving a surviving child and a surviving spouse not the parent of the child

in both Louisiana and Scotland can recognise the inadequacies of their own system both in terms of preference and protection.

Fourth and finally, one of the reasons that the study of comparative law is important is "to facilitate the time-honoured practice of theft".[126] So what do Louisiana and Scotland, which to a large extent share the same values of preference and protection regarding the surviving spouse, have to steal from each other? Most notably, Louisiana should steal Scotland's idea of granting intestate inheritance rights to civil partners. Scotland took this step in 2004; Louisiana has made no move in that direction at all. Although the Civil Partnership Act is much broader than mere intestacy law, insofar as it applies in the family law context, there is no reason why Louisiana could not recognise inheritance rights of same-sex partners in the successions context. A variety of ample ways exist in which to implement this suggestion, not the least of which is a registered domestic partner scheme allowing inheritance rights for those so designated via a simple state-provided registration procedure.[127] Several other American states have adopted a domestic partner registration scheme of this kind.[128] As discussed above, empirical evidence suggests that Americans feel strongly that the same-sex marriage prohibition should not affect succession law, and as long as such a registration scheme provides only limited intestate inheritance rights, the system should not run afoul of Louisiana's prohibition on recognising "[a] legal status identical or substantially similar to that of marriage for unmarried individuals".[129]

Conversely, Scotland can learn much from Louisiana's community property system. First, as is the case in Louisiana, on the death of one spouse, the

---

is "only one of many situations where the surviving spouse is not a parent of all the issue". 2007 Discussion Paper para 2.68. Other situations might involve surviving children from both marriages. 2007 Discussion Paper para 2.68. This problem is also not insurmountable. One solution could involve decreasing the size of the share that the surviving spouse would receive and increasing the size of the share that each of the children would receive because "the decedent's descendants who are not descendants of the surviving spouse are not natural objects of the surviving spouse". Uniform Probate Code § 2-102, cmt.

126 T Bingham, "Foreword", in B Markesinis, H Unberath, and A Johnston, *The German Law of Contract: A Comparative Treatise*, 2nd edn (2006).

127 See generally R Brashier, *Inheritance Law and the Evolving Family* (2004) 60 at 80-84. Although the execution of an olographic will is an easy way in which an individual can grant inheritance rights to a civil partner, many have argued that there is still significant psychological reluctance today to will-making because it forces an individual to contemplate his own mortality. See, e.g., G Beyer, "Statutory Will methodologies – incorporated forms vs fill-in forms: Rivalry or peaceful coexistence?" (1990) 94 DickLRev 231 at 238.

128 See, e.g., Haw Rev Stat Ann § 572c-2 (2004); Cal Prob Code § 6401 (West 2002); Cal Fam Code § 297 and 297.5 (West 2004); Me Rev Stat Ann title 18-A §§ 2-102 and 2-103 (2003); NJ Stat Ann 26: 8A-4 (2007); Wash Res Code Ann 26.60.030 (2007). Arizona recently considered similar legislation. See, e.g., H R 2710, 47th Leg, 1st RE.g. Sess (Ariz 2005).

129 La Constitution art 12 § 15.

surviving spouse should receive the entirety of the deceased spouse's estate, provided no children exist.[130] Scotland's current law, which requires a spouse to share property with a deceased's sibling or parent, is contrary to majoritarian preference in Scotland.[131] Beyond that, however, it is not immediately evident how Scottish law can learn from Louisiana's community property regime because in Scotland all property is separate. Moreover, Scottish property law, unlike Louisiana property law, does not maintain a conception of the usufruct. Although some regard a liferent as a personal servitude, modern thinking considers it a separate estate in land.[132] The similarities between the Civil Law usufruct and the Scottish liferent are substantial insofar as "[t]he overriding principle in both systems is that the property should be enjoyed … without encroaching on the substance or capital of the subject liferent", but substantial differences remain.[133] Most notably, a Scottish liferent cannot exist over consumable or fungible things.[134] The nature of a liferent is that it must be *"salva rei substantia"*.[135] Thus, as Erskine writes, they cannot exist over things that "perish in use".[136]

In attempting to mirror the benefit of Louisiana's community regime, this paper does not suggest altering the structure of Scotland's property law nor does it recommend resurrecting the Scottish liferent in heritage, which was abolished in 1964.[137] Instead, it recommends a searching inquiry into the function of Louisiana's community property regime at the death of one spouse. In the inheritance context, it should be remembered, the community regime serves both the preferential function (i.e., property is distributed first to one's spouse) and the protective one (i.e., each spouse owns all assets in indivision, even if all assets are titled in the name of one spouse). This prefer-

130   The Scottish Law Commission has taken the same position, Report on Succession (n 1) para 2.5.
131   2007 Discussion Paper, para 2.18 (stating 88% of respondents either "agreed" or "strongly agreed" that a surviving spouse should receive the entire estate in the absence of descendants). See also Intestate Succession and Legal Rights (Scot Law Com Con Mem No 69, 1986) Appendix 2.
132   Walker, *Scottish Private Law* (n 41) vol 3 at 138.
133   W M Gordon and M J de Waal, "Servitudes and real burdens", in Zimmermann, Visser and Reid, *Mixed Legal Systems* 753-757 (considering differences between usufruct in South African law and liferent in Scottish law).
134   Walker, *Scottish Private Law* (n 41) vol 3 at 140; W M Gloag and R C Henderson, *Introduction to the Law of Scotland*, 12th edn by Lord Coulsfield and H L MacQueen (2007) para 42.30; S C Styles, "Liferent and fee", in SME vol 13 (1992) para 1604.
135   Stair, *Inst* 2.6.4.
136   Erskine, *Inst* 2.9.40. Although this is true, Scottish courts have "interpreted enduring assets broadly." See, e.g., Styles, "Liferent and fee" (n 134) para 1604; *Rogers v Scott* (1867) 5 M 1078 (holding that a liferent could exist over corporeal moveables on a farm).
137   2007 Discussion Paper, para 2.40. The Scottish Law Commission has also recently rejected the suggestion that a liferent be awarded to a surviving spouse in intestacy. 2007 Discussion Paper, para 2.40.

ence, however, exists only with regard to assets acquired during marriage, not to separate property. Thus, if *A* and *B* marry young, enter a community regime, and *A* dies forty years later, under the laws of community property, *B* will obtain the vast majority of the community (i.e., *B* will retain his half and have usufruct over *A*'s). On the other hand, if *A* and *B* marry later in life, enter a community regime, and *A* dies one year later, the rules of intestacy still grant *B* the bulk of the community, but the pool of community assets is likely to be much smaller since the community existed only for one year.

The Uniform Probate Code, in an attempt to model the inheritance effects of the community property system, has developed a procedure that achieves effects similar to the benefits of community property in a separate property regime. It provides a spouse with 50% of an escalating percentage interest in the decedent's augmented estate (starting with 3% for those newly married and increasing to 100% after fifteen years of marriage).[138] This proposal has benefits because, in the situation involving a long marriage between *A* and *B*, it likely fulfills *A*'s preference by providing *B* with half of the property acquired during the marriage. In case of a short marriage between *A* and *B*, it duplicates preference by providing less overall property to *B* after *A*'s death and by allowing *B* to retain freedom to distribute property to others, such as children from a prior marriage. This system, like community property, does double work insofar as it "is the first step in the overall plan of implementing a partnership or marital sharing theory of marriage, with a support theory backup".[139]

This proposal has been recently considered by the Scottish Law Commission and rejected as "sophisticated but complex".[140] Instead, the Commission has advanced a German-style approach that would allow a surviving spouse or civil partner to claim a fixed percentage (i.e., 25%) of what he or she would have inherited in intestacy.[141] Although the Commission's recommendation is certainly an improvement on the current situation, its one-size-fits-all approach leaves something to be desired because it affords the same protection to spouses who were married for ten days or ten years. The proposal outlined here makes that nuanced but important distinction, while at the same time affording adequate protection to the surviving spouse.

F. CONCLUSION

138   Uniform Probate Code § 2-203 (as amended 2008).
139   Uniform Probate Code § 2-202, cmt.
140   2007 Discussion Paper, para 3.41.
141   2007 Discussion Paper, para 3.47; Report on Succession (n 1) para 3.6.

In conclusion, both Scottish and Louisiana law have very different inheritance rights for the surviving spouse, although both attempt to achieve the same general purposes of fulfilling a decedent's preference and at the same time protecting the surviving spouse from arbitrary disinheritance. Part of this difference in the law, of course, is a product of history. This is not surprising because, as Watson suggests, law "to a truly astounding degree … is rooted in the past".[142] Both systems still retain antiquated protective devices such as aliment or the marital portion, which create illusory protections at best. Even the more common provisions of each system's inheritance law, however, are anchored in history. Louisiana's intestacy law is tied to its conception of property law and, more specifically, to its marital property law. Revisions to the law of intestacy have been infrequent and conservative, the most significant of which occurred in the mid-1800s and early 1900s with only a clarifying and minor revision in 1981. Similarly, the continued distinction in Scottish law between inheritance rights in personal and heritable property is a highly criticised element that goes back to earliest Scottish law. Scotland's inheritance law was most recently revised in 1964, some forty-five years ago, and calls have been made for its overhaul.

As a rule, a law's connection to the past is not a bad thing. In fact, the stability provided by history can often be good, as uncertainty or lack of clarity in intestacy law can be detrimental not only to confidence in the protective force of the law, but also to the decisions of individuals. With inheritance law, however, an overly rigid connection with the past can thwart progress and advancement. Such progress is essential for the rules of inheritance, which to be relevant must keep apace with societal preferences. To the extent inheritance rules attempt to implement a decedent's presumed preference, the above conclusion is obvious. Less obvious, but equally important, is the need for the protective function of inheritance rules to pay close heed to changes in society, at least to the extent that these protective rules are designed to implement mandatory *societal* goals from which individuals may not deviate, such as preventing the disinheritance of the surviving spouse. The extent to which Scotland and Louisiana have achieved those goals is subject to debate, but the above discussion suggests much work remains to be done. In that vein, this work has attempted to provide creative, new, and sometimes foreign ways in which to implement the goals of preference and protection in each mixed system.

---

142 A Watson, *Legal Transplants: An Approach to Comparative Law*, 2nd edn (1993) 95.

5 Ownership of Trust Property in Scotland and Louisiana

*James Chalmers**

A. ARE TRUSTS EVEN NECESSARY?
B. TRUST PROPERTY AND INSOLVENCY IN LOUISIANA
C. WHO OWNS TRUST PROPERTY IN LOUISIANA?
D. WHO OWNS TRUST PROPERTY? THE SCOTTISH STORY
E. COMPETING THEORIES: TRUSTEE OR BENEFICIARY AS OWNER?
F. CONCLUSION

Trusts make those accustomed to Civilian property systems uncomfortable, given that they seem to rely on the peculiar Common Law separation of legal and equitable ownership. Equity, it seems, is a concept to be avoided at all costs. (This is not always true. The very first sentence of Mackenzie Stuart's book on the Scottish law of trusts explains that a trust is "nothing except a confidence reposed by one person in another, and enforceable in a Court of Equity",[1] but few if any Scottish writers would be comfortable making this sort of statement today.)

For that reason, one would expect both Scotland and Louisiana to have some difficulty with the trust. And those expectations would be met, although in very different ways. In Scotland, the law has followed practice: trusts exist, and questions of what they are and why they work have been seen as of secondary importance. Hence the Trusts (Scotland) Act 1921 laconically informs the reader that, for the purposes of the statute, the word "trust" includes "any trust".[2] The leading textbook on the subject includes a section headed "Definitions of trust", which reviews five different possible definitions of a trust in order to inform the reader that they are all incorrect.[3] The

* The author acknowledges with gratitude the support of the British Academy through its Overseas Conference Grant scheme.
1 A Mackenzie Stuart, *The Law of Trusts* (1932) 1. The definition is a quote from *In re Williams: Williams v Williams* [1897] 2 Ch 12 at 18 per Lindley LJ.
2 Section 2(a).
3 W A Wilson and A G M Duncan, *Trusts, Trustees and Executors*, 2nd edn (1995) para 1-54 ff.

authors do then offer a definition of their own, and the present writer has kept up the tradition by arguing that this definition is itself defective.[4]

Over time, the question of who owns trust property has caused considerable confusion, with writers and the courts vacillating between various positions: first, that the trustee is the owner of the property, then, that both the trustee and beneficiary are simultaneously the owners of the property, then, that the beneficiary is the owner, and now (full circle) that the trustee is the owner.[5] More recently, that has led academic writers to ask why it is, if the trustee is the owner, that the beneficiary's right is protected against the creditors of the trustee – a point which was established over a century ago, but on the theory of the beneficiary-as-owner.[6] That has led to the development of the "dual patrimony" theory, the argument being that a trustee has a distinct private patrimony and a trust patrimony, the assets in which cannot normally be transferred *inter se*.[7]

In Louisiana, by contrast, the trust has met with rather more resistance, being gradually facilitated by legislation. That has meant that trust legislation in the two jurisdictions has been very different in nature. There has never been anything approaching a code of trust law in Scotland, but the prohibition of *fidei commissa* and substitutions in Louisiana law meant that the recognition of trusts required enabling legislation, first for charitable trusts (in 1882) and then for private trusts (in 1920), the law in both areas having been gradually liberalised over time to allow for wider use of the device.[8] Resistance to the trust seems to have stemmed from a more acute awareness of the difficulties the concept posed for a Civilian system of property. As Pascal argued:[9]

> because of its juridical structure – a division of legal and equitable titles – it simply does not fit into the symmetry of our legal system any more than an armature for an electric motor would fit into a steam engine. There was really no room for dividing

4 J Chalmers, *Trusts: Cases and Materials* (2002) 2.

5 See below, section D. An alternative approach would be to regard the trust as a legal person of some sort and *itself* the owner of the trust property. That approach is not considered further here, because it would seem to require statutory intervention and could not therefore explain the trust as it currently exists. See M Cantin Cumyn, "The Quebec trust: A Civilian institution with English law roots", in J M Milo and J M Smits, *Trusts in Mixed Legal Systems* (2001) 73, 76.

6 *Heritable Reversionary Co Ltd v Millar* (1892) 19 R (HL) 43.

7 K G C Reid, "Patrimony not equity: the trust in Scotland" (2000) 8 ERPL 427; G L Gretton, "Trusts without equity" (2000) 49 ICLQ 599. See also Scottish Law Commission, Discussion Paper on the Nature and the Constitution of Trusts (Scot Law Com DP No 133, 2006) paras 2.16-2.18.

8 For a review, see K V Lorio, "Louisiana trusts: The experience of a Civil Law jurisdiction with the trust" (1982) 42 La LR 1721.

9 R A Pascal, "Some ABC's about trusts and us" (1952-1953) 13 La LR 555, 557.

the legal and equitable ownership in property in our system and thus it would have been a violation of the *ordre publique* to recognise the validity of a trust.

A. ARE TRUSTS EVEN NECESSARY?

None of this really mattered, Pascal argued, because "there was and is no need for the trust in the Civil Law to accomplish most of that which could and can be accomplished in Anglo-American law by the trust alone".[10] It is true that most of what is done by way of trust could be done by way of contract instead. Indeed, in the Scottish courts, Lord President Inglis once asserted that "a trust is a contract made up of the two nominate contracts of deposit and mandate".[11]

But if contract law could do *everything* a trust could do, surely a trust would be irrelevant except as a mere convenience? In Scotland, the answer is found in a conjunction of two principles. First, the rule that a property held in trust cannot be seized by the personal creditors of the trustee. This principle is often attributed to the 1892 decision in *Heritable Reversionary Co. Ltd. v Millar*,[12] although it can in fact be traced back almost sixty years earlier.[13] The significance of *Millar* is that the House of Lords was prepared to go so far as to apply this principle even to heritable property which had been registered in the name of the trustee without any mention of the trust's existence.[14]

The second principle is the rule that the trustee is the owner of trust property. Despite the fact that this was *not* the basis on which *Millar* was

10 Ibid.
11 *Croskery v Gilmour's Trs* (1890) 17 R 697 at 700. Considerable doubt was expressed about this theory in *Allen v McCombie's Trs* 1909 SC 710, although the claim that it was "rejected" (W A Wilson, "The trust in Scots law", in W A Wilson (ed), *Trusts and Trust-Like Devices* (1981) 237, 238) goes too far. See also F H Lawson, *A Common Lawyer Looks at the Civil Law* (1953) 201, who considered that in Scots law "the trustee becomes owner and the beneficiary acquires a contractual right against him". Certain aspects of trust law can, however, be illuminated by reference to contract, and Langbein has argued in favour of a "contractarian analysis" of the trust, albeit one which avoids "fold[ing] the law of trusts into the law of contract": J H Langbein, "The contractarian basis of the law of trusts" (1995) 105 Yale LJ 625, 630.
12 (1892) 19 R (HL) 43. See W A Wilson and A G M Duncan, *Trusts, Trustees and Executors*, 2nd edn (1995) paras 1-12 to 1-22.
13 To *Paul v Jeffrey* (1835) 1 Sh & Macl 767. See K G C Reid, *The Law of Property in Scotland* (1996) para 694.
14 That is, the trust was latent rather than patent. See Reid, *Property* para 694. The decision is problematic in that a creditor who relied on the Register of Sasines might therefore be misled, although the seriousness of the problem depends on whether it would be regarded as legitimate for the creditor to rely on the Register. Cf *Cameron's Trs v Cameron* 1907 SC 407 at 413 per the Lord President (Dunedin) (denying that registration is "publication to the whole world"), but see now, e.g., Scottish Law Commission, Discussion Paper on *Sharp v Thomson* (Scot Law Com DP No 114, 2001) paras 2.11-2.14 and Discussion Paper on the Nature and the Constitution of Trusts (n 7) paras 4.29-4.42.

decided (the court thought that the beneficiary owned the property, in which case it was clearly not available to the trustee's creditors),[15] it remains the case that where a trustee becomes bankrupt, the trust property is not available to his creditors.[16] That, it has been argued – and this might be termed the "insolvency thesis" – is the one thing that makes a trust distinctive from contract in Scots law. A trust can offer protection against creditors; contract cannot.[17] Of course, an institution could be established – whether as a matter of law or practice – where ownership of trust property did not vest in the "trustee", who simply came under contractual obligations of management, but such an institution would be "more akin to a contract of agency specific to certain assets"[18] rather than a trust as that term is normally understood.

B. TRUST PROPERTY AND INSOLVENCY IN LOUISIANA

So, what makes a Louisiana trust distinct from a contractual arrangement? Does the insolvency thesis hold in this jurisdiction? Surprisingly, the issue of the trustee's insolvency has received very little attention in Louisiana.[19] The only decision which seems to address the point is the 1935 Supreme Court decision in *Daugherty v Canal Bank and Trust Co.*[20] The facts in that case were straightforward: the Bank held the sum of $1,665.62 in trust for Mrs Daugherty, and went into liquidation. Mrs Daugherty sued for the entire sum; the bank contended that she was only entitled to be recognised as an ordinary creditor and paid in due course of liquidation.

For the majority of the court, the bank's status as a trustee seemed to make little difference to the point. Instead, the case turned on whether Mrs Daugherty's property could be specifically identified. The court asserted that the funds belonged to Mrs Daugherty,[21] and seemed to treat the situation as a contract of deposit. Under the Civil Code, a depositor remains the owner of the thing deposited and in the event of insolvency is preferred to other creditors of the depositary, provided that "the thing reclaimed be identically

---

15 See *Millar* at 46-47 per Lord Watson, quoted at n 61 below.

16 See *Sharp v Thomson* 1995 SC 455 at 479 per the Lord President (Hope).

17 G L Gretton, "Constructive trusts" (1997) 1 EdinLR 281, 288.

18 E Reid, "The law of trusts in Russia" (1998) 24 *Review of Central and East European Law* 43, 51.

19 L Oppenheim and S P Ingram, *Louisiana Civil Law Treatise: Trusts* (1977) § 131 assert that "it is extremely doubtful that property held in trust can be seized to satisfy a trustee's personal creditor", but without citing authority.

20 180 La 1003 (1935).

21 *Daughtery* at 1015.

the same which he deposited".[22] On that basis, given that the funds had been intermingled, Mrs Daugherty was merely an ordinary creditor.

The court went on to consider whether this result, which was consistent with prior authority, was affected by 1920 legislation recognising the validity of private trusts.[23] The court suggested that the effect of the statute was at most to require the bank *not* to intermingle the trust fund with its own. And even if that was the case, it remained the fact that the funds had been intermingled, and while Mrs Daugherty might have a remedy for the breach of this obligation, she remained an ordinary creditor. What is instructive is the fact that at no time did the majority contemplate the possibility that the bank had been the owner of the funds "as trustee": in its view the intermingling "changed plaintiff's legal status from that of the owner of the funds to that of a depositor or creditor of the bank".[24] The decision attracted some criticism from a single commentator, who pointed out that: [25]

> There must be a fundamental difference between a trust and an ordinary mandate. If there be no substantial difference then we have always recognized trusts in Louisiana, the Civil Code and the decisions of the courts to the contrary notwithstanding. This fundamental distinction will be found in the sacred and inviolable status of trust property in the hands of a trustee as contrasted with the power of an agent to subject assets in his hands in that capacity to the payment of his debts.

That argument would seem attractive to a Scots lawyer, but it seems to have had little traction in Louisiana. Insolvency does receive some specific attention in the Trust Code itself: there, it is said that the creditor of a beneficiary may seize only the beneficiary's "interest in income and principal", rather than the trust property itself.[26] But that provision could be interpreted in two different ways: it may be an application of the rule that the beneficiary is *not* the owner, or it might alternatively be necessary as an exception to the normal consequences of ownership.

---

22 Civil Code art 3222.
23 1920 La Acts No 107.
24 *Daugherty* at 1020.
25 J D Miller, "Preference rights of *cestui* for collection of trust income in hands of trustee" (1934-1935) 9 Tulane LR 416, 420. The decision seems to have been largely ignored in the literature and case law thereafter.
26 La RS 9:2004. The creditor can only seize the interest if it is itself subject to voluntary alienation or the beneficiary has donated property to the trust (and then only to the extent of that donation).

C. WHO OWNS TRUST PROPERTY IN LOUISIANA?

In 1915, R W Lee wrote that:[27]

> wherever the Common Law penetrates, it carries with it its younger sister Equity along with the whole apparatus of Trusts and the distinction of legal and equitable ownership – things utterly incomprehensible to the civilian mind. What then is a judge to do in a Civil Law jurisdiction confronted with such a monstrosity as a common law settlement? There is only one thing to do – to capitulate.

In Louisiana, there is no hint of any such capitulation in the Trust Code. According to article 1781, a trustee "is a person to whom title to the trust property is transferred to be administered by him as a fiduciary". This seems at first glance, to provide – if only indirectly – that the trustee is the owner; what else could it mean to say that he has "title" to the property? But according to Professor Yiannopoulos, it does indeed mean something different:[28]

> according to doctrine and jurisprudence, the "title" of the trustee is merely a power of administration and disposition rather than ownership. Despite the broad legislative formulation, the ownership of the trust property is vested in the principal beneficiary.

Given the authority cited, the claim is a brave one, and the supporting footnote itself deserves quotation: "See Reynolds v Reynolds, 365 So 2d 530 (La App 3d Cir 1978) … But see Reynolds v Reynolds, 388 So 2d 1135 (La 1979)".[29] The authority for this proposition is a Court of Appeal decision that has been overruled by the Supreme Court, but it is the Court of Appeal decision which Professor Yiannopoulos asks us to take as authoritative.[30]

Why so, and why does it matter who owns trust property anyway? The answer to the second question is that in many cases it matters less than might be thought, but *Reynolds* is an exception. Here, Margaret Romero (as she originally was) was one of four grandchildren named as beneficiaries under a trust created in 1962. In 1966, while the trust was still in existence, she married Glynn Reynolds: they were judicially separated in 1970. At that time,

27 R W Lee, "The Civil Law and the Common Law – a world survey" (1915) 14 *Michigan Law Review* 89, 99-100.

28 A N Yiannopoulos, *Louisiana Civil Law Treatise; Property*, 4th edn (2001) § 236. For a similar claim, see A N Yiannopoulos, "Trust and the Civil Law: the Louisiana experience", in J M Milo and J M Smits, *Trusts in Mixed Legal Systems* (2001) 55, 70.

29 Ibid ("cf" citations following the first *Reynolds* citation have been omitted).

30 See also A N Yiannopoulos, "Trust and the Civil Law: The Louisiana experience", in V V Palmer (ed), *Louisiana: Microcosm of a Mixed Jurisdiction* (1999) 213, 229, where an identically-worded claim is made under reference to the Court of Appeal decision and the Supreme Court's decision is not cited. (In terms of La Civil Code art 1, jurisprudence is not a source of law, so there is no reason in principle why the view expressed by a Court of Appeal should not be endorsed, even though the Supreme Court adopted a different approach.)

a total of $11,989 in trust income had accrued to Mrs Reynolds. Most of this was held by the trustee as undistributed earnings, but $555 had been distributed and was held by Mrs Reynolds in a bank account.[31]

The problem was this. Under article 2386 of the Civil Code, the "fruits of the paraphernal property of the wife" fell to be treated as community property.[32] If the trust property belonged to Mrs Reynolds, then the $11,989 was the "fruits of paraphernal property" and formed part of the community property to be settled on the parties' divorce. But if the trust property belonged to the trustee, the $11,989 was *itself* paraphernal property and so not community property.

The question had been the subject of conflicting decisions: in *United States v Burglass*,[33] the Fifth Circuit had held that while legal title to trust property was in the trustee, ownership of the property was in the beneficiaries. But that approach, distinguishing between "legal title" and "ownership", looks barely different from the Common Law theory, and the Court of Appeal rejected it in *Dunham v Dunham*,[34] arguing that it had been "unnecessary for the Court in the Burglass case to hold that title and ownership were divided".[35] In the *Dunham* court's view, the language of Louisiana trust law "clearly and unmistakably" vested both title and ownership in the trustee.[36]

Did *Reynolds* resolve this conflict? According to a plurality of the court on rehearing, Mrs Reynolds had a "beneficial interest" in the trust, something which was itself an incorporeal right and formed part of her paraphernal estate.[37] On that basis, the court distinguished between the undistributed and distributed trust income (something which neither of the courts below, nor the Supreme Court on original hearing had done): the distributed trust income was a fruit of the paraphernal estate and so fell into community property; the undistributed trust income was not.[38] Chief Justice Dixon's opinion (concurring in part and dissenting in part) similarly focused on the question of what amounted to fruits: in his view, the interest afforded to Ms Reynolds under the terms of the trust was not a right to fruits, but instead an

31 See *Reynolds* at 1136-1137. A much larger sum ($11,913) had been paid into the bank account over the course of the marriage, but most of it had been spent by the time of dissolution of the community.

32 Unless an "affidavit of paraphernality" had been executed and recorded, something which had not been done.

33 172 F 2d 960 (5th Cir 1949).

34 174 So 2d 898 (La App 1st Cir 1968).

35 At 907.

36 Ibid.

37 *Reynolds* at 1142.

38 At 1141-1142. The basis for this conclusion was that Ms Reynolds "had no right to this money until the trustee decided to distribute it".

annuity or alimentary pension. But in his view, the trustee was to be regarded as the owner of the trust property,[39] and he cautioned against rethinking the law of ownership:[40]

> The trust is permitted by the Constitution (Article 12, s 5) and the statutory scheme is as complete as it need be. Absolutely no impediment to the function of the trust will occur by the application of the accepted Civil Code concept of ownership. The unknown factor in this case would be the effect of holding that the income beneficiary and the trustee both have ownership interests in the property constituting the corpus.[41]

Reynolds has been regarded as leaving the position unclear, in that the plurality of the court referred to Ms Reynolds right as being "clearly less than full ownership".[42] While such ambiguity is unhelpful – does this mean some *form* of ownership, or something else? – the court is clear elsewhere that Ms Reynolds "did not own the corpus of the trust",[43] and it must follow from the court's conclusion regarding the undistributed trust income that Ms Reynolds was not an owner.[44] The clear position taken by the court provides no basis for preferring the lower court's decision, at least without further argument.

This approach receives some incidental, if not clear-cut, support from another Louisiana decision. In *St Charles Land Trust v Amant*,[45] a woman died domiciled in California as the beneficiary of a trust which held immoveable property in Louisiana. The court had to decide whether her interest was to be characterised as incorporeal immoveable property or incorporeal moveable property: if the former, it was subject to Louisiana succession taxation. Implicit in this discussion was an assumption that the deceased could not be seen as an owner of the trust property *itself*, although the majority of the court shied away from describing the trustees as owners, preferring instead to describe them as having "legal title".[46] The possibility of distinguishing between ownership and title in order to explain the Louisiana trust is noted towards the end of this chapter.[47]

39 At 1148.
40 As Dennis J (dissenting) had argued on both original hearing and rehearing: see *Reynolds* at 1140 (distinguishing title from the "form of ownership" afforded to the beneficiary) and at 1151 (reiterating earlier reasons).
41 At 1149.
42 At 1141. See Lorio (n 8) 1735.
43 *Reynolds* at 1142.
44 It is not clear, therefore, why Lorio (n 8) 1735 n 119 regards *Reynolds* as "somewhat incongruous" with *St Charles Land Trust v St Amant* 253 La 243 (1968).
45 253 La 243 (1968).
46 At 389.
47 Section E. below.

D. WHO OWNS TRUST PROPERTY? THE SCOTTISH STORY

As noted earlier, the progress of the trust has been very different in Scotland.[48] The trust has never been prohibited, nor introduced by statute: to oversimplify, practitioners have simply made use of the trust device and the courts and legal writers have had to deal with it. In one special case, the courts even had to capitulate to the practitioner's reluctance to modify his practice.[49] At least by the eighteenth century, the practice had developed of conveying property to X in liferent (usufruct) and his children in fee (naked ownership). This, of course, made little sense if X *had* no children at the time of the conveyance, and so the courts held that such a conveyance simply gave ownership to X.[50] But conveyancers did not change their practice. Undeterred – or, as Gretton puts it, "rather like lemmings"[51] – they altered their practice only to the extent of adding the word "allernally" (only) to the liferent. And at this point the courts gave in, recognising a form of trust called the "fiduciary fee", whereby X would hold the property for himself in liferent and his children in fee.[52] That device was subsequently recognised in statute[53] and remains competent today.[54]

For the Institutional writers, the position was clear: the trustee was the owner of the property.[55] (Significantly, Bell described it as a "separate estate in the person of the trustees".)[56] But Lord McLaren threw that into doubt in the late nineteenth century by arguing that the trustee and beneficiary were *both* the owners of the trust property.[57] In taking this position, he appears to have been concerned that the Institutional writers had characterised the

---

48   For a review, see K G C Reid, "The idea of mixed legal systems" (2003) 78 Tulane LR 5, 29-31.
49   See G Gretton, "Trusts", in Reid and Zimmermann, *History*, vol 1, 481, 513.
50   *Frog's Creditors v His Children* (1735) Mor 4262.
51   Gretton (n 49) 513.
52   *Newlands v Newlands' Creditors* (1794) Mor 4289.
53   Trusts (Scotland) Act 1921 s 8. For an argument that the statutory provision is in part defective, see W Jardine Dobie, *Manual of the Law of Liferent and Fee in Scotland* (1941) 34.
54   It is, however, difficult to see what advantage there would be in using it rather than a trust "proper", given that a fiduciary fiar ("X" in the example in the text) does not have the usual powers of a trustee: Trusts (Scotland) Act 1921 s 8(2). Gretton (n 45) 513 remarks that "such conveyances are never now used". Cf K McK Norrie and E Scobbie, *Trusts* (1991) 60, who introduce the topic of fiduciary fees by stating that "[w]hen a liferent and fee are set up it is competent, indeed common, to confer the right to the fee on a person or persons not yet born", but this must be treated as a general statement about liferent and fee rather than the specific device of a fiduciary fee.
55   Stair, *Inst* 1.13.7.
56   Bell, *Prin* §§ 1992 and 1994.
57   *Hay's Trs v Hay* (1890) 17 R 961 at 964 (describing the beneficiary's right as a "concurrent estate"); *Govan New Bowling Green Club v Geddes* (1898) 25 R 485 at 492 (referring to a "beneficial estate").

beneficiary's right as a mere *jus crediti* (right of credit),[58] when it was surely something stronger than this. Extrajudicially, he coined the phrase "personal right of property"[59] to explain the beneficiary's right, a description which would be attractive but for the fact that it is incoherent.

Matters took a different tack a few years later when Lord Watson went further and argued that the trustee was not the owner of the property at all.[60] In *Heritable Reversionary Co Ltd v Millar*, he said there could be:[61]

> no doubt that according to the law of Scotland the [trustee], though possessed of the legal title, and being the apparent owner, is in reality a bare trustee; and that the [beneficiary], to whom the whole beneficial interest belongs, is the true owner.

That approach has now been rejected, and it is clearly understood that in Scots law the trustee is the owner of the trust property. It may be noted, however, that the distinction posited between "title" and "ownership" is one which has been invoked much more recently to explain the trust in Louisiana.[62]

E. COMPETING THEORIES: TRUSTEE OR BENEFICIARY AS OWNER?

Why might the trustee-as-owner theory not find favour? Its most obvious difficulty is that – at first sight – it fails to explain why the beneficiary's right is not in competition with the creditors of the insolvent trustee. But, as noted above, that difficulty can be addressed by means of the dual patrimony theory.[63] For that reason, it does not provide a basis for objecting to the trustee as owner. Alternatively, the objection can be made at a seemingly more intuitive level, that it simply does not "feel right" to describe the trustee as an owner:[64]

---

58 See Bell, *Prin* § 1996. See also *Inland Revenue v Clarke's Trs* 1939 SC 11 at 22 per the Lord President (Normand) ("nothing more than a personal right to sue the trustees and to compel them to administer the trust … ").

59 McLaren, *Wills and Succession*, vol 2, s1527.

60 Except, of course, in a system where ownership of land is registered, this is utterly irreconcilable with the trustee being registered as the owner. This is doubtless why Lord Watson resorts to a distinction between "apparent ownership" and "true ownership" in the passage quoted. On the use of concepts of constrained or restricted ownership to explain the trustee's right, see M J de Waal and R R M Paisley, "Trusts", in Zimmermann, Visser and Reid, *Mixed Legal Systems* 819, 833-834.

61 (1892) 19 R (HL) 43 at 46-47.

62 Section E. below.

63 See n 7 above and accompanying text.

64 D W Gruning, "Reception of the trust in Louisiana: the case of *Reynolds v Reynolds*" (1982) 57 Tulane LR 89, 120.

the principal beneficiary seems more like an owner than does the trustee, who resembles an owner only in his power to manage the corpus. A trustee may be removed by a court for cause. He may be appointed by a court, even provisionally and on the court's own motion. And although the trust is defined as a transfer of title to the trustee, his acceptance is unnecessary to its existence. Therefore, if the Civil Law insists on finding an owner, the principal beneficiary seems the necessary choice.

What does it mean to "resemble an owner"? The Louisiana Civil Code states that an owner may "use, enjoy, and dispose" of property,[65] but reference to this definition of ownership does not provide a solution. One writer appears to have viewed the right to "enjoy" the property as key,[66] in which case it probably would be the beneficiary who comes closest to being regarded as an "owner". But many people who are not owners in law are, from time to time, given rights to "enjoy" property without owning it.

If it is sought to shoehorn either the trustee or beneficiary into this definition of ownership, it is surely the trustee who fits best – if nothing else, he has control over the way in which the property is used and enjoyed, even if that power is curtailed by the terms of the trust. Most significantly, he has the power to dispose of the property, a right not enjoyed by the beneficiary. Rather than focusing on enjoyment, an alternative approach would be to say that it is the person who has the right to alienate the property who most resembles the owner. Consistent with the principle *nemo plus juris ad alium transferre potest quam ipse haberet*, only an owner has this power. Alienation implies ownership; enjoyment does not.[67]

These possible objections, it is suggested, are far from convincing. More importantly, the objections to the beneficiary-as-owner theory are fatal to that approach.

One reason why the beneficiary-as-owner theory would not be workable in Scots law is the issue which arose in respect of fiduciary fees (discussed earlier): a beneficiary in a Scottish trust can be unascertained: for example, a

---

65 La Civil Code art 477 defines ownership as "the right that confers on a person direct, immediate, and exclusive authority over a thing. The owner of a thing may use, enjoy, and dispose of it within the limits and under the conditions established by law." That definition is not of great assistance in answering this question, as both a trustee and a beneficiary could be said to satisfy it in part but not wholly.

66 G Le Van, "Louisiana counterparts to legal and equitable title" (1980-1981) 41 La LR 1177, 1184.

67 The characterisation of a Louisiana beneficiary as bearing a greater "resemblance" to the owner than the trustee is further impeded by 1997 legislative amendments providing for "spray trusts": that is, giving the trustee discretion to allocate income between beneficiaries. (See K A Weiss, "Drafting Louisiana income 'spray' trusts: After the 1997 Trust Code amendments" (1998) 72 Tulane LR 1329.) If the beneficiary's right can be varied by the trustee in this way, it seems to look rather less like a right of ownership.

trust can be validly created for A's children even if A has (and may never have) any offspring. But this objection may not carry the same weight in Louisiana law, where it is generally required that all beneficiaries be designated and vested from the inception of the trust. An exception applies in respect of "class trusts", but even there at least one member of the class must be in being at the time the trust is created.[68]

Perhaps, therefore, this difficulty is not fatal to the theory in respect of the Louisiana trust, but the second cannot be argued away in this fashion. That is this: how can the trustee, if he is not the owner of the trust property, deal with it? Specifically, how can he transfer good title to a third party? Both Scots law and the Louisiana Civil Code adhere to the principle of *nemo plus juris ad alium transferre potest quam ipse haberet* (or *nemo dat quod non habet* – "no one can give what he does not have"), which would seem to preclude the non-owner trustee from transferring title to the trust property.[69] It is possible, of course, for an agent to alienate property on behalf of an owner, and at first glance this might appear to provide a solution. In some ways a trustee is similar to an agent: for example, just as an agent is entitled to reimbursement from a principal,[70] so is a trustee entitled to reimbursement from the trust estate.[71] These rights are, however, different in nature: the trustee's right is to make a claim on the trust funds and not to pursue the beneficiary personally.[72] If the trust were in a legal person and owner of the property, a relationship of agency would explain the trustee's position. But absent such an approach, agency will not solve the problem: the trustee simply does not have the relationship with a *beneficiary* which agency would require.

There are two further possible responses, neither satisfactory. The first is that suggested by Lord Watson in *Heritable Reversionary Co Ltd v Millar*,[73] to resort to the doctrine of personal bar. Lord Watson suggested that "a true owner who chooses to conceal his right from the public, and to clothe his trustee with all the *indicia* of ownership, is thereby barred from challenging rights acquired by innocent third parties for onerous considerations under

---

68 See E F Martin, "Louisiana's law of trusts 25 years after adoption of the Trust Code" (1990) 50 La LR 501, 512-513.

69 In Louisiana, see Civil Code art 2452: "The sale of a thing belonging to another does not convey ownership."

70 L Macgregor, "Agency and mandate", in *The Laws of Scotland: Stair Memorial Encyclopaedia*, Reissue (2002) para 122.

71 A Mackenzie Stuart, *The Law of Trusts* (1932) 358; L Oppenheim and S P Ingram, *Louisiana Civil Law Treatise: Trusts* (1977) § 423.

72 So where a trustee breaches trust at the request of a beneficiary, the Trusts (Scotland) Act 1921 s 31 only goes so far as to allow the court to apply the beneficiary's interest in the trust by way of indemnity to the trustee, not to create a right against the beneficiary.

73 (1892) 19 R (HL) 43.

contracts with his fraudulent trustee".[74]

But while that solution might have worked (at least partially) on the facts suggested in *Millar*, it is difficult to see it as a full solution. First, it is doubtful that (for example) underage or otherwise incapable beneficiaries could be held to have personally barred themselves from challenging the rights of a third party in this way, not least because they will have had no say in the initial creation of the trust. Secondly, even if the beneficiary is prevented from challenging the third party's right in this way, this will not serve to confer a real right on the third party, and so if his property falls into the hands of another, he may be left without a remedy.

The alternative response, as found in the Louisiana literature, is that suggested by Professor Yiannopoulos:[75]

> In Louisiana, there is neither need nor room for a fragmentation of ownership into the components of legal title and equitable interest. The trustee has a real right that permits him to manage and dispose of the trust property. The beneficiary has likewise a real right, which is ownership subject to trust, that is, ownership without power of administration and disposition. Thus, functionally, the trust device has been accommodated in Louisiana without the implications of a split ownership that is unknown to Civil Law.

So, in order to avoid distinguishing between legal and equitable ownership, we instead distinguish between the trustee's real right ("title") and the beneficiary's real right ("ownership subject to trust"). It is true that this avoids using any form of the dreaded word "equity", but that is mere wordplay. Gretton has observed that it is unlikely any English lawyer would claim that a trustee has ownership, "though they might say that he had 'title'".[76] At least insofar as terminology is concerned, the solution offered by Yiannopoulos adopts exactly the distinction which it seeks to resist. Granting both the trustee and the beneficiary real rights is, in effect, a separation of legal and equitable ownership, and asserting that it is in fact something different is not a solution.

F. CONCLUSION

This chapter has sought to address a narrow but important point relating to the nature and constitution of trusts, and one which appears to have been satisfactorily resolved in Scots law but unsatisfactorily addressed in Louisiana. To that extent, therefore, there may be benefits to Louisiana in

---

74 At 47.
75 A N Yiannopoulos, *Louisiana Civil Law Treatise: Property*, 4th edn (2001) § 236.
76 Gretton (n 17) 282.

looking to the Scottish approach – not as a model for legal change, but as a model for understanding how a trust can satisfactorily operate in a Civilian property system. This approach, however, depends on adopting the theory of "dual patrimony", which has been developed at length elsewhere and is not explored here.[77] Although that theory (it is thought) satisfactorily explains the Scottish position, it has not yet been judicially endorsed, and the Scottish Law Commission has suggested that it be put on a statutory footing for the avoidance of doubt.[78] Neither jurisdiction could claim to have solved the problem with any finality, but Scotland is – at present – some considerable way closer to doing so.

77 See references at n 7 above.
78 Discussion Paper on the Nature and the Constitution of Trusts (n 7) para 2.28.

6 The Legal Regulation of Adult Domestic Relationships

Kenneth McK Norrie

A. INTRODUCTION
B. TWENTIETH CENTURY DEVELOPMENT
(1) Getting married
(2) Personal consequences of marriage
(3) Property consequences of marriage
(4) Succession rights of spouses
(5) Divorce
(6) Financial consequences of divorce
C. TWENTY-FIRST CENTURY PARTING OF THE WAYS
(1) Cohabitation, or unregistered relationships
(2) Same-sex relationships
(3) Covenant marriage
D. CONCLUSION

INTRODUCTION

Family law, perhaps more than any other area of law, reflects the society it serves. This is not surprising since, after all, society at heart is made up of families, of groupings of individuals bound by ties of blood and affection who share their private lives together and who present to the public as "belonging" to each other. As society and family forms change, so too does family law change: the profound historical shifts in social structures between the beginning and the end of the twentieth century in both the jurisdictions under consideration in this book find their reflection in equally profound legal changes. So, for example, the changes to the position of women in society led inexorably to a fundamental restructuring of the husband-wife relationship in both Scotland and Louisiana with various practical legal consequences;[1] the development of a previously unimagined diversity of methods by which children can be – and are – brought into existence today has forced both

---

1 See K Lorio, "The changing concept of family and the effect on Louisiana succession" (2003) 63 La LR 1161.

146

jurisdictions to alter ages-old perceptions of parenthood;[2] the secularisation of marriage and the virtual evaporation of the unquestioned acceptance that marriage, good or bad, must be enjoyed or endured for life, has not only increased the number of divorces in fact but has also led to the liberalisation of the grounds for divorce in law. The process continues. As "gay liberation" from the 1970s transformed itself into "gay pride" in the 1990s, most societies across the western world rejected their previous abhorrence of same-sex relationships and moved to a state of tolerance, acceptance and (in some places) celebration of sexual diversity. All legal systems have had to respond to the vastly increased visibility and assertiveness of the LGBT[3] community. Some have responded positively, some negatively, but all have responded in some way.

The examination of the legal regulation of adult domestic relationships presented in this chapter will illustrate how, in Scotland and Louisiana, social changes such as those mentioned above led to the domestic legal rules in these jurisdictions developing in parallel ways for much of the twentieth century. We will also see that towards the end of that century, and throughout that part of the twenty-first already experienced, the legal response to contemporary social shifts in how family life is led has diverged widely in these two juris-dictions. Yet the social phenomena of family breakdown and reconstitution, and of non-marital relationships, are increasingly common in both Scotland and Louisiana, and further legal change is inevitable as a response to the pressures created by these phenomena. The long-term maintenance of the present state of divergence is certainly not an historical inevitability – it is not even, I suggest, particularly likely.

The analysis presented here is not, it perhaps needs to be recorded, partic-ularly connected to the two jurisdictions' heritage as mixed legal systems and would apply equally to many other (western) legal systems. This is because family law's roots are far older than the division of the western world into legal "families" and the similarities and differences are explained more readily by religious than legal heritage.[4] So the comparative examination that follows may be taken as representative of a divergence in approach where today's fault line is politico-religious rather than strictly legal. Louisiana follows a

2 This affects succession rights too: see R Trahan, "Successions and donations" (2004) 64 La LR 315.

3 Lesbian, gay, bisexual, transsexual. The law governing transsexuals is beyond the scope of this chapter. For in-depth coverage of the position in North America, the UK and Australasia, see R Sharpe, *Transgender Jurisprudence* (2002).

4 A point illustrated, and elaborated, elsewhere in this book: see R Trahan, "Prerequisites to marriage in Scotland and Louisiana: An historico-comparative investigation", ch 7 infra.

path adopted by a significant number of jurisdictions within the United States of America while Scotland follows a path typical (now) of much of Europe, Australasia, Canada and South Africa.

B. TWENTIETH CENTURY DEVELOPMENT

For much of the twentieth century, regulation of adult domestic relationships was effected exclusively through the institution of marriage, and there was a high level of agreement in both jurisdictions as to the very purpose of that institution. For that reason it is not surprising that, while the structures sometimes differed, the effects of the rules were usually substantially similar.

(1) Getting married

Both jurisdictions see marriage as an institution that creates a status and which is itself created by a contract. Article 86 of the Louisiana Civil Code defines marriage as "a legal relationship between a man and a woman that is created by civil contract". Fraser says much the same for Scotland: "Marriage is a contract, in so far as it requires the consent of two persons, but it is very much more than this. It is an institution or status".[5] That status can be created only when the contract is concluded at a public marriage ceremony, at which the free consent of the parties is expressed, these parties being free from legal impediment.[6] The state must grant its permission through the issuance of a marriage licence (marriage schedule in Scotland). There must be witnesses to the ceremony, and recording of the contract in the public registers.[7] In both jurisdictions the parties must be present, the ceremony is to be conducted by a person authorised by the state,[8] and there are limitations on who may marry whom, a matter that is given detailed consideration in another chapter of this book.[9] In both countries it is a matter of the greatest importance that marriage be freely entered into. Consent to marry is not regarded as free (and the marriage, therefore, is void) if it has been given under duress[10] or by a party too young to give consent.[11] Neither jurisdiction requires consummation.

---

5 P Fraser, *A Treatise on Husband and Wife*, 2nd edn (1876-1878) vol 1 156.
6 La Civ Code art 87.
7 The Vital Records Registry in Louisiana and the General Registers of Scotland.
8 La Civ Code art 91; Marriage (Scotland) Act 1977 ss 8 and 18.
9 Trahan, "Prerequisites to marriage" (n 4).
10 La Civ Code art 93; Marriage (Scotland) Act 1977 s 20A(2), as inserted by the Family Law (Scotland) Act 2006 s 2.
11 On a curious difference between Scotland and Louisiana in this respect, see Trahan, "Prerequisites to marriage" (n 4) at 193.

(2) Personal consequences of marriage

Throughout the twentieth century in jurisdictions across the western world the personal consequences of being a married person diminished very substantially.[12] It would, however, be a serious mistake to interpret this "retreat of law" as signifying any legislative intent to reduce the social importance of marriage. The phenomenon is, rather, a response to crucial changes in society and in particular the position of women. Throughout the vast majority of its history, marriage operated as a private law means of regulating the individual relations between two socially, economically and legally very different, and very unequal, persons: a man (who was master) and a woman (who had duties of obedience).[13] This of course reflected the expectations of individuals and the economic circumstances of society as it was then structured. The twentieth century, however, saw a radical transformation in the position of women – illustrated starkly by the removal during the Second World War of the rules in fully half the states of the USA that prohibited the employment of married women – and the rules designed to emphasise male dominance in the private domain had to change to reflect this. We no longer accept the injunction (to Eve) in *Genesis* 3, 16 and the conception of marriage moved from a relationship of power and dependency to one of mutuality, a change that has been felt across the world.[14] So the rules that applied in both Louisiana and Scotland bringing a wife – and, crucially, her property – within the control of her husband were removed as no longer reflecting society's needs and expectations. This occurred in Louisiana with the Married Women's Emancipation legislation between 1916 and 1928, and in Scotland with the Married Women's Property (Scotland) Acts 1881 and 1920. Thereafter, in both jurisdictions, a wife who was under the age of majority remained subject to her husband's legal authority in relation to contracts, but the minor wife escaped even this remaining element of control,

---

12 For Scotland, see E Clive, *Husband and Wife,* 4th edn (1997) and J Mair, "A modern marriage?" (2006) 10 EdinLR 333; for Louisiana see K Spaht, "The last one hundred years: The incredible retreat of law from the regulation of marriage" (2003) 63 La LR 243.

13 See A Gautier, "Legal regulation of marital relations: An historical and comparative approach" (2005) 19 Int J Law Pol & Fam 47.

14 Art 16(1)(c) of the Convention on the Elimination of All Forms of Discrimination Against Women (CEDAW) (adopted by the UN General Assembly Resolution 34/180 on 18 December 1979) provides that States "shall ensure, on the basis of equality of men and women … the same rights and responsibilities during marriage and its dissolution". Of the 186 signatories to this Convention, 185 have ratified it. The USA has not, and although some signatories – predominantly Muslim countries – have entered reservations to art 16, the USA remains the only western country that does not formally accept the aspirations contained in CEDAW for gender equality.

in 1974 in Louisiana[15] and in 1984 in Scotland.[16] Another rule designed to emphasise the mastery within marriage of the male partner, that choice of residence rested with the husband, remained part of the law of Scotland until 1984[17] and the law of Louisiana until 1985.[18] Similarly the obligation of support, which was originally as gendered as the society it was designed to serve, became gender-neutral as social expectations and state policy shifted from male dominance to mutuality in relationships.[19]

In neither Scotland nor Louisiana, however, is the process of equalising the husband and wife relationship complete. Marriage remains a gendered institution and there still exists in both jurisdictions detritus from a previous age. In Louisiana one of the few remaining rules preferencing men over women is found in Article 216 of the Civil Code, which governs parental authority over children and provides that in the event of differences between the parents the authority of the father prevails.[20] As well, there are special rules governing the married woman's surname,[21] a matter the law of Scotland is entirely indifferent to. In Scotland, the common law rule that a married woman cannot be convicted of resetting stolen goods when her husband was the thief, nor of harbouring her husband while a fugitive from justice, has never been abolished, and was affirmed as recently as 1982.[22] These rules are based on the proposition that a wife's duty to obey her husband is higher than her duty to obey the law.

(3) Property consequences of marriage

A major structural difference between the two jurisdictions is that Louisiana adopts, but Scotland rejects, a community property regime on marriage. Here, perhaps, we do see a manifestation of different legal as opposed to religious traditions, for community property regimes are characteristic of Civil Law systems. Most jurisdictions in the US, a predominantly Common Law country, adopt separate property regimes, and the handful of states with community of property are mostly those whose early law was based on the Civilian systems of France and Spain. The effect in Louisiana is that a married person's property will be classified as either community property or

15 1974 La Acts No 89.
16 Law Reform (Husband and Wife) (Scotland) Act 1984 s 3(3).
17 Ibid, s 4.
18 1985 La Acts No 271.
19 See now La Civ Code art 98; Family Law (Scotland) Act 1985 ss 1-7.
20 This is not so in Scotland: Children (Scotland) Act 1995 s 2(2).
21 La RS 9: 292.
22 See *Smith v Watson* 1982 SLT 359; *Miln v Stirton* 1982 SLT (Sh Ct) 11.

separate property.[23] Community property comprises the property acquired during the existence of the legal regime (that is to say during the marriage) through the effort, skill or industry of either spouse, including property acquired through the use of community property, property donated to the spouses jointly, damages for any loss or injury to community property, "and all other property not classified by law as separate property".[24] The effect of the community property regime is that during its subsistence, each spouse owns a present undivided one-half interest in the community property[25] and each spouse acting alone may manage, control or dispose of community property,[26] subject to certain limitations.[27] Separate property, on the other hand, belongs to the individual spouse exclusively and cannot be accessed by the other spouse's creditors. This primarily comprises property acquired by either spouse prior to the establishment of the community property regime (i.e., before the marriage) and property inherited by or donated to one spouse alone.[28] Damages for personal injury sustained during the existence of the community property regime remain separate property,[29] though punitive damages will be community property.[30] A separate property regime may be established by a matrimonial agreement to that effect, either before or during the marriage.[31] But the default position in law is community property and this applies to a large majority of married couples in Louisiana. The community property regime terminates on divorce, retroactively to the date of the filing of the petition for divorce;[32] it also terminates on the death of one of the spouses, a declaration of death, a judgment of separation of property or by a matrimonial agreement that terminates the community.[33]

Scotland does not adopt a system of community property and there is indeed an express statutory provision to the effect that marriage shall not

---

23 La Civ Code art 2335.
24 Ibid art 2338.
25 Ibid art 2336.
26 Ibid art 2346.
27 Such as the alienation of immovables or furnishings of the family home (La Civ Code art 2347) and donations of property to a third party (La Civ Code art 2349).
28 La Civ Code art 2341.
29 Ibid art 2344. Damages for solatium in Scotland are effectively treated in the same way in relation to the division of "matrimonial property": *Skarpass v Skarpass* 1993 SLT 343.
30 *Morris v Morris* 685 So 2d 673 (La App 3 Cir 1996).
31 La Civ Code art 2370. The "matrimonial agreement" requires to follow very specific provisions before it will be effective in ousting the community property regime, and there has been much litigation on whether a contract between spouses amounts to a matrimonial agreement. See K Rigby, "Matrimonial agreements: Recent developments" (2006) 67 La LR 73.
32 La Civ Code art 159.
33 Ibid art 2356.

affect the respective property rights of the parties to the marriage[34] (subject to a relatively minor exception in relation to "household goods", where there is a (rebuttable) presumption that such goods are jointly owned by both spouses[35]). Nevertheless, the two systems, though structurally distinct, are not so far apart in effect. For the major consequences of a community property regime arise at the end of the marriage, either by death or divorce. And the effect the regime achieves in Louisiana at these points is, as we will see, substantially similarly to that achieved in Scotland, though by a different route.

(4) Succession rights of spouses

It has long been a Civilian tradition that the surviving spouse has a protected right of succession, exercisable even against the terms of a will.[36] Scotland and Louisiana continue to reject the principle of free testation, which characterises most Common Law systems and, though the details of the protection afforded to surviving spouses differ in important respects, the pressures and the aims are substantially the same.

As is described more fully elsewhere in this book,[37] Scots law confers a complex mix of protections and preferences on a surviving spouse by a set of rules laid down, by and large, in the Succession (Scotland) Act 1964. These rules have not, at the level of principle, altered since that date. They were designed for, and work well in the context of, a stable single family unit – which was overwhelmingly the sort of family that existed in 1964. The rules have become far more problematical in a world where reconstituted families, second (and subsequent) marriages, and step-relationships are common. In 2007 the Scottish Law Commission questioned whether the balance between spouse and children of a deceased should be different depending upon whether there had been family reconstitution or not.[38] The application of the current rules strongly favours the surviving spouse, as Scalise shows.[39] This position is almost universally supported when either there are no surviving children or the children are children of the marriage.[40] But when the surviving spouse is a second (or subsequent) spouse and step-parent to the deceased's children, a rule preferencing that spouse over these children to the same

---

34 Family Law (Scotland) Act 1985 s 24.
35 Ibid s 25.
36 See R Scalise, "Inheritance and the surviving spouse", ch 4 supra.
37 Ibid.
38 See Discussion Paper on Succession (Scot Law Com DP No 136, 2007) paras 2.65-2.70; Report on Succession (Scot Law Com No 215, 2009).
39 Scalise "Inheritance and the surviving spouse" (n 36).
40 See n 38 above at para 2.37.

extent is far less obviously right.[41]

In Louisiana the need to recalibrate the balance between surviving spouse and children to take account of varying family forms has been more readily recognised. Since 1844 the surviving spouse has had a usufruct[42] over the community property inherited by the issue of the marriage[43] and a right to succeed to the deceased's share of the community property if there were no surviving issue.[44] The surviving spouse also had a claim over the separate property owned by the deceased on death, varying depending upon relative wealth and the existence and number of children.[45] The rules governing usufruct have changed over time, especially in relation to the surviving spouse who is step-parent rather than parent of the surviving children.[46]

So both systems recognise the need to balance the competing interests of surviving spouse and children of the deceased, and in both the historical movement has been towards both simplification and greater protection of the spouse. There are two curious results here: (i) as family relationships become more complex the rules of succession are becoming more simplistic; and (ii) while the legal consequences of marriage are gradually being reduced, in succession law the practical significance of marriage is increasing.

(5) Divorce

Divorce has been available in Louisiana since 1827,[47] and in Scotland since the Reformation in 1560.[48] In both jurisdictions, the remedy was for a long time available only on a showing of fault on the part of the defender, consti-tuted by the "violation of marital obligations" in Louisiana, and by the canon law offences of adultery or desertion in Scotland. However, in both, the last quarter of the twentieth century saw "no-fault" divorce added to fault-based divorce whereby marriage could also be terminated on proof that the marital relationship has broken down: in both jurisdictions this is shown simply by the fact that the couple no longer live together and have not done so for a specified period. This is recognition that living together, rather than sex or procreation, is the ultimate defining characteristic of the marital relationship

---

41 See Lorio, "The changing concept of family" (n 1); K Norrie, "Reforming succession law: Intestate succession" (2008) 12 EdinLR 77.
42 Defined in La Civ Code art 535 as "a real right of limited duration on the property of another".
43 1844 La Acts No 152 §2; La Civ Code (1870) art 916, now art 890.
44 La Civ Code art 889. See *Malone v Cannon* 41 So 2d 837 (La 1949).
45 La Civ Code arts 2432-2434.
46 See 1975 La Acts No 680; 1981 La Acts No 911.
47 1827 La Acts §4.
48 See Clive, *Husband and Wife* (n 12) para 20.001.

in contemporary society and this, at heart, is the basis for the conservative dislike of no-fault divorce. In Louisiana the requisite period of non-cohabitation is normally 180 days but is 365 days where there are minor children (unless the defender has physically or sexually abused the person seeking the divorce or a child of one of them).[49] The remaining fault-based grounds are adultery and conviction of a felony and sentence to death or imprisonment at hard labour.[50] In Scotland the Divorce (Scotland) Act 1976 added non-cohabitation for the requisite period to the existing fault grounds of adultery, desertion and unreasonable behaviour and, since 2006, the periods of non-cohabitation are one year if the defender consents to the divorce and two years otherwise.[51]

A crucial feature of the modern divorce law in Scotland is that the grounds of divorce are insulated from the other matters that the divorce court will normally be asked to resolve, such as the financial settlement and future care of children. It is irrelevant to a residence dispute on divorce, for example, who was to blame for the breakdown of the relationship, for the paramount consideration is the welfare of the child[52] and it is considered that blame for the marital failure will normally have no direct bearing on that issue.[53] And conduct (including whose "fault" it is that the marriage broke down) is also ignored in Scotland in determining the financial settlement on divorce, except (i) when it would be manifestly inequitable to leave conduct out of account and (ii) when the conduct in question has adversely affected the financial resources available for redistribution.[54] In Louisiana, on the other hand, while marital fault is not a determining factor in a custody dispute,[55] it does affect the financial settlement that the court can make: future periodic support is available only to a spouse "who is free from fault",[56] a phrase that is wider than "fault" as a ground of divorce.[57]

---

49 La Civ Code art 103.1. The extension to 365 days was introduced by 2006 La Acts No 743.
50 La Civ Code art 103.
51 Divorce (Scotland) Act 1976, as amended by the Family Law (Scotland) Act 2006 s 11.
52 Children (Scotland) Act 1995 s 11(7).
53 Though of course behaviour that does affect children, e.g. domestic violence, will be central to any residence dispute. See Children (Scotland) Act 1995 s 11(7A) and (7B), as inserted by the Family Law (Scotland) Act 2006 s 24; La RS 9:364.
54 Family Law (Scotland) Act 1985 s 11(7).
55 "Our jurisprudence has long recognised that a good mother should not be deprived of the custody of her children, if in *their* interests, simply because she has been at fault in marital difficulties which cause the parties to separate" (*Stelly v Montgomery* 347 So 2d 1145, at 1149 (Sup Ct La, 1977)).
56 La Civ Code arts 111 and 112.
57 *Currier v Currier* 599 So 2d 456 (La App 2 Cir 1992).

(6) Financial consequences of divorce

Under Louisiana's community property regime, divorce brings that regime to an end, retroactively to the date of filing the petition for divorce,[58] and the property is distributed equally between the (now ex-) spouses. They each, in other words, take away 50% of the property that came into their joint ownership between the date of the marriage and the date of the commencement of the divorce proceedings. Though structurally very different, Scots law achieves virtually the same result. On divorce the primary claim that may be made is for a fair share of "the matrimonial property",[59] defined as all the property either or both spouses own which was acquired between the date of the marriage and the date of separation (except property inherited by or gifted to one spouse alone).[60] There is a very close identity here with the definition of community property in Louisiana.[61] A "fair" share is presumed to be an equal share[62] though either party may seek to persuade the court that fairness requires something other than a fifty-fifty division.

In addition to a 50% share of the community property or matrimonial property, other claims may be made in both jurisdictions. Louisiana permits an award of periodic support[63] to be made to an ex-spouse who is in need of support. This obligation is automatically terminated by the death of either party or the remarriage of the obligee, or a judicial determination that the obligee has cohabited with another person "in the manner of married persons".[64] And in addition a spouse who made financial contributions during the marriage to the education or training of his or her spouse that increased that spouse's earning power may be awarded a sum "to the extent that the claimant did not benefit during the marriage from the increased earning power".[65] Scotland permits a sum to be awarded if necessary to redress an imbalance in the financial and non-financial contributions the spouses made to their family life, to ensure a fair sharing of ongoing child-care costs, to fund retraining, and to avoid serious financial hardship.[66] Importantly, the Scottish courts are constrained in ordering a financial adjustment of the assets of the parties to

---

58 La Civ Code art 159.
59 Family Law (Scotland) Act 1985 s 9(1)(a).
60 Ibid s 10(4).
61 La Civ Code arts 2338 and 2341.
62 Family Law (Scotland) Act 1985 s 10(1).
63 La Civ Code arts 111-112.
64 Ibid art 115. Remarriage includes, for this purpose, a marriage that is absolutely null: *Keeney v Keeney* 30 So 2d 549 (La 1947).
65 Ibid art 121. E.g., in the context of similar legislation in Washington, *In Re Marriage of Washburn* 677 P 2d 152 (Wash 1984).
66 Family Law (Scotland) Act 1985 s 9(1)(b)-(e).

achieve if possible a "clean break" and ongoing support is discouraged: this may only be awarded when the claimant shows that a one-off payment would be inappropriate or insufficient in the circumstances.[67] Ongoing support is seen as maintaining an unhealthy dependency. This fear finds no reflection in the law of Louisiana.

C. TWENTY-FIRST CENTURY PARTING OF THE WAYS

(1) Cohabitation, or unregistered relationships

Not every couple marries. Some – an increasingly large percentage in most western countries – live together in admittedly conjugal partnership, without the state sanctioning their relationship through the institution of marriage. Many such couples lead their lives in ways indistinguishable from the typical married couple, sharing their social lives, amalgamating resources, being sexually intimate, and procreating together. This phenomenon raises the question of how the law should deal with such unregistered relationships.[68] Now, the concept of "family" is a social construct, unlike marriage which is a legal construct, and it follows that cohabiting couples may form social units, properly called families, even outside of the legal institution.[69] The law, of course, responds to factual circumstances as well as to its own constructs and few legal systems today ignore cohabitants entirely. It has been suggested that the extent to which a legal system does respond to the factual circumstance of a couple living their family life outside the constraints of marriage depends very much upon whether a response is perceived to be a danger to the institution of marriage.[70] The validity of this proposition may be tested against the very different approaches of the legal systems in Scotland and Louisiana to the social phenomenon of non-marital cohabitation.[71]

The common law of Scotland gave no recognition to the relationships between adults who lived together in a conjugal but unmarried state, but

---

67 Ibid s 13(2).

68 For a US review, see M Mahoney, "Forces shaping the law of cohabitation for opposite-sex couples" (2005) 7 J L & Fam Stud 135; M Brinig and S Nock, "Marry me, Bill: Should cohabitation be the (legal) default option?" (2004) 64 La LR 403.

69 This has clearly been recognised in Europe, where the European Court of Human Rights has held that the "family life" protected by art 8 ECHR is not confined solely to families based on marriage and may encompass other *de facto* relationships: *Marckx v Belgium* (1979) 2 EHRR 330; *Kroon v Netherlands* (1995) 19 EHRR 263. The responses of different European countries (and even of different UK jurisdictions, where Scotland is far ahead of England) have been diverse. See A Barlow, "Regulation of cohabitation, changing family policies and social attitudes: A discussion of Britain within Europe" (2004) 26 *Law & Policy* 57.

70 See Mahoney, "Forces shaping the law" (n 68).

71 In this section, consideration is limited to opposite-sex couples.

this is unlikely to have been motivated by the perceived need to protect marriage from challenge. Rather, in the medieval and early modern period, marriage acted as a means of regulating property relationships and those with no property had need for neither marriage nor its legal regulation. A more moralistic tone manifested itself in the nineteenth century, during which it was understood that contracts between cohabitants would be contrary to public policy as a form of prostitution and illicit intercourse.[72] However, few in contemporary Scotland would argue that this is a realistic or appropriate way to describe the vast majority of cohabiting couples today and the law has clearly moved on. Statute has long recognised cohabitants in the UK as family couples for tax and social security reasons where it worked to the couples' disadvantage. This does not compromise the state's continuing preference for marriage, since failure to recognise the relationship would in fact make it more attractive to live in an unmarried relationship.[73] Recognition in this context implied no state endorsement of the validity or acceptability of non-marital relationships. Nor was there any such endorsement implicit in the next extension of statutory rules to cohabiting couples, contained in the 1981 legislation that provided protection against domestic violence and family home protection.[74] This is better regarded as recognition of particular vulnerability rather than an acceptance of the worth of unmarried relationships. More significant, however, was the amendment to the wrongful death legislation which gave a surviving cohabitant title to sue on the negligently caused death of his or her partner.[75] The law of delict is founded on the compensation of losses, that is, those diminutions of values that the law regards as worth protecting. This is a recognition, therefore, that the loss suffered by the survivor is of something valuable and that the relationship has the same emotional and even social worth as the relationship of marriage. In truth, it was this Act that first signalled the legally sanctioned legitimacy of non-marital relationships in the UK, and which made further recognition inevitable.

That further recognition, when it came, struck a careful balance between stated government policy to retain marriage as a special and legally preferred institution and the social fact that non-marital cohabitation was continuing

72 *Graham v Kennedy* (1860) 22 D 560.
73 Cohabitation recognition has, in fact, a long history in the UK when the state has more pressing concerns than the valorisation of marriage: see R Probert, "Unmarried wives in war and peace" (2005) 17 *Child and Family Law Quarterly* 1, in which she discusses legislation passed in 1914 allowing "unmarried wives" to receive separation allowances when their partners volunteered for war.
74 Matrimonial Homes (Family Protection) (Scotland) Act 1981.
75 Damages (Scotland) Act 1976, amended to include cohabitants by the Administration of Justice Act 1982.

to increase in both incidence and social acceptability.[76] Two major new rights were conferred on cohabitants by the Family Law (Scotland) Act 2006, but they were explicitly designed to be less valuable than the analogous rights enjoyed by married couples. The first is the right to claim succession from an intestate estate.[77] That this is less valuable than the spouse's claim is ensured in three ways: (i) unlike the surviving spouse, the surviving cohabitant does not have an automatic right to a share of the deceased's estate, but simply a right to ask the court, in its discretion, to award a portion thereof; (ii) the intestate estate from which the claim may be made is net of any rights possessed by any spouse surviving the deceased; and (iii) the total amount awarded by the court must never exceed that which could have been claimed had the survivor been a spouse rather than simply a cohabitant. The second claim permitted under the 2006 Act is for financial settlement on separation.[78] This is again more limited than the claim a spouse can make on divorce, in that there is no entitlement to any share of property, nor a claim for ongoing support, but simply a claim for a one-off lump sum to redress any financial and other imbalances that arose during the relationship, and for sharing child-rearing costs fairly.

By these means, the Scottish Parliament follows a policy of ensuring that marriage remains the legally preferred institution, while recognising that some couples do not marry but deserve nevertheless to be protected in some circumstances. It is important to note that this approach does not imply a status model for the regulation of unregistered family relationships. There is no "status" of cohabitant. Rather, there is a legal response to a factual situation. Marriage remains a construct of the law, and consequences flow automatically from the status created thereby; cohabitation is a factual scenario the consequences of which are determined by the justice of the individual claim, once the claimant has proved the existence of the scenario.

In Louisiana, other than basic protection against domestic violence[79] (which as pointed out above can be extended to individual cohabitants without

---

76 The 24th *British Social Attitudes Report* (2008), by the National Centre for Social Research, reports that 66% of the UK population believes there is no social difference between married and unmarried couples, and that only 28% believe that the former make better parents than the latter.

77 Family Law (Scotland) Act 2006 s 29. The Scottish Law Commission has now recommended the extension of cohabitants' claims to testate estates; see Report on Succession (n 38) para 4.9.

78 Ibid s 28. The 24th *British Social Attitudes Report* (2008) indicates that 89% of the UK population believe that cohabiting couples should have a right to financial provision on separation, though the figure falls to 38% if the relationship has lasted less than two years and involves no children.

79 La RS 46: 2132 where "household member" entitled to special protection includes "any person of the opposite sex … living with the defendant as a spouse, whether married or not". Notice the protection is deliberately withheld from same-sex couples.

implying any recognition of the validity or worth of the relationship itself), cohabitants have no statutory rights or obligations and are treated as individuals who happen to share an address.[80] Louisiana's policy is not only one of encouraging and preferencing marriage but also of actively discouraging non-marital relationships. So instead of following Scotland and providing that the legal consequences of cohabitation are less valuable than the consequences of marriage, Louisiana law actively punishes cohabitation through the complete withholding of benefits that family relationships might otherwise attract. The fear is strong that giving any benefit to cohabitation would undermine marriage as the state's preferred structure within which family life ought to be led. Even as late as 1983 we find the Court of Appeal of Louisiana holding that a domestic contract between cohabitants was "unenforceable because it is an unlawful contract for meretricious services".[81] The Court concluded that "the state is justified in encouraging the legitimate (marriage) over the illegitimate (concubinage), for to do otherwise is to spread the seeds of destruction of a civilised society".[82] As usual, however, if recognition disadvantages a couple in the way that marriage would disadvantage them,[83] then recognition is granted to the "illegitimate" because this achieves the primary aim of encouraging the "legitimate" but it can hardly be denied that there is, indeed, relationship recognition. For it is naive to see marriage solely in terms of rights. Marriage imposes obligations as invariably as it confers rights, and to recognise cohabitation for the purpose of imposing obligations is to recognise cohabitation as surely as recognising it for the purpose of confer-

---

80 This is by no means atypical in the US, where many states used to and some still in fact *criminalise* non-marital cohabitation, an astounding fact to European eyes – and indeed to anyone who has read the US Supreme Court judgments in *Griswold v Connecticut* 381 US 479 (1965) and *Lawrence v Texas* 539 US 558 (2003). In *Martin v Ziheri* 607 SE2d 367 (2005) the Supreme Court of Virginia struck down a law criminalising non-marital sexual activity on the basis of *Lawrence*.

81 *Schwegmann v Schwegmann* 441 So 2d 316 (La App 5th Cir 1983). Here Louisiana *is* atypical in the US, for most states now follow the seminal Californian case of *Marvin v Marvin* 557 P2d 106 (1976) in enforcing domestic contracts between cohabitants. Beyond this, only a very few states (e.g., Hawaii, California and Oregon) have enacted domestic partnership laws for cohabitants who register their relationship, though rather more municipalities permit local registrations to confer local benefits: see C Bowman, "Legal treatment of cohabitants in the United States" (2004) 26 *Law & Policy* 119. Systems of registered relationships assume a status model, leaving those who do not register without any recognition *because*, it would seem, of a lack of status. An equity-based response to individual circumstances outside the law of contract is effectively unknown in the US.

82 But see the concurring opinion of Calogero CJ in *Forum for Equality v McKeithen* 893 So 2d 715 (La 2005) at 737 to the effect that "nothing in the majority opinion would prohibit an unmarried couple from contracting to be co-owners of property, from designating each other agents authorised to make critical end of life decisions, or from leaving property to each other through wills".

83 See, e.g., La Civ Code art 115, where both marriage and cohabitation extinguish any spousal support obligations imposed upon an ex-spouse by a divorce court.

ring rights. The point, however, is to give out a signal of state disapproval which Louisiana law-makers, one assumes, hope will translate into social disapproval. This is social engineering through the politics of superiority. At least it is not the politics of hate.

(2) Same-sex relationships

Originally there was express prohibition in neither Scotland nor Louisiana on same-sex couples marrying, due to the unquestioned assumption that marriage was, axiomatically, an opposite-sex relationship. However, explicit bars on same-sex couples marrying were enacted at around the same time in both jurisdictions, though the legislative motivations for putting in words a rule that had for very many centuries before then been quite unquestioned were probably different. In Scotland the bar was made explicit in the Marriage (Scotland) Act 1977.[84] At that time, male-male sexual activity remained a criminal offence in Scotland, though seldom prosecuted, but by then (ten years after decriminalisation in England)[85] it was realised that this position was unsustainable and that the firewall criminalisation provided against relationship recognition would soon be removed.[86] A pre-emptive answer to claims for marital rights (which had never, in fact, been made) was thought useful and manifested itself in the 1977 Act. Louisiana legislators, who had no intention of decriminalising male-male sexual activity, saw a threat from another source – sister states in the US (and the Full Faith and Credit Clause of the Federal Constitution). In other states claims for relationship recognition had begun to be made[87] though, at that time, these had little hope of success.[88] But Louisiana legislators can act quickly when they want to and, like their Scottish counterparts, they pre-emptively barred persons of the same sex from marrying each other, through an amendment to the Civil Code.[89]

These amendments generated little comment at the time in either jurisdiction, probably because they were perceived as doing no more than placing beyond any doubt that which was hardly doubtful, and which in any case

---

84 S 5(4), in listing the impediments to marriage, included for the first time that the parties were of the same sex.
85 Sexual Offences Act 1967.
86 In fact, this occurred with the Criminal Justice (Scotland) Act 1980 s 13.
87 See *Baker v Nelson* 191 NW 2d 185 (Supreme Court of Minnesota 1971); *Jones v Hallahan* 501 SW 2d 588 (Kentucky App Ct 1973); *Singer v Hara* 522 P 2d 1187 (Court of Appeals of Washington 1974); *Adams v Howerton* 673 F 2d 1036 (9th Cir 1982); *De Santo v Barnsley* 476 A 2d 952 (Pa Super 1984).
88 It would not be until *Baehr v Lewin* 852 P 2d 44 (Haw 1993) that a US court first held the exclusion of same-sex couples from marital rights to be unconstitutional.
89 La Civ Code art 86, as amended by 1975 La Acts No 361.

enjoyed majoritarian support. For some years afterwards the idea that gay
and lesbian people could enter into civil relationships with each other,
involving legally enforceable rights and responsibilities, was met with uncom-
prehending resistance in both jurisdictions by legislators and, indeed, society
as a whole. As late as 1988 the UK Parliament can be found declaring in
statutory (though probably unenforceable) form that "homosexuality" was
no more than a "pretended family relationship".[90] Yet by the end of the
century things were changing in the United Kingdom, and changing fast.
The watershed came in 1999 when the House of Lords held for the first
time that a statute referring to cohabitants could and should be interpreted
to include same-sex couples.[91] As a matter of narrow statutory interpretation
the practical effect of this decision was limited, but its symbolic importance,
in terms of state disavowal of discrimination against or even disapproval
of same-sex relationships, was profound.[92] Since then, in European terms,
the principle of non-discrimination on the ground of sexual orientation has
become fairly pervasive.[93] This new mindset is reflected in Scottish family
law. The Scottish Parliament, since its re-establishment in 1999, has been
assiduous in ensuring that all its legislation conferring rights and responsibilities on cohabiting couples explicitly includes within its terms same-sex
couples.[94] Formal equality in law between same-sex and opposite-sex cohabitants has thus been achieved in Scotland. And this position has caused little
social dismay in Scotland, though some religious people remain irreconcilably

90 Local Government Act 1986 s 2A, as inserted by the Local Government Act 1988 s 28. The aim
    of this grammatically illiterate provision was the same as the Colorado Amendment held uncon-
    stitutional by the US Supreme Court in *Romer v Evans* 517 US 620 (1996). See A Campbell and
    K Norrie "Homosexual rights in *Romer v Evans*: Animus adverted" (1998) 27 Anglo-American
    L Rev 285. This Act was repealed (in Scotland) by the revealingly entitled Convention Rights
    (Compliance) (Scotland) Act 2001.
91 *Fitzpatrick v Sterling Housing Association* [1999] 4 All ER 705.
92 See K Norrie, "We are family (sometimes): Legal recognition of same-sex relationships after
    Fitzpatrick" (2000) 4 EdinLR 256.
93 Art 14 ECHR was extended to include sexual orientation discrimination by the European Court
    of Human Rights in *Da Silva Mouta v Portugal* (2001) 31 EHRR 47. In the fields of employment
    and provision of goods and services such discrimination is banned: see the Employment Equality
    (Sexual Orientation) Regulations 2003, SI 2003/1661 and the Equality Act (Sexual Orienta-
    tion) Regs 2007, SI 2007/1263. For discussion of the overall European position, see A Morris,
    "Constitutionalising equality in the EU: Tolerance and hierarchies" (2005) 8 Int J Discrim L 33.
    The European Court of Justice ruled in April 2008 that civil partners, if in a legal relationship
    comparable to that of spouses, required to be afforded the same pension entitlements as spouses.
    Council Directive 2000/78/EC on Equal Treatment in Employment [2000] OJ L303/16 has as
    one of its aims, the Court confirmed, to combat discrimination on grounds of sexual orientation:
    Maruko v Versorgungsanstalt der Deutschen Buhnen [2008] 2 CMLR 32.
94 See, e.g., the Adults with Incapacities (Scotland) Act 2000; Protection from Abuse (Scotland)
    Act 2001; Agricultural Holdings (Scotland) Act 2003; Housing (Scotland) Act 2004; Family Law
    (Scotland) Act 2006; Adoption and Children (Scotland) Act 2007.

opposed and plead that it is discrimination on the ground of religious belief to remove their right to discriminate on the basis of sexual orientation.[95]

The prohibition on same-sex marriage contained in the Marriage (Scotland) Act 1977 remains and there is no political will – nor, it needs to be said, activist pressure – to change that. Nevertheless, an equivalent institution, termed civil partnership, was created for same-sex couples by a UK statute, the Civil Partnership Act 2004,[96] which confers much the same rights and responsibilities on registered same-sex couples as on married (i.e. opposite-sex, registered) couples.[97] That this new statutory institution is not to be seen (by the law, at any rate) as a form of marriage is emphasised in a number of ways. First and most importantly, opposite-sex couples are excluded from accessing the Civil Partnership Act 2004, just as same-sex couples are excluded from accessing the Marriage (Scotland) Act 1977. The two institutions are designed for what are regarded as two different forms of couple. This is a "separate but equal" regime so disliked in some US states,[98] in Canada[99] and in South Africa.[100] Secondly, civil partnership is explicitly and completely a secular institution, unlike marriage. It is to be remembered that in both England and Scotland there are established (state) churches, respectively the Episcopalian Church of England and the Presbyterian Church of Scotland. Marriage, for many long centuries controlled by the established church, remains in large part a religious institution.[101] And thirdly, civil partnership is desexed with the result that the major legal differences in effect between the separate institutions

95 An argument to this effect was accepted by an Employment Tribunal in *Ladele v London Borough of Islington* (case no 2203694/2007, 8 July 2008) where a registrar of "orthodox Christian beliefs" was held to be discriminated against when her employers refused to excuse her from registering civil partnerships, although this decision was overturned on appeal (Employment Appeal Tribunal, Appeal No UKEAT/0453/08/RN, 19 Dec 2008) on the basis that "the Tribunal ha[d] fallen into the trap of confusing the council's reasons for treating the claimant as they did with her reasons for acting as she did" (para 69).

96 The Scottish provisions are contained in ss 85-136.

97 See C Stychin, "'Las Vegas is not where we are': Queer readings of the Civil Partnership Act" (2006) 25 *Political Geography* 899; N Bamforth, "'The benefit of marriage in all but name'? Same-sex couples and the Civil Partnership Act 2004" (2007) 19 *Child and Family Law Quarterly* 133.

98 *Goodridge v Department of Public Health* 798 NE 2d 941 (Mass 2003); *Lewis v Harris* 908 A 2d 196 (Su Ct NJ 2006); *In Re Marriage Cases* 183 P 3d 384 (Sup Ct Cal 2008); *Kerrigan v Commissioner of Public Health* (Sup Ct Conn 2008); *Varnum v Brien* (2009) 763 NW 2d 862.

99 *Halpern v Attorney General of Canada* (2003) 225 DLR (4th) 529.

100 *Fourie v Minister for Home Affairs and Ors* 2006 (1) SA 524.

101 Indeed it was only in 1929 that Scotland introduced civil marriages, that is to say marriages created by secular state officials rather than by clerics. See J Mair, "Public ceremony and private belief: The role of religion in the Scots law of marriage" 2007 JR 279. The Louisiana Civil Code, on the other hand, has always treated marriage as a secular institution: see art 86 which emphasises that marriage is created by *civil* contract (although it has always recognised the church celebration of marriage).

of marriage and civil partnership relate to the role of the sexual act within the relationship – adultery is not a ground for dissolving a civil partnership, though it remains one for dissolving a marriage;[102] incurable impotency is not a ground upon which a civil partnership can be annulled, though it is the sole ground for nullifying an otherwise valid marriage.[103]

Whatever the specific differences between marriage and civil partnership (and whatever it is called), the fact remains that in Scotland same-sex couples have a legal means for the registration of their relationship which is functionally equivalent to the legal means afforded to opposite-sex couples by the process called marriage. Civil partnership, though a separate regime from marriage, is designed to achieve a status with virtually the same legal effect – and social significance – as marriage.

It is very different in Louisiana. Same-sex relationships (marriage or any equivalent, and unregistered relationships) conducted within state borders are given no direct statutory recognition.[104] Indeed, the very idea of same-sex registered relationships (whether as marriage or as a separate but equivalent institution) is perceived by many to be a larger threat to marriage than the legal recognition of cohabitation.[105] The second President Bush, for example, called for an amendment to the US constitution to protect "marriage" from the threat he saw same-sex unions posing to it.[106] Yet no "Defense of Marriage Act" has ever been proposed in order to face down the "threat" posed by cohabitants' rights. It is difficult to see the logic behind the fear that led to DOMAs being enacted across the US. Opening marriage to same-sex couples does not challenge the special and preferred place afforded by the law to the institution, for it does not involve offering couples an alternative and lesser

---

102   Divorce (Scotland) Act 1976 s 1(2)(a).

103   Clive, *Husband and Wife* (n 12) paras 07.063-07.077; see also Trahan, "Prerequisites to marriage" (n 4).

104   Though it has to be said that certain quasi-marital benefits may be contractually conferred on same-sex couples by insurers and employers, including some of the largest employers in the US.

105   K Spaht, "Revolution and counterrevolution: The future of marriage in the law" (2003) 49 Loy L Rev 1, purports to see the threat to marriage of same-sex relationship recognition as being on a par with the threat posed by no-fault divorce. One can readily accept that divorce might compromise marriage, but the logic of the claim that extending marriage threatens marriage is not easy to see. L Wardle, "Is marriage obsolete?" (2003) 10 Mich J Gender and L 189, and "The attack on marriage as the union of a man and woman" (2008) 83 N Dakota LR 1365, eschews the need for a causative connection when he points out that marriage rates are declining in countries with same-sex marriage. It cannot be denied that divorce rates in the US have risen since Elizabeth II ascended her throne, but it would, surely, be unfair to blame the woman unless a causative link to her reign were established.

106   See press release, 24 Feb 2004, at *http://www.whitehouse.gov/news/releases/2004/02/20040224-2. html*.

choice, as cohabitation recognition does.[107] Instead, it allows more people to benefit – gay people – and this reveals that it is not marriage *per se* that is under threat by same-sex relationship recognition but the preference shown to heterosexuality itself. Yet I have never understood why heterosexuality is regarded as such a weak and sickly thing that it needs state protection. Another oft-expressed fear is that extending marriage to same-sex couples will change the institution beyond its natural boundaries. This presupposes that there is something "natural" and not socially constructed in marriage. This is error: swans mate, they do not marry; bull walruses with their harems of cows are not polygamists. It also ignores the great changes that marriage has undergone throughout its long history. So for example the introduction of divorce brought an end to the medieval idea that marriage was necessarily for life (in fact it restored a far older – and early Christian – notion of marriage[108]). The reduction of male dominance that characterised much of the twentieth century resulted in the gradual evolution of marriage into a relationship of equals which for thousands of years previously would have been regarded as palpable and self-evident nonsense – perhaps even more absurd than the idea of two men or two women marrying each other.[109] The ban on interracial marriage that applied in Louisiana for well over 200 years was jettisoned when society grew to accept the equal moral worth of persons irrespective of skin colour, and the institution of marriage was not irreparably damaged thereby:[110] rather, marriage yet again revealed its flexibility by adapting to the changing values of society. Nor does the longevity of the rule, often pled in support of maintaining it, add anything of weight to the

107 This may be the reason why English law, e.g., has been able to give extensive recognition to same-sex couples in the Civil Partnership Act 2004, but has not yet been able to accommodate comprehensive provision for cohabitants. This is unfortunate, but logical.

108 Some Rabbinical traditions have Adam divorcing his first wife Lilith before being provided with the more compliant Eve, in a story, beloved of modern-day feminists (because of Lilith's refusal to be sexually submissive), that did not survive the final cut of what became the Old Testament in the Christian Bible.

109 If, as Trahan points out ("Prerequisites to marriage" (n 4) at 180) Diocletian purported to marry a man, it is as well to note that there never was, in the 1,450 years from Augustus to Constantine XI, a female emperor of Rome ruling in her own right. (In fact, we cannot today tell the nature of the "blood brotherhood" Diocletian entered into with Maximian when he made him co-emperor. Of all the near 300 emperors of Rome, Diocletian was the only one who abdicated of his own volition and retired to his garden. He was a good man (leaving aside the Persecutions, that is)).

110 The US Supreme Court held such a ban to be unconstitutional in *Loving v Virginia* 388 US 1 (1967) and it was removed from the Louisiana Civil Code by 1972 La Acts No 256. In California a similar ban had been removed twenty-five years earlier, in *Perez v Sharp* 32 Cal 2d 711 (1948), and this decision was used by the Supreme Court of California as a direct analogy that demanded the same result in *In Re Marriage Cases,* n 98 above, where the ban on same-sex marriage was held unconstitutional in that state.

argument. "It is revolting", Oliver Wendel Holmes famously said over 100 years ago, "to have no better reason for a rule of law than that it was laid down in the time of Henry IV".[111] Nevertheless, the debate whether this latest social change should be reflected by legal change has been by far the most polarising throughout the US.[112] There is something more than a *kulturkampf* at play here. There is, it seems to me, a genuine *fear* of homosexuals, or at least of their socially destructive potential.[113] Such a fear is properly termed homophobia and it can avoid the charge of bigotry only through proof – and not presumption – that such destructive potential actually exists.

Louisiana is a fairly typical example within the US of how this fear has found voice in legislation. Marriage has since 1975 been defined as "a legal relationship between a man and a woman".[114] Further, by a 2004 constitutional amendment,[115] Louisiana state officials and courts are forbidden from recognising "any marriage contracted in any other jurisdiction which is not the union of one man and one woman".[116] So couples who contract, out of state, a same-sex union will not be permitted within Louisiana to access any state benefit (or, presumably, suffer any obligation) attaching to marriage. Further, officials and courts are forbidden from construing the Constitution or any state law as requiring that "marriage or the legal incidents thereof be conferred upon any member of a union other than the union of one man and one woman. A legal status identical or substantially similar to marriage for unmarried individuals shall not be valid or recognised." This constitutional

111 "The path of the law" (1897) 10 Harvard LR 457 at 459. Tradition was rejected as a sufficient ground to maintain the rule that marriage is limited to opposite-sex couples by both the Supreme Court of California in the *In Re Marriage Cases* and the Supreme Court of Connecticut in *Kerrigan v Commissioner of Public Health* (both n 98 above). The latter is perhaps the most carefully argued of all the US decisions on the issue.

112 By far the most detailed and most up-to-date (June 2008) exposition of the legal position of same-sex couples in each of the fifty states in the USA may be found in I and S Curry-Sumner, "Is the union civil? Same-sex marriage, civil unions, domestic partnerships and reciprocal benefits in the USA" (2008) 4 *Utrecht Law Review* 236. But in this fast-moving area this article was (as this chapter doubtless will be) substantially out of date a year after publication.

113 The debate over "Proposition 8", the successful Ballot Initiative during the 2008 Presidential Election designed to overturn the Californian Supreme Court's decision in *In Re Marriage Cases* (n 98 above), was conducted in "stunningly apocalyptic terms" (*International Herald Tribune* (Japan edition) 28 October 2008, 5). Opening marriage to same-sex couples would "destroy marriage" and with it western civilisation. It is difficult to believe that many of those who voted in favour of Proposition 8 truly believed this would be the result.

114 La Civ Code art 86, as amended by 1975 La Acts No 361.

115 La Const art 12 §15, as amended by 2004 La Acts No 926. The Louisiana Supreme Court rejected a challenge to the validity of this amendment in *Forum for Equality v McKeithen* 893 So 2d 715 (La 2005).

116 In US terms, this is not unusual. It was reported by M Medina in 2004 that at that time thirty-six states in the US had "Defense of Marriage Acts": see "Of Constitutional Amendments, Human Rights and Same-Sex Marriage" (2004) 64 La LR 459 at n 41.

provision is designed to cut off the threat of judicial activism that has seen same-sex marriage and civil partnership introduced in other US states, in Canada and in South Africa. Louisiana state policy, at the legislative level, is clearly against same-sex unions. Indeed, the Civil Code expressly states, in the context of its Conflict of Laws rules, that "marriage between persons of the same sex violates a strong public policy in the state of Louisiana".[117]

It may, however, be that the visible froth of these legislative waves hides more powerful currents in the waters beneath. The US Supreme Court has a history of deep suspicion of limitations on freedom to marry,[118] however tightly and blindly states cling to them. And that Court has always required more than majoritarian preferences to justify differential treatment, which is why the plebiscite that endorsed Colorado's Amendment 2 did nothing to save it when it was challenged.[119] The reason is not difficult to identify, and was perhaps best expressed by Baroness Hale in the House of Lords: "Race discrimination was always wrong, long before the world woke up to that fact. Sex discrimination was always wrong, long before the world woke up to that fact".[120] These judicial attitudes, taken with the failure of opponents (to their immense frustration) to persuade courts around the world that there is good, secular, reason to exclude same-sex couples from the civil effects of marriage, suggest that the ban in Louisiana on same-sex relationship recognition is not, perhaps, as secure as it might appear. "Secular", in this context, means reasoning based on social good and harm, and not reasoning which, at heart, amounts to nothing more than the following:

(i) the doctrinal interpretations of my religion are against same-sex relations, *and*
(ii) my religion is better than your religion, *therefore*
(iii) I am right and you are wrong, *and therefore*
(iv) the law should reflect my view and not yours.

Unregistered cohabitation in Louisiana by couples of the same sex is ignored by the law, just as cohabitants of the opposite sex are – even, wickedly,

---

117 La Civ Code art 3520(B), as amended by 1999 La Acts No 890.

118 See *Loving v Virginia* 388 US 1 (1967); *Zablocki v Redhail* 434 US 374 (1978).

119 *Romer v Evans* 517 US 620 (1996). This was a voter initiative passed on the day of President Clinton's election; Proposition 8 in California, passed on the day of President Obama's election, is no safer, though its constitutionality was upheld by the Supreme Court of California in *Strauss v Horton* 2009 WL 1444594. In *Citizens Against Rent Control v Berkeley* 454 US 290 (1981) the Supreme Court explicitly stated that "it is irrelevant that the voters rather than a legislative body enacted [the challenged law], because the voters may no more violate the Constitution by enacting a ballot measure than a legislative body may do so by enacting legislation" (per Burger CJ at 295).

120 *Secretary of State for Work and Pensions v M* [2006] 2 FLR 56 at 61.

to the extent of denying them special protection from domestic violence.[121] However, as so often happens, such relationships might be recognised as having legal effect if this is to the couple's disadvantage.[122] The justification predictably offered, that this is necessary to ensure that same-sex couples are not better off than opposite-sex (married) couples, serves to obscure but does not completely disguise the acceptance that there is, indeed, a couple whose relationship has legal consequence. So the law in Louisiana does, sometimes, respond to the factual environment that exists. The difference compared with Scotland is that in limiting the scope for response to circumstances in which the couple are clearly disadvantaged, the Louisiana legislature is quite deliberately sending out a clear message of its strong disapproval of same-sex couples and of homosexuality itself. It may well be, as Trahan predicts,[123] that legal change will be forced upon a reluctant Louisiana from outside: if so, it is sobering to remember that the religiosity of supporters of anti-miscegenation legislation has not saved their memories from charges of bigotry.

(3) Covenant marriage

One of only three states in the United States (and the first) to create a separate form of marriage that was hoped to be more stable than standard marriage, Louisiana introduced the "covenant marriage" into its law in 1997.[124] The very name is designed to emphasise the solemnity of marriage and, though there is no religious requirement, to reflect a sacramental perception of the institution. Couples have a choice of whether to enter a standard marriage or a covenant marriage, though it is reported that only around 2% of marrying couples in Louisiana choose the latter.[125]

Professor Kathleen Spaht, the leading writer in Louisiana on covenant

---

121 See n 79.

122 See La Civ Code art 115 where an ex-spouse enjoying spousal support after divorce loses that entitlement by cohabiting with another person *of either sex* in the manner of married persons. But see *Succession of Bacot* 502 So 2d 1118 (La App 4th Cir 1987) which concerned the rule in La Civ Code 1481 that those who lived together "in open concubinage" could not donate to each other either mortis causa or inter vivos more than one tenth of their moveable estate. Concubinage was held to be a state of heterosexuality and so the testamentary limitation did not apply to the same-sex couple in the present case. The decision was enthusiastically endorsed (to the disadvantage of a same-sex couple) by the Ohio Court of Appeals in *Gajovski v Gajovski* 610 NE 2d 431 (1991).

123 Trahan, "Prerequisites to marriage" (n 4) at 175 and 204

124 1997 La Acts No 1380. The rules are contained in La RS 9:272-309. Louisiana's innovation was followed by Arizona and Arkansas: see Ariz RS §§ 25-901 to 25-906; Ark Code Ann §§ 9-11-801 to 9-11-808. Attempts in many other states to introduce covenant marriage have failed.

125 S Nock et al, "Covenant marriage turns five years old" (2003) 10 Mich J Gender and L 169 at 170.

marriage, identifies the three principal respects in which it differs (in Louisiana)[126] from standard marriage.[127]

First, to enter a covenant marriage the couple must participate in premarital counselling covering the nature of marriage and its seriousness, and they must submit to the counsellor a Declaration of Intent that their marriage will be for life and that they have disclosed to each other everything that would affect the decision to marry.[128] If it is subsequently established that full disclosure has not been made (let us suppose, that one of the parties had already been married, or had a child from a previous relationship) it would seem that the marriage remains valid, and indeed remains a covenant marriage. Spaht argues[129] that if one adopts a contractual analysis of marriage then such non-disclosure could be used to have the marriage declared void. There are, however, at least three problems with this. First, all marriages are created by contract but breach of that contract is not in itself an alternative ground for divorce. Indeed, and secondly, it would be illogical to characterise breach of contract as an additional means of escaping a covenant marriage, if the very purpose of the covenant is to make that sort of marriage harder to escape from. And thirdly, of course, a contract analysis of marriage simply does not work (unless marriage is cheapened to a commercial transaction involving the transfer of assets in return for bodily services). Spaht attempts to address this point by limiting the contractual elements of covenant marriage to the Declaration of Intent, so that "a covenant marriage represents a status combined with permissible contractual agreements between the spouses".[130] If this is so then covenant marriage is reduced to little more than a standard marriage with an ante-nuptial agreement attached: if the agreement is breached the validity of the marriage remains untouched and any financial result is a matter of contract law and not family law. The "covenant" becomes a commercial transaction, which is hardly consistent with the sacramental

126   The regimes created in Arizona and Arkansas have different rules.

127   K Spaht, "Covenant marriage seven years later: Its as yet unfulfilled promise" (2005) 65 La LR 605 at 612-613. This article starts with an attack on same-sex marriage and ends with an attack on *Lawrence v Texas* 539 US 588 (2003), indicating the author's bizarre perception of covenant marriage as a defence to the "threat" posed by homosexuality. See also to similar effect her "Revolution and counterrevolution" (n 105 above). The present writer considers it unlikely that the availability of covenant marriage will turn gay people straight. To be fair to Spaht, her earlier work valorising covenant marriage focused on "the sake of the children": see Spaht (n 129 below) and "For the sake of the children: Recapturing the meaning of marriage" (1998) 73 Notre Dame LRev 1547.

128   La RS 9:273.

129   K Spaht, "Louisiana's covenant marriage: Social analysis and legal implications" (1998) 59 La LR 63.

130   Ibid 105.

ideals it aspires to.

The second special effect of a covenant marriage identified by Spaht is that the spouses owe each other love and respect and commit to a community of living together, satisfying each other's needs;[131] they must live together unless there is good cause otherwise;[132] the spouses must educate their children and prepare them for the future.[133] In addition, they must agree to take all reasonable steps to resolve differences if their marriage is in difficulties, including marriage counselling.[134] These explicit obligations (basically, to lead a good family life and work at it in times of trouble) are implicit in any genuine marriage and none can be directly enforced by court order. With both standard and covenant marriage, the remedy for failure to love or to live together or to try to resolve differences is divorce, not damages.

The third and, it seems to me, only truly substantive difference between the two forms of marriage available in Louisiana is that while the fault grounds for divorce are the same,[135] the no-fault ground is rather stricter. Instead of a non-cohabitation period of six months (or one year) justifying a divorce, the waiting period required in case of covenant marriage is two years.[136]

Scotland has no equivalent concept to the covenant marriage. If a couple wish to marry in Scotland they have a choice of method for entering into the institution – by religious ceremony or by civil solemnisation – but they have no choice of regime to govern the relationship once created. Nevertheless, marriage in Scotland is clearly understood to involve a number of social and personal obligations above and beyond those directly enforceable in a court of law, such as the obligation to love and respect, to live together, and to provide a suitable and supportive environment for children of the family. This brings the idea of marriage in Scotland close to the Louisiana law of covenant marriage. Indeed, given that the two-year period of non-cohabitation required for non-consensual no-fault divorce in Scotland is the same as that required for no-fault divorce in a covenant marriage, it is not implausible to conclude that marriage in Scotland has a closer affinity to Louisianan covenant than standard marriage.

The idea of a single jurisdiction with more than one conception of marriage is not unique to Louisiana and this occurs in all countries where family law follows a person's religious affiliation rather than their nationality or domicile,

131 La RS 9:294.
132 La RS 9:295.
133 La RS 9:298.
134 La RS 9:271.1
135 La Civ Code arts 103 and 103.1 for standard marriage; La RS art 9:307 for covenant marriage.
136 La RS 9:307(A)(6).

as in (for example) Israel and India.[137] For at least a millennium many countries in the world have recognised and permitted, side by side, monogamous and polygamous marriages. South Africa now maintains a complex mix of traditional (colonially designed) civil marriage,[138] customary marriage[139] (which is often polygamous) and Civil Union marriage.[140] And if marriage is defined by its incidents, then Louisiana itself, and all other jurisdictions with optional community property regimes, has long offered a choice of type of marriage to opposite-sex couples. Covenant marriage, it would seem, simply widens the choice of governing regime and is nothing more nor less than a opt-in scheme for longer waiting periods for divorce.

D. CONCLUSION

Family law reflects the society it serves. Social conservatism, a powerful force in Louisiana, bolstered by the overt religiosity of its people, finds reflection in the law's refusal to accommodate non-marital and same-sex relationships and its attempts, through covenant marriage, to recover at least some of the ground lost to that paradigm of liberalism, no-fault divorce. In Scotland, on the other hand, the liberal ascendancy in society has allowed the law to shake free from the dominance of the church, and family law has responded in the ways described in this chapter. Neither jurisdiction, however, is entirely free from the influences of the wider polities of which it is a member, and majoritarian preferences are never sufficient on their own either to conserve existing or to develop new legal rules and institutions. Both are subject, in other words, to constitutional constraints not of their own making. The differences in legal regulation of adult domestic relations described in this chapter may be explained to a large degree by the fact that the US as a whole remains socially conservative while Europe as a whole is predominantly liberal. Conservatism has given law- and policy-makers in Louisiana (conservative, even by the standards in American "red" states) the confidence to tell people, through its regulation of family law, how they *ought* to lead their private lives. Liberalism has encouraged law- and policy-makers in Scotland to step

---

137   See S Mitra and A Fischer, "Sacred laws and the secular state: An analytical narrative of the controversy over personal laws in India" (2002) 1 *India Review* 99.

138   Under the Marriage Act 25 of 1961.

139   Under the Recognition of Customary Marriages Act 120 of 1998.

140   A curious beast, introduced by the Civil Union Act 17 of 2006 which creates two separate institutions: civil partnership for those who want all the consequences but not the name of marriage, and marriage for those who want all the consequences and the name of marriage *and* an institution that is open equally to opposite-sex and same-sex couples.

back from a similar role and to accept the social reality that same-sex and other non-marital relationships not only exist but are today viewed by society as legitimate family structures, deserving recognition, protection and even respect.

More than this, the comparison offered in this chapter reveals a profound difference in legal philosophy between the two jurisdictions under consideration in relation to the fundamental question: what is family law actually for? It seems that in Louisiana family law is explicitly an instrument of state policy that can – and, many believe, should – be used to structure society in a particular way. So a formalist approach is adopted, with state benefits and inter-spousal obligations accruing only to those whose family lives satisfy the formal requirements of (traditional) marriage. In Scotland on the other hand family law exists to regulate private lives *as they are led* and it eschews any ostensible social engineering purpose: this is a more functionalist approach which focuses on the functions families perform in society rather than their outward appearances. The adoption by Louisiana of a state policy of active encouragement of its population to pursue one form of family life over another is rational only if (i) people choose a particular family form for its legal consequences and (ii) people know with a fair degree of accuracy what these legal consequences are. Neither proposition is particularly plausible and it is submitted that Scotland's approach in this area of law is by far the wiser. Indeed, the present writer is not persuaded that marriage can bear all the weight that is claimed for it, in terms of stabilising society and ensuring the optimal upbringing of children. Too often, legal comparisons of the lives led by married and unmarried couples ignore the social realities of economic standing, educational opportunities, and race.[141] And they always ignore the political values of choice and free will.

Spaht[142] accepts that Louisiana society no longer sees marriage as an instrument for "the aculturisation of children"[143] but rather as a means of furthering the aspirations of the parties themselves. The same comment would be apposite in Scotland. But Scots law has moved to reflect this change in social attitude in a way that Louisiana has not. The political imperative of conservatism has presently trumped legal logic in Louisiana, but it is unsustainable. Spaht's conclusion that the law's "abandonment" of the regulation of marriage "played a significant role in changing society's understanding of marriage"[144]

141 See W Duncan, "The social good of marriage and legal responses to non-marital cohabitation" (2003) 82 Or L Rev 1001.
142 Spaht (n 12).
143 Ibid 244.
144 Ibid 247.

is fatally flawed, for she mistakes effect for cause. In truth, it is changes in the position of women that removed the need for many of the rules of marriage designed to deal with the consequences of gender inequality in the law. And it is also gender equality that makes same-sex relationship recognition inevitable: for turning marriage into a relationship of equals removes the definitional imperative for a relationship of opposites. Moreover, cohabitation recognition is inevitable, for people will never be socially equal in economic or other power terms and, even when couples avoid marriage, the law is still required to deal with the social consequences of continued inequality both within and outwith marriage. Even Louisiana accepts this, if reluctantly and only if the couple are free from the sin of same-sexism, in the field of domestic violence protection. Yet family law, if it is to retain credibility, needs to be capable of performing wider social functions than this, and in fields as diverse as succession, taxation and evidentiary privilege needs to avoid being reduced to a formalistic examination of whether the relationship at hand fulfils the requirements of "traditional" marriage.

Marriage can change. It has been an astoundingly flexible institution across the centuries, and for that reason alone the conservatism that seeks to freeze it in its mid-twentieth century manifestation will either fail in that endeavour or destroy that which it seeks to preserve. For an institution that does not serve the needs of the people is an institution that the people will increasingly ignore. Conservatives and liberals, if for different reasons, may yet agree that it is worth trying to avoid such an outcome.

7 Impediments to Marriage in Scotland and Louisiana: An Historical-Comparative Investigation

J-R Trahan

A. INTRODUCTION
B. THE COMMON SUBSTRATE: THE ROMAN CATHOLIC CANON LAW OF MARRIAGE
(1) The Roman law of marriage
(a) Absolute impediments
(i) Impuberty
(ii) Impotence
(iii) Existing marriage
(b) Relative impediments
(i) Relationship
(ii) Status
(iii) Identity of sex
(2) Christian adaptations of and supplements to the Roman law of marriage
(a) Absolute impediments
(i) Impuberty
(ii) Impotence
(iii) Existing marriage
(b) Relative impediments
(i) Relationship
(ii) Status
(iii) Identity of sex
C. SCOTS LAW
(1) From the Reformation until the late twentieth century
(a) Absolute impediments (impuberty, impotence, existing marriage)
(b) Relative impediments
(i) Relationship
(ii) Status

(iii) Identity of sex

(2) From the late twentieth century up to the present

(a) Absolute impediments

(i)   Impuberty

(ii) Impotence

(iii) Existing marriage

(b) Relative impediments

(i)   Relationship

(ii) Status

(iii) Identity of sex

D. LOUISIANA LAW

(1) The first French period (1715-1762)

(2) The Spanish period (1762-1800)

(3) The second French period (1800-1803)

(4) The American period part 1 (1803-1987)

(a) Absolute impediments

(i)   Impuberty

(ii) Impotence

(iii) Existing marriage

(b) Relative impediments

(i)   Relationship

(ii) Status

(iii) Identity of sex

(5) The American period part 2 (1987-present)

(a) Absolute impediments

(b) Relative impediments

(i)   Relationship

(ii) Status

(iii) Identity of sex

E. CONCLUSIONS

(1) Patterns: similarities and differences

(2) Explanations for the patterns

(a) Similarities

(b) Differences

(3) Projections based on the patterns

A. INTRODUCTION

The historical development of the law of impediments to marriage in Scotland and Louisiana has proceeded and continues to proceed on closely parallel tracks. In both jurisdictions, the earliest law seems to have been one or another version of the "sacred" law of the Roman Catholic Church (the so-called "canon law"),[1] which, in turn, was in large part but a re-working, in the light of Biblical teaching and Christian moral theology, of post-classical (and, in some respects, even classical) Roman law. In both jurisdictions, this "sacred" law was eventually replaced by "secular" law, a change that, at least at first, had little impact on the actual content of the law. But then, over time and especially in the twentieth century, the secular law of each jurisdiction has progressively been purged of many of the elements within it that were of distinctively canonical origin and of even a few of its Roman law elements. On top of that, in both jurisdictions, the elements that have been so purged, on the one hand, or preserved, on the other, turn out to be very much the same. Still, there remain a few differences, several conspicuous. Examples include the following: (1) Scotland alone continues to recognise the traditional Roman/canon law "impediments" to marriage of "impotence" and "impuberty"; (2) the remaining vestiges of the traditional Roman/canon law impediment of "close relation" vary somewhat from one jurisdiction to the other; and (3) though both jurisdictions continue to recognise the traditional Roman/canon law impediment of "identity of sex", the rationale for and the strength of commitment to this decision vary widely between the two jurisdictions. In the future, further convergence between the laws of the two jurisdictions can be expected, though acceptance of "same-sex marriage" (something that is almost inevitable in both jurisdictions) is not likely to come as quickly in Louisiana as in Scotland.

My aim in this chapter is to survey the past, the present, and the future (to the extent I can predict it) of the law of impediments to marriage in Scotland and Louisiana. In the course of this survey I shall highlight the similarities and differences between the development of that law in Scotland and the development of that law in Louisiana and, both for these similarities and for these differences, offer up at least some tentative explanations.

---

1 A Esmein, *Le Mariage en droit canonique* (1968, reprint of original 1891 edn), vol 1, 63-64.

B. THE COMMON SUBSTRATE: THE ROMAN CATHOLIC CANON LAW OF MARRIAGE

(1) The Roman law of marriage

In Roman law, the prerequisites to marriage were gathered under three headings: (1) *connubium*, (2) *pubertas*, and (3) *consensus*.[2] The concepts of *connubium* and *pubertas*, which the Romans thought of in affirmative terms of power or eligibility to marry, can be described in modern terms[3] as the "absence of 'impediments' to marriage".[4] These impediments can be divided into two broad categories: (1) absolute impediments – those that prohibited the affected person from marrying *anyone at all*; and (2) relative impediments – those that prohibited the affected person from marrying only *this or that person* or a member of *this or that set* of persons.[5]

(a) Absolute impediments

(i) Impuberty

From the very beginning, Roman law seems to have required that both parties to the marriage had reached the age of "puberty".[6] Though the Romans themselves seldom, if ever, expressed the reason for this requirement, that reason is not difficult to discern. In the Roman mind, "procreation of children" was among the essential purposes of marriage.[7] And so, for the Romans, a marriage of persons still too young to procreate would have made no sense.

The manner in which the Romans assessed puberty varied over time. Under early Roman law, puberty was a matter of fact, one to be found out by "inspection" of the would-be spouses. Later, however, the age of puberty

---

2 L F Miravite, *Handbook for Roman Law* (1970) 79; P F Girard, *Manuel élémentaire de droit romain*, 8th edn by F Senn (1929), vol 1, 168.

3 The re-conceptualisation of *connubium* and *pubertas* in the negative form of "impediments to marriage" seems to have originated in the high Middle Ages. See J Gaudemet, *Le mariage en Occident* (1987) 195-197; P C Augustine, *A Commentary on the New Code of Canon Law*, vol 5 (1919) "Marriage Law, Matrimonial Trials" 81.

4 The concept of *consensus* corresponds to the modern concept of "consent to marry" or, more precisely, the manifestation of that consent, mental capacity to give that consent, and vices of that consent. S M Treggiari, *Roman Marriage* (1991) 37-80; P E Corbett, *The Roman Law of Marriage* (1930) 24-67; Gaudemet (n 3) 44-46 and 48-52; M Kaser, *Roman Private Law*, 3rd edn (1980) § 8 at 284-293; Miravite (n 2) 79-84; Girard (n 2) 168-174.

5 This binary classification is a standard feature of scholarly treatments of the law of impediments to marriage in the Civil Law tradition. See, e.g., Gaudemet (n 3) 197.

6 J Inst 1.10 pr; see also Treggiari (n 4) 39-43; Corbett (n 4) 51; Gaudemet (n 3) 48-49; Kaser (n 4) § 58 at 287; Girard (n 2) 171; J Crook, *Law and Life of Rome* (1967) 100.

7 D 1.1.1.3; see J A Brundage, *Law, Sex and Christian Society in Medieval Europe* (1990) 33; Crook (n 6) 99.

seems to have been fixed by reference to the calendar: for boys, at fourteen years of age; for girls, at twelve years of age.[8]

(ii) Impotence

Under Roman law, certain sexually impotent persons, in particular, *castrati* (eunuchs) were disqualified from marrying.[9] Regarding the reason behind the rule, the Roman law sources are disappointingly silent. One possibility is that the Romans disqualified *castrati* for the same reason they disqualified prepubsecent children: *castrati* could not procreate. But if that were the reason, then the Romans, one would suppose, would have disqualified not only *castrati* but also all persons who, for whatever reason, were impotent. That, however, was not the case, that is, the Romans did not consider impotence itself to be a cause of nullity of marriage.[10] And so one must look for another explanation. One possibility that presents itself is this: to avoid "divided loyalties" or "conflicts of interest". Most *castrati* had positions of high administrative responsibility, for example tending to the concubines of high-ranking political officials or watching over some governmental treasury.[11] Perhaps the prohibition on marriage by *castrati* was designed to ensure that these important administrators never developed an allegiance that might rise above that which they owed to the political superiors whom they served.

(iii) Existing marriage

In the minds of the Romans, marriage had to be monogamous.[12] The Roman jurisconsults took it for granted that "[t]he same woman cannot be married to two men, nor the same man have two wives."[13] But this rule, at least at first, seems to have rested less on a judgment about public morality (bigamy was *not* a crime in Rome until the post-classical period)[14] than upon a judgment about private intention. Given the way the Romans understood marriage itself, they "simply assumed that people could not have the necessary intention to live as man and wife with more than one partner".[15] And so it was that the Romans, when presented with a person who seemed to have "married" first one person

---

8 J Inst 1.22 pr; C 5.4.24; C 5.60.3; see also Treggiari (n 4) 39-42; Corbett (n 4) 51-52; Gaudemet (n 3) 48-49; Kaser (n 4) § 14 at 81-83; Girard (n 2) 171; Crook (n 6) 100.

9 D 23.3.39.1; see also Corbett (n 4) 53; Kaser (n 4) § 58 at 287; Brundage (n 7) 37.

10 Esmein vol 1 (n 1) 232; Brundage (n 7) 37.

11 See "Eunuch", *Britannica online Encyclopedia* (*http://www.britannica.com/EBchecked/topic/195333/eunuch*).

12 Crook (n 6) 101; see also Kaser (n 4) § 58 at 285 and 288; Brundage (n 7) 37.

13 Gai Inst 1.63; J Inst 1.10.7; see also D 3.2.1 and 3.2.13.1-4; Cod 9.9.18.

14 Brundage (n 7) 37; Crook (n 6) 101.

15 Crook (n 6) 101.

and then another, inferred that not bigamy but rather something else had occurred – either (1) the apparently bigamous spouse had tacitly divorced the first (something that Roman law allowed)[16] before marrying the second or (2) the relationship between the apparently bigamous spouse and the second was one of mere concubinage.[17]

(b) Relative impediments

(i) Relationship

From the start, the Romans placed restrictions on the kinds of "relatives" who could enter into marriage.[18] Under Roman law, persons related to each other in the direct line (for example, parent and child or grandparent and grandchild) were never allowed to marry.[19] The situation with respect to collaterals (for example, siblings or uncles and nieces) was slightly different. In the early Republic, collaterals in the fourth degree (e.g., first cousins) and perhaps even more distant collaterals were prohibited from marrying. But by the early part of the Empire, this prohibition had been relaxed, so that the prohibition no longer applied to collaterals beyond the third degree (that is, only marriages between siblings and between uncles/aunts and nieces/nephews were prohibited).[20]

These prohibitions applied without limitation to consanguinous relatives. In the case of adoptive relatives, only the prohibition on marriages in the direct line was applied without qualification: marriages in the collateral line (e.g., siblings by adoption) were permitted once the person who had created the adoptive relation had died.[21] With respect to affinitive relatives (those related by marriage), only the prohibition in the direct line was applied at first; later, however, that in the collateral line was also applied, though in that case the prohibition was limited to the second degree.[22]

These restrictions on intra-familial marriage reflect the peculiar Roman version of a phenomenon that is universal to all human cultures: the so-called "incest taboo".[23] Regarding the ultimate genesis of this taboo, there has

16 Brundage (n 7) 39.
17 Id; Kaser (n 4) § 58 at 288; Crook (n 6) 101.
18 Brundage (n 7) 36.
19 Gai Inst 1.59; J Inst 1.10.1; see also Gaudemet (n 3) 49; Kaser (n 4) § 58 at 288; Crook (n 6) 100.
20 Gai Inst 1.60,61,62,63; J Inst 1.10.2,3,4; see also Gaudemet (n 3) 49; Kaser (n 4) § 58 at 288-289; Girard (n 2) 173; Crook (n 6) 100.
21 Gai Inst 1.61; J Inst 1.10.2; see also Kaser (n 4) § 58 at 289.
22 Gai Inst 1.63; Inst. Just 1.10.6,7; see also Kaser (n 4) § 58 at 289; Gaudemet (n 3) 50.
23 See generally J H Turner and A Maryanski, *Incest: Origins of the Taboo* (2005); A P Wolf and W H Durham (eds), *Inbreeding, Incest, and the Incest Taboo: The State of Knowledge at the Turn of the Century* (2004); C Lévi- Strauss, "The family", in J Middleton (ed), *Studies in Social & Cultural Anthropology* (1968) 128.

been, still is, and undoubtedly will continue to be much disagreement. Most contemporary social scientists posit some sort of "utilitarian" basis for the taboo, that is, the primitive originators of the taboo are said to have created it consciously rather than unconsciously and to have done so for the purpose of promoting this or that perceived social good, for example, to avoid the heightened risk of birth defects (or perhaps of low birth rates) that is associated with procreation between close consanguinous relatives, or to build alliances between families within the social group, families that, but for these alliances, might have perceived themselves as rivals. But one cannot really know for sure. What one can know for sure, however, is that by the time that Roman civilisation reached the point at which it could boast an intellectual culture, those intellectuals who undertook to explain why the taboo existed gave a profoundly different account of it than any of these utilitarian accounts, namely, one that was moral and religious: for them, it was "just plain wrong" and this because it was against "the will of the gods".[24]

(ii) Status

In many cases, the "status" of one or both of the parties, for example, his ethnicity, his class, his standing as "freeborn" or "slave" or "freed", or his religion, stood as an obstacle to the contemplated marriage. The impediments of this order included the following: marriage was prohibited (1) between Roman and non-Roman;[25] (2) between patrician and plebeian (in very ancient times);[26] (3) between master and slave;[27] (4) between slave and slave;[28] (5) between freeborn person and freed slave;[29] and (6) between Christian and Jew (during the later Empire).[30]

(iii) Identity of sex

There are no official sources of Roman law that even raise the question of the propriety of same-sex marriage, much less answer it.[31] Even so, it is clear that, at least as a matter of customary law, such a marriage would have been

---

24 See generally T Mommsen, *Le droit pénal romaine* (1907) no 682 at 406-407 and n 1; cf Plato, *De Legibus* 8.838 ("[T]hese things [instances of incest] are said to be wrong, and are considered as hateful before God, and the foulest of the foul.")

25 Gai Inst 1.56,57,67,75; Kaser (n 4) § 58 at 288.

26 See *Lex Canuleia* (abrogating the former impediment); Livy 4.1; Kaser (n 4) § 58 at 288.

27 Ulpian, *RE.g.* 5.5; see also Kaser (n 4) § 58 at 288.

28 J Inst 1.10; Brundage (n 7) 36.

29 See D 23.2.23 (abrogating the former impediment).

30 Cod 1.9.6; Girard (n 2) 174.

31 One possible exception is a constitution issued by Constantine in 342 AD, Cod Theod 9.7.3. Its meaning, however, is less than entirely clear.

an impossibility. Though it is true that the Romans tolerated homosexual conduct under certain circumstances,[32] this tolerance seems not to have extended to conduct between women and, even as to conduct between men, seems to have been mixed with contempt, for the "passive" partners in homosexual anal intercourse were regarded as unmanly.[33] Perhaps even more telling in this regard is the public reaction that was provoked when certain of the emperors, notably Nero and Diocletian, purported to "marry" men: these "marriages" were universally considered to be merely farcical.

(2) Christian adaptations of and supplements to the Roman law of marriage

To say that the Christian conception of marriage differed profoundly from that of the Romans is an understatement. For the Christian, marriage was much more than "just" a social relationship: it was, at once, a *simulacrum* of the relationship between Christ and his church[34] and a *sacramentum*,[35] that is, a special means whereby God was thought to mediate his grace to those in the church.[36] Given the gulf between these conceptions of marriage, one might have expected there to be quite a gulf between the Roman and the Christian laws of marriage. With respect to some issues, such as whether and, if so, on what grounds a marriage could be dissolved by "divorce", that was certainly the case. But with respect to many other issues, it was not the case. And among these "other" issues were those pertaining to the prerequisites to marriage. In developing its own law on the prerequisites of marriage, the church, especially its Western branch, seems to have taken Roman law (in post-classical form) as its starting point and then to have added to or subtracted from that law only where and to the extent that the church's moral theology so required.

(a) Absolute impediments

(i) Impuberty

The canonists, for the most part, retained the late Roman law rules of puberty (they set the ages of puberty at fourteen for boys and twelve for girls),[37] but

---

32 Brundage (n 7) 48.
33 Brundage (n 7) 49.
34 J Witte, Jr, *From Sacrament to Contract: Marriage, Religion, and Law in the Western Tradition* (1997) 17-18.
35 Id at 22-23 and 26-30; Esmein vol 1 (n 1) 63-64.
36 Witte (n 34) 27.
37 St Thomas, S T, Supp Tert Pt, Q 58, Art 5 (Benziger Bros, New York, 1949); see also Gaudemet (n 3) 197; Esmein vol 1 (n 1) 212 (quoting and explicating the works of various canonists, including Panormitanus); Augustine vol 5 (3) 163.

with this modification: if one of the spouses was an *impuberius* or *impuberia*, the marriage would nevertheless be recognised as valid provided that he or she was able (1) to engage in sexual relations[38] (physical criterion), and (2) to understand the act that he or she had accomplished[39] (psychological criterion).[40] To some extent, then, the canonists seem to have revived the early Roman law rule.

(ii) Impotence

Expanding the Roman law rule according to which *castrati* lacked *connubium*, the canonists made of sexual impotency itself (*impossibilitatis coeundi*),[41] regardless of its cause, an impediment to marriage.[42] Whatever may have been the rationale for the more limited Roman law rule, the rationale for the more expansive canon law rule is clear. As the canonists understood marriage, it required of the parties thereto that they engage in sexual relations with each other.[43] The performance of this duty was considered to be a means to two ends, one positive – procreation – and the other negative – avoidance of immoral sexual conduct.[44] For the canonists, then, impotency defeated the very purpose of marriage.[45]

(iii) Existing marriage

The canonists retained the Roman law rule that a person who is presently married can not contract a second marriage.[46] But their reason for retaining that rule differed dramatically from that which had led the Romans to establish it. For the canonists, polygamy represented a perversion of marriage as God had originally established it, a perversion attributable to the corruption

38 Esmein vol 1 (n 1) 212 (quoting and explicating the works of various canonists, including Panormitanus).
39 Gratian, Part 2, C.30 q.2 c.1; see also Esmein vol 1 (n 1) 212.
40 St Thomas, S T, Supp Tert Pt, Q 58, Art 5; see also Esmein vol 1 (n 1) 212-216; Augustine vol 5 (n 3) 163.
41 See e.g., Gratian, Part 2, C.9 q.2 c.29, at 1071; see also Esmein vol 1 (n 1) 232.
42 Gaudemet (3) 198; Esmein vol 1 (n 1) 232-241 (quoting and explicating the works of various canonists, including Panormitanus).
43 St Thomas, S T, Supp Tert Pt, Q 64, Arts 1 and 2. This notion – that of a "conjugal debt" – can be traced all the way back to St Paul himself. See 1 Cor 7:3.
44 See Rev R D Lawler et al, *Catholic Sexual Ethics: A Summary, Explanation, and Defense*, 2nd edn (1998) 53; E Boissard, *Questions théologiques sur le mariage* (1948) 17-19 and n 3; Augustine vol 5 (n 3) 16 (citing and explicating the works of various early Church Fathers, including Chrysostom and Augustine).
45 See, e.g., St. Thomas, S T, Supp Tert Pt, Q 58, Art 1; see also Esmein vol 1 (n 1) 236-239 (quoting and explicating the works of various canonists, including Hincmar of Reims).
46 St Thomas, S T, Supp Tert Pt, Q 66, Arts 1 and 2; see also Esmein vol 1 (n 1) 267-268; Augustine vol 5 (n 3) 173 and 174-176.

of humankind that followed the Fall.[47] As Jesus himself had stated, God's original plan contemplated a union of just one man and just one woman, united in such a way that "they are no longer two, but one flesh".[48]

It bears noting that the canon law rule was, in practice, far more rigorous than was the Roman law rule. This additional rigour sprang from the canon law rule of "indissolubility" of marriage,[49] according to which divorce was prohibited, save in the most extraordinary circumstances.[50] And so, whereas under Roman law one might escape the impediment of existing marriage by either death *or divorce*, under canon law one could escape it only by death.[51]

(b) Relative impediments

(i) Relationship
That the canonists generally approved of the Roman system of prohibitions on intra-familial marriage (the "anti-incest" impediments) hardly comes as a surprise. After all, the Christian Scriptures condemned such marriages in no uncertain terms.[52] Nevertheless, the canonists faulted the Roman system for "not going far enough", and this in three respects.[53]

First, the canonists over time extended the Romans' prohibition against intermarriage between consanguinous relatives well beyond the third degree. At its height, the canon law prohibition even reached as far as what the canonists called the "seventh degree".[54] This extension was even more extreme than it seems, for the canonists counted degrees of relationship differently than did the Romans. In the canonical computation system a "degree" included all those persons who were in the same generation from the common ancestor, so that, for example, first cousins were considered to be related in the second, rather than the fourth, degree.[55] And so, to use Roman terminology, the canon law prohibition at this point extended out to the *fourteenth* degree![56] Eventually this extreme rigour was tempered slightly. At the Fourth Lateran Council, held in 1215, the church cut the impediment back to the "fourth degree",[57] that is, in Roman terms, the eighth degree.

47 Lawler (n 44) 130; see also St Thomas, S T, Supp Tert Pt, Q 65, Art 1, Obj 6 and Rep to Obj 4.
48 See Matt 19:6.
49 See generally Esmein vol 1 (n 1) 64; Gaudemet (n 3) 240.
50 Esmein vol 2 (n 1) 45; see also Gaudemet (n 3) 258-259.
51 See generally St Thomas, S T, Supp Tert Pt, Q 66, Art 1; Esmein vol 1 (n 1) 268.
52 See, e.g., Lev 18:6-18 and 20:11-21; Deut 27:20-23; and 1 Cor 5:1.
53 See generally Esmein vol 1 (n 1) 336; J-P Lévy, *Cours d'histoire du droit privé (la famille)* (1966) 34-37.
54 Esmein vol 1 (n 1) 341-43; Gaudemet (n 3) 205.
55 Esmein vol 1 (n 1) 344-46; Lévy (n 53) 35.
56 Esmein vol 1 (n 1) 348-49; Lévy (n 53) 35.
57 Esmein vol 1 (n 1) 355; Gaudemet (n 3) 205.

Second, the canonists decided to treat affinitives no less leniently than consanguinous relatives. Thus, marriages between affinitives were at one time prohibited out to the "seventh degree" (by the canonical reckoning), but in the end only out to the "fourth degree" (by the same reckoning).[58]

Third, the canonists added yet another category of "relative" alongside consanguinous and affinitive relatives – "spiritual" relatives.[59] The term refers to those to whom one becomes related though one's baptism or confirmation.[60] Even at its height, the prohibition on intermarriage between spiritual relatives never reached as far as did the prohibition on intermarriage between consanguinous and affinitive relatives. The only forbidden matches were these: between (1) godparent and godchild (*paternitas*), (2) godparent and biological parent of the godchild (*compaternitas*), (3) spouse of the godparent and biological parent of the child (*compaternitas indirecta*), (4) godchild and biological child of his godparent (*fraternitas*).[61]

To the canonists' general tendency to expand the Romans' anti-incest impediments there was only one exception. It concerned adoptive relatives.[62] Though many of the early canonists affirmed the late Roman law rule (three degrees by the Roman reckoning),[63] later canonists took a more lenient position, namely, that the prohibition should extend no further than the second degree (same reckoning).[64]

(ii) Status

During the early Middle Ages, the church recognised none of the late Roman law status-based impediments to marriage, not even that of "disparity of cult", that is, the prohibition on marriage between Christians and Jews.[65] That the early canonists found little merit in the impediments related to slavery is easy enough to understand: those impediments were out of kilter with the notion of Christian equality.[66] But why the early canonists failed to latch on to the impediment of disparity of cult probably had less to do with principle than with practical reality, namely, that because Christianity had not yet attained the status of "universal" religion of the civilised world, marriages between

---

58 Gaudemet (n 3) 211-12; Lévy (n 53) 35 and 36; G LePointe, *La famille dans l'ancien droit*, 4th edn (1953) 144 and 145.

59 Esmein vol 1 (n 1) 362-363; Gaudemet (n 3) 209.

60 Esmein vol 1 (n 1) 362; Gaudemet (n 3) 209.

61 Esmein vol 1 (n 1) 364-373; Gaudemet (n 3) 209-211.

62 See generally Gaudemet (n 3) 207-209.

63 Esmein vol 1 (n 1) 359.

64 Esmein vol 1 (n 1) 359; Gaudemet (n 3) 203.

65 Gaudemet (n 3) 201-204 and 215-218; Esmein vol 1 (n 1) 216-217 and 317-325.

66 Gaudemet (n 3) 1; Esmein vol 1 (n 1) 317 and 325.

Christians and non-Christians were still rather common.[67]

This early tolerance of cross-cult marriages waned during the later Middle Ages.[68] At that time, the canonists undertook to deal not only with marriages between Christians and Jews, but also with marriages between Christians and heretics. Eventually, all canonists came round to the conclusion that cross-cult marriages of the former kind (Christian and Jew) were null.[69] Regarding cross-cult marriages of the latter kind (Christian and heretic), there was, by contrast, less than complete agreement. Nearly all authors counted at least some of these marriages as null.[70] But some authors carved out exceptions to this rule for marriages to "baptised" heretics and/or to heretics whose views, though condemned by the church, were not thought to warrant the extreme sanction of excommunication.[71]

(iii) Identity of sex

When it comes to determining whether canon law permitted marriage between persons of the same sex, we are in much the same position as we were when we raised this question of Roman law and for the same sort of reason: there is no canon law source which provides, in so many words, that "persons of the same sex cannot contract marriage". There can be no doubt, however, that this was in fact "the law", if only as a matter of custom. Penitentials dating from the Middle Ages make it clear that homosexual conduct was considered to be inherently and without exception sinful and, not only that, but among the worst of sins.[72] As we have already seen, the canonists taught that marriage, almost by definition, required that the parties thereto have sex with each other.[73] How could they have recognised a form of marriage that, at its very foundation, required what they considered to be immoral acts?

C. SCOTS LAW

The "oldest" Scots law of marriage of which any noticeable vestiges still remain today is that which began to develop in the twelfth century.[74] It was

---

67 Gaudemet (n 3) 200-201; see also Esmein vol 1 (n 1) 216-217. This is not to say that the early church did not frown on such marriages; it certainly did. But the only sanction imposed on those who entered into them was penitential.
68 Esmein vol 1 (n 1) 216 and 217-219; Gaudemet (n 3) 201-204.
69 Esmein vol 1 (n 1) 218; Gaudemet (n 3) 201 and 204.
70 Esmein vol 1 (n 1) 218-219; Gaudemet (n 3) 203-204.
71 Esmein vol 1 (n 1) 219; Gaudemet (n 3) 203-204.
72 Brundage (n 7) 166-168; Lawler (n 44) 55-56.
73 See text at nn 43-45 above.
74 J W Cairns, "Historical introduction", in Reid and Zimmermann, *History*, vol 1, 14 at 16-18; M C Meston et al, *The Scottish Legal Tradition* (1991) 31-39.

at that time that the so-called "Celtic Church" was, at last, more or less assimilated into mainstream Roman Catholicism.[75] With that development came the introduction into Scotland of Roman Catholic ecclesiastical courts, applying more or less "pure" Roman Catholic canon law.[76]

(1) From the Reformation until the late twentieth century

At the time of the Reformation in 1560[77] the Scottish Parliament, under the influence of John Knox, outlawed Roman Catholicism[78] and established the "Reformed" church[79] as the national church of Scotland.[80] This development was full of portent for the future of Scottish marriage law. In the Reformers' eyes, the Roman Catholic canon law consisted, in large part, of "man-made doctrine", the product of extra-Biblical and, at some points, contra-Biblical speculation. The Reformers' aversion to canon law extended even to, indeed, especially to, that part of it which concerned marriage,[81] although, whether in Germany, Switzerland, or Scotland, they did not set aside *all* of that law. The Reformers rejected, first, the *sacramental theology* that had provided part of its theoretical underpinning.[82] In addition, they rejected certain *procedural* aspects of that law, for example, that part of it that gave jurisdiction over marriage to ecclesiastical courts.[83] But insofar as the *substantive* canon law of marriage was concerned, the Reformers found most of it to be in accord with Scripture or, at the very least, with the notion that marriage arises from a contract, a notion that the Reformers seem to have taken over uncritically from the canon law.[84]

(a) Absolute impediments (impuberty, impotence, existing marriage)

In the Reformation's aftermath, the Scots retained nearly all of the canon law pertaining to absolute impediments to marriage. First, the Scots kept the impediment of impuberty[85] (which the Scots came to call "nonage").

---

75 Cairns (n 74) 29; see generally Meston (n 74) 39-40.
76 E M Clive, *The Law of Husband and Wife in Scotland*, 4th edn (1997) para 01.003; Cairns (n 74) 30; Meston (n 74) 41.
77 E Cameron, *The European Reformation* (1991) 386; E Simon et al, *The Reformation* (1966) 62; J D Woodbridge (ed), *Great Leaders of the Christian Church* (1988) 250-251.
78 Cameron (n 77) 386; Simon (n 77) 63; see also Clive (n 76) para 01.003.
79 M Collins and M A Price, *The Story of Christianity: 2000 Years of Faith* (2003) 136-137.
80 Simon (n 77) 63; see also Cameron (n 77) 387.
81 Witte (n 34) 42-43.
82 Witte (n 34) 42-43, 51-52, 74, 79-80 and 94-95.
83 Witte (n 34) 42-43, 80.
84 Witte (n 34) 44.
85 Though the Scots did, indeed, keep the age impediment, they denatured it, or so it seems to me.

The general rule required that the male be fourteen and the female twelve. But, following the canon law, the Scots recognised the possibility that a child below this age might be deemed free of the impediment if he were able to copulate.[86] There is at least some authority for the proposition that the problem could be cured and the marriage validated if, after the younger party were to reach puberty, the couple were to continue cohabiting.[87] Second, the impediment of impotence remained unaltered.[88] Third, the impediment of existing marriage was also retained,[89] but with this significant variation: under Scottish law, after the Reformation, the impediment could be escaped not only by death, but also by divorce. The only one of these impediments that thereafter underwent any significant change was impuberty. In the Marriage Act 1929, the minimum age for marriage was raised to sixteen for both sexes.

(b) Relative impediments

(i) Relationship

One of the few points in the law of marriage at which post-Reformation Scotland broke with canon law is that which concerns impediments based on relationship. The cause of the break is easy to identify. When the Reformers compared the anti-incest prohibitions of the canon law with those of Scripture, they found that the former were far more rigorous than the latter. Convinced that the canonists, by going beyond Scripture, had departed from it, the Reformers determined to set things aright by devising new rules based solely on the latter.[90] Under these rules, only the following matches were prohibited: (1) relatives in the direct line, regardless of degree; (2) relatives in the collateral line who "stand in place of parents and children to one another" (i.e., aunts/uncles and nieces/nephews). These prohibitions were applied to affinitives no less than to consanguinous relatives.[91] But the prohibitions were

---

As understood by the Romans and by the canonists, the "age requirement" for marriage was not thought of as a requirement of "capacity for" marriage, certainly not "mental capacity" (Augustine vol 5 (n 3) 163-164). It was not so with the Scottish Institutional writers. The significance of a potential spouse's being "of age", they wrote, was that it created a "presumption" that he or she was "capable of consent" to marriage (Erskine, *Inst* 1.6.2; Stair, *Inst* 1.4.6). For these authors, then, age served as a "proxy" for mental capacity.

86 Bankton, *Inst* 1.5.26; Erskine, *Inst* 1.6.2; Mackenzie, *Inst* 1. 6. 3; Stair, *Inst* 1.4.6.

87 See Erskine, *Inst* 1.6.2; see also Clive (n 76) para 07.015.

88 Bankton, *Inst* 1.5.27; Erskine, *Inst* 1.6.4; Mackenzie, *Institutions* 1.6.17; Stair, *Inst* 1.4.6.

89 Bankton, *Inst* 1.5.52; Erskine, *Inst* 1.6.5; Stair, *Inst* 1.4.2-3.

90 *APS* iii 26, c 15 ("Anent thame that committis incest"); Stair, *Inst* 1.4.6; see also K McK Norrie, *The Family Law (Scotland) Act 2006: Text and Commentary* (2007) 2.

91 Bankton, *Inst* 1.5.45-48; Erskine, *Inst* 1.6.4; Mackenzie, *Institutions* 1.6.5 and 17; Stair, *Inst* 1.4.4 and 6.

not applied to adoptive relations, for there were no such relations to which they might have been applied: Scotland did not authorise "adoption" until the late date of 1930.[92]

(ii) Status

Insofar as status-based impediments to marriage are concerned, the Scots, during the post-Reformation era, took a step "backward" in time, specifically, back to the days of early canon law. The Scots, perhaps because they could find no warrant for them in Scripture, rejected both the old Roman status-based impediments and the late mediaeval canon law impediments of disparity of cult (those that prohibited marriage between Christians and heretics and between Christians and Jews).

(iii) Identity of sex

As is true of the Roman law sources and the canon law sources considered above, the Scots law sources of the post-Reformation era make no mention of any impediment of "identity of sex", at least not in so many words. Here, one encounters yet another case of the matter being so settled by custom that no one – no legislator, no judge, no scholar – thought it necessary to address the issue.[93]

(2) From the late twentieth century up to the present

(a) Absolute impediments

(i) Impuberty

The Marriage (Scotland) Act 1977 retained the impediment of impuberty (nonage) and, further, the age of impuberty that had been established in the Marriage Act 1929 – sixteen for both sexes.[94] Though the matter is perhaps not entirely free from doubt,[95] the better view is that an underage marriage can no longer be "validated" later by virtue of the parties' continued cohabitation after the younger party has reached the minimum age for marriage.

(ii) Impotence

In recent years Scots have debated whether the traditional impediment of impotency is worth retaining. The Scottish Law Commission has taken the

---

92 P G B McNeill, *Adoption of Children in Scotland*, 3rd edn (1998) 1.

93 J M Thomson, *Family Law in Scotland*, 4th edn (2002) 32; Clive (n 76) para 07.016.

94 Marriage (Scotland) Act 1977, s 1 ("A marriage solemnized in Scotland between persons either of whom is under the age of 16 shall be void."); see also Thomson (n 93) at 26-27; Clive (n 76) paras 07.014-07.015.

95 See the discussion in Clive (n 76) para 07.015.

position that nullity of marriage because of impotency is an oddity that can lead to unnecessary difficulties. The Commission considered that, in cases of marriage breakdown for which impotency might be the cause, divorce should be the more satisfactory and logically defensible civil remedy. For these reasons, the Commission recommended that the impediment be dropped.[96] But this recommendation was not incorporated into the Family Law (Scotland) Act 2006. Under current Scots law, impotency of a spouse renders the marriage merely voidable,[97] as opposed to void.[98]

(iii) Existing marriage

In 1992 the Scottish Law Commission proposed that the traditional impediment of existing marriage (a marriage is void if either party to it is, at the time of the marriage, already married) be enacted in legislative form.[99] This recommendation was not heeded, but this impediment can (still) be introduced as an objection to marriage pursuant to section 5(4) of the Marriage (Scotland) Act 1977.

(b) Relative impediments

(i) Relationship

The current Scottish law of marriage maintains in force the anti-incest impediments of the old, though with a few modifications, some subtle, others more profound. Section 2(1) of the Marriage (Scotland) Act 1977 provides that a marriage between a man and any woman related to him in a degree specified in column 1 of Schedule 1 to the Act, or between a woman and any man related to her in a degree specified in column 2 of that Schedule, "shall be void". The list is exhaustive in the sense that where the relationship is not mentioned in the Schedule, the parties may validly marry. The prohibited relationships arise from (1) consanguinity, (2) affinity, and (3) adoption.

In the case of *consanguinous* relationships, intermarriage is prohibited in both the direct and the collateral lines up through the third degree (that is, a person cannot marry his or her parent, grandparent, or great-grandparent;

---

96 Report on Family Law (Scot Law Com No 135, 1992) para 8.26.
97 On the competence of an action of nullity at the instance of the impotent party, see *S G v WG* 1933 SC 728. On the meaning of "voidable", see S Styles and N R Whitty (eds), *Glossary of Scottish and European Union Legal Terms and Latin Phrases*, 2nd edn (2003) 178. In Louisiana, one would say "relatively null". La Civ Code art 2031.
98 On the meaning of "void", see *Glossary* (n 97) 178. In Louisiana, one would say "absolutely null". La Civ Code art 2030. This is the only ground for which a marriage is voidable, as opposed to void, in Scottish law, as the Scottish jurisprudence has recognised. *C B v A B* (1884) 11 R 1060 per Lord Young at 1067, affd (1885) 12 R (H L) 36.
99 Report on Family Law (Scot Law Com No 135, 1992) para 8.3.

child, grandchild or great-grandchild; brother or sister; uncle, aunt, nephew or niece).

In the case of relationship by *affinity*, not all marriages are prohibited. Quite the contrary. Persons who are related within the degrees of affinity in paragraph 2 of the Schedule may marry provided that both parties have attained the age of twenty-one at the time of the marriage and the younger party has not at any time before attaining the age of eighteen lived in the same household as the other party and been treated by the other party as a child. One example of a case to which this restriction might apply is that of step-parent and step-child.[100]

Recent changes were made to the restrictions on persons who are related within the degrees of affinity in paragraph 2A of the Schedule. Prior to 2006, certain affinitives were required to wait until the deaths of their former spouses and of those through whom they had come to be related by marriage before they could marry each other: (1) in the case of a man who wanted to marry his mother-in-law or his daughter-in-law, the couple had to wait until after the deaths of his former wife and her father or the deaths of his son and his son's mother; and (2) in the case of a woman who wanted to marry her father-in-law or her son-in-law, the couple had to wait until after the deaths of her former husband and his mother or the deaths of her daughter and her daughter's father. The Family Law (Scotland) Act 2006 amended the Marriage (Scotland) Act 1977 to remove these special requirements.[101]

Regarding intermarriage of *adoptive* relatives, the Marriage (Scotland) Act 1977 established a quite modest set of impediments. Among such relatives, the only prohibited intermarriages are those in the direct line and in the first degree (that is, an adoptive parent and child cannot marry each other). Other possible matches, for example, between siblings by adoption, are permitted.[102]

(ii) Status
Like the old Scottish law of marriage, the current law recognises no status-based impediments (e.g., impediments based on race or religion).

(iii) Identity of sex
Today as yesterday marriage in Scottish law continues to be defined as a union between a man and a woman. A marriage will therefore be void if the parties purporting to marry are of the same sex.[103] It is now possible, however, for

100 Norrie (n 90) 3.
101 Norrie (n 90) 2-3.
102 Thomson (n 93) 27-32; Clive (n 76) para 03.011.
103 Thomson, (n 93) 32; Clive (n 76) para 07.016.

parties of the same sex to form a "civil partnership", following the enactment of the Civil Partnership Act 2004 in the UK. Parties of the same sex, who are not already in an existing civil partnership or lawfully married, who are not within the prohibited degrees of relationship, and are both aged sixteen years or over, may enter into this newly-established form of legal relationship. Same-sex couples who form a civil partnership receive parity of treatment with those opposite-sex couples who enter into marriage, that is, enjoy the same legal rights and privileges as do married couples. Even so, "civil partnership" is not "marriage".

The Scots' omission thus far to extend access to *marriage* to same-sex couples seems to have rested on several considerations. First, some Scots apparently consider such an extension to be "unnecessary", inasmuch as such couples can get the "same" benefits by way of civil partnership.[104] Second, in the minds of some Scots, "marriage", properly so called, is an institution that, almost as a matter of definition, is about uniting male and female[105] and/ or about procreation.[106] Third, like various members of the UK Parliament, some Scots may fear that allowing same-sex couples to enter "marriage" might offend the sensibilities of those persons, now admittedly a minority, who would object to such marriages on religious grounds.[107] Fourth, a good number of Scots who are "gay" or "lesbian" do not, in fact, want access to marriage, which they fault for being too "patriarchal" and/or "religious".[108]

D. LOUISIANA LAW

(1) The first French period (1715-1762)

The history of Louisiana's private law, including that of marriage, dates back to the time of the French colonisation of Louisiana. In 1712, the French king made "Our Edicts, Ordinances & Customs and the Usages of the Provostry and Viscounty of Paris" applicable to the colony.[109]

---

104 Scottish Executive, *The Consultation on Civil Partnership Registration: An Analysis of the Responses* (2004) § 4.23, at 21 (available at *http://www.scotland.gov.uk/Resource/ Doc/47210/0025544.pdf*).

105 Scottish Executive, *Civil Partnership Registration: A Legal Status for Committed Same-Sex Couples in Scotland* (2003) § 5.8, at 17 (available at *http://www.scotland.gov.uk/consultations/ justice/cprs.pdf*).

106 Scottish Executive, *Consultation on Civil Partnership Registration* (n 104) § 4.4, at 16.

107 *The Civil Partnership Bill [HL]: Background and Debate* (House of Commons Research Paper 04/64, 7 September 2004) 47, quoting Lord Lester, HL Deb 12 May 2004, col 178GC.

108 Scottish Executive, *Consultation on Civil Partnership Registration* (n 104) § 4.23, at 21.

109 J-R Trahan, "The continuing influence of *le droit civil* and *el derecho civil* in the private law of Louisiana" (2003) 63 La LR 1019 at 1021.

Because the France of that day was a Roman Catholic state, one would suppose that French marriage law was nothing more nor less than the Roman Catholic canon law of marriage. And, with some exceptions that are not important here, that was true. But *this* "Roman Catholic canon law" was not quite the same as that which we examined earlier. By the time that the French colony of Louisiana was born, the Roman Catholic Church had re-stated and, in some respects, modified its canon law of marriage. The precipitating cause of this development was the challenges that the Reformers had presented to the Roman Catholic theology of marriage and, with it, the Roman Catholic Church's regulation of marriage.[110] This restatement and modification of the traditional canon law of marriage was accomplished at the Roman Catholic Church's great "counter-reformation" council, the Council of Trent.[111]

Insofar as the law of impediments to marriage is concerned, the Council, in the end, made only a few innovations, but what innovations it made were significant. These innovations concerned "spiritual" relatives. Oversimplifying somewhat, the change can be stated as follows: the scope of the impediment was scaled back so that it thereafter prohibited marriage only (1) between the spiritual child (baptisé(e) or confirmé(e)), on the one hand, and his or her spiritual parent (godfather or godmother), on the other, and (2) between a spiritual parent (the godfather or godmother), on the one hand, and a biological parent (mother or father), on the other.[112] The reason for this change seems to have been simply that the more extended prohibition had served no truly useful purpose.

This, then, was the "French law of marriage" that ended up being put into effect in Louisiana by virtue of the French king's decree of 1712. It was largely identical to the Roman Catholic canon law of marriage that had formed the original Scottish law of marriage, save in this respect: it included the innovations of the Council of Trent reducing the ambit of the impediment of relationship as applied to spiritual relatives.

In the remainder of the French period, no major developments in the law of impediments to marry took place, save one. This development was brought about through the enactment, by means of French royal decree, of Louisiana's infamous *Code Noir* in 1724. This code forbade, first, marriages between blacks and whites and, second, marriages between slaves and freemen.[113] In addition, the code obviated the "problems" of marriages between Chris-

---

110 See Witte (n 34) 37; Gaudemet (n 3) 277; 2 Esmein, vol 2 (n 1) 121 and 137.
111 On the decrees and canons of the Council of Trent regarding marriage, see, in general, Witte (n 34) 36-41; Gaudemet (n 3); Esmein, vol 2 (n 1) 137-368.
112 Witte (n 34) 38; Esmein, vol 2 (n 1) 261.
113 *Le Code Noir de la Louisiane* art VI.

tians and Jews and between Christians and heretics (such as Protestants), respectively, by (1) expelling all Jews from the colony,[114] and (2) outlawing all religions other than the "Catholic faith".[115]

(2) The Spanish period (1762-1800)

After Spain acquired Louisiana from France in 1762 the Spanish authorities put "Spanish law" into effect in Louisiana.[116] This "Spanish law", however, was not exactly the same as that which was then in force in the mother country (Castille). To be sure, much of the law of Castille was also brought to Louisiana. But alongside that law were a number of other laws that had been designed for all of Spain's colonies in general and, in some instances, for the colony of Louisiana in particular. Among the parts of the law of Spanish colonial Louisiana that were also in effect in Castille were the decrees and canons of the Council of Trent concerning marriage,[117] which the Spanish crown had adopted (subject to certain reservations that are not important here) in 1564.

Among the parts of the law of Spanish colonial Louisiana that were not in effect in Castille was the "slave law". Now, in specifying just what, if anything, this slave law had to say on the subject of impediments to marriage, we encounter a profound difficulty, namely, that it is not entirely clear of what the "slave law" of Spanish Louisiana consisted.[118] On the one hand, the second Spanish governor of Louisiana, O'Reilly, did issue a decree that maintained Louisiana's French *Code Noir* in force, at least at first. On the other hand, O'Reilly later put into effect a number of rules that were drawn from the slave law in place in most of Spain's other colonies. Not only that, but some of the decisions handed down by the Louisiana courts late in the Spanish era seem to have rested on the assumption that *all* the provisions of Louisiana's *Code Noir*, not just those specifically contradicted by O'Reilly's decrees, had somehow ceased to be effective. This assumption may explain why, during the Spanish period, marriages between blacks and whites were generally permitted.[119] The fate of the *Code Noir*'s prohibition against marriages between slaves and freemen is even less clear.

---

114   Id, art 1.
115   Id, art 3.
116   See J-R Trahan (n 109) 1022.
117   As demonstrated in H Baade, "Marriage contracts in French and Spanish Louisiana: A study in 'notarial' jurisprudence" (1978) 53 Tulane LR 1 at 43-44; see also Witte (n 34) 41.
118   The problem has been examined in H W Baade, "The law of slavery in Spanish Luisiana, 1769-1803", in E F Haas (ed), *Louisiana's Legal Heritage* (1983) 43.
119   K S Hanger, *Bounded Lives, Bounded Places: Free Black Society in Colonial New Orleans, 1769-1803* (1997).

(3) The second French period (1800-1803)

Spain retroceded Louisiana to France in 1800, though the formal transfer of possession of the colony was postponed until November 1803. Between 1800 and the time at which France re-transferred Louisiana to the United States, which occurred only one month after the French had assumed possession, the French government left the law of Louisiana, including that of marriage, as it was.[120]

(4) The American period part 1 (1803-1987)

(a) Absolute impediments

(i) Impuberty

After Louisiana was acquired by the United States, the Spanish colonial rule regarding the impediment of impuberty was retained, at least at first.[121] In 1934, however, the legislature raised the minimum marriageable ages for males and females from fourteen and twelve to eighteen and sixteen, respectively.[122] About a decade later, the Louisiana courts concluded that the rule on impuberty was merely "directory"; that is, violating it might expose the violaters to liability for a fine but did not cause the marriage to be null.[123] That decision effectively removed impuberty from the list of absolute impediments to marriage in Louisiana law.

(ii) Impotence

During the American period, Louisiana, at least at first, apparently retained the Spanish colonial rule regarding the impediment of impotence, for the Digest of 1808 (Louisiana's first civil code) did not expressly abolish it and, it seems, did not impliedly abrogate it, as it was not inconsistent with any of the Digest's provisions. But the rule was expressly repealed less than two decades into the American period.[124] With that, the ages-old absolute impediment of impotence dropped out of Louisiana law.

(iii) Existing marriage

From the very start of the American period, "existing marriage" stood as a bar to a subsequent marriage.[125] On this point, then, the Spanish law rule was retained.

---

120 See J-R Trahan (n 109) 1023.
121 *Digest* bk 1, tit 4, art 6 at 24 (1808); CC art 93 (1825); CC art 93 (1870).
122 1934 La Acts 140.
123 *State v Golden* 26 So 2d 837 (1946); *In re State in Interest of Goodwin* 39 So 2d 731 (La 1949); M B Hubert, "The annulment of marriages in Louisiana" (1949) 24 Tulane LR 217 at 226.
124 CC art 116 (1825).
125 Act of 6 Apr 1807 § 10; *Digest* bk 1, tit 4, art 7 at 24 (1808); CC art 94 (1825); CC art 93 (1870).

(b) Relative impediments

(i) Relationship

As the American period began, the Spanish colonial rule regarding incestuous marriages was retained for the most part, but with this important qualification: the prohibition in the collateral line was cut back to three degrees (by the Roman reckoning).[126] In time, the prohibition on the marriage of "spiritual" relatives was eliminated, perhaps by as early as 1807 (the legislation of that year concerning the impediment of relationship does not mention it)[127] but certainly no later than 1825.[128] And then in 1902 the legislature pushed the prohibition back out to four degrees.[129]

(ii) Status

Early in the American period, the status-based impediments concerning race and slavery that had been recognised under the French *Code Noir* were re-established.[130] Louisianans of the American period eventually gave up both of these impediments, though at first only reluctantly. The prohibition on slave-free unions was not abolished until the mid-nineteenth century and then only thanks to the Civil War; the prohibition on black-white unions was not abolished until the late date of 1972, and then only because the federal Supreme Court had concluded that such prohibitions violated the Fourteenth Amendment to the federal constitution.[131] Though these changes in the law were resisted at first, they now enjoy widespread acceptance.

The status-based impediments concerning religion (which, arguably, had remained operative during the Spanish colonial period) – those that forbade marriage between Christians and Jews and between Christians and heretics – were gone by 1808 at the latest.[132] Those impediments, it seems safe to speculate, were considered to be inconsistent with the principle of "separation of church and state" inscribed in the First Amendment to the federal constitution.

---

126 Act of 6 Apr 1807 § 15; *Digest* bk 1, tit 4, art 10 at 26 (1808); CC art 97 (1825); CC art 95 (1870).
127 Act of 6 Apr 1807 §§ 15 and 16.
128 CC art 98 (1825).
129 1902 La Act No 120.
130 See, e.g., *Digest* bk 1, tit 4, art 8 at 24 (1808); ("Free persons and slaves are incapable of contracting marriage together; ... it is the same with respect to the marriages contracted by free white persons with free persons of color.")
131 1972 La Acts 256. See *Loving v Virginia* 388 US 1, 87 S Ct 1817 (1967).
132 The prohibition is absent from the list of impediments set out in the Digest of 1808.

(iii) Identity of sex

During most of the American period, it evidently was assumed, as a matter of custom, that persons of the same sex could not contract marriage with each other. In 1975, the legislature cast this traditional understanding in legislative form.[133] According to the folklore that has grown up concerning the enactment, the sponsors of the legislation were reacting to news that legislators in some state "out west" had proposed legislation that, if enacted, would have extended access to marriage to same-sex couples.

(5) The American period part 2 (1987-present)

Louisiana's current law of prerequisites to marriage took shape in 1987. It was at that time that the Louisiana Legislature comprehensively revised the parts of the Louisiana Civil Code in which those prerequisites are set forth.

(a) Absolute impediments

Like Louisiana's old law of marriage, the current law recognises only one of the traditional absolute impediments, namely, that of "existing marriage". According to Civil Code article 88, "[a] married person may not contract another marriage". The other two traditional absolute impediments – those of impuberty and impotence – remain as they were under the old law in its final state: unrecognised.[134]

(b) Relative impediments

(i) Relationship

Current Louisiana marriage law maintains the anti-incest impediment of the old, but with certain modifications. Under Civil Code article 90, marriage is prohibited between ascendants and descendants, regardless of degree, and between collaterals "within the fourth degree". The full force of this impediment, however, falls only on consanguinous relations. As to affinitives, it does not apply at all. For adoptive relations, there is an important exception: collaterals within the fourth degree can marry each other if they can satisfy a court that their marriage would not threaten "family harmony".[135]

---

133 1975 La Acts 361.

134 Some critics have faulted the revisors of the Civil Code articles on impediments to marry for failing to resuscitate the impediment of impuberty, which, as we saw earlier, the Louisiana jurisprudence had killed back in the 1940s. See supra n 123. Without such an impediment, the critics charge, there is nothing to stop, say, two prepubescent children from contracting a valid marriage. The criticism is misplaced, for reasons I shall provide below. See below, text accompanying n 157.

135 La Civ Code art 90, para 4, sent 2 and cmt (d).

(ii) Status
In continuity with Louisiana law of the immediate past, current Louisiana law recognises no status-based impediments (e.g., impediments based on race or religion).

(iii) Identity of sex
Louisiana's current law, like the old, prohibits marriages between persons of the same sex. This prohibition has been enshrined in several sources of law. At first, the prohibition was set out only in "mere" legislation. New Civil Code article 89, entitled "Impediment of same sex", provides that "[p]ersons of the same sex may not contract marriage with each other". This rule, we are told in yet another Civil Code article, rests on a "strong public policy of the state".[136] More recently, the prohibition has been added to the Louisiana Constitution. Article XII, § 15, enacted in 2004, reads as follows:

> Marriage in the state of Louisiana shall consist only of the union of one man and one woman. No official or court of the state of Louisiana shall construe this constitution or any state law to require that marriage or the legal incidents thereof be conferred upon any member of a union other than the union of one man and one woman.

Unlike Scotland, Louisiana, as yet, has made no "alternative" arrangements for same-sex couples, such as civil partnerships. Indeed, the same state Constitutional amendment that bars same-sex couples from marriage goes on to prohibit any such alternative arrangements: "A legal status identical or substantially similar to that of marriage for unmarried individuals shall not be valid or recognized."[137]

It should be clear, then, that whatever considerations may have underlain Louisiana's decision to exclude same-sex couples from access to marriage, those considerations had to differ, at least in part, from those that underlay Scotland's decision to leave such couples without access to marriage. And, indeed, they *were* different. Some of the justifications offered for Louisiana's decision were what one might call "secular". First, there was the "definitional" argument: marriage, by definition, is about "uniting male and female" and/or "procreation". Second, there was the "defence of marriage" argument: opening marriage to same-sex couples would "undermine" the institution of marriage in various ways, for example, it would reinforce the (supposedly false) idea that marriage is about nothing but the self-gratification of the spouses, a mere way to meet *their* needs for emotional and sexual intimacy,

136   See La Civ Code art 3520.B.
137   La Const (1974) art XII, § 15, sent 3 (amend 2004).

or would send the (supposedly false) message that two men or two women are "just as good as" a mother and a father when it comes to raising children. Still other justifications, however, were more or less openly "religious": same-sex marriage presupposes homosexual relations; homosexual relations are immoral; therefore, to allow same-sex marriage is to allow immorality. That such religious considerations played a role in Louisiana's decision hardly comes as a surprise: Louisiana remains a deeply religious jurisdiction (at least by comparison with the states of Europe, Scotland included), a fact about which I shall have more to say later,[138] and the most vocal supporters of both the Civil Code articles and the Constitutional amendment noted above included the Roman Catholic bishops and the pastors of innumerable conservative Evangelical Protestant churches.[139]

E. CONCLUSIONS

(1) Patterns: similarities and differences

Within the results of my study of the development of the law of impediments to marriage in Scotland and Louisiana, it is possible to discern a number of patterns. There are, to start with, a number of significant similarities between the two jurisdictions.

Comparing developments in the marriage law of the two jurisdictions *synchronically*, one notes that, at any given point in history, Scotland and Louisiana (or its "founding" countries, France and Spain) have had more or less the same requirements for marriage. As time has marched on, most of the changes made to these requirements in one jurisdiction have been mirrored in the other, and at roughly the same time. The one exception to this generalisation – and it is a glaring one – concerns the impediment of "difference of race" (the anti-miscegenation rule). Though this impediment was never recognised in Scotland, it was established in Louisiana fairly early on and was not suppressed until a generation ago.

Comparing developments in the marriage law of the two jurisdictions *diachronically*, one notes a couple of patterns. First, in both jurisdictions there has been a steady decline in the number of impediments. Second, in

138 See below, text accompanying nn 150-155.
139 The religious justification for the 2004 constitutional amendment was on open display as the proposed amendment to the state constitution wended its way through the legislative process. On the first day of the legislative session, the sponsors of the bill appeared at a massive news conference alongside the pastors of a number of conservative Evangelical mega-churches and representatives of the Roman Catholic Archdiocese of New Orleans to explain the purpose of the bill, a purpose described, in part, as upholding "Christian morality".

both jurisdictions many of the remaining impediments have been relaxed.

Alongside these similarities, however, there remain a few differences, some of which are striking. First, Scotland continues to recognise two of the traditional absolute impediments to marriage that Louisiana set aside sometime back: the impediments of impotence and impuberty (nonage). Second, Scotland's and Louisiana's respective anti-incest impediments differ in scope at several points: (1) as to consanguinous relatives, whereas Scotland prohibits matches in the collateral line only out through the third degree (aunt and nephew, for example), Louisiana prohibits matches in that line out through the fourth degree (first cousins, for example); (2) as to affinitives, whereas Scotland still prohibits marriages between step-parent and step-child in at least some circumstances, Louisiana does not; (3) as to adoptive relatives, whereas Scotland permits all matches save that of adoptive parent and children, Louisiana still prohibits, as well, matches between adoptive grandparents and grandchildren and allows matches between adoptive siblings only after court approval. Third, though both Scotland and Louisiana continue to regard "identity of sex" as an impediment to marriage, Scotland's reasons for doing so differ markedly from Louisiana's – in Louisiana, but not in Scotland, religious reasons play a significant role – and Scotland's commitment to doing so is not nearly so strong as is Louisiana's.

(2) Explanations for the patterns

(a) Similarities

In the search for an explanation of the *similarities* between the histories of the law of impediments to marriage in Scotland and Louisiana, one candidate soon presents itself: in both jurisdictions, the common understanding of the nature and purposes of marriage has changed and, it seems, has changed along the very same lines.[140] But this "cause" undoubtedly rests on some still more fundamental cause. What is it?

One obvious possibility is the phenomenon of "secularisation",[141] which has spread throughout Western culture, Scotland and Louisiana included, during the past several centuries. In the West, secularisation has involved two more or less simultaneous and closely interrelated developments:

---

140 K S Spaht, "The last one hundred years: The incredible retreat of law from the regulation of marriage" (2003) 63 La LR 243.

141 There is now a considerable literature on the topic of "secularisation". See, e.g., D Martin, *On Secularization: Towards a Revised General Theory* (2005); C J Sommerville, "Secular society / religious population: Our tacit rules for using the term 'secularization'" (1998) 37 *Journal for the Scientific Study of Religion* 249; M Chaves, "Secularization as declining religious authority" (1994) 72 *Social Forces* 749.

(1) "de-Christianization",[142] that is, a decline in the number of persons who adhere to Christianity[143] and / or who recognise Christian teaching as "authoritative",[144] and (2) what I shall call, for want of a better word, "Enlightening", that is, an increase in the number of persons affiliated with one or another of the various traditions that arose from the so-called "Enlightenment", which was in large part a reaction against Christianity,[145] such as the "Marxist" tradition or the now much more popular "liberal" tradition.[146]

This "secularisation thesis",[147] at least at first glance, seems to explain a good bit of what has happened to the law of impediments to marriage in both Scotland and Louisiana through the years. The thesis certainly can account for many of the changes that occurred in both Scotland and Louisiana with respect to the impediment of "relationship", in particular, the elimination of any impediment as to "spiritual" relatives as well as the scaling back of the impediment as to consanguinous and affinitive relatives. Further, the thesis may be able to explain why it was that Louisiana eventually gave up – or, to be more accurate, reconciled itself to the loss of – its status-based impediments to marriage, beginning with those based on religion and ending with those based on the slave/free dichotomy and, much more recently, the black/white dichotomy. Among the values most prized by those who share the Enlightenment worldview are (1) getting religion out of the business of making of positive law; (2) expanding the "liberty" of persons to do what they want to do (including to marry whomever they may want); and (3) assuring the "equality" of all persons. But this secularisation thesis may prove too much. My doubts have less to do with what has happened in Scotland than with what has happened in Louisiana. The source of my doubts is evidence which suggests that Louisiana, in contrast to Scotland, may not be all that secular

142 Sommerville (n 141) 251; see also Witte (n 34) 197-198.
143 Sommerville (n 141) 251.
144 Chaves (n 141) 750 and 754.
145 See B Ramm, *The Evangelical Heritage: A Study in Historical Theology* (1973) 67-70.
146 I use the expression "liberal tradition" here in its broad sense to include not only "classical" liberalism, such as that associated with John Locke or F A Hayek, but also "social justice" liberalism, such as that associated with Maynard Keynes or John Rawls. Despite their differences, these variations on liberalism have this in common: they privilege liberty (at least "personal" liberty) above all other values and maintain that restrictions on liberty must be rigorously justified. See generally "Liberalism", in *Stanford Encyclopedia of Philosophy* (2007) (available at *http://plato.stanford.edu/entries/liberalism/*).
147 I refer to the thesis stated earlier – that the cause of the changes in the law of impediments to marry in Scotland and Louisiana over the last few centuries is the secularisation of Scottish culture and Louisianan culture. This thesis has little relation to a (now largely discredited) thesis of the same name of which sociologists of religion are wont to speak, namely, that as a culture advances economically, politically, and socially, "religion" inevitably declines. See, e.g., Sommerville (n 141) 252; Chaves (n 141) 749-750.

yet, at least not secular enough for the secularisation thesis to be of great explanatory power there.

Though one might measure the extent of secularisation in other ways, one reasonable way, it seems to me, is to look at rates of adherence to what might be called, for lack of a better term, "traditional Christianity". When one uses this measure, one finds some rather startling differences between, on the one hand, the extent of secularisation in Scotland and, on the other, the extent of secularisation in Louisiana.

Let us start with rates of religious identification. According to the most recent Scottish census, 65% of Scots still identify themselves as "Christian", of which 42% identify with the "Church of Scotland",[148] 16% with the Roman Catholic Church, and 7% with "other churches"; and 28% claim no religion at all (5% simply refused to answer).[149] In Louisiana, according to a recent poll conducted by the Pew Institute, the religious identification statistics break down as follows: 89% Christian, of which 31% are "Evangelical Protestant", 28% are Roman Catholic, 20% are "African-American", and 9% are "mainline Protestant";[150] 8% are unaffiliated; and less than 0.5 % had "no answer".[151] Though the differences between the raw Scottish figures and the raw Louisiana figures are themselves stunning, they hardly tell the whole story. As I have indicated, the overwhelming majority of Scots who describe themselves as "Christian" identify with the Church of Scotland. Now, from the standpoint of traditional Christianity, the Church of Scotland appears to be a rather "secularised" church, meaning that it seems to have appropriated much of "Enlightenment" values, especially on matters of "moral theology". To take just one example, there is within the Church of Scotland today a strong and growing movement to permit clergy to "bless" same-sex unions.[152]

---

148 I.e. Presbyterian.

149 Scottish Executive, *Analysis of Religion in the 2001 Census: Summary Report* (2005) table 1.1, at 6 (available at *http://www.scotland.gov.uk/Publications/2005/02/20757/53568*).

150 I.e. "Anglican", "Presbyterian", "Methodist", "Lutheran", etc.

151 Pew Institute for Religion and Public Policy, *US Religious Landscape Survey*(2008) App 1 at 98 (available at *http://religions.pewforum.org/*).

152 In May 2006, the General Assembly of the Church of Scotland approved a policy according to which "a minister or deacon who conducts any service marking a civil partnership does not commit a disciplinary offence" (R Nowell, "Church of Scotland approves blessing gay unions", *Presbyterian News Service*, 26 May 2006, at *http://www.pcusa.org/pcnews/2006/06289.htm*). Though this policy never took effect, due to its later having been voted down by the majority of presbyteries (M Mackay, "Church of Scotland Presbyteries overwhelmingly reject same-sex blessings", *Christian Today*, 11 December 2006, at *http://www.forwardtogether.org.uk/20061211christiantoday.pdf*), the proponents of the policy, who have not left the church, continue to agitate for its adoption (M Mackay, "Division after new Kirk Moderator promises fight for gay blessings", *Christian Today*, 20 November 2006, at *http://www.christiantoday.com/article/division.after.new.kirk.moderator.promises.fight.for.gay.blessings/8391.htm*).

Further, one suspects that the typical member of the Church of Scotland, unlike, say, the typical Scottish Roman Catholic, subscribes to the Enlightenment notion that religious arguments should for the most part be kept out of the "public square". Let us compare the Louisiana figures. In Louisiana, the overwhelming majority of self-described Christians identify themselves as Evangelical Protestants, Roman Catholics, or adherents of various Protestant African-American denominations. For the most part, these groups, in contrast to the Church of Scotland, still subscribe to a very "traditional" or "conservative" moral theology – one that, for example, condemns homosexual relations without qualification.[153] Moreover, these groups are notorious for *not* keeping their religious convictions "private".

With regard to rates of active church participation the contrast between the two jurisdictions is truly astonishing. Only 11% of Scots "regularly" attend church, according to a recent study conducted by the Church of Scotland.[154] But according to a recent Gallup poll, a full 58% of Louisianans attend church "nearly every week" if not "every week".[155]

These data show not only that Louisiana is still far less secularised than Scotland, but also – and this is the truly important point – that it is not really all that secular (not yet). And so, one is forced to consider whether there might not be some other explanation, aside from the secularisation thesis, for the developments in Louisiana's law of impediments to marriage that I earlier attributed to secularisation.

These alternatives are not difficult to come by. Consider, first, the developments that concerned the impediment of relationship (elimination of "spiritual" relativity; scaling back of the degrees of relationship). Such developments might be explained not by reference to the ascendancy of Enlightenment thinking over Christian thinking but rather by reference to the dramatic increase in the ratio of Protestants to Catholics in Louisiana during the American period. Moreover, the developments concerning the impediment of difference of race might be explained on the theory that what ultimately triumphed was not Enlightenment notions of "equality and liberty", but

153   For Roman Catholicism, see Catechism of the Catholic Church no 2357 (1994) ("Basing itself on Sacred Scripture, which presents homosexual acts as acts of grave depravity, tradition has always declared that 'homosexual acts are intrinsically disordered'."). For conservative Evangelical Protestantism, see, e.g., Southern Baptist Convention, Resolution, *On the California Supreme Court Decision to Allow Same-Sex Marriage* (2008) ("Any action giving homosexual unions the legal status of marriage denies the fundamental immorality of homosexual behavior.").

154   A Clark, "Churches defend Scotland's level of faith", *Christian Today*, 14 October 2004, at *http://www.christiantoday.com/article/churches.defend.scotlands.level.of.faith/1569.htm*.

155   F Newport, "Church attendance lowest in New England, highest in South", *Gallup News Service*, 26 April 2006.

rather Christian notions of "equality and brotherly love", as exemplified in the teachings and practices of the African-American Protestant leader Martin Luther King, Jr and the Evangelical Protestant leader Billy Graham.

In raising these questions about the viability of the secularisation thesis as applied to Louisiana, I do not mean to suggest that the thesis explains *nothing* at all. On the contrary, I believe that the thesis explains or at least helps to explain at least some of those developments: the Louisiana of today is certainly more secular than the Louisiana of a century ago. My point, rather, is simply that, in the case of Louisiana, secularisation may not have been the only, or the most important, force at work.[156]

(b) Differences

With respect to the *differences* between Scotland and Louisiana in terms of the historical evolution of the law of impediments to marriage, explanations not surprisingly vary from difference to difference. Let me consider these differences one after the other.

That Scotland has retained the impediment of impotence strikes me as anomalous. Perhaps the best explanation for it is simply political "inertia":

156 One might argue, as some have argued, that there is still "something else" at work in Louisiana, at least insofar as continued support for the same-sex impediment is concerned, namely, "homophobia", that is, an irrational fear of or hatred toward homosexuals. See, e.g., K McK Norrie, "The legal regulation of adult domestic relationships" (ch 6 above). There is certainly some merit to this contention. In many cultures and for many years, including in western culture at least since the Roman era, many people have had this fear or have harboured this hatred. The same has been and still is true in Louisiana. Though homophobia is, then, undoubtedly "a" factor in Louisiana's opposition to same-sex marriage, it would be a serious mistake to conclude that it is "the" factor or, for that matter, even "the most important" factor. My judgment rests on two considerations. First, homophobia is notoriously difficult to measure. Until sociologists figure out how to measure this phenomenon and conduct the appropriate studies, we can only guess how many Louisianans oppose same-sex marriage because they are homophobic, rather than for some other reason, e.g., genuine religious conviction that same-sex unions are immoral, or genuine concern that permitting same-sex marriages would harm the institution of marriage itself and, in so doing, interfere with its important social functions. Second, my own experience causes me to question whether homophobia has much to do with the matter. When I have asked opponents of same-sex marriage to explain the "reasons" for their opposition, their answers have *never* been to the effect that homosexuality is distasteful, or of the form "Gays and lesbians make me uncomfortable". Rather, most of the answers given by most of these people have included "religious" arguments of the following form: (1) there is a God; (2) He has communicated His will to us through the Scriptures (the Roman Catholics add "and Tradition"); (3) in those Scriptures He has made it clear that homosexual acts are immoral; (4) inasmuch as marriage is (again, according to Scriptures) an inherently "sexual" relationship, for the polity to extend access to marriage to same-sex couples would, in effect, be for the polity to condone homosexual acts, making the polity an accomplice in that immoral behaviour; and (5) therefore, the polity ought not to extend access to marriage to same-sex couples. It seems to me, then, that if any sort of "phobia" motivates people such as these to oppose same-sex marriage, it is not "homophobia" (fear of homosexuals) but fear of God.

because so few couples were affected by the impediment and because divorce provided an adequate remedy for those few who were, no organised political opposition to the impediment ever took shape.

Though Louisiana's decision to eliminate the impediment of impuberty seems, at least at first glance, to be no less inexplicable than Scotland's decision to retain the impediment of impotence, there may be, in Louisiana's case, some method behind the apparent madness. The problem at which that impediment has historically been aimed is that of "underage marriage", specifically, marriages between persons at least one of whom is still too immature to engage in sexual relations. Now, there is more than one way of dealing with this issue. According to revised Civil Code article 87, "free consent" is required for a valid marriage. Revised Civil Code article 92 provides that "consent" is "not free" when it is given by a person who is "incapable of discernment". Among the examples of persons "incapable of discernment" given in comment (d) to that article is "a person who is too young to understand the consequences of the marriage celebration". Chances are that no one acquires the ability to "understand the consequences of the marriage celebration" until, at the earliest, late adolescence, long after he or she has acquired the capacity to engage in sexual relations. Thus, Louisianans presently use "psychological maturity" as a proxy for "physical maturity".[157]

Regarding the differences between the two jurisdictions' anti-incest impediments, which are quite slight in any case, the explanation is probably that of varying reasonable "judgment calls" with respect to acceptable and unacceptable risks. Consider the differential treatment of matches between consanguinous first cousins. That Louisiana prohibits them while Scotland allows them probably reflects no more than the fact that the Louisiana lawmakers were just slightly more averse to the low risk of birth defects in children of such unions than were their Scottish counterparts. Or, consider the differential treatment of matches between step-parents and step-children. That Scotland prohibits them in some circumstances while Louisiana allows them probably reflects no more than the fact that the Scottish lawmakers were just slightly more averse to the low risk to "family harmony" that such unions pose than were their Louisiana counterparts.

Last, but not least, there are between the two jurisdictions differences in terms of the justifications given for and the tenacity of commitment to retaining the impediment based on "identity of sex". For this difference, an

---

157 Recall that the Scots, after the Reformation, did something similar, that is, used physical maturity as a proxy for psychological maturity. See n 85 above.

explanation is ready at hand: compared to the progress of secularisation in Scotland, that in Louisiana is "way behind".

(3) Projections based on the patterns

Insofar as the development of the law of impediments to marriage is concerned, part of the "what has already happened", is, as we have seen, the march of secularisation. If that phenomenon continues – if, that is, the Enlightenment traditions continue to gain ground against the Christian tradition in both Scotland and Louisiana (though this is not a foregone conclusion, it is nevertheless likely), the "retreat" from the regulation of marriage[158] in both jurisdictions is likely to proceed apace. But as between the two jurisdictions, there will, of course, be different starting points for any such further developments.

In Scotland, where secularisation is already well-advanced, this development might be manifested in any number of respects. I can think of at least four possibilities, which I shall present in what, to my mind, is an order of declining probability. The first is the demise of the impediment of impotence. It will be recalled that the justification for that impediment in canon law was that marriage necessarily presupposes procreation or, at the very least, sex that is "open" to procreation. To many who have an Enlightenment worldview, this justification is no longer compelling, and for the simple reason that the understanding of marriage on which it rests – an understanding that most "Enlightened" people consider to be religious – is no longer compelling. The second possibility is the elimination of the impediment of "identity of sex". True, the ostensibly secular "definitional" defences that have already been mounted in Scotland in support of this impediment – that marriage is "inherently" about a "male and female" relationship and/or "procreation" – may remain persuasive to some. But to others – and, I predict, they will eventually form the majority – these defences will, in time, cease to be compelling. The reason, again, is that, most persons who have an Enlightenment worldview believe that these defences rest on hidden religious premises, premises that, to their minds, can no longer be taken seriously. Evidence for this prediction can be found in the experience of other relatively secular jurisdictions (for example, the Netherlands) that, at first, provided only civil partnerships for same-sex couples, but eventually gave them access to marriage itself. Third, there is the possibility of the further scaling back of the anti-incest impediment. What remains of the prohibition against marriage between

---

158   See Spaht (n 140) 300 ff.

consanguinous relatives can perhaps be justified on the secular ground that such relationships, if they are procreative, may result in children who exhibit a heightened frequency of birth defects. But what about marriages between step-parent and step-child or, for that matter, even marriages between consanguinous relatives that are *not* open to procreation, such as where one or the other party has been sterilised or where the female has passed menopause? Perhaps one could, even then, still justify the prohibition on the secular ground of "preserving family harmony". But for that argument to be persuasive one would have to conclude that the value of "avoiding offence to other close family members" outweighs the value of "permitting each person to marry whomever he wishes", and that is a balance that a child of the Enlightenment – with a love for "individual liberty" – is unlikely to strike. Finally, it is possible that the anti-polygamy impediment will be eliminated or at least curtailed. The obstacle to the realisation of this possibility is the undeniable fact that, at least for this impediment, a powerful "secular" justi-fication remains, namely, that it defends the important Enlightenment value of "equality", as that value concerns women. The defenders of the impedi-ment rightly note that throughout human history the most common form of polygamy has been polygyny and, further, polygyny has always brought with it a kind of "second class" status for women. Nevertheless, in the UK a small, but growing, number of political and religious leaders[159] have recently begun calling for legal recognition of polygamous marriage, at least within those UK subcultures in which such marriage is common practice (e.g., among Muslims). The rationale behind these calls seems to be two-fold. First, there is the practical: since lots of couples are entering into such marriages anyway, the law ought to take care to regulate their effects. Second, there is the theoretical: it is wrong, our Enlightenment traditions teach us, for us to "impose our 'Christian' values", including those that pertain to marriage, on adherents of non-Christian faiths.

If given sufficient time, Louisiana might, on its own, end up taking the same steps with respect to impediments to marriage as I have just predicted Scotland will take (save for that concerning the impediment of "impotence", which Louisiana has already taken). But I doubt whether Louisiana will be given sufficient time. As we have seen, Louisiana is far behind Scotland on the "curve" of secularisation. For Louisiana, without outside interference, to reach the point at which Scotland will shortly find itself might well require decades and decades. Many scholars of United States constitutional law have

---

159 J Petre and A Porter, "Adopt Sharia law in Britain, says Archbishop of Canterbury Dr Rowan Williams", *The Daily Telegraph*, 9 February 2008.

predicted that the United States Supreme Court will before too much longer
end up ruling that prohibitions on same-sex marriage are unconstitutional.[160]
Others have predicted that, once that happens, it will just be a matter of time
before that Court will strike down prohibitions on at least some forms of incestuous marriage and perhaps even prohibitions on polygamous marriage.[161]
If these predictions prove to be correct, then Louisiana will, indeed, end
up opening access to marriage to same-sex couples and, later, to some close
relatives and perhaps even multiple parties, but only under compulsion and
with reluctance, just as Louisiana, a generation ago, gave up its prohibition
on marriage between black and white. What will happen to the opposition
to such marriages after that is anyone's guess. I doubt, however, that such
opposition will ever cease to exist. Further, I feel confident that it will long
remain open and public, unlike opposition to interracial marriage, which, to
the extent it still exists, is now largely kept private. As I have shown, opposition to same-sex, incestuous, and polygamous marriage is deeply rooted in
traditional Christian faith. That was not true of the opposition to interracial
marriage. Now, as secularisation continues its onward march in Louisiana,

160   Consider, e.g., the following remarks of Professor Larry Tribe, noted authority on American
       constitutional law: "The process that might move the Supreme Court from *Lawrence* [*v Texas*]
       to the invalidation of restrictions on same-sex marriage might not be a speedy one. It took the
       Supreme Court thirteen years to move from *Brown v Board of Education* to *Loving v Virginia*,
       and in the interim the Court's silence was deafening. Perhaps that glacial pace was understand-
       able; there is only so far an institution famously lacking both the sword and the purse can push
       without incurring either lawful defiance in the form of a campaign to amend the Constitution
       or unlawful defiance in the form of violent resistance. But setting aside these political consid-
       erations, the principle behind *Loving* now seems clear. Similar arguments resting on fear for
       unit-cohesion and morale were made to keep military units racially separate and to keep women
       in the lower, noncombat ranks. Eventually, the thinness of that rationale became apparent. It is
       hard to imagine that the trajectory of same-sex marriage rights will not follow the same path."
       ("*Lawrence v Texas*: The 'Fundamental Right' that dare not speak its name" (2004) 117 Harvard
       LR 1893 at 1947.) See also M Coles, "*Lawrence v Texas* and the refinement of substantive due
       process" (2005) 16 Stan L & Pol'y Rev 23 at 26 (contending that "*Lawrence*, fairly applied,
       makes the end of the [same-sex] marriage exclusion constitutionally inevitable, unless the Court
       abandons its approach to the protection of implicit rights, or creates an unprincipled excep-
       tion …"); R H Bork, "The necessary amendment", *First Things: A Monthly Journal of Religion
       and Public Life*, August/September 2004, 17 (proposing that the US Constitution be amended
       to define marriage as a relationship between one man and one woman "before our Supreme
       Court has done the inevitable", that is, declared prohibitions on same-sex marriage unconstitu-
       tional).
161   See, e.g., G Dent, "How does same-sex marriage threaten you?" (2007) 59 Rutgers L Rev 233
       at 257 ("In light of the nullification of criminal sodomy laws in *Lawrence v Texas*, laws barring
       polygamy are already constitutionally indefensible. If SSM [same-sex marriage] be recognized,
       it will be impossible in principle not to validate polygamy as well. Endogamy does not yet
       enjoy such support, but it, too, already has some enthusiasts."); see also W N Eskridge and D
       R Spedale, *Gay Marriage: For Better or for Worse? What We've Learned from the Evidence*
       (2006) 24 ("Slippery slope objections have become almost boilerplate in speeches or books that
       oppose same-sex marriage.").

the number of persons who identify with traditional Christianity and/or the number of persons for whom traditional Christianity is authoritative will, of course, fall off, eventually to the point that these persons will lose their "majority" status. But chances are that they will long remain a large and vocal minority.[162] And within this minority, opposition to same-sex, incestuous, and polygamous marriages is unlikely ever to fade away.

---

162 Already the rate of decline in adherence to traditional Christianity in the United States, Louisiana included, has itself declined to a marginal level (see generally Sommerville (n 141), Chaves (n 141)) due, at least in part, to concerted efforts now being made by traditional Christian organisations to keep their traditions alive.

8 Contracts of Intellectual Gratification – A Louisiana-Scotland Creation

Vernon Valentine Palmer

A. INTRODUCTION
B. THE SCOTTISH ADVANCE: SOLATIUM IN DELICT
(1) Introduction
(2) Stair, Erskine and Hume
C. THE DELAYED AWAKENING – SOLATIUM *EX CONTRACTU*
D. LOUISIANA'S CODAL APPROACH – AN ORIGINAL CONTRIBUTION
(1) Introduction
(2) Mistaken translations and doubtful interpretations
E. THE JURISPRUDENCE – SOME HIGHLIGHTS
(1) The *Meador* interpretation and modern interpretation
(2) Code revision in 1985 and later jurisprudence
F. CONCLUSION

A. INTRODUCTION

Numerically at least, the impersonal trades and barters of the marketplace constitute the majority of our contracts. In these we primarily seek lucrative ends and the satisfaction of basic needs. They no doubt affect our pocketbooks more than our minds, though those worlds are never wholly separate. There is, however, a different type of contract that directly envisions the advancement and development of an individual's personality interests. Here the salient reason for contracting is to obtain an intangible nonpecuniary asset that enriches our lives in some way, whether it be peace of mind, intellectual pleasures, peer recognition or perhaps social standing. Such contracts are in effect vessels of self-expression and self-realisation, as when a young artist's works will be exhibited by a prestigious museum,[1] or a music lover

---

1 See the "young architect" example provided in the Unidroit *Principles of International Commer-*

obtains a ticket to hear a renowned artist, or a philanthropist buys an historic property to preserve it from demolition, or a person makes pious donations to comply with a sense of religious duty or inner conscience. Of course contracts primarily affecting the personality need not always seem noble and high-minded. A great number of them are simply embedded in daily life, our calendar, our rites of passage, and so forth. Thus our weddings, burials, gradu-ations, vacations, philanthropy, schooling, seasonal diversions, and reunions are intensely personal and important events in which a host of crucial services and suppliers are involved behind the scenes (caterers, photographers, funeral directors and so forth). These engagements are rife with intangible interests at stake. A breach in the performance may impair some aspect of the promisee's personality interests – affective, social or physical.[2]

As early as 1825 Louisiana's codifiers[3] came to the conclusion that contracts of this kind have "intellectual enjoyment" as their aim and nonpecuniary damages are appropriate upon breach. What the codifiers envisioned was a category that we may call "contracts of intellectual gratification". Here is the original provision:[4]

> Where the contract has for its object the gratification of some intellectual enjoy-ment, whether in religion, morality or taste, or some convenience or other legal gratification, although these are not appreciated in money by the parties, yet damages are due for their breach; a contract for a religious or charitable founda-tion, a promise of marriage, or an engagement for a work of some of the fine arts, are objects and examples of this rule.

In modern times, a parallel doctrine has been recognised in Scotland. Under Scots (and English) case law arising in the 1970s, nonpecuniary losses or mental distress could be awarded for breach of contract whenever "a major or important object of the contract is to give pleasure, relaxation or peace of mind".[5] The description of the contract's nature in Scotland is somewhat

---

cial Contracts art 7.4.2 (illustration 6) wherein an award of nonpecuniary damages is approved for international commercial transactions.

2 See E Reid, "Protection for rights of personality in Scots Law: A comparative evaluation" (2007) 11(4) EJCL (at *http://www.ejcl.org/114/art114-1.pdf*); A Bucher, *Personnes physiques et protec-tion de la personnalité* (1985) 125-127; J Carbonnier, *Droit civil*, vol 1, *Les personnes*, 17th edn (2000) 147-148, 163-164; A Popovici, "Personality rights – A Civil Law concept" (2004) 50 Loy L Rev 349; S Strömholm, *Right of Privacy and Rights of Personality: Comparative Survey* (1967).

3 The three jurisconsults were Louis Moreau-Lislet, Pierre Derbigny and Edward Livingston. There has been debate concerning which parts of the Code each was primarily responsible for. See V V Palmer, *The Louisiana Civilian Experience* (2005) 63-65. It is usually said that Edward Livingston had responsibility for the contractual provisions in Book III.

4 La Civ Code art 1928, § 3 (1825). The provision was revised in 1985. See art 1998 (1985), set forth infra at 228.

5 *Farley v Skinner* [2002] 2 AC 732 per Lord Steyn at para 24.

differently worded than the text in the Louisiana Civil Code, and yet the exceptional category that each system has in mind is essentially the same and has given rise to quite comparable results.

For example, on the basis of the 1825 code provision Louisiana courts awarded immaterial damages when a millinery establishment failed to deliver trousseau dresses in time for a wedding,[6] when a telegraph company failed to deliver a message warning of a son's grave illness and approaching death,[7] when a contractor failed to construct a uniquely-configured swimming pool to fit the dimensions of promisee's yard,[8] when an "elegant and commanding marble fireplace" was defectively installed,[9] and when a couple's "dream house" turned out to be their *cauchemar*.[10] On the other hand, in Scotland and the United Kingdom a bride received solatium for a photographer's breach of his agreement to take photos of her wedding ceremony;[11] a vacationer was awarded immaterial damages for disappointment and distress when his Alpine holiday was ruined;[12] a homeowner was awarded damages when his swimming pool was built to the wrong depth, though the mistake had no effect upon the market value of his property;[13] and a purchaser who sought to buy a gracious home in a quiet setting was awarded immaterial damages where the surveyor's report failed to note the constant noise intrusion from airplane traffic overhead.[14] It appears that substantially the same principles, reasoning and results occur in Scotland and Louisiana.

Moral damages may strike some as an ephemeral, second-rate remedy, but it is indispensable to the enforcement of this type of agreement. One reason for this is that an action for specific performance (or specific implement in Scotland) may simply be unavailable or impracticable, even when the action is favoured by legal tradition.[15] Specific performance is sometimes moot

---

6 *Lewis v D H Holmes* 34 So 66 (La 1903). See also *Garther v Tipery Studios, Inc* 334 So 2d 758 (La App 4th Cir 1976) (shoddy wedding photos) and *Mitchell v Shreveport Laundries, Inc* 61 So 2d 539 (La App 1952) (suit not cleaned by wedding day).

7 *Graham v Western Union Tel Co* 109 La 1070 (La 1903).

8 *CLB Enterprises v Kittok* 575 So 2d 834 (La App 5th Cir 1991).

9 *B & B Cut Stone Co, Inc v Resneck* 465 So 2d 851 (La App 2nd Cir 1985).

10 *Thomas v Desire Community Housing Corp* 773 So 2d 755 (La App 2000).

11 *Diesen v Samson* 1971 SLT (Sh Ct) 49.

12 *Jarvis v Swan's Tours Ltd* [1973] 1 QB 233; also *Jackson v Horizon Holidays* [1975] 1 WLR 1468; [1975] 3 All ER 92.

13 *Ruxley Electronics Ltd v Forsyth* [1996] AC 344.

14 *Farley v Skinner* (n 5 above).

15 In Scotland, specific implement is considered the pursuer's "right". See L Macgregor, "Specific implement in Scots law", in J Smits, D Haas and G Hesen (eds), *Specific Performance in Contract Law: National and Other Perspectives* (2008) 67. In Louisiana specific performance is also in theory considered the primary contractual remedy, and treated by the Code as a "right" at least in particular circumstances, though the right is defeasible if the remedy is "impracticable".

even though the performance is technically "possible". Once the moment for the delivery of a wedding dress or a telegram has arrived and been lost, or a vacation has already been ruined, the remedy is of no use. A related problem is that the type of engagement (for example that of a portraitist) may involve obligations "to do" that are considered "strictly personal" and may not be assigned, inherited or compelled.[16] In addition, the value of the performance to the promisee is typically idiosyncratic and there is no substitute in the market.[17] Consequently a legal system prepared only to repair the actual pecuniary loss caused by a breach of contract appears to be offering incomplete justice. No pecuniary damage may have resulted, yet the plaintiff has not received the essential benefit he paid for. An award of nonpecuniary damages, if allowed, is perhaps the only means of expressing or redressing the plaintiff's intangible loss. But such relief is not allowed everywhere. In some legal systems it is altogether barred in contract. In Louisiana and Scotland it is confined to the contracts of intellectual gratification.

Louisiana and Scotland are mixed systems, and the action for solatium *ex contractu* must face the crosscurrents and headwinds within the dual traditions. Arguments and attitudes both pro and con have affected its progress and shaped its journey. One persistent objection is that the action introduces an unacceptable degree of uncertainty into the law of contract. It is said that contracting parties cannot foresee when mental distress will result from a breach, and it is impossible to measure this kind of harm, much less determine if the claim is genuine.[18] The alleged imprecision and uncertainty of the damage is urged as a foundation for barring recovery altogether or permitting it only exceptionally.[19] Maintaining amount certainty (which is perhaps a prime value in a system that began by enforcing bargains, not promises) seems to be a core policy, even if it is obscured in the technical grammar of "unforeseeability" and "remoteness of damage".[20] There are, however, Civil

---

See art 1986. Nevertheless, the remedy is not fully buttressed by robust injunctive relief. See *J Weingarten Inc v Northgate Mall* 404 So 2d 896 (La 1981).

16 It may be a "strictly personal" obligation on the part of the obligee and the obligor. See La Civ Code art 1766.

17 J Tomain, "Contract compensation in nonmarket transactions" (1985) 46 U Pitt L Rev 867.

18 See H McGregor, *McGregor on Damages*, 17th edn (2003) § 1838; J Lewis, "Can damages buy you happiness? Damages for distress after *Farley v Skinner*" (2008) 19 *King's Law Journal* 113 at 130. The alleged unpredictability and unforeseeability of moral damages may make them disfavoured by proponents of the theory of efficient breach of contract. P S Atiyah claimed "All such damage awards could be multiplied or divided by two overnight and they would be just as defensible or indefensible as they are today." *Accidents, Compensation and the Law*, 7th edn (2006) 162.

19 See *Restatement Second of Contract* § 353; Aggravated, Exemplary and Restitutionary Damages (Law Com No 247, 1997) paras 1.26-1.39.

20 Even so, it is difficult to explain how foreseeability should operate in contractual situations where

Law systems that award moral damages without distinction as to whether the claim originates in contract or tort, and without making recourse to the foreseeability principle as a limitation on recovery.[21] Thus the headwind from one tradition may be compared to the smoother seas in another.

A second objection is that to allow recoveries for nonpecuniary losses in contract may unleash a floodgate of liability. The fear is that claims of distress, or even mere vexation, might become routine appendages in pleadings, thus submerging the courts in litigation. This version of the floodgates argument is clearly borrowed from the law of tort where it has considerable appeal in Anglo-Saxon legal cultures.[22] Some judges, as if bracing for an impending deluge, adopt the stoical position that contract breaking must simply be accepted as an ordinary risk of commercial life "which players in the game are expected to meet with mental fortitude".[23] In Civilian systems permitting the award of moral damages more freely we would probably hear no mention of the floodgates.

A third objection to the action (and the list is by no means exhaustive) reveals a difference of perspective about the nature of nonpecuniary damages. Common Lawyers frequently think of moral damages as a form of punitive damages. This conflation is historically embedded and has produced a tendency to see damages in binary terms – as either compensatory or punitive, with "compensation" taken to mean patrimonial loss only. It has been said that "the very idea of punishment is anathema to the law of contract", but "punishment" may cover anything that is not "compensation".[24] Under a crude "compensate or punish" approach, non-patrimonial loss will normally be unrecoverable.[25] In contrast, the Civil Law tradition tends to say

the advancement of a nonpecuniary interest is the main objective of the contract. In that event the nonpecuniary loss resulting from breach is inevitably something more than merely a "foreseen" consequence of the breach. It is the inherent consequence of the breach.

21 Reliance will be placed upon "certainty" of proof, rather than "foreseeability" or remoteness.

22 For the three strands of the floodgates argument and its variable influence within certain legal cultures, see M Bussani and V V Palmer, "The notion of pure economic loss and its setting", in M Bussani and V V Palmer (eds), *Pure Economic Loss in Europe* (2003) 3 at 16-20.

23 *Johnson v Gore Wood & Co* [2002] 2 AC 1 per Lord Cooke at 49. American judges have sometimes urged a stiff upper lip as well: "Life in the competitive world has at least equal capacity to bestow ruin as benefit, and if is presumed that those who enter this world do so willingly ... Absent clear evidence to the contrary we will not presume that the parties to a contract such as the one before us meant to insure each other's emotional tranquility." *Hatfield v Max Rouse & Sons Northwest* 606 P 2d 944 (1980) per McFadden J at 952.

24 P-W Lee, "Contract damages, corrective justice and punishment" (2007) 70 MLR 887.

25 The equation of nonpecuniary loss with punishment is embedded in the House of Lords decision in *Addis v Gramophone Co Ltd* [1909] AC 488 (usually regarded as the leading English authority against the award of "punitive" damages in contract). See particularly Mummery LJ's account in the Court of Appeal in *Farley v Skinner* of the policy considerations against moral damages: [2000] PNLR 441 paras 32-35, rev'd [2002] 2 AC 732. To some extent Louisiana and Scottish

that moral damages are compensatory by nature and punitive damages have no legitimacy in private law, including the law of contract. They compensate for a loss to a protected personality interest. This difference in perspective is not merely semantic. It derives in part from the more comprehensive development of personality rights on the continent where nonpecuniary awards are viewed as standard means of protection.

On this subject, therefore, the two traditions have not pulled in the same direction, and it may not be happenstance that Louisiana and Scotland developed an approach that lies approximately midway along the spectrum. A scan of the legal horizon reveals three models. On the one extreme are systems, such as the South African, that permit no recovery of solatium in actions for breach of contract. Rights of personality must be vindicated delictually under the aegis of the *actio iniuriarum* and the Aquilian action. An action for immaterial harm *ex contractu* is categorically excluded unless the contract itself contains a liquidated damages clause to protect that interest.[26] On the opposite extreme is the laissez-faire approach in jurisdictions such as France and Quebec. Here moral damages are freely available in contract, as in tort.[27]

jurists have resisted this influence but they have not completely escaped it. In a 1981 meeting of the Council of the La Law Institute, the Council rejected a recommendation to extend the availability of nonpecuniary damages to all kinds of contracts, partly in fear, it was said, of opening the door to punitive damage awards. See June Minutes at 6, 8-11. For a summary of nineteenth-century attitudes, see *Dirnmeyer v O'Hern* 39 La Ann 961 (La 1887) and *Underwood v Gulf Refining Co of Louisiana* 128 La 968 (1911). See also *Black v Carrollton R R Co* 10 La Ann 33 (La 1855) (Ogden J concurring). In Scotland this influence is sometimes seen in decisions such as *Hogg v Gow* 27 May 1812 FC, especially the opinion of Lord Justice Clerk Boyle, and even in the *European Code of Contract* (revised English text by H McGregor in (2004) 8 EdinLR (special issue). Regarding the unrecoverability of such damages in American contract law, see UCC s 106; *Williston on Contracts*, 3rd edn (1968) s 1340; *Corbin on Contracts*, (interim edn 2002) vol 11, s 1077.

26 See *Administrator, Natal v Edouard* 1990 (3) SA 581 discussed in E Clive and D Hutchison, "Breach of contract", in Zimmermann, Visser, and Reid, *Mixed Legal Systems* 176 at 186; also in K McK Norrie, "Wrongful birth in South African law" (1991) 40 ICLQ 442. Originally the German Civil Code also took a restrictive position on the recovery of nonpecuniary damage ex contractu. The BGB provided that nonpecuniary harm should be granted only in cases expressly provided by law (§ 253). Such recovery was exceptionally permitted under the rules of tort (§ 847) but nothing was provided under the rules of contract. See H Koch, "The law of torts", in M Reimann and J Zekoll (eds), *Introduction to German Law*, 2nd edn (2005) 210. Under the revised German law of obligations (2002), the texts have been slightly liberalised, but the effect may not be significant in terms of relaxing the barrier in contract. A redrafted § 252.2 states that nonpecuniary loss is compensatable in any case of "injury to body, health, freedom and sexual self-determination". See U Magnus, "The reform of German tort law", *Indret* Working Paper no 127 (2003) 5 (*http://www.indret.com/pdf/127_en.pdf*). The implication is that such recovery is no longer tied exclusively to the law of torts or the fault principle.

27 The Quebec Civil Code regards moral damage as a matter of contractual compensation. Under art 1458, "he is liable for any bodily, moral or material injury he causes to the other contracting party". According to Baudouin, the scope of compensation is therefore the same both contractually and extracontractually. J-L Baudouin and P Deslauriers, *La responsabilité civile*, 6th edn

No categorical exclusion is recognised since the harm caused by the violation of a contract is considered identical to the harm suffered by the commission of a delict.[28] There is no restriction concerning the type of contract or the nature of *l'objet* of the obligation and therefore no exceptional niche has been carved out for noncommercial contracts intimately connected to personality interests. Indeed the range of cases in which nonpecuniary loss is recoverable in France has been continuously extended by what some writers regard, and frequently deplore, as "the inflation" of rights to personality and "the absorption" of the law of obligations by personality rights.[29] Even inconvenience, vexation and worry resulting from the breach of an ordinary commercial contract may be compensated.[30]

The moderate approach of Louisiana and Scotland falls somewhere between these extremes. The two jurisdictions have reached, by different paths and different chronology, a position "in the centre". This may strike the reader as a puzzling case of "convergence without communication", for there is no sign of reciprocal influence or borrowing from one another. This could be a case of spontaneous co-invention, shaped by common problems and mixed-jurisdiction similarities, but we also know that legal ideas travel by intriguing and mysterious channels, and certainly we do have not access to them all. In the absence of connecting evidence, my paper cannot reach a conclusion on this broader question. My aim, necessarily more modest, is to explore and analyse the comparative history and development of this interesting subject on both sides of the Atlantic and draw attention to the role that contracts of intellectual gratification play in the protection of personality interests.

B. THE SCOTTISH ADVANCE: SOLATIUM IN DELICT

(1) Introduction

Theodore Sedgwick, an American author, produced in 1847 a rather panoramic study of the Common and Civil Law on the subject of damages. The work attracted a wide audience in the United States, and to a surprising

---

(2003) s 1326 at 875. Tancelin, however, takes a dim view of moral damage in Quebec. According to him it plays a secondary, marginal role. M Tancelin, *Des obligations: contrat et responsabilité*, 4th edn (1988) s 555 at 337.

28 P Malaurie and L Aynès, *Cours de droit civil: Les obligations*, 6th edn (1995) 480. The notion of "unity of harm" is grounded upon the general principle of *réparation intégrale* (art 1149) which is thought to be the same goal in both tort and contract.

29 X Pradel et al, *Le préjudice dans le droit civil de la responsabilité* (2004) 123 ff.

30 See, e.g., Cour de Cass 3ème, 15.02.1972, Bull III, no 102.

degree, it was frequently used and cited by the Civilians in Louisiana. The influence on Louisiana is especially ironic because Sedgwick, at least in his first edition, completely ignored the Civil Law of Louisiana and was unaware of the important contribution the Louisiana Civil Code had made to his subject.[31] His comparative law interest was indeed cosmopolitan – but entirely offshore. In addition to canvassing Civilian writers such as Domat, Pothier, Toullier, Du Moulin, Merlin and others, Sedgwick studied Scots law closely and made numerous references to its writers and cases. In a sense his book would have been a connecting bridge between Scots and Louisiana lawyers seeking answers to questions about damages. Louisiana lawyers cited the work to show that Lord Kames called Pothier's rule on consequential damages "resulting damage";[32] and to show that Scots law granted "solatium" for mere affronts and injurious words.[33] Yet the book did not unite audiences in the two mixed jurisdictions, because Sedgwick neglected Louisiana law entirely, and an early opportunity for a fruitful exchange between the mixed systems was missed.

Sedgwick certainly did not disguise his admiration for Scots law:[34] "The Scotch law", he wrote, "is the only one, so far as I am aware, which has endeavored practically to analyze the elements of injury. By the jurisprudence of Scotland, in actions for personal torts, the damages are divided into special damages, the actual pecuniary loss, and solatium, solace or recompense for the wounded feelings." He understood solatium in the context of delict, and it was not viewed as a penalty or a form of exemplary damages. He did not suggest that it might be awarded in contract actions, and in this he correctly appreciated the law at that time. With the possible exception of a promise of marriage, neither Scots nor Anglo-American law in the mid-nineteenth century had extended nonpecuniary damage into that realm.

In praising Scots law for its clear analysis, Sedgwick argued that Scots law had made an advance on other systems. Apparently pain and suffering (incidental to personal injury claims) and reparation for verbal insults came

---

31 See T Sedgwick, *A Treatise on the Measure of Damages, Or, An Inquiry into the Principles which Govern the Amount of Compensation Recovered in Suits at Law* (1847, reprint Arno Press 1972). The work was cited about a dozen times by court or counsel in the first ten years after publication, and in subsequent years more than 100 times. While the 1847 edition failed to mention Louisiana law, the 1852 edition quoted, in footnote and with little discussion, the text of art 1928. The text dryly commented, "Louisiana is the only State, I believe, in the Union where an effort has been made to reduce the subject of damages to statutory limits." 2nd edn (1852) 208-209.

32 *Goodloe v Rodgers* 10 La Ann (La 1855), citing Lord Kains [sic], *Principles of Equity*.

33 *Daly v Van Benthuysen* 3 La Ann 69 (La 1848).

34 *Treatise on the Measure of Damages* (1847) 36.

into the Scottish system at an earlier date (in the period 1750-1800)[35] than in England or the United States, thus making Scots law appear precocious, at least by English standards where even pain and suffering accompanying physical injury did not become actionable until around the mid-nineteenth century.[36] It did not, however, extend into contractual actions. Many Civilian writers disapproved of this, and any gravitational influence from English law argued against it as well. The wheels of Scots contract law turned very slowly and there was no development until the next century.

(2) Stair, Erskine and Hume

Writing in the late seventeenth century Stair divided the subject of damages by the various interests that were to be protected. There were four interests outlined in his scheme: (1) life, members, and health; (2) liberty; (3) fame, reputation and honour; and (4) content, delight or satisfaction.[37] If we pass over for a moment his first grouping, which deals primarily with physical interests, the remaining interests would seem to have in common an intangible quality, namely fame, honour, reputation, content, delight and satisfaction, whose protection, one might think, could require awards of nonpecuniary damages. Yet Stair does not mention solatium in his *Institutions*, and one may well wonder by what means he expected these interests to be protected. In part the answer seems to be that he circumvented the issue and had no need of the concept because he already accepted *pretium affectionis* as the measure of patrimonial loss. He was prepared to measure patrimonial loss, on oath, by the "singular affection to, or our opinion of, the value or worth of anything that owners have". This subjectivised account of recovery recognised that "the special affection and opinion of the owner is a piece of his interest and enjoyment". This method was broad enough to incorporate nonpecuniary damages without ever creating a distinct category. It is tempting to argue from the placement of these remarks that Stair was thinking primarily delict-ually rather than contractually, for his discussion of *pretium affectionis* occurs within title 9 of book 1: "Reparation … Delinquences and Damages Thence

---

35 See J Blackie (n 39 below). By 1751 Bankton mentions solatium in the context of personal injury: *Inst* 1.10.35.

36 The recovery of pain and suffering in England began perhaps not sooner than the 1840s. W R Cornish and G de N Clark, *Law and Society in England 1750-1950* (1989) 493. As late as 1862 an English judge said, "In my personal judgment, it is an unmanly thing to make such a claim." *Theobald v Ry Passengers Assurance Co* (1854) 15 Jur 583 per Pollock CB at 586. Compare J O'Connell and R J Bailey, "Payment for pain and suffering: Who wants what, when and why" (1972) *University of Illinois Law Forum* 1 at 87, stating that such awards in England and the United States were not explicitly recognised before the *late* eighteenth century.

37 *Inst* 1.9.4.

Arising". Nevertheless, it is clear from title 10, "Obligations Conventional", that his conception of patrimonial loss applied to both delict and contract.[38] Arguably, a sharp divide between contractual and delictual damages was not a feature of his thought. Still, an explicit conception of solatium appears to be missing.

To judge by Erskine's *Institute*, written in 1754, solatium had not yet entered the vocabulary of Scots lawyers. Erskine's treatment in fact took little notice of nonpecuniary interests of any kind.[39] In treating "delinquency" he thought of damages in pecuniary terms – it is "Everything by which a man's estate is lessened". He dismissed the Stair's notion of *pretium affectionis* because it was too subjective: "All are agreed, that the extent of the damage, where the delinquency is not attended with fraud, ought to be estimated by its real worth, and not by the pretium affectionis, or imaginary loss that the sufferer is pleased to set upon it: agreeably to the rule of the lex Aquilia."[40] Given this view of delictual damage, it seems relatively certain that he gave no place to nonpecuniary awards in the field of contract.[41] Even in discussing seduction and promise of marriage, Erskine made no mention of awards for suffering, distress or anguish. To the contrary a deserted fiancée was deprived of this recovery because of "our close adherence to the rule, Matrimonia debent esse libera".[42] A telling sign of the state of development, assythment was still anchored in the law of crime and was not even a civil action at that time. Erskine observed, "No instances are to be found upon record, of recovering an assythment in a judicial way".[43]

By the time of Hume's *Lectures*, delivered in 1821-1822, there has been substantial movement. Solatium had gained a firm footing, being frequently employed as a synonym for nonpecuniary awards in delict. Obviously in the seventy-five years following Erskine's first edition, the Scots law of delict had made strides in enlarging the protected interests. As Hume put it:[44]

> The law is not content with thus protecting individuals from what may endanger them in their persons, or their patrimonial concerns. It further attempts to guard their character in all points of morality, where an attack upon it might disturb their

---

38 Inst 1.10.14 (reparation for breach of permutative contracts is *secondum pretium affectionis*).
39 According to John Blackie, solatium as a distinct element of the claim was not available until the 1760s: see "Defamation", in Reid and Zimmermann, *History*, vol 2, 633 at 676.
40 Bankton said as well that estimations of damage by party oath in litem were not the law of Scotland: *Inst* 1.10.28.
41 *Inst* 3.3.86.
42 *Inst* 1.6.3. Today actions for breach of promise of marriage are statutorily barred. Law Reform (Husband and Wife) (Scotland) Act 1984 s 1(1).
43 *Inst* 4.4.105.
44 *Lectures*, vol 3, 136-137.

peace, – or hurt their enjoyment of life, – or materially lessen their estimation, or usefulness, their consideration in their circle of society.

Hume now referred to solatium in a range of contexts. A tradesman who has been assaulted and disabled from working at his trade, in addition to recovering his patrimonial damage and the expense of his cure, could claim a sum of money in solatium for his pain and distress: "He has, I say, as good a right to this, as the Procurator Fiscal has to a fine to His Majesty's use." A husband could receive solatium for the seduction of his wife.[45] It was also available for damage to reputation in actions for scandal and for wounded feeling due to insults and affronts.

Interestingly moral damage for insult was considered a new development in Hume's day ("in our later practice … a thing of latter introduction"), the judicial precedents dating only from the early nineteenth century.[46] Assythment, an ancient feature of the criminal law, had been transposed into an ordinary civil action. Hume called it the money given to the widow or child "in solatium partly of their patrimonial loss, and partly of their grief and distress on the occasion".[47]

When Hume turned the discussion to actions based on negligence, however, his account became somewhat tentative, and understandably so. Around the time of his *Lectures* liability for accidental wrongful death and injuries was only beginning to include the recovery of immaterial loss.[48] In a series of cases in the years 1795-1812, however, the Court of Session engrafted the old action for assythment upon the Aquilian action. This now permitted the close relatives of a decedent who was negligently killed to recover for lost economic support, as well as for their suffering and grief.[49]

Thus by the early nineteenth century the patrimonial and non-patrimonial elements were finally blended into a workable action called *solatium*. It comprehensively referred to both pecuniary and nonpecuniary loss and yet did not require animus or mens rea for the recovery of nonpecuniary

---

45 *Lectures*, vol 3, 131.

46 *Lectures*, vol 3, 155-156.

47 A comparable position was reached two centuries earlier in the Netherlands. For Grotius's position in the *Inleidinge* (1620), 3.34.2, see R Feenstra, "Réparation du dommage et prix de la douleur chez les auteurs du droit savant, du droit naturel et du droit romano-hollandais", in B Durand, J Poirier, and J-P Royer (eds), *La douleur et le droit* (1997) 411 at 418-422. See also Voet, vol 2, 9.2.11 (according to custom an assessment for scarring, pain and disfigurement is recoverable).

48 See H MacQueen and W D H Sellar, "Negligence", in Reid and Zimmermann, *History*, vol 2, 517 at 526 ff.

49 See *Gardner v Ferguson* (1795) (unreported) Hume, *Session Papers*, vol 87 no 97; *Innes v Magistrates of Edinburgh* (1798) Mor 13189 and 13967; *Blacks v Cadell* 9 February 1804 FC, (1804) Mor 13905; (1812) 5 Pat App 567; *Brown and Children v Macgregor* 26 February 1813 FC. See also *Dow v Brown and Co* (1844) 6 D 534; *Greenhorn v Addie* (1855) 17 D 860.

harm. In effect the merger created a composite that simultaneously eased the limitations on the Aquilian action (only pecuniary loss covered) and on the *actio iniuriarum* (animus required) and lifted the criminal law restrictions (mens rea) on the customary law of assythment. Some terminological confusion attended its birth. A leading judge[50] erroneously christened it "an actio injuriarum" which, as Robert Black has shown, it could not possibly have been.[51] It was not the classic *actio iniuriarum* as understood by the Scots writers of the previous century.[52] It was more accurately a transformed assythment stripped of ancient criminal law connotations and assimilated to the Aquilian action.

It was apparently on the basis of this achievement that Sedgwick thought Scots law was more advanced than other systems he had studied. And the epilogue was that solatium continued to flourish in the Scottish law of delict, but in contract it slumbered on for more than 100 years.[53] Only in the late twentieth century was there an awakening.

C. THE DELAYED AWAKENING – RECOGNISING SOLATIUM *EX CONTRACTU*

The exceptional category ... is not the product of Victorian contract theory but the result of evolutionary developments in case law from the 1970s. (Lord Steyn.)[54]

Down to the 1970s, Scots law was dominated – if not immobilised – by the authority of the House of Lords decision in *Addis v Gramophone Co* in 1909.[55] Though an English appeal, *Addis* was typically treated as the law in both Scotland and England. In that case an employee was wrongfully dismissed by his employer in a harsh and humiliating manner. The jury awarded him £600 on this account alone. On appeal to the House of Lords, however, the

---

50 *Eisten v North British Railway Co* (1870) 8 M 980 per Lord President Inglis at 983-984.

51 "The fact that solatium was not competent under the lex Aquilia blinded them to the fact that it was the true basis of the Scottish action, and that the element of solatium was a native customary law accretion on the Roman law governing damnum injuria datum." R Black, "A historical survey of delictual liability in scotland for personal injuries and death" (1975) 8 CILSA 46 at 50, 189 at 195 (n 31).

52 Cf Lord Kames in *Graeme and Skene v Cunningham* (1765) Mor 13923.

53 *Lockhart v Cunninghame* (1870) 8 SLR 151 might be regarded an isolated exception to this statement, but the court did not speak of solatium in fashioning relief (breach in selling and not returning pursuer's favourite chestnut mare – *pretium affectionis* allowed to cover the pursuer's feelings). The court's approach resembled that taken by Stair. See n 37 above and text thereafter.

54 *Farley v Skinner* (n 5 above).

55 [1909] AC 488. Even today writers on Scots law carefully qualify their views because *Addis* has never been overruled.

claim was disallowed, stressing the necessity of maintaining a high wall of separation between contract and tort remedies. They rejected any use of "exemplary damages" (as an award of solatium was conceived) in an action based on breach of contract.

Lord Atkinson noted there were three narrow exceptions to the policy prohibiting this recovery, and said he was unwilling to create a fourth.[56] The principal objection was that if nonpecuniary damages were recoverable in contract, it would lead to confusion and uncertainty in commercial affairs. Motives, he argued, are properly taken into account in aggregating or mitigating damages in tort, and they might be allowed where there is concurrent tort liability as in a breach of contract attended by malice, fraud, defamation or violence. But once the action is brought in contract, then the motives or intentions behind the breach are irrelevant. Common debts were not to be lessened or increased because a creditor is "harsh, grasping or pitiless" or because the debtor failed to perform due to personal misfortune. Amount certainty and objective calculation were primary values. The creditor is to be paid what he would have received under the contract, neither more nor less.[57] This categorical exclusion of the claim obviated any need to use the test of "foreseeability", namely whether the plaintiff's humiliation or mental distress resulting from the breach was within the parties' contemplation at the time of the contract. Insult to feelings was apparently not actionable even if it was a "foreseeable" consequence of reprehensible conduct.

After *Addis* the question for the future was whether any new exceptions or distinctions could be admitted to undermine or circumvent the basis of this reasoning. The case that led the way arose in Scotland in 1971.

In *Diesen v Samson*[58] a professional photographer was engaged to take photographs of the pursuer's wedding, but he forgot all about the engagement and did not appear at the church. The bride was distressed by the loss of a pictorial record of her marriage. According to the Sheriff-Substitute, "the real issue in the case is whether it can ever be proper for a court to award damages for injury to feelings resulting from breach of contract".[59] Noting that Scottish writers frequently cited the case of *Addis*, he observed, "It would seem that the law of Scotland is the same as the law of England on the subject, and that English textbooks may be of assistance." He then quoted

---

56 At 495. These were actions against a banker for refusal to pay a customer's cheque; actions for breach of promise of marriage; and actions where a vendor of land fails to provide good title.
57 At 496.
58 1971 SLT 49. *Diesen* has been credited with starting the trend in English law. See D Harris, A Ogus and J Phillips, "Contract remedies and the consumer surplus" (1979) 95 LQR 581.
59 At 49.

at length a key passage in the leading English treatise on damages, *Mayne and McGregor on Damages* (in its twelfth edition of 1961) wherein it was argued that an exception to the rule in *Addis* should be made when a contract was not of a commercial nature and when the parties had damages for mental suffering in contemplation.[60] In referencing a *noncommercial* contract the authors meant one that affected the personal, social and family interest of the claimant, rather than his or her business interests. The Sheriff-Substitute found cogency in the reasoning and employed the distinction urged by the authors: "The contract in the present case would seem to be one of the kind envisaged by these authors, because it was not commercial in that sense and was exclusively concerned with the pursuer's personal, social, and family interests and with her feelings."[61] He awarded £30 to the bride in solatium.

There are several interesting aspects to this decision. Certainly the use of an English treatise to fashion a doctrine that was already immanent in the Scots Civilian heritage is somewhat ironical. Further, the judge's statement that the law in Scotland and England was "the same" appeared at first to be the familiar refrain in mixed jurisdictions when Common Law assimilation is about to take place.[62] But in this instance, the laws were apparently "the same" in a different sense. He apparently meant that if *Addis* was properly distinguishable on these facts, then both systems would have a precedential gap that needed to be filled. And instead of Common Law assimilation occurring, it seems that the decision correlated to Scottish legal traditions, extending a distinctive Scottish concept into a contractual setting. To the foreign observer it is perhaps surprising that a decision by a Scots court at local level would help alter the course of English law and even Common Law systems abroad.[63] According to William McBryde, Diesen "has had more influence on other jurisdictions than any other recent decision of a court in Scotland on matters of contractual remedies".[64]

Diesen v Samson immediately influenced several English decisions involving disappointed holidaymakers whose holidays were ruined by massive nonperformance of package-tour agreements. In *Jarvis v Swan's Tours Ltd*

---

60 For these authors, the amount of recoverable damage was subject to the ordinary rules of remoteness in *Hadley v Baxendale* (H McGregor, *McGregor on Damages*, 17th edn (2003) § 3-020, n 92; § 3-030).

61 *Diesen* at 50.

62 On the customary pretexts for the reception of Common Law in mixed jurisdictions, see V V Palmer, *Mixed Jurisdictions Worldwide – The Third Legal Family* (2001) 54-57.

63 According to W W McBryde, "Remedies for breach of contract" 1996 EdinLR 43 at 72, the decision has also been followed in Northern Ireland and Canada.

64 McBryde at 72, n 178.

(1973)[65] and *Jackson v Horizon Holidays* (1975)[66] the holidaymakers received not only the difference in value between what they paid and the services they actually received, but a further sum to salve their injured feelings.[67] In 1976 in *Heywood v Wellers,* the Court of Appeal awarded nonpecuniary damages against solicitors who breached their undertaking to protect the client from being molested by the defendant with whom she was engaged in litigation.[68]

This emerging category, which as mentioned had its genesis in an unprepossessing Scottish case, began to receive considerable attention from English authors. Writing even before *Jackson* and *Heywood* were decided, Gunther Treitel argued that the operative principle should be that contracts by tour operators, wedding photographers or bridal car hirers are such that[69]

> one of the main objects of the contract is to provide enjoyment or some sentimental benefit; and it is therefore reasonable to award damages for injured feelings against a party who defeats that object. [Apart from this] damages cannot be recovered for the "anxiety" which a breach of contract may cause to the injured party.

In this passage Treitel implicitly accepted the idea of making an exception to *Addis* for noncommercial contracts, yet he articulated the basis of the exception more teleologically. He framed it around a "main object" or aim of the contract, much as the Louisiana codifiers did in 1825.

In 1976 Lord Bridge articulated a formula in which he emphasised the "sole purpose" of the contract.[70] An article by Bernard Jackson in 1977 argued that Gunter Treitel and Lord Bridge were on the right track in stating the basis for an exceptional category of contract. Jackson's view was that nonpecuniary damages are justified when the creation or alleviation of a mental state was a primary object of the plaintiff in entering the contract.[71] He suggested that English law should look to France for help in understanding this question, particularly the French jurisprudence on *dommage moral* where the obligee failed to obtain a nonpecuniary advantage for which he contracted. Jackson did not refer to the Louisiana Civil Code or Louisiana cases in his article, but another article published that year quoted the full text of the Louisiana Civil Code and made the observation that "The Civil Law systems have shown much

---

65 [1973] QB 233; [1973] 1 All ER 71.
66 [1975] 3 All ER 92; [1975] 1 WLR 1468.
67 Bernard Jackson noted that Lord Denning's decision in *Jarvis* was largely decided on policy grounds; *Hadley v Baxendale* was not cited. See "Injured feelings resulting from breach of contract" (1977) 26 ICLQ 502 at 504.
68 *Heywood v Wellers* [1976] QB 446.
69 *The Law of Contract,* 4th edn (1975) 660 ff.
70 *Heywood v Wellers* [1976] 1 QB 463 at 464A.
71 B S Jackson, "Injured feelings resulting from breach of contract" (1977) 26 ICLQ 502.

greater readiness to award 'non-material' or 'nonpecuniary damages ...'[72]

In 1991 Lord Bingham framed the issue in terms that would be frequently quoted by subsequent judges. In *Watts v Morrow* he identified two exceptional situations in contract where nonpecuniary losses are recoverable.[73] He began by noting the policy that a contract-breaker is not in general liable for feelings of distress, frustration, anxiety, displeasure, vexation, tension or aggravation that are felt by the innocent party. Then came the exceptions:[74]

> But the rule is not absolute. [1] Where the very object of a contract is to provide pleasure, relaxation, peace of mind or freedom from molestation, damages will be awarded if the fruit of the contract is not provided ... If the law did not cater for this exceptional category of case it would be defective ... [2] In cases not falling within this exceptional category, damages are in my view recoverable for physical inconvenience and discomfort caused by the breach and mental suffering directly related to that inconvenience and discomfort.

Thus far it has suited my purposes to follow only the development of Lord Bingham's first exception ("the very object of a contract") but we should note that the second exception ("physical inconvenience") is also well-recognised in Scotland and deserves some explanation. Both jurisdictions have distinguished awards for "inconvenience" from damage awards under the object of the contract. Inconvenience has traditionally meant serious physical discomfort that falls short of personal injury.[75] Dating from the nineteenth century, it was apparently one of the earliest forms of recoverable nonpecuniary loss in a breach of contract action.[76] It is actionable as a general head of damages in contract, even with respect to commercial contracts that would not satisfy the first exception.[77] Though masquerading as a distinct concept, it is simply one example of nonpecuniary damage embraced within the concept of

---

72 D Harris, A Ogus and J Phillips, "Contract remedies and the consumer surplus" (1979) 95 LQR 581.

73 [1991] 1 WLR 1421.

74 See also *Bliss v SE Thames Health Authority* [1985] IRLR 308 on the point that in order to receive damages, the contract must be to provide pleasure or prevent pain.

75 See *Watts v Morrow* [1991] 1 WLR 1421; *Fraser v DM Hall & Son* 1997 SLT 808. See A Chandler and J P Devenney, "Breach of contract and the expectation deficit: inconvenience and disappointment" (2007) 27 *Legal Studies*, 126 at 145; A Bowen, "*Watts v Morrow* and the consumer surplus" 2003 SLT 1.

76 Chandler and Devenney (n 75) at 127, note 9, citing *Burton v Pinkerton* (1867) LR 2 Exch 340 and *Hobbs v London and South Western Railway Co* (1875) LR 10 QB 111. An early Scots case granting an award for inconvenience and trouble was *Webster & Co v Cramond Iron Co* (1875) 2 R 752.

77 See *M'William & Sons v Fletcher* (1905) 13 SLT 455 (contract to supply a ship to carry coal). Recovery for inconvenience in a commercial context is clearly subject to the rules of remoteness. See *Watts* (n 75) at 1445; *Mills v Findlay* 1994 SCLR 397 (inconvenience of eighty visits to the property in effort to resell it after purchaser's breach).

solatium.[78] It may play a significant role as an alternative ground in cases where the nature of the contract cannot be said to be one of pleasure, relaxation and so forth.[79]

Meanwhile, north of the Tweed the development of the exception recognised in *Diesen* continued apace in the case of *Colston v Marshall* (1992).[80] The pursuers entered into agreements whereby the defender would furnish "a residential caravan site of the highest amenity" for a weekly rent of £48, but the defender failed to provide a site of that quality and they suffered upset and distress and sought solatium. The sheriff dismissed the cause without trial, but on appeal Sheriff Principal Macleod ruled that the pursuer should be permitted to proceed to proof. He noted that the caravan agreements could be viewed as "social in character" in that they sought to provide "a particular degree of mental and physical satisfaction to the occupants of the caravans". This particular phrasing obviously reflected the cumulative influence of the English authorities.[81] He concluded that if the trier of fact found that mental upset or distress for failure to provide the promised amenity was within the contemplation of the parties when the agreements were entered into, then damages in solatium could be awarded. In a 1994 case a member of a bowling club was wrongfully suspended from membership. Solatium was awarded as compensation for pursuer's injured feelings and loss of privileges.[82]

At the turn of the century the House of Lords refined and clarified the scope of the exception in two important cases. In *Ruxley Electronics Ltd v Forsyth* (1996)[83] the House of Lords approved an award for loss of amenity where a swimming pool was incorrectly constructed in the diving area to a depth of six feet, instead of to the specified depth of seven feet, six inches. The breach had no effect on the market value of the property but the court compensated the homeowner for his reduced enjoyment or his disappointment. Lord Lloyd of

---

78 See *Mack v Glasgow City Council* 2006 SC 543, where the pursuer suffered the "inconvenience" of having to live for over two years in a house with severe water penetration, dampness and mould, per Lord Macfadyen delivering the Opinion of the court at para 17: "It is unfortunate that the pursuer's pleadings use the term 'solatium'; … we must look behind the language and examine the true nature of the pursuer's claim." See also *Purdie v Dryburgh* 2000 SC 497. Cf *Buchan v North Lanarkshire Council* 2000 Hous LR 98.

79 See n 76 above and accompanying text.

80 1993 SLT (Sh Ct) 40; 1993 SCLR 43.

81 "No Scottish authorities in point have been cited to me, but the English cases contain dicta that command my respect" (at 42).

82 *Graham v Ladeside of Kilbirnie Bowling Club* 1994 SLT 1295. Whether solatium lies in a claim for breach of warrandice (warranty) arising from a defective title to heritage does not seem to be settled: *Palmer v Beck* 1993 SLT 485; but see *Watson v Swift & Co's Judicial Factor* 1986 SLT 217.

83 [1996] AC 344.

Berwick referred to the "well-established" exception when *"the* object of the contract is to afford pleasure" (emphasis added).[84]

When a similar question was presented in *Farley v Skinner*,[85] Lord Steyn adjusted the phrasing and widened the exception. In that case a successful businessman wanted to buy a gracious country residence for his retirement. One of his principal objectives was to purchase a property offering peace and tranquility. He located a prospective property and specifically instructed a surveyor, the defendant, to investigate whether the home would be affected by aircraft noise since it was situated in the vicinity of Gatwick airport. The defendant's report stated that there was no indication of a noise problem. After the property was purchased and extensive renovations were completed, the plaintiff discovered the property lay in a flightpath for the airport, not far from a navigation beacon. The noise intrusion was constant, substantial and annoying. The trial judge awarded £10,000 for disappointment and inconvenience, even though the plaintiff could not prove he had paid too much for the property or had suffered any pecuniary loss.[86] The Court of Appeal, following the formulation of Bingham J in *Watts v Morrow*, quoted above, reversed the award on the ground that firstly, the plaintiff's pleasure, relaxation and peace of mind were not "the very object" of the purchase contract and secondly, the aircraft noise did not reach the threshold of physical inconvenience.

Finding the reasoning on the first ground too narrow, Lord Steyn said that the test should be whether the surveyor's obligation to investigate aircraft noise was "a major or important part of the contract".[87] He rejected the proposition that the entire object had to be of this type. "It is sufficient," he wrote, "if a major or important object of the contract is to give pleasure, relaxation or peace of mind." Particularly interesting from a cross-Atlantic perspective was his reason for rejecting the narrower approach. He argued that if an architect was employed only to design a pleasurable amenity like a wide staircase, then the breach of such a distinct obligation would certainly result in an award. But if that same obligation were contained in a general contract to design a

---

84 For analogous forms of nonpecuniary loss, see *Malik v BCCI* [1998] AC 20 where a bank employee recovered for "stigma damage" in circumstances where his employer engaged in organised crime activites and he was unable to find work in the financial sector again. See also discussion of the "performance interest" in *St Martins Property Corp Ltd v Sir Robert McAlpine & Son Ltd* [1994] 1 AC 85.

85 [2002] 2 AC 732.

86 No pecuniary damages were proved, since the expert evidence indicated that despite the noise intrusion the property was worth what plaintiff had paid for it. Thus the case resolved into the issue of the claim for nonpecuniary loss of amenity.

87 He accordingly called for the overruling of *Knott v Bolton* (1885) 11 Const LJ 375 where damages were denied against an architect who failed to design an impressive entrance and wide stairway to a home that the owners had desired.

house, then the entire object test would not be satisfied. He found this was too technical and merely elevated form over substance.[88]

Lord Steyn's opinion was significant in several ways. Firstly, the award for immaterial harm was not conceived as exemplary or punitive but as compensatory damage. The old conflation between moral damage and punitive damage – clearly reflected in *Addis* – seems to have played no part in his thinking. Secondly, unlike certain judges and writers, his opinion avoided the issues of *Hadley v Baxendale*: his formulation stands independent of remoteness rules.[89] Similarly, it played no part in Lord Denning's decision in *Jarvis v Swan's Tours Ltd* nor in Lord Bingham's reasoning in *Watts v Morrow* (*Hadley* was not cited). Yet remoteness is an interesting and important issue for English, Scots and Louisiana law, and I will close this section by a brief look at that question.

We saw earlier in the cases of *Diesen* and *Colston* that the Scottish judges granted solatium for disappointed expectations based upon the exceptional nature of the contract. The treatise which they relied upon, however, adverted to the contemplation test as a further condition for recovery.[90] That further condition was formulaically repeated in the Scottish cases (but not in English cases decided by Lord Denning or Lord Steyn). Even when it was repeated, however, there was no application of the rule to the facts. This perfunctory and inconsistent treatment is curious, until it is recognised that the remoteness test has no reason to operate in this context. Since the recovery of solatium is restricted *by judicial rule* to "social" contracts in which a main objective of the parties was to obtain pleasure, relaxation and the like, then the nonpecuniary loss arising from breach is, by hypothesis, the fruit or benefit that was bargained for. Under the first rule of *Hadley v Baxendale*,[91] the aggrieved party may recover those damages "as may fairly and reasonably be considered... arising naturally". Of course the contractual objective of the parties makes this part of the Hadley test tautologous. It is in fact circular to reason that nonpecuniary damages arise "naturally" when there is the breach of a contract whose main objective is to produce nonpecuniary benefits. As to the second rule in *Hadley*, (a rule incidentally that was received in Scotland well before

88 Referring to the alternative ground of inconvenience, Lord Steyn and three other Lords of Appeal were prepared to hold that the aircraft noise had sufficient intensity to produce actionable physical discomfort and that the trial judge had ground for an award on that basis.

89 Compare the view of Lord Scott of Foscote whose opinion in *Farley* indicated that both limbs of *Watts v Morrow* are concerned with questions of consequential loss and are subject to the principles of *Hadley*. It must be noted, however, that he stressed the remoteness hurdle only when considering the head of inconvenience and discomfort ([2002] 2 AC 732 at 767-768).

90 See n 60 above and accompanying text.

91 (1854) 156 Eng Rep 145.

it was adopted in England)[92] the pursuer may recover consequential damages (which means damage affecting plaintiff's "other property") that were "in the contemplation of both parties". Here again the exceptional nature of the contract erases the condition, at least wherever the nonpecuniary objective of the parties should be apparent or will have been communicated. Thus it appears that both rules in Hadley have been eclipsed by the "main-objective" requirement, and so long as that requirement continues to define the area within which solatium *ex contractu* is recoverable, those tests will involve superfluous and circular reasoning.[93] This seems to be why leading English and Scottish decisions were properly silent on the remoteness question.

Interestingly, in 1999 the Scottish Law Commission proposed a bold alternative that would rely exclusively upon the remoteness test to determine recoverability of solatium in contract, in stark contrast to the present approach of Scots law. In a report entitled "Remedies for Breach of Contract"[94] the Law Commission proposed legislation declaring that there should be no bar to the recovery of nonpatrimonial loss in contract actions, other than the "normal rule" disallowing damages for losses which are too remote. In other words, under the Commission's proposal, all types of contracts would be open to claims for solatium, but every claim would be screened by the remoteness principle.[95] The Commission said it preferred this approach to the "arbitrary" distinctions courts had drawn between inconvenience and distress on the one hand, and between commercial and social contracts on the other.[96] I am not informed as to why the recommendations were not enacted, but of course any proposal to sweep away the entire judicial *oeuvre* stretching from *Addis* to *Farley* could encounter resistance from different quarters. I would

---

92 I have not been able to look at earlier editions, but the contemplation rule was already found in the 1816 4th edition of Bell's *Commentaries on the Laws of Scotland*, vol 1, 359. Bell took his source from Pothier's *Traité du contrat de vente* no 73 which he quoted at length. Pothier's rule was later borrowed by the English judges in *Hadley*. See A W B Simpson, "Innovation in nineteenth century contract law" (1975) 75 LQR 247 at 274-277; R Danzig "*Hadley v Baxendale*: A study in the industrialization of the law" (1975) 4 J of Leg Studies 249 at 257-258.

93 For further analysis in reference to Louisiana law, see n 98 below and accompanying text.

94 (Scot Law Com No 174, 1999) (available at *http://www.scotlawcom.gov.uk/downloads/rep174. pdf*).

95 As stated in the Report (para 3.1, n 1) "Under this normal rule damages will be limited to the loss which the defender might reasonably have contemplated at the time of the contract, taking into account any special circumstances made known to the defender by the pursuer."

96 See n 78 above. In *Mills v Findlay* 1994 SCLR 397 at 399 Sheriff Principal Cox questioned the validity of these distinctions and disallowed solatium for the financial embarrassment of the seller after the buyer refused to go through with the sale: "the distinction may not be between 'social' and 'commercial' contracts. The true distinction may be that in these cases the defenders must have contemplated distress to the other contracting party if they did not fulfil their bargain. Damages for distress might in these circumstances be an implied term of the contract."

only observe that as the rule of remoteness would become the sole check on recovery for solatium *ex contractu*, conservative judges, who traditionally feared expanding the role of moral damages in contract, might easily adopt a policy-driven interpretation of the contemplation rule as a means of checking expansion or even of doing away with the exceptional category. Or it might be envisaged that the contracts of intellectual gratification would rather routinely satisfy the remoteness test (for the tautologous reasons discussed above), while commercial contracts generally would not. If so, this might leave Scots law approximately in its present position, but for changed and less transparent reasons.

D. LOUISIANA'S CODAL APPROACH – AN ORIGINAL CONTRIBUTION

Article 1928 § 3 CC (1825)[97]
Revised Article 1998 CC (1985)
Damages for nonpecuniary loss may be recovered when the contract, because of its nature, is intended to gratify a nonpecuniary interest and because of the circumstances surrounding the formation or the nonperformance of the contract, the obligor knew, or should have known, that his failure to perform would cause that kind of loss.

   Regardless of the nature of the contract, these damages may be recovered also when the obligor intended, through his failure, to aggrieve the feelings of the obligee.

(1) Introduction

Article 1928, § 3 (1825) was the first legislation regulating nonpecuniary damages in Louisiana and, to my knowledge, it was the first statutory regulation of this kind anywhere. Its origins are unclear. No direct source has been found, though many, including the present author, have scoured diligently. We can only assume it is an original creation of the authors of the Civil Code. There was no earlier source in the Code of 1808, nor in France's Civil Code of 1804.

During the Civil Code revision in 1985 the provision was modified and substantially reshaped, as comparison of the two texts reveals. Interestingly the Supreme Court takes the position that the Legislature in 1985 intended no fundamental change in the law, which allows the Court to maintain that its previous interpretation was not legislatively overruled and continues to be relevant under the new provision. The court's position minimises the

---

97 For the text of the provision, see n 4 above and accompanying text.

fact that there are striking new features in the revised provision. Firstly, the exceptional category has been reconceived. In place of contracts of "intellectual gratification" the new provision covers contracts intended "to gratify a nonpecuniary interest". The latter is arguably a far broader category, even if it is not so broad as the Reporter's reputed desire to extend moral damages to every kind of contract.[98] Secondly, for the first time a type of "contemplation" test has been subjoined to the exception ("and because of circumstances … the obligor knew, or should have known, that his failure to perform would cause that kind of loss"), so that the test of whether moral damages is available has now become a double test.[99] Thirdly, new language was added allowing moral damages to be recovered whenever the obligor *intended* to aggrieve the feelings of the obligee, regardless of the type of contract involved and regardless of what the parties contemplated at formation. Here the equivalent of the *actio iniuriarum* has been recognised in the contractual setting, thus permitting moral damages on the basis of a scienter independent of the shared objectives of the parties. An intentional aggrievement would constitute an imposition on the innocent party in violation of the duty of good faith. The importance of these changes can best be seen by examining the original scope and purpose of § 3 in the 1825 Civil Code.

Originally, article 1928, § 3 created an exception to the familiar rules on the reparation of contractual damage, including the famous "contemplation" rule, a limitation on damages enunciated by Pothier and found in both the French and Louisiana codes.[100] Article 1928 § 3 expressly declared that it creates "exceptions and modifications" to the foregoing rules on damnum emergens, lucrum cessans and remoteness of damage. Thus as a matter of system and structure contracts of intellectual gratification were not governed by the usual rules on pecuniary damages, nor were they intended to be subject to the principle of remoteness of damage. The logic behind this position is straightforward. If a contract's very purpose is to obtain nonpecuniary benefits, how can the loss of such benefits ever be too remote from the contemplation of the parties? Logically, the *raison d'être* of a contract is never remote.

It is also important to emphasise, however, that § 3 had wider purposes. It also authorised the recovery of nonpecuniary damages in the adjacent fields of tort and quasi contract. It stated that "In the assessment of damages under this rule, *as well as in cases of offenses, quasi offense, and quasi contracts,*

---

98 Minutes of the June 1981 Louisiana State Law Institute Council Meeting at 8, discussed in *Young v Ford Motor Co Inc* 595 So 2d 1123 at 1131-1133 (La 1992).

99 Though one of doubtful utility, for the reasons explained at nn 91 above and 100 below and accompanying text.

100 See French *Code civil* art 1150.

much discretion must be left to the judge or jury ..." (emphasis added). This authorisation was general and not restricted to particular types of torts. Thus it gave broader protection to personality interests in tort than in contract where recovery was confined on an exceptional basis.[101] Given this difference in scope, the impact of article 1928, § 3 was initially felt more in the field of delict than in contract. The article clearly allowed recovery for plaintiff's pain and suffering in personal injury cases[102] and for injury to feelings, honour and dignity caused by verbal insults or defamation.[103]

(2) Mistaken translations and doubtful interpretations

It is generally known that serious errors were made in translating the original French text, and that when those mistakes are revealed the scope of the contractual exception may not be as wide as the English version, quoted above, would suggest. The text in French, the language of redaction and deemed more authoritative, read as follows:

> Lorsque le contrat a pour but de procurer à quelqu'un une jouissance purement intellectuelle, telle que celles qui tiennent à la religion, à la morale, au goût, à la commodité ou à toute autre espèce de satisfaction de ce genre, quoique ces choses n'aient pas été appréciées en argent par les parties, des dommages n'en seront pas moins dus pour la violation de la convention. Un contrat, qui a pour but une foundation religieuse ou charitable, une promesse de marriage, ou l'entreprise de quelqu'ouvrage appurtenant aux beaux arts, offre l'exemple d'un cas auquel cette règle peut s'appliquer.

Two errors are relatively clear. First, the French adjective "purement" (first line) does not appear anywhere in the English translation. A weaker modifier ("some") was inserted in its place, thus not only altering the emphasis but opening up the scope of the exception. There is a considerable difference in degree between a contract *purely* for intellectual enjoyment, and one in which *some* intellectual enjoyment can be derived. Secondly, the French noun *"but"* (first line), which signifies the "end" or "purpose" of the contract, was rendered as the contract's "object", which is a patent confusion of the *objet* of an obligation with its "purpose" or *causa*.[104] Now it appeared that a contract of intellectual gratification was revealed by examining the performance(s)

---

101 This also opened a zone of concurrent contract/tort liability (beyond the category of intellectual gratification) in which the obligor's breach could be alternatively regarded as a tort.

102 *Black v Carrollton R R Co* 10 La Ann 33 (La 1855).

103 *Miller v Holstein* 16 La 389 (La 1840).

104 A few sentences earlier, in § 1 of art 1934, the word "objet" was translated as "object", so now within the same text one English word bore two entirely different meanings. The same conflation appears in Professor Litvinoff's translation of the provision. See "Moral damages" (1977) 38 La LR 1 at 8-9.

to be rendered (namely, its *"objet"*) rather than by looking at the reason and purposes for wanting a performance (namely, the party's *cause*).

Errors of translation aside, the scope of the provision was never clear in any event. As pointed out by Wolbrette,[105] arguments can be made for a strict, a broad, and a liberal reading.

> First, the language might be strictly construed so that in order to recover nonpecuniary damages the object of the contract must be exclusively intellectual enjoyment, as opposed to partially intellectual and partially physical gratification. Second, the language could be given a broader interpretation so that if any part of the object was intellectual enjoyment damages could be recovered, even though the object also contained physical elements. Third, the language could be read very liberally to require no intellectual elements whatsoever, but only that the object of the contract provide some physical convenience not appreciable in money.

The dominant interpretative approach of the Supreme Court has been to reject the extremes. There are practical and textual reasons for taking this position. Under a strict reading, a purchaser who desired to own a luxurious home could be denied nonpecuniary damages against the breaching party because even homes of the highest aesthetic quality provide shelter and safety and cannot be described as "exclusively" devoted to nonpecuniary enjoyment. Moreover, a strict reading cannot be justified by the article's own examples. The examples mentioned – a contract for a religious or charitable foundation, a promise of marriage, the commissioning of a work of art – are not necessarily contracts of intellectual enjoyment exclusively. A collector may buy art partly for art's sake and partly for its investment value; the buyer of an antique car might use it for daily transportation. The examples, therefore, may be seen as prototypes of mixed-purpose contracts in which nonpecuniary and pecuniary interests meet and blend, and both should be protected in accordance with the drafters' intent. The word "exclusive" was not used in either the French or English versions of the article.[106] Obviously purposes are rarely pure. In the making of a work of art or the playing of a concert, the artist's cause may be partly pecuniary (his salary), partly intellectual (his cultural statement). The artist expects to be paid but surely that does not sum up the essence of why he performs. It would seem strained to hold that moral damages are recoverable by a disappointed patron but not by the

---

105 "Damages ex contractu: Recovery of nonpecuniary damages for breach of contract under Louisiana Civil Code article 1934" (1974) 48 Tul L Rev 1160 at 1161 ff.

106 Professor Litvinoff has pointed out that the redactors of the French text took care to write the adverb "purely" before the word intellectual, and surely they would have written the adjective "exclusive" before the noun "purpose" if they had so intended. "Moral damages" (1977) 38 La LR 1 at 11.

artist.[107] It follows that a *contract's* purpose cannot be exclusively for intellectual enjoyment, but is always mixed. The strict interpretation is therefore at odds with the drafters' expression "Lorsque le contrat a pour but de procurer a quelqu'un une jouissance purement intellectuelle...."

Another difficulty is the elusiveness of the expression "intellectual gratification". Does the exception embrace only an elevated conception of "intellectual contract" or does it simply include contracts in which parties seek psychic enjoyment to any significant degree? The purchase of a Rolls Royce or a villa by the lake may satisfy the patrician conception of intellectual gratification, but a mass-produced automobile or a row cottage may generate equal anticipation or psychic satisfaction for more humble folk. It may be that the codifiers were not attempting to delineate the things which give intellectual gratification, but the gratification that things may give. Put another way, is the category bounded by the object or by the eye of the beholder?[108] It is at least arguable that the exception should encompass any contract where pleasure is a significant element of the obligee's cause.

Louisiana courts have silently battled over the point just discussed, sometimes objectifying the exception into a set of things in accordance with its elevated examples, at other times regarding it as a flexible, open-ended, causa-determined category that embraces the less exalted tastes of the average man. The 1985 revision was an opportunity to make a definite choice in this regard, but no choice was actually made. It seems the new provision simply hovers between the two possibilities. It allows recovery "when the contract, because of its nature is intended to gratify a nonpecuniary interest ...". The unofficial comment ventured to describe a nonpecuniary interest as an interest of a "spiritual order", which leaves matters neither official nor clear.

E. THE JURISPRUDENCE – SOME HIGHLIGHTS

It was not until 150 years had passed that Louisiana's unique dispensation received systematic analysis. When that analysis finally took place, problems of translation and interpretation rose to the surface for the first time. As

---

107 For this fundamental error, see *Kosmala v Paul and the Baton Rouge Symphony* 644 So 2d 856 (1st Cir 1994). ("Where a contract is for performance of an artistic work such as a concert given by a musician, a portrait made by a painter, or a wedding dress sewn by a seamstress, and the artisan breaches the contract, the patron has an action for nonpecuniary loss; however the artisan does not ... if the patron breaches the contract.")

108 To David Hume, "Beauty is no quality in things themselves. It exists merely in the mind which contemplates them."("Of the standard of taste", in E Miller (ed), *Essays Moral, Political and Literary* (Indianapolis 1987) 1.23.8.

previously mentioned, there was little or no development in Scotland either before the 1970s, though solatium had deep roots in the Scottish system. This delayed flowering suggests that Scotland's and Louisiana's experiences do present, both chronologically and analytically, interesting parallels for comparative study.

One might begin by noting that in both jurisdictions the first cases to award moral damages in a contract setting involved a promise of marriage. The context seems like an anachronistic place to begin, for it was always unlikely to produce doctrine capable of generalisation. The action for breach of *fiançailles* was regarded as *sui generis* and a shaky base from which to project analogical growth and development.[109] True, a marital engagement arose from the consent of the parties, but by the turn of the nineteenth century jurists were reconsidering the propriety of a contractual viewpoint. For one thing, a promise of marriage was no longer subject to specific enforcement, though two centuries earlier specific implement was common in Holland and perhaps France.[110] Further, though the breaking of the promise might occasion some pecuniary damage, the claim would not encompass *lucrum cessans*, namely, the profit that the disappointed party would have gained had the promise been kept.[111] It therefore came to be regarded, as Malaurie and Aynès point out, as an anomalous contract (*"un contrat qui n'en est pas un"*).[112] Indeed it was finally decided in France that fetters should not be placed on the "unlimited" freedom to marry, and that all such promises, from a contractual standpoint, were null and unenforceable.[113] Similar solicitude for the open character of marriage once flourished in eighteenth-century Scotland where it became the principal objection against the award of solatium to a deserted fiancée.[114]

The shifting assessment of this *sui generis* contract offers a clue as to the origins of Louisiana's code provision. As early as 1807, a Louisiana statute

---

109 According to F P van den Heever, the remedy has features in common with an action on contract and an action in delict. *Breach of Promise and Seduction* (1954) 28.

110 In Voet's time (1647-1713), threat of civil imprisonment was used to compel performance or a judgment taking the place of a ceremony might be issued (vol 4, 13.1.12).

111 The *Code Napoléon's* silence on the subject of engagements led Merlin to conclude that they were subject to the ordinary rules governing contracts, yet he noted special restrictions on their enforcement. See Dalloz, *Répertoire universel et raisonné de jurisprudence* (1812), vol 5, s v "Fiançailles", para 6 at 208.

112 See n 28 above.

113 B Beignier, *L'honneur et le droit* (1995) 452-453.

114 Erskine, n 42 above. English law made the withdrawing party more heavily accountable, awarding the *lucrum cessans* as well as possibly imposing vindictive or exemplary damages. See H Berindoaque, *Des dommages interest en matière contractuelle et delictuelle dans le droit Anglais* (Paris 1923, thèse) 86.

declared that "As the law considers marriage in no other view than that of a civil contract, it sanctions all those marriages as valid where the parties at the time of making them were 1stly, Willing to contract; 2dly, Able to contract, and 3dly, Did contract pursuant to the forms and solemnities prescribed by law."[115] It was reasonable to deduce that if marriage is a contract, then a promise of marriage must likewise be binding as a contract. Pothier said in his *Traité* that by nature "des fiançailles, ... sont un contrat synallagmatique". Damages recoverable upon breach might include not only the expenses incurred by the aggrieved party but also a sum for the affront that may have been inflicted ("L'affront que souffre la partie à qui l'on a manqué de foi …").[116] Thus at the time Louisiana's Code of 1825 was drafted, reparations for breach of promise to marry were still awarded upon a contractual basis in France.[117] It was not until 1838 that the Cour de cassation definitively broke with that tradition out of respect for the freedom of marriage. Thereafter a broken promise would not give rise to liability in contract. It might entail tort liability under article 1382 but the breaching party's behaviour had to be considered culpable.[118] This chronology suggests that the codifiers of 1825 caught the last flicker of France's expiring contractual approach, and on its basis constructed a limited theory of moral damages – the contracts of intellectual gratification. This early commitment to a limited category, however, meant that Louisiana judges would not be in a position to follow the full flowering of *dommage moral* in French jurisprudence in the second half of the nineteenth century.

The Louisiana Supreme Court's first encounter with an action for breach of promise of marriage arose in the case of *Morgan v Yarborough* (1850).[119] Here the nature of the claim was already becoming a source of confusion. The trial judge based his award to the aggrieved lady upon the delictual article of the Civil Code. This meant that Mr Yarborough's repudiation of his engagement to Ms Morgan was conceived as tortious, which, as already explained, was the approach taken in France since 1838. In the Supreme Court Justice Slidell upheld the award of damages, but placed the liability squarely on a

---

115 An Act Concerning the Celebration of Marriages, 6 April 1807. This act was taken bodily into the Digest of 1807. The source of the statute was the Projet du Gouvernement of 1800 rather than the French *Code civil* of 1804.

116 *Traité du contrat de mariage* (1813) 38, 41-42.

117 In the decision of the Cour d'appel of Colmar, 13 May 1818, the court categorised a promise to marry as a contract, but grounded an award of damages under art 1382 CC.

118 30 May 30 1838, S 1838.I.493. As Ganot viewed the change, "De contractuelle, la faute est devenue délictuelle" (*La réparation du préjudice moral* (Rennes 1924, thèse) 133). See also A Colin and H Capitant, *Cours élémentaire de droit civil français*, 3rd edn (1920), vol 1, § 2 at 128-129.

119 5 La Ann 316 (La 1850).

contractual foundation: "But our legislation has not left this matter in doubt. The article 1928 C C speaks expressly of a promise of marriage. It is there treated as a contract, and a measure of damages for its breach is given."[120] In subsequent cases this characterisation was consistently followed, and there were successful actions of this type as late as 1962. But it is evident that by the late twentieth century public opinion and judicial attitudes greeted such actions with scepticism. Thereafter such actions would not succeed without proof of exceptional circumstances.[121]

In Scotland the first marriage cases awarding solatium theorised that a wrong had been done to the feelings, reputation and marital chances of the lady (quaintly described as her "loss of market"). In *Johnston v Paley* (1770) the court proceeded to allow recovery on a delictual basis,[122] and the Court of Session followed that approach in the leading case of *Hogg v Gow* (1812).[123] In that case the Court found that damages for breach of a promise to marry could embrace solatium for "the unutterable anguish" the pursuer must have suffered. The defender's repudiation was described as a "wrong" against the lady.[124] The speech of Lord Bannatyne alluded to an earlier time in Scottish history when the action was refused in principle because it was conceptualised contractually: "Our early lawyers seem to have made a mistake on the subject in point of principle. Marriage should be free; but it does not follow that if one of the parties leads the other to entertain hopes which are disappointed, and hurts the mind beyond all computation, that he shall not be obliged to repair the damage." If this "mistake" of principle actually occurred, the action in Scotland changed its stripes far earlier than in France, but for the same reason.

Near the end of the nineteenth century, Louisiana courts began to face claims for moral damages in a variety of situations. One of the first cases to arise involved an undelivered telegram containing a grave message from a husband to his wife advising of their son's illness and approaching death.

120 At 322.
121 See *Glass v Wiltz* 551 So 2d 32, 33 (4th Cir 1989). This decline was not evident to commentators before 1950. See, e.g., H Cohen, "Breach of promise to marry" (1950) 24 Tulane LR 501.
122 15 December 1770 FC 188. The pursuer, a twenty-five-year old, brought suit in vindication of her character against a seventy-five-year old who offered his hand and then changed his mind. The Commissaries awarded her a palinode, a fine and £500 in damages. The Commissaries found various wrongs committed by the defender, including insult and slander of her character.
123 27 May 1812 FC 654.
124 Thus Lord Meadowbank: "I do not understand the principle on which it can be said that there has been no wrong done, or that a breach of promise is a wrong of such a kind that no damages are due on account of it. Is it no wrong to inflict perhaps the severest distress that the human mind can suffer?" Lord Justice Clerk Boyle: "The principles of justice authorise us to award the most exemplary damages." Lord Robertson: "For every wrong there must be a remedy."

The message was sent but never received, thus causing the wife exceptional distress.[125] The intermediate appellate court held that there was no cause of action for her suffering, relying upon the "great weight of authority in the states of the Union and in England".[126] The Louisiana Supreme Court reversed this judgment. Justice Nicholls wrote: "It is useless for us to refer to decisions of courts exercising functions where the common law prevails upon a subject-matter to which we have to be controlled by local law." Referring to French authorities on *"préjudice moral"* (a heading that was by then well developed in France)[127] the court held that the Louisiana code provision permitted relief on these facts.[128] Nevertheless, as a logical matter, it was not by any means self-evident why a contract to deliver a telegram could be classified as a contract to procure intellectual gratification. The Court's answer to that problem, however, was to subsume the case within the Code article on the basis of *a fortiori* argument. It reasoned that a Code provision catering to the loss of intellectual enjoyment and anticipated pleasure must cover the negative as well as the positive side of the coin – i.e. the infliction of mental suffering due to negligent breach of contract. Moral damage therefore had both a positive and negative side – indifferently – under the Code provision.

In 1903 a bride-to-be claimed moral damages for the non-delivery of her wedding trousseau dresses.[129] Described as a woman of "wealth and high social standing", she ordered a number of dresses to be ready by the wedding day. The dresses were intended to be worn on a wedding tour in which she would meet her husband's friends and relatives in various cities. Having nothing appropriate to wear, she was forced to forego and decline all invitations and entertainments planned in her honour in the cities she visited, allegedly causing her mortification and humiliation. The Supreme Court was satisfied that the defendant clearly understood that the purpose of the contract was to provide dresses necessary to social engagements after her wedding: "D H Holmes must be held to have known that, if the dresses were not finished by that day, the bride would be keenly disappointed." In emphasising the defendant's awareness of the plaintiff's plans, the court apparently realised

---

125   *Graham v Western Union Tel Co* 109 La 1070 (La 1903).

126   The court canvassed the objections raised in common law authorities, including the difficulty of estimating the damages, the increased litigation the action would engender, and the possibility of "great oppression" upon the defendant (at 1071).

127   Ganot, n 118.

128   Art 1934 (1870) (formerly art 1928 CC (1825). The change in numbering occurred in the code revision of 1870.

129   *Lewis v D H Holmes* 34 So 66 (La 1903).

that article 1934 operates much like the conception of cause in a contract. An obligee's purpose, to be actionable, must be shared with the obligor. This requirement is relatively easy to satisfy in contracts bearing on weddings, funerals, birthdays and other major life events, since the purpose is generally signalled by the *objet* of the performance itself. When a wedding cake, inscribed as such, is not delivered by a certain day or photographs depicting a wedding are of unprofessional quality, the *objet*, perhaps without more, proclaims the purpose.[130] In other cases, however, a special communication of the purpose may be necessary in order to inform the obligor.[131]

In passing, it may be noted that article 1934 was applied in the cases of the undelivered telegram and trousseau dresses without the courts ever inquiring whether the contract's purpose was *exclusively* intellectual. It will be recalled that a strict reading of the provision may invite this question, but the courts apparently applied what Wolbrette called a "broader interpretation" to the provision. These contracts clearly had mixed purposes: elegant dresses for a wedding tour may have been critical items for a bride's position in life, involving a sense of dignity, self-esteem and social standing, but they are also garments that serve the usual physical and utilitarian purposes as well. The courts properly realised that there are no contracts in the abstract that are, on the one hand, solely intellectual, or on the other hand, solely physical.

The need for communication on object and cause, at the stage of consent, was the central issue in an 1895 railway case.[132] The plaintiff purchased a ticket to travel to a certain destination, but due to the conductor's error, the train did not stop at the appointed station. The plaintiff walked 2.1 miles back to the correct station. There was not, however, any pecuniary loss resulting from this inconvenience. The lower court awarded plaintiff the sum of $50, apparently as moral damage. Justice McEnerny for the Supreme Court disagreed, stating that while the contract of transport had unquestionably been violated, and an award of nominal damages might be appropriate, the plaintiff was not entitled to any sum for moral damages.[133] He rejected the plaintiff's argument that in purchasing a passenger ticket, "pleasure of visits to friends necessarily entered into the contemplation of the parties" by saying:

---

130 See *Garther v Tipery Studios Inc* 334 So 2d 758 (4th Cir 1976).
131 See *Mitchell v Shreveport Laundries Inc* 61 So 2d 539 (2nd Cir 1952) (wedding suit lost by laundry, causing groom the humiliation of wearing a soiled garment; the laundry was informed of the client's purpose).
132 *Judice v Southern Pacific Co* 47 La Ann 255 (La 1895).
133 Had the same case arisen in England or Scotland, however, an award might have issued under the heading of the "inconvenience" of walking to the correct destination. See authorities cited, n 75 above and following, and accompanying text.

> It would be an unreasonable construction of the contract of carrying passengers that the defendant company should know the objects and purposes of each passenger boarding the train, and an implied contract should spring from such imputed knowledge. The contract was to carry the plaintiff safely to Burke Station.... The defendant violated *this* contract.[134]

The court thus effectively read into the Code provision the need for plaintiff to show that intellectual gratification was intersubjectively understood, not entertained by plaintiff alone.[135] Presumably if the purpose of plaintiff's journey had been to attend a concert or social event in another town, and that purpose was shared with the railway's servants, the court would have upheld a claim for moral damages.

(1) The *Meador* interpretation and modern interpretation

The leading case of *Meador v Toyota of Jefferson Inc* (1976)[136] marked the first time that the Louisiana Supreme Court analysed the scope of the exception with precision. Ms Meador, eighteen years old, owned a new Toyota, her first automobile. The car was damaged in an accident and she brought it to the Toyota dealership for repairs. It was not returned to her until seven months later. There was no question that the dealer had breached the implied obligation to repair within a reasonable time and that the delay had caused certain pecuniary damages. The trial court awarded plaintiff compensation for her pecuniary losses, and also awarded $700 for aggravation, distress and inconvenience. The Court of Appeal, however, disallowed the nonpecuniary award entirely, and the Supreme Court affirmed this judgment. In refusing a nonpecuniary award, Justice Calogero gave a broad reading to the article:[137]

> Thus we would interpret Article 1934 (3) as follows: Where an object, the exclusive object, of a contract is physical gratification (or anything other than intellectual gratification) nonpecuniary damages as a consequence of nonfulfillment of that object are not recoverable. On the other hand where a principal or exclusive object of a contract is intellectual enjoyment, nonpecuniary damages ... are recoverable.

The court found there was no more than an incidental intellectual object at stake in the case of repairs to a Toyota vehicle:[138]

134 Ibid.
135 This requirement is now explicit in the revised provision art 1998 CC (above).
136 332 So 2d 433 (La 1976).
137 The court reaffirmed that the moral damages may be both negative and positive, as previously held in the case of the undelivered telegram, n 125 above. Thus plaintiff might recover for the lost enjoyment and the mental distress, aggravation and inconvenience resulting from the denial of enjoyment (*Meador* at 437).
138 At 437.

We conclude that plaintiff is not entitled to recover...because the procuring of intellectual enjoyment, while perhaps an incidental or inferred contemplation of the contracting parties, was not a principal object of the contract to have the car repaired...with its consequent utility and physical gratification.

The Court's opinion has something in common with the Book of Genesis,[139] for from out of the deep came three categories:

Exclusively physical	Exclusively intellectual	Mixture of physical and intellectual
No recovery	Recovery	Conditional recovery

According to this interpretation, when the contract's object is "exclusively physical", nonpecuniary damage cannot be recovered. When the contract's object is "exclusively intellectual", moral damage can clearly be recovered. If the contract's object is a mixture of the two (partly physical *and* partly intellectual), then moral damages may be recovered, provided the anticipated intellectual benefits formed at least "a principal object". If such benefit were only an incidental object, moral damages cannot be awarded.

The Court here invented a vocabulary not found in the Code provision. It charted a universe in which every contract's purpose (object) is either physical enjoyment or intellectual enjoyment, or a mixture of the two. The Court did not attempt to define what the word "intellectual" means today or in historical terms. It was taken to mean the opposite of physical enjoyment. One may wonder whether that division presents a practical test, or whether that line is worth drawing.[140] It is submitted that the court approached the question as if it were classifying the *objets* (the performances) rather than the purposes or motives of the parties. As previously argued, the Code provision calls for a categorisation in accordance with the motives of the parties, rather than an essentialist classification of objets. The *objet* could be used of course as a sign or guide to party purpose, but if it becomes the basis of classification, then the promisee's purpose becomes secondary or possibly

139 "When God began creating the heavens and the earth, the earth was at first a shapeless chaotic mass, with the Spirit of God brooding over the dark vapors" (Genesis 1.1-2).
140 Is consuming one kind of food (hamburger) "physical enjoyment" and consuming another kind (caviar) "intellectual enjoyment"? Would it be material that one enjoys the former and dislikes the latter? This issue inheres in the Court's antique car example, n 144 below and accompanying text.

irrevelant. Another important feature of the court's interpretation is the use of the qualifying words "exclusive", "physical" and "principal". These words are not in the Code article. They were added to mark the threshold degrees of intellectual enjoyment that trigger nonpecuniary damages (or preclude them). They give the court a flexible way of dealing with mixed purpose contracts. In this schema, an "incidental" nonpecuniary object is too insignificant to trigger recovery. A "principal" nonpecuniary object (this qualifier was borrowed from the provisions dealing with error as a vice of consent)[141] meets the threshold requirement. An "exclusive" intellectual object meets and exceeds it. An "exclusive" physical object, on the other hand, precludes relief.

(2) Code revision in 1985 and later jurisprudence

Difficulties administering the court's interpretation persisted throughout the post-*Meador* jurisprudence. Both the lower courts and the Supreme Court itself vacillated in the aftermath.[142] As mentioned previously, the conceptual framework was legislatively revised when the Code article was re-enacted and newly numbered in 1985, though the Supreme Court felt justified in superimposing its prior jurisprudence on to the new provision. The new provision distinguishes between nonpecuniary and pecuniary interests, and permits moral damages when "a" nonpecuniary interest was contemplated by the parties. In *Young v Ford Motor Co Inc* (1992)[143] the Court interpreted this to mean that a *significant* nonpecuniary interest must be present. It denied recovery in that case because the plaintiff's interest was not significant but merely incidental. Refusing to acknowledge that there was any reason to change the *Meador* analysis, the Court merely substituted the modifier "significant" in place of "principal".

In *Young* the plaintiff was purchaser of a new pickup truck that he intended to use in connection with his service station and for recreation and pleasure. Use of the vehicle soon disclosed multiple latent defects and after more than a dozen unsuccessful repair attempts, plaintiff brought an action in redhibition to rescind the sale, recover the price, expenses, attorney fees,

---

141 See generally arts 1823-1846 (1870). See, e.g., art 1823 (1870): "It is not every error that will invalidate it [the contract]. To have that effect the error must be in some point which was a principal cause for making the contract."

142 For inconsistency in the circuits, see G P Graphia, (Comment) "Nonpecuniary damages: A guide to damage awards under Louisiana Civil Code article 1998" (1990) 50 La LR 797. For inconsistency by the Supreme Court, compare *Ostrowe v Darensbourg* 377 So 2d 1201 (La 1979) and *Sanders v Zeagler* 686 So 2d 819 (La 1997).

143 595 So 2d 1123 (La 1992).

and obtain damages for mental anguish. A jury awarded damages on all these heads, including $3,750 for mental anguish. The Court of Appeal disallowed the latter award and the Supreme Court affirmed.

In refusing an award of moral damages, the court ruled that plaintiff had not sought to gratify "a significant nonpecuniary interest by way of the contract". In examining whether plaintiff's interest was significant, the Court looked to the "nature" of this contract and to the evidence of his purpose. It stated:[144]

> Although purchase of a new truck or car may be prompted by both the pecuniary interest of securing transportation and the nonpecuniary interest relating to enjoyment, taste, and personal preference of owning and driving the chosen vehicle, the nature of the contract is primarily pecuniary (unless other factors evidence a different conclusion).

The nature of the contract was therefore pecuniary (physical), despite the evidence of plaintiff's recreational plans. The court provided illustrations of "other factors" which it had alluded to:[145]

> Contrast the contract of purchase made in a standard new car sale with a contract for purchase of an antique car that, while it might be driven on the streets, represents the obligee's desire to own, and perhaps to show, a distinctive, unique automobile. Or, contrast the traditional new car purchase with a contract for purchase of a specially designed, custom-built vehicle.

The tendency to essentialise the *objet*, I submit, still dominates the approach of the court.[146]

Yet experience continues to show that the centre may not hold, and the way around holdings stressing the nature of the *objet* is to document the special desires of the plaintiff. Take for example the case of *Thomas v Desire Community Housing Corp* (2000) which begins as follows:[147]

> Hendrick Thomas grew up in the Desire Housing Project in a family of eleven. All of the boys slept in one room and all the girls in another. In 1979 he married Lois Hughes ... In pursuit of the American Dream, Mr and Mrs Thomas longed for a house of their own, their "Dream House" as they referred to it.

The house the defendant constructed, however, received no construction permit from the city and was massively deficient. The trial court, in addition to $30,000 to repair construction defects, awarded nonpecuniary damages of $15,000. The appellate court affirmed, opining that revised article 1998 had

---

144 At 1133.
145 At 1133.
146 As remarked in *B & B Cut Stone Co Inc v Resneck* 465 So2d 851, "it is interesting to consider how the result in *Meador* would have differed had the plaintiff been driving an antique Bentley ... or anything more elevated than the proletarian Toyota".
147 773 So 2d 755 (4th Cir 2000).

liberalised the award of nonpecuniary damages.[148] "No longer, then, must a nonpecuniary object be the principal or exclusive object of the contract. The obligee simply must want to satisfy a significant nonpecuniary interest." The court concluded: "To the Thomases this was the culmination of a life-long dream to improve the quality of their lives, by rising from the housing projects to homeownership. It was to be the fulfillment of the American Dream for them. We find this to be a significant nonpecuniary interest."

F. CONCLUSION

The study of contracts of intellectual gratification in Scotland and Louisiana shows that moral damages *ex contractu* play an unappreciated role in the protection of personality interests. Historically, tort law has been more closely identified with protecting personality interests, and to be sure it remains the dominant way these rights are thought about. Through a tort prism we see personality rights as rights *erga omnes*, namely, as absolute subjective rights that others must not invade. This is quite different from a contractual viewpoint. A contractual vision of personality interests allows an individual the freedom to stipulate for those interests he or she wishes to create, secure or enjoy, even if no legislator or judge has thought fit to declare such interests worthy of protection. These need not be particularised categories like privacy, honour and dignity, but relative interests of various weights. In this sense contract concerns the pro-active personality creating interests through the agreements parties enter into. Here we may think of personality rights as plastic and varied as the parties may conceive.

Both Louisiana and Scotland have steered a middle course in creating an exceptional category of contract in which these personality interests receive protection. Louisiana codified the exception in the early nineteenth century, while Scotland created it through a decisional breakthrough in the 1970s. It is interesting to observe, however, how little difference these starting points made in the final analysis. The judges labouring with an old code text arrived, despite a mistranslated code, at approximately the same position reached by their their distant brethren operating without any text at all. The latter found a gap in the "common law" of Scotland and filled it with a series of precedents, while the former encountered gaps in an ambiguous code and poured in new meaning. Yet the Scottish judge might not have recognised the existence of any gap unless he was already informed, at a deeper level,

---

148 It commented that previously nonpecuniary damages were not recoverable for breach of a contract to build a home.

by the liberal Scottish tradition on solatium, and the Louisiana judge might never have perceived the gaps in the text without the context provided by the code and the tradition. The judges in both systems next faced the issue of stating the boundaries of the exception with clarity and of keeping the category stable and within reasonable limits. Both employed the "object" of the contract as the basis for recognising contracts of intellectual gratification. In Louisiana the object evokes the wider connotation of "the cause" of the contract, while in Scotland it would not have that overtone, yet this produced little or no divergence in approach. A common problem was to settle upon the exact qualifiers shaping the parameters of the exception. The reasoning was almost identical. The judges realised that the object of a contract is typically of mixed purpose, and it would be overly restrictive to require the plaintiff to prove that his or her exclusive, sole or entire purpose was to seek intellectual gratification. Accordingly, the Scottish and English cases say it is sufficient if "a major or important object" of the contract is to give pleasure, relaxation or peace of mind. The Louisiana judges say it is enough if the plaintiff seeks to gratify "a significant" interest of that type. The Louisiana judges found the qualifier in the guise of interpreting the legislative will; the Scottish and English judges found theirs in the course of an inductive search for the correct principle. What we seem to have witnessed is the creative process in two mixed jurisdictions which balanced their dual traditions in similar ways and with similar results.

9 The Effect of Unexpected Circumstances on Contracts in Scots and Louisiana Law

Laura J Macgregor[*]

A. INTRODUCTION
(1) Scope of the analysis
(2) Structural differences in the law of contract
B. IMPOSSIBILITY AND FRUSTRATION
C. COMPARISON: IMPOSSIBILITY IN LOUISIANA LAW AND FRUSTRATION IN SCOTS LAW
(1) Foreseeability of the event in question
(2) The role of fault and the causal analysis
(3) The assumption of risk
(a) Louisiana law
(b) Scots law
(4) Conclusion
D. POSSIBLE CONGRUENCE? FAILURE OF CAUSE AND FRUSTRATION OF PURPOSE
(1) Cause in Scots law and Louisiana law
(a) Scots law
(b) Louisiana law
(2) Frustration of purpose in Scots law
(3) Comparison
(4) Conclusion
E. THE CONSEQUENCES OF UNEXPECTED CIRCUMSTANCES
(1) Louisiana law
(2) Scots law
(3) Comparison
F. CONCLUSION

[*] I would like to express my sincere thanks to Adam McKinlay for his excellent research assistance. I would also like to thank all of the participants in the Scotland-Louisiana project for their helpful comments on a previous draft of this chapter, in particular Professors Vernon Palmer and David Snyder.

A. INTRODUCTION

In times of economic stability, long-term contracts may, in theory, act as an efficient tool of financial planning. They provide a means for buyers of goods or services to achieve certainty of supply, and for sellers to achieve a guaranteed income stream. In times of instability, long-term contracts take on an altogether less attractive mien. Contracting parties and their lawyers are prompted to re-read contract terms in search of escape routes. Most – possibly all – legal systems refuse to release parties from contracts solely on the ground that they have become economically less attractive to perform. However, there are more deserving cases, where radical and unprecedented changes of conditions make it unfair to hold parties to their original bargains. As is often the case, the task lies in developing clear rules which can be used to distinguish deserving from non-deserving cases.

In the current climate of global economic instability, naturally, the question of unexpected circumstances comes to the fore once more. And, of course, other phenomena have a similar effect. Natural events such as Hurricane Katrina affect people's lives as well as their business transactions. In some respects times have changed. Parties to commercial contracts will probably use *force majeure* or hardship clauses, which seek to anticipate and regulate the consequences of such events. Such clauses do not, however, provide a water-tight solution. In low-value transactions where clients do not seek advice from solicitors or legal advisers, such clauses may not be used. Even where the contract does contain a clause, it may contain phrases such as "fortuitous event" which require to be interpreted by reference to a Civil Code (in Louisiana) or the common law (in Scotland).

This chapter analyses the legal rules governing unexpected circumstances in contract law in the mixed legal systems of Louisiana and Scotland. The subject lies at the heart of commercial law, and one of the most interesting issues is likely to be whether the influence of the United States and England, world-leading commercial systems, has been dominant. The subject poses challenges to the comparatist. Louisiana, like many other legal systems, employs more than one legal concept in this area. By contrast, in Scots law, the unitary concept of frustration is applied to all cases. Other obstacles to be overcome include structural differences in the law of contract, and the difficult boundary between unexpected circumstances and error. Despite these difficulties, this chapter concludes that the two mixed legal systems can indeed learn from one another, in particular by drawing on the best parts of the different sources available to them.

(1) Scope of the analysis

The description "unexpected circumstances" has been used rather than "changed circumstances". "Unexpected" communicates the unanticipated nature of the sequence of events which has occurred, a factor which is important in both legal systems. Implicit in this description is that the unexpected event occurs after formation, during the life of the contract. Factors in existence but not known to the parties at the point of formation tend, in both systems, to lie within the ambit of error. As is explored below, in Louisiana law (but not in Scots law) there appears to be an overlap between the rules on error and unexpected circumstances.[1] In other systems too, these two areas of law have a close relationship.[2]

Unexpected circumstances are obviously more problematic in long-term as opposed to short-term contracts: the longer the duration of the contract, the more likely it is that an unexpected event will occur. Aside from this point, there is an intimate relationship between long-term contracts and unexpected circumstances. In long-term contracts at the point of formation parties must assess the risks inherent in the relationship and set the price accordingly. Fixed price contracts insulate parties from fluctuations in market price. Not surprisingly therefore, a key question in long-term contracts is whether a particular party assumed the risk that a particular event would occur. Notwithstanding this close relationship, there seems no reason in principle to omit contracts of shorter duration from consideration. Only the executed contract, performed instantly, is omitted from this enquiry, because problems of unexpected circumstances do not arise.

(2) Structural differences in the law of contract

French influence on Louisiana law has ensured that the concept of fault has played, and continues to play, a key role in breach of contract. In French and Louisiana law, liability for breach is based on fault.[3] By contrast, fault is thought to be irrelevant in common law systems of breach of contract. Although Scots law has a mixed system of breach of contract, it has not received the Civilian emphasis on fault as an aspect of breach.[4] Faced with

---

1 See D.(1)(b) below.
2 E.g., German law, where mistaken assumptions at the point of formation are governed not by the law of error but by the law on changed circumstances. See B Markesinis, H Unberath, and A Johnston, *The German Law of Contract* (2006) 342.
3 La Civ Code art 1994. Professor Reinhard Zimmermann notes that this is the tradition of the *ius commune*: *The Law of Obligations, Roman Foundations of the Civilian Tradition* (1990) 814.
4 See H L MacQueen, "Remedies for breach of contract: The future development of Scots law in its European and International context" 2007 EdinLR 200.

a relevant case, a Scottish court will not assess the degree to which the party in breach is at fault: liability is virtually strict.[5] In systems such as French and Louisiana law, where liability for breach is based on fault, a party in breach who is not at fault ought to be released. Non-performance may be due to a supervening event, and if this is so, there is no fault. Impossibility of performance therefore acts as an excuse for non-performance.

Differences also lie in the attitude of each system to the concept of cause. Cause is a significant aspect of Louisiana law, defined in the Civil Code as the reason why a contracting party obligates himself.[6] Additionally, an obligation cannot exist without a lawful cause.[7] Where a cause has "failed" due to unexpected circumstances, as explored below,[8] the parties are released from their contractual obligations. Modern Scots contract law, by contrast, possesses no concept of cause. These structural differences relating to breach and cause have an impact on the analysis of unexpected circumstances. Whilst they play a key role in Louisiana law, that is not the case in Scots law.

A further "structural" difference is the role played by good faith in the two systems. Whilst a central aspect of Louisiana contract law,[9] the concept remains little developed in Scots law.[10] The duty of good faith may even be "enhanced" in contracts of long duration in Louisiana, where parties are thought to pursue a common end.[11] One might have expected this difference to be significant here. Good faith is, after all, the bedrock upon which certain systems have built their rules on unexpected circumstances.[12] However, in

5 Unexpected circumstances being the exception, in which strict liability may not apply.
6 La Civ Code art 1967.
7 La Civ Code art 1966.
8 See D.(1)(b) below.
9 La Civ Code art 1759: "Good faith shall govern the conduct of the obligor and the obligee in whatever pertains to the obligation".
10 Receiving recognition from Lord Clyde in the House of Lords in the Scottish case, *Smith v Bank of Scotland* 1997 SC (HL) 111 at 118. More recently, another Scottish House of Lords judge, Lord Hope, described it as "an underlying principle of an explanatory or legitimating rather than an active or creative nature": see *R v Immigration Officer at Prague Airport, ex parte European Roma Rights Centre* [2004] UKHL 55, [2005] 2 AC 1 at para 60. For analysis see H L MacQueen, "Good Faith", in H MacQueen and R Zimmermann, (eds), *European Contract Law: Scots and South African Perspectives* (2006) 43.
11 S Litvinoff, *"Force majeure,* failure of cause and théorie de l'imprévision: Louisiana law and beyond" (1985) 46 La LR 1 at 37, citing R A Hillman, "Policing contractual modifications under the UCC: Good faith and the doctrine of economic duress" (1979) 64 Iowa L Rev 849. In view of the essentially adversarial nature of negotiation of commercial contracts in Scotland, it is doubtful whether the Scots lawyer would agree that long-term contracts involve the pursuit of a common end.
12 See, e.g., in German law the concept of *Störung der Geschäftsgrundlage* or the doctrine of the foundation of the contract, as in BGB § 313, "Disturbance of foundation of transaction" (and see Markesinis, *German Law of Contract* (n 2) 319-346); and in French law the administrative law doctrine of *imprévision* (described below at B.) which is thought to be based, at least in part, on art 1134 of the *Code civil* on good faith.

neither legal system is the concept of good faith of particular importance in unexpected circumstances cases. Rather, there is an emphasis in both systems of underlying ideas of fairness or equity. This is certainly true of Scots law, where ideas of *naturalis aequitas* have underpinned the rules on frustration, particularly those applying following frustration of contract.[13] So too article 4 of the Louisiana Civil Code of 1870 contains the following more general statement:

> When no rule for a particular situation can be derived from legislation or custom, the court is bound to proceed according to equity. To decide equitably, resort is made to justice, reason, and prevailing usages.

Article 4 strikes a familiar chord with Scots lawyers, to such an extent that it would not look out of place in the works of Stair and Erskine and the Scottish Institutional writers, who drew extensively on natural law ideas.

Modern developments are also relevant. Scotland, part of a member state of the European Union, is affected by European Union law. A significant recent development in European contract law is the publication of the Draft Common Frame of Reference or, to use it its full title, *Principles, Definitions and Model Rules of European Private Law*, ("DCFR").[14] The DCFR is a purely academic initiative, intended to act as a "toolbox" of terms, and thus as an inspiration for European and possibly also national legislatures. Moves are underway to develop the DCFR into a political common frame of reference. There is every reason to suppose that the DCFR will be influential in Scotland, particularly given the Scottish Parliament's legislative competence over the law of obligations.[15] The DCFR provisions on unexpected circumstances are therefore referred to throughout this chapter.

B. IMPOSSIBILITY AND FRUSTRATION

The idea that parties may be released from long-term contracts because of a change in circumstances was recognised by Roman law. The maxim *rebus sic stantibus* described a doctrine which "made the validity of a contract depend on the continuance of the circumstances obtaining at the time of its formation".[16] However, in more recent history a competing idea was

---

13 T M Cooper, "Frustration of contract in Scots law" (1946) 28 *Journal of Comparative Legislation* 1 at 1 and 3.
14 *Principles, Definitions and Model Rules of European Private Law, Draft Common Frame of Reference, Interim Outline Edition*, produced by the Study Group on a European Civil Code and the Research Group on EC Private Law (2008).
15 Scotland Act 1998 ss 28-29 and 126(4)(c).
16 K Zweigert and H Kötz, *An Introduction to Comparative Law*, 3rd edn tr T Weir (1998) 518.

emphasised, namely the binding nature of contracts: *pacta sunt servanda*. The unstable economic conditions brought about by two World Wars led to a resurgence of interest in *rebus sic stantibus*, particularly in Germany where it was used to combat the effects of dramatic inflation.[17] In French law art 1148 of the *Code civil* provided that parties are not liable in damages where prevented from performing due to either *cas fortuit* or *force majeure*.[18] This provision was applied strictly, the courts requiring absolute impossibility. The strict approach was, however, tempered by the *Conseil d'Etat* in administrative contracts. This occurred through use of *imprévision*, which allows the court to revise contracts affected by change of circumstances, in order, not to release parties from their contracts, but rather to "re-balance" obligations.[19] That concept has remained confined to public law contracts, the civil courts refusing to follow the lead taken by the *Conseil d'Etat*. *Imprévision* can therefore be seen as a tool used, for example, to ensure continuity of supply of public utilities, and not one which is available to private parties to help resolve their disputes.

The original article of the Louisiana Digest of 1808 governing unexpected circumstances was in terms almost identical to article 1148 of the Code Napoléon of 1804.[20] English translations of the Digest of 1808 and Code of 1825 referred to *cas fortuit* and *force majeure* as "fortuitous event" and "irresistible force".[21] The article currently in force uses only the former expression.[22] By the time of the Code of 1825, the general rule which saved an obligor from payment of damages in cases of *force majeure* or *cas fortuit* had been made subject to two exceptions, neither of which is found in the original French source. The development of those exceptions is discussed below.[23] The article currently in force in Louisiana, article 1873, provides

---

Professor Saúl Litvinoff provides the full text as follows: *Contractus qui habent tractus succesivum et dependentiam de futurum, rebus sic stantibus intelligentur*, translating this as "Contracts providing for successive acts of performance over a future period of time must be understood as subject to the condition that the circumstances will remain the same" (*The Law of Obligations*, 5 *Louisiana Civil Law Treatise* 2nd edn (2001) § 16.72 n 3). See also D 50.17.23 on impossibility.

17 Markesinis, *German Law of Contract* (n 2) 319-346.

18 *Code civil* art 1148. These concepts are undefined in the French Code. M Hunley suggests the following definition: "unforeseeable events not imputable to the obligor which present an insurmountable obstacle to his performance" ("Supervening impossibility as a discharge of an obligation" (1947) 21 Tulane LR 603 at 606).

19 Perhaps most famously in the *Gaz de Bordeaux* case, Conseil d'État, 30 March 1916, DP 1916 3.25.

20 See La Civ Code of 1808 art 48 p 268 and *Code Napoléon* 1804 art 1148.

21 La Civ Code of 1809 art 48 p268; La Civ Code of 1825 art 1933. From 1870 the Code became available only in English.

22 La Civ Code art 1873.

23 See C.(2) and (3)(a) below.

that an obligor is not liable for his failure to perform when it is caused by a fortuitous event that makes performance impossible. Impossibility, which must be absolute,[24] is a key issue. More detailed analysis of article 1873 can be found below.[25] For the moment it is sufficient to note only the French source of the Louisiana provisions and the central role played by the concept of impossibility.

Some of the earliest Scottish cases could be classed as examples of the release of parties from contracts on grounds of supervening impossibility, although that term was not actually used. Balfour notes two examples from the sixteenth century involving the non-payment of teinds.[26] In the first case non-payment was excused where the failure to harvest crops had occurred because of fear that enemy troops would burn down barns.[27] In the second it was excused where crops were destroyed by violence which a contracting party was unable to resist.[28] These Scottish cases stand in marked contrast to the infamous English case, *Paradine v Jane*,[29] occurring almost 100 years later, in which the unhappy tenant was held bound to pay two years' rent despite being ejected from the premises during this time by Prince Rupert's invading army. Indeed, it was only in 1863 with *Taylor v Caldwell*[30] that the English principles of frustration began to emerge. Underlining the earlier development of the Scottish principles, Cooper suggested that frustration in Scotland developed around two bodies of case law: that concerning the obligation of restitution (in effect, the *condictio causa data causa non secuta*); and that concerning *rei interitus*, or the destruction of the subject matter of a contract. The latter idea was developed in cases concerning contracts of lease, sale and *locatio operis*.[31]

References to supervening impossibility can be found in more recent cases, as for example the following from a judgment of Lord Sorn in 1951:[32]

---

24 La Civ Code art 1873: revision comment (d) 1984, A N Yiannopoulos (ed), Louisiana Civil Code, 2005 Edition, 396.

25 See C. below.

26 Teinds were the right of the local parish to a tenth of the land, later converted into a monetary payment, now abolished: see K G C Reid, *The Abolition of Feudal Tenure in Scotland* (2003) para 10.20.

27 Balfour, *Practicks*, 146, cvii, citing *The Chaptour of Glasgow v the Laird of Cesfurde*, 29 July 1563.

28 Balfour, *Practicks*, 146, cviii, citing *Abbot of Halyruidhous v the Laird of Inverleith* 20 January 1549.

29 (1647) Aleyn 26.

30 (1863) 3 B & S 826.

31 Cooper, "Frustration of contract" (n 13) 1-2.

32 *Union Totaliser Co Ltd v Scott* 1951 SLT (Notes) 5.

What is meant by "supervening impossibility", as I understand it, is the emergence of a new state of affairs, due to subsequent legislation or other supervening events, in which the performance of the contract has become either impossible, or something fundamentally different from what was originally contemplated. The essence of it is that the situation giving rise to the impossibility should be a situation not envisaged by the parties when making the contract.

Despite these words, impossibility plays a much reduced role in modern Scots law. Whereas in 1929 it formed the main chapter-heading in the leading textbook,[33] in the modern text it has been relegated to a minor chapter-heading, preceding an analysis of less than two pages.[34] "Frustration" has taken over as the term of art.

With reference to the words of Lord Sorn, frustration includes not only actual impossibility, but also cases where the contract becomes one which is "fundamentally different from what was originally contemplated". Thus, frustration is wider than impossibility. Scottish judges now tend to adopt the following definition from the speech of Lord Radcliffe in an English House of Lords case, *Davis Contractors Ltd v Fareham WDC*:[35]

> frustration occurs whenever the law recognizes that without default of either party a contractual obligation has become incapable of being performed because the circumstances in which performance is called for would render it a thing radically different from that which was undertaken by the contract. Non haec in foedera veni. It was not this that I promised to do.

Although Scottish frustration appears to be wider than impossibility in Louisiana, initial conclusions may be misleading. Much depends on the manner in which article 1873 is applied by the Louisiana courts. The section immediately below compares the content and application of article 1873 with the Scottish doctrine. The comparison looks beyond terms such as "impossibility" and "frustration" to the component parts of the concepts as applied by the judiciary in each legal system.

---

33 W M Gloag, *The Law of Contract*, 2nd edn (1929) ch 19.

34 See W W McBryde, *The Law of Contract in Scotland*, 3rd edn (2007) paras 21-26–21-29. In H L MacQueen and J Thomson, *Contract Law in Scotland*, 2nd edn (2007) it appears as a minor chapter heading preceding an analysis of the destruction of the subject matter of the contract (*rei interitus*): see paras 4.72 and 4.73. Forte goes as far as to conclude that "'Impossibility' is a misnomer under Scots and English law" (A D M Forte, "Economic frustration of commercial contracts: A comparative analysis with particular reference to the United Kingdom" 1986 JR 1 at n 1).

35 [1956] AC 696 per Lord Radcliffe at 729. The seeds of this approach were, however, sown in the speeches of Lords Wright and Porter in an earlier Scottish House of Lords case, *James B Fraser & Co v Denny, Mott & Dickson* 1944 SC (HL) 35.

C. COMPARISON: IMPOSSIBILITY IN LOUISIANA LAW AND FRUSTRATION IN SCOTS LAW

(1) Foreseeability of the event in question

Article 1873 excuses the obligor from failure to perform when that failure is caused by a fortuitous event that makes performance impossible. A fortuitous event is defined as one that, at the time the contract was made, could not have been reasonably foreseen.[36]

A key question is whether foreseeability is applied in a subjective or an objective sense. A different part of the Civil Code provides that a contractual object is possible or impossible according to its own nature and not according to the parties' ability to perform,[37] which is suggestive, perhaps, of an objective approach. However, according to the Court of Appeal, the attitude of the Louisiana courts is rather more subjective in nature: "[they showed] ... more concern for the reasonableness of the parties' foresight in a given situation rather than the objective foreseeability of a particular event".[38]

Events such as hurricanes and flooding are a fact of life in Louisiana. Being eminently foreseeable, even probable, one might expect difficulty in persuading the Louisiana courts of their classification as fortuitous events. Although there are indeed examples of a strict approach,[39] in a significant case, *Viterbo v Friedlander*, the US Supreme Court (applying Louisiana law) concluded that the frequency of occurrence of the breaking of the Mississippi through the levees did not take it out of the class of *cas fortuit*.[40]

Scottish judges tend not to use the word "foreseeable" in this context, although Lord Sorn in the passage quoted above indicated that the situation must be one which was "not envisaged by the parties when making the contract".[41] It may be that the requirement is so obvious that it goes without saying. There is certainly a difference of emphasis in the Scottish cases, where, as is explored immediately below, the focus lies on the nature of the event itself and the contracting party's inability to resist that event.

---

36 La Civ Code art 1875. See Litvinoff who indicates that a superior force is an accident that human prudence cannot prevent, *Obligations* (n 16) § 16.16.

37 La Civ Code art 1972.

38 *McElroy v Dynasty Transport Inc* 907 So 2d 69 (La App 1 Cir 3/24/05); see also Revision Comment (b) to article 1873 in A N Yiannopoulos (ed), Louisiana Civil Code, 2005 edition, 396, which cites *Farnsworth v Sewerage & Water Board of New Orleans* 173 La 1105, 139 So 638 (1932).

39 See *Vinson v Graves* 16 La Ann 162 (1861) where the court exhibited this attitude to the overflowing of the Mississippi River.

40 120 US 707 7 S Ct 962, 30 L Ed 776 (1887) at 733, discussed in detail at D.(1)(b) below.

41 See n 32 above.

(2) The role of fault and the causal analysis

In the introduction to this chapter the different role played by fault in breach of contract in the two systems was noted. The reasoning displayed by French courts (identifying fault as a necessary part of breach, and releasing parties in cases of unexpected circumstances because of the lack of fault) is not applicable in Scots law. Not surprisingly, therefore, references to the fault of the parties in Scottish cases are difficult to find.[42] Rather, the focus lies on the application of principles of causation. A supervening event has been defined as "outside the control of the party founding on it"[43] and "[not due] to the act of either of the parties, but arising from circumstances beyond the control of either".[44] The irresistible nature of the event is also emphasised.[45] Where a party can exercise control over an event but fails to do so, non-performance can be attributed to his inaction, rather than to the event itself. Thus, in Scots law a party may be released from his obligations where non-performance is truly unavoidable.

Issues of causation are also brought to the fore in Louisiana law in the three exceptions to article 1873 (exceptions in the sense that their effect is to hold the obligor liable). Two exceptions were contained in the Code of 1825, and the third was added following revision to the Code in 1985. Under the fourth paragraph of article 1873 a contracting party remains liable "when the fortuitous event that caused his failure to perform has been preceded by his fault, without which the failure would not have occurred". In *Sickinger v Board of Directors of Public Schools for Parish of Orleans*, the Supreme Court of Louisiana indicated that both this exception and the exception in the second paragraph of article 1873 are founded on the idea that "the fortuitous event that prevented a carrying out of the contract was a danger that might reasonably have been contemplated by the parties to the contract".[46] A contracting party is at fault in failing to anticipate the event, and this fault becomes the real cause of non-performance. The phraseology suggests simple "but for" causation.

---

42 Cf W W McBryde "Frustration of contract" 1980 JR 1 at 13. Although examples are noted by McBryde (*Duncan v Arbroath* (1668) Mor 10075 and *Jacksons (Edinburgh) Ltd v Constructors John Brown Ltd* 1965 SLT 37) it is hard to concur with his view that fault is referred to in most cases.

43 McBryde, *Contract* (n 34) para 21-04.

44 Gloag, *Contract* (n 33) 67.

45 See *James B Fraser & Co Ltd v Denny, Mott & Dickson Ltd* 1944 SC (HL) 35 per Lord MacMillan at 41; *Cantiere San Rocco v Clyde Shipbuilding and Engineering Co* 1923 SC (HL) 105 per Lord Birkenhead at 108 and 111. One can find similar emphasis in Louisiana law – see Litvinoff who indicates that a superior force is an accident that human prudence cannot prevent, *Obligations* (n 16) § 16.16.

46 147 La 479, 85 So 212 (1920) per O'Niell J at 487.

As already stated, none of the exceptions was present in the equivalent article of the French *Code civil*, article 1148.[47] In 1883 the Supreme Court of Louisiana in *Eugster & Co v Joseph West & Co*[48] commented on the exceptions contained in article 1873's fourth and second paragraph as follows:[49]

> It cannot seriously be doubted that the rule of the French law was modified in the redaction of our Code with the purpose of bringing it more in accord with that system from which we derive our commercial law, and the authorities from the common law we have cited therefore derive additional force from that circumstance. They are thus safe guidelines in construing the provisions of our Code upon the subject in hand.

With regard to the other exceptions, that contained in the third paragraph of article 1873, the most recent in date, provides that the obligor is liable "when the fortuitous event occurred after he has been put in default".[50] In Louisiana law a contracting party can recover damages for delay only once he has put the party in breach "in default".[51] This can be achieved in a number of ways, for example, through a written request for performance, but also by a specific provision in the contract itself.[52] Scots law contains no such rule, and the issue of whether a party is entitled either to rescind or to claim damages for delay would be decided by asking whether the delay amounted to a material breach. The effect of the exception in the third paragraph of article 1873 is therefore to ensure that a contracting party already put in default cannot rely on a later fortuitous event to absolve him from his obligation to pay damages. Professor Litvinoff explains that putting in default involves a "devolution of the risk to [the obligor]",[53] supporting his view by reference to *Eugster & Co v Joseph West & Co*, cited above.[54] In that case the defendant was bound to ship grain to the plaintiff using a barge. He delayed in doing so, and the subsequent freezing of the river meant that he became unable to deliver the goods on time. The court concluded that the defendant's default, occurring before the potentially fortuitous event, prevented him from alleging that the event was fortuitous. However, technically, the defendants were not in breach of contract before the freeze occurred. They failed to commence shipment within a period of eleven days prior to the

---

47 Although French doctrine recognises the possibility of parties expressly assuming the risk of a fortuitous event through contractual stipulation, see Litvinoff, *Obligations* (n 16) § 16.42.
48 35 La Ann 119 (1883) 1 at 6.
49 35 La Ann 119 (1883) 1 at 3.
50 La Civ Code art 1873(3).
51 La Civ Code art 1989.
52 La Civ Code art 1991.
53 See Litvinoff, *Obligations* (n 16) § 16.46.
54 35 La Ann 119 (1883) 1 at 6 (cited at n 48). There are also references, at 2, to the defendants' "neglect" to ship the goods while conditions were favourable.

freeze when the contract provided them with twenty days in which to do so. The case can be explained by identifying the probable onset of a freeze as a factor which placed a positive duty to act on the defendants. Their subsequent failure to act shifted the risk to them.

Perhaps not surprisingly for a case-based system, Scots law lacks the depth of analysis found in Louisiana law regarding the impact of a breach preceding the unexpected event. It seems clear that degrees of behaviour falling short of fault in Scots law will not prevent a party from raising a plea of frustration.[55] Additionally, the definition of frustration appearing in Sheriff Guthrie's seventh edition of Bell's *Principles of the Law of Scotland* includes the requirement that neither party should be in default.[56] The impact of a prior breach may depend on the attitude of the innocent party to the breach. He has alternative responses to breach: he may accept the breach and rescind (terminate) the contract; or he may ignore the breach (even if material) and continue performance. Where he has accepted the breach and rescinded, a post-breach supervening event is irrelevant. Where he has opted to continue performance, there is at least an argument that the breach can no longer be legally relevant. As a result, the effect of a breach which precedes a frustrating event is an issue which, in Scots law, might require to be analysed on a case-by-case basis.

To conclude this part, one could say that there is similarity of approach in the two legal systems to the extent that, in general, neither system would allow a contracting party to avoid paying damages where he is in breach of contract prior to the occurrence of the unexpected event.

(3) The assumption of risk

(a) Louisiana law

The exception contained in the second paragraph of article 1873 provides that a contracting party will be liable for his failure to perform when he has assumed the risk of such a fortuitous event.[57] Assumption may be express or implied[58] and so is, essentially, a question of interpretation of the contract. Risks can be expressly assumed, even where the fortuitous event is described as "extraordinary".[59] Where the occurrence of the event is highly probable,

---

55 See *London and Edinburgh Shipping Co v The Admiralty* 1920 SC 309.

56 Bell, *Principles*, 7th edn by W Guthrie (1876) § 31. A later version of this same text, appearing in the 10th edn, §29, also edited by Guthrie, was approved by the House of Lords in *James B Fraser & Co v Denny, Mott & Dickson* 1944 SC (HL) 35.

57 La Civ Code art 1873.

58 La Civ Code art 1873 Revision comment (b) 1984 in A N Yiannopoulos (ed), Louisiana Civil Code, 2005 edn, 396.

59 *Losecco v Gregory* 108 La 648, 32 So 985 (1901).

the claimant is likely to be found to have assumed the risk of its occur-rence. This is illustrated by a case in which a subcontractor unsuccessfully argued that heavy rainfall constituted a fortuitous event when, at the time he entered into the contract, the building site was already under water.[60] So too in *Sickinger* a school board had undertaken to move a house and reconstruct it on a new location.[61] At the time of formation of the contract, the board was unaware that a tropical storm was due to hit the area. Nevertheless, recon-struction was due to take place during hurricane season, and so damage from a hurricane would be possible, perhaps even probable. When the storm hit, the house was practically destroyed. The court held that, because the danger of a storm during the hurricane season was well known to the school board, they had assumed the risk of it occurring. They were under an obligation either to move the house before the commencement of the season during which such storms were likely to occur, or move it in such a way as to avoid the danger.

Unless a party has expressly assumed the risk of an extraordinary event in the contract, he is unlikely to be taken to have impliedly assumed such a risk. Events falling into the category of "extraordinary" have included "abnormal and unprecedented" rainfall which prevented performance.[62] There is (as was acknowledged by the court in *Sickinger*) a link between the assumption of risk and foreseeabilty. If a risk is foreseeable, a party will be taken to have assumed it. Where the event is foreseeable in theory but highly unlikely to occur, a party will not be taken to have assumed the risk of its occurrence.

The court in *Eugster*[63] identified the source of the exceptions contained in the second and fourth paragraphs of article 1873 as the common law. US influence was clearly significant during this period: two years previously the decision was taken, for fear of a resultant lack of consistency with US commercial law, not to enact a draft Louisiana Commercial Code produced by the Revision Committee.[64] The assumption of risk does indeed play a role in the current article 2 of the Uniform Commercial Code, although this is one of the articles of the UCC which has not been adopted into Louisiana law.[65] Assumption of risk also plays a role in the *Restatement (Second) of Contracts*.[66] Inspiration for the two exceptions may indeed lie in US law,

---

60 *Harper v Home Indem Co* 140 So 2d 653 (La App 2d Cir 1962)

61 See n 46 above.

62 *Farnsworth v Sewerage & Water Board of New Orleans* 173 La 1105, 139 So 638 (1932).

63 See n 54 above.

64 A N Yiannopoulos, "Requiem for a civil code: A commemorative essay" (2003) 78 Tulane LR 379 at 388.

65 See UCC § 2-509, §§ 2-509 and 2-510.

66 *Restatement (Second) of Contracts* § 268.

although there are now few similarities between the exceptions on the one hand and the terms of either the UCC or the Restatement (Second) on the other. The exceptions seem not to have been drawn word-for-word from a US source. Rather, they can be characterised as "home-grown".

Assumption of risk arguments are highly visible in so-called "economic frustration" cases, that is, where a party seeks to be released from contractual obligations which have become financially punitive. Such arguments are unsuccessful in Louisiana law, financial impossibility not being classed as a legally relevant type of impossibility. Obligations must be performed "at any cost, whatever the sacrifice".[67] Such cases are more accurately described as involving economic *impracticability*.[68] A contract is never impossible to perform on economic grounds alone, funds or goods always being theoretically obtainable. However, the Louisiana District Court in 1985 rejected what it described as the "Common Law" doctrine of economic impracticability.[69] This US doctrine, found in the *Restatement (Second) of Contracts*, was an attempt to widen the grounds on which parties could be released from contracts, including "unreasonable difficulty, expense, injury or loss".[70] However, even under the *Restatement*, increased cost alone will not have this effect.[71] As is the case in Louisiana, in the Scots courts too the doctrine of economic impossibility or impracticability has been rejected.[72]

The courts base their rejection of economic impossibility on the obligation incumbent on a contracting party to assess risks inherent in a long-term contract at the point of formation and price accordingly.[73] The very purpose of entering into such a contract is to insulate the parties from fluctuations in price. The event occurring during the "life" of the contract may be a shortage (with resultant high market prices) or a glut (with resultant low market prices). The overall effect is the same: for one contracting party the contract becomes drastically uneconomic to perform. To take into account arguments

---

67 The statement is Litvinoff's, *Obligations* (n 16) § 16.17, approved by the US District Court in *US Bancorp Equipment Finance Inc v Loews Express LLC* (E D La, 9 January 2008). This case is commented on in more detail below.

68 This is the term used in UCC § 2-615 and *Restatement (Second) of Contracts* § 261.

69 *Superior Oil Company v Transco Energy Company* 616 F Supp 98 (1985). UCC § 2-615, "Excuse by failure of presupposed conditions" refers to cases in which performance has been made "impracticable by the occurrence of a contingency the non-occurrence of which was a basic assumption on which the contract was made ..." See also *Restatement (Second) of Contracts* § 261.

70 *Restatement (Second) of Contracts* § 261, cmt d.

71 *Hong Kong and Whampoa Dock Co v Netherton Shipping Co Ltd* 1909 SC 34; UCC § 2-615, cmt 4.

72 *Davidson v Macpherson* (1889) 30 SLR 2.

73 See *Marrioneaux v Smith* 163 So 206 (1935) at 208; *Hanover Petroleum Corp v Tenneco* 521 So 2d 1234 (1988).

of economic impossibility would be to release parties from a bad bargain. Refusal to do so is, arguably, economically efficient.

Catastrophic events such as hurricanes create situations of economic collapse in which parties may be unable to perform for a number of different reasons: goods may be in chronically short supply; or parties may lack the finances to perform, whether because of non-payment under other contracts, or due to an unwillingness of banks to lend. Not surprisingly, a number of relevant cases have been raised in the aftermath of Hurricane Katrina. In one such case, the business of a bus tour company, Loews Express, was effectively destroyed by the hurricane. Different factors contributed to Loews' financial collapse: not simply the fact that the tourists had stopped coming to New Orleans, but also the disruption of business caused when buses were commandeered to help evacuate the flooded city.[74] Loews became unable to pay charges due for hire/lease of the buses. The court refused to free them from their obligations under the leases, Judge Fallon commenting:[75]

> the defendants' argument, taken to its logical extreme, would allow anyone financially harmed by Hurricane Katrina to avoid their contractual obligations altogether. Such a result is obviously untenable and it is one that this Court believes the Supreme Court of Louisiana would reject.

Times of economic instability lead to similar crops of cases. It is no accident that the approaches of French and German law to unexpected circumstances cases developed significantly in the aftermath of the World Wars. Fluctuations in oil prices have had a particularly onerous effect on long-term oil and gas supply contracts in Louisiana.[76] The assumption of risk plays an important role in such cases. Thus we see refusals to release parties from "take or pay" contracts, in terms of which the purchaser must take, or pay for if he does not take, a certain quantity of oil or gas in each year.[77] At a much earlier stage, the

---

74 *US Bancorp Equipment Finance Inc v Loews Express LLC* (E D La, 9 January 2008). For other cases decided in the aftermath of hurricanes see *Schenk v Capri Construction Co* 194 So 2d 378 (1967); *Associated Acquisitions v Carbone Properties of Audubon* 962 So 2d 1102 (2007); *Payne v Hurwitz* 978 So 2d 1000 (La App 1 Cir 2008).

75 This case was decided by a federal trial court, the United States District court. Federal jurisdiction is based on "diversity of citizenship between the parties", in other words, the fact that the parties are citizens from different states. The court is applying Louisiana state law to the substantive issues in the case, i.e. making an *"Eerie* guess" as to how the Supreme Court of Louisiana would decide this case (*Eerie R Co v Tompkins* 304 US 64 (1938)).

76 See the interesting discussion by C Morrison Hopkins, "The energy crisis and economic impossibility in Louisiana fuel requirements contracts: A gameplan for reform" (1975) 49 Tulane LR 605.

77 See *Hanover Petroleum Corp v Tenneco* 521 So 2d 1234 (1988) in which Judge Guidry explained, at 1238, the necessity of pricing risks into a contract: "shifting supply and demand and changing governmental regulations are normal factors considered in any business transaction. By the clear

Great Depression provoked a similar rash of litigation.[78]

The results in some of these cases seem harsh. Although in *Loews* the court concluded that Hurricane Katrina was a fortuitous event, the plaintiff was ultimately unsuccessful because the court applied settled case law which refuses to recognise economic impossibility. It is difficult to see how Loews could, factually, have performed in the circumstances following Hurricane Katrina. However, the decision is justified by policy reasons, particularly the need to avoid upsetting commercial transactions in times of economic instability. The clarity of the legal rules is unlikely to prevent the occurrence of a further series of cases in the wake of the current global economic crisis.

(b) Scots law

According to Professor William McBryde, the assumption of risk is of fundamental importance in unexpected circumstances cases in Scots law, pre-dating the development of rules on frustration: "Long before the term 'frustration' was used Scots lawyers were asking – on whom does the risk of a supervening event fall?"[79] McBryde's views are consistent with those of Lord Cooper, the latter referring to the cases contained under the title "*Periculum*"[80] in Morison's *Dictionary of Decisions* (of the Court of Session from 1540 until 1808). Indeed, McBryde exhorts the Scots lawyer to "ignore dicta in English cases", and "follow the approach of his predecessors".[81] He indicates, correctly, it is suggested, that the court in allocating risk does more than interpret the contract, deciding an issue of policy.[82] As is the case in Louisiana law, it is not difficult to find Scottish examples of parties seeking unsuccessfully to be released from contracts in times of economic depression. In refusing to release a tenant from his obligation under a lease to clear waste ground, the Lord Justice Clerk, Lord Macdonald, explained:[83]

---

and unambiguous terms of the remainder of the contract, the plaintiff accepts the supply risk, the defendant accepts the market risk, and both parties adopt the risk of changed governmental regulations." See also *Kenny v Oak Builders Inc* 256 La 85, 235 So 2d 386 (1970); *Exxon Corp v Columbia Gas Transmission Corp* 624 F Supp 610 (W D La 1985); *Superior Oil Company v Transco Energy Company* 616 F Supp 98 (1985).

78 *Dallas Cooperage & Woodenware Co v Creston Hoop Co* 161 La 1077, 109 So 844 (La 1926); *Marrioneaux v Smith* 163 So 206 (La App 1935).

79 McBryde "Frustration of contract" (n 42) at 4; Forte, "Economic frustration" (n 34) at 4, n 13; McBryde, *Contract* (n 34) para 21-02; Cooper, "Frustration of contract" (n 13) at 2.

80 Cooper, "Frustration of contract" (n 13) at 2.

81 McBryde "Frustration of contract" (n 42) at 5.

82 McBryde "Frustration of contract" (n 42) at 5.

83 *Davidson v Macpherson* (1889) 30 SLR 2 at 5. See also *Blacklock & Macarthur Ltd v Kirk* 1919 SC 57; and *Hong Kong and Whampoa Co Ltd v Netherton Shipping Co Ltd* 1909 SC 34.

If that is to be a defence to an obligation of this kind it would simply result in this, that every lease will be interfered with against the landlord when prices are low, but that the tenant may hold the farm and get the advantages of it when prices are high.

In a similar vein, the leading Scottish contract author, Gloag, concluded in 1929: "So far as the existing authorities go no change in economic conditions, however serious and however deeply it may affect the contract, can amount to frustration such as to avoid it."[84]

However, one finds less emphasis on the assumption of risk in modern Scottish cases. The emphasis lies rather on the test in English cases, in which parties are released where changed circumstances have rendered the contract so radically different in nature that the parties can no longer be held to it. The test in the English case, *Davis Contractors v Fareham UDC*,[85] is applied in Scottish cases. The approach based on the assumption of risk so admired by Cooper and McBryde may now lie beyond the reach of the Scottish courts.

(4) Conclusion

The conclusion initially reached remains true: frustration in Scots law is wider than impossibility in Louisiana law. Looking at these concepts themselves, there are similarities and differences of approach. Forseeability, a key concept in Louisiana law, is not emphasised in Scots law. The carefully drafted exceptions to article 1873 can be contrasted with rather vague statements on the same issues in Scottish cases. Perhaps the most significant conclusion, however, relates to the assumption of risk. Established as a significant factor in Scots law at an early stage it is no longer emphasised. Not present in the French *Code civil*[86] it became part of Louisiana law through later revision of the Code, probably due to Common Law influence. Louisiana law here displays the type of mixing one might expect of the mixed legal system. By contrast, the Scottish story seems to be the dominance of English law. The central role within the Draft Common Frame of Reference for the assumption of risk at least ensures that it remains on the agenda in Scotland for contract law reform.[87]

---

84 Gloag, *Contract* (n 33) 354.
85 [1956] AC 696. For other influential English cases see *British Movietone News LD v London and District Cinemas* [1952] AC 166; *Tsakiroglou & Co v Noblee Thorl* [1962] AC 93; *Ocean Tramp Tankers Corporation v V/O Overact (The Eugenia)* [1964] 2 QB 226; *Pioneer Shipping v BTP Tioxide* [1982] AC 724, where Lord Roskill remarked (at 752): "[Frustration is] not likely to be invoked to relieve parties of the normal consequences of imprudent commercial bargains."
86 Although, as stated, it appears to have been discussed in French legal writings.
87 This concept also appears as part of the formulation of the rules in the DCFR, art III. – 1:110(3)

D. POSSIBLE CONGRUENCE? FAILURE OF CAUSE AND FRUSTRATION OF PURPOSE

(1) Cause in Scots law and Louisiana law

(a) Scots law

Cause is entirely absent from modern Scots contract law, although it may not always have been so. According to Mackenzie Stuart it played a "considerable" role in the sixteenth and seventeenth centuries.[88] More recently, Professor Lubbe noted that, in the Scottish Statutes of Robert I a plea of debt required a statement of *causa pro qua debentur*[89] in order to be valid. He drew *inter alia* on this requirement as the basis of a possible link between Scots law and "the medieval continental notion that the customary written instrument attesting to the existence of a stipulation between the parties had to state the cause for which it had been undertaken".[90] He thus links Scots law with the wider, canonist conception of *causa*.[91] Professor Lubbe discusses early cases in which *causa* was a requirement of promise, until *Deuchar v Brown* in 1672, in which the Court of Session accepted that "a promise for whatever cause is valid and obligatory".[92] Stair played a significant part in cutting the ties between Scots law and the canonist notion of *causa*, by focusing rather on whether the parties intended to conclude legal relations.[93] Thus, Scots law was set on a path of adherence to *pacta sunt servanda*, which necessarily dictates a narrow approach to frustration.

(b) Louisiana law

Cause plays a prominent role in Louisiana law: "An obligation cannot exist without a lawful cause."[94] According to Professor Litvinoff cause has been understood over time as the "motive, purpose, end or reason" why a party obligates himself,[95] the current Civil Code defining it by reference to only

---

(c): "Variation or termination by court on a change of circumstance". The court has the power to vary the terms of the contract affected by change of circumstances only if "the debtor did not assume, and cannot reasonably be regarded as having assumed, the risk of that change of circumstances".

88 A J Mackenzie Stuart, "Contract and quasi-contract", in G C H Paton (ed), *Introduction to Scottish Legal History* (Stair Society vol 20, 1958) 241 at 244.

89 "Purpose for which the debt is undertaken" (author's translation). The statute identified by Lubbe is 1318 c 16; APS, I, 471 (c 15).

90 G Lubbe, "Formation of contract", in Reid and Zimmermann, *History*, vol 2, 1 at 12.

91 Lubbe, "Formation of contract" at 12.

92 (1672) Mor 12386. Lubbe notes that the report closely accords with Stair, *Inst* 1.10.10.

93 Mackenzie Stuart, "Contract" (n 88) 252-253; Lubbe, "Formation of contract" 18.

94 La Civ Code art 1966.

95 S Litvinoff, "Still another look at cause" (1987-1988) 48 La LR 3 at 14.

the last of these words.[96] He identifies the common factor in each idea as "something which stimulates the will".[97] Parties may, however, have many reasons for entering into a contract, not all of which are sufficiently important to constitute cause. Deciding what is, on the one hand, cause, and, on the other, a legally irrelevant motive, although not an easy task, is essentially a factual enquiry.

The purpose of cause is not, as a Common Lawyer might imagine, to act as an additional requirement to be satisfied before an obligation can be binding. After all, cause is presumed to exist where none is expressed.[98] Rather, it is a reflection of the tendency in Civilian systems to give primacy to the will of the contracting parties. It is closely related to the reasons why a legal system would choose not to give effect to an obligation, such as error, duress, misrepresentation and illegality. Rather than an extra requirement, it is a reason why one might not give effect to obligations.[99]

Litvinoff is a strong exponent of the greater use of cause in unexpected circumstances cases. Causes fail, and when that occurs, the parties ought to be released from their obligations. The idea of failure of cause[100] has been explained by Denson Smith as follows:[101]

> realization of the principal cause or motive is understood to be the *basis upon which consent is given* and it therefore becomes a tacit condition of the contract. This is because the final and principal motive for assuming an obligation must lie in the obvious end being sought … *If this cause fails, the will is vitiated and the contract falls*.

Litvinoff also explains the link between dissolution by reason of impossibility under article 1876[102] and cause:[103]

---

96   La Civ Code art 1967. The previous version defined cause as "motive" why a party obligates himself. In *St Charles Ventures LLC v Albertsons Inc* 265 F Supp 2d 682 (2003) District Judge Duval explained, at 688: "In the Revision Comments of 1984, it is noted that this article changed the prior code article to define cause in terms of 'reason' rather than 'motive' for 'the importance of judicial discretion in characterizing an obligation as enforceable'."
97   Litvinoff, "Still another look" (n 95) 14.
98   La Civ Code art 1969: "An obligation may be valid even though its cause is not expressed."
99   Litvinoff, "Still another look" (n 95) 3.
100 Express references to "failure of cause" were contained in articles 1897-1899 of the Civil Code of 1870. Those references are not present in the current Civil Code, although it is thought that their removal did not signify any change in the law: see Litvinoff, "Still another look" (n 95) 26.
101 (Emphasis added). J Denson Smith, "A refresher course in cause" (1951-1952) 12 La LR 2 at 10-11, approved by Sanders J in *Del Cryer v M & M Manufacturing Company* 273 So 2d 818 (1973).
102 Art 1876 reads: "Contract dissolved when performance becomes impossible. When the entire performance owed by one party has become impossible because of a fortuitous event, the contract is dissolved. The other party may then recover any performance he has already rendered."
103 Litvinoff, "Still another look" (n 95) 8; Hunley also links dissolution to failure of cause, "Supervening impossibility" (n 18) 616.

where the entire performance owed by one party becomes impossible because of a fortuitous event, the obligation of the other party comes to an end as the contract is dissolved. That is so because obtaining his co-contractant's performance is the reason why the other party bound himself, a reason, or cause, that failed – ceased to exist – when that performance became impossible.

Failure of cause developed in French law in "exceptional cases"[104] in which the courts proved willing to release parties where the facts did not extend to impossibility. An example is *Aguado v Bearn* in which land was leased on the understanding that it would be used for hunting.[105] Following a government decree banning hunting, the lessee was found entitled to a reduction of rent. The clearest expression of this idea in Louisiana law occurred in a case decided by the Supreme Court of the United States in 1887, *Viterbo v Friedlander*.[106] A lessee successfully argued that he should be released from his obligations under a lease of a sugar plantation after the plantation was subject to serious flooding by the Mississippi River. The flood destroyed not only most of the crop, but also the parts required to grow new plants. The receding waters left a layer of silt which effectively obliterated drainage ditches. The case was decided using articles of the Code which operate to release the parties where the subjects are totally destroyed by a fortuitous event. Looking to the spirit rather than the letter of these articles in the French *Code civil*, Mr Justice Gray applied the same approach to this particular case, where, although there had been no actual destruction of the leased subjects, the purpose for which the lease had been entered into had been destroyed. The decision was reached following a careful and lengthy analysis of Civilian sources including the *Digest*, and the works of Domat,[107] Pothier,[108] and Troplong.[109]

This solution is, to Litvinoff, flexible, and preferable to the "all or nothing" approach of impossibility. His views received judicial approval from the United States District Court in *St Charles Ventures LLC v Albertsons Inc*.[110] Commenting on article 1873, the court stated:[111]

104 M D Aubry, "Frustration reconsidered – some comparative aspects" (1963) ICLQ 1165 at 1174.
105 *Aguado v de Bearn et Consorts*, Cour de Paris, 1 May 1875, (1875) 2 D 204. See also *Estève v Dubois et Lacoste*, Trib Toulouse, 1 June 1916, (1916) 2 D 1128.
106 120 US 707 7 S Ct 962, 30 L Ed 776 (1887). See also P Du Plessis, "Of mice – and other disasters – and men: Rent abatement due to unforeseen and uncontrollable events in the Civilian tradition" (2002) Tul Civ LF 113-149.
107 *Les lois civiles dans leur ordre naturel, suivies de droit public*, pt 1, lib, 1, tit 4, § 3, No 3 and § 4, No 6 (1703).
108 *Traité du contrat de louage*, No 74 (1806).
109 *Le droit civil expliqué suivant l'ordre des articles du Code de l'échange et du louage: commentaire des titres VII et VIII du livre du Code civil*, Nos 204, 206-207, 211, 225, 695-697, 756 (1840).
110 265 F Supp 2d 682 (2003) at 697.
111 At 697. Like *US Bancorp Equipment Finance Inc v Loews Express LLC* discussed above at n 74, this is another "diversity case".

That article, however, is inserted in a special section now devoted to impossibility of performance. When read together, the articles in that section disclose that there exists between impossibility of performance and the theory of cause a connection that was less explicit in the Louisiana Civil Code of 1870. When properly understood, that connection may serve as a foundation for a more flexible approach to force majeure.

Failure of purpose cannot be fully analysed without taking into account the role of error in Louisiana law. In Scots law the ambit of error is narrow, releasing a party from a contract by reason of unilateral error very rarely, if at all.[112] In Louisiana law, error[113] is intimately connected to cause and, as a result of that connection, to failure of cause.[114] Indeed, it has been judicially recognised that the two concepts overlap.[115] Judging by the reported case law, it is common for parties in unexpected circumstances cases to base their pleadings on three alternatives:[116] failure of cause;[117] impossibility of performance;[118] or error of cause.[119]

In *Marcello v Bussiere*[120] the buyers agreed orally to buy a bar-lounge business and become tenants of the premises. They were unaware that the lounge had a poor reputation, and had lost its liquor licence six months previously. It was also highly unlikely to be granted a licence in the future. The buyers took possession and began extensive renovation works. Finding that a licence would not be granted to them, the renovations ceased. Although the act of sale and lease were never executed, the buyers received demands for rent. Allegations of fraud against the seller were not proven. The Supreme Court of Louisiana found that the determining motive for the contracts was to secure a going bar-lounge business and that this motive was either known to, or ought to have been known, to the seller. Because the purchasers received no going business concern, nor could they obtain a licence, the court held that there was an error in the principal cause of the contract.[121] The purchasers,

---

112 McBryde, *Contract* (n 34) para 15-41.
113 La Civ Code art 1949: "Error vitiates consent only when it concerns a cause without which the obligation would not have been incurred and that cause was known or should have been known to the other party." See also art 1950: "Error may concern a cause when it bears on the nature of the contract, or the thing that is the contractual object or a substantial quality of that thing, or the person or the qualities of the other party, or the law, or any other circumstances that the parties regarded or should in good faith have regarded as a cause of the obligation."
114 La Civ Code arts 1948-1952.
115 *St Charles Ventures LLC v Albertsons Inc* 265 F Supp 2d 682 at 697 (2003) at 688.
116 E.g., *St Charles Ventures LLC v Albertsons Inc* 265 F Supp 2d 682 at 697 (2003) at 697.
117 La Civ Code arts 1966-1967.
118 La Civ Code arts 1873-1878.
119 La Civ Code arts 1948-1950.
120 284 So 2d 892 (La 1973).
121 284 So 2d 892 (La 1973) at 895.

ignorant of the poor reputation of the bar and likely problems in obtaining a licence, were mistaken in their belief (present at formation) that they could run a bar-lounge business.[122] The outcome in this case is somewhat surprising to a Scots lawyer, more used to a narrower concept of error. Arguably, releasing the buyer in such circumstances is over-protective of his interests, and fails to strike a balance between the interests of both contracting parties. The purchaser could, of course, have protected himself by appropriate drafting.

A further case illustrative of the close relationship between error and failure of cause is *St Charles Ventures LLC v Albertsons Inc.*[123] Albertsons, a supermarket operator, had agreed to lease new supermarket premises. The unexpected opening of Walmart close to the proposed Albertsons super-market had, according to Albertsons, destroyed its motive for entering into the lease, and amounted to failure of cause. Duval J referred with approval to Litvinoff's identification of a fortuitous event where the entire performance becomes impossible as the primary example of error of cause.[124] The court found that one of the motives for entering into the transaction was indeed the improbability of a competing retail outlet entering into the market. This was a "calculated risk, a motive, but not a cause".[125] This being the case, Albertsons' argument of failure of cause was unsuccessful.

There appears to be little judicial concern over a possible overlap between error and failure of cause in these cases. As is illustrated by *St Charles Ventures*, the assumption of risk is a component part of both analyses.[126] This is significant, ensuring that error of cause does not provide an easy alterna-tive to the stricter test of failure of cause. It is perhaps not significant which of the two concepts is used by the Louisiana courts in these situations. What is significant is that Louisiana law supplements its otherwise strict test of impossibility with a further legal concept, providing a contracting party with an "escape route" where that party's cause cannot be brought to fruition.

122 See also *Gisclair v Matmoor, Inc* 537 So 2d 876 (La App 5th Cir 1989) in which a purchaser was released from a contract where his principal cause for entering into the transaction was to develop the land for heavy commercial use. It transpired that this was impossible because the land was designated as wetlands (and had been so designated at the point of formation). *Gisclair* differs from *Marcello* in that the purchaser had made the purchase conditional on use for commercial purposes. See also *Louviere v Meteye* 260 So 2d 377 (La App 4th Cir 1972).

123 265 F Supp 2d 682 (2003) at 697. See also *Carpenter v Williams* 428 So 2d 1314 (La App 3d Cir 1983), and in particular the approval of the statement of Dennis J in *O'Neal v Cascio* 324 So 2d 539 (La App 2nd Cir 1975) at 542.

124 At 688.

125 At 695.

126 See *Hanover Petroleum Corp v Tenneco Inc* 521 So 2d 1234 (La App 3rd Cir 1988) where the court rejected the argument that the plaintiff should be released from its obligations because they had been undertaken without knowledge of the impending economic collapse. As explored above (C.(3)(a)), the assumption of risk was an important factor in the court's decision.

(2) Frustration of purpose in Scots law

As already stated, cause is no longer part of Scots law. Nevertheless, Scots law, in common with Common Law systems, may contain a concept which resembles failure of cause: frustration of purpose. This resemblance has been noted by Litvinoff, amongst others.[127] Frustration of purpose releases parties where unexpected circumstances have rendered performance by party A of no practical value to party B.

In English law, the most famous expression of frustration of purpose occurred in the "coronation cases".[128] Those cases, prompted by the cancellation of King Edward VII's coronation celebrations, have been fully analysed elsewhere and will not be discussed here, although it may be noted that the source of the doctrine was, unusually, Roman law.[129] The solution applied was, in effect, an implied term that the continuation of a state of affairs or continued existence of a thing was the "basis and foundation" of the contract.[130] However, this example of the development of an English concept based on Roman law was destined to be short-lived. Divergence from the Roman source occurred when, in *Chandler v Webster*,[131] the court indicated that the doctrine released parties from future performance, and did not return them to their previous positions. Subsequently, the authority of the coronation cases has been doubted in England[132] and in Scotland.[133] If a Scottish doctrine of frustration of purpose exists, it must arise from Scottish case law.

Although McBryde is doubtful about the existence of frustration of purpose as a category, there are cases which may have established it as such.[134] One is *Tay Salmon Fisheries Co Ltd v Speedie*[135] which concerned a lease of salmon

127 *"Force majeure"* (n 11) 12; Markesinis, *German Law of Contract* (n 2) 342.
128 *Krell v Henry* [1903] 2 KB 740; *Civil Service Co-Op Society v General Steam Navigation* [1903] 2 KB 756; *Herne Bay Steam Boat v Hutton* [1903] 2 KB 638; *Chandler v Webster* [1904] 1 KB 493; and see E Peel (ed), *Treitel on the Law of Contract*, 12th edn (2007) paras 19-041-19-043.
129 *Krell v Henry* [1903] 2 KB 740 per Vaughan Williams LJ at 747-748, although this solution had been developed at an earlier stage in *Taylor v Caldwell* (1863) 3 B & S 826, where Lord Blackburn cited (at 834) Pomponius, D 45.1.33.
130 Ibid. The resemblance to modern German law is notable: see BGB § 313(2) "Disturbance of foundation of transaction".
131 [1904] 1 KB 493
132 See doubts expressed in the House of Lords in *Joseph Constantine SS Line Ltd v Imperial Smelting Corporation Ltd* [1942] AC 154; *Larrinaga & Co Ltd v Société Franco-Americaine des Phosphates de Médulla* (1923) 39 TLR 316 per Viscount Finlay at 318; and the Privy Council in *Maritime National Fish Ltd v Ocean Trawlers Ltd* [1935] AC 524.
133 Gloag, *Contract* (n 33) 352-353; Cooper, "Frustration of contract" (n 13) 3; T B Smith, *A Short Commentary on the Law of Scotland* (1962) 849, all relying on the Scottish case of *Trevalion & Co v Blanche & Co* 1919 SC 617.
134 McBryde, "Frustration" (n 42) 12.
135 1929 SC 593.

fishings to endure for nineteen seasons. During the course of the lease a bye-law was passed converting the greater part of the subjects of lease into a danger zone for the purpose of aerial gunnery and bombing practice. Limited occupation of the area for the purposes of fishing remained possible: the order was effective only for four days a week and use of the power required advance notice. However, the nets were heavy and difficult to set up and dismantle. Commenting that "There is no exact precedent for the present case; and it is not immediately clear on what principle the tenant's claim rests",[136] Lord President Clyde equated "the complete expulsion of a tenant from possession of the subject of his lease" with "*practically* complete expulsion from it resulting from the operation of statutory bye-laws".[137] Importantly, he paraphrased and distinguished the usual test for frustration in Scots and English law ("such as to make the contract a different one from what it originally was").[138] He therefore appears to suggest that the usual test for frustration would not assist the pursuer in this case. The issue here was rather that "possession secured by a lease cannot any longer be enjoyed".[139]

A further example is *Mackeson v Boyd*,[140] a case involving a mansion house let on a furnished basis. It was requisitioned by military authorities during the Second World War, excluding the tenant from the premises. As in *Tay Salmon*, the court equated the facts with legal eviction and held that the tenant was entitled to abandon the lease. Is this possibly a case of impossibility since the tenant had no access to the premises whatsoever?[141] Reference too could be made to *Smith v Riddell*[142] in which an elderly farmer, Smith, leased his farm, including stock and crops to Riddell. In return, Riddell agreed to support Smith for the rest of Smith's life. Unexpectedly, Riddell died before Smith, and the question which arose was whether Mrs Riddell was entitled to the stock and crops under the lease. Lord Justice Clerk Moncreiff, delivering the opinion of the court, stated: "I think it would be against reason and against conscience that this agreement should be enforced against this old man when the only consideration for which he undertook it has become impossible of fulfilment."[143] The case poses difficulties (not least in the puzzling reference to

---

136 At 600.
137 At 601 (emphasis added).
138 At 601.
139 At 601.
140 1942 SC 56.
141 Neither *Tay Salmon* nor *Mackeson* is cited by McBryde as an example of frustration of purpose (although they are discussed by him in a special section devoted to frustration and contracts relating to land, see McBryde, *Contract* (n 33) para 21-35).
142 (1886) 14 R 95.
143 (1886) 14 R 95 at 98, quoted in McBryde, *Contract* (n 33) para 21-34.

consideration). The contract involved *delectus personae*[144] so that Mrs Riddell arguably had no right to be a party to it. Like *Mackeson,* it may actually be a case of impossibility, performance by the deceased Riddell being impossible. Nevertheless, the court's references to "reason" and "conscience" as factors underlying their refusal to enforce are interesting. This is evidence of the underlying equitable basis of the Scottish principles.

Finally the Scottish House of Lords case *James B Fraser & Co v Denny, Mott & Dickson* may be an example of frustration of purpose.[145] Wartime legislation rendered illegal the sale of timber. It was held that a lease of the timber yard was so intimately connected to the contract of sale that the lease too was frustrated. Performance of the lease was not absolutely impossible: the tenant could have used the premises for a different purpose. This case can be contrasted with the earlier case of *Hart's Trs v Arrol*[146] in which a shop was let for the duration of ten and a half years, the use clause stipulating use as a wine and spirit merchants. It was held that the lease was not brought to an end by the termination of the licence. Lord McLaren's approval of part of the Lord Ordinary, Lord Robertson's, opinion is interesting:[147]

> on principle I can see no reason why, apart from express agreement, a failure of the purpose for which a tenant leases a house or shop should, even if this purpose is expressed in the lease, liberate the tenant from his obligations. A tenant may take a lease of business premises intending to apply them to purposes of a highly speculative character with which the landlord has nothing to do. The landlord is only bound by what is expressed in the agreement with him, and if the speculation should fail, that is the misfortune of the person who enters the speculation.

This strict approach is clearly motivated by a concern for the possible repercussions of giving effect to unexpressed purposes. To the same effect is the Scottish House of Lords case *McMaster & Co v Cox, McEuen, & Co.*[148] The buyer intended his purchase to be exported, but subsequent legislation had rendered exports illegal without a licence. It was held that the seller could not have known of the intended purpose, even though the contract specifically provided that the goods were to be supplied in the type of packaging normal for export. The courts refused to release the buyer from his order.

Drawn together, these cases do provide a basis for the development of a concept of frustration of purpose. It must be conceded, however, that they provide only an uncertain basis for this doctrine.

---

144 See the definition of the strictly personal obligation contained in La Civ Code art 1766, which resembles the Scots idea of *delectus personae.*
145 1944 SC (HL) 35.
146 (1903) 6 F 36.
147 At 40.
148 1921 SC (HL) 24.

(3) Comparison

Litvinoff's suggestion that failure of cause in Civilian systems resembles failure of purpose in Common Law systems can now be tested by reference to Louisiana and Scots law. Essentially, the question is whether like cases will be treated alike regardless of which test is applied.

A key issue in both legal systems is the extent to which party B must be aware of party A's purpose/cause before that knowledge becomes legally relevant. In Louisiana law, error vitiates consent only where it concerns a cause without which the obligation would not have been incurred and that cause was known *or should have been known to* the other party.[149] In Scots law the purpose need not be common,[150] but it seems that communication of A's purpose by A to B must take place.[151] Scots law contains no presumption similar to that found in Louisiana law and is therefore narrower in comparison. This is a significant difference: Louisiana law, but not Scots law, would release party A where party B ought, in good faith, to have known of A's cause/purpose.

Some of the outcomes of Louisiana cases seem surprising from a Scots perspective, creating suspicion that the courts are giving effect to motives rather than causes. One such case is *Carpenter v Williams*.[152] Williams had received orders from his employer, Transco, to move closer to his place of employment. Seeking to buy a new house, Williams approached Carpenter, a builder, and a contract was eventually concluded between the parties to buy a house in Lake Charles. During the course of the discussions Williams explained to Carpenter that he already had a house in Lafayette, but that he was moving home to comply with Transco's instructions. Transco however rescinded its instructions, rendering Williams' removal unnecessary. Carpenter sought to enforce his contract with Williams. The Court of Appeal refused to enforce, finding that "the principal, and only, cause or motive Williams had for entering into the buy-sell agreement with Carpenter was

---

149 La Civ Code art 1949; also art 1950, reproduced at n 113 above. See further Litvinoff, "Still another look" (n 95) 17, where he describes the process by which a motive becomes a legally relevant cause as "inter-subjectivity".

150 The purpose was an individual one in both *Tay Salmon Fisheries Co Ltd v Speedie* 1929 SC 593 and *Mackeson v Boyd* 1942 SC 56.

151 *McMaster & Co v Cox, McEuen & Co* 1921 SC (HL) 24, McBryde, *Contract* (n 33) para 21-33.

152 428 So 2d 1314 (La App 3d Cir 1983). See also the US case, *Vines v Orchard Hills Inc* 181 Conn 501, 435 A 2d 1022 (1980) on similar facts. Mr Vines (the equivalent of Mr Williams) was held in breach but entitled to restitution of a down-payment on the sale price. I am grateful to Professor David Snyder for bringing this case to my attention.

to comply with Transco's orders".[153] According to the court, Carpenter was aware of that fact, and it therefore reasoned that "when Transco rescinded its order to Williams, the cause or motive for entering into the contract ceased to exist or failed and the contract became unenforceable".[154]

Carpenter is a controversial case, the court being criticised for confusing error of cause with error in motive. A Scottish court would almost certainly have held that Mr Williams, by concluding an unconditional contract, had assumed the risk of his employer changing his instructions. Like *Marcello*, *Carpenter* is another case which seems, from a Scottish perspective, over-protective of the interests of the party pleading failure of cause, at the expense of the interests of the other contracting party. In both cases under Scots law the buyer would have been expected to protect himself by appropriate drafting. The Scottish case of *Hart's Trs v Arrol*[155] is an example of the court's strict attitude towards this type of case. These differences in the law in the two systems can only properly be understood if one also takes into account possible differences in drafting methods. Scottish contracts are long, each party attempting as far as possible to cover all eventualities. One could even say that parties attempt through drafting to minimise any recourse to the common law. Purposes which are not expressed in the written contract are simply not relevant. In Louisiana perhaps lawyers are more content to rely on sources outside of the contract, principally, of course, the Civil Code. In such a context, it is more understandable that unexpressed purposes can be legally relevant.

(4) Conclusion

This comparison casts doubt on Litvinoff's suggestion that failure of cause in the Civil Law resembles failure of purpose in the Common Law. Certainly, this part of the chapter suggests that different outcomes will be reached by applying the Scottish and Louisiana concepts to the same sets of facts. Through use of both failure and error of cause, Louisiana law displays a wider approach than Scots law. The differences between the two systems are more extreme when one takes into account the uncertainty over whether Scots law actually contains a category of frustration of purpose. Can Scots law learn from the experience of another mixed system here? There may be concerns that the Louisiana approach is too lenient. The potential unfairness to the

---

153 428 So 2d 1314 (La App 3d Cir 1983) at 1318.
154 At 1318. This case was discussed with approval in *Carpenter v Williams* 428 So 2d 1314 (La App 3d Cir 1983) at 1318.
155 (1903) 6 F 36, discussed at D.(2) above.

contracting party not pleading failure of purpose was highlighted by T B Smith. Referring to the coronation cases (which he ultimately concluded should not be binding in Scotland) he stated:[156]

> If seats are let in a shop window to view a procession, and it does not take place owing (say) to illness of a personage in whose honour it is held, the shopkeeper is deprived of the use of the window for normal purposes. Moreover, had the parties contemplated the event at the time of contracting, it is probable that the purchaser of the seats would have been willing to accept the risk of the procession being cancelled.

Smith emphasises the potential loss to the seller/hirer, and advocates a finding that the buyer/lessee has assumed the risk of the subsequent event.

Some might argue that Scots law does not need a separate doctrine of frustration of purpose, the usual test of frustration being sufficiently wide to cope with examples of frustration of purpose. This is, however, not the case. Even taking into account the wide approach to interpretation currently adopted by both Scottish and English courts, it seems unlikely that the courts would feel able to "read into" the contract a purpose which is not stated in the contract.[157] And yet the Scottish cases which arguably constitute a doctrine of frustration of purpose are sensible and practical decisions. Relevant case law exists, and to reject it seems a backwards step. It is perhaps significant that other European legal systems deploy more than one concept in unexpected circumstances cases. It may be too much to expect a single concept (such as frustration) to deal satisfactorily with all cases. That is not to say, however, that a doctrine of frustration of purpose will be easy to apply. It will, of course, be difficult to distinguish between legally relevant purposes and non-legally relevant motives. The level of difficulty alone does not justify rejection of the class as a whole. Nor is it necessarily significant to the development of a Scottish doctrine that the Louisiana courts may have reached outcomes which appear to Scots lawyers to be overly lenient to the party pleading failure/error of cause, for example by elevating a motive to the level of cause (*Carpenter*) or applying a more lenient doctrine of unilateral error (*Marcello*). The Scots doctrine of frustration of purpose could be developed in a manner which takes into account other Scottish contractual concepts, and also methods of drafting.

This section closes with one final observation on Louisiana law, which is that the concept of cause is alive and well. Whether by accident or intention,

---

156   *Short Commentary* (n 133) 849.
157   See the speech of Lord Hoffmann in *Investors Compensation Scheme Ltd v West Bromwich Building Society* [1981] 1 All ER 98 at 114-115.

it remains a central concept in unexpected circumstances cases. This factor may strengthen ties with French law, despite linguistic differences. The influence of US law has been insufficient to dislodge cause from its central position. This is indeed surprising, especially considering that unexpected circumstances cases tend to operate in the commercial field where US law exerts such a dominant influence.

E. THE CONSEQUENCES OF UNEXPECTED CIRCUMSTANCES

(1) Louisiana law

As a general rule, dissolution of a contract in Louisiana law involves the restoration of the parties to the situation that existed before the contract was made.[158] Not surprisingly, this general effect is qualified for contracts involving continuous or periodic performance, so that the effect of dissolution is not extended to any performance already rendered.[159]

Following dissolution, under article 1876 the "other party may then recover any performance he has already rendered".[160] Litvinoff comments that this remedy is available in respect of a "performance rendered in the expectation of receiving another one in return".[161] He likens it to payment of a thing not due.[162]

A further article, article 1877, deals with partial impossibility, providing the court with two options: to declare the contract dissolved; or to reduce the other party's counter-performance proportionately.[163] Litvinoff suggests that this remedy is available only where "the parties' reciprocal performances can be divided into equivalent proportions".[164] Where this is not possible, the contract price may be proportionately reduced only where partial performance has been "substantial".[165] Where a non-substantial partial performance has occurred, which cannot be returned by the party enriched, that party must compensate the other.[166]

---

158 La Civ Code art 2018.
159 La Civ Code art 2019.
160 La Civ Code art 1876(2).
161 Litvinoff, *Obligations* (n 16) § 16.61.
162 Ibid. Thus, Litvinoff characterises the remedy as what would be, to a Scots lawyer, the *condictio indebiti*. This is not the remedy used in this context in Scots law. Scots law uses, rather, the *condictio causa data causa non secuta*.
163 La Civ Code art 1877.
164 Litvinoff, *Obligations* (n 16) § 16.63.
165 Ibid, relying inter alia on *O & M Const Inc v State, Div of Admin* 576 So 2d 1030 (La App 1st Cir 1991), writ denied, 581 So 2d 691 (La 1991).
166 La Civ Code art 2298.

The remedies applicable in cases of partial impossibility contained in article 1877 are of relatively recent vintage, appearing for the first time in the Civil Code in 1985.[167] The revision comments make clear that the aim was to achieve an outcome which is fairer than either full dissolution or validity of the contract.[168]

(2) Scots law

In contrast to the position under Louisiana law, identifying the effect of frustration on a contract in Scots law is not an easy matter. Frustration has been described as bringing the contract to an end.[169] This should not, however, be taken as an indication that the contract is void. On the contrary, certain contractual clauses survive frustration, notably, of course, *force majeure* clauses, but also arbitration clauses.[170] Rather, the effect of frustration is to free both parties from their obligations to be performed in the future, with effect from the frustrating event.[171] Rights accrued under the contract remain and can be litigated.

In Scots law, the remedy available to redress unjustified enrichment following frustration is the *condictio causa data causa non secuta* ("CCDCNS"). This remedy applies where someone has given money or property to another on the understanding that the recipient will make a counter-performance.[172] Where that counter-performance does not materialise, the remedy is the return of the money or property. This is the contracting party's only remedy. In its use of the CCDCNS, Scots law differs from English law, where a statutory solution is applied.[173]

Because Scots law applies a remedy drawn from unjustified enrichment here, the initial observation might be that Scots law should be aligned with the Civil Law systems. All is not as it seems, however. As has been widely documented in Scottish legal scholarship, the presence of the CCDCNS

---

167 La Civ Code art 1877 Revision Comment (c), in A N Yiannopoulos (ed), Louisiana Civil Code, 2005 edn, 396.

168 La Civ Code art 1877 Revision Comment (c), in A N Yiannopoulos (ed), Louisiana Civil Code, 2005 edn, 396.

169 See McBryde, "Frustration" (n 42) 15-16. Twenty-seven years later he adopted different phraseology: "Frustration ends parties' rights and obligations to future performance under the contract" (*Contract* (n 34) para 21-44).

170 *Scott & Sons v Del Sel* 1923 SC (HL) 37.

171 McBryde, *Contract* (n 34) para 21-44; MacQueen and Thomson, *Contract* (n 34) para 4.68.

172 See, e.g., *Watson v Shankland* (1871) 10 M 142, in which Lord President Inglis applied the CCDCNS in order to find prepaid freight to be recoverable when the cause upon which it had been given failed to materialise.

173 The Law Reform (Frustrated Contracts) Act 1943.

here is something of an anomaly. Its adoption into Scots law is relatively modern, occurring in 1923 with the case of *Cantiere San Rocco SA v Clyde Shipbuilding & Engineering* Co.[174] In Roman law, the remedy operated in non-contractual contexts. According to Professor MacCormack the remedy predates the recognition of agreements as distinct sources of legal obligations.[175] The path of its adoption in contract in Scots law begins with its discussion in the works of the Institutional writers, Erskine and Bell. Although both recognised its non-contractual nature, they referred not to the giving of money or property for a "cause" which fails, but rather for a "consideration" which fails. The use of the word "consideration," with its English contractual connotations, prepared the ground for the application of the remedy in a contractual context. This development then occurred in the Scottish House of Lords case, *Cantiere*. Despite forceful criticism of the operation of this remedy in a contractual context,[176] it is nevertheless embedded in Scots law. It is, however, a rather misleading indicator of Scot law's Civilian roots.

Prior to adoption of the CCDCNS, Scots law contained a different solution drawn from unjustified enrichment. This solution had its source in the equitable underpinnings of Scots law. Lord Cooper (writing after *Cantiere* was decided) noted:[177]

> The germinal ideas of frustration appeared in Scotland not in answer to the question whether a contract should be dissolved by operation of law by reason of certain supervening changes of circumstances, but in answer to the far wider question how the relations of the two parties should be *equitably readjusted* by the Court when the one has been unintentionally enriched at the expense of the other.

Thus Cooper suggests that the Scottish court possessed the ability equitably to re-adjust relations between the parties. The benefits of this flexible approach were not lost on later writers.[178] Nevertheless, a modern Scottish court is likely to react with surprise to the suggestion that it possesses such a power. *Cantiere* is entrenched as the governing authority. The loss of equitable re-adjustment is regrettable, not least because the CCDCNS suffers from a significant

---

174 1923 SC (HL) 105.

175 G MacCormack, "The *Condictio causa data causa non secuta*", in R Evans-Jones (ed), *The Civil Law Tradition in Scotland* (1995) 253.

176 See R Evans-Jones, "Unjust enrichment, contract and the third reception of Roman law in Scotland", (1993) 109 LQR 663; idem, *Unjustified enrichment*, vol 1, (2003) ch 4.

177 Cooper, "Frustration of contract" (n 13) at 1 (emphasis added). Cooper notes as significant Craig's explanation of the reasons underlying a vassal's forfeiture of his feu where he has failed to obey the call to arms of a feudal superior. The grant of the feu is the "consideration" or reason for the grant of the feu. This, Craig notes, is an example of the CCDCNS (*Jus Feudale*, vol 2, 3.5.23).

178 Smith, *Short Commentary* (n 133) 846-850; Forte, "Economic frustration" (n 34) 12 and 17.

limitation: it is available only where an actual transfer of a tangible benefit has been made by one contracting party to the other prior to the frustrating event. Where a contracting party has expended effort which has not resulted in such a transfer, the CCDCNS cannot be used. That party is left with no remedy. Thus, the Scottish solution is limited, and contains no parallel to the powers open to a Louisiana court in cases of partial impossibility.

(3) Comparison

The effect of impossibility/frustration is, in essence, the same in the two legal systems: the parties are released from their contractual obligations. In Louisiana law this is the direct result of the operation of the doctrine of cause: failure of cause extinguishes the reciprocal obligations. The reason for the release of the parties from a frustrated contract in Scots law is more difficult to identify. The test of frustration looks to the radically different nature of the obligations of the parties in changed circumstances. There is a close link with interpretation – the courts construe the written contract to determine whether it applies in the changed circumstances.[179] As expressed by Lord Watson:[180]

> the meaning of the contract must be taken to be, not what the parties did intend (for they had neither thought nor intention regarding it), but that which the parties, as fair and reasonable men, would presumably have agreed upon if, having such possibility in view, they had made express provision as to their several rights and liabilities in the event of its occurrence.

The contracting parties are released from their obligations when there has been "such a change in the significance of the obligation, that the thing undertaken would, if performed, be a different thing from that contracted for".[181]

The significant limitations of the enrichment remedy which applies following frustration of contract have already been noted. These lie in stark contrast to the flexible solution available to Louisiana courts under article 1877. Unlike the Louisiana court, the Scottish court cannot order proportionate reduction of the price, nor award compensation where performance is not substantial, and cannot be returned. The question arises, therefore,

---

179 *British Movietonenews LD v London District Cinemas LD* [1952] AC 166, per Viscount Simon at 181.

180 *Dahl v Nelson* (1880-81) LR 6 App Cas 38, approved by Lord Radcliffe in *Davis Contractors Ltd v Fareham Urban District Council* [1956] AC 696 at 728.

181 *Davis Contractors Ltd v Fareham Urban District Council* [1956] AC 696, per Lord Radcliffe at 729

whether Scots law would benefit from a solution similar to that contained in article 1877. This article is an example of a judicial power, present in some Civilian systems, to revise a contract.[182] It provides, however, only a limited power of revision: in effect, it allows part of the price to be allocated to corresponding obligations within the contract. Examples of such powers are so rare in Scots law as to be practically non-existent.[183] They tend to be viewed as an unwarranted intrusion into the autonomy of the contracting parties. Nevertheless, there is a strong argument that this approach would allow the court to reflect the intentions of the parties more closely. Commercial parties are likely to prefer an amended version of the contract to no contract at all (should frustration operate), or the contract as drafted (should the court refuse to find the contract frustrated).

It is, of course, possible in Scots law too to identify obligations which are counterparts of one another. This is required before the Scottish remedy of retention can operate: party A faced with breach by party B may retain contractual performance in order to encourage B to perform. A may only retain performance of a specific obligation where it is the counterpart of the obligation breached by B.[184] This remedy rests on the concept of mutuality. Thus, the Scottish courts already identify counterpart obligations in the same way as the Louisiana courts do in the context of article 1877. Article 1877 may, therefore, be based on a conceptual framework which is already part of Scots law. A Scottish version of article 1877 could operate efficiently, particularly in a construction context where contracts are usually structured on an instalment basis.[185] The construction sector has been badly hit by the UK economic downturn, and may need a more sophisticated approach to frustrated contracts than is currently available.

Like Louisiana law, the DCFR contains a judicial power to vary the contract to make it reasonable and equitable in the new circumstances.[186] Additionally, the court may terminate the obligation at a date and on terms to be determined by the court.[187] There are limitations on these powers: the change of circumstances must be "exceptional" and the power to vary may be

---

182 E.g., German law under BGB § 313 "Disturbance of foundation of transaction".

183 One isolated example, the court's power to re-open an extortionate credit bargains under the Consumer Credit Act 1974 s 138, was recently repealed, never having been used by a Scottish court. This section has been replaced with new powers to regulate unfair bargains, see Financial Services and Markets Act 2000 ss 140A-C, and comment by F Davidson and L Macgregor, *Commercial Law in Scotland*, 2nd edn (2008) para 3.8.7.

184 *Bank of East Asia v Scottish Enterprise* 1997 SLT 1213 (HL).

185 *Bank of East Asia v Scottish Enterprise* 1997 SLT 1213 (HL).

186 DCFR III – 1:110(2)(a).

187 DCFR III – 1:110(2)(b).

utilised only where it would be "manifestly unjust" to hold that party to the contract.[188] The Louisiana solution as a balanced and more limited solution, is more attractive to Scots lawyers than the surprisingly radical solution offered by the DCFR.

F. CONCLUSION

The most striking aspect of Louisiana law (to the Scottish observer) is the strongly Civilian character of the rules on unexpected circumstances. This is due, to a great extent, to the significant role of cause. Undoubtedly, there has been US influence. Evidence of this can be found in two of the exceptions to article 1873 which are inspired by US law. Further evidence is provided by the fact that Louisiana legislators decided not to enact a commercial code in Louisiana for fear of departing from US commercial law.[189] However, the *private* law rules contained within the Civil Code are what govern this area of law. Other relevant considerations include the fact that article 2 UCC, which governs unexpected circumstances in sale of goods, has not been enacted in Louisiana law. One must assume also that the concept of economic impracticability found in the *Restatement (Second) of Contracts* has been insufficiently attractive to have a greater influence on Louisiana law. As a result, one might say that there has been relatively limited US influence on the terms of the Civil Code which govern unexpected circumstances.

What has occurred in Louisiana is a process which takes place in other mixed legal systems: the shaping of commercial law by private law concepts which are Civilian in nature. Commercial law rules in mixed legal systems tend to be classified as Common Law in nature,[190] and perhaps not worthy of study by comparatists. However, private law concepts play an important role in commercial contexts and can in some cases admit Civilian influence into commercial law through the back door. So the Louisiana rules on unexpected circumstances are Civilian in character because they stem from the Civil Code.

Nicholas suggested that, in the field of unexpected circumstances, Civilian systems are characterised by the application of rules on impossibility, whereas Common Law systems are characterised by the interpretation of the contract.[191] Looked at this way, Louisiana law seems to be Civilian in nature. But although

---

188   DCFR III – 1:110(2).
189   See text at n 64 above
190   See K G C Reid, "The idea of mixed legal systems" (2003) 78 Tulane LR 5 at 25.
191   B Nicholas, "Rules and terms – Civil and Common Law" (1974) 48 Tulane LR 946 at 954.

article 1873 of the Louisiana Civil Code was undoubtedly inspired by article 1148 of the French *Code civil*, the Louisiana rules are far from a direct copy of their French source. The exceptions to article 1873 are a significant innovation on the equivalent French rules. Louisiana law is a mixture: gumbo rather than US stew or French ragout.

The Scots rules on unexpected circumstances are, in comparison, more difficult to identify. English influence has dominated, resulting in the rejection of an early approach based on the assumption of risk in favour of a test of frustration drawn from an English case.[192] However, the legal basis of frustration in English law is far from clear,[193] and so the use of English precedents in Scotland is not likely to lead to clarity. Whether Scots law contains a concept of frustration of purpose is subject to doubt. Such a concept, if it does exist, is narrower than the Louisiana equivalent (in requiring actual communication of a purpose.)

Seeking to identify the tradition to which the Scots rules belong, one might conclude from the emphasis placed by Nicholas on interpretation, that Scots law lies within the Common Law tradition.[194] Although there has been extensive Common Law influence, this conclusion would not be correct. It ignores both the enrichment rules and the strong undercurrent of equity. Scots law too is a mixture.

It is suggested that the two mixed legal systems analysed here can learn from one another, although Scots law would be the major beneficiary in this process. Louisiana law provides a model of an efficient use of the assumption of risk. Courts clearly make policy decisions in this area and the assumption of risk approach at least recognises that this is the case. In other respects, Louisiana law is a less attractive model for the Scots lawyer. It could be criticised for an over-expansive idea of cause, sometimes elevating to the level of cause a purpose which appears to be a motive only. Outcomes in some cases seem surprising to Scots eyes because of a more lenient approach to unilateral error. Louisiana law clearly has the upper hand, however, when it comes to enrichment remedies. The provisions on partial impossibility are particularly attractive to the Scots lawyer who is left to lament the loss of the courts' powers equitably to re-adjust the contract, a power which led Lord Cooper to characterise Scots law as possessing a "high degree of flexibility and adaptability".[195]

---

192 *Davis Contractors Ltd v Fareham District Council* [1956] AC 696.
193 See discussion of this point in *National Carriers Ltd v Panalpina (Northern) Limited* [1981] AC 675.
194 B Nicholas, "Rules and terms" (n 191) 954.
195 Cooper, "Frustration of contract" (n 13) 5.

The experience of this comparison may also shed light on generally-held views on mixed legal systems. Professor du Plessis commented:[196]

> Due to political and linguistic variables, some mixed legal systems, like Scotland and Louisiana, have gravitated towards the Common Law tradition, while others, like Cyprus and Québec, still hold on strongly to the Civil Law.

Although there has been gravitation in both systems, such broad statements are perhaps misleading. Despite the fact that few Louisiana lawyers are now fluent in French, this has not prevented cause from thriving in Louisiana law. In the political arena in Scotland there has been recent change. Scotland's government is now a minority nationalist government, and the Scottish parliament has the power to legislate over the field of obligations. Independence seems more likely now than at any other time in recent history. The level of English influence on the law of obligations may be decreasing.

Looking to other supposed attributes of mixed legal systems, is there evidence of either system exercising a choice between solutions offered by the Civil and the Common Law?[197] One would answer this in the negative for Scots law, where rules have developed in an *ad hoc* manner, solutions being formed in the courts with little thought of the impact on the underlying foundations. There is more evidence of selection taking place in Louisiana law, in the grafting of exceptions inspired by the Common Law on to the French-influenced basis of article 1873.

It is, however, difficult to discern the process of "mixing" here. Legal systems appear to have coalesced, to such an extent that it is difficult to characterise a school of thought as either "Civilian" or "Common Law". Modern German law,[198] the US *Restatement (Second) of Contracts*,[199] and, historically, English law,[200] have all employed the idea of the continuation of the basis of the transaction as a solution. A further example is the assumption of risk: originally part of Scotland's (Civilian?) past, it now receives little emphasis there. Not originally part of Louisiana's French-inspired system, it was adopted through US influence. To which tradition do these concepts belong? The source of the rules may not, however, be the most significant issue. As this comparison has illustrated, the same concepts may react in different ways when applied within different national frameworks.

---

196 J du Plessis, "Comparative law and the study of mixed legal systems", in M Reimann and R Zimmermann (eds), *The Oxford Handbook of Comparative Law* (2006) 477 at 506.

197 The debate is summarised by J Smits in *The Contribution of Mixed Legal Systems to European Private Law* (2001) 10-11.

198 BGB § 313.

199 § 261.

200 *Taylor v Caldwell* (1863) 3 B & S 826.

Perhaps the most significant question is the direction each of these mixed legal systems is likely to take in the future. Having, to a large extent, resisted the influence of US commercial law, and retaining emphasis on cause, Louisiana is likely to continue along its currently Civilian route. The influence of English law on Scots law has been much stronger and the vestiges of the Civilian approach are increasingly obscured. One hopes with MacQueen that the future in Scotland will indeed be one of "mixedness".[201] Intriguing possibilities are opened up by the Draft Common Frame of Reference, as discussed in the first section of this chapter:[202] a predominantly Civilian body of law which is likely to be influential in Scotland, and elsewhere in Europe. Although the Scottish rules have, in the past, developed with little regard to their theoretical foundations, the same mistakes need not be made in the future.

---

201 H L MacQueen, "Looking forward to a mixed future: A response to Professor Yiannopoulos" (2003) 78 Tulane LR 411 at 417.

202 At section A.(2) above.

10 Hunting Promissory Estoppel

David V Snyder[*]

A. APOLOGIA FOR A DOCTRINAL STUDY OF PROMISSORY
    ESTOPPEL
B. FUNDAMENTALS
(1) Promissory estoppel in the United States and England
(2) A historical introduction to promissory estoppel in Louisiana law
(a) Cause and consideration in Louisiana law
(b) Promissory estoppel in Louisiana
(3) Promise and personal bar in Scotland
(a) The Scots law of promise
(b) Personal bar and allied doctrines
C. DOCTRINAL MIXING
(1) Stair, Europe, the centuries, and the smoke ball
(2) Codification in Louisiana
D. PROMISSORY ESTOPPEL JOBS
E. THEORETICAL DEDUCTIONS
(1) The nature of liability
(2) Formalities and their functions
(3) Doctrines with elbows in a jostling world
F. CONCLUSION

Promissory estoppel came into Louisiana silently, as it pervaded the rest of the United States, under the guises of other doctrines. Even after Williston discovered the hidden current in the American case law and named

* Thanks for research assistance go to Rémi Auba Bresson, Drew Cutler, Janette Hays, and Diana Verm. I am grateful as always to the amazingly resourceful Adeen Postar of the Pence Law Library and to the other fine professionals there, particularly Y Renée Talley-Cuthbert. I would like to note my special gratitude to Hector MacQueen and Elspeth Reid, my mentors in this project; Laura Macgregor, who made a special effort to help me understand Scots law and its institutions; as well as to Vernon Palmer and the other organisers and participants in the Louisiana-Scotland project, who provided more assistance than can be catalogued here. Many errors no doubt remain, and they are mine alone. In keeping with the editors' injunction, I have endeavoured to minimise footnotes. In that effort I have often relied on certain central sources acknowledged prominently but not repeatedly, and discussion and citations in those sources are not necessarily reiterated in the present contribution. Readers should realise that this practice may depart from the usual conventions in American legal writing.

it "promissory estoppel" (to distinguish it from equitable estoppel), the doctrine remained unacknowledged in Louisiana. With its Civil Law heritage Louisiana had no need to fix Common Law problems, it was thought, and promissory estoppel was only a tool for Common Law repairs. This thinking turned, though, and the state has now enshrined promissory estoppel in the Civil Code. In Scotland, on the other hand, a distinctive law of promise had been introduced centuries earlier. Even Adam Smith and David Hume interested themselves in promises and their place in the law, and in Smith's case, in Scots law particularly.[1] This doctrine would seem to leave no room for promissory estoppel, which has therefore been kept out. This background, and these differing results, made promissory estoppel an enticing prospect for a study of two mixed jurisdictions, each of which is characterised by its own internal relationship between Civil Law and Common Law. The story told here, comparing Louisiana and Scotland, is an examination of the intricate relationship between these two sets of relationships.

A. APOLOGIA FOR A DOCTRINAL STUDY OF PROMISSORY ESTOPPEL

Promissory estoppel is marked by three characteristics that make it peculiarly interesting for comparative study. Its father was the strict doctrine of consideration, and its mother was the just pressure to decide cases fairly despite technical strictures. Its growing up was shaped by the death of its old-fashioned but generous grandparent the seal, which honoured gratuitous promises only if sufficiently cloaked in formality. This ancestry, comprised of distinguishing doctrines of the Common Law and the case method of legal development, seemed to destine promissory estoppel for a life only within Common Law systems. Yet its presence in Louisiana law over many decades, and its introduction into the Civil Code in the late twentieth century, might have been thought to indicate that the doctrine was sufficiently powerful to be propelled into the worlds of mixed jurisdictions at least, and perhaps the Civil Law itself.

Second, promissory estoppel is the closest that the Common Law comes to recognising the moral core of a promise. With the consideration doctrine, the Common Law seems to hold that a promise is only worthwhile if someone else is paying for it. Moreover, its worth is typically defined only in monetary terms. In American scholarship the latter point has become sharpened by

---

1 W W McBryde, "Promises in Scots law" (1993) 42 ICLQ 48 at 57-59.

the literature that spins contracts into options either to perform or to pay damages.[2] How systems outside the relatively pure jurisdictions in England and the United States treat unbargained-for promises may cast light on the presence or absence of moral fibres running through the legal treatment of promises, and the strength and orientation of those sometimes hidden threads.

The moral implications of promise can be seen in two ways: the moral need for the promisor to adhere to the promise, and the moral impetus to protect a promisee harmed by a broken promise. Put this way, the third point becomes apparent, as promissory estoppel can be conceived more as a doctrine of tort than of contract. The issue seems legal and technical, but stripped of its legal jargon it begs the question as to whom, and what interests, the law seeks to protect. A close look, then, might reveal the law's choices: the promisor's duty, which is a consequence of his own freedom and the dignity of his will, is woven through the promisee's right, which is itself a consequence of the promisee's injury, whether real, potential, or conceptual. The law's treatment of unbargained-for promises seems an attractive path for research, enabling a better understanding of systemic commitments in different jurisdictions.

Admittedly, this project is unusual in its formulation. The centre of the enquiry is a doctrine, and this design would seem to ignore the insights offered by Rudolf Schlesinger and the followers of the Cornell method.[3] This study, though, while unorthodox in its doctrinal focus, does not disregard their teachings. The focus is on the kinds of "jobs" expected of promissory estoppel or its equivalents in Louisiana and Scotland. The examination, of course, will take place in a doctrinal light inevitably filtered through the omnipresences of American and English Common Law, with which both smaller jurisdictions have to contend.

The greater project here is a bilateral comparison, and the mixed nature of the systems compared is a key component. In this regard, a fourth point can be added to the three characteristics of promissory estoppel mentioned above: the Louisiana and Scottish law relating to unbargained-for promises allows an extraordinary insight into the mixing of policies, doctrines, and attitudes, along with the peculiar sources of law in these two mixed jurisdictions. In Stair's Institutional analysis of promises and contracts, and in the Louisiana State Law Institute's careful debate on promissory estoppel, observers may witness just the kind of mixing that imports select ingredients, alters them to

2 See, e.g., A W Katz, "The option element in contracting" (2004) 90 VaLRev 2187.
3 See generally R B Schlesinger (ed), *Formation of Contracts: A Study of the Common Core of Legal Systems* (1968).

suit local taste, and lets the transformation of the import take the flavour of its new environment. This story is what I have been hunting, and I believe I have found it in the law of promises, whether couched in terms of promissory estoppel and detrimental reliance or unilateral obligations and personal bar.

FUNDAMENTALS

The relation of promissory estoppel to some of the basic tenets of legal systems –consideration, cause and promise – is part of the attraction of this enquiry. To understand these relationships, the components in each system need to be established and evaluated. We begin with the Common Law, especially the American law of promissory estoppel, but with some reference to its English counterpart. With that foundation, the mixed approaches in Louisiana and Scotland can be examined.

(1) Promissory estoppel in the United States and England

Promissory estoppel appears in its most important current formulation in the *Restatement (Second) of Contracts* (1981):

> § 90. *Promise Reasonably Inducing Action or Forbearance*
>
> (1) A promise which the promisor should reasonably expect to induce action or forbearance on the part of the promisee or a third person and which does induce such action or forbearance is binding if injustice can be avoided only by enforcement of the promise. The remedy granted for breach may be limited as justice requires.
>
> (2) A charitable subscription or a marriage settlement is binding under Subsection (1) without proof that the promise induced action or forbearance.

A promise and detrimental reliance on it are both required, except in cases involving charitable subscriptions (and the now rare marriage settlement), and the equitable and exceptional nature of the rule appears plainly. This provision in the second *Restatement* builds on the influential introduction of the doctrine in the first *Restatement* (1932), and while the evolution of the doctrine is both interesting and important, current constraints do not allow lengthy exploration.[4]

---

4 Much of the information on the history of promissory estoppel in the US and in Louisiana can be found in more detail in my earlier article, "Comparative law in action: Promissory estoppel, the Civil Law, and the mixed jurisdiction" (1998) 15 ArizJIntl&CompL 695 (1998), reprinted in V V Palmer (ed), *Louisiana: Microcosm of a Mixed Jurisdiction* (1999) ch 10. This previous article takes into account two early and prominent articles on the introduction of detrimental reliance into Louisiana: C Larroumet, "Detrimental reliance and promissory estoppel as the cause of

The standard story may be rehearsed briefly: promissory estoppel, as hinted before, is the child of the strict consideration doctrine. How consideration came to be understood according to a rigid bargain theory is a curious matter, but however it happened, the development was crystallised in the first *Restatement of Contracts*. Consideration required a bargain. At about the same time, formal contracts ceased to matter as the seal became outmoded. Thus there could be no consideration, and no enforceable contract, unless both parties were seeking the other's promise or performance. So put, though, the results of countless cases could not be explained. In recognition of this trend within the common law, the honest Restatement recognised a doctrine of promissory estoppel. To be enforceable, then, a promise would have to be part of a contract supported by consideration (meaning a bargained-for exchange) or lie within the saving reach of the newly legitimised promissory estoppel. The sponsors of the Restatement saw that the courts applying the common law would not be rigidly constrained by an inflexible bargain theory, and promissory estoppel provided an escape in sufficiently compelling cases.

The doctrine has of course grown. For a time some influential thinkers restricted it to use outside business transactions, reasoning that in a commercial setting consideration should present no difficulty, and the parties could protect themselves through contracts. "[I]t does not in the end promote justice", Learned Hand wrote, to protect "those who do not protect themselves".[5] This restriction withered with the generation that propounded it, though, and by the time of Justice Traynor, it had perished. The California Supreme Court in *Drennan v Star Paving Co*[6] was perfectly willing to bring promissory estoppel to the rescue of general contractors disappointed by the withdrawal of a subcontractor's bid – the very context of which Judge Hand had written. No longer confined to promises of family members and grateful employers, then, promissory estoppel for a time seemed destined to displace consideration.[7]

Consideration and the seal are not the only relevant doctrines. Rigid formal requirements could create similar pressure for escape. Some contracts, to be enforceable, must be in writing under the Statute of Frauds and its progeny,

---

contract in Louisiana and comparative law" (1986) 60 Tulane LR 1209, and M Y Mattar, "Promissory estoppel: Common Law wine in Civil Law bottles" (1988) 4 Tul Civ LF 71, as well as a number of other scholarly works on the subject. Full citations and collections of authorities can be found in the notes of the earlier article. For the most part, the treatment of these issues is not reprised here.

5 *James Baird Co v Gimbel Bros* 64 F 2d 344 at 346 (2d Cir 1933).

6 333 P2d 757 (Cal 1958).

7 G Gilmore, *The Death of Contract* (1974).

but sometimes strict adherence to writing requirements seems to lead to injustice. A number of exceptions to the statute were eventually made, but such situations also led some courts to allow a more general residual escape based on promissory estoppel. This phenomenon received express recognition in section 139 of the second *Restatement*; it had not appeared in the first *Restatement*,[8] although the case law to support the idea was arguably present already.

Given its potential relevance to the Scottish side of this project, promissory estoppel in England also deserves mention.[9] The middle of the nineteenth century witnessed liberalisation in various English doctrines of estoppel,[10] but that case law saw little use in the twentieth century until Lord Denning's judgment in *Central London Property Trust Ltd v High Trees House Ltd*.[11] Later cases, including prominent opinions from Lord Denning, developed the doctrine, although it retained its roots in estoppel and thus could not ground a cause of action.[12] Although this kind of estoppel, referred to occasionally as "promissory estoppel", is now well established,[13] it remains tethered to its defensive conception and is therefore often said to be a shield rather than a sword.[14] English law arguably employs a less constricted doctrine of consideration than American law, though, which may diminish the need for offensive promissory estoppel.[15] Nevertheless, some suggest that under the influence of Australian law, itself influenced by the American Restatements, English law may move toward an expanded notion of promissory estoppel closer to American lines.[16]

8   *See Restatement (Second) of Contracts* § 139 reporter's note.
9   I have primarily followed J M Ngugi, "Promissory estoppel: The life history of an ideal legal transplant" (2007) 41 URichmondLRev 425 at 466 ff, as my source on English law.
10   See particularly *Hughes v Metropolitan Ry Co* [1877] 2 AC 439 (HL), and *Birmingham & Dist Land Co v London & NW Ry Co* (1889) LR 40 Ch D 268 (CA).
11   [1947] KB 130 at 134 f.
12   *See Combe v Combe* [1951] 2 KB 215 (CA).
13   *See Ajayi v R T Briscoe (Nigeria) Ltd* [1964] 1 WLR 1326 (PC).
14   *See First Natl Bank PLC v Thompson* [1996] Ch 231 at 236 (CA) (rejecting unitary approach to estoppel, which would allow offensive use of the doctrine to protect promises); see also *Republic of India v India S S Co* [1998] AC 878 at 914 (HL). Compare *Amalgamated Inv & Prop Co v Texas Commerce Intl Bank Ltd* [1982] QB 84 at 122 (CA) (Denning MR) (Estoppel was "limited by a series of maxims: estoppel is only a rule of evidence, estoppel cannot give rise to a cause of action, estoppel cannot do away with the need for consideration, and so forth. All these can now [after 150 years of evolution] be seen to merge into one general principle shorn of limitations."). For the armorial analogy, see *Combe* per Birkett LJ at 224.
15   See A T Denning, "Recent developments in the doctrine of consideration" (1952) 15 MLR 1 at 1-3.
16   The seminal Australian case is *Waltons Stores (Interstate) Ltd v Maher* (1988) 164 CLR 387, and the English courts have begun to cite it and its progeny, see Ngugi (n 9) at 492 and n 411. See generally ibid at 485-493. The expansiveness of proprietary estoppel seems to afford considerable

(2) A historical introduction to promissory estoppel in Louisiana law

(a) Cause and consideration in Louisiana law

Louisiana, it might be said dogmatically, has no doctrine of consideration, so one might think that promissory estoppel would have no role in the state. The dogma, however, is misleading, and it can be traced most clearly to sources other than the Civil Code for the vast majority of the state's legal history. The problem, indeed, was that the Civil Code itself contained the problematic word *consideration*, both in the central definition of cause and elsewhere. In particular the Civil Code of 1870 provided that "By the *cause* of the contract "is meant the consideration or motive for making it."[17] The Civil Code of 1825 was the source for the 1870 provision, and the 1825 French version gave this definition: "On entend par la cause du contrat ... la considération ou le motif qui a engagé à contracter."[18] If this were not enough, consideration received another explicit mention in the Code just where it creates some of its most obstreperous problems in the Common Law: with respect to options (the minor differences between options and irrevocable offers are ignored in this chapter, and both are referred to as "options"). From the early twentieth century until 1985, the relevant language read, "One may purchase the right, or option to accept or reject, within a stipulated time, an offer or promise to sell, after the purchase of such option, for any consideration therein stipulated, such offer, or promise cannot be withdrawn before the time agreed upon ..."[19]

All of this fomented a fair amount of Civilian angst in Louisiana. Nevertheless, efforts were made to reconcile these mentions of consideration with the indisputably Civilian notion of cause. In general, Professor Litvinoff sought to show, "consideration" as used in the Code could be read to be "at times synonymous with 'cause', and other times with 'onerous cause'".[20] He argued that the consideration requirement would be satisfied in virtually every option, given that the parties are interested in buying or selling, particularly since the flexible "any consideration therein stipulated" formulation replaced the

---

offensive capacity, not far removed from American promissory estoppel. See, e.g., *Wayling v Jones* [1995] 2 FLR 1029; E C Reid and J W G Blackie, *Personal Bar* (2006) 95 f.

17 La Civ Code art 1896 (1870).

18 See art 1887 of the Civil Code of 1825. Where the Code of 1825 is the source, the French version is more authoritative than the English versions of either 1825 or 1870: e.g. *Ross v La Coste de Monterville* 502 So 2d 1026 at 1029-1030 (La 1987).

19 The quoted text reflects amendments through 1920 to article 2462 of the Code of 1870. See generally J Dainow (ed), *Compiled Edition of the Civil Codes of Louisiana* vol 2 (1972) 105-106.

20 S Litivinoff, *Obligations* vol 2 (1975) s 107.

earlier, stricter requirement that the option be "purchase[d] ... for value".[21] Despite such scholarly arguments, Louisiana courts unhesitatingly required that an option be supported by consideration, much as at Common Law.[22]

At the same time, Louisiana did recognise certain kinds of conventional obligations without any consideration, as long as formal requirements were met. Although the American Common Law had lost an efficacious seal, Louisiana retained the possibility of a valid gratuitous contract, that is, a promise of a donation, if appropriate formalities were observed. The English version of the article did include a defining reference to consideration ("without any profit or advantage, received or promised as a consideration for it"), but this was not entirely faithful to the original French ("sans aucun profit ni avantage stipulé en faveur de l'autre partie").[23] In any event, the reference to consideration did not cause difficulty in this case, and Louisiana law recognised even a fully gratuitous contract as a donation inter vivos as long as the intent was expressed in a so-called authentic public act (i.e., a writing "passed before a notary public and two witnesses"[24]) and the promise was accepted.[25] Louisiana here followed the French idea of cause, classifying the obligation as gratuitous but still allowing it, with formal requirements. Still, mentions of consideration in other contexts muddied the Louisiana waters on whether the courts would follow the doctrine of cause exclusively or would revert to ideas of consideration. The legal situation in Louisiana was decidedly mixed.

Clean-up occurred in the 1985 revision of the Civil Code, reflecting the mid- to late-twentieth-century Civilian renaissance. References to consideration were excised, and consideration doctrine was expelled. After requiring cause and defining it, without reference to consideration, the comment to the revision states: "Under this Article, 'cause' is not 'consideration'".[26] With

---

21 The "value" requirement appeared in the 1910 version, although similar ideas of consideration go back in Louisiana law at least to the early nineteenth century. See *Heirs of Cole v Cole's Exrs* 7 Mart (ns) 414 (La 1830) ("defendants denied the consideration, and the court below being of opinion, that none had passed between the parties, gave judgment").

22 *See Goodyear Tire & Rubber Co v Ruiz* 367 So 2d 79, 81 (La Ct App 4th Cir 1979) (option invalidated as nudum pactum); *McCarthy v Magliola* 331 So 2d 89 (La Ct App 1st Cir 1976) (upholding option supported by consideration);*Glover v Abney* 106 So 735 (La 1925) (option without consideration not binding); *Moresi v Burleigh* 127 So 624 (La 1930) (holding $100 sufficient consideration); *Davis v Bray* 191 So 2d 774 (La Ct App 2d Cir 1966) (same).

23 The English text is the same in the Codes of 1825 (art 1766) and 1870 (art 1773). The French text comes from the 1825 Code.

24 La Civ Code arts 1536, 1538. French law is similar, requiring a notarial act. See *Code civil* art 931.

25 La Civ Code arts 1540–1543.

26 Arts 1966 (requiring cause), 1967 (defining cause) and cmt (c).

respect to options, the revision requires no consideration, and the comment states, with a certain amount of gumption, that it "does not change the law".[27] Anyone reading the new article on the irrevocability of offers would not know of the consideration difficulties of three-quarters of a century. And the reference to consideration in the article on gratuitous contracts was also removed, without mention, with the usual comment that the revised article "does not change the law".[28]

(b) Promissory estoppel in Louisiana

As in the Common Law states, promissory estoppel got its start in nineteenth-century case law in which the equities of the case seemed to require enforcement of a promise that did not amount to the usual kind of contract. In *Choppin v Labranche*, the Louisiana Supreme Court enforced a promise to leave in peace the remains of the plaintiff's ancestor.[29] A number of cases also enforced promises on grounds that could be rationalised under the terms of promissory estoppel. To be sure, the cases did not use the "promissory estoppel" label; courts arrived at these results through a variety of devices but this name had not yet been invented. So promissory estoppel percolated quietly through the cases, as elsewhere in the country.

The more interesting development occurred in the 1950s, when the Louisiana Supreme Court considered promissory estoppel in *Ducote v Oden*. By that time the doctrine had not only a name but also a renowned imprimatur from the American Law Institute. After repeating counsel's argument, sounding the very words of the Restatement, the court remarked that "[s]uch a theory is unknown to our law" and could not be found in the "provisions of the Civil Code".[30] The court, however, also emphasised the weakness of the plaintiff's allegation: the promise took place in a "casual ... conversation in the stages of discussion",[31] and even courts which accepted the doctrine would likely have found that the elemental "promise" had not been shown. Nevertheless, for many years *Ducote* was taken as a rejection of the Common Law doctrine, perhaps coming to stand for a broader and more certain holding than the court had originally intended.

Eventually, this position would be reversed by the Civil Code. The Louisiana State Law Institute included promissory estoppel in the 1984 revision, and

27 Art 1928 and cmt (a).
28 Art 1910 and cmt (a).
29 20 So 681 at 682 (La 1896).
30 *Ducote v Oden* 59 So 2d 130 at 132 (La 1952).
31 At 131-132.

in particular, in the central definition of *cause*. How this shift occurred is examined in more detail below. For the moment, it is enough to see the product of the Institute debates, which appears in the current Civil Code:

> *Art 1967. Cause defined; detrimental reliance*
>
> Cause is the reason why a party obligates himself.
> A party may be obligated by a promise when he knew or should have known that the promise would induce the other party to rely on it to his detriment and the other party was reasonable in so relying. Recovery may be limited to the expenses incurred or the damages suffered as a result of the promisee's reliance on the promise. Reliance on a gratuitous promise made without required formalities is not reasonable.

The revision comments say that *Ducote* "is thus overruled", and since the revision, innumerable cases have applied or considered article 1967.

(3) Promise and personal bar in Scotland

The doctrinal landscape in Scotland shares certain core characteristics with Louisiana but is in some ways considerably different. The law of promise and of personal bar are the doctrines most relevant to this enquiry. The law of promise is intriguing but slender. The scope of personal bar, which in American terms seems like all of estoppel and waiver rolled into one (although this perception oversimplifies matters), is vast.[32] We begin with a short look at promise.

(a) The Scots law of promise

Although promises are central to legal systems of obligations, the naked promise, unadorned by consideration or even acceptance, is a special creature. For hundreds of years Scots law has recognised the binding force of at least some promises, even if unaccepted by the beneficiary and unsupported by consideration. Indeed, the lack of acceptance, or any need for it, is the only way to distinguish a promise from a contract in Scots law, since there is no requirement of consideration even for a contract.[33] The distinctive Scots law of promise, at least at first, would seem to preclude any place for promissory estoppel or its analogues.[34] Until 1995, however, gratuitous

---

32 Reid and Blackie, *Personal Bar* (n 16) at 54-69.
33 Unlike Louisiana, Scotland has not generated great doctrinal or theoretical confusion in this regard, but consideration is not entirely irrelevant. E.g. in *Gordon v East Kilbride Development Corp* 1995 SLT 62 Lord Caplan, at 64, declined to find a promise partly because the lack of consideration made a true obligatory promise too unlikely.
34 On promise see W W McBryde, *The Law of Contract in Scotland*, 3rd edn (2007) ch 2, and on proof

promises had to be proved by writ or oath. So perhaps they were not so naked after all. Moreover, particular kinds of commercial obligations might have to be constituted or proved formally, such as cautionary obligations (i.e., contracts of suretyship).[35] These formal requirements would seem to beg for an antidote in appropriate cases.

(b) Personal bar and allied doctrines

Before 1995, two common law rules sometimes rescued obligations suffering from formal defects in their constitution. If the promisee, with the promisor's knowledge, relied on the defective agreement as valid, then the promisor was bound as long as his conduct was "unequivocally referable to the agreement".[36] This rule was called *rei interventus* and sounds quite similar to promissory estoppel when used to cure defects arising from the statute of frauds. A second rule, homologation, bound the promisor when he himself showed that he accepted the defective contract as valid. It sounds similar to the American and English rules on ratification.

Homologation and *rei interventus* were limited, however, to defects in the constitution of the obligation – not defects in proof. This meant that some obligations, which did not legally exist without writing, could nonetheless be deemed to exist. Other obligations – including gratuitous promises – did not require writing for their constitution, but had to be proved by writ or oath. For that reason, homologation and *rei interventus* could not save the distinctive Scottish promise if there was no writing to prove it or it was not confessed under oath.[37] This would seem to tie Scots law to Louisiana law: both systems allow enforceable gratuitous promises, unlike the Common Law, because no consideration is required. A formality, however, is necessary (and, in the case of Louisiana, so is acceptance). Since the law in both places allows promises

---

by writ or oath, the 1ˢᵗ edition (1987) paras 2-42 to 2-47 and 27-20; McBryde (n 1); W D H Sellar, "Promise", in Reid and Zimmermann, *History*, vol 2 (2000) 252; H L MacQueen and J Thomson, *Contract Law in Scotland*, 2ⁿᵈ edn (2007) paras 1.52, 2.54-2.63; M Hogg, *Obligations*, 2ⁿᵈ edn (2006) ch 2; R Zimmermann and P Hellwege, "Belohnungsversprechen: 'pollicitatio', 'promise' oder 'offer'?: Schottisches Recht vor dem Hintergrund der europaischen Entwicklungen" 1998 ZfRV 133. On personal bar see Reid and Blackie, *Personal Bar* (n 16), which I believe supersedes J Rankine, *The Law of Personal Bar in Scotland* (1921). See also H L MacQueen and W D H Sellar, "Scots law: Ius quaesitum tertio, promise and irrevocability", in E J H Schrage (ed), *Ius Quaesitum Tertio* (2008) 357. J P Dawson's famous *Gifts and Promises: Continental and American Law Compared* (1980) has helped shape my interest and approach.

35 Mercantile Law Amendment (Scotland) Act 1856 ch 60 s 6.

36 Bell, *Prin* § 26.

37 See Reid and Blackie, *Personal Bar* (n 16) ch 7, especially 123-124. This statement appears true at least if the promise were not ancillary to a contract susceptible of proof by parole. See McBryde, *Contract*, 1ˢᵗ edn (1987) (n 34) paras 2-44 to 2-47 at 24 f.

unhampered by rules on consideration, promissory estoppel and analogous rules like homologation and *rei interventus* might be thought unnecessary.

In another light, though, the state of affairs in Scotland seems surprising. Homologation and *rei interventus* were recognised sometimes, after all. A person could be deemed bound although he was not in fact obligated in the eyes of the law, provided the elements of homologation or *rei interventus* were satisfied. Yet in the eyes of the law he was released from a real and validly constituted obligation, simply for want of adequate proof, even if the elements of homologation or *rei interventus* were satisfied. This result is more remarkable in that it flows from a purely technical distinction between the constitution and the proof of an obligation.[38]

The most prominent point though is that the rule in Scotland was not softened if there had been detrimental reliance on the promise.[39] This result might be explained away, though, on two grounds. I am only aware of a few cases so holding, almost all of which are old (1911 and 1928) or even antique (1771 and 1861). Views of the equities of promises and reliance may have changed over periods that can best be measured in centuries. Also, the more recent Court of Session decisions (1911 and 1928), as well as the sheriff court case that is the sole decision in memory (1997), all concerned wills, and as Lord President Dunedin observed in one of them, it would "be a most extraordinary result" if promises to make wills could be informal when wills themselves had to be written.[40]

Homologation and *rei interventus* were not the only tools at the disposal of the courts. The memorably named doctrine of "Melville Monument liability" can also come to the rescue.[41] In the seminal case, Walker and his father were developing the New Town of Edinburgh on Walker's estate. Milne led a group of subscribers who planned to erect a monument to Viscount Melville and, with Walker's permission, broke the land and undertook other preparations. They also interfered with Walker's plan for the development of the estate before deciding to put the monument elsewhere, in St Andrew Square,

---

38 This distinction is not present in Louisiana. See La Civ Code art 1536 (donation must be in proper form "under penalty of nullity"), 1538 (donation "will not be valid" without requisite form); see also Civil Code of 1825, arts 1523 ("sous peine de nullité"), 1525 ("ne sera valable").

39 *Gray v Johnston* 1928 SC 659; *Smith v Oliver* 1911 SC 103; *Edmondston v Edmondston* (1861) 23 D 995; *Millar v Tremamondo* (1771) Mor 12395. The only recent case is from the sheriff court: *McEleveen v McQuillan's Ex'x* 1997 SLT (Sh Ct) 46. On proof by writ or oath, see A G Walker and N M L Walker, *The Law of Evidence in Scotland* (1964), most particularly para 130, but also ch 11 in general, at 113-134.

40 *Smith v Oliver* 1911 SC 103 at 111.

41 *Walker v Milne* (1823) 2 S 379 (2nd edn 338). See generally MacQueen and Thomson, *Contract* (n 34) paras 2.93-2.96.

where it still stands. When Walker sued, Milne objected that the contract involved heritage (rights in land) and was invalid because it was unwritten. The court nevertheless allowed Walker to recover any expenditure he had wasted on account of the relocation of the monument.

Melville Monument liability looks very much like promissory estoppel, especially on the facts of *Walker v Milne*. One of the long-time jobs of promissory estoppel is to solve problems caused by writing requirements, which are precisely the problem in *Walker*. The facts of the case highlight two other points as well. First, the case concerns not a promise but an invalid contract, the parties having proceeded by mutual agreement as opposed to unilateral declaration. This semantic nicety does not distinguish it from American promissory estoppel, however, but merely reflects a different usage. Scots law limits *promise* to unilateral obligation, while American law often speaks of contractual agreements in terms of (reciprocal) promises. Certainly many promissory estoppel cases involve apparent agreements rather than simple unilateral declarations.

Second, the facts suggest charity or gratuity. The agreement could possibly be characterised as being supported by consideration, or as an onerous and synallagmatic contract. Perhaps Walker wanted to grace the New Town development with an attractive monument to Lord Melville, and thought it would add value to the venture. Milne and the subscribers certainly wanted a site for the monument, and perhaps the parties agreed to a bargain based on those desires. But the erection of a monument supported by subscriptions and Walker's dedication of land without payment indicate that this undertaking was essentially eleemosynary. This fact-situation is a second way in which Melville Monument liability, in this case, could be seen as a kind of promissory estoppel. It is doing one of promissory estoppel's classic jobs in a context that typified other promissory estoppel cases, especially early ones.

While *Walker v Milne* was followed in the nineteenth century, current judicial attitudes regard liability as exceptional, declaring that "any tendency to extend the scope of the remedy is to be discouraged".[42] This sceptical judicial view can be detected early, as in *Gray v Johnston*, where the majority saw Melville Monument liability subsisting in the cold shadow of the defective contract,[43] and where the only sympathetic treatment came in Lord Justice Clerk Alness's dissent.[44] Liability should be limited, recent authority holds, to situations where the promisor has at least impliedly assured the other party

---

42 *Dawson Intl plc v Coats Patons plc* 1988 SLT 854 at 865, affd 1989 SLT 655.
43 1928 SC 659 at 672 per Lord Ormidale.
44 At 676f.

that there is a binding contract,[45] not where the parties are still negotiating. So it seems that the potential for Melville Monument liability remains as a saving doctrine for defective contracts, but just barely. It might be conceived as a slender branch of personal bar,[46] but even so, it is a delicate curiosity instead of a powerful lever.[47]

As for personal bar more generally, recent scholarly work has done much to rationalise the very broad doctrine, which provides a largely defensive remedy for inconsistent conduct that causes unfairness. It is summarised in the following schema by Elspeth Reid and John Blackie:[48]

(A) INCONSISTENCY
(1) A person claims to have a right, the exercise of which the obligant alleges is barred.
(2) To the obligant's knowledge, the rightholder behaved in a way which is inconsistent with the exercise of the right. Inconsistency may take the form of words, actions, or inaction.
(3) At the time of so behaving the rightholder knew about the right.
(4) Nonetheless the rightholder now seeks to exercise the right.
(5) Its exercise will affect the obligant.

(B) UNFAIRNESS
In the light of the rightholder's inconsistent conduct, it would be unfair if the right were now to be exercised. Any of the following is an indicator of unfairness:
(1) The rightholder's conduct was blameworthy.
(2) The obligant reasonably believed that the right would not be exercised.
(3) As a result of that belief the obligant acted, or omitted to act, in a way which is proportionate.
(4) The exercise of the right would cause prejudice to the obligant which would not have occurred but for the inconsistent conduct.
(5) The value of the right barred is proportionate to the inconsistency.

If Scotland did observe some kind of promissory estoppel, it would fall reasonably neatly within this schema, with one possible exception.

The main difficulty is point (A)(3), suggesting that the promisor must know that his promise is not legally binding before his acts can count against him and hold him to his promise. To the extent that legal knowledge is a strict requirement, it could in principle differentiate personal bar from promissory

---

45 *Dawson* 1988 SLT 854 at 862-865.
46 *Gray v Johnston* 1928 SC 659 at 676 (Alness LJC dissenting); Reid and Blackie, *Personal Bar* (n 16) at 96 n 82; see also J Blackie, "Good faith and the doctrine of personal bar", in A D M Forte (ed), *Good Faith in Contract and Property* (1999) 129 at 153-155 (noting that personal bar is generally only a shield from liability while the Melville Monument theory is not so limited, suggesting that the latter is perhaps closer to promissory estoppel than to personal bar).
47 Since *Dawson*, the doctrine has made only token reappearances, as in *Bank of Scotland v 3i Plc* 1990 SC 215 and in *McMillan v Ghaly*, unreported, Dundee Sh Ct, 9 September 2002 (available at *http://www.scotcourts.gov.uk/opinions/A1350_99.html*).
48 *Personal Bar* (n 16) 30.

estoppel. Scottish cases, old and new, do seem to treat legal knowledge as fundamental, holding that "no man can be barred from the assertion of a legal right by acts done in ignorance of his legal rights".[49] I know of no promissory estoppel cases in which the court even enquires into this point, which would suggest that the issue is immaterial. On the other hand, the Scots requirement of legal knowledge seems generally to be presumed, and the presumption is strengthened by the rule, subject to exception, that ignorance of the law is not a good rejoinder to a plea of personal bar.[50] This requirement thus may not distinguish personal bar from promissory estoppel in a way that would make a difference in many cases.

Moreover, the knowledge requirement is omitted from the Requirements of Writing (Scotland) Act 1995,[51] which gives many of the ideas of personal bar, and thus of promissory estoppel, statutory form insofar as they provide an exception to formal requirements. The statute would seem to give these principles greater authority and clarity than could be achieved through sporadic common law development. At least four moves happen in its provisions. They abolish any requirement that promises be proved by writ or oath, requiring instead that they be constituted in writing. They clarify that the formal requirement applies only to gratuitous promises outside a business context, not to any promises in the course of business and not to non-gratuitous promises outside the business context. (It may be doubted whether a unilateral obligation can be anything but gratuitous, as there is "no counterpart obligation",[52] or even acceptance. If the promise is made in recognition of a natural or moral obligation, however, or is meant to repay a past debt, it might not best be characterised as gratuitous: donative intent – *animus donandi* – is lacking. The promisor may instead intend to fulfil and discharge an obligation, imperfect though it may be.)[53] Most importantly for

---

49 *Lauder v Millars* (1859) 21 D 1353 at 1357 per Lord Justice Clerk Inglis; also *Porteous' Trs v Porteous* 1991 SLT 129; *Strathclyde Regional Council v Persimmon Homes (Scotland) Ltd* 1996 SLT 176.

50 See Reid and Blackie, *Personal Bar* (n 16) at 41-42.

51 See Requirements of Writing (Scotland) Act 1995 s 1; Reid and Blackie, *Personal Bar* (n 16) para 2-34.

52 H L MacQueen, "Constitution and proof of gratuitous obligations: A comment on Scottish Law Commission Memorandum No 66" 1986 SLT (News) 1 at 2, sets forth the view that all promises are gratuitous essentially for this reason.

53 Cf La Civ Code arts 1523-1526 (so-called donations that are sufficiently remunerative are not treated as donations), and on remuneratory donations in Scots law, see W M Gordon, "Donation", in SME vol 8 (1992) para 608. Note that an imperfect obligation, while not binding in a legal tribunal, is nevertheless binding *in foro conscientiæ*, as Stair knew, see *Inst* 1.10.4. McBryde, noting that many promises occur in a commercial context, also holds that "not all promises are gratuitous" (McBryde (n 1) at 48). This conclusion may be bolstered by the presumption against donations: "It is a rule in law, *donatio non præsumitur*; and therefore, whatsoever is done, if it

present purposes, the statute provides that the promise be constituted, not merely proved, in writing. This last move opens the way for exceptions to formal requirements based on the principles underlying homologation and *rei interventus*. The modern statute abolishes those two common law rules and substitutes its own formula.

To simplify, then, where one party has materially relied, the other party may not withdraw if doing so would result in material harm. The lack of formality is forgiven. Although the statutory language is lengthy and convoluted, this Scottish statute essentially states the principle of promissory estoppel as applied to problems posed by the statute of frauds – a principle stated explicitly in section 139 of the second *Restatement* of Contracts. The Act requires that the reliance take place with the promisor's "knowledge and acquiescence", however. What is meant by these words is less than clear. Professors MacQueen and Thomson suggest that actual knowledge is necessary, although acquiescence is likely to be presumed.[54] But is the requirement satisfied if the reliance is foreseeable,[55] perhaps even expected and desired,[56] yet the promisor has not been informed that it has actually taken place? It will be informative to observe whether the old stance on knowledge under *rei interventus* doctrine is continued.[57] Certainly the promisor's knowledge and acquiescence would always be relevant to promissory estoppel, if for no other reason than the relevance of injustice.[58]

Finally, the Act applies its reliance principles to variations. Contract modifications have traditionally raised the very two problems in the common law that promissory estoppel has characteristically attacked. Because of the pre-existing duty rule – a corollary of the bargain theory of consideration – modifications often lack consideration and may be deprived of force for that reason. In addition, not only may the usual requirements of the statute of frauds fell the modification, but the parties may add their own statute of frauds by requiring that all contract modifications be in writing. Although

---

can receive any other construction than donation, it is constructed accordingly" (Stair, *Inst* 1.8.2). See also n 180 below (commercial payment adjustments that are neither donative nor onerous nor synallagmatic). The difference of opinion noted here seems to centre on what is meant by *gratuitous*, a fine point that might have broad implications for the basis of legal obligation. For further discussion, see H MacQueen and M Hogg, "Donation in Scots law", in M Schmidt-Kaessel (ed), *Donation in Europe* (forthcoming); Hogg, *Obligations* (n 34) paras 2.06-2.11.

54 MacQueen and Thomson, *Contract* (n 34) para 2.49.

55 As in the formulation in *Restatement (Second) of Contracts* s 90.

56 As in the classic promissory estoppel cases like *Ricketts v Scothorn* 77 NW 365 (Neb 1898), and *Greiner v Greiner* 293 P 759 (Kan 1930).

57 For the pre-statutory standard, see *Danish Dairy Co v Gillespie* 1922 SC 656.

58 The principle is most familiar from the land cases like *Greiner* and is encapsulated in *Restatement (Second) of Contracts* § 129 (reliance on "continuing assent").

these "no oral modification" clauses were invalid at American common law, article 2 of the Uniform Commercial Code validates them, but subjects them to an exception based on the ideas of estoppel.[59] The 1995 Act thus aligns itself with American notions of promissory estoppel, although these notions are more salient in American law generally than in Louisiana in particular.

C. DOCTRINAL MIXING

One of the great attractions of studying promises in Louisiana and Scotland is the chance to observe doctrinal mixing. The work in Louisiana is relatively recent – it concluded about twenty-five years ago – and the drafts of proposals and minutes of meetings are available. The relevant work in Scotland occurred centuries ago, but historical and doctrinal analysis have revealed how the mixture took place.

(1) Stair, Europe, the centuries, and the smoke ball

The Scots law on promises has excited considerable interest at least since Professor Sir Thomas Smith brought attention to it in the mid-twentieth century. Its career since then has been no less remarkable, now being taken into the *Principles of European Contract Law* and the *Draft Common Frame of Reference*.[60] The starting place is considerably earlier, however, and begins with Stair's great work of the seventeenth century, his *Institutions of the Law of Scotland*.[61]

Stair treats promises in his title, "Obligations Conventional, by Promise, Paction, and Contract". In his scheme, the promise leads to an obligation, which restricts our liberty because of "our will and consent", and so in modern terms might be denominated a *consensual* obligation.[62] One of the most unusual features of the Scots law of promise is that no agreement or

---

59 *See* UCC § 2-209. See generally D V Snyder, "The law of contract and the concept of change: Public and private attempts to regulate modification, waiver, and estoppel" 1999 WisLRev 607.

60 "A promise which is intended to be legally binding without acceptance is binding" (*Principles of European Contract Law* art 2:107); similarly, see *Draft Common Frame of Reference for European Contract Law*, bk 2, arts 1:103(2), 4:301-4:303. See also T B Smith, "Pollicitatio – promise and offer" 1958 *Acta Juridica* 141, reprinted in T B Smith, *Studies Critical and Comparative* (1962) 168; T B Smith, "Unilateral promise (pollicitatio)", in *A Short Commentary on the Law of Scotland* (1962) ch 32.

61 6th edn by D M Walker (1981). The account here is simplified, even as Stair himself offered a simplified analysis of a complex dispute within the civil law, canon law, and the *ius commune*. Stair is the primary source, but Sellar's history of promise (n 34) contains much of the information, and the complexity of the debate within the *ius commune* comes through most clearly in MacQueen and Sellar (n 34) at 358-365.

62 Stair, *Inst* 1.10.1.

coming together is required (so it is not *conventional*). The exercise of the will results in an "engagement [that] is a diminution of freedom, constituting that power in another, whereby he may restrain, or constrain us to the doing or performing of that whereof we have given him power of exaction". Stair's next point states a qualification to the general principle: "But it is not every act of the will that raiseth an obligacion, or power of exaction".[63] Instead, he distinguishes between "desire, resolution, and engagement". Only the last of these gives rise to an obligation, even if there be clear proof of a resolution "by word and writ", and he cites a case to this effect.[64] So even a written resolution is not the same as a promise – a point that will resonate in a case in 2007[65] – and this raises two questions: first, what is the difference between a resolution and a promise, and second, what happens if someone is injured by this clear resolution? The second question is answered with an exception, as it appears that Stair would find an obligation if "the resolution be holden forth to assure others".[66] This, it would seem, is related to the notion of personal bar, although not so termed, and it seems based essentially on the interests of the "others", as the resolution by itself is insufficient, although Stair does not require any reliance, at least explicitly.

Stair appears to answer the first question with a circular definition,[67] but of greater interest here is his explanation of the promise, not just because of the significance for promissory estoppel but also because of its mixture of sources. "[A] promise is that which is simple and pure, and hath not implied as a condition, the acceptance of another".[68] Stair thus distinguishes an obligation based on a promise from an obligation based on a contract, which "is the deed of two, the offerer and the accepter".[69] This distinction draws on roughly four categories of sources: natural law, canon law, civil (Roman) law, and Scots law. Stair begins by considering and rejecting Grotius's requirement of acceptance.[70] Unaccepted promises "now are commonly held obligatory, the canon law having taken off the exception of the civil law, *de nudo pacto*".

Here can be observed the authority of the civil (Roman) law, but as updated and even superseded by canon law. The reference to canon law is not expounded, but it appears slightly later with respect to proof. Stair explains

---

63 Ibid.
64 Ibid 1.10.2 (citing *Kincaid v Dickson* (1673) Mor 12143, 2 Stair 181).
65 *Countess of Cawdor v Earl of Cawdor*, discussed at nn 158-162 below and accompanying text.
66 Stair, *Inst* 1.10.2.
67 Ibid ("the only act of the will, which is efficacious, is that whereby the will conferreth or stateth a power of exaction in another, and thereby becomes engaged to that other to perform").
68 Ibid 1.10.4.
69 Ibid 1.10.3.
70 Ibid 1.10.4 (citing Grotius, *de jure belli*, lib 2 cap II §14).

the position of Roman rules of *nudum pactum*, but says, "We shall not insist in these, because the common custom of nations hath resiled therefrom, following rather the canon law, by which every paction produceth action, *et omne verbum de ore fideli cadit in debitum*."[71] The reliance on canon law is explicit, and the choice may seem less surprising given that ecclesiastical courts maintained an important role in Scotland even after the Reformation; the Court of Session was itself largely ecclesiastical in its conception, character, and outlook.[72] Stair also cites the views of Petrus Gudelinus and of Corvinus, and we here find a reference to "the common custom of nations", in Latin possibly rendered as *ius gentium*, although here probably better denominated *ius commune*, meaning the post-antique custom of nations rather than the *ius gentium* of the Roman law. By this point, then, we find Stair's sources include the law of nature, as represented by Grotius, the law of ancient Rome, the law of the medieval Church, and the custom of nations – meaning, notably, Continental nations.

But these sources were not all, for Stair also included Scots practice, represented by case law in the paragraph on promise, and later, by what he says is a statute. Three cases are marshalled to give the Scots law of promise. Further research has shown that Stair accurately represented contemporary law, although the statute he had in mind is slightly vexing,[73] and an examination of Hope suggests that despite Stair's assertion, Scots law had not entirely gone down the path of the canon law, at least when Hope was writing. Hope's view, while sympathetic to the canon law idea, says that the "comone law" of Scotland differed from the canon law.[74] We might thus detect an element of advocacy in Stair's selective choice of sources – assuming no significant change in the "comone law" between Hope and Stair. Also noticeably absent is the law of England. However it is considered, then, the law propounded by Stair was a gourmand mixture, drawing on sources crossing centuries and crossing the Continent (but not dipping south into England).

---

71 Ibid 1.10.7 (citing C.1 & 3 *de pactis*). The reference is to *Dectretales Gregorii* IX 1.35.1, 3, or more technically X 1.35.1, 3 (referring to the *Liber Extra*, added by Gregory IX to the *Decretum* of Gratian). These canons, I am told, are the locus classicus of the Canonist idea that all agreements must be kept. The *Glossa Ordinaria*, which appears in the margins of the *Dectretales*, notes that the civil law is different, as Stair does, although Stair is oversimplifying the Canon Law. (Many thanks to Professor James Gordley for illuminating all of these points.) Stair's Latin aphorism does not appear in this source, and perhaps he was the aphorist himself, giving his own "version of the canonist *pacta servanda sunt*". See H L MacQueen, "Good faith in the Scots law of contract: An undisclosed principle?", in A D M Forte (ed), *Good Faith in Contract and Property Law* (1999) 5 at 14 n 40.

72 Sellar, "Promise" (n 34) at 264-266.

73 Ibid at 260-261.

74 Ibid at 264, citing Hope, *Practicks*, vol 1, 98.

In addition, as might be guessed from the exposition above, Stair discusses the problem of proof. Here the case law is brought to bear. Promises, he says, cannot be proved by witnesses, even for small amounts – unlike contracts. He suggests an exception where the promises "are parts of bargains about moveables", but otherwise the general rule is unyielding, and a writ would be necessary. Just as "the Roman law gave no action upon naked pactions, to prevent the mistakes of parties and witnesses in communings", Scots law sought to prevent such mistakes, particularly since writing had become "so ordinary" and those who failed to avail themselves of "so easy a method" could not resort to legal process. In such cases, the promise could be recognised only in the conscience of the promisor – a formulation that evokes the imperfect obligation of the natural law writers.[75] So again careful mixing, cutting, and adapting can be seen.

Although this mixing can be observed in the seventeenth century, awareness of its importance in modern law can be credited to the twentieth-century work of Smith and the "neo-Civilian revival" that took place after the Second World War.[76] Two of Smith's works brought the Scots law of unilateral promise out of obscurity. Part of his work took on the fusion (or confusion) of English and Scots law on promises and contracts, particularly with respect to options and rewards.[77] Possibly the leading edge on which English law worked its way into Scotland was the memorable case of *Carlill v Carbolic Smoke Ball Co*.[78] With that case, Smith demonstrated how the unwieldy English requirements of offer, acceptance and consideration were brought into the Scots law of rewards and options.[79] The law of unilateral promise that Stair had justified with his careful mixture was eroded by cases that followed the English approach of *Carlill* and that tried to make promises into contracts with acceptance and consideration.[80] The Scots law remained, as the 1899 case of *Morton's Trustees v Aged Christian Friend Society*[81] shows, in rather

---

75 Stair, *Inst* 1.10.4.
76 MacQueen and Sellar (n 34) 380.
77 Smith, *Studies Critical* (n 60) 178-182.
78 [1892] 2 QB 484, affd [1893] QB 256.
79 The terminology is troubling here, as many of the "reward" cases are about undertakings by publishers and their insurers to pay if an individual should die in a railway accident while carrying a particular newspaper or diary. Similarly, an "option" sounds like shorthand for an "option contract", but only a price said to be good for a set period is meant. Writing in English brings in English connotations, yet using Scottish legal terminology is too narrow given the mixing involved. The failure of language to fit is an interesting point in itself with regard to mixed jurisdictions, from the standpoint of linguistics or linguistic anthropology.
80 Smith, *Studies Critical* (n 60) at 179 cites *Law v Newnes* (1894) 21 R 1027; *Hunter v Hunter* (1904) 7 F 136; *Hunter v General Accident etc Corp* 1909 SC 344, affd 1909 SC (HL) 30.
81 (1899) 2 F 82.

a sorry state; *Morton's Trustees* brings in the law of promise when offer and acceptance is the accurate analysis.[82] Smith laid bare the problems of the assimilation of Scots law to English law and the confusing consequences for common fact patterns like options and modifications.[83]

Smith then illustrated the elegance of the Scottish (i.e., non-English) solution, and he placed it into a comparative context that gave it both pedigree and gravitas. His work took into account the Civil Law families of French and German law and in particular Roman-Dutch and South African law. He explained where the Scots solution fitted among those traditions, and demonstrated its superior doctrinal simplicity. This is work of mixture and comparison as well as scholarship and advocacy.

Perhaps the best way to appreciate Smith's success is to look at the doctrine now. Professor MacQueen followed Smith a generation or so later with a similar analysis, noting an English case in which trustees had committed to accepting the highest bid[84] and showing again how Smith's Scottish treatment of the smoke ball case, using the law of unilateral promise, produced the right result with a simpler and more accurate legal characterisation of the facts.[85] Admittedly the necessity for MacQueen's article shows that Smith was not complete in his success; while several cases took the Scottish road to enforcing options as unilateral obligations,[86] some (notably Professor Walker) seemed instead to follow English law.[87] The echoes of Smith and the smoke ball explanation continue, appearing still in Professor McBryde's standard work,[88] and evidencing what may be unavoidable for a mixed jurisdiction like Scotland or Louisiana: a distinctiveness in the smaller jurisdictions (Scotland and Louisiana) that is defined by difference from the dominant jurisdiction (England and the United States).

So Scotland came to have its doctrine of the unilateral promise. But it was a complex concatenation that led to this simple result. Stair drew on natural law and canon law and civil law – in short, the complex of the *ius commune* – and found a protection for a unilateral promise. Further mixing

---

82 E.g. McBryde, *Contract* (n 34) para 2-24. There may also have been an element of *rei interventus*. See *Wick Harbour Trs v The Admiralty* 1921 2 SLT 109 at 112 per Lord Sands (OH).

83 *A & G Paterson v Highland Ry* 1927 SC (HL) 32.

84 *Harvela Investments v Royal Trust Co of Canada* [1984] 2 All ER 65, revd [1985] Ch 103 (subsequently rev'd [1986] AC 207).

85 H MacQueen, "Offers, promises and options" 1985 SLT (News) 187.

86 *Sichi v Biagi* 1946 SN 66; *Scott v Morrison* 1979 SLT (Notes) 65; *Stone v MacDonald* 1979 SLT 288; W M Gloag, *The Law of Contract*, 2nd edn (1929) 166.

87 MacQueen (n 85) at 189. Walker apparently followed *Hamilton v Lochrane* (1899) 1 F 478, a case from the period where Smith identifed most confusion.

88 McBryde, *Contract*, 3rd edn (2007), (n 34) above, paras 2-05 and 2-27. Compare the 2nd edn (2002) and McBryde (n 1) at 63-64.

and further imports from English law followed, until Smith and his followers were able to write the doctrine that recited a more purely Scottish rule – or more accurately, a less English one – and marked a return to Stair.

(2) Codification in Louisiana

Some of the most interesting mixing to be observed in Louisiana occurs centuries after Stair, and of particular interest is the Civil Code revision.[89] The Council of the Louisiana State Law Institute wanted to remove consideration from Louisiana obligations law and to add promissory estoppel. This desire was made explicit when the Council "instructed the reporter to draft an article that would make it quite clear that 'cause' is not 'consideration' in the common law sense, and, further, to introduce a concept analogous to 'detrimental reliance' or 'promissory estoppel'".[90] The developments with respect to cause and consideration have been summarised above, but here the introduction of promissory estoppel deserves specific examination.

The model for promissory estoppel, patently, was the *Restatement (Second) of Contracts* section 90. The earliest available draft defines cause, distinguishes it from consideration, and provides for promissory estoppel. The draft reproduces section 90 of the *Restatement* below the proposed Code wording, along with previous Code articles defining cause. The irony is double-edged: not only did Common Law notions define cause, positively and negatively, but promissory estoppel was imported at the same time that the chief doctrine making it necessary was deported. This could all be achieved by legislative fiat, but this was not enough. The reporter was further "instructed to make detrimental reliance compatible with cause".[91] This he endeavoured to do by a wording change that might seem insignificant. Cause, instead of being the "motive" for the contract (as in the old article) could be said to be the *reason* for making the promise. Then one might say, as the draft does, that "[c]ause is the reason that makes an obligation enforceable".

This sleight of hand would turn cause around entirely. Observe the switch: cause began as the motive for making the contract. The cause of a contract, then, may be illegal, in which case the contract would not be enforceable. Still, the contract would have a cause, albeit an illegal one that could not

---

89 This section draws on Snyder (n 4) at 706-723.
90 Louisiana State Law Institute, *Revision of the Louisiana Civil Code of 1870*, book 3 – Obligations Revision – "Cause", at 3 (20 April 1979) (prepared for Meeting of the Committee, 20 April 1979, but hand-dated "3-13-79" suggesting a date of 13 March) (Saúl Litvinoff, Reporter) (henceforth April 1979 Draft).
91 Ibid at 2-3.

support a valid contract. In the proposed formulation, however, cause works differently. If the promise is supported by cause, it is for that very reason enforceable, by definition. There could be no such thing as an illegal or invalid cause. Cause, then, is made to serve the same function as consideration. At Common Law, if there is consideration the promise is enforceable, and otherwise not. Under the proposed formulation, if there is cause, the promise is enforceable, and otherwise not. This proposition is a far cry from the original scheme in which cause served a classficatory function (donative, onerous, legal, illegal, etc), and merely having a cause was not sufficient to make a contract enforceable. While the proposal is Civilian in its adherence to a cause that is not identical to bargain, it is working like Common Law consideration doctrine: having a cause or a consideration makes a contract enforceable, and lacking it makes the contract unenforceable. Common Law and Civil Law are mixed, intricately and intimately.

Mixing is also apparent in the three-fold justification for the introduction of promissory estoppel, which the draft links to the Louisiana (and French) Code, to Louisiana case law, and to learned Civilian doctrine. Promissory estoppel, the reporter says, is consonant with principles in the existing Code, including its Napoleonic general article on delictual obligation: "Every act whatever of man that causes damage to another obliges him by whose fault it happened to repair it."[92] In addition, promissory estoppel is found in the case law. This proposition was problematic in light of the Louisiana Supreme Court decision in *Ducote v Oden*, as mentioned above,[93] but the reporter identified the undercurrent of cases that applied the principle *sub rosa* both before and after *Ducote*.

Perhaps the most remarkable argument is the last: that promissory estoppel is in essence a Civil Law doctrine anyway. Likened to delictual and quasi-delictual obligations, it is linked particularly to *culpa in contrahendo*, the primarily German doctrine providing a remedy against one whose fault in the contracting process damages the other party.[94] It is also linked to "the binding force of a unilateral declaration of will",[95] the same idea observed in Scotland, and most clearly in Stair. The crowning glory, though, goes to the assertion that estoppel is descended from the Roman law doctrine of *venire*

---

92 The quotation comes from art 2315 of the Code of 1870, although this paragraph remains essentially unchanged in the current Code. It is the same (except for a typographical error) as art 1382 of the Code Napoléon.

93 At n 30.

94 The doctrine is discussed in Snyder (n 4) at 703–706.

95 April 1979 Draft (n 90) at 6–7.

contra factum proprium.[96] The assertion that promissory estoppel is not a Common Law invention after all, and is instead Roman and thus quintessentially of the Civil Law, is contentious. *Venire contra factum proprium* is more generally viewed as being based on facts rather than executory promises, and is therefore closer to equitable estoppel (i.e., estoppel in pais) rather than promissory estoppel. Moreover, *venire contra factum proprium* is probably better attributed to the *ius commune*, and perhaps Bartolus originally, rather than Rome, as earlier research has shown.[97] But these are scholastic points. The impetus came from the American Common Law and the Restatement. The revision draft reproduces section 90, not a text from the Digest or from Bartolus, neither of which is very clearly about promissory estoppel anyway.

So we see mixing, and machinations, in three ways. First, the rule of the American Common Law is taken from the Restatement and paraphrased into the Civil Code. Second, the juxtaposition of Common Law and Civil Law thinking drove efforts (ultimately unsuccessful) to define cause in a way that would have been consonant with promissory estoppel and that would have made cause serve the same function as consideration, albeit not requiring a bargain. Third, the attempt to justify promissory estoppel as a doctrine of Civil Law, and even Roman law, shows the kind of Civilian striving expected only when Common Law thinking seems uncomfortably – even threateningly – close.

D. PROMISSORY ESTOPPEL JOBS

Discussing and comparing doctrines in the abstract can lead to a disembodied logic, as well as to errors born of finding cognate doctrines that sound similar but are used differently. One way to check that the doctrines under examination bear comparison is to consider what jobs they do.[98] Promissory estoppel in Louisiana worked in many of the same sorts of jobs associated with promissory

---

96 Ibid at 7 ("It is worthwhile to mention that, after all, neither estoppel in pais nor promissory estoppel are common law inventions. The notion of estoppel descends directly from the Roman *venire contra factum proprium*." Citation is made to J Puig Brutau, *Estudios de Derecho Comparado* (1951) 97).

97 See D 12.4.5.pr (Ulpian, Diputationum 2), 4.3.34 (Ad Sabinum 42), 19.5.16.1 (Ad Sabinum 22), 17.1.15 (Paul, Ad Sabinum 2); also Gai Inst 3.160; M Schwaibold, *Brocardica* (1985) 43 (under "Neminem debere venire contra factum suum et si non valeat quod fecit"). The quotation from Bartolus is "non potest quis venire contra factum suum ad sui commodum etiam ex persona alterius" (Commentaria ad D 12.6.2). The texts are parsed and further sources cited in Snyder (n 4) at 712-713 n 100.

98 On law-jobs see K N Llewellyn, "The normative, the legal, and the law-jobs" (1940) 49 Yale LJ 1355.

estoppel in the rest of the United States,[99] and this situation continues. Subcontractor bids led to some of the classic cases of promissory estoppel in Louisiana as elsewhere.[100] These cases usually concern option contracts, irrevocable offers, and the like. The more general problem of so-called "precontractual" liability can itself be a source for promissory estoppel claims, and again Louisiana has seen its share, including disputes about options.[101] The cases in Louisiana, as in the United States more widely, often revolve around claims that insurers have granted insurance in some provisional but binding way (at least temporarily), or that a lender has committed to making a loan. There have now been legislative efforts to quash the latter effect in Louisiana,[102] and since the Louisiana Supreme Court has made clear that it will broadly and strictly enforce this special statute of frauds for credit agreements,[103] the loan cases may dissipate. One prominent job for promissory estoppel would thus be eliminated, but it is nevertheless a limited exception.

In addition, promissory estoppel claims are sometimes asserted instead of contract claims. When this phenomenon was perceived it excited much scholarly comment in the United States as it seemed to bolster the earlier claim that contract was dead, not only because promissory estoppel had killed consideration, but because promissory estoppel was a more viable general cause of action than the technically constrained contract action. Further studies, however, have shown these effects to have been exaggerated,

---

99 The cases for the first dozen years of promissory estoppel in the Civil Code are collected and classified in Snyder (n 4) at 734-747.

100 E.g., *Drennan v Star Paving Co* 333 P 2d 757 (Cal 1958).

101 For cases involving potential precontractual liability issues, see *Suire v Lafayette City-Parish Consol Govt* 907 So 2d 37 (La 2005); *Baker v LSU Health Scis Ctr, Inst of Professional Education* 889 So 2d 1178 (La Ct App 2004); *Hibernia Nat'l Bank v Antonini* 862 So 2d 331 (La Ct App 2003) (loan case, claimed promise of permanent funding); *Holt v Bethany Land Co* 843 So 2d 606 (La Ct App 2003) (option holder was using the land); *Magic Moments Pizza, Inc v Louisiana Restaurant Assn* 819 So 2d 1146 (La Ct App 2002) (insurance coverage through detrimental reliance); *Haring v Stinson* 756 So 2d 1201 (La Ct App 2000). See also *Gangi Seafood, Inc v ADT Security Services* 2005 US App LEXIS 4 (5th Cir 2005) (alarm service); *Rogers v Brooks* 122 Fed Appx 729 (5th Cir 2004); *Becnel v Whirley Indus* 2003 US Dist LEXIS 21575 (D La 2003) (precontractual liability and confidentiality); *Starco Meats, Inc v Bryan Foods, Inc* 2003 US Dist LEXIS 4452 (D La 2003); *Jobe v ATR Mktg, Inc* 1998 US Dist LEXIS 18171 (D La 1998) (option). Cases involving problems of agency or mandate might also be put in this category, or perhaps deserve a classification of their own. See *Freeman Decorating Co v Encuentro Las Americas Trade Corp* 2005 US Dist LEXIS 18313 (D La 2005); *Dan Rhodes Enters v City of Lake Charles* 857 So 2d 1256 (La Ct App 2003).

102 Since 1989, credit agreements must be in signed writings. La Rev Stat Ann § 6:1122, per 1989 La Acts no 531, § 1. Although not relevant to the point in the text, surely it must be remarked that the new statute requires a written expression of "consideration"!

103 *Jesco Constr Corp v Nationsbank Corp* 830 So 2d 989 at 992 (La 2002) (holding that the writing requirement for credit agreements bars all actions, including detrimental reliance, based on unwritten loan agreements).

primarily because promissory estoppel claims rarely win. The courts are generally unsympathetic to promissory estoppel, and contract is a considerably firmer ground for recovery.[104]

Similarly, in Louisiana a number of cases asserting promissory estoppel claims could be put into the "completed contract" category, creating the idea that promissory estoppel is supplanting contract, or other more specific rules. Sometimes, indeed, this observation is accurate,[105] and sometimes a detrimental reliance claim can even seem to displace or at least supplement a contract.[106] Because the courts can be so stringent in their approach to promissory estoppel, though, such claims often fail. For that reason the later American studies just mentioned have found contract very much alive, with promissory estoppel being the last resort it was conceived to be,[107] and some Louisiana cases suggest this mindset.[108] While some cases bring promissory

104 See S W DeLong, "The new requirement of enforcement reliance in commercial promissory estoppel: Section 90 as Catch-22" 1997 WisLRev 943; R A Hillman, "Questioning the 'new consensus' on promissory estoppel: An empirical and theoretical study" (1998) 98 ColumLRev 580. The main articles forming the brief "new consensus", which had been proclaimed in R E Barnett, "The death of reliance" (1996) 46 JLegalEduc 518 at 522, were D A Farber and J H Matheson, "Beyond promissory estoppel: Contract law and the 'invisible handshake'" (1985) 52 UChiLRev 903, and E Yorio and S Thel, "The promissory basis of section 90" (1991) 101 Yale LJ 111 at 129. The classic kernel of the now debunked "new consensus" is of course Gilmore, *Death of Contract* (n 7).

105 *Woodard v Felts* 573 So 2d 1312 at 1315-16 (La Ct App 2d Cir 1991), and *Kethley v Draughon Business College, Inc* 535 So 2d 502 at 506-507 (La Ct App 2d Cir 1988), use article 1967 instead of the specifically applicable article 1952 on determining damages when consent is vitiated by error.

106 *See Water Craft Mgmt LLC v Mercury Marine* 361 F Supp 2d 518 (D La 2004) (competitor/franchise); *Comprehensive Addiction Programs v Mendoza* 50 F Supp 2d 581 (D La 1999) (sales contract that did not close for lack of a loan); see also *Industrias Magromer Cueros y Pieles SA v Louisiana Bayou Furs*, 293 F 3d 912 (5th Cir 2002) (finding twin contract and detrimental reliance claims based on the same operative facts).

107 The subsidiarity of promissory estoppel to contract is reinforced as a practical matter by the results of the DeLong and Hillman studies (n 104) showing that promissory estoppel, while easily asserted, rarely wins in comparison to contract claims, and this empirical finding only buttresses the theoretical conception of the doctrine as it has typically been understood. See J M Feinman, "The last promissory estoppel article" (1992) 61 FordhamLRev 303 at 309 ("Look first for the contract that meets traditional requirements; if and only if it is not available, look for a section 90 cause of action").

108 *Condrey v SunTrust Bank of Ga* 429 F 3d 556, 565-566 (5th Cir 2005) (where parole evidence is inadmissible to vary a contract, detrimental reliance doctrine is inapplicable (citing *Omnitech Intl v Clorox Co* 11 F 3d 1316 at 1330 (5th Cir 1994)); *Drs Bethea, Moustoukas and Weaver LLC v St Paul Guardian Ins Co* 376 F 3d 399 (5th Cir 2004) (insurance contract: no detrimental reliance possible within the scope of integrated contract); *McDermott Intl v Indus Risk Insurers*, 2003 US Dist LEXIS 22286, concl of law paras 22-24 (D La 2003) (insurance contract: sophisticated party should not rely on assertions outside the contract); *Ark Entertainment, LLC v C J Gayfer & Co* 2000 US Dist LEXIS 3867 (D La 2000) (real contract precludes detrimental reliance); *In re Horn* 827 So 2d 1241 (La Ct App 2002) (ultimately uses public records doctrine rather than detrimental reliance).

estoppel into the realm of completed synallagmatic contracts,[109] others hold that where there is a synallagmatic contract, that contract provides the rights of the parties rather than alleged promises and detrimental reliance.[110] Likewise courts seem unlikely to find reasonable reliance when the alleged promisor has not made a promise that rises to the level ordinarily associated with a contract or guarantee.[111]

In the completed bargain cases, sometimes a lack of formalities causes the move into promissory estoppel. At first the Louisiana courts appeared poised to join the states that resisted the general rule, encapsulated in the special section of the Restatement (section 139, as opposed to the usual section 90), that promissory estoppel could defeat a defence under the statute of frauds. More recent Louisiana cases point in the other direction, however, and several have followed the general rule that promissory estoppel under article 1967 can trump a writing requirement. The strength of these holdings is uncertain, however, as all arose in securities transactions;[112] while there had been an applicable writing requirement when the operative events occurred, the writing requirement had been abolished by the time that the cases were decided. The strict enforcement of the new writing requirements for loan agreements should also be recalled.[113]

The main qualification when Louisiana is compared to the American Common Law is in the area of family promises and gifts. These cases arguably gave rise to the doctrine in the first place, but Louisiana refused to follow, retaining its Civil Law authentic act as a way of making an enforceable promise to make a gift – a legal device that the American Common Law lost when the seal fell into desuetude. Nevertheless, this has proved a fertile breeding ground for promissory estoppel claims in Louisiana, although they have been unsuccessful.[114]

---

109   See *Shreveport Plaza, LLC v Dollar Tree Stores, Inc* 196 Fed Appx 320 (5th Cir 2006), in addition to the cases cited above (n 106).

110   *Condrey* 429 F 3d at 565-566; *Drs Bethea* 376 F 3d 399 (integrated contract, therefore no detrimental reliance possible within scope of contract); *Ark Entertainment* 2000 US Dist LEXIS 3867 (real contract precludes detrimental reliance).

111   *Miller v Loyola Univ of New Orleans* 829 So 2d 1057 at 1062 (La Ct App 2002).

112   *Rhoads v Quicksilver Brokers Ltd* 801 So 2d 1284 at 1289 (La Ct App 2001); *Dugas v Guillory* 719 So 2d 719 at 726 (La Ct App 1998). The Louisiana Supreme Court addressed similar issues earlier, but article 1967 had not yet become effective at the relevant time and the court did not apply it. See *Morris v Friedman* 663 So 2d 19 (La 1995), construed in Snyder (n 4) at 729-731; see also *Cenac v Hart* 741 So 2d 690 at 695 (La Ct App 1999) (not applying promissory estoppel exception because it had not yet become effective).

113   *Jesco Constr Corp v Nationsbank Corp* 830 So 2d 989 at 992 (La 2002).

114   In addition to cases cited earlier see *Moncrief v Succn of Armstrong* 939 So 2d 714 (La Ct App 2006); *Crosby v Stinson* 766 So 2d 615 (La Ct App 2000).

Just as article 1967 has taken on the promissory estoppel jobs in Louisiana, a combination of the doctrines of promise and bar serves the same functions in Scotland. Since Smith, MacQueen has probably done as much as anyone to promote the use of promise, and he has suggested several jobs for it. Following Smith, he suggests its use in reward cases, and, more practically, in gratuitous promises in commercial contexts as well as familial and charitable ones. A variety of commercial transactions would fit well within the scheme of promissory estoppel jobs set out above. With respect to gratuitous commercial promises, for example, he suggests a hypothetical (reminiscent of *A & G Paterson v Highland Railway*,[115] about which Smith had also written) in which a lessor agrees to lower the rent but only during the time the tenant is experiencing financial difficulties. The hypothetical also echoes some of the estoppel-based contract re-adjustments classified in the "completed bargain" category of Louisiana cases.[116]

Of course the doctrine is often suggested in the context of irrevocable offers and options,[117] particularly where advertising is involved (e.g., "lowest tender accepted" or "first offer over £Y secures").[118] More broadly, in this category of precontractual liability, a variety of cases would match the Louisiana case law. MacQueen notes the problems common in large construction contracts, particularly when public bidding, final negotiation, and subcontract arrangement are involved. Frequently "letters of intent" are used in this context in the United Kingdom, and while that is not the typical practice in the United States, the problems generated by the complex undertakings and the need for preparation before finalising the general contract provide the perfect ground for the use of promise.[119] Scottish law and Louisiana law appear to have a close fit in this regard. In the postcontractual context, guarantees made after the purchase of goods might best be analysed under a promissory rubric.[120]

On the other hand, two transactions suggested by MacQueen do not fit with Louisiana cases. The first, in relation to requirements contracts, is not put forward with great vigour.[121] The second suggestion concerns the potential role of promise in explaining the enforceability of bankers' letters of

---

115 1927 SC (HL) 32. *Central London Property Trust Ltd v High Trees House Ltd* [1947] KB 130 also comes to mind.
116 Compare *Shreveport Plaza, LLC v Dollar Tree Stores, Inc* 196 Fed Appx 320 (5th Cir 2006).
117 See MacQueen and Thomson, *Contract* (n 34) para 2.61.
118 MacQueen, "Gratuitous obligations" (n 52) 4.
119 Ibid at 3. This assumes that the letter of intent indicates a promise, i.e., a commitment to be bound, not a mere expression of a future plan. See Hogg, *Obligations* (n 34) para 2.74.
120 Hogg, *Obligations* (n 34) para 2.84 lists a number of potential jobs for promise.
121 Ibid at 4.

credit and the like.[122] In the United States these issues have been governed by statute for about fifty years, since article 5 of the Uniform Commercial Code came into widespread use. Louisiana has adopted article 5, evidence again of mixing in the contractual and commercial law of Louisiana. To the extent that other questions arise about similar instruments, Louisiana also has enacted articles 3 and 4 of the UCC on negotiable instruments and bank deposits. Enforceability therefore does not raise troubling issues in this connection.

Other commercial contexts have proved ripe for analysis along the lines of promise. The facts of *Krupp Uhde GmbH v Weir Westgarth Ltd*[123] suggest one: large contracts often necessitate not only re-adjustments between the parties, but also adjustments with others. Once lending is brought into the analysis the possibilities become obvious, as one of the parties may need to obtain additional financing or may wish to refinance. Because of the demands of that party's lender, relatively minor but crucial re-adjustments may be needed, as with payment instructions: a subcontractor's lender may well insist that the general contractor pay the lender directly instead of relying on the subcontractor to receive payment and then forward the money to the lender in repayment of the loan. A binding undertaking from the general contractor to pay the lender directly can make the lender considerably more secure, and the failure of the general contractor to comply with its undertaking could be the difference between the lender being repaid in the millions or instead getting nothing at all.

The law of promise can work here, as suggested by counsel for the pursuers in *Krupp Uhde*, although the court eventually decided that assignation of the payment right was a better interpretation of the transaction. The real question was whether the lender was entitled to full payment or instead only the payment due to the subcontractor after deductions were made because of problems in the subcontractor's performance. There was little doubt that the lender should get only what the subcontractor itself was entitled to receive; the more interesting point is the legal device used. It would have been perfectly feasible to find a promise, but to interpret the promise as a commitment to pay the lender only what the subcontractor was owed. Assignation of whatever payment right the subcontractor had, however, not only achieves the same result but could have the added benefit of giving the lender the better security that it seemed to want. A mere promise to pay L

---

122 MacQueen, "Gratuitous obligations" (n 52) 3.
123 Unreported, OH, Lord Eassie, 31 May 2002, available at *http://www.scotcourts.gov.uk/opinions/ eas1505.html*. Note a similar Louisiana case, *Boyte v Wooten* 2006 US Dist LEXIS 45098 at °12-°16 (D La 2006) (reliance possible on letter regarding payments).

what is due to S arguably keeps the payment right in S, while an assignation of S's payment right to L may shift the property in the payment right from S to L. In that case, should S go bankrupt – the very possibility this arrangement contemplates – L will have better grounds to argue that the payment should still be made to L and is not a right that is part of S's bankruptcy estate. The parties might thus achieve their undoubted goal of bankruptcy remoteness. *Krupp Uhde*, then, is something of a parable about the law of promise: the doctrine is potentially so broad that it might be used beyond the bailiwick in which it works best.

Other commercial contexts, however, would be better suited to promise. In American commercial practice, for example, the work ("due diligence") before a merger often requires the parties to obtain consent from contractual partners of the merging parties, assuring that the merged entities will have the benefit of those pre-existing contracts. "Estoppel letters" are obtained from the key contracting partners, promising not to object to the merger, and perhaps consenting to the assignment of the contract. These letters can give rise to promissory estoppel, and lawyers treat them as enforceable. Estoppel, however, requires reliance, which could be difficult to prove to a court with a sceptical view (a frequent occurrence). Would the parties really have foregone the merger in the absence of the estoppel letter? Often it may be shown that the merger went forward without letters from some contracting parties. Were this situation to arise in Louisiana, as it certainly does, the position would be far from certain given the lack of demonstrable reliance. The Scots law of promise offers a considerably better analysis.

So far the exploration of jobs in Scots law has focused on the law of promise, but personal bar and its allied doctrines are also crucial. The Requirements of Writing (Scotland) Act 1995 abolishes the need for proof by writ or oath in relation to all promises, and does not impose a writing requirement for the constitution of business promises. The Law Revision Commission thought business promises, though possibly gratuitous, were likely to be "very far from being rash or impulsive gestures,"[124] and MacQueen and Hogg suggest that there ought not to be "formal impediments to commercial activity".[125] As a business promise might be found in many contexts, as with payments involved in home improvements,[126] this exception may prove wide-ranging.

---

124 Report on Requirements of Writing (Scot Law Com No 112, 1988) paras 2.23-2.24.
125 MacQueen and Hogg, "Donation" (n 53) at 9.
126 *Morrison v Leckie* 2005 GWD 40-734 per Sheriff M P Anderson. I have relied on a case summary and have not seen the judgment. Depending upon the view taken of the *Morrison* decision, the idea of business promises may need rethinking. Compare the narrow view evinced by Hogg, *Obligations* (n 34) para 2.22.

In addition, a reliance-based exception is generally available, as discussed above, for other promises. It would seem, then, at least in theory, that the laws of promise and bar do the promissory estoppel jobs in Scotland, with some qualifications, in much the same way that article 1967 works in Louisiana.

The case law in Scotland is considerably thinner than in Louisiana, but the cases found in the past fifty years confirm this impression. Many fall into the category I have called the cusp of contract (preferring that phrase to the more precise but less accurate "precontractual" liability). *J W Soils (Suppliers) Ltd v Corbett*[127] involves an alleged promise to pay for expenses incurred as the parties considered a real estate development that would turn Rowallan Castle into a hotel and leisure centre. *Stone v Macdonald*[128] is about an option problem, and although it may be a contract case rather than a case of promise (there is some conflict here),[129] it is at least founded on a case of promise.[130] Other option cases include *Miller Homes Ltd v Frame*[131] and a sheriff court case in which the promised option had prescribed.[132] *Mason v A & R Robertson & Black* involves efforts to close a sale where the contract was already agreed by missives; the alleged promise came from a third party, the solicitor, who undertook to take care of the transaction should the parties go forward.[133] But while cases can be found, the courts are careful about finding a promise too easily.[134] If the parties contemplate a transaction like a sale, which involves bilateral rather than unilateral obligation, the courts generally expect to see offer and acceptance and are unlikely to find a unilateral promise.[135]

127 1991 GWD 32-1891, 1991 CLYB 4533.
128 1979 SC 363.
129 Sellar, "Promise" (n 34) at 278 and McBryde, *Contract* (n 34) para 2-04 treat it as a promise.
130 Lord Justice Clerk Ross, who sat in *Stone v Macdonald*, later characterised it as a contracts case, albeit founded on a case of promise (*Chapman v Aberdeen Construction Group Plc* 1993 SLT 1205 at 1213 –*Sichi v Biagi* 1946 SN 66 being the case of promise on which *Stone v Macdonald* was based). Another option case implicating ideas of promise, according to Hogg, *Obligations* (n 34) para 2.63, is *McCall's Entertainments (Ayr) Ltd v South Ayrshire Council* 1998 SLT 1403.
131 2001 SLT 459 para 14 per Lord Hamilton.
132 *Smith v Stuart* 2004 SLT (Sh Ct) 2 per Sheriff D J Cusine.
133 1993 SLT 773 at 778 per Lord Cameron; see also *Digby Brown & Co v Lyall* 1995 SLT 932. *Uniroyal Ltd v Miller & Co Ltd* 1985 SLT 101 might also be mentioned; it involves a construction contract and preparations for it. A letter of intent that had been issued might have been understood within the doctrine of promise, but the court did not discuss the doctrine at all, and indeed, such a letter of intent may also in appropriate circumstances be understood instead as a contract (accepted when the builder commences work) rather than a promise. See *Robertson Group (Construction) Ltd v Amey-Miller (Edinburgh) Joint Venture* 2005 SCLR 854 affd 2006 SCLR 772.
134 McBryde, *Contract*, 2nd edn (2001) (n 34) para 2.04 notes, "In recent years there have been only three known cases which have been decided on the basis of an alleged promise" (citing *Bathgate v Rosie*; *Stone v MacDonald*; and *J W Soils (Suppliers) Ltd v Corbett*).
135 See *Anderson v Anderson* 1961 SC 59 per the Lord Ordinary, Lord Walker, at 62-63; *Haldane v Watson* 1972 SLT (Sh Ct) 8.

Similarly, most of the relevant cases of statutory bar fall into the "cusp of contract" category, reflecting deals that are partially but not wholly completed. *Advice Centre for Mortgages v McNicoll* involves a lease in which the parties had agreed to possession, term, and rent, and the tenants allegedly even moved in, paid rent, and improved the property. The court found that the parties regarded a purchase option as significant, however, and since they had failed to reach agreement on that point, there was no agreement that could give rise to bar.[136] The court was unsympathetic towards the parties' failure to comply with the necessary formalities – the promissory estoppel exception to the statute of frauds, in American terms: "If parties do not adhere to the very simple requirements [of writing] that are now prescribed, they have only themselves to blame."[137] Another cusp-of-contract case, *Park Lane Developments (Glasgow Harbour) Ltd v Jesner*[138] involved an alleged agreement about conveying a parking place. The buyer seemed to think he was getting a conveyance outright, but the developer offered only common ownership, which the buyer (after considerable delay) rejected. A further recent case was, like so many of the promise cases, about an option.[139] These cases suggest that arguments about statutory bar are being pressed – not necessarily successfully – in much the same context in Scotland as in Louisiana.

In the completed contract category, a distinction between the Scottish and Louisiana law should be noted. In Louisiana, because of concern about the reliability and therefore the primacy of the contract, some courts have turned away promissory estoppel claims. This is made possible by the reliance element of promissory estoppel; a court can well hold that relying on promises not contained in the contract (or in *a* contract, as in *Miller v Loyola University*) is unreasonable. In Scots law, as a promise is a unilateral obligation requiring no reliance, this reasoning is not possible. Rather, counsel may argue that a promise has been made entirely outside the contract, and if the wording is sufficiently clear, a promise ought to be found. This point appears not only in *Krupp Uhde* but also in the similar case of *Ballast Plc v Laurieston Properties Ltd*,[140] and other authorities.[141] Proof of the promise needs to

---

136   [2006] CSOH 58, 2006 SLT 591.

137   Per Lord Drummond Young at para 16.

138   Unreported, Glasgow Sheriff Court, Sheriff CAL Scott, 3 May 2006, available at *http://www. scotcourts.gov.uk/opinions/CA458_05.html*.

139   *Ben Cleuch Estates Ltd v Scottish Enterprise* 2008 SC 252, discussed further at n 154 below.

140   [2005] CSOH 16, unreported, OH, Lady Paton, 25 January 2005, available at *http://www. scotcourts.gov.uk/opinions/CSOH16.html*.

141   McBryde, *Contract* (n 34), at 20 and nn 38-39 refers to the finding of guarantees and back letters as "frequent," although only one case is cited, *East Anglian Electronics Ltd v OIS Plc* 1996 SLT 808.

be quite clear, however, and the courts will be "looking for a commercially sensible construction" with some explanation as to why a reasonable person would think that a legally binding guarantee (as had been argued) had been made through, as in *Ballast*, a letter about a mechanism of payment.[142] Such explanations are often lacking. In this category of cases, therefore, we find Louisiana and Scottish courts exercised by similar concerns, and reaching similar results, although on somewhat different grounds.

Aside from these relatively fertile areas, cases can be found elsewhere. The classic category of family promises, though often unsuccessful, can still come in for treatment akin to promissory estoppel under the Scots doctrine of promise.[143] Not all cases can be so neatly lined up into typical categories, however. *Bathgate v Rosie*[144] involves seemingly quotidian facts that do not often make their way into the case law. A mother promised to pay for a window her son had broken, and the law held her to her promise. One might be tempted to classify this promise as founded on a natural or moral obligation, but a natural or moral obligation does not itself constitute the necessary promise.[145] In any case, as a residual doctrine promissory estoppel and its cognates always have odd cases to settle.[146] *Lord Advocate v City of Glasgow DC* may also fall into this residuum.[147] Other cases involving public authorities, which may involve an indeterminate creditor or in any event a lack of a formal acceptance, might prove amenable to analysis as promise cases. This possibility is suggested by *Commissioners of Northern Lighthouses v Edmonston* (the "Muckle Flugga Lighthouse case") although the court there held that the pursuers were the creditors of a contractual obligation.[148]

Although many Scottish and Louisiana cases have not been noticed here, by Louisiana standards the Scottish case law, particularly on promise, seems

142 At para 105.
143 See *De Lathouwer v Anderson* 2007 SLT 437. For less successful attempts, see discussion of *Smith v Oliver* and similar cases, *supra*, and in the family category, *Countess of Cawdor v Earl of Cawdor* 2007 SC 285 *infra*.
144 1976 SLT (Sh Ct) 16.
145 McBryde, *Contract* (n 34) para 2-04 (citing *J W Soils (Suppliers) Ltd v Corbett*, n 127 above).
146 On the Louisiana side, see *Law v City of Eunice* 626 So 2d 575 at 577-78 (La Ct App 3d Cir 1993) (criminal defendant's bargain with police officer: because a plea bargain does not create a conventional obligation, court hesitates on contract action but suggests detrimental reliance).
147 1990 SLT 721.
148 1908 SLT 439. Professor MacQueen has pointed out to me that the jobs assigned to the promise doctrine could well be keyed to the lack of acceptance, which is one of its defining features. He suggests cases when no one can accept (a promise to an indeterminate or incapable person, or a non-entity); too many could accept (as with rewards); or when the acceptance comes after the promisor is dead, incompetent, or insolvent. This theory is appealing and accords with Stair's refutation (1.10.4) of Grotius but also seems rather more coherent than what is found in the cases.

almost vanishingly thin. I have considered cases in Louisiana since article 1967 became effective in 1985, focusing in this particular chapter primarily on cases from the past ten years or so, when there have been countless cases on promissory estoppel. In Scotland I have looked for cases from the past five decades, a considerably longer period. The entry on promise in *The Laws of Scotland: Stair Memorial Encyclopaedia* (1996) cites only one case from the past fifty years[149] (with no supplemental entry) and Gloag and Henderson's *The Law of Scotland* another one,[150] and only a limited number of more recent cases have emerged, as can be seen above. MacQueen has pointed out that the concept of unilateral promise is "little utilised",[151] and on the side of statutory bar, Reid has observed "surprisingly little litigation".[152] The implication is not necessarily that the doctrine per se is different or differently used, as larger differences in litigation patterns may provide a better explanation. But the discrepancy is certainly remarkable.

A related point should also be made. In the cases that there are, the courts on both sides of the Atlantic often enforce the legal requirements stringently, one might even say with a vengeance. The facts of *Advice Centre for Mortgages* have already been mentioned, but the cases could be multiplied. Reliance must be clear, and if it is as referable to one state of affairs as another, the statutory element for bar is not met.[153] Even when the reliance is clear, it needs to be "reasonable" under the statute.[154] Similar concerns are apparent in Louisiana. Some courts, at least, carefully enforce the requirements of a promise and reasonable, detrimental reliance on it. For that reason, many cases deny recovery based on promissory estoppel. The trend of probing judicial scrutiny of promissory estoppel claims is clear enough,[155] but perhaps nowhere as clearly as in the at-will employment cases.

---

149 Vol 15, para 615, citing *Bathgate v Rosie* 1976 SLT (Sh Ct) 16.

150 W M Gloag and R C Henderson, *The Law of Scotland*, 12th edn, by Lord Coulsfield et al (2007) para 5.02, citing *Hunter v Bradford Property Trust* 1970 SLT 173.

151 MacQueen and Thomson, *Contract* (n 34) para 2.61.

152 E Reid, "Personal bar: Three cases" (2006) 10 EdinLR 437 at 437.

153 *Tom Super Printing Supplies Ltd v South Lanarkshire Council* 1999 GWD 31-1496.

154 See *Ben Cleuch Estates Ltd v Scottish Enterprise* 2008 SC 252 in which the tenants held an option under a lease from the pursuers. Various correspondence, however, was sent by a subsidiary of the pursuers, and the tenant sent its notice of exercise of the option to the subsidiary. The tenant's reliance on the correspondence as indicating where to send the notice was found to be reasonable, although at first instance the Lord Ordinary had decided otherwise (2006 GWD 8-154).

155 *Peoples State Bank v GE Capital Corp* 2007 US App LEXIS 6055 (5th Cir 2007); *Showboat Star Partnership v Slaughter* 789 So 2d 554 at 561-63 (La 2001); *Moroux v Toce* 943 So 2d 1263 (La Ct App 2006); *Lakeland Anesthesia, Inc v United Healthcare of Louisiana* 871 So 2d 380 (La Ct App 2004); *Marshall v First Bank & Trust* 848 So 2d 660 (La Ct App 2003); *Miller v Miller* 817 So 2d 1166 (La Ct App 2002); *Butler v Sudderth* 784 So 2d 125 (La Ct App 2001); *Jackson*

An employee at-will cannot reasonably rely on a different state of affairs, it seems, almost no matter what – absent an old-fashioned contract.[156] This trend, observed in both Louisiana and Scotland, appears consistent with the studies of promissory estoppel more generally in the United States.[157] While employment claims have met with particular hostility from the bench, the courts seem keen more generally to assure that promissory estoppel remains in its secondary status, safely behind contract.

Even aside from reliance issues, which after all are not relevant in the Scots law of promise, the attitude is the same. Possibly the best illustration of this attitude is the recent case of *Countess of Cawdor v Earl of Cawdor*.[158] Apparently there had been a long-running dispute between the Dowager Countess and her step-son the Earl and Thane.[159] At issue were some pension-fund transfers arranged by the trustees with respect to the Countess and her husband, the late Earl. The pension trustees determined at a meeting to effect transfers from one pension scheme to another. The meeting had been formal, the trustees had taken legal and financial advice, and a written minute was duly entered and signed. The Earl then died, and the trustees and the Dowager Countess with the apparent consent and help of the new Earl completed some but not all of the transfers. The issue for the court to decide was whether there had been an enforceable promise to effect the remainder.

Lord President Hamilton quoted Stair.[160] Neither desire nor resolution is enough to constitute an obligation, he observed, but some greater exercise of the will is required: a promise. A legally binding promise was certainly possible, as counsel suggested, based on the leading case of *Macfarlane v*

---

v *Lare* 779 So 2d 808 (La Ct App 2000). On the promise requirement, see *Roxco Ltd v Harris Specialty Chems* 85 Fed Appx 375 (5th Cir 2004) (disclaimer); *Peoples State Bank, supra*, as well as some treatment of the question in *Shreveport Plaza, LLC v Dollar Tree Stores, Inc* 196 Fed Appx 320 (5th Cir 2006); *Brookshire Bros Holding, Inc v Total Containment, Inc* 2006 US Dist LEXIS 46061 (D La 2006); *Freeman Decorating Co v Encuentro Las Americas Trade Corp* 2005 US Dist LEXIS 18313 (D La 2005); *Dorsey v N Life Ins Co* 2005 US Dist LEXIS 17742 (D La 2005); *LeMarie v Lone Star Life Ins Co* 2000 US Dist LEXIS 16595 (D La 2000); *Ark Entertainment, LLC v C J Gayfer & Co* 2000 US Dist LEXIS 3867 (D La 2000); *Serv Steel & Pipe v Guinn's Trailer Sales, Inc* 850 So 2d 902 (La Ct App 2003); *see also Miller v Loyola Univ of New Orleans* 829 So 2d 1057 (La Ct App 2002).

156 *May v Harris Mgmt Corp* 928 So 2d 140 (La Ct App 2005) (note dissent's point that majority was sidetracked into consideration analysis); *Robinson v Healthworks Intl* 837 So 2d 714 (La Ct App 2003); *Trigg v Pennington Oil Co* 835 So 2d 845 (La Ct App 2002); *McJamerson v Grambling State Univ* 769 So 2d 168 (La Ct App 2000).

157 DeLong (n 104).

158 2007 SC 285.

159 See T Judd, "Heir of Macbeth loses legal battle in Cawdor Castle feud", *The Independent*, 8 November 2002.

160 At para 15, citing *Inst* 1.10.2, 1.10.4.

Johnston.[161] Lord President Hamilton's reading of the minute did not indicate this level of commitment by the trustees, however, "but rather an intention, in the light of the advice received, to make in due course a transfer". This was a plan but not a promise.[162] The courts hesitate to construe legally binding obligations, whether the parties involved are trustees resolved to transfer significant monies or, more simply, a doctor reassuring a patient.[163]

E. THEORETICAL DEDUCTIONS

(1) The nature of liability

Putting together Scottish and Louisiana law has thrown a number of points into relief. The most prominent is how the theoretical underpinning of promissory liability differs between the systems, based largely on the history and source of the doctrine, and possibly on the moral commitments of the legal systems. Scots law largely has drawn its law of promise from Stair, who in turn drew on canon law and (less clearly) the Scottish common law and the *ius commune*, to the exclusion of civil law. Although Stair disclaimed the notion that every act of will could give rise to an obligation, he still came down firmly with the thinkers who grounded liability on consent or will – not on the more delictual notion of reliance. Not even acceptance is required. Of course on the personal bar side delictual notions are more prevalent, and Stair's treatment of promise conceded that there could be liability even in the absence of a promise if a resolution "be holden forth to assure others".[164] But this exception takes little from the main point, for a robust law of promise little needs promissory estoppel or personal bar,[165] except in cases where a lack of formalities or some other defect gets in the way.

The Louisiana side is weighted in the other direction. Certainly the promise is crucial, and the obligation may therefore be said to be based on consent and the individual will. Indeed, the early draft legislation recognised that a basis for introducing promissory estoppel into the Civil Code was to validate "the binding force of a unilateral declaration of will".[166] And the prominence of promise as the basis for liability has led to formal characterisation of the liability as contractual rather than delictual. The placement of

---

161   (1864) 2 M 1210.
162   *Cawdor* paras 14-17.
163   *Dow v Tayside University Hospitals NHS Trust* 2006 SLT (Sh Ct) 141 per Sheriff M J Fletcher at 145.
164   Stair, *Inst* 1.10.2.
165   McBryde, *Contract* (n 34) para 2-02.
166   Apr 1979 Draft (n 90) at 6-7.

the key provision in the Civil Code articles on contracts in general, and even in the article on cause in particular, confirms this choice, and the courts have generally followed this formal allocation.[167]

Nonetheless, the Louisiana law seems decidedly delictual in comparison to the Scottish law of promise. "Detrimental reliance" in Louisiana is all about the promisee's reliance. Louisiana, after all, took its law not from the lawyers of the Church, concerned for the soul of the promisor, but from the *Restatement* of the American Common Law, concerned with equities when the requirement of consideration or the disappearance of the seal visited injustice on relying promisees. Given the equitable nature of these concerns, to protect against the harm done to the promisee, the reliance is required just as much as the promise, and the reliance must be reasonable and detrimental. Liability is hardly based on consent alone, therefore, and the element of tort is quite strong in comparative terms.

(2) Formalities and their functions

Interestingly, Scotland and Louisiana made similar moves at roughly the same time, between 1985 and the early 2000s. Scotland during that period moved away from its requirement of proof by writ or oath for promise, a requirement that did not admit an exception even if there was detrimental reliance. At the same time the Louisiana Civil Code and the case law interpreting it recognised a reliance-based exception to some formal requirements, although not all of them. Too much can be made of similar moves at similar times, but their occurrence should at least be recorded, and some of the implications considered.

When admitting some device to circumvent formal or other requirements for promises, the courts in Louisiana and Scotland have shown great care, as those requirements are generally thought to serve some important function. Typically American thought, following Lon Fuller, turns to evidentiary, cautionary, and signalling or channelling functions.[168] Stair expresses the same idea, although without breaking it down into particular functions aside from the avoidance of mistakes.[169]

Let us begin with the evidentiary function. Writing serves as clear evidence of what was said, and whether it was indeed a promise. It is not obvious whether Stair (or the Scottish courts) recognise as much, but reliance can do

---

167 *Stokes v Georgia-Pacific Corp* 894 F2d 764 at 770 (5th Cir 1990); *Flynn v Nesbitt* 771 F Supp 766 at 768 (E D La 1991).
168 L L Fuller, "Consideration and form" (1941) 41 ColumLRev 799 at 800-803.
169 Stair, *Inst* 1.10.4.

the same, albeit less clearly. Reliance is probative to a degree, as substantial reliance seems less likely in the absence of some commitment. The reliance becomes quite probative if it occurs with the knowledge, and perhaps even cooperation, of the promisor.

The "cautionary" (in the American sense, having nothing to do with suretyship) and signalling or channelling functions are related, but significantly different. A writing or an authentic act before a notary and witnesses should focus the attention of the promisor, ensuring that a commitment is made only after appropriate deliberation. The Scottish Law Commission was certainly sensitive to this point,[170] and it is recognised (although not expressly) in current case law.[171] In addition, a writing or authentic act demarcates the promise as a legally binding one, not only cautioning the promisor but signalling to the world in general, and the courts more particularly, that the promisor intended to enter into legally binding relations, rather than informal relations not subject to legal compulsion.

In some ways each of these functions can be seen as protecting promisors. Promisors are prevented from acting too hastily and are protected against misconstruction of their words and actions. Their position with respect to legal relationships is clarified. But some of these functions can be otherwise served, and in a way that aids the promisee. A court might hold, for instance, that where there is enough reliance by the promisee with the knowledge and cooperation of the promisor, then the promisor has received all of the protection it needs. If the promisor let a tenant enter the premises, accepted rent, and acquiesced in changes to the property, one might think that the landlord knew what it was doing and was willing for there to be legal effects.[172] Finding the *function* of the required formality (writing) to be satisfied by reliance, the court might hold for the tenant. The Scottish courts, however, have seemed hesitant.

The Scottish courts may be particularly concerned with signalling or channelling functions, which protect the parties, the courts, and society in general. If we read the case law as requiring a clear demarcation between friendly and even cooperative relations on the one hand and legal ones on the other, it makes better sense. Although the landlord admitted the tenant,

---

170 Report on Requirements of Writing (Scot Law Com No 112, 1988) paras 2.21, 2.24; see also MacQueen, "Gratuitous obligations" (n 52) at 2 (construing Constitution and Proof of Voluntary Obligations and Authentication of Writings (Scot Law Com Con Memo No 66, 1985)).

171 *McEleveen v McQuillan's Ex'x* 1997 SLT (Sh Ct) 46 (Sheriff Principal N D Macleod) emphasises cautionary functions especially at 48, while recognising evidentiary and signalling functions as well, e.g., at 50.

172 Discussion based on *Advice Centre for Mortgages v McNicoll*, nn 136-137 above.

the parties were not yet ready to be bound. A writing is simple enough, and "ordinary"[173] – hardly unusual in an age of forms and general literacy. Friendly banter between friends on their way out for an evening of bingo should not normally be turned into a contractual relationship about the splitting of winnings.[174] Even trustees in a formal meeting may announce and record their intentions, and carry some of them out, without being held committed to all of them.[175]

So it seems to appear to the Scots courts. The commitment must be unmistakably clear. Perhaps this is no more than Erskine said in the eighteenth century,[176] but that his dictum remains as important now as in his time is remarkable. If it still remains true, as Stair had said earlier, that *omne verbum de ore fideli cadit in debitum*,[177] then the *verbum* must be ever so plain, and *fideli* must carry a heavy and manifold meaning. It seems that Stair more aptly described the landscape, in Louisiana as well as Scotland, in English: "But it is not every act of the will that raiseth an obligation."[178]

(3) Doctrines with elbows in a jostling world

The Scots law of promise, augmented by the law of personal and statutory bar, raises a question in Louisiana that arose during the revision of the Code. Does Louisiana need promissory estoppel? The answer at the time was that Louisiana had sufficient Civil Law doctrine to take care of promissory estoppel jobs, but that promissory estoppel itself would provide a more direct approach to the typical problems.[179] Furthermore, promissory estoppel might be a more approachable doctrine, the mix in Louisiana being such that the *Restatement* is in far easier reach than sources on *venire contra factum proprium* or *culpa in contrahendo*. This would seem particularly true for adjustments in commercial relationships that are not donative but that are not easily classified as onerous or synallagmatic contracts (for example,

---

173 Stair, *Inst* 1.10.4.
174 The general rule and possibility of exception based on considerable testimonial proof is shown in *Robertson v Anderson* 2003 SLT 235, admittedly a contract case.
175 *Countess of Cawdor v Earl of Cawdor*, n 158 above.
176 *Inst* 3.3.90 (a promise must be "made in words proper to express a present act of the will, such as, 'I promise', or 'I oblige myself to give', or 'make over in a present'"), cited in MacQueen and Hogg, "Donation" (n 53) at 2, 6.
177 Stair so recites the canon law, which he adopts (*Inst* 1.10.7, citing C.1 & 3 *de pactis* [C.2, 3, 1 and 3]).
178 *Inst* 1.10.1; see also S Litvinoff, "Still another look at cause" (1987) 48 La LR 3 at 4 ("In spite of emphatic declarations ... the fact is that consent alone is not enough to engender legal binding force").
179 April 1979 Draft (n 90) at 7.

undertakings to pay a counterparty's financier instead of the counterparty itself, as in *Boyte* or *Krupp Uhde*).[180] Promissory estoppel has elbowed its way into Louisiana. Perhaps fear about the offensive powers of its elbows has caused the courts to keep the doctrine in careful check.

Those elbows may be thrust in other directions. Promissory estoppel may stifle innovation in recognising the efficacy of declarations of the will that could be enforceable without reliance. The same idea carries greater weight in Scotland, but in the other direction. Recognition of a legally enforceable promise, with the relatively permissive requirement of a simple writing (as opposed to a deed), seemingly slowed the development of reliance-based exceptions. Even though these were given statutory recognition in 1995, the courts appear reluctant to put them into play.

This result seems too bad. Before a legally binding relationship is recognised a promisor ought to be cautioned, the courts ought to have good evidence, and the line between the merely social and the coercively legal should be brightly marked. But these statements are ideal, and justice involves balance. The law might intervene not only because of consent but also because of harm to another. Certainly the case for legal interference is stronger when there is both consent by the defendant and harm to the plaintiff, as suggested, at least, by Fuller and Perdue's construction of Aristotle.[181] Accordingly, justice may be served if there is heavy reliance, with the foresight, and perhaps even knowledge and cooperation, of the promisor, even if the promise is not stated in ideal terms.

F. CONCLUSION

The mixed nature of the law in Scotland and Louisiana has proved fertile for comparison. As usual the stories become more intricate as they involve elements from different places, with complicated histories and traditions and languages. At the same time, the sensible concerns of courts applying different but analogous doctrines can be observed across jurisdictional boundaries. Pervading the complex learning and borrowing are similar notions of justice and congruent policies oriented around practicality. When deciding at what

---

180   *Boyte v Wooten*; *Krupp Uhde GmbH v Weir Westgarth Ltd* (both n 123 above).
181   Aristotle, *Nicomachean Ethics* 1132a-1132b, construed in L L Fuller and W R Perdue Jr, "The reliance interest in contract damages" part 1 (1936) 46 Yale LJ 52 at 56-57. The more problematic implications of this construction are not treated here. Cf J Gordley, "Enforcing promises" (1995) 83 CalLRev 547; J Gordley, *The Philosophical Origins of Modern Contract Doctrine* (1991); generally, J Gordley, *The Foundations of Private Law* (2006) ch 13, 289-306. Compare McBryde (n 1) at 55 (on Molina), 66 (on St Thomas Aquinas).

point, in the absence of an ordinary contract, persons have bound themselves to each other, these sorts of concerns ring especially clearly. This, I hope, is what we have discovered as we have hunted for promissory estoppel in places where it is rather an exotic beast.

11 Unjustified Enrichment, Subsidiarity and Contract

Hector L MacQueen[*]

A. INTRODUCTION
B. THE FRENCH TRADITION: LOUISIANA
(1) The French background
(2) Development of general action in Louisiana
(3) Subsidiarity in Louisiana
(4) Enrichment and contract in Louisiana
C. SCOTLAND: JURISTIC AND JUDICIAL RECONSTRUCTIONS
(1) Historical development of an enrichment taxonomy
(2) Subsidiarity of recompense
(3) A reconfigured enrichment taxonomy
(4) Enrichment and contract
D. COMPARISON OF LOUISIANA AND SCOTS LAW

INTRODUCTION

Until recently one could say with some confidence that acceptance of a general principle against unjustified enrichment was one of the hallmarks of a Civilian system of law. The emergence in Common Law systems of "unjust enrichment" as an important head within the law of obligations has qualified but not altogether eliminated the truth of the observation. Certainly one can still be sure that unjustified enrichment in mixed legal systems is an indicator of the Civilian rather than the Common Law dimension in their development, and that the current state of enrichment law in such systems is a benchmark against which to test the strength or otherwise of that element in the modern mix. But one should not fall into the error of thinking that unjustified enrichment questions are approached in the same way in all Civilian systems. In a classic article published in the *Tulane Law Review* in 1962,[1] the late

---

[*] I would like to acknowledge with gratitude comments made on an earlier draft by Martin Hogg, Laura Macgregor, Vernon Palmer and Niall Whitty, but am of course alone responsible for errors of fact, law and opinion that remain.

1 "Unjustified enrichment in the Civil Law and Louisiana law" (1962) 36 Tulane LR 605; (1962)

Barry Nicholas distinguished between contemporary French and German approaches, noting that under the former the Code recognised only specific obligations to reverse enrichment in certain defined situations, while the BGB took the general principle as its starting point and developed a regime around that single concept. Although in France jurisprudence and doctrine had developed a general enrichment principle, its extra-codal character meant that it performed only a limited, gap-filling or subsidiary role; whereas in Germany there were no such limits, and the relationship between enrichment and other branches of the law was a matter for substantive and doctrinal analysis of their respective domains.

In a previous paper I attempted to analyse the approaches of some of the major "mixed" legal systems to the law of unjustified enrichment.[2] The principal feature brought out by the study was that all the systems had recently made progress towards some form of a general action for the recovery of unjustified enrichment as part of their law. This overall conclusion clearly applied to both Louisiana and Scotland, but there were also significant differences between them corresponding respectively to a considerable degree to the distinct French and German approaches. It is not surprising to find Louisiana in the French camp. As will be shown in more detail below, the structure of Louisiana enrichment law originates from, and remains heavily influenced by, the French Civil Code of 1804, while French jurisprudence continues to be significant in the law's development. As will be illustrated in this paper, Scots enrichment law was also shaped to some degree by French influence in the nineteenth century, but a radical re-conceptualisation of the whole law by jurists and judges in the 1990s was driven above all by more general approaches to the analysis of enrichment law, in particular that developed in and from the German Civil Code of 1900. The debate sparked in the English law of restitution by the writings of the late Peter Birks and a number of important decisions by the House of Lords in cases on the subject also played an influential role.[3] The upshot is that the French pattern is almost wholly invisible in contemporary expositions of Scots enrichment law.

The story is thus one of parallel development through different approaches during which time there has apparently been no contact between the respective systems, save in a very limited way through the medium of some common

---

37 Tulane LR 49 (two parts). A note by J Beatson at (2004) 120 LQR 354 gives some interesting background on the composition and influence of this article.

2 "Unjustified enrichment in mixed legal systems" [2005] RLR 21.

3 See further H L MacQueen, "Peter Birks and Scots enrichment law", in A Burrows and Lord Rodger of Earlsferry (eds), *Mapping the Law: Essays in Memory of Peter Birks* (2006) 401.

sources in the nineteenth century.[4] There is also the crucial difference that where Louisiana private law is codified, Scots law is not. Thus it is clear that a general enrichment action exists in Louisiana, because the Code now so provides. In Scotland, by contrast, the matter depends upon a small number of judicial decisions in the late 1990s and the acceptability of their interpretation by legal writers. On the other hand, the specificity of codal provision as against the flexibility of case law and juristic analysis has an important effect on the law's response to particular questions like the one to be addressed in this paper, the relationship between unjustified enrichment and other branches of the law such as contract.

One important, originally French concept in Louisiana law is the subsidiarity of the general enrichment action in relation to other branches of the law, as a way of controlling its scope within particular limits. Subsidiarity in this sense was also found in Scots enrichment law before its reconstruction in the 1990s, and has been used since then by the courts, albeit subject to academic criticism. It is not however found in any strong way in German law.[5] This paper therefore explores the concept of subsidiarity, looking critically at the role it seems to play in Louisiana law and testing the extent to which its use is still appropriate in the remodelled Scots law.[6] The relationship between enrichment and contract provides a helpful context for this discussion.

B. THE FRENCH TRADITION: LOUISIANA

(1) The French background

The merest glance through the Digest and Codes of 1808, 1825 and 1870 shows the dominance of the traditional French approach to enrichment in the history of Louisiana law. All of these texts followed the French Civil Code of 1804 in content, which itself followed, it would seem, the restricted approach of Pothier to the subject.[7] Articles 1375 and 1376 of the French Code lay

---

4 Note however that the first treatment of the problem of indirect enrichment in Scots law, by N R Whitty (see below, n 93), drew directly upon the analytical model proposed by Nicholas (n 1 above) for Louisiana law.

5 For the very limited role of subsidiarity in German law, see R Zimmermann and J du Plessis, "Basic features of the German law of unjustified enrichment" [1994] 2 RLR 14 at 36-38.

6 On subsidiarity in general, see B Nicholas, "Unjust enrichment and subsidiarity", in F Santoro Passarelli and M Lupoi (eds), *Scintillae iuris: Studi in memoria di Gino Gorla* (1994) 2037; R Grantham and C Rickett, "On the subsidiarity of unjust enrichment" (2001) 117 LQR 273; L Smith, "Property, subsidiarity and unjust enrichment", in D Johnston and R Zimmermann (eds), *Unjustified Enrichment: Key Issues in Comparative Perspective* (2002) 588; J Beatson and E Schrage, *Cases, Materials and Texts on Unjustified Enrichment* (2003) ch 7; D Visser, *Unjustified Enrichment* (2008) 56-60.

7 Pothier dealt with *negotiorum gestio* as an appendix to his *Treatise on Mandate*, and the *conditio*

down rules for, respectively, the management of another's affairs (*negotiorum gestio*) and the repayment or return of a payment or performance rendered when it was not due – *répétition de l'indu* or the *condictio indebiti* of the Civil Law.[8] Although Pothier had recognised that both these actions rested on a general principle against unjustified enrichment,[9] none of that found its way into the *Code civil*. The consequent lack of a general enrichment action in the Code was eventually remedied, on the basis of "the principle of equity which forbids enrichment at the expense of another", by the French courts. The *arrêt Boudier* in 1892 developed the *actio de in rem verso* for this purpose.[10] In this case a landlord who had resumed possession of a farm from a defaulting tenant and had gained the standing crop in part-settlement of the tenant's debt was held liable under the *actio* to a merchant who had supplied the tenant with fertiliser before the termination of the lease but had not been paid. The Cour de cassation held that the decision did not violate the principle of privity of contract (found in Art 1165 of the *Code civil*) and ruled:

> Considering that the action *de in rem verso* derives from the principle of equity which forbids one to enrich oneself at the expense of another and has been regulated by no text of our laws, its exercise is subject to no fixed condition ... [I]t is sufficient that the plaintiff alleges and offers to establish the existence of an advantage which, by a sacrifice or an act, he has conferred on the other party.

The potential breadth of the enrichment principle thus stated by the Cour de cassation was immediately observed by the *arrêtiste* Labbé: the court "simply invoked the principle of equity ... [T]here could be nothing more vague and less precise".[11] Labbé stressed the merchant's lack of a remedy against the tenant and the need for the landlord's enrichment to be without cause as the true underpinnings of the *Boudier* decision. The scope of the enrichment principle has since been controlled in the jurisprudence and doctrine by concepts that only enrichment without lawful cause falls to be reversed; that

---

indebiti in a *Treatise on Quasi-Contract called Promutuum and on the Action Condictio Indebiti*. See also his *Treatise on Obligations* 1.1.2.1 (para 113) for brief reference to each topic under the heading "Of quasi contracts".

8 On French law I have relied particularly on J P Dawson, *Unjust Enrichment* (1951) 92-107; E Schrage and B Nicholas, "Unjust enrichment and the law of restitution: A comparison", in E J H Schrage (ed), *Unjust Enrichment: The Comparative Legal History of the Law of Restitution* (1995) 21-24; J Bell, S Boyron and S Whittaker, *Principles of French Law* (1998), 398-430. See also the article by Barry Nicholas on Louisiana enrichment law, n 1 above.

9 See Pothier, *Obligations*, 1.1.2.3 (para 123); *Condictio Indebiti*, paras 134, 140 (all citing Pomponius' maxim in the Digest, *jure naturae aequum est neminem cum alterius detrimento fieri locupletiorem*).

10 *Julien Patureau-Miran v Boudier* Cass req 15 June 1892, S 1893.1.281, note Labbé, D P 1892.1.596. Translations of both texts accessible in Beatson and Schrage (n 6) 39-42.

11 As translated in Beatson and Schrage (n 6) 41.

the enrichment must normally be direct in the sense that it arises from some sort of transaction between the impoverished and the enriched parties rather than being mediated (as in the *Boudier* case itself) through a third party; and, above all for present purposes, that the general action has a subsidiary nature, reflecting its extra-codal character as a gap-filler in relation to the rest of the law. This means that it cannot be used to evade or circumvent other rules of law, or where there is another remedy available. In simple terms:[12]

> the action for unjustified enrichment can only be admitted if there is no other action open to the plaintiff; … in particular it cannot be admitted in place of another action which the plaintiff cannot bring because of prescription, a forfeiture, a foreclosure, or because of the effect of res judicata, or because he cannot produce the evidence necessary for the success of the action, or because of any other obstacle of law.

Obstacles of law fall however to be distinguished from obstacles of fact. Thus if one's ordinary claim in law is as a matter of fact not useful – for example, because, as in the *Boudier* case, one's contractual partner is insolvent – then the enrichment claim may still be brought despite the theoretical presence of another remedy. The indirectness of the enrichment claim in the *Boudier* case is overcome by the fact that the tenant's surrender of the crop to the landlord assumed that the latter would pay for the fertiliser, although there are still difficulties in that the material did nevertheless pass into the tenant's patrimony and was put into the land by the tenant in his own interest and not as a mere instrument of the landlord.[13] It is therefore far from clear whether the landlord's enrichment was at the expense of the supplier of the fertiliser, or that the impoverishment of the latter was without cause.

(2) Development of general action in Louisiana

Louisiana was not able to follow these post-Code steps of French law until quite late in the twentieth century, although from the very beginning in 1808 its judges were empowered, "where there is no express law … to decide according to equity" (the Directory Clause).[14] From 1825 the Code also included a reference to "the moral maxim of the law that no one ought to enrich himself at the expense of another".[15] But the Digest and Codes otherwise

---

12 This is the formulation of the Cour de cassation in *Dame Masselin v Decaens* Cass civ 29 April 1971, Gaz Pal 1971.2.554, D 1971 Somm 197, JCP 1971.IV.145, as translated in Beatson and Schrage (n 6) 428.

13 See the discussion in Nicholas "Unjustified enrichment (I)" (n 1) 629-630.

14 This is art 21 in the 1808 Digest and all subsequent Louisiana codes until becoming art 4 in the most recent (1993) revision. See further V V Palmer, *The Louisiana Civilian Experience: Critiques of Codification in a Mixed Jurisdiction* (2005) ch 7.

15 1825 Code art 1960; 1870 Code art 1965.

simply laid down rules for management of another's affairs and recovery of undue performances.[16] It was only in 1967 that Louisiana had its equivalent of the *arrêt Boudier* in *Minyard v Curtis Products Inc.*[17] *Minyard* was a case arising out of a construction project, in which the plaintiff sub-contractor had been found strictly liable in contract for a defective product used in its work and sought indemnity from the defendant manufacturer of the product in question. There had been no direct contractual relationship between the plaintiff and the defendant, the product having reached the plaintiff via a third party, in respect of whom any contractual claim had prescribed. The Supreme Court of Louisiana held that the action for indemnity rested upon principles of unjust enrichment, which the Civil Code did not restrict to the transaction of another's business or the payment of a thing not due. Drawing upon the *Boudier* case and the comparative analysis of French and Louisiana law by Barry Nicholas published in 1962,[18] the court found that the remedy provided in France by the *actio de in rem verso* was "not unlike" that allowed by the action for indemnity in Louisiana jurisprudence, and that it was compatible with the principles of the Civil Code.[19] The plaintiff's claim was therefore allowed and was found not to be barred under the rules of prescription applying to quasi-contracts. *Boudier* and the recognition in French law of a general principle against unjustified enrichment were referred to in support of the court's conclusions.

In *Minyard* the Supreme Court of Louisiana followed French law as analysed by Barry Nicholas, in identifying five prerequisites within which the general enrichment action was confined, these being: (i) an enrichment; (ii) an impoverishment; (iii) a correlation between the enrichment and the impoverishment; (iv) the absence of justification; and (v) the absence of any other remedy.[20] The influence of French doctrine and jurisprudence is clearly apparent in this list. The Louisiana court elaborated its requirement

16 1825 Code arts 2274, 2279, 2280; 1870 Code arts 2295 (*negotiorum gestio*), 2301, 2302 (restoration of the undue).

17 251 La 624, 205 So 2d 422 (1967).

18 N 1 above.

19 This somewhat tentative approach to the general enrichment principle reflects difficulties made apparent in subsequent discussion: see *Edmonston v A-Second Mortgage Co* 289 So 2d 31 (La 1971); A Tate, "The Louisiana action for unjustified enrichment" (1976) 50 Tulane LR 883; idem, "The Louisiana action for unjustified enrichment: A study in the judicial process" (1977) 51 Tulane LR 446; B Nicholas, "The Louisiana law of unjustified enrichment through the act of the person enriched" (1991-92) 6/7 Tul Civ LF 3, 10-13.

20 Nicholas, "Louisiana law" (n 1) at 13, remarks that "in retrospect it can perhaps be seen as unfortunate that the five propositions were laid down by the court categorically as prerequisites, whereas in the article from which they were derived they were no more than the headings under which the requisites of the action were to be discussed."

of "absence of any other remedy" as follows: "simply an aspect of the principle that the action must not be allowed to defeat the purpose of a rule of law directed to the matter at issue. It must not, in the language of some writers, 'perpetrate a fraud on the law'".[21] But it is striking that the plaintiff in *Minyard* was allowed to make his enrichment claim even although his contractual one against a third party had prescribed, which seems to go further than French law would allow. The emphasis seems to fall more upon the availability of practical alternatives to the enrichment action than upon the formal legal alternatives which the plaintiff might at some stage have had. There was no discussion of the indirectness of the enrichment and its mediation through a third party.

These judicial developments formed important background to the Code revision processes which were also under way in Louisiana, and now, unlike its mother French system, the Louisiana Code identifies "unjust enrichment" as a source of obligations imposed by law,[22] and, more significantly still, contains a general enrichment article.[23] Article 2298 is headed "Enrichment without cause: compensation":

> A person who has been enriched without cause at the expense of another person is bound to compensate that person. The term "without cause" is used in this context to exclude cases in which the enrichment results from a valid juridical act or the law. The remedy declared here is subsidiary and shall not be available if the law provides another remedy for the impoverishment or declares a contrary rule. The amount of compensation due is measured by the extent to which one has been enriched or the other has been impoverished, whichever is less. The extent of the enrichment or impoverishment is measured as of the time the suit is brought or, according to the circumstances, as of the time the judgment is rendered.

Article 2298 is placed after a chapter of articles (2292-2297) dealing with "management of affairs" (i.e. *negotiorum gestio*). Article 2298 is the first in a new chapter entitled "Enrichment without cause", and is the only article in a section named "General principles". This is then followed by a further section of seven articles (2299-2305) dealing with "Payment of a thing not owed".[24]

---

21 251 La 652 (1967).

22 La Civ Code art 1757.

23 So in Louisiana it has been judicially recognised that because the new article "expresses principles based on existing civilian doctrine and jurisprudence" it governs transactions occurring before its effective date (*Willis v Ventrella* 674 So 2d 991 (La 1996), noted [1997] 5 RLR 219).

24 Arts 2299-2301 are dealt with in more detail below. Art 2302 deals with mistaken payment of another's debt. Art 2303 concerns the bad faith recipient's liability to restore the undue performance with fruits and products. Art 2304 relates to the recipient's obligation to restore the thing itself if it exists or, if it has been destroyed, damaged or become un-returnable, its value if in good faith and loss caused by recipient's fault; bad faith recipient liable for value even if loss not caused by fault. Art 2305 sets out the recipient's liability if the thing has been alienated: if in good faith, the value obtained, if in bad faith, the same plus damages.

Thus, while the general enrichment article is placed at the beginning of the Code's provisions on enrichment, the most detailed treatment continues to be given to reversing the payment of the undue, or the *condictio indebiti*. In Louisiana, therefore, the structure of articles 1375 and 1376 of the French Civil Code remains influential, and even the seemingly strong position of the general enrichment article in the revised Louisiana Code is undercut by its express limitation as a subsidiary remedy, exactly like the *actio de in rem verso* in France.

(3) Subsidiarity in Louisiana

Subsidiarity, involving as it does questions of the relationship between unjusti-fied enrichment and other parts of the law, has attracted considerable atten-tion in Louisiana. Barry Nicholas and Justice Albert Tate were both of the view that, as it had been expressed in *Minyard*, subsidiarity's role in Louisiana enrichment law was very limited.[25] This could be reinforced by its non-opera-tion where, as in *Minyard* itself, an alternative claim had prescribed. But the appearance of subsidiarity in the text of the revised Code does mean that it still features in current cases in its own right, in which the courts also frequently stress the role of the general enrichment action as a mere "gap-filler" in relation to the rest of the law. There are numerous decisions making use of the concept to deny enrichment recovery. So, for example, a supplier whose materials had been put into a newly-built home could not recover by way of an enrichment claim against the owner of the home when left unpaid by the main contractor, since there was a statutory regulation of claims and privileges against immoveables in such cases which had not been used by the supplier.[26] Again, a client from whom an accountant had stolen funds to repay another client was not allowed to recover from the other client because she had received partial settlement from banks and also had a restitutionary judgment against the accountant; this, it was held, precluded her from using the subsidiary enrichment action as well, although it was unlikely that her judgment against the accountant would be of much practical use to her.[27]

Subsidiarity in Louisiana can therefore preclude an enrichment claim where there is another remedy available against, not the enriched, but a third party. In *Coastal Environmental Specialists Inc v Chem-Lig International*

25 Tate, "Louisiana action (I)" (n 19) 886-890; Tate, "Louisiana action (II)" (n 19) 457-466; Nicholas, "Louisiana law" (n 1) 13-14.
26 *Builders Supply of Ruston Inc v Qualls* 750 So 2d 427 (2000).
27 *Soileau v ABC Insurance Co* 844 So 2d 108 (2002), rehearing denied, writ denied 855 So 2d 313 (2003).

Inc,[28] for example, an environmental clean-up company contracted with a lessee of land to clean up soil contaminated by a chemical spill by the now insolvent lessee. The clean-up company claimed against the lessor on the basis of unjustified enrichment. The Court of Appeal held that the clean-up company had a remedy of law against the lessee and this precluded any enrichment claim against the lessor. With reference to the lessee's insolvency and the small likelihood that the remedy against the lessee would be of practical value, the court added that "whether [the company] can succeed in recovering and collecting in its suit against [the lessee] is not determinative".[29] In *Carriere v Bank of Louisiana*[30] a landlord claimed unjust enrichment of a bank that under a mortgage had foreclosed on a tenant's restaurant but continued to operate the business from the premises. It having been held that as a matter of law the bank had no obligation to pay rent, it was further decided that any enrichment claim was excluded by the landlord's continuing claim for rent from the tenant, and that it did not matter that the tenant's insolvency meant that in fact the landlord would remain unpaid. The court also referred to an action that the landlord could have raised under article 493 to require the bank to remove its buildings and other improvements permanently attached to the land.

In all these cases the Louisiana courts follow what Lionel Smith has dubbed a "strong" form of subsidiarity,[31] under which an enrichment claim is refused when some other legal principle applies, even if claims under that principle fail. In this Louisiana again goes beyond the French position, under which, as we have seen, the existence of an "obstacle of fact" to the realisation of another claim that might be made will allow the enrichment claim to go ahead. The Louisiana approach is thus rather more akin to the Italian understanding of subsidiarity (which concept is likewise found in the Italian Code rather than the jurisprudence of the courts), which distinguishes "abstract" subsidiarity –excluding the general enrichment action whenever another action is in principle available even if the plaintiff can in fact obtain no value from it – from "concrete" subsidiarity, where the enrichment action remains open if the other possible action is ineffective as a practical matter.[32]

---

28 818 So 2d 12 (La 2001).

29 The Court also held that the contract with the lessee precluded the clean-up company's recovery from the lessor under *negotiorum gestio*.

30 702 So 2d 648 (1996); rehearing denied 31 October 1997; reconsideration denied 30 January 1998, 709 So 2d 692.

31 Smith, "Property, subsidiarity and unjust enrichment" (n 6) 596-609. "Weak" subsidiarity merely directs the plaintiff towards the correct claim.

32 Nicholas, "Unjust enrichment and subsidiarity" (n 6) 2038.

As Nicholas points out, in comparison with concrete subsidiarity "the abstract meaning leaves little scope for the action of unjust enrichment".[33]

It is finally worth noting that in Louisiana subsidiarity applies only to the general enrichment action and was apparently placed there by the legislature.[34] The concept plays no role in the other articles about unjustified enrichment or management of another's affairs. Thus the commentary on article 2299 (Payment of a Thing not Owed) remarks:

> The remedy that Article 2299 provides is not subsidiary; this remedy is available even if other remedies are also available but there can be no double recovery. A plaintiff who may avail himself of several theories of recovery, one of which is the delivery or payment of a thing not owed, may choose the theory of recovery that best suits his interests … Thus, a plaintiff may choose to bring an action in revendication, an action in tort, an action grounded on enrichment without cause, or an action grounded on Article 2299 for the return of a thing not owed.

Presumably however where there were several such alternatives on one set of facts, the action grounded on enrichment without cause would generally fail on subsidiarity grounds.

(4) Enrichment and contract in Louisiana

Subsidiarity apart, the approach in Louisiana appears to focus principally on enrichment connected to impoverishment for neither of which there is legal cause or justification. Legal cause or justification is explained primarily in terms of valid contracts or the operation of law, rather than by examination of specific reasons or factors making an enrichment unjustified. So lessors were held not unjustifiably enriched by their receipt of fire insurance proceeds on a policy purchased by sub-lessees, although the latter had also paid for repair of the fire-damaged premises, because the terms of the lease and sub-lease required the sub-lessees not only to repair the leased premises, but also to pay insurance premiums and furnish a policy naming the lessors as designated loss payees. The contract terms thus provided "legal cause" or "justification" for the lessors' enrichment.[35]

Barry Nicholas and Justice Albert Tate were both of the view that there is considerable overlap between subsidiarity and the requirement of absence of cause.[36] So, for example, in the *Carriere* case already discussed above

33 Nicholas, "Unjust enrichment and subsidiarity" (n 6) 2039.
34 A N Yiannopouolos (ed), *Louisiana Civil Code*, vol 1 (2008), commentary to art 2298.
35 *Edwards v Conforto* 636 So 2d 901 (La 1994). See also, e.g., the complex building contract case *Century Ready Mix Corp v Boyte* 968 So 2d 893 (La App 2 Cir 2007).
36 Tate, "Louisiana action (I)" (n 19) 886-890 and "Louisiana action (II)" (n 19) 457-466; Nicholas, "Louisiana law" (n 1) 13-14.

as an instance of the application of subsidiarity, the court also rejected the landlord's claim on grounds of justification or cause of both the enrichment and the impoverishment. The bank's enrichment arose both by operation of law (the rules of mortgage foreclosure) and the landlord's impoverishment by a valid juridical act, the lease contract, signed by the landlords, which had expressly permitted the tenant to create mortgages over the lease subjects. Thus it is not clear that the concept of subsidiarity was either necessary or decisive in this case. Nor was there any need for the court to refer to the indirectness of the bank's enrichment to justify its decision. Likewise in the *Coastal Environment* case also noted above, the claim could be disposed of without reference to the enrichment having come about via a third party.

Where a contract is void, there is no cause to support any enrichment, and claims may accordingly be made.[37] Contracts initially valid but which subsequently fail may give rise to enrichment claims unaffected by the limitations of subsidiarity. In *Simon v Arnold*[38] parties entered a contract under which they agreed to an immediate exchange of occupancy of their respective homes pending an exchange of titles to be completed in twelve months' time. One of the parties also agreed to take over the other's mortgage payments immediately, with that mortgage to be formally assumed at the same time as the titles were eventually exchanged. The arrangement thus made in fact continued for seven years without the title position ever being regularised, and the relationship then broke down. The court held that the initial agreement was subject to a suspensive condition which had failed to materialise, and the contract therefore failed. The party whose mortgage payments had been taken over was enriched at the other party's expense because the amount of her mortgage indebtedness had been reduced by some $7,000. The impoverished party was held entitled to recover this (rather than the $33,000 apparently paid to the lender) along with what he had spent on improvements to the property he had occupied under the initial agreement, found to amount to some $4,000.

Since subsidiarity does not apply to actions for payment of a thing not owed under article 2299, the relationship of that article to contract has to be considered in other ways. An obvious example of an undue payment or performance would be one under a void contract, and article 2300 reinforces this by saying that "a thing is not owed when it is paid or delivered for the discharge of an obligation that does not exist".[39] Account must, however, be taken of the

---

37 *Baker v Maclay Properties Co* 648 So 2d 888 (La 1995).
38 727 So 2d 699 (La 1999).
39 The ultimate source of this article, which has no parallel in the *Code civil* but reproduces the substance of arts 2304 and 2305 of the Louisiana Civil Code of 1870, appears to be Pothier, *Prêt de Consomption*, 3.2.1, n 143.

Code's other provisions on nullity of obligations. They distinguish between absolute and relative nullity, the former arising when a contract violates a rule of public order, or when the object of a contract is illicit or immoral,[40] the latter when the contract violates a rule intended for the protection of private parties, such a party's lack of capacity or the invalidity of a party's consent.[41] In both cases the contract is to be treated as never having existed, and the parties must be restored to the situation that existed before the contract was made.[42] But in cases of absolute nullity, the right of restoration is limited:

> [A] performance rendered under a contract that is absolutely null because its object or its cause is illicit or immoral may not be recovered by a party who knew or should have known of the defect that makes the contract null. The performance may be recovered, however, when that party invokes the nullity to withdraw from the contract before its purpose is achieved and also in exceptional situations when, in the discretion of the court, that recovery would further the interest of justice.[43]

Thus developers who carried out work for a city under contracts which were null and void as violations of statute were nonetheless able to recover their costs from the city, the contracts being *malum in prohibitum* rather than *malum in se*, and fraud or bad faith being absent.[44] But in general nullity arising from illegality does not lead to restoration unless a party has withdrawn from the contract before completing performance, or the court thinks that, exceptionally, justice will be better served by allowing recovery.[45]

Another type of contract case in which use is frequently made of article 2299 is that of overpayment or over-performance by a contracting party, where the excess can generally be recovered as undue.[46] Article 2301 also states that "a thing is not owed when it is paid or delivered for discharge of an obligation that is subject to a suspensive condition";[47] but the case law does not show any examples of successful claims on this basis apart from the decision of

40 Art 2030. Note also art 1966, laying down that all contracts must have a lawful cause, and art 1968, declaring the cause of a contract to be unlawful when it produces a result prohibited by law or against public policy.

41 Art 2031.

42 Art 2033.

43 Art 2033.

44 *Coleman v Bossier City* 305 So 2d 444 (1974). See also *Progressive Bank & Trust Co v Vernon A Guidry Contractors Inc* 504 So 2d 997 (1987).

45 See also *"We the People" Paralegal Services v Watley* 766 So 2d 744 (2000).

46 See, e.g., *Dynamic Exploration Inc v Sugar Bowl Gas Corp* 367 So 2d 18 (1978); *New Orleans Public Service Inc v Vanzant* 580 So 2d 533 (1991), writ denied 584 So 2d 1168; *Johnson v Hospital Affiliates Intern Inc* 416 So 2d 207 (1982).

47 Again, the ultimate source of this article, which has no parallel in the *Code civil* but reproduces the substance of arts 2308 and 2309 of the Louisiana Civil Code of 1870, appears to be Pothier: *Prêt de Consomption*, 3.2.1, notes 150 and 151.

Simon v Arnold already mentioned above.[48] Nor is there any specific provision for performance rendered under a resolutive condition which subsequently materialises, presumably because in principle the performance was owed when made. The courts have been careful, however, to follow the Code in distinguishing between, on the one hand, such conditional obligations, where the happening of the condition is uncertain, and, on the other, obligations subject to a term – for example, a period of time which may be certain (e.g. payment becomes due on a given date) or uncertain (e.g. life insurance policy becomes payable upon the beneficiary's death).[49] Article 2301 does not enable the recovery of early performances rendered under contracts subject to a term, and article 1781 specifically provides that "although performance cannot be demanded before the term ends, an obligor who has performed voluntarily before the term ends may not recover the performance".[50]

The requirement of the payor's error, found in article 2299's predecessor, no longer applies. In *Head v Adams*,[51] a case decided under the 1870 Code's requirement of error, a prospective purchaser recovered $2,450 paid to the prospective vendor in anticipation of successful completion of a purchase of property under a sale that was never completed. To the Scots lawyer, however, this looks more like misprediction of future events than an error about present facts, as well as being a payment made in the knowledge that it was not owed, which should take this case out of the "undue" category and into the realms of the *condictio causa data causa non secuta* if anywhere.[52] But there is nothing of that kind in articles 2299 et seq of the Louisiana Civil Code, and presumably such matters would therefore have to be dealt with under the general enrichment claim of article 2298.

Under the heading "Effects of Dissolution", article 2018 of the Louisiana Civil Code reads as follows:

> Upon dissolution of a contract, the parties shall be restored to the situation that existed before the contract was made. If restoration in kind is impossible or impracticable, the court may award damages.
> If partial performance has been rendered and that performance is of value to the party seeking to dissolve the contract, the dissolution does not preclude recovery for that performance, whether in contract or quasi-contract.

---

48 See for examples of unsuccessful claims *McDonald v Barker Auto Sales Inc* 810 So 2d 1242 (2002) (a garage repairs case); *Penny v Spencer Business College* 85 So 2d 365 (1956).

49 For suspensive and resolutive conditions, see art 1767; for obligations subject to a term see arts 1777-1785.

50 See, e.g., *Texas General Petroleum Corp v Brown* 408 So.2d 288 (1981); *In re Dowden* 207 B R (*Bankruptcy Reporter*) 514 (1997).

51 275 So 2d 476 (1973).

52 See further below 346-348.

Dissolution of a contract may come about when a party fails to perform,[53] which may happen through impossibility of performance, or in cases of partial or incomplete performance arising from breach of contract. The notes to article 2018 explain that "under this article, if an obligor can no longer perform after rendering a substantial part of the performance, he is entitled to recover for that performance according to the terms of the contract, and the other party is entitled to damages for the unperformed part". But "if dissolution takes place after less than a substantial part of the performance has been rendered, the obligor, if that performance is of value to the obligee, is entitled to recover the equivalent of the obligee's enrichment". On the other hand, "if dissolution takes place after the obligor has rendered a part of the performance which is of no value to the obligee, the obligor is entitled to no recovery". Article 2019 further limits the possibilities for recovery by providing that "In contracts providing for continuous or periodic performance, the effect of the dissolution shall not be extended to any performance already rendered".[54]

There are several examples in Louisiana jurisprudence of the application of article 2018 to the classic case of the building completed with defects. If the builder's performance is substantial, then it may claim the contract price, subject to a deduction of the cost of repair or completion of the work.[55] If however the builder's performance is not substantial, then its only claim is to what used to be termed a *quantum meruit*, while the client can recover against the builder the costs of completion or repair.[56] The client may go further and require the removal of the building along with restoration of the land to its prior state if the defects can only be corrected by removal and replacement.[57] It is not clear how the Louisiana courts would deal with the *Boomer v Muir* problem,[58] where the defendant's breach allowed the plaintiff contractor to terminate and recover $250,000 as the value of his work, although the contract price was $20,000. If the contractor's performance is

53 Art 2013.
54 A lease is an example of a contract providing for continuous performance, an outputs contract one for periodic performance.
55 See, e.g., *Richard v Gary Matte Builders Inc* 944 So 2d 725 (2006); *Neel v O'Quinn* 313 So 2d 286 (1975), writ denied 319 So 2d 440; *Lawson v Donahue* 313 So 2d 263 (1975); *Florida Ice Machinery Corp v Branton Insulation Inc* 290 So 2d 415 (1974); *Airco Refrigeration Service Inc v Fink* 134 So 2d 880 (1961).
56 See, e.g., *Stephenson v Smith* 337 So 2d 570 (1976); *Henson v Gonzalez* 326 So 2d 396 (1976). In *Baker v Maclay* 648 So 2d 888 (1995) the Louisiana Supreme Court made clear that the use of *quantum meruit* should be confined to the case of the measure of compensation or price unstated in a contract. See also *"We The People" Paralegal Services v Watley* 766 So 2d 744 (2000).
57 *Neel v O'Quinn* 313 So 2d 286 (1975), writ denied 319 So 2d 440.
58 24 P (2d) 570 (1933).

of no value to the client, recovery is denied to the contractor.[59] Neither the article nor the case law make clear whether the assessment of value here is objective or subjective; that is to say, whether it matters what the client as a matter of fact thinks of the quality of the contractor's work.

Finally on article 2018, a Louisiana contract case which is extremely well known in the United Kingdom as a result of the attention drawn to it by English restitution lawyers is *City of New Orleans v Fireman's Charitable Association*.[60] The city contracted with the association for the provision of fire services over a period of several years. After the contract expired, the city discovered that the association had not maintained resources at the level needed to provide the services contracted for in the event of fire, and sued for damages for non-performance. It was held that as the city had suffered no loss, no substantial damages were recoverable. The association's savings of over $40,000 might be an enrichment, but such gains by the contract-breaker were irrelevant to liability for breach of contract. The question of whether article 2018 might change this outcome depends on whether it is possible to treat a contract already discharged by expiry of its term as one that can now be dissolved within the meaning of article 2013 ("When the obligor fails to perform, the obligee has a right to the judicial dissolution of the contract or, according to the circumstances, to regard the contract as dissolved"), and on whether the remedial scope of article 2018 could be extended to what would be in effect price reduction akin to the *actio quanti minoris*. It is worth noting that in any event the court also denied the city full restitution of what it had paid, on the basis that the services required under the contract had been provided.

In conclusion, the relationship between enrichment and contract is quite well worked out in Louisiana law, not so much as a matter of subsidiarity but more in terms of both general principle and a number of specific codal provisions on null and dissolved contracts. Indeed, the existence of these specific provisions may well be part of the reasoning underpinning the deployment of subsidiarity in the general enrichment claim allowed by article 2298: this is not to be allowed to upset the checks and balances established elsewhere in the Code.

---

59 *Toepfor v Thionville* 299 So 2d 415 (1974); *Home Services v Marvin* 37 So 2d 413 (1948).
60 9 So 486 (1891). See, e.g., discussions by G Jones, "The recovery of damages gained from a breach of contract" (1983) 99 LQR 443 at 459; J Edelman, *Gain-Based Damages: Contract, Tort, Equity and Intellectual Property* (2002) 176.

C. SCOTLAND: JURISTIC AND JUDICIAL RECONSTRUCTIONS

(1) Historical development of an enrichment taxonomy

The history of the development of enrichment law in Scotland has been the subject of much research since 1990, but it is clear that the study is not yet complete. For example, most work has begun with the writings of Stair in the late seventeenth century, although there must be an earlier story to be uncovered.[61] Stair himself divided the law under two broad headings. The first was *restitution*, for when a party was obliged to return property or money received from another, either because it belonged to the other (and so not strictly an enrichment obligation, in modern terms), or because the situation was one in which the "cause" by which a thing became one's property "ceased" (i.e. the retention of it was *sine causa*, or without legal justification). Examples of the latter were drawn from some of the Roman law *condictiones* such as the *condictio ob non causam (finitam)*, the *condictio causa data causa non secuta*, or (in a more restricted way) the *condictio ob turpem causam*.[62] The obligation of restitution also extended to *indebite solutum* "when any party through error delivereth or payeth that which he supposeth due, or belongeth to another"[63] – that is, the territory of the *condictio indebiti*. The second heading was *recompense*, which for Stair was about obligations of gratitude, including those arising from *negotiorum gestio* and receipt of a donation as well as claims arising from improvements carried out to another's property. A legal obligation to recompense an enrichment arose when it occurred at the expense of another who had no intention to donate.[64]

Eighteenth and early nineteenth-century writings narrowed the content of restitution and recompense down to pure enrichment cases, although *negotiorum gestio* continued to be linked with recompense.[65] The classic definition of recompense, seemingly derived from Stair, was given by Bell,

---

61 For pre-Stair references see H L MacQueen and W D H Sellar, "Unjust enrichment in Scots law", in E Schrage (ed), *Unjust Enrichment: Comparative Legal History* (1995), at 291-292. See also D Reid, "Thomas Aquinas and Viscount Stair: The influence of scholastic moral theology on Stair's account of restitution and recompense" (2008) 29 *Journal of Legal History* 189-214, for an argument that Stair's distinction of the obligations of "restitution" and "recompense" (see further below) is drawn from canonist doctrine and Thomist philosophy.

62 Stair, *Inst* 1.7.7-8 (referring to all three *condictiones* mentioned).

63 *Inst* 1.7.9.

64 *Inst* 1.8. Note that for Stair the ingratitude of the donee made a gift void and obliged its return to the donor (*Inst* 1.8.2). See further H L MacQueen and M A Hogg, "Donation in Scots law", in M Schmidt-Kaessel (ed), *Donation in Europe* (forthcoming).

65 See Bankton, *Inst* 1.8 and 9; Erskine, *Inst* 3.1.10 and 11; Hume, *Lectures*, vol 3, 165-185; Bell, *Prin* §§ 525-542 (first four editions, 1829-1839); J S More, *Lectures on the Law of Scotland* (1864) ch 3 (Quasi Contracts).

Professor of Scots Law at the University of Edinburgh: "Where one has gained by the lawful act of another, done without any intention of donation, he is bound to recompense or indemnify that other to the extent of the gain."[66] As with the definition of the scope of the *actio de in rem verso* in the *arrêt Boudier*, Bell's definition of recompense was later criticised as incomplete and as it stood too wide: for example, because it made no reference to a requirement of the gain being at the other party's expense, while donation was not the only possible case in which an enrichment recovery would be excluded.[67]

Influence from France in juristic analysis became apparent in Bell's writing. He claimed to have been the first to bring Pothier's work into Scotland,[68] and was criticised by his students for lecturing on French rather than Scots law.[69] Certainly the treatments of restitution and recompense in his *Principles of the Law of Scotland* (first published 1829) cite not only Pothier's treatise on obligations and the *condictio indebiti* but also the *Code civil* (article 1377) and (in the 1839 fourth edition) Toullier's *Droit civil français* (1833).[70] It was however Bell's brother-in-law and posthumous editor, Patrick Shaw, who in the middle of the nineteenth century broke restitution down into what became two rather independent categories, one (still called restitution) dealing with cases about corporeal (generally moveable) property, the other entitled repetition and covering mainly cases that had hitherto been listed under the heading of the *condictio indebiti*.[71] Although Stair had used the term "repetition",[72] its redeployment in the mid-nineteenth century as a specific category of Scots enrichment law surely owes everything to the *répétition de l'indu* of Pothier and the *Code civil*. The structure of the "three Rs" (restitution, repetition and recompense) which had thus emerged would hold its grip on the subject until the 1990s.[73]

---

66 Bell, *Prin* § 538.
67 See, e.g., *Edinburgh and District Tramways Co Ltd v Courtenay* 1909 SC 99 per Lord President Dunedin at 105.
68 See K H Nadelman, "Joseph Story and George Joseph Bell" 1959 JR 31 at 37.
69 See T StJ N Bates, "Mr McConnachie's notes and Mr Fraser's confessional" 1980 JR 166 at 176.
70 Bell also cites Voet, Vinnius, Huber and a number of English as well as Scottish cases.
71 The first instance of this taxonomy that I have found is in Shaw's *Treatise on the Law of Obligations and Contracts* (1847), at 223-234. Shaw later carried the taxonomy over into the fifth (1860) edition of Bell's *Principles of the Law of Scotland*, which he edited: see further P Hellwege and R Evans-Jones, "Some observations on the taxonomy of unjustified enrichment in Scots law" (1998) 2 EdinLR 180 at 185, and R Evans-Jones, "Unjustified enrichment", in Reid and Zimmermann , *History*, vol 2, 369 at 376-377. Further on Shaw see the life in the *Oxford Dictionary of National Biography* and comments in D M Walker, *The Scottish Jurists* (1985), at 128, 337, 345, 375, 388, 394, 397, 400-401; neither of these treatments is satisfactory in doing justice to Shaw's admittedly highly derivative authorial work.
72 *Inst* 1.7.2. See further Reid, "Aquinas and Stair" (n 61) 206-207, note 165.
73 See, e.g., the three *Encyclopaedias of Scots Law* produced between the 1890s and the 1930s,

This structure of Scots law was not unlike that of contemporary French and, following that source, Louisiana law. Since in practice most enrichment cases were about transfers of money between the parties, repetition was the one of the three Rs having most content and significance. The Roman *condictiones* formed an important route map for the courts in determining which transfers should be reversed, and amongst these the most commonly referred to was the *condictio indebiti*. Recompense covered cases not involving transfers of money or property, in particular ones of improvement to another's property, and was recognised as depending on more general ideas of unjustified enrichment, embodied in the Pomponian maxim *nemo debet locupletari ex aliena iactura*. *Negotiorum gestio* had an established place in the law, and while its primary function was as a remedy enabling an intervener to claim his own expenses, there were cases where it gave rise to an enrichment claim against the person whose affairs had been managed by the intervener.

(2) Subsidiarity of recompense

There was nothing explicit within the structure of nineteenth-century Scots law to compare with the concept of subsidiarity in French jurisprudence. But in *Commissioners of Northern Lighthouses v Edmonston*[74] in 1908 the idea began to emerge in a case where the Commissioners had a contract with a landowner whose property lay next to a shore station serving their Muckle Flugga lighthouse. The contract obliged the landowner to maintain an access road to the shore station, but despite pressure from the Commissioners he failed to carry out his obligations. Accordingly the Commissioners carried out the work at their own hand, and claimed the expense of it from the landowner by way of an action of recompense. Lord Johnston rejected their claim, explaining that the proper course of action "would have been to have raised an action declaratory of Mr Edmonston's obligation under his contract, and for implement of the contract, with an alternative crave that, failing implement, the road should be repaired at the sight of the Court and at Mr Edmonston's expense".[75] While neither the word "subsidiarity", nor any equivalent or paraphrase, appeared in his judgment, Lord Johnston clearly

---

all of which contain separate articles on Recompense, Repetition and Restitution, and nothing on Unjustified Enrichment or any similar title (although both editions of the first two (*Green's Encyclopaedia*) had short articles on the *condictio causa data causa non secuta* and the *condictio indebiti*). Note also the successive editions of Gloag & Henderson's *The Law of Scotland* from 1927 down to 2001 (although significant revision began under the hand of Alan Rodger in the 10th edn of 1995).

74 (1908) 16 SLT 439.
75 At 442.

found unacceptable the idea that a party with a contractual entitlement and remedies following from that can instead choose self-help and in effect thrust an obligation of recompense on the other contracting party.

A more generalised approach towards a concept of subsidiarity in Scots enrichment law first began to emerge in the 1970s, starting with a decision of the Second Division of the Court of Session, *Varney v Burgh of Lanark*.[76] The facts were that a local authority, in breach of its statutory duty, refused to construct sewers to connect a contractor's housing development to the general sewage system in the area. The contractor instead undertook the work itself, and then claimed recompense from the authority. The contractor was unaware that under both statute and common law it had had a right to obtain a court order compelling the authority to fulfil its duty. The majority of the Second Division held that the recompense claim, being "equitable" in nature, must fail where the pursuer had available an alternative, "legal" remedy, even if it was ignorant of that at the relevant time. Since Scots law traditionally does not distinguish law from equity, or between legal and equitable remedies, this approach seems contrary to principle and is accordingly controversial. But like Lord Johnston in the Muckle Flugga case, the judges were clearly concerned about the possibility of enrichment remedies springing from self-help when a more orderly and controlled procedure was available. The third judge in *Varney*, Lord Fraser, shared these concerns, but expressed himself in narrower and more cautious terms than his brethren:[77]

> I do not know that it is absolutely essential to the success of an action for recompense that the pursuer should not have, and should never have had, any possibility of raising an action under the ordinary law, but in my opinion it would at least require special and strong circumstances to justify an action of recompense where there was, or had been, an alternative remedy open to the pursuer.

This view – that where an alternative remedy exists in a given situation, recompense is available only in "special and strong circumstances" – seems to have been preferred to the legal/equitable dichotomy in subsequent decisions of the courts.[78] But it was clear that recompense occupied a subordinate position in the law, albeit that once the legal/equitable theory was jettisoned the basis of principle for so relegating the obligation was left quite opaque.

---

76 1974 SC 245.
77 At 259-260.
78 See *Lawrence Building Co v Lanark County Council* 1978 SC 30 (where on facts very similar to *Varney* recompense was held relevant); *Trade Development Bank Ltd v Warriner and Mason (Scotland) Ltd* 1980 SC 74; *Cliffplant Ltd v Kinnaird* 1981 SC 9 at 28; *City of Glasgow District Council v Morrison McChlery & Co* 1985 SC 52; *Trans Barwil Agencies UK Ltd v John S Braid & Co Ltd* 1989 SLT 73 at 78; *Property Selection & Investment Trust Ltd v United Friendly Insurance plc* 1999 SLT 975 at 985.

Subsidiarity arguments featured in at least two contract cases after *Varney*. In *Bennett v Carse*[79] a claim for the repayment of money was based in the alternative on either an oral contract or recompense. The defender argued on the one hand that since there was no proof of the agreement by way of his writ or oath the contract claim must fail; on the other hand, in the light of *Varney* the availability of a contract claim, albeit one that could not be realised for lack of the required evidence, meant that there could be no recompense. Had this argument been successful, it would have supported the existence of a strong form of subsidiarity in the law of recompense, similar to the French idea of an "obstacle of law"; but the recompense claim was held to be relevant. A somewhat similar argument appeared in *NV Devos Gebroeder v Sutherland Sportswear Ltd*,[80] where the pursuer first raised a contract action for payment in respect of the supply of goods. This failed because the pursuer was itself in breach, the goods supplied having been defective. Since the defender had retained and used the goods, the pursuer next turned to recompense, but was met by a defence of prescription, since it was more than the statutory five-year prescriptive period since the goods had been supplied. The pursuer argued that the running of the prescriptive period had been interrupted in terms of the prescription statute by a "relevant claim", namely the contract claim. The argument was rejected by the First Division, on the basis that contract and recompense were distinct areas of law, even although the claims arose from the same set of facts. Subsidiarity emerged in the opinion of Lord President Hope who, having cited *Varney*, continued: "The obligation of recompense is a remedy which is independent of contract, so much so that it is excluded if the matter in question is the subject of a contract which can still be enforced."[81] At least, however, this recognised that the mere existence of a contract is not enough to preclude recompense, which can come in if for some reason the contract is unenforceable. But the pursuer in *Devos* should have followed the example of *Bennett v Carse* and put the claims in the alternate, so that the recompense claim remained alive while the enforceability of the contract was judicially tested.

79 1990 SLT 454.
80 1990 SC 291.
81 At 303-304.

(3) A reconfigured enrichment taxonomy

Three major cases,[82] coupled with a rich outburst of academic writing and Scottish Law Commission analysis, led to a transformation of Scots enrichment law in the second half of the 1990s. The details have been fully explored elsewhere,[83] and here a brief overview will suffice. The three Rs have been re-characterised as remedies rather than as obligations or actions, the scope of each being defined by the ways in which enrichment is reversed. So restitution is about the restoration of corporeal property, repetition is about the return of money, and recompense is about paying for other forms of enrichment. Scots law has now reached a position where in principle an enrichment is said to be unjustified and one which should be reversed if its retention is supported by no legal ground. Examples of "legal grounds" or justifications for enrichments include receipt under a gift or in performance of a valid contract. In Scots law, then, before an enrichment can be reversed or paid for, its retention by the enriched person has to be unjustified.

The general starting point is, however, that enrichments will remain where they are unless a reason can be shown for their reversal. Scots law could simply say that, unless the enrichment is justified by a legal ground, such as a valid contract or gift, it falls to be reversed; but it has not committed itself quite so far. Considerations such as protecting possession and the security of transactions so that, once carried through, the law will need weighty reasons to undo them, have pointed in an opposite direction: it is for the person who wants to reclaim an enrichment to show reasons why that should be allowed. There is accordingly now controversy as to whether Scots law is truly based upon "absence of a legal ground", or is rather a system in which one has to point first, in the Common Law manner, to other factors, over and beyond the absence of, say, a valid contract, before an enrichment liability will exist. As has been pointed out, "absence of a legal ground" can only be a necessary rather than a sufficient basis for identifying reversible enrichment. There have also to be excluded incidental enrichments, where one incurred expenditure for one's own purposes and, as it were by a side-wind, benefitted another; and knowing imposition of a benefit without contract or intention to donate.[84] The suggestion that as a result a "third way" has been created

82 See *Morgan Guaranty Co of New York v Lothian Regional Council* 1995 SC 151; *Shilliday v Smith* 1998 SC 725; *Dollar Land (Cumbernauld) Ltd v CIN Properties Ltd* 1998 SC (HL) 90.

83 See most recently M Hogg, "Unjustified enrichment in Scots law twenty years on: Where now?" [2006] RLR 1.

84 See Appendix by E Clive to Scottish Law Commission Discussion Paper, Judicial Abolition of the Error of Law Rule and its Aftermath (Scot Law Com DP No 99, 1996), 50-56.

in Scots law, in which both absence of a legal ground and a factor (such as error) making retention of the enrichment unjust must be present in some shape or form,[85] may not sufficiently appreciate that the Civil Law absence of legal ground approach has always also brought in additional requirements such as a liability error or a defence of knowledge. The key difference from the Common Law is that the factor in question must be related to the legal ground, as for example with a liability error.[86]

Three types of situation have been identified by writers as ones in which enrichments may be open for reversal. The influence of German analysis will be clear from the following summary. The first situation is where the enrichment is transferred to the enriched person by the impoverished one. Here the Roman *condictiones* still play an important role, as descriptions of type-situations in which an enrichment of any kind would be seen as unjusti-fied – for example, because the transfer was undue, or made for a purpose which subsequently failed to materialise. The second case is enrichment by imposition, the term given where the impoverished person carries out actions for the improvement of the enriched's property or performs obligations lying upon the enriched. The third and final case is where the enriched person acquires the enrichment by its own actions rather than those of the impover-ished party: for example, by taking and using property without permission or by otherwise invading or interfering with the impoverished person's rights.

It remains unclear whether subsidiarity has been carried over from its old role in recompense, and whether it can or will play any role in limiting innovation within the new dispensation. If the German model is followed, the answer should be in the negative.[87] But if subsidiarity does still have any appli-cation, then obviously that role cannot be limited to those cases where the remedy of recompense happens to be sought by the pursuer. Instead we have to look at the different typologies of facts in which claims arise, and assess whether subsidiarity questions may arise in any of them and, if so, how they should be handled. As Niall Whitty argues in the most detailed discussion of

---

85 N Whitty and D Visser, "Unjustified enrichment", in Zimmermann, Visser and Reid, *Mixed Legal Systems* 412; Visser, *Unjustified Enrichment* (n 6) 175-193.

86 See N Whitty, "Mapping the law" [2008] RLR 241 at 246, and references there given; and further J du Plessis, "Towards a rational structure of liability for unjustified enrichment: Thoughts from two mixed jurisdictions" (2005) 122 SALJ 142, also published in R Zimmermann (ed), *Grund-strukturen eines Europäischen Bereicherungsrechts* (2005) 175. Visser, *Unjustified Enrichment* (nn 6 and 85) responds to these arguments.

87 Note that in *Macadam v Grandison* [2008] CSOH 53 Lord Hodge observed that "it is no longer appropriate to speak of recompense as a ground of action. Nor is it necessary, as in the past, to aver what were the five elements or prerequisites [*thus including subsidiarity*] for recompense" (para 35).

the current position, "a doctrine of subsidiarity cannot be general throughout enrichment law but must be justified in particular contexts by pertinent evaluations of policy and principle".[88] On such an analysis, he argues, the only case for the application of subsidiarity is that of unauthorised performance of another's obligation (not including payment of another's money debt) – that is, cases such as the Muckle Flugga lighthouse decision and *Varney* – where the concept regulates the power of one party to thrust new obligations upon another.[89] This line is followed in the most recent (2007) edition of Gloag & Henderson's *The Law of Scotland*,[90] while Martin Hogg has gone further to argue that the cases excluding enrichment remedies for unauthorised performance of another's non-money contractual obligations are to be explained not so much by concepts of subsidiarity as by principles against interference with another's contractual rights.[91]

At least one post-1990s case has raised the issue of subsidiarity in a contractual context. In the sheriff court decision of *Renfrewshire Council v McGinlay*[92] R leased a shop to J, who subsequently ceased to trade and handed the shop over to M, who occupied it without a lease for three years. R upon discovery of the situation attempted unsuccessfully to obtain rent from J (but did not sue him) before finally giving him notice to quit. R also attempted to negotiate a lease with M, but this too failed and M eventually quit the property after being called upon to do so by R. R then sued M for recompense for the three years' use of the property. The claim failed on the basis that, following *Varney*, R should first have sued J for rent or damages under the lease. The court was moved by the risk that if recovery was allowed against M, R might still have its contractual entitlement against J. The decision none the less seems a wider application of subsidiarity than anything in the previous law. There seems to have been no consideration of whether J was solvent or worth suing. Further, this is not a case where the impoverished person imposed a benefit upon an unwilling other, which, as has just been argued above, is or should be the main instance of the application of subsidiarity in Scotland, but is rather one where the enriched person unauthorisedly used and got benefit from the impoverished person's property.

88 (2006) 10 EdinLR at 130.
89 And also the case which prompted the Whitty commentary, *Transco plc v Glasgow City Council* 2005 SLT 958.
90 W M Gloag and R Candlish Henderson, *The Law of Scotland*, 12th edn by Lord Coulsfield and H L MacQueen et al (2007) para 9.06. The present writer is responsible for the chapter (25) on unjustified enrichment and *negotiorum gestio*. See para 25.19.
91 *Obligations*, 2nd edn (2006) paras 4.111-4.122.
92 2001 SLT (Sh Ct) 79, criticised by R Evans-Jones, *Unjustified Enrichment*, vol 1, (2003) paras 7.44, 8.117.

It is, however, significant that the subsidiarity was found to arise because there was or might be a claim against a third party as well as against the enriched person if the enrichment action was allowed. An alternative explanation for the decision in the case might therefore be that it is actually one of indirect enrichment in a multi-party situation, of a kind where in general Scots law, again like its German counterpart, has been reluctant to permit recovery.[93] R relied on the faith and credit of the party with whom it contracted (J), and should not in terms of principle and policy be allowed to convert M, with whom it otherwise has no connection, into a guarantor of J's debts, especially when the possibility exists of recovery from the principal debtor. We will return below to the Scots law view of indirect enrichment, but may note here the possibility that ideas of subsidiarity, if given space beyond their scope, can overlap significantly with other ways of ensuring that enrichment liability does not over-reach itself.

(4) Enrichment and contract[94]

How then may the question of the relationship between enrichment and contract be approached in the new Scottish scheme of things? At least one point seems immediately clear from the general principles of enrichment law. An enrichment received under a contract is a justified one, since the contract provides a "legal ground" for the enrichment. While this proposition requires some qualifications to be discussed below, it does mean that there is no question of investigating a contractual exchange of performances on the basis that one party received more or less than some abstract equality of value in the process. The question is closed off for enrichment law by the very definition of the subject.[95]

On the other hand, where there is no contract, then enrichment law may have full play. Thus transactions between parties negotiating a contract but without ultimate success may be dealt with as potentially unjustified enrichments, whether they result from transfers, impositions or takings.[96] It is perhaps less likely that in such pre-contractual relationships impositions or takings will be unauthorised ones but the possibility cannot be ruled out; and even if authorised they may well have been understood and intended

---

93 See generally N R Whitty, "Indirect enrichment in Scots law" (in two parts) 1994 JR 200 and 239; Evans-Jones, *Unjustified Enrichment* (n 92) ch 8; and further below, 349-350.

94 I have been greatly assisted in the preparation of this section of the paper by consideration of Visser, *Unjustified Enrichment* (n 6) 90-113.

95 *Dollar Land (Cumbernauld) Ltd v CIN Properties Ltd* 1998 SC (HL) 90.

96 See, e.g., *Shetland Islands Council v BP Petroleum Development Ltd* 1990 SLT 82.

to be non-gratuitous. The same principles apply to parties negotiating the extension or renewal of an established contractual relationship: should the negotiations fail, performances outside the existing or previous contract will be remediable by enrichment law.[97]

Again, the parties may appear to conclude a contract but the law determines that it is void or null so that no contract comes into existence. Performances under this relationship are, as in Louisiana, clearly subject-matter for treatment under enrichment law, since they were undue or without a legal cause.[98] But, once more, as in Louisiana law, there are specialities where the nullity or unenforceability (as the case may be) of the contract arises from its illegality or its being contrary to public policy. Despite acceptance from the time of Stair of the *condictio ob turpem causam*, the courts will, in general, not allow the party who has rendered performance in terms of an illegal contract to recover his or her performance: *in pari delicto potior est conditio defendentis (possidentis)*.[99] It is debated whether, like Louisiana (and also English law), the law makes an exception to this for the party who repents before full performance of the illegal contract.[100] But a distinction, first drawn by the authoritative text writer Gloag and subsequently approved in the courts, has been made between agreements which the law will not allow to operate as contracts, and contracts which are contrary to law.[101] The gist of this seems to be that in the first case the transaction may still have legal effects between the parties, while in the second case performance will not be enforced and losses will be left to lie where they fall. The first case is illustrated by *Cuthbertson v Lowes*.[102] Statute declared void contracts of sale using customary rather than imperial weights and measures, but the court held that the purchaser in a bargain for the sale of potatoes by the "Scotch acre", while not liable for the contract price, was nonetheless bound to account for the value of the potatoes he had acquired. The statute did not make the transfer of potatoes for value unlawful. In *Jamieson v Watt's Trustee*,[103] by contrast, work for which a licence was required by statute could not be made the basis of any claim for payment when it had been done without the necessary licence having been obtained. Gloag's distinction is difficult to apply consistently, and may merely disguise

---

97 See, e.g., *Rochester Poster Services Ltd v A G Barr plc* 1994 SLT (Sh Ct) 2.
98 See, e.g., *Morgan Guaranty v Lothian Regional Council* 1995 SC 151.
99 W W McBryde, *The Law of Contract in Scotland*, 3rd edn (2007) paras 19.17-19.26; Evans-Jones, *Unjustified Enrichment* (n 92) ch 5.
100 Gloag and Henderson, *The Law of Scotland* (n 90) para 9.06. Cf Evans-Jones, *Unjustified Enrichment* (n 92) paras 5.91-5.104.
101 W M Gloag, *The Law of Contract*, 2nd edn (1929) 550; *Jamieson v Watt's Tr* 1950 SC 265.
102 (1870) 8 M 1073.
103 1950 SC 265.

the reality of making choices based upon the justice of the individual case and public policy considerations, and weighing the factors involved against each other.[104] The Louisiana Code appears a more transparent account of the law in this regard.

There are cases where performances rendered under a contract that was valid at the time can be recovered through enrichment law. Where a contract exists but there is over-performance by one of the parties – over-payment or double payment, for example – such performance is not required by or due under the contract and its retention by the other party is unjustified; the case for recovery will be strengthened if that party makes profitable use of what has been received.[105] Gloag & Henderson's *The Law of Scotland* states the following as an instance of the *condictio causa data causa non secuta*: "Where the contract is subject to a suspensive condition which does not materialise, and as a result the defender comes under no obligation to supply the consideration, the pursuer can recover any prepayment."[106] The basis for this conclusion is that the pursuer's payment was made for a future purpose, although the footnote to the text quoted introduces a note of doubt on this point.[107] Louisiana law would take the view, noted earlier, that this is simply a case of an undue performance. Evans-Jones argues that where a transfer is made under a contract subject to a resolutive condition which then materialises to dissolve the contract, the transfer falls to be restored under the *condictio ob causam finitam*, the purpose of the transfer having existed when it was made and ceased to do so afterwards.[108] This would seem to go further than Louisiana law has done to date.

Contracts may be voidable in Scots law, that is to say, valid until a ground of invalidity, such as fraud, undue influence or misrepresentation, is successfully invoked in a court action of reduction or as a defence to a claim of specific implement. The distinction between void and voidable, which is essentially drawn from the Common Law strand of the Scottish legal heritage, is thus not at all the same as that between absolute and relative nullity in Louisiana

---

104 For another, recent, example, see *Dowling & Rutter v Abacus Frozen Foods Ltd* 2002 SLT 491.

105 See, e.g., *Chisholm v Alexander* (1882) 19 SLR 835. *Smiths Gore v Reilly* 2003 SLT (Sh Ct) 15 seems to be wrongly decided in this connection.

106 Gloag & Henderson (n 90) para 25.13 (4), citing Voet 12.6.3 and *Brown v Nielson* (1825) 4 S 271.

107 Most probably because in South Africa it has been held that the *condictio indebiti* applies rather than the *condictio causa data causa non secuta*: see Whitty and Visser, "Unjustified enrichment" (n 85) 425-426. See also Evans-Jones, *Unjustified Enrichment* (n 92) paras 3.130-3.131 and 4.14 (but note failure of a suspensive condition does not necessarily make the whole contract void).

108 Evans-Jones, *Unjustified Enrichment* (n 92) paras 4.14, 4.18, 6.07.

law. Voidable contracts present something of a conundrum in Scots law, in that the requirement and remedy of *restitutio in integrum* applies: that is, it is at once a condition and a consequence of reduction that the parties may be restored to their pre-contractual position. It is disputed whether this is a contractual or an enrichment remedy, the protagonists being Evans-Jones and Saul Miller.[109] The issue is again that so far as pre-avoidance performances constitute enrichments they are justified by the contract as it is still valid. Once more the *condictio ob causam finitam* seems most likely to be relevant if the recovery is to be seen as enrichment-based.

Most discussion has however focused on cases where obligations of performance under contracts are terminated before completion, the main examples being frustration by supervening events and material breach of contract, leaving the question of whether the gains and losses arising at termination can or are to be dealt with under enrichment law. The House of Lords held in 1923 that the consequences of frustration could be handled by the *condictio causa data causa non secuta* and, despite much academic criticism, there is little sign of this approach being reversed.[110] There may well be a case here again for applying the *condictio ob causam finitam*. The position on termination for material breach is complicated by the concurrent availability of damages claims for the innocent party, but there is a view that this party has a general right to restitution of all benefits transferred to the other party under the contract pre-termination at least so far as not reciprocated by the counter-performance,[111] while there is much authority holding that the contract-breaker too has an enrichment claim in respect of benefits conferred on the other side but not paid for.[112] As in Louisiana, the classic case is the completed but defective building: in general, the builder has a contract action for the price subject to a deduction for the cost of remedial works, but where the failure is material, the builder's only action is for recompense.

Scots law has not yet addressed the case of the defective work that is of no value to the recipient, or where the cost of a performance greatly exceeded the contract price (the *Boomer v Muir* situation). Other unresolved questions are (1) whether or not the innocent party's right of restitution is derived from

---

109 S Miller, "Unjustified enrichment and failed contracts", in Zimmermann, Visser and Reid, *Mixed Legal Systems* 437 at 460-466; Evans-Jones, *Unjustified Enrichment* (n 92) paras 9.125-9.134. Visser, *Unjustified Enrichment* (n 6) 91-112, is highly relevant to this debate.

110 *Cantiere San Rocco SA v Clyde Shipbuilding and Engineering Co* 1923 SC (HL) 105. See further Evans-Jones, *Unjustified Enrichment* (n 92) ch 4; Miller, "Unjustified enrichment and failed contracts" (n 109) 440-460.

111 H MacQueen & J Thomson, *Contract Law in Scotland*, 2nd edn (2007) paras 5.48-5.53

112 Ibid paras 6.55-6.60.

the law of unjustified enrichment and, as in the frustration cases, the *condictio causa data causa non secuta* (or, perhaps, the *condictio ob causam finitam*), or is rather a contractual remedy which happens to prevent enrichment but is principally about protecting the innocent party from loss; and (2) the basis for the contract-breaker's enrichment claim: does it depend upon transfer and if so, upon which *condictio*; or is it an imposition which was clearly not intended to be gratuitous; or does the liability depend upon the recipient taking over and making use of what the contract-breaker did under the now-aborted contract? The last seems the likeliest, given that it has been held in a building case that the client can reject the defective work altogether and require its removal from the site by the builder.[113]

One further possible case arising in the context of breach of contract is the claim an innocent party might make to the contract-breaker's gains derived from the breach, the enrichment basis for this being interference or invasion with the innocent party's rights. Relatively old Scottish House of Lords authority is, like the New Orleans firemen case, against this kind of claim[114] but is perhaps being undermined by growing English recognition of the validity of such an enrichment-based action, albeit as a form of damages for breach of contract rather than as an enrichment (or, in standard English terms, restitution) claim.[115] As an enrichment claim it could be fitted into the new taxonomy as a form of invasion of or interference with another's rights, while in contract law terms it supports the general entitlement to performance which is a characteristic of Scots contract law.

As already noted in the discussion above of *Renfrewshire Council v McGinlay*, a final point arises from the complex body of cases dealing with indirect enrichment and multi-party situations, where the existence of contracts somewhere in the chain of links between the impoverished person (I) and the enriched one (E) is often a reason for the customary denial of recovery in such cases.[116] Where, for example, I has contracted with a third party (T) and from that contract a benefit flows to E, the courts have

---

113 *Ramsay v Brand* (1898) 25 R 1212.

114 *Teacher v Calder* (1899) 1 F (HL) 39.

115 The leading case is *Attorney General v Blake* [2001] 1 AC 268, commented on by J Thomson, "Restitutionary and performance damages" 2001 SLT (News) 71. See also *Experience Hendrix LLC v PPX Enterprises Inc* [2003] EMLR 25; *WWF World Wide Fund for Nature v World Wrestling Federation Entertainment Inc (No 2)* [2007] EWCA Civ 286, [2008] 1 WLR 445, [2008] 1 All ER 74. For Scots law perspectives see M Hogg, *Obligations*, 2nd edn (2006) paras 4.123-4.131.

116 For what follows see Whitty, "Indirect enrichment" (n 93) and Evans-Jones, *Unjustified Enrichment* (n 92) ch 8. See also the comparative analysis in Visser, *Unjustified Enrichment* (n 6) 193-217.

tended to hold that I relied on the credit of T rather than E in performing the contract, and hence has no recovery from the latter. Sometimes this is expressed as a matter of I having suffered no loss, or as E's benefit being incidental; only occasionally is it a matter of the contract's existence being as such an absolute bar to an enrichment claim. The existence of a contract between T and E may also have an effect: if T uses moneys obtained from I to perform his contract with E, the latter cannot be enriched by payment of what he was owed by T, nor should he be exposed to a second claim by I having given value for what he received, albeit to the middleman T rather than I. Nor should E be unfairly deprived of defences good against T but not I. So in multi-party cases enrichment claims between remote parties in an "enrichment chain" are often restricted or excluded by the presence of contracts. But this is seldom so simply because of any perceived subsidiarity; rather, there are factors present, linked to the contract, which mean that, at least as between I and E, the enrichment is not unjustified, or has not been gained by E at the expense of I.[117]

D. COMPARISON OF LOUISIANA AND SCOTS LAW

Despite their different histories and the rather different structures of enrichment law which are the outcome of those histories, similarity is the most immediately striking point to arise from a comparison of results in Louisiana and Scotland when questions arise about the relationship between enrichment and contract. It is clear in both systems that enrichment arising from a valid contract is justified and not reversible, while performances under a contract that is void or never formed may give rise to enrichment claims. In both systems there are a number of cases where enrichment-based claims may be allowed despite the presence of a contract between the parties: for example, when suspensive conditions fail; when the contract becomes impossible or is frustrated by supervening events; or in certain cases where a contract is terminated for breach or non-performance.

Additionally, both systems recognise a principle of subsidiarity which is sometimes interpreted as meaning that enrichment recovery is excluded whenever there is a contract, whether between the parties or between one of the parties and a third person. It is significant, however, that in both systems there is controversy as to the need for (or scope of) this subsidiarity, even if one's ambition is to fence in enrichment liability within the overall structure

---

117 Whitty, "Indirect enrichment" (n 93) (1) 216-217, criticises the deployment of subsidiarity in multi-party cases.

of the law. Can the limitations imposed by subsidiarity be worked out better, and more in accord with coherent legal principle, by way of further analysis of when enrichments are unjustified? The detailed discussion of the enrichment/contract relationship in the foregoing suggests that the answer to this question is very often "Yes". This need not mean the elimination of subsidiarity from discussions of enrichment in general, but the doctrine need not be treated expansively, or indeed as an easy escape route from some difficult questions.

In any event, how easy is it to find subsidiarity? Comparative examination of the Louisiana material confirms just how unsystematic and un-thought through the Scottish approach to the subject has been until very recently, when Niall Whitty became the first to tackle the many unanswered questions left by the case law. We do not know, for example, whether in Scotland the alternative to enrichment must be one which is practically, as opposed to theoretically, available to the impoverished party. We do not know how far the impoverished party, or indeed the court, must search for an alternative remedy before launching an enrichment claim. Is it only necessary to look for a remedy against the enriched party, or must possible remedies against a third party (or indeed fourth and fifth parties and beyond) be taken into account as well? Again, we do not know whether the enrichment claim must avoid being a "fraud on the law", or a circumvention of other rules of law such as prescription and the law of evidence (*Bennett v Carse* might suggest not but as an Outer House decision it can scarcely be determinative of the question.). What may perhaps be said is that subsidiarity is most likely to be deployed where enrichment has been imposed upon a person without consent, in order to ensure that solutions to difficulties are sought through due legal process rather than by way of self-help. Sometimes that may involve specific implement of a contractual obligation, and it may be of some importance here that specific implement is an entitlement in Scots law, albeit subject to a degree of control by the court.[118]

Daniel Visser has argued that "to recognise a general action which is subsidiary to the currently existing actions is probably the safest route for any jurisdiction newly introducing a general action".[119] His discussion is directed principally at the relationship between the general action and any more specific enrichment actions recognised in a system, and Louisiana has clearly

---

118   See L J Macgregor, "Specific implement in Scots law", in J Smits, D Haas and G Hesen (eds), *Specific Performance in Contract Law: National and Other Perspectives* (2008) 67.
119   Visser, *Unjustified Enrichment* (n 6) 58; see also his contribution "Unjustified enrichment", in J M Smits (ed), *Elgar Encyclopaedia of Comparative Law* (2006) 771.

followed this approach. In Scotland the issue is rather different. It is not so much a question of the co-existence of the general with the other actions as the takeover of the specific actions by a general principle in terms of which the whole system of enrichment law is to be explained and understood. This context means that subsidiarity becomes more about the relationship between unjustified enrichment and other branches of law such as contract. Here, as Visser remarks, "the debate around subsidiarity is really about the role that a legal system wants to give to unjustified enrichment".[120] With regard to contract, it is not simply that the presence of one justifies an enrichment, while the absence of a contract makes an enrichment recoverable. It may be that the principle against unjustified enrichment at most informs the response which contract law makes to situations such as partially performed contracts, whether the partial performance comes about as a result of non-performance by one or both parties or through supervening external circumstances. Or it may be that such situations become the province of the general action, since contract law's focus is on the fulfilment of the performance or expectation interest and is therefore to be seen as reaching its limits in cases where that cannot happen.

Even more complex is the situation where the contract is between not the impoverished and the enriched parties, but between one or other of them and a third party – the problem of indirect enrichment. Visser observes that subsidiarity is only a relevant concept in this context if the law states that a party may raise an enrichment claim only after the possibility of gaining satisfaction from its contractual partner has been exhausted; if the rule is instead to the effect that only one of the possible actions is ever allowed, it is one of alternativity rather than subsidiarity.[121] It seems – and the Louisiana law rather confirms this – that it may be better to tackle the problem of indirect enrichment by asking whether the gain of the enriched party is really at the expense of the loss-maker or, putting it another way, whether the loss of the impoverished party is without legal justification or cause. In entering any contract, a party takes a risk, in particular that of the insolvency or untrustworthiness of the other party; the law of unjustified enrichment, as distinct from, say, the institution of the guarantee or the rules of relief, is not to be a means of avoiding the risks inherent in contractual relationships. Visser argues accordingly that the "right approach to any multi-party situation is … to apply the basic elements of enrichment in each case", while identifying

---

120 Visser, *Unjustified Enrichment* (n 6) 57 note 281; Visser, "Unjustified enrichment" (n 119) 772.
121 Visser, *Unjustified Enrichment* (n 6) 57 note 281; Visser, "Unjustified enrichment" (n 119) 772.

which of a range of policy factors is the most relevant to the facts in hand.[122] This approach has the merit of maintaining the basic coherence of the law's general principles while linking them firmly to appropriate policy considerations. At present, it is suggested, Louisiana law is closer to this model than is Scots law.

Finally, we may ask what, if any, light this comparison of Louisiana and Scotland throws on the nature of mixed legal systems. Unjustified enrichment is, as indicated at the outset of this chapter, a hallmark of the Civilian dimension in a mixed system, while the absence of any developed concept in Common Law systems meant that the opportunity for mixing was relatively slight. In Scotland the most visible signs of Common Law influence were the error in law bar to recovery of which the law rid itself in *Morgan Guaranty v Lothian Regional Council* in 1994, and some tendency to equate the *conditio causa data causa non secuta* with failure of consideration,[123] while in Louisiana the notions of "waiver of tort" and *quantum meruit* were applied in claims for what a German-influenced Scots lawyer would see as cases of unjustified takings and restitution after breach of contract respectively.[124] But with the possible exception of the error in law bar in Scotland, none of these examples affected the fundamental character of enrichment law in either system; and indeed, just as Scotland has given up the error in law rule, so Louisiana has moved away from a Common Law to a Civil Law understanding of the notion of *quantum meruit*.

Much more significant to the shape of the two systems is the kind of Civilian influence to which each of them has at different times been exposed. The French influence has been decisive for Louisiana and has remained so through successive revisions of the Code. The same French influence played its part in the nineteenth-century reshaping of Scots enrichment law, but that reshaping took the form of juristic writing based on case law rather than a Code, and so lay open to the rethinking and recasting on German lines which ultimately took place in the late twentieth century and is still going on early in the twenty-first. There were several ironies in that development.[125] The catalyst for change was the writings of an English lawyer who happened at that time also to be the Professor of Civil Law at Edinburgh University and looked at Scots law mainly with a view to forcing English law to recognise unjust enrichment as a source of obligation. Subsequently in one of the

---

122 Visser, *Unjustified Enrichment* (n 6) 193-217.
123 MacQueen and Sellar, "Unjust enrichment" (n 61) 317-318; R Evans-Jones, "Unjust enrichment, contract and the third reception of Roman law in Scotland" (1993) 109 LQR 663.
124 See Nicholas, "Unjustified enrichment" (n 1) 51-62.
125 For what follows, see MacQueen, "Peter Birks and Scots enrichment law" (n 3).

key House of Lords cases in which English law made that move, *Woolwich Building Society v Inland Revenue Commissioners*,[126] the two Scottish judges dissented, forcing other Scots lawyers to begin at last to look at their law in a critical and comparative way. So England played its part in the Scottish enrichment revolution. Mixing, it may be concluded, is a more subtle and contingent process than one of merely borrowing or transplanting, and much depends upon the basic formal structures of the mixing system as well as upon persons, opportunities and the system's open-ness to change.

126 [1993] AC 70.

12 Causation as an Element of Delict/Tort in Scots and Louisiana Law

Martin A Hogg

A. INTRODUCTION
(1) Procedural differences between the two jurisdictions
(2) Analytical differences between the two jurisdictions
B. SEPARATION OF CAUSE-IN-FACT FROM MATTERS AFFECTING THE SCOPE OF LIABILITY ("LEGAL CAUSATION")
C. CAUSE-IN-FACT
D. SCOPE OF LIABILITY
(1) Louisiana
(2) Scotland
E. SPECIFIC CAUSAL DIFFICULTIES
(1) Indeterminate causation generally
(2) Asbestos-related injuries generally
(3) Pleural plaques
F. CONCLUSIONS

A. INTRODUCTION

At first glance, causation may not seem an obvious subject of enquiry for a comparative work on Scots and Louisiana private law. There is a tendency to assume that every jurisdiction takes the same approach to causation, and that in consequence there is little point to comparative causal analysis. As will be seen in this chapter, while this assumption may be true of the basic principles of causation, specific jurisdictional developments in Scotland and Louisiana have led to the adoption of different analyses in respect of certain causal problems, even if the result turns out to be the same in some of the problems. Causation may also seem an unusual topic for examination in that, unlike the other subjects covered in this volume, the Louisiana Civil Code contains no provision relating to causation, the law resting upon, and having been entirely developed by, the common law. This non-legislative approach to causation is found in Scotland too. Does this suggest that neither jurisdiction considers causation an especially important part of the delictual analysis? Not at all. Both jurisdictions view the causal issue as a crucial stage in a delict/tort action, and one to which their highest courts have turned their attention at various points. Indeed, although Scotland is a small jurisdiction, it was two Scottish appeals to the House of Lords, *Wardlaw v Bonnington Castings*[1] and *McGhee v National Coal Board*,[2] which were largely instrumental in defining the approach of courts across the United Kingdom to causation-in-fact in the twentieth century.[3] Such judicial inventiveness has also been a hallmark of the Louisiana courts, which developed the so called "duty-risk" analysis to the attribution of responsibility to causes-in-fact at a time when the Common Law jurisdictions of the United States were still languishing in the juristic darkness of "proximate cause" thinking. Causation can thus be argued to be a topic worthy of inclusion in this volume both because of interesting jurisdictional peculiarities of approach as well as because it is a topic which shows the courts of the two systems at their creative best, even if, as is suggested below, that judicial creativeness has been somewhat selective and is in need of further exercise.

In order to understand the way in which causation as a requirement of the analysis of delict/tort is treated in both Scotland and Louisiana, it is useful at the outset to appreciate certain important procedural as well as analytical differences between the two systems in their general treatment of actions for negligence.

(1) Procedural differences between the two jurisdictions

A number of procedural differences between the two jurisdictions are worthy of comment. Firstly, there is the theoretical distinction between a system like Scotland, which recognises the doctrine of judicial precedent (*stare decisis*), and one like Louisiana, where courts are not generally bound by individual judicial decisions but will show deference to an established body of case law (*jurisprudence constante*). Such a distinction can be overstated, however. In fact, Louisiana does recognise what may be called "vertical" stare decisis, that is, the doctrine that inferior courts are bound by the jurisprudence of the Supreme Court, even if this extends only to a single decision of that

---

1 1956 SC (HL) 26; [1956] AC 613.
2 1973 SC (HL) 37; 1973 SLT 14.
3 In particular, through development of the "material contribution" and "material increase in risk" tests in causation-in-fact, discussed below.

court on an issue.[4] Furthermore, it seems clear that Louisiana's *jurisprudence constante* approach has permitted several established causal rules to become generally accepted within the law. These judicially recognised doctrines are important, given that the idea of causation is not explained in any way in the Civil Code.[5] One should not, therefore, overplay the significance of the *stare decisis/jurisprudence constante* divide.

Secondly, negligence cases are for the most part disposed of in Louisiana by way of jury trial, in Scotland by way of a judge sitting alone. It is usually impossible to know what juries thought about issues of fact, including the question of precisely how causation-in-fact was established (or not) on the facts of a case. To be sure, we have the interrogatories, or instructions to the jury as they are styled in Scotland, given by the judge, which explain to some extent what the court's view of the idea of causation-in-fact entails, but we do not have reasoning explaining how causal doctrines were applied by the jury to the facts of the case. The prime role of such interrogatories in the process of determination of a case make it vitally important that these are framed correctly by the judge. There has been much academic writing on how such interrogatories ought to be framed.[6] Inevitably, different understandings of the law of tort have impacted upon views as to how a judge ought to approach the exercise of drawing up interrogatories.

Thirdly, and tempering to some extent the frustrating absence of written determination of the facts which more frequent use of jury trials creates, both matters of fact and law may be reviewed by Louisiana courts.[7] In Scotland, *per contra*, findings of fact are very rarely disturbed by civil appeal courts. It is startling to a Scots lawyer in just how many negligence cases Louisiana

---

4 See further V Palmer (ed), *Mixed Jurisdictions Worldwide: The Third Legal Family* (2001) at 283 f.

5 CC art 2315(A) states: "Every act whatever of man which causes damage to another obliges him by whose fault it happened to repair it." Other provisions use the language of "occasion" rather than fault, for instance CC art 2316 which states: "Every person is responsible for the damage he occasions not merely by his act, but by his negligence, his imprudence, or his want of skill." No practical effect seems to turn on which of the terms "cause" or "occasion" is adopted.

6 D Robertson considers this question at length in "The vocabulary of negligence law: Continuing causation confusion" (1997) 58 La LR 1. He cites, for instance, the case of *Bannerman v Bishop* 688 So 2d 570 (La App 2 Cir 1996) a road traffic injuries case in which, in his view, the fact that a rehearing was needed may have been due to poor interrogatories being given at the first hearing. Robertson favours separate instructions being given in relation to cause-in-fact and "legal cause", on which point T C Galligan, "Cats or gardens: Which metaphor explains negligence?" (1997) 58 La LR 35, agrees.

7 The Louisiana Constitution states that "the jurisdiction of the supreme court in civil cases extends to both law and facts" (art 5 § 5(C)). The same jurisdiction applies to other courts of appeal (art 5 § 10 (B)).The effect in Louisiana of this appellate jurisdiction has been to reduce the importance of trial by jury, since the upper court judges can more easily review the errors of fact finding. Counsel may therefore not choose trial by jury to begin with.

appeal courts are willing to re-open questions of fact, or indeed to order a rehearing of the case after an initial hearing and determination.

Lastly, it is worth mentioning that, in Louisiana, a distinction is made between cases of negligence per se, which involve breach of a statute, and cases of ordinary negligence, that is of non-statutory negligence. In the latter, negligence must be proven as a failure to show reasonable care under a common law duty of care. In the former, breach of the statute is presumed to amount to negligence. Such a distinction between negligence per se and ordinary negligence is not made in Scotland.[8] Some Scottish (or United Kingdom) statutes impose strict liability and some fault-based liability. In those which impose fault-based liability, negligence must still be proven by the pursuer.[9]

(2) Analytical differences between the two jurisdictions

The issue of analytical differences between the way in which delictual, in particular negligence, actions are conceived in the two jurisdictions is relevant for a discussion on causation as there are a number of theories as to how causation should be fitted in to the negligence equation. Competing theories of negligence have been supported by different academics and applied by different courts at various times. The level of theoretical discussion of these different theories of negligence liability among the Louisiana judiciary is startling to the Scots lawyer. One does not find in the Scots cases a serious ongoing debate as to a choice of theories of negligence (or delict in general) which courts might apply.

In Scotland, the accepted judicial view is, broadly, that there was a pre-*Donoghue* way of understanding the general action for reparation in delict, based upon the twin ideas of fault and harm, and a post-*Donoghue* approach based upon duty of care, negligence, causation, and harm (or damage). In the post-*Donoghue* case law there have in addition been noticeable, and essentially UK-wide, shifts in general judicial delictual policy over time, principally:

(i)   1970s/early 1980s expansionist attitude to liability based upon the idea that foreseeability of harm should lead to liability unless some other factor mitigated against imposing it;[10]

(ii) a mid/late 1980s onwards policy that delictual liability should expand only incrementally, by analogy with existing recognised categories; and

---

8 However in Scotland (as in Louisiana) some circumstances give rise to a presumption of negligence under the doctrine of *res ipsa loquitur.*

9 See, e.g., the Occupiers' Liability (Scotland) Act 1960.

10 A policy which reached its apogee in *Anns v Merton London Borough Council* [1978] AC 278.

(iii) a further policy, following the decision of the House of Lords in *Caparo v Dickman*[11] in 1990, that foreseeability of harm alone will be insufficient to establish a duty of care in many types of action (especially those involving pure economic loss), but rather the demonstration of "proximity" (a close relationship between the parties) will also be required in such cases, as well as a demonstration that imposition of a duty is consistent with considerations of justice, fairness and reasonableness.

These shifts in policy have, as a result of the operation of *stare decisis*, taken effect across the courts generally (with perhaps a few maverick exceptions). Thus, the continuing debates which one sees among the Louisiana bench on the preferred model of tort[12] are missing from judicial considerations in Scotland, although such debates continue to take place among the academic community.

Each of the competing models of tort in Louisiana shares certain common-alities, principally an understanding that the elements in the tortious equation include at least the following stages:

(i)   proof that the defendant's substandard conduct was a cause-in-fact of the plaintiff's injuries (the cause-in-fact element);
(ii)   proof that the defendant's conduct failed to conform to the appropriate standard (the breach element);
(iii) proof that the defendant had a duty to conform his conduct to a specific standard (the duty element);
(iv)   proof that the defendant's substandard conduct was a legal cause of the plaintiff's injuries (the scope of liability or scope of protection element); and
(v)   proof of actual damage (the damages element).[13]

These basic elements of the negligence analysis are also shared by Scots Law, although some of the terminology traditionally used to describe them differs from the Louisiana terms, and two of the stages are usually conflated. The typical Scottish approach is to analyse a negligence case by considering the following elements:

(i)   the existence of a duty of care on the part of the defender towards the pursuer (the duty of care element);
(ii)   breach of that duty of care by the defender (the standard of care or breach element);

---

11 [1990] 2 AC 605.
12 Robertson has identified six models, viz: (i) a Keetonian model (based upon the theories of Prosser & Keeton); (ii) a Cardozo model; (iii) a Leon Green model; (iv) a Holmsian model; (v) a "judicial legislator" model; and (vi) an "absorbing the breach inquiry into the duty issue" model, each of which is explained more fully in D Robertson, "Allocating authority among institutional decision makers in Louisiana state-court negligence and strict liability cases" (1997) 57 La LR 1079.
13 Per Kimball J, for the majority of the Supreme Court, in *Perkins v Entergy Corp et al* 782 So 2d 606 (La 2001). See, to similar effect, Robertson, n 12, at 1091.

(iii) proof that the defender's breach of duty was both a factual and a legal cause of the pursuer's injuries (the causation element); and

(iv) the injury/harm sustained must not be "too remote" from the harmful conduct (the remoteness of damages element).

The Scottish analysis thus considers cause-in-fact and so-called legal causation under a single causal umbrella, although the two enquiries may be, and preferably are, considered separately. It should also be noted that there is a tradition in Scotland of further breaking down the duty element into two subordinate questions: (a) whether the duty of care alleged was of a kind which is capable of arising, and (b) whether, in the specific circumstances of the case, the injury was of a kind which was too remote from the duty (the remoteness of injury issue). The terminology of "remoteness of injury", apart from being confusingly similar to that of the "remoteness of damages" under stage (iv), will be quite unfamiliar to Louisiana lawyers, who may justifiably wonder what purpose it serves. In fact, the issues of so-called legal causation and "remoteness of injury" seem to be in large part about the same thing, namely whether the type of harm which arose in the circumstances was of a kind for which the law should provide recovery (a normative question).

The Scottish analysis is far from unproblematic. Not only will it be argued later that a number of Scottish causal ideas require to be judicially overhauled, but the general approach to the other elements in the delictual equation might also be said to be in need of such an overhaul. In this respect, the Louisiana analysis seems, from an outsider's perspective, to have been more carefully considered and developed, although this may be more providential than by design.

B. SEPARATION OF CAUSE-IN-FACT FROM MATTERS AFFECTING THE SCOPE OF LIABILITY ("LEGAL CAUSATION")

In both jurisdictions there is recognition that causation-in-fact (that is, causation as it operates in the real world) and matters affecting the scope of liability for consequences (what has traditionally been called "legal causation") should be considered separately. Terminology, however, continues to confuse.

In general the following can be said:

(i) Scotland continues the tradition of bringing within the topic of "causation", widely drawn, the separate enquiries of causation-in-fact and matters affecting the scope of liability for consequences, referring to the latter as "legal causation".[14] There is a growing academic view that the bunching of

14 While there remains a greater tendency to adopt the language of legal causation in Scotland,

these two quite different enquiries under a general heading of causation is unhelpful and productive of confusion,[15] although this academic shift in opinion has yet to be reflected in judicial attitudes.[16]

(ii) Louisiana has for the most part abandoned the terminology of "legal cause", and has moved to a "duty/risk" analysis of matters affecting the scope of liability for consequences. The duty/risk approach asks whether the risk and the harm caused were within the scope of protection afforded by the duty breached.[17]

I have argued elsewhere,[18] along with others, that the use of the term "legal causation" is unhelpful, and masks essentially normative, policy-driven considerations.[19] The Louisiana preference for the language of "duty/risk" and "scope of liability" enables a clearer understanding of the policy nature of the scope of liability for consequences question. As was said in *Roberts v Benoit*,[20]

> The most critical issue in the instant case is whether the injury plaintiff sustained was within the contemplation of the duty discussed above. There is no "rule" for determining the scope of the duty. Regardless if stated in terms of proximate cause, legal cause, or duty, the scope of the duty inquiry is ultimately a question of policy as to whether the particular risk falls within the scope of the duty.

Such a clear policy base to this consideration is often lost sight of in Scotland, where the "legal cause" analysis typically involves consideration of the issue

---

the term has been used on occasion by the Louisiana courts, not always helpfully. One may note the comments of Sanders J in *Dixie Drive It Yourself* 242 La 471, 137 So 2d 298 (La 1962) who remarked (La 471 at 481-482) that "[t]here is no universal formula for the determination of legal cause. In the instant case it bifurcates into two distinct inquiries: whether the negligence of the obstructing driver was a cause-in-fact of the collision; and whether the defendants should be relieved of liability because of the intervening negligence of the driver of the Dixie truck." This comment seems to suggest a styling of the total causal enquiry as one of "legal cause", with causation-in-fact as one subset of this enquiry. Such an approach is not shared in other decisions or by Louisiana commentators in general.

15 See, for instance, R Wright, "Once more into the bramble bush: Duty, causal contribution, and the extent of legal responsibility" (2001) 53 Vanderbilt LR 1071; J Stapleton, "Unpacking causation", in P Cane and J Gardner (eds), *Relating to Responsibility* (2001) 145; M Hogg, "The role of causation in delict" 2005 JR 89; M Hogg, "Re-establishing orthodoxy in the realm of causation" (2007) 11 EdinLR 1.

16 In a public address given at a Conference on "Causation in the law", University of Birmingham, 28 April 2007, Lord Hoffmann, the leading British judge with an interest in causation, made it clear that he prefers an analysis by which all matters affecting both causation-in-fact and the scope of liability are analysed under the single head of (legal) causation, asserting that causation is always contextual to the discipline (such as law) in which it is applied. See, to similar effect, his earlier published remarks in "Causation" (2005) 121 LQR 592, itself the published text of a prior conference address.

17 See, for instance, Hall J in *Roberts v Benoit* 605 So 2d 1032 (La 1991) at 1051.

18 M Hogg, "The role of causation in delict" (2005) JR 89.

19 This argument is considered further below, at section D.

20 Per Hall J, 605 So 2d 1032 (La 1991) at 1044.

of whether a supervening cause (*novus actus interveniens*) has "broken the chain of causation" between the harm and the cause-in-fact under examination such as to exculpate that cause from any responsibility for the harm. The tenor of the language used in that consideration suggests a policy-free, scientific investigation, which in reality is not the case.

There is some debate among Louisiana commentators as to whether determination of the scope of the duty, and whether the risk and harm fall within the scope of that duty, should lie with the court or with the jury.[21] In Professor Robertson's view, scope of duty questions in common law negligence cases, while policy-based, are best left to juries, for the reason (in his view) that:[22]

> the rule whose scope of protection is tested by the legal cause inquiry comes … from the trier of fact itself. The rule's proper scope of protection is a "question of policy," all right. But it is the trier of fact's own policy.

To Scottish eyes this view – that it is, in effect, "the people" who decide the scope of duties of care – seems somewhat idealistic, deriving perhaps from a different conception of constitutional theory. A Scots lawyer would be more likely to say that common law duties imposed upon us by the law of delict derive from formulation of such by the courts, albeit with regard to the expectations of society at large. Robertson's view is not shared by other Louisiana commentators. Professor Crawford, referring to the policy approach enunciated in *Roberts v Benoit* in the earlier quotation, has argued that "it is well-recognized that questions of policy are for the court, while questions of fact are for the jury".[23] Professor Galligan, while agreeing that for the most part juries are the appropriate bodies to decide scope of protection questions, takes the view that, in a not inconsiderable number of cases, judges should feel free to decide upon the matter, noting that:[24]

> Louisiana, arguably more than any other state, has a rich and vibrant tradition, inspired by Wex Malone, such that it is appropriate for judges to decide the scope-of-duty issue. It seems a shame to abandon that tradition when it still has current meaning to many judges in many cases.

---

21 Art 1812 (C) of the Louisiana Code of Civil Procedure (CCP) states that "In cases to recover damages for injury, death, or loss, the court *at the request of any party* shall submit to the jury special written questions inquiring as to (1) Whether a party from whom damages are claimed, or the person for whom such party is legally responsible, was at fault, and, if so: (a) *Whether such fault was a legal cause of the damages*" (emphasis added). All that the CCP thus tells us is that in *some* cases the jury is to determine legal causation; this leaves the position in other cases undetermined.

22 D Robertson, "The vocabulary of negligence law: Continuing causation confusion" (1997) 58 La LR 1 at 20.

23 W Crawford, *Tort Law (Louisiana Civil Law Treatise*, vol 12) (2000) ch 1, para 1.16.

24 Galligan, "Cats or gardens" (n 6) at 61.

Galligan supports his argument by reference to a number of cases which were decided according to the so-called "Green-Malone" model of tort, under which scope of duty questions are a matter for the judge.[25]

This judge/jury debate is, of course, of somewhat limited importance for the Scottish legal system, where virtually no negligence cases are determined by way of jury trial. The Scottish judiciary exclusively determine the scope of duties of care, and thus the breach to which any harm must be causally linked.

C. CAUSE-IN-FACT

In both jurisdictions, in common with all other western legal systems, the basic test of causation-in-fact is the *sine qua non* or "but for" test. In both jurisdictions this test has been developed by the courts, for, while Louisiana possesses a Civil Code and Scotland does not, the former's codal provisions provide only that "[e]very act whatever of man that causes damage to another obliges him by whose fault it happened to repair the damage",[26] without specifying the test by which causation-in-fact is to be determined.

The operation of this test, by the use of counterfactual analysis, is well documented in other commentaries on causation.[27] So too is the inability of this basic test to provide an acceptable answer in a number of causally problematic scenarios, an inability which has prompted both Scotland and Louisiana to develop alternative (not wholly satisfactory) tests. Among such scenarios two archetypal situations are those where two or more antecedent causes combine to produce an outcome which could have been produced by any one of the causes operating alone (cases of so-called "over-determined" causation, such as the "double-hit hunters" cases),[28] and cases where a sole cause has produced an outcome but it is unclear which of a number of possible causes was the operative one (cases of indeterminate causation, such as the so-called "single-hit hunters" cases).[29] Both jurisdictions struggle to provide a clear analysis of how to approach such cases.

---

25 Galligan cites, inter alia, *Francisco v Joan of Arc Inc* 692 So 2d 598 (1997 La App), and *Tassin v State Farm Insurance Co* 692 So 2d 604 (1997 La App). He also cites in this respect what he calls "Louisiana's most famous Green/Malone duty/risk case", *Hill v Lundin & Associates Inc* 260 La 542, 256 So 2d 620 (1972), discussed below at section D.

26 CC Art 2315 (A). In failing to specify a specific test for causation, the Louisiana Code is similar to the French Code.

27 See, e.g., explanation of counterfactual analysis in Wright, Stapleton, or Hogg, n 15 above.

28 So-called by reference to the scenario of a plaintiff who is killed by bullets from two or more weapons, the impact of any of the bullets alone being sufficient to have resulted in the death.

29 So-called by reference to the scenario of a plaintiff who is killed by a single weapon, but it is unclear which of a number of possible weapons was responsible.

In order to deal, it is said, with cases falling within the first of these two types (over-determined outcomes), the Louisiana courts have developed an alternative test to the *sine qua non* test, namely the "substantial factor" test. One asks, in applying this test, whether the defendant's conduct was a substantial factor in bringing about the outcome. This appears to mean (on one view, and there are several) whether the conduct made a significant contribution to the outcome. Problematically, however, there has been a tendency to employ this test not merely in cases of over-determined outcomes but generally in cases where more than one antecedent factor (whether occurring concurrently or consecutively) is considered a potential cause-in-fact of an outcome. Its use in such cases of multiple, but not over-determined, causation, may be seen in a number of decisions of the Louisiana courts.[30] It is difficult to see what assistance the substantial factor test may be thought to provide to courts in cases other than those of over-determined causation, or indeed why "but for" cannot provide a satisfactory answer to such cases. As the reporter to the Tentative Draft of the *Restatement (Third) of Torts* put it:[31]

> With the sole exception of multiple sufficient causes, "substantial factor" provides nothing of use in determining whether factual cause exists ... Recognition that a factual cause does not have to be the sole cause of harm ... obviates any need for substantial factor as a test for causation. Indeed, the substantial-factor standard is no better, and perhaps worse, than but-for in avoiding the misconception that a single cause must be found for an outcome: the key appreciation is that any cause need only be one of many, whether one uses but-for or substantial-factor language, and the latter may lead a jury erroneously to believe that it must search for a single or most significant factor.

This criticism is well made. Recognising that a "but for" cause may contribute to harm, without its having been necessary for the harm to have occurred at all, is surely sufficient to deal with cases where a cause is not necessary for an outcome but can be shown to have contributed to a portion of the overall harm caused. This is recognised in Scots law by the recognition that to be a cause-in-fact, a factor need not have been the sole cause of an outcome, but merely have materially contributed to that outcome.[32]

Whatever the merits of employing substantial factor in cases of over-determined causation (and I have argued elsewhere that the NESS test of

---

30 See, e.g., *Dixie Drive It Yourself v American Beverage* 242 La 471, 137 So 2d 298 (1962); *Roberts v Benoit* 605 So 2d 1032 (La 1991); *Perkins v Entergy* 782 So 2d 606 (La 2001); *Andry v Murphy Oil* 935 So 2d 239 (La 2006); *Thibodeaux v Stonebridge LLC* 873 So 2d 755 (La 2004); *Toston v Pardon* 874 So 2d 791 (La 2004).

31 *Restatement (Third) of Torts: Liability for Physical Harm* (Basic Principles) (Tentative Draft no 2, 25 March 2002) § 26, cmt j.

32 *Wardlaw v Bonnington Castings* 1956 SC (HL) 26, [1956] AC 613.

causation-in-fact would be better suited to solving such cases),[33] or indeed in multiple factor cases in general (where "but for" seems perfectly capable of dealing with many of the cases), its employment in the second common causally problematic case, that of causal indeterminacy, is even more troublesome. A good recent example of the substantial factor test being brought to play in such a case of indeterminacy – where the court was unsure, using the "but for" test, which one of (or perhaps several of) a number of possible causes had produced an injury – is the decision of the Fourth Circuit of the Louisiana Court of Appeal in *Andry v Murphy Oil*.[34] The case concerned the complex events leading up to an explosion at an oil refinery, beginning with a lightning strike and followed by attempted repairs undertaken by employees both of the oil company (Murphy) and of an energy company (Entergy). Applying substantial factor analysis, Tobias J said of the question whether the actions of the employees of the energy company had been a cause-in-fact of the explosion:[35]

> We find that the trial court had sufficient evidence to find that the negligence of Entergy's employees played so important a role in producing the explosion and fire that responsibility should be imposed on Entergy, even if we cannot say definitely that the harm would not have occurred "but for" its employees actions.

This is a somewhat problematic statement. If the behaviour of Entergy's employees was not to be considered a "but for" cause of the injury, it is unclear precisely how the court saw their behaviour as playing "so important a role" in the explosion that it was a cause of it. It may be that the court felt intuitively that the actions of the defendant's employees must have been important to the outcome, and thus inferred as much,[36] without being able to furnish a clear statement as to the precise basis on which causal connection was established, but, if so, adoption of the concept of substantial factor merely masks the judicial reasoning. If this was indeed simply a case of an intuitive judicial sense that a cause must have contributed to an outcome, it could be said to bear comparison with the approach of the House of Lords

33 The NESS test asks whether a cause-in-fact was a Necessary Element for the Sufficiency of a set of antecedent conditions Sufficient for the occurrence of the outcome (the capitalised letters explaining the acronym NESS): see further Hogg, articles at n 15 above.

34 935 So 2d 239 (La App 4 2006).

35 At 259.

36 In fact, Tobias J, having just stated that but for causation in relation to the behaviour of Entergy was not established, goes on to state (at 259) that "Certainly, all three elements, namely the switching errors [the behaviour of Entergy's employees], the defective valve, and relighting efforts [the behaviour of Murphy's employees], were necessary components leading to the explosion and fire." If that is so, then the behaviour of Entergy's employees *was* a *sine qua non* of the explosion. In this respect, the analysis of Tobias J seems somewhat confused.

in the Scottish appeal *Wardlaw v Bonnington Castings*,[37] which established causation-in-fact on the basis of the defender's "material contribution" to an injury, even though the evidence supporting such a material contribution seems to have been inferred rather than demonstrably proven.[38]

If the court in *Andry* was indeed making such an inference of causal connection, a comparison might also be drawn with the approach adopted in Louisiana personal injury cases where plaintiffs are permitted to make use of the so-called "Housley presumption" in establishing causal connection.[39] This rebuttable presumption holds that[40]

> a medical condition producing disability is presumed to have resulted from an accident if, before the accident, the injured person was in good health, but shortly after the accident, the disabling condition manifested itself – providing that the medical evidence shows there to be a reasonable possibility of causal connection between the accident and the disabling condition. In order to defeat this presumption, the defendant must show some other particular incident caused the injury.

This expression of the Housley presumption is noteworthy in its reference to the plaintiff's demonstration of a "reasonable possibility" of causal connection between harm and medical condition, which is not the same as actually demonstrating such causal connection. So long as this reasonable possibility of causal connection can be shown, the burden of proof will then be transferred to the defendant. In a case in which the presumption was applied,[41] it was held applicable because the medical condition (a lumbar hernia following a traffic accident) was capable of arising after the type of accident in question, and because of a lack of any other realistic alternative cause of the injury. This sort of reasoning arguably equates to what the court in *Andry* was doing, even though the *Housley* presumption was inapplicable in *Andry* given that the injury caused was not the subsequent development of a medical condition.

The Scottish courts never explicitly make use of a *Housley*-type presumption, and would say if asked that the burden of proving causation (and not of simply showing a reasonable possibility of causal connection) always rests on

---

37 1956 SC (HL) 266, 1956 SLT 135.

38 See M Jones, *Medical Negligence* (2003), who comments (at para 5-020) of the decision: "the courts were willing to draw an *inference* of fact that there had been a material contribution when it was in reality impossible to say whether there had been any such contribution".

39 After its formulation in *Housley v Cerise* 579 So 2d 973 (La 1991). The presumption was applied recently in *Michelle Detraz v Victor Lee D/B/A Virgin Nails* 950 So 2d 557 (La 2007), a decision of the Louisiana Supreme Court in which an original finding in fact by the jury that causation had not been made out by the plaintiff was reinstated on appeal.

40 As summarised by Victory J in *Michelle Detraz v Victor Lee D/B/A Virgin Nails* 950 So 2d 557 (La 2007) at 560.

41 *Marlo Dabog v John Deris* 625 So 2d 492 (La 1993).

the pursuer. Nevertheless, they may arguably be achieving a similar result by finding for the pursuer in a case where a negligent act, capable of resulting in a harm, is indeed followed by such harm, albeit that an unknown alternative factor might instead have caused the harm. In reaching such a conclusion, however, they will, where loss of a chance analysis is not employed, justify their decision by stating that the presence of the antecedent operative factor under examination must be taken to have made a material contribution to the outcome. Such was the reasoning in the *Wardlaw* decision, referred to above.

Substantial factor can thus, in some Louisiana cases, be equated to the Scots idea of material contribution. In other cases, however, where a substantial factor has "played an important role" in an outcome, the Louisiana courts seem to come close to regarding it as having "materially increased the risk of injury". A case in point is *Roberts v Benoit*,[42] which pre-dates *Andry*. In discussing whether the negligence of the Sheriff's Department was a cause-in-fact of an injury sustained when a firearm was discharged by an improperly promoted and poorly trained deputy sheriff (Benoit), Cole J said (on a rehearing):[43]

> It is likely that this accident might have occurred had Benoit, who already owned a weapon, never been commissioned. Thus, it is impossible to say with any degree of certainty, "but for" the sheriff's conduct, this accident would not have happened. Nonetheless, inasmuch as the sheriff's actions can be said to have appreciably enhanced the chance of the accident occurring, they are a cause-in-fact of the accident.

Here substantial factor is equated with increasing the risk of injury, an explanation which immediately draws comparison with the analysis of the House of Lords in the Scottish appeal *McGhee v NCB*[44] that a material contribution to an injury might (in a limited class of case) be constituted by a factor which materially increases the risk of that injury occurring. This approach was recently recast by the House of Lords in *Barker v Corus*[45] in terms of liability for loss of a chance.

This risk-creation usage of substantial factor as an alternative test to "but for" in some cases of causal indeterminacy was however criticised in the commentary to the draft *Restatement of Torts Third*, which argued that:[46]

---

42 605 So 2d 1032 (La 1991).

43 At 1052.

44 1973 SC (HL) 37.

45 *Barker v Corus (UK) plc* [2006] UKHL 20; [2006] 2 AC 572.

46 *Restatement (Third) of Torts: Liability for Physical Harm* (Basic Principles) (Tentative Draft No 2, 25 March 2002) § 26, cmt j.

> To be sure, courts may decide, based on the availability of evidence and on policy grounds, to modify or shift the burden of proof for factual cause, as they have when multiple tortfeasors act negligently toward another but only one causes the harm ... Courts may, for similar reasons, decide to permit recovery for unconventional types of harm, such as a lost opportunity to avoid an adverse outcome. Nevertheless, the substantial-factor rubric tends to obscure, rather than to assist, explanation and clarification of the basis of these decisions. The element that must be established by whatever standard of proof is the but-for or necessary-condition standard ...

The decision in *Barker* that causal indeterminacy in such cases is best addressed by a finding of loss of a chance, at least answers this criticism and avoids the unorthodox approach previously taken in *McGhee* that risk creation could be equated to material contribution.

The complexity of the substantial factor debate does not end there, as "substantial factor" has in fact been employed in some decisions not as an alternative test of causation-in-fact but simply as a synonym for a necessary, or "but for", cause. This only serves to obfuscate matters further. Such synonymous application is found in the leading Louisiana case on *sine qua non* causation, *Dixie Drive It Yourself System v American Beverage*.[47] The case concerned a road traffic accident caused when the defendant's vehicle, which had negligently been parked on the highway, was struck from behind by a second vehicle owned by the plaintiff. One of the questions for the court was whether the defendant's actions had been a cause-in-fact of the harm, a question answered by the Supreme Court in the affirmative. In relation to the issue of causation-in-fact, Sanders J stated:[48]

> Negligent conduct is a cause-in-fact of harm to another if it was a substantial factor in bringing about that harm. Under the circumstances of this case, the negligent conduct is undoubtedly a substantial factor in bringing about the collision if the collision would not have occurred without it. A cause-in-fact is a necessary antecedent.

While the reference to a cause-in-fact's being a necessary antecedent is a clear reference to the *sine qua non* test, a test given a strong foundation in this decision, the equation of *sine qua non* with the idea of substantial factor confuses and adds nothing to the analysis. Nonetheless, the Supreme Court of Louisiana still continues to issue judgments in which substantial factor and *sine qua non* are used interchangeably. In the recent case of *Toston v Pardon*[49] the Supreme Court summed up the causal enquiry thus:[50]

---

47 242 La 471, 137 So 2d 298 (La 1962).
48 At 482.
49 874 So 2d 791 (La 2004).
50 At 799.

A party's conduct is a cause-in-fact of the harm if it was a substantial factor in bringing about the harm ... The act is a cause-in-fact in bringing about the injury when the harm would not have occurred without it ... While a party's conduct does not have to be the sole cause of the harm, it is a necessary antecedent essential to an assessment of liability.

Given the multifarious roles which substantial factor has been asked to play, one is forced to conclude that the phrase does not seem susceptible of any clear definition. It has been used as a synonym for "but for"; it seems to have been used to mean something similar to what Scottish courts have called material contribution – a factor as a contributing but non-necessary cause; and it has been used to indicate a factor which increases the risk of injury occurring, as in the Scottish material increase in risk concept. This suggests that the Louisiana courts are somewhat at sea in their analysis of causation-in-fact. "Substantial factor" has taken on the appearance of a shibboleth, produced on any occasion when causal problems arise, allowing a court simply to act intuitively without recourse to any clear explanation of the basis for its decision. Adoption of a more robust test would not only give clearer guidance to the courts in determination of causation-in-fact, but would allow clearer analysis to be made by jurists. In Scotland, while the material contribution test is clearly established, and *Barker v Corus* has rescued factual causation from a dubious increase-in-risk approach, the courts too struggle to analyse the hard cases in a clear and principled way.

As the present time, both the Scottish and Louisiana courts seem hesitant to develop the rules in relation to proving causation-in-fact in ways which reflect academic development of the law in this field. This may be because courts are timid of a subject perceived as full of logical pitfalls. If that is so, then the legal academic community needs to convince the judiciary that a more developed analysis of causation-in-fact is both possible and practicable.

D. SCOPE OF LIABILITY

In both jurisdictions the terminology of legal causation remains in use, although Louisiana is demonstrating a growing preference for abandoning it in favour of the terminology of "scope of liability". I have previously argued, in common with other commentators, that Scots (and indeed English) Law would be immeasurably improved were it to follow such a revisionist course. The language of legal causation is apt to confuse, suggesting as it does that what are essentially normative, policy issues should be treated as if they were logical matters of cause and effect.[51] The Scottish courts, however, unlike those of Louisiana, have not decisively broken with the language of "legal causation": the legacy of Hart and Honoré[52] remains, in this respect, influential in Scots legal thinking.

(1) Louisiana

In Louisiana the language of "proximate cause" to describe those causes-in-fact deemed sufficiently important to attract responsibility for harm, language traditionally popular in Common Law state jurisdictions, is absent from the modern law, a development which has been generally welcomed by the academic and judicial community alike. The move away from proximate cause terminology, a shift now also gaining ground in Common Law state jurisdictions,[53] began with the *Dixie Drive It Yourself* case.[54] The Court of Appeal had expressly adopted proximate cause analysis:[55]

> Whatever negligence may have been involved on the part of the driver of the defendant vehicle had become passive and too remote to be a contributing cause of the accident. The sole proximate cause thereof was the negligence of the driver of the plaintiff truck. The defendant is not liable because the negligence of its employee-driver was not a proximate cause of the accident.

Such language, however, was specifically criticised by the Supreme Court, as well as the idea that the party who had the last opportunity to avoid an injury ought to be held solely responsible for it. It commented:[56]

> The thrust of this formulation of law is toward relieving all but the last wrongdoer of liability to an innocent victim in torts involving intervening negligence. This restrictive doctrine finds little support in legal theory. We do not subscribe to the formulation as applied in this case.

The Supreme Court emphasised that the proper consideration of the significance of possible causes was instead to be found in a duty/risk analysis, Sanders J commenting:[57]

---

51 See Hogg, "The role of causation in delict", also Stapleton and Wright (all at n 15 above).
52 H Hart and T Honoré, *Causation in the Law*, 2nd edn (1985).
53 Influential in this respect are the current draft *Restatement* provisions which have abandoned "proximate cause" terminology in favour of "scope of liability" terminology: see *Restatement (Third) of Torts: Liability for Physical Harm* (Proposed Final Draft no 1), ch 6 ("Scope of Liability"), "Special note on proximate cause". On the other hand, the US Supreme Court is still adopting the terminology of "proximate cause": see, e.g., its recent deployment in *Dura Pharmaceuticals Inc v Broudo* 544 US 336, 342 (2005).
54 See n 47 above.
55 128 So 2d 841 (La App 1961) per Samuel J at 843.
56 242 La 471 (La 1962) at 488.
57 242 La 471 (La 1962) at 488.

The essence of the present inquiry is whether the risk and harm encountered by the plaintiff fall within the scope of protection of the statute. It is a hazard problem. Specifically, it involves a determination of whether the statutory duty of displaying signal flags and responsibility for protecting traffic were designed, at least in part, to afford protection to the class of claimants of which plaintiff is a member from the hazard of confused or inattentive drivers colliding with stationary vehicles on the highway.

The decision in *Dixie Drive It Yourself* did not mark a clear-cut end to the use of proximate cause terminology. Five years later, in *Pierre v Allstate Insurance*,[58] the Supreme Court was still describing its conclusions in terms of "the primary direct and proximate cause of the accident" being the negligence of the driver of a vehicle.[59] Despite this hiccup, the rejection of "proximate cause" terminology laid down in *Dixie Drive It Yourself* was confirmed by the Louisiana Supreme Court in *Roberts v Benoit*, where the Court pointedly noted that "[t]he very term 'proximate cause' is fraught with confusion, as it has nothing to do either with cause or proximity".[60] Adding support to the view that the language of causation should be restricted to causation-in-fact alone, the Court observed that "[o]nce it is determined the conduct is a cause-in-fact of the injury, all causation inquiries are complete".[61]

The Louisiana courts have given further consideration to the scope of liability question through the idea that the matter may be tested by reference to "ease of association", in other words by asking whether the harm which befell the plaintiff is easily associated with the type of conduct engaged in by the defendant.[62] This doctrine stems from the important case of *Hill v Lundin*.[63] In that case, a maid fell over a ladder on the premises of her employer. The ladder belonged to a construction company doing work at the premises. Its employees had left the ladder standing against a wall. An unknown person subsequently placed the ladder on the ground. Although the maid had noticed the ladder on the ground, in her haste to stop a child of the family running over it, she tripped over the ladder and was injured. The maid sued the construction company. The Supreme Court held that the company was not liable for the maid's injuries. Barham J said:[64]

> The basic question, then, is whether the risk of injury from a ladder lying on the ground, produced by a combination of defendant's act and that of a third party,

58 257 La 471, 242 So 2d 821 (La 1971).
59 257 La 471 (La 1971) at 481.
60 605 So 2d 1032 (La 1991) at 1052.
61 605 So 2d 1032 (La 1991) at 1052.
62 See judgment of Cole J in *Roberts v Benoit* 605 So 2d 1032 (La 1991) at 1054.
63 260 La 542, 256 So 2d 620 (La 1972).
64 260 La 542 at 548-549; 256 So 2d 620 at 622.

is within the scope of protection of a rule of law which would prohibit leaving a ladder leaning against the house.

Foreseeability is not always a reliable guide, and certainly it is not the only criterion for determining whether there is a duty-risk relationship. Just because a risk may foreseeably arise by reason of conduct, it is not necessarily within the scope of the duty owed because of that conduct. Neither are all risks excluded from the scope of duty simply because they are unforeseeable. The ease of association of the injury with the rule relied upon, however, is always a proper inquiry.

How does one decide whether an injury can be "easily associated" with conduct? Foreseeability of the result appears in the eyes of the courts to play some part in the matter, but not by any means an exclusive role.[65] Even just considering the question of foreseeability, however, what does one have to foresee: is it that conduct is likely to cause an injury? Or that it is very likely so to do? And what considerations other than foreseeability are relevant, or may override that of foreseeability? More content requires to be given to the ease of association concept if it is to serve as a useful test.

There is no established equivalent to this ease of association analysis in Scotland, and it must be questionable whether such a single and somewhat vague concept can adequately address all the matters that a legal system would wish to consider when determining whether causes-in-fact are to be deemed sufficiently significant to attract liability.[66] Additionally, if as Professor Robertson argues, the ease of association idea is designed to answer the question whether the rule of law violated by the defendant was designed to protect the plaintiff's general class of persons against the harm the plaintiff suffered, the further problem arises that, in Scots Law at least, this is a question which, while doubtless affecting consideration of the traditionally styled "legal cause" issue, has also been thought appropriate for consideration under the earlier stage of analysis of the scope of the duty of care (especially the so-called "remoteness of injury" question, alluded to earlier). Deciding where, in the analysis of delict, to consider such policy questions has troubled Scots Law, so that there has been no single way of analysing these issues, as will now be seen.

(2) Scotland

While reliance upon the doctrine of "last opportunity" rejected in *Dixie Drive It Yourself* has also been departed from in Scotland, the phraseology

---

65 "Although ease of association encompasses the idea of foreseeability, it is not based on foreseeability alone" (*Roberts v Benoit* 605 So 2d 1032 (La 1991) per Hall J at 1045).

66 Stapleton, Wright and the present author, among others, have suggested a number of different considerations which ought properly to inform the scope of liability question in their respective legal systems (see literature cited at n 15).

of "proximate cause" is still encountered in the Scottish courts (although less frequently so than in England). Use has also been made in Scotland of similar terms such as "direct", "real" or "decisive" cause, or *causa causans* ("causing cause"), terminology which expresses a similar underlying idea.[67] While it is mostly in the pre-1980s case law that one finds references to "proximate cause" in the judgments,[68] the use of the term *causa causans* is still frequently encountered in the submissions of counsel and in judgments at all levels.[69]

The clearest Scottish example of reliance on proximate cause terminology in the twentieth-century case law is probably the famous decision of the House of Lords in *Grant v Sun Shipping Company Limited and Another*,[70] concerning liability for injuries sustained by a stevedore who fell through an uncovered hatch on a ship upon which he was working. The injured man sued both the shipowners, for their failure to fence off the uncovered hatch, and a company which had been carrying out repairs on the ship, the party responsible for having uncovered the hatch. In the Court of Session, it was held that "the true *causa causans* ... and the actual *causa proxima* was the extreme negligence of the pursuer himself",[71] whose case was consequently dismissed. The House of Lords overturned this decision, holding that both the shipowners and the ship repairers were liable for the man's injuries. One of the questions considered by the House of Lords was whether the failure of the shipowners to fence off the hatch was a *novus actus interveniens* between the negligence of the repairers and the injuries sustained by the pursuer. It is common for the Scottish courts to resolve the so-called legal causal question by asking whether, between the cause under enquiry and the harm suffered, a new, intervening cause, or *novus actus interveniens*, has arisen. Holding in this case that there was no *novus actus interveniens*, Lord Porter remarked:[72]

---

67 See further, for discussion of such terms, D Walker, *The Law of Delict in Scotland*, 2nd edn (2001) 207 f. Walker makes liberal use of the idea of proximate causation.

68 See, e.g., *Keenan v Rolls-Royce Ltd* 1969 SC 322; *Bruce v John Toole & Son (Cable Contractors) Ltd and others* 1969 SLT (Notes) 61; *Walker v Scottish & Newcastle Breweries Ltd* 1970 SLT (Sh Ct) 21; *O'Donnell v Murdoch McKenzie & Co Ltd* 1967 SC (HL) 63; *Hunter v Robert Baird & Sons and Others* 1962 SLT 166; *Linden v Ministry of Supply and Another* 1949 SLT (Notes) 59; *Boyle v The Corporation of Glasgow & Another* 1949 SC 254; *Hutson v Edinburgh Corporation* 1948 SC 668.

69 See, e.g., *McKie v Macrae* 2006 SLT 43; *Robb v Dundee City Council* 2002 SC 301; *McFarlane v Tayside Health Board* 1997 SLT 211, revd 1998 SC 389, revd in part 2000 SC (HL) 1; *Leeds Permanent Building Society v Walker Fraser & Steele* 1995 SLT (Sh Ct) 72; *Harvey v The Singer Manufacturing Co Ltd* 1960 SC 155.

70 1948 SC (HL) 73.

71 See the judgment of Lord Mackay at 81.

72 At 89.

I see no break in the chain of causation existing between the negligence of the second defenders [the ship repairers] and the subsequent accident. At the vital moment the hatch-covers were off and the light down. That negligence never ceased to operate nor were the second defenders entitled to rely upon someone afterwards coming to put it right … it was still their negligence which directly caused or contributed to the accident.

In considering whether an action or omission amounts to such a *novus actus intevrniens* it has typically been stated that the quality of the intervening conduct, in particular whether it was unforeseeable, unreasonable or unwarrantable, is a relevant consideration. This does not provide much by way of additional assistance, however. Like the concepts of proximate cause and *causa causans*, the doctrine of *novus actus interveniens* has been similarly criticised for suggesting that somehow the decision which of a number of causes-in-fact should attract liability is a neutral, causal question, when it is (or ought to be) an exercise largely based upon normative considerations.[73]

Does anything turn on the fact that, in the post-1980s Scottish cases, it has been mostly counsel who have employed the language of proximate cause rather than the judiciary?[74] For instance, in both *McFarlane v Tayside Health Board*[75] and *Sabri-Tabrizi v Lothian Health Board*,[76] the phrase was employed in counsels' submissions to the court but not by the judges. This might be thought to suggest that the concept of "proximate cause" has fallen out of favour with the Scottish bench. However, given the frequent judicial use of the similar notion of *causa causans*, it seems clear that the Scottish courts continue to adhere to a traditional view of causation as comprising both cause-in-fact as well as legal causation, and that they consider that the question of legal causation is properly addressed using causal language of some kind. In this respect, a clear distinction may be drawn with the scope of liability approach taken by the Louisiana courts, with its "ease of association" language, language which is not expressly causal but appears, as discussed earlier, to embody an underlying idea of foreseeability of result, among other unspecified considerations.

The Scottish approach is in need of reform. Such reform, if it is to happen, would best be accompanied by a wider reflection on when the various stages

---

73 See Hogg and Stapleton (n 15).

74 Use of the phrase has not been wholly confined to counsel: in *Bell v Lothiansure Ltd* 1993 SLT 421, an understanding between pursuer and defender that the phrase "arising from" in an insurance document meant "proximately caused by" was accepted without demur by the Inner House of the Court of Session, who then spent some time considering authorities on proximate causation.

75 1998 SC 389, reversing 1997 SLT 211, and revd in part by 2000 SC (HL) 1.

76 1998 SC 373.

of the delictual analysis are to be employed in specific cases. A new general theory of delict, based upon a proper understanding of the relationship between the constituent elements of a claim, is required. Until that happens, judges will remain unclear as to which of the elements is to be used to explain the decision in particular cases. It is unsurprising that, at the present time, the Court of Session finds itself having to remark in its determination of a negligence claim that:[77]

> the test to be applied has been expressed in various different ways. Sometimes the court has referred to the question of reasonable foreseeability, sometimes the court has referred to remoteness of damage, sometimes the court has asked whether there has been *novus actus interveniens*, and sometimes the court has looked for the *causa causans*.

Such uncertainty concerning the proper approach to the analysis of the facts of delictual claims ought to give rise to concern. There is a compelling case for development of a new academic consensus on the proper approach to the analysis of delict. While such an enterprise cannot be ventured in this paper, it may at least be said that the Louisiana consensus that causal language is inappropriate to the question of the significance of causes would make a good start for Scots law, even if its "ease of association" doctrine seems as yet an unproven and undeveloped way to advance matters.

E. SPECIFIC CAUSAL DIFFICULTIES

(1) Indeterminate causation generally

An indication of how Louisiana courts deal with some issues of causal indeterminacy has already been given earlier in this paper. It was seen that the substantial factor test has been employed not simply in cases of over-determined causation, but also on occasion in cases of multiple consecutive causes where it is unclear, on a "but for" basis, which of the antecedent factors has contributed to the outcome. This was the case in both *Andry v Murphy Oil* and *Roberts v Benoit*, in both of which the court expressed doubts that a finding of causation-in-fact would have been possible on a pure "but for" basis. In *Andry*, however, there were contradictory statements

---

77 The comments are those of Lord Justice Clerk Ross in *Bell v Scottish Special Housing Association* 1987 SLT 320 at 321E. To similar effect, albeit within a contractual context, are comments of Lord Reed in *Douglas Shelf Seven Ltd v Co-operative Wholesale Society Ltd and another* [2007] CSOH 53, who remarked (at para 599) that "[t]here are often different possible ways of rationalising restrictions on liability: lines can be drawn in terms of the scope of the obligation, or causation, or remoteness. The central problem is usually deciding where to draw the lines, rather than which conceptual route to follow."

from the bench indicating that "but for" causation was proven, so that the decision ought not to be taken as solidly establishing the use of substantial factor as a solution to any problem of indeterminacy. However, the adherence in *Benoit* to the idea that increasing the chances of injury is sufficient for establishing causation-in-fact does indicate a willingness to create a solution to a problem of causal indeterminacy. Nevertheless, *Benoit* has not created a substantial judicial shift in favour of the loosening of the "but for" requirement in cases of indeterminacy. There has been no adoption of a general test of material increase in the risk of injury which might be employed in defined and controlled circumstances, such as occurred in Scotland following *McGhee v NCB*. *Benoit* was unlikely to be a *McGhee*, as there was no attempt in the *Benoit* judgments to provide a coherent rationale for the loosening of the "but for" requirement; instead one senses that the result was driven by a specific policy of discouraging inappropriate appointments in the realm of law enforcement.

As described below in the specific context of asbestos liability, the Louisiana cases suggest that there is no appetite for developing any conceptual analysis to cope with indeterminate causality in general, other than by means of the recognition of a limited exception in respect of over-determined causation, an exception based upon the unhelpful and vague concept of substantial factor. Scotland, on the other hand, while failing adequately to provide a coherent test to deal with cases of over-determined causation, did choose to create a radical solution to indeterminate causation by developing the material increase in risk test. This has been subject to recent House of Lords' re-alignment in *Barker v Corus*, discussed below, such that material increase in risk as an alternative test of causation-in-fact has been recast as liability for loss of a chance. This is a solution which prefers permitting a claim for a different type of harm (a lost opportunity of avoiding harm) rather than a loosening of the orthodox rule that a causal connection must be shown between the wrongful behaviour and a real world harm.

(2) Asbestos-related injuries generally

Courts are only too aware of the complexities and varieties in asbestos litigation. As one Louisiana judge put it, "asbestos litigation is like a box of chocolates – the outer covering is familiar, but the taste inside is different, and one never knows what one is going to get".[78] One complexity of Louisiana law, not

---

78 *Hoerner v ANCO Insulations Inc* 812 So 2d 45 (La 2002) per Judge Steven Plotkin (of the Fourth Circuit) at 52.

present in the Scots law, is that claims by employees against employers for work-related injury fall within the regime of workers' compensation claims, a quite distinct category of law from negligence claims.[79] There have been a number of reported cases relating to asbestos exposure falling within this regime.[80] At the present time, Louisiana, unlike other states which have been preferred *fora* for asbestos plaintiffs,[81] has not adopted any legislative measures to limit asbestos claims (for instance, by requiring a present physical injury to be shown before a claim may be raised). The analytical treatment of asbestos-related injuries provides a clear area of contrast between the two jurisdictions, even if the result achieved is broadly the same.

In Scotland, in common with England, liability for divisible, dose-related asbestos injuries (pneumoconiosis, asbestosis) proceeds from the position that causation-in-fact must be shown on a traditional "but for" basis for a non-negligible portion of the injury before the party responsible for that portion may be found liable (solely and not *in solidum*) for such portion.[82] In relation to indivisible asbestos-related injuries (mesothelioma), liability *in solidum* was traditionally imposed for the totality of the injury upon all parties who caused more than a non-negligible exposure of the pursuer to asbestos.[83] That position was briefly altered, following the decision in *Barker*

---

79 The relevant legislation, which since 1952 has included occupational diseases like asbestosis, silicosis, dermatosis, and pneumoconiosis within its ambit, is found at La RS 23:10. It should be noted that so-called "take-home" claims, i.e. by the family of employees who have brought home noxious substances like asbestos into the family home, are not covered by workers' compensation legislation. Such take-home claims have increased in popularity since 2000: see, e.g., *Chaisson v Avondale Industries* 947 So 2d 171 (La App 2006). See further on the popularity of take-home claims, P M Hanlon and E Runyan Geise, "Asbestos reform – Past and future", *Mealey's Litigation Report: Asbestos*, April 2007, vol 22, part 5, 1 at 10-11.

80 See, e.g., *White v Johns-Manville Sales Corp* 416 So 2d 327 (La App 1982); *Howard v Johns-Manville Sales Corp* 420 So 2d 1190 (La App 1982); *Kramer v Johns-Manville Sales Corp* 459 So 2d 642 (La App 1984); *Carmadelle v Johns-Manville Sales Corp* 459 So 2d 621 (La App 1984); *McDonald v New Orleans Private Patrol* 569 So 2d 106 (La App 1990); *Atkinson v Celotex Corp* 633 So 2d 383 (La App 1994); *Adams v Asbestos Corporation Ltd* 914 So 2d 1177 (La App 2005).

81 Ohio, Texas and Florida are prime examples, accounting for 35% of all US asbestos claims in the period 1998-2000. Each of these states has adopted legislation to delimit the boundaries of asbestos claims: Ohio Rev Code Ann §§ 2307.91 to 2307.98 and 2502.02); Tex Civ Prac & Rem Code Ann §§ 16.0031 and 90.001 to 90.012); Fla Stat ch 774.201 to 774.209). See, for further commentary, Hanlon and Runyan Geise (n 79). Such legislative developments were driven in part by the American Bar Association, which voted in 2003 in favour of restricting asbestos claims by unimpaired litigants (Resolution of the House of Delegates of the American Bar Association, February 2003).

82 *Wardlaw v Bonnington Castings* 1956 SC (HL) 26; [1956] AC 613, which in fact imposed liability *in solidum* on the facts of the case, a result widely thought to be an aberration in an otherwise impressive decision.

83 *Fairchild v Glenhaven Funeral Services* [2003] 1 AC 32.

v Corus (UK) plc[84] (strictly only applicable in England, but likely to have been followed by the Scottish courts), such that liability was only imposed singularly ("severally" is the Scots term) upon each defender responsible for a non-negligible exposure to asbestos in respect of the magnitude of the chance of injury created by such exposure. This development attracted widespread criticism from asbestos victims' groups, who successfully lobbied for legislative change to re-impose solidary liability in such cases. This was achieved under section 3 of the Compensation Act 2006,[85] which re-instated solidary ("joint and several" in Scottish and English terms) liability in respect of the causation of asbestos-related mesothelioma of the pleura.[86] Under the legislation, defenders may continue to seek an apportionment of liability *inter se*, and awards may be reduced in respect of contributory negligence.[87] Additionally, in order to protect properly insured defenders from bearing the burden of liability in cases where co-defenders may not be similarly insured, and thus potentially unable to meet their liability, the statute provides for Treasury regulations creating a compensation fund from which defenders may seek a contribution in respect of the portion of total liability due by co-defenders unable to pay.[88] These changes in respect of mesothelioma claims were effected without undoing the general re-alignment made in *Barker* of material increase in risk causation as lost chance recovery.

The Louisiana courts have, by contrast, used the "substantial factor" criterion to create a single judicial response to asbestos exposure, whether the injuries sustained are divisible or indivisible. The Louisiana approach, consistent with the approach taken in other state jurisdictions, follows that taken by the US Federal Court of Appeal in *Borel v Fibreboard Paper Prods Corp*,[89] in which a single approach to divisible and indivisible asbestos-related injuries was taken.

The first case of asbestos-related injury in Louisiana worthy of note is *Quick v Murphy Oil Co*,[90] in which the plaintiff had contracted asbestosis (a divisible injury). He sued a number of parties. One such defendant argued

---

84 See n 45 above.

85 The Act received Royal Assent on 25 July 2006, and s 3, on liability for mesothelioma, came into force on the same day. S 3 is given retrospective effect, although without effecting claims settled before 3 May 2006 (s 16(3),(4)).

86 S 3(1), (2). The exposure caused by the defender must have been the result of negligence or breach of statutory duty (s3(1)(a)), and the cause of the mesothelioma must, "because of the nature of mesothelioma and the state of medical science", be indeterminate (s3(1)(c)).

87 S 3(3).

88 S 3(7). The relevant regulations are the Compensation Act 2006 (Contribution for Mesothelioma Claims) Regulations 2006, SI 2006/3259.

89 493 F 2d 1076 (5th Cir 1973).

90 643 So 2d 1291 (La App 1994).

that exposure to its asbestos-containing product was minimal, such that it should not be held to have been a cause-in-fact of the plaintiff's asbestosis. The court agreed, holding that the exposure for which the defendant was responsible was minimal, and noted that the medical evidence indicated a "very high" probability that Quick would have developed asbestosis without the exposure in question. Thus the exposure in question was neither a "but for" cause of his injury, nor was it sufficiently serious to amount to a substantial factor in the causation of that injury.

Explaining the basis for its decision, the court in *Quick* held that in multiple defendant asbestos cases "courts have analysed the cases under concurrent causation, a doctrine which "proceeds from the assumption that more than one defendant substantially contributed to the plaintiff's injury".[91] In other words, a presumption is created in multiple defendant asbestos cases, using the substantial factor concept, that, where there is concurrent exposure from more than one source of asbestos, each source is assumed to contribute to the resultant injuries. The defendant may demonstrate, however, that the exposure caused by it was not a "substantial factor" in the plaintiff's injuries, which was precisely what happened in *Quick*.

There is a contrast here with the result in the Scottish case *Wardlaw v Bonnington Castings*.[92] In that case, where one of three noxious-dust-producing machines was demonstrated to have contributed only an insignificant amount of dust in comparison to the total to which the pursuer had been exposed, it was discounted as a cause of injury; whereas the other two machines, producing significant quantities of dust, were assumed to have contributed to the pursuer's pneumoconiosis. While both cases share an assumption of causal connection in respect of two or more non *de minimis* concurrent causes, *Quick* goes further in asking the defendant to demonstrate that the concurrent causal effect for which it was responsible was *not* substantial. In Scotland, there is no such assumption that a concurrent cause will be substantial: it is for the pursuer to demonstrate that a cause was sufficiently "material" (in the Scots terminology) to constitute a cause-in-fact of the injury.

The Louisiana courts subsequently chose to extend the *Quick* approach to indivisible injuries. In *Egan v Kaiser Aluminum & Chemical Corp*,[93] the plaintiff contracted a mesothelioma of the pleura as a result of exposure to asbestos. He sued a former employer for whom he had worked for seventeen

91 Per Barry J at 1294.
92 1956 SC (HL) 266.
93 677 So 2d 1027 (La App 1996).

years (the first-named defendants), as well as a number of manufacturers of asbestos-containing products to which he had been exposed during his working life. One of the defendant manufacturers, OCF, appealed against a finding of liability on the basis that the plaintiff had been exposed to its products for a maximum of one year out of his working life, and that this exposure ought not therefore to be deemed a substantial factor in the causation of his mesothelioma. Citing the *Quick* asbestosis decision, the Fourth Circuit dismissed OCF's argument, holding that:[94]

> Simply because the plaintiff was exposed to OCF's asbestos-containing product over a relatively short period of time, and had considerable long-term exposure to other products, it cannot be said that the exposure to Kaylo [the defendant's product] could not have been a substantial contributing factor in his development of mesothelioma. The evidence supports a finding that his exposure to Kaylo was a substantial contributing factor in his development of the disease.

This statement demonstrates the impact of an assumption of substantial causal effect, as laid out in the earlier *Quick* case, and shows the heavy burden which it imposes on defendants when applied in a case of an indivisible injury like mesothelioma. The court in *Egan* is, in effect, saying that because the defendant cannot show that its product could *not* have been a substantial factor in the causation of the plaintiff's indivisible injury, it will be assumed to be such a factor. Of course there is no way that most defendants will be able to demonstrate this in cases of indivisible injury, as such injuries could have been triggered by a single unknown fibre of asbestos inhaled during a short period of exposure. The effect of the assumption that anything other than a *de minimis* period of exposure is a substantial factor in asbestos-related cases of indivisible injury effectively ensures that any defendant who cannot show that it was responsible for only a *de minimis* level of exposure will be held to bear a share of the responsibility for the plaintiff's injury. While a causal link is often also found in Scottish mesothelioma cases, the difference is that in Scotland it is for the pursuer to demonstrate which exposures were sufficiently material.

The *Egan* approach was more drastic in its effect in the period before the Civil Code was altered to curtail dramatically the imposition of liability *in solidum*.[95] Prior to that date, the result achieved in Louisiana was similar to the finding of solidary liable made in *Fairchild*, and now entrenched in the provisions of the Compensation Act 2006.

The decision in *Egan* has been followed in a later decision of the Fourth

---

94 Per Armstrong J at 1035.
95 The current codal provision is CC art 2323.

Circuit in *Vodanovich v A P Green Industries Inc*,[96] albeit the plaintiff's claim was rejected in that case.[97] Most recently of all, its status has been cemented through the approval of the Louisiana Supreme Court in its decision in *Adams v Owens-Corning Fiberglas Corp*.[98]

(3) Pleural plaques

In *Gregg v Scott*,[99] the House of Lords rejected a claim against a doctor who was said negligently to have caused a reduction in a patient's life expectancy, because, inter alia, such loss was not tied to any existing demonstrable injury. Courts in England and Scotland have consistently shown themselves unwilling to permit such claims for mere loss of a chance of avoiding a future personal injury.[100] Such a position has created an imperative to find new categories of demonstrable existing loss on to which claimants can attach medical lost chance claims.

One such category of arguable existing injury is asymptomatic pleural plaques triggered by exposure to asbestos. Consideration of whether such pleural plaques constitute recognisable injury appears not to have received the same judicial attention in Louisiana as it has in Scotland and England. This may, in the recent past, have been because asymptomatic exposure to asbestos would have given a right to damages in Louisiana so long as the risk of developing a consequential asbestos-related illness was more than merely slight. This entitlement resulted from a number of reported decisions[101] taken together with a prior version of Article 2315(B) of the Civil Code. However, the text of that Article has, since a 1996 amendment, excluded liability in damages for the costs of "future medical treatment, services, surveillance, or procedures of any kind unless such treatment, services, surveillance, or procedures are directly related to a manifest physical or mental injury or disease". This amendment has brought Louisiana law into line with Scots

---

96 869 So 2d 930 (La App 4th Cir 2004).
97 On the basis that "the plaintiff has failed to establish any direct or circumstantial evidence of exposure to asbestos fibers released by the defendants' activities".
98 923 So 2d 118 (La App 1st Cir 2005). In relation to certain claims of maritime exposure to asbestos a more liberal regime applies under a special statute, the Jones Act, the criteria of which are easier to satisfy for plaintiffs: all the plaintiff need do is prove exposure to asbestos aboard the employer's vessel, but not demonstrate *whose* asbestos he was exposed to; moreover, the plaintiff need not prove "substantial causation". He is required only to prove "slight causation" (in other words, the negligence of the employer must only have been *a* cause of injury, no matter how slight a cause). See, e.g., *Torrejon v Mobil Oil Co*, 876 So 2d 877 (La App 4 Cir).
99 [2005] UKHL 2; [2005] 2 AC 176.
100 See further Hogg, "Re-establishing orthodoxy" (n 15).
101 *Bourgeois v A P Green Industries Inc* 716 So 2d 355 (La 1998); *Bonnette v Conoco Inc* 837 So 2d 1219 (La 2003).

law, where damages may not be sought in relation to the risk of future illness unless such risk relates to a demonstrable existing physical injury. Evidently this new position raises for Louisiana, as well as for Scotland, the question of whether the presence of pleural plaques constitute existing physical injury.

In a couple of Outer House cases decided in the late 1990s, the Court of Session decided that asymptomatic pleural plaques constituted actionable damage of themselves.[102] This position, however, was reached without any consideration of the arguments surrounding the question, the Court in both cases merely accepting the assumption of both sides that pleural plaques were injurious per se. By contrast, in recent high-profile English litigation, the House of Lords took the contrary view that asymptomatic pleural plaques are *not* actionable damage per se,[103] a view which one judge in the Outer House subsequently took to be determinative of this question in Scots Law.[104] The decision of the House of Lords was entirely consistent with orthodox principles of what constitutes damage, but it produced an emotional response from the asbestos litigants' lobby, so much so that in Scotland the governing party decided to introduce a Bill to the Scottish Parliament in June 2008 to exclude the effect of this decision and to permit claims by those suffering from pleural plaques (as well as pleural-thickening and asymptomatic asbestosis) despite the lack of any symptoms.[105] This development was a questionable victory for interest group lobbying of politicians in the face of principle and precedent. It may be contrasted with recent legislative developments in those US states which have chosen to exclude claims by the "worried well", who have merely been exposed to asbestos, in favour of claims by those suffering demonstrable harm, in order that the limited funds of defendants are channelled to those most in need.[106] The Bill singularly fails to address the question of how the quantum of damages for an asymptomatic condition like pleural plaques or pleural thickening is to be assessed, given that such conditions produce no sensation of pain nor have any deleterious effect upon health.

What then is the view of Louisiana law on pleural plaques? Given the nature of pleural plaques as merely cellular change without any necessary

102   *Nicol v Scottish Power plc* 1998 SLT 822; *Gibson v McAndrew Wormald* 1998 SLT 562 (see in particular Lord Maclean's comments at 563).

103   *Johnston v NEI International Combustion Ltd*, *Grieves v F T Everard & Sons Ltd* [2007] UKHL 39; [2008] 1 AC 281.

104   See comments of Lord Uist in *Wright v Stoddard International plc* [2007] CSOH 173; 2008 Rep LR 37.

105   Now enacted as the Damages (Asbestos-related Conditions) (Scotland) Act 2009, asp 4. See for comment on the Bill, M Hogg, "Asbestos related conditions and the idea of damage in the law of delict" 2008 SLT (News) 207.

106   See Hanlon and Runyan Geise (n 79) at 3-4.

attendant pain or suffering, one might have thought that the decision in *In re Rezulin Products Liability Litigation*,[107] a case heard before a New York court but applying, in part, Louisiana law, would have been influential in Louisiana pleural plaque litigation. In the *Rezulin* case, it was held that asymptomatic sub-cellular changes produced by ingestion of a pharmaceutical product were not actionably injurious under Louisiana law, the court stating that "there is no evidence that plaintiffs' alleged injuries have manifested any clinically observable detriment".[108] This, taken with the fact that any future harm which might occur was merely speculative, led the court to conclude that the plaintiffs' alleged injuries were not "manifest injury" for the purposes of a claim under the Louisiana Products Liability Act. Such reasoning seems applicable to asymptomatic pleural plaques. However, it has not been the position adopted by the Louisiana courts.

To begin with, it is worth noting that an examination of the Louisiana cases in which plaintiffs have been identified as suffering from pleural plaques indicates that some of the medical evidence presented to the courts has not been entirely helpful. In *Hoerner v ANCO Insulations Inc*,[109] for instance, the Fourth Circuit summarised the plaintiff's medical practitioner's evidence as being to the effect that "Mr Hoerners' x-rays show the presence of pleural plaques, which indicate that he has asbestosis",[110] a finding which was not criticised by the court. This is a medically erroneous statement: the presence of pleural plaques has no necessary connection with asbestosis. Many persons exposed to asbestos who develop pleural plaques never go on to develop asbestosis, and, where they do, the asbestosis is not causally connected to the presence of the pleural plaques. A similarly misleading medical statement had been made by the Fourth Circuit in the earlier case of *In re Asbestos Plaintiffs v Bordelon Inc*,[111] when the court described pleural thickening or pleural plaques as "tumors or cancers of the pleura".[112] This misleading terminology of disease when applied to pleural plaques will tend to produce the view that pleural plaques are, of themselves, injurious. This has on occasion been the view adopted by juries in Louisiana litigation, although the picture is rather mixed.

In the *Bordelon* multi-party litigation, one plaintiff (Naquin) had been diagnosed by a physician as suffering from pleural plaques, and "pleural

107   361 F Supp 2d 268 (SDNY 2005).
108   At 278.
109   812 So 2d 45 (La 2002).
110   Per Steven R Plotkin J at 74.
111   726 So 2d 926 (La App 4ᵗʰ Cir 1998).
112   Per Jones J at 938.

and pulmonary asbestosis, and hypertension". On the other hand, another examining physician had found "no definite evidence of asbestosis, but alluded to the possibility of pleural plaques". On the basis of this conflicting evidence, the jury concluded that Naquin was not suffering from an asbestos-related disease. The Fourth Circuit did not overturn this finding, concluding that it was "not manifest error nor clearly wrong from our review of the record before us".[113] One might speculate that the jury took the view that, given the evidence least favourable to the plaintiff, the mere possibility of the presence of pleural plaques was insufficient to demonstrate actual injury, but this would indeed be mere speculation. However, in the later multi-party litigation of *Abadie v Metropolitan Life Insurance Co*,[114] the Fifth Circuit upheld a jury award to one plaintiff (Quave) of $12,800 in respect of asbestos exposure, the medical evidence indicating that the exposure had resulted in chronic inflammation of the left lung and a "possible pleural plaque" on the same lung. In respect of another plaintiff in the same case (Robin), the Fifth Circuit upheld a jury award of $76,500 in respect of asbestos exposure diagnosed variably upon medical examination as having caused either "bilateral pleural plaques" or "some pleural change". The award to Robin certainly suggests that a Louisiana jury is willing to take the view that mere pleural change is sufficient to constitute manifest and actionable injury.

The use of juries to determine the injurious or otherwise nature of pleural plaques, with the consequent lack of reasons being given as to when and why manifest injury has been sustained through inhalation of asbestos, is frustrating for the jurist. The mixed picture of success before juries may in part be the result of contradictory and sometimes incorrect medical testimony. The problems of such unhelpful testimony are exacerbated by misleading judicial comments, such as that of the Fourth Circuit in *Bordelon*, referred to earlier, that pleural plaques are a form of "cancer". If courts are to understand the contents of "the box of chocolates" which is asbestos litigation, they need to have a clearer understanding of the aetiology of the various asbestos-related medical conditions and to express this aetiology correctly to juries and in their appeal judgments.

F. CONCLUSIONS

Some conclusions may be drawn in relation to the approach of the two systems to causation in delict/tort, both by way of similarity as well as of difference.

---

113 Per Jones J at 967.
114 784 So 2d 46 (La App 5th Cir 2001).

As noted at the outset, comparison is rendered more difficult by the standard usage of jury trials to settle civil claims in Louisiana, so that we often have no stated reasons for specific outcomes being reached.

A number of parallels may be drawn as follows.

(i) Both recognise that causation-in-fact is properly to be separated from considerations affecting the scope of liability for consequences (or "legal" or "proximate" causation as it has traditionally been called), albeit that in Scotland continuing legal cause terminology can somewhat muddy the waters.

(ii) Both adopt a basic *sine qua non* test of causation-in-fact, but have yet to develop a test (such as the academically popular NESS test) which would deal with certain complex problems of factual causation, including over-determined outcomes, which cannot be solved using the *sine qua non* test.

(iii) Both suffer from continuing terminological difficulties, Louisiana with its unhelpful "substantial factor" test and Scotland with its continued reliance on "legal cause" terminology to describe what are essentially normative considerations. Both systems would benefit from further reflection on such terminological usage.

(iv) Both systems would also benefit from giving deeper consideration to the factors which should be recognised as generally affecting the scope of liability for consequences. The normative, policy issues which have often influenced decisions require to be given more explicit and considered recognition.

(v) Both might possibly – and Scotland might certainly – benefit from a re-assessment of the general analysis of the law of delict/tort. There is continuing doubt as to the proper stage at which to consider certain matters, and how therefore certain factual situations should be analysed. Similar facts can produce different analyses in different cases, sometimes by reference to duty of care, sometimes to standard of care, and sometimes to causation. Courts tend to muddle uncertainly through, and while they may reach the right decision, it can be without much clarity of thought.

There are also however differences, both in style and approach, between the two systems.

(i) There is a greater willingness amongst the Louisiana judiciary to engage in academic and philosophical debate about theories of delict, and of causation in particular. Scottish judges have typically eschewed such debate, although the recent upsurge in cases dealing with causal issues, itself perhaps a result of a new attitude amongst the judiciary in the past twenty or so years of engaging with, rather than politely ignoring, academics, may suggest that this is changing.

(ii) While the Scottish (and English) courts originally developed material increase in risk analysis, and now loss of a chance, to deal with cases of causal indeterminacy, Louisiana courts have been unwilling to move beyond the limited confines of "substantial factor" coupled with a scientifically questionable (albeit pro-plaintiff) unitary treatment of divisible and indivisible injuries. The Scottish analysis could prove beneficial in developing Louisiana law in this respect.

(iii) While a number of Louisiana decisions on pleural plaque liability have suffered from questionable expert medical evidence, in Scotland the difficulty has lain with a too-ready willingness to treat pleural plagues as actionable harm without considering that question in any depth. Whilst the considered view of the House of Lords, following the *Grieves* litigation,[115] is that pleural plaques are *not* actionable harm, in Scotland this decision has been overturned by legislative provision, a development which, it has been suggested, marks a triumph of emotionalism over principle. What the effects of these developments will be upon the Louisiana consideration of this type of remains to be seen, but, if any, they are likely to be slight, as changes in asbestos policy are largely driven by jurisdiction-specific concerns.

In both systems it is fair to say that one detects a degree of reticence among members of the judiciary in delving into causal issues. This may well be the result of a perception that the topic is a complex one, apt to muddy the waters of litigation. If that is indeed the case, it may be one very good reason why courts faced with causal questions might benefit from showing greater reliance on the lead given by academic discussion in the way which they have undoubtedly done in other legal fields. Such an academic-judicial partnership would be likely to assist in the development of the law in both jurisdictions in relation to the specific causal conundrums with which each continues to wrestle.

115   See n 103 above.

13 Personality Rights: A Study in Difference

Elspeth Christie Reid

A. INTRODUCTION
B. LOUISIANA: THE GENERAL CLAUSE AND THE INTENTIONAL TORTS
C. SCOTLAND: THE CIVILIAN HERITAGE WITHOUT A CODE
D. THE "GRAVITATIONAL PULL" OF THE COMMON LAW
E. DIFFERENT COMMON LAW TRADITIONS?
F. PUBLICITY RIGHTS: SURVIVAL OF CIVILIAN ANALYSIS?
G. DIFFERENT CONSTITUTIONAL "MOMENTS"
H. CONCLUSION

A. INTRODUCTION

Over the past century, in both the Civil Law[1] and the Common Law,[2] the concept of "personality rights" has evolved to encompass that bundle of rights which protects the integrity and inviolability of the individual. Von Bar, for example, writing on European tort law, lists as personality rights the right to protection of life, and to be protected against injury to the body or health, and deprivation of liberty,[3] as well as "the right to one's name, the right to one's image, and the right to honour and self-esteem", and the right to protection

---

1 In France, the contents of Raymond Lindon's classic text, *Les Droits de la Personalité* (1974), included: la vie privée et l'image, le nom, la sépulture, les souvenirs de famille, les lettres missives, la défense de la considération, le droit moral de l'auteur" (suggesting less emphasis than von Bar upon aspects of physical integrity). For the perspective from another mixed jurisdiction see J Burchell, *Personality Rights and Freedom of Expression* (1998); J Neethling, J M Potgieter and P J Visser, *Neethling's Law of Personality*, 2nd edn (2005).

2 An English definition similarly concentrates primarily upon privacy and reputation: for Thomas Gibbons personality rights encompass "various interests in privacy, reputation, intellectual property, and moral choice" ("Personality rights: The limits of personal accountability", in E M Barendt (ed), *Yearbook of Media and Entertainment Law 1997/98* 53 at 53.) For an early American discussion see R Pound, "Interests of personality" (1915) 28 Harvard LR 343 (part 1), 445 (part 2), describing the interests of "the individual and physical existence" (349) – more specifically the interest in physical integrity and personal liberty, honour and reputation, and belief and opinion.

3 C von Bar, *The Common European Law of Torts* vol 2 (2000) paras 46 ff.

against unlawful disclosure of personal information and interference with family life.[4] A succinct working definition is found in the non-exhaustive listing in article 3 of the Quebec Civil Code:

> Every person is the holder of personality rights, such as the right to life, the right to the inviolability and integrity of his person, and the right to the respect of his name, reputation and privacy. These rights are inalienable.

In summary, there are rights which "protect the attributes of the human person", and thus concentrate upon "the être – the being – in contrast with the avoir – the having".[5] But while the category is recognised in both Scotland[6] and Louisiana,[7] and an abundant literature has formed on both sides of the Atlantic, there are significant variations – even within the Civil or Common Law groupings – with regard to the private law remedies by which personality rights may be vindicated. This chapter considers how the interaction of Civil Law and Common Law traditions has shaped protection of personality rights in the mixed legal systems of Louisiana and Scotland.

The key feature of Common Law/Civil Law difference in the law of tort/delict was famously stated, in the pages of the *Tulane Civil Law Forum*, to lie "in the plural".[8] The legacy of the forms of action is the Common Lawyer's conceptualisation of tortious liability in discrete categories or "torticles".[9] This contrasts with the Civil Lawyer's vision of delict (in the singular) resting on a single general principle of delictual liability, as exemplified in article 1382, the "general clause" of the French *Code civil*.[10]

---

4 Ibid paras 93-94.
5 A Popovici, "Personality rights – a Civil Law concept" (2004) 50 Loy L Rev 349 at 352.
6 However, the concept of "absolute rights of individuals" encompassing protection against physical harm, seduction, wrongous imprisonment and injury to reputation is of course familiar: see, e.g., Bell, *Prin* §§ 2026-2057; and see now N R Whitty and R Zimmermann (eds), *Rights of Personality in Scots Law: A Comparative Perspective* (forthcoming 2009, Dundee University Press).
7 Professor Yiannopoulos lists "name, likeness, liberty, personal integrity, and honor" as the "incidents of human personality" (*Louisiana Civil Law Treatise*, "Property", at § 17). Stone noted the use of the term "interest of personality", *Louisiana Civil Law Treatise*, "Tort doctrine" (1977 edn) at § 125, but observed that "Louisiana is fortunate in that article 2315 speaks simply of 'damage to another' and is not bothered, as was the common law, to find an appropriate writ or label to justify a remedy".
8 B Rudden, "Torticles" (1991) 6&7 Tul Civ L F 105 at 109.
9 The "pigeon-hole" structure of torts is set out in W Page Keeton (ed), *Prosser and Keeton on Torts*, 5th edn (1984) § 1 at 3, and although the authors suggest that "there is no necessity whatever that a tort have a name", they find "objectionable" "the single broad principle, that any harm done to another is a wrong" (at 4).
10 See F P Walton, "The comparative law of the right to privacy" (1931) 47 LQR 219 at 220: a French court is "in no way bound to bring the case under any one of the familiar heads of categories of wrongs familiar to English lawyers, such as trespass or defamation, for no such categories exist in the French civil law. The only question is whether fault on the part of the plaintiff caused the damage."

It follows that a fundamental distinction is evident in the process by which primary rights generate secondary obligations. The Common Lawyer attempts to extend liability to new situations not by reference to general organising principle but by analogy with situations for which remedies already exist.[11] So, for example, in the absence of a pre-existing privacy tort, the English courts acknowledge "privacy as a value which underlies the existence of a rule of law" but have not given independent status to "privacy as a principle of law in itself".[12] Compliance with article 8 of the European Convention on Human Rights, which imposes a positive obligation to secure respect for private life, has been achieved piecemeal, partly by limited legislative provision and partly by reference to torts such as trespass, nuisance, defamation, passing-off and also breach of confidence.[13] No new tort of privacy has been created.

In the Civil Law, by contrast, fresh areas of liability are approached by reasoning deductively from the general organising principle represented, in France, by article 1382. If a right is recognised as worthy of protection, its infringement constitutes "dommage" for the purposes of article 1382,[14] and "faute" is likely to be discerned in the defendant's conduct, unless the defendant may be regarded as acting lawfully in exercising his or her own privilege or liberty. Thus recognition of the right to protect private life in article 9 of the *Code civil* means that infringement of privacy is "dommage", and the person responsible is *prima facie* deemed to be at fault, subject to that person's own privilege of freedom of expression. As Walton observed four decades before the "Brigitte Bardot" law of 1970 set the seal on judicial recognition of privacy by inserting article 9 into the *Code civil*, "a new 'tort'

11 *Kingdom of Spain v Christie, Manson & Woods Ltd* [1986] 1 WLR 1120 per Sir Nicolas Brown-Wilkinson at 1129: "In the pragmatic way in which English law has developed, a man's legal rights are in fact those which are protected by a cause of action. It is not in accordance ... with the principles of English law to analyse rights as being something separate from the remedy given to the individual ... in the ordinary case to establish a legal or equitable right you have to show that all the necessary elements of the cause of action are either present or threatened." (See also *Stovin v Wise* [1996] AC 923 per Lord Hoffmann at 949 on extension of duty of care in the law of negligence, "starting with situations in which a duty has been held to exist and then asking whether there are considerations of analogy, policy, fairness and justice for extending it to cover a new situation".)
12 *Wainwright v Home Office* [2004] 2 AC 406 per Lord Hoffmann at para 31.
13 For a "restatement" of the English law of confidentiality a decade after the passing of the Human Rights Act 1998, see P Stanley, *The Law of Confidentiality* (2008).
14 The idea of an infringement of a legally protected interest is built in to the concept of reparation: "La lésion d'un intérêt juridiquement protégé, donc légitime, est inhérente à la notion même de dommage réparable" (B Starck, H Roland, L Boyer, *Obligations: 1, Responsabilité délictuelle*, 5th edn (1996) 53). For these purposes, "Il n'y a pas de différence de nature entre l'atteinte à un droit et l'atteinte à un intérêt légitime juridiquement protégé" (ibid). In the German BGB, § 823(1), the focus is similarly the infringement of certain recognised rights.

has an easier passage in France than in England … though no special name for it has become generally accepted, and though it is not easy to define the limits of the right".[15]

Nonetheless, it is perhaps unsurprising to find that, in this area at any rate, liability based upon the general clause has developed incrementally, and that analysis is structured around categories which bear a strong resemblance to "delicticles".[16] Raymond Lindon, author of the classic French text on *Les droits de la personnalité*, explains that a grand concept "n'a pas, à la façon de Minerve sortie tout armée du cerveau de Jupiter, été enfantée soudain par un juriste de génie".[17] Instead, remedies for particular types of infringement have evolved often through the medium of judicial decisions,[18] and Lindon's own text is broken down into chapters devoted to separate interests.

There is admittedly an important formal distinction to be drawn between the status of Civil Law *jurisprudence constante* and that of Common Law precedent, in terms of the potential binding status of a single Common Law case as compared with the persuasive status of a line of Civil Law judgments. However, one need only look at the development of privacy law in France to appreciate the practical force of judge-made law in shaping new areas of liability.[19] The secondary obligations to abstain from infringement of personality rights may derive from the general clause, article 1382, but this overarching principle is given content by extensive commentaries explaining

---

15 F P Walton, "The comparative law of the right to privacy" (1931) 47 LQR 219 at 220.

16 See H S Daggett et al, "A reappraisal appraised: A brief for the Civil Law of Louisiana" (1937) 12 Tulane LR 12 on the importance of *jurisprudence constante*.

17 *Les droits de la personnalité* (n 1) 2-3 ("has not, like Minerva emerging ready-armed from Jupiter's skull, been given birth to by a jurist of genius") .

18 E.g., the amendment of the *Code civil* to include the right to privacy in art 9 is widely regarded as codifying well-established judge-made law (Law 70-643 of 17 July 1970). (In a similar way, the listing of protected interests in BGB § 823(1) was expanded in the second half of the twentieth century to include personality rights by reference to the post-war Constitution.) The introduction to *Les droits de la personnalité* (at 8) promised that it would contain "une profusion de jugements et d'arrêts, dont le nombre permet de mieux suivre l'évolution des tâtonnements et des progrès de la pensée des juges". See also N S Marsh, "Deduction and induction in the law of torts: A comparative approach" (1951) 33 *Journal of Comparative Legislation and International Law* 59 at 61: "in French, as in English law, the law of torts is not … to be found in legislative principles but in judge-made law, from which the principles, if any, must be induced".

19 See note 15 above; also Lindon, *Les droits de la personnalité* (n 1) 64-67; H Beverley-Smith et al, *Privacy, Property and Personality* (2005) 147-153. Such cases would include, e.g., *Olivier Philippe*, CA Paris, 13 March 1965, 1965 *JurisClasseur Périodique* II 14223; *Bardot*, CA Paris, 27 February 1967, D 1967 Jur 450. On the role of the judges in developing protection for rights of personality in German law, see R Zimmermann, *The Law of Obligations: Roman Foundations of the Civilian Tradition* (1990) 1092-1094; H Rösler, "Harmonizing the German Civil Code of the nineteenth century with a modern constitution – the Lüth Revolution 50 years ago in comparative perspective" (2008) 23 Tul Civ L F 1 at 27-29; H Beverley-Smith et al, *Privacy, Property and Personality* (2005) 113.

the meaning of "faute" in particular contexts and by reference to judicial decisions. Neither the volume of case law cited, nor its specificity, nor even its persuasiveness, should be regarded necessarily as indicators of Common Law influence.

B. LOUISIANA: THE GENERAL CLAUSE AND THE INTENTIONAL TORTS

In Louisiana, liability for infringement of personality interests, like all damage caused by the fault of another, is subordinated to the framework of the general clause of the Civil Code, article 2315: "Every act whatever of man that causes damage to another obliges him by whose fault it happened to repair it." As in the equivalent clause of the *Code civil* (article 1382), therefore, fault is the central concept and is left undefined. Professor Palmer has commented that in order to achieve structure and limits the open-textured formulation of the general clause invites specific listing of protected interests.[20] And indeed while the concept of intentional torts was not fully accepted until relatively recently in Louisiana,[21] the basic nomenclature does not now differ noticeably from that applied in other US states. Torts are itemised in the plural, and fault is understood, in principle, as encompassing all conduct falling below a reasonable standard, including intentional harm,[22] although in practice it may be analysed differently according to the specific interest protected.[23]

Thus liability for wrongful deprivation of liberty is grounded in the general clause, article 2315;[24] but in order to determine how the requirement of fault

20 V V Palmer, "The collapse of the general clause", in *The Louisiana Civilian Experience* (2005) 191 at 196. More specifically, Professor Crawford has pointed out that since this article appeared in the chapter on "offenses and quasi-offenses", it is not surprising that some of the elements of the Common Law definitions upon which the criminal law was based informed the understanding of fault in relation to torts such as "battery". 12 *Louisiana Civil Law Treatise* "Tort Law" (Westlaw – current through 2007-2008 Update) § 12.2.

21 See F L Maraist and T C Galligan, *Louisiana Tort Law* (looseleaf) § 2.01. The terminology of intentional torts appears to have gained currency due to amendment of the worker's compensation laws in 1975 (LSA-RS 23:1032B) to provide that certain immunities did not extend to "an intentional act". "Intentional" conduct is also now significant in being excluded from the cover offered by some insurance policies.

22 *Veazey v Elmwood Plantation Associates, Ltd* 650 So 2d 712 (La 11/30/94) per Justice Kimball at 718: "'fault' under civilian theory clearly includes more than just negligence; it extends the gamut from strict liability to intentional torts"; also Stone, "Tort doctrine" (n 7) § 61.

23 In relation to battery, for example, the plaintiff must prove "all prima facie elements of the tort, including lack of consent to the invasive conduct". *Landry v Bellanger* 851 So 2d at 954 (La 5/20/03); *Touchet v Hampton* 950 So 2d 895 at 898 (La App 3rd Cir 2/7/07), 950 So.2d 895, 898; *Johnson v Bergeron* 966 So 2d 1059 (La App 5th Cir 2007).

24 See M I Schwartzman, "Tortious liability for false imprisonment in Louisiana" (1942) 17 Tulane LR 81.

is met in particular cases it is usual to "pigeon-hole"[25] fact sets under the headings of malicious prosecution, false imprisonment or false arrest. In malicious imprisonment the detention, being made under due legal process, is *prima facie* lawful, and so is actionable only if the means used were coloured by malice.[26] On the other hand false imprisonment and false arrest are made without legal authority and therefore unlawful.[27] The key considerations for wrongful imprisonment and wrongful arrest are factual or turn on local rules of criminal procedure[28] – such as whether the degree of restraint constituted confinement, and whether the circumstances were inadequate to justify arrest without a warrant. As Schwartzmann explains:[29]

> The good faith of the person who causes the arrest is not of importance, because the only question involved is whether there was legal authority for the imprisonment. Hence the question of malice is immaterial except as it may affect the question of damages.

In practice, therefore, the abstract principle of the general clause is deconstructed into a range of subsidiary "torticles". But as in French law this need not necessarily detract from the status of the general clause as the primary reference point in developing new areas of liability:[30]

> [I]t becomes clear that in the decision of a case in tort or delict in Louisiana, the court first goes to that fountainhead of responsibility, articles 2315 and 2316, and in applying those articles it goes to the many other articles in our Code as well as statutes and other laws which deal with the responsibility of certain persons, the responsibility in certain relationships, and the responsibility which arises due to certain types of activities. Just as we have found in the Code many standards of conduct, many statutes and local ordinances also detail standards of conduct which courts may apply per se, impliedly or by analogy.

In consequence, recognition of a right as worthy of protection entails that, in principle, a remedy should lie for its unjustified infringement. In Stone's words: "Article 2315 speaks simply of 'damage to another' and is not bothered … to find an appropriate writ or label to justify a remedy".[31]

---

25 The term used by Schwartzman, ibid at 82.

26 Ibid at 85-86.

27 See *Restatement (Second of Torts)* § 35. (§ 44 states that "If an act which causes another's confinement is done with the intention of causing the confinement, the actor is subject to liability although his act is not inspired by personal hostility or desire to offend.")

28 See Criminal Code LSA-RS 14.46: "False imprisonment is the intentional confinement or detention of another, without his consent and without proper legal authority."

29 "Tortious liability for false imprisonment in Louisiana" at 84.

30 *Langlois v Allied Chemical Corporation* 258 La 1067, 249 2D 133 (1971) at per Justice Barham 1077/137.

31 "Tort Doctrine", in the *Louisiana Civil Law Treatise* at § 125.

C. SCOTLAND: THE CIVILIAN HERITAGE WITHOUT A CODE

The importance of the Civil Law element in the Scots legal mix is similarly not in doubt.[32] An outline account of liability for infringement of personality rights – although the term is not, of course, used – can be found in the "Institutional" writings of the seventeenth and eighteenth centuries. Stair listed attacks on life, health, liberty, fame, reputation and honour as "delinquencies" which were not only crimes but also *"iniuria"* attracting civil liability.[33] Bankton similarly noted that fame and reputation might be harmed by "real" and "verbal" injuries.[34] But, prior to the nineteenth century, injuries to the person, including even verbal injuries, were regarded primarily as criminal offences against public order, justiciable in either the criminal or the commissary (ecclesiastical) courts.[35] Although a handful of civil cases were reported before this period, it was only after 1800, and in particular after the institution of Jury Courts in 1816[36] with jurisdiction to hear "all actions on account of injury to the person, whether real or verbal, as assault and battery, libel or defamation",[37] that civil claims began to be reported in significant numbers. It is unsurprising, therefore, that Bell's *Principles*, first published in 1829, gave a noticeably fuller treatment to interests of the person than earlier Institutional writings. In the four editions for which Bell himself was responsible, statements of principle were accompanied by reference to a growing case-law. As in Louisiana there was a tendency to conceptualise infringement of personality rights (and other intentional delicts) on the basis of the discrete offences observed in that case-law – in effect as "delicticles".

Take the case of wrongful deprivation of liberty, considered in the previous section. This was already the subject of clear treatment in the Institutional writers,[38] and indeed one of the final statutes of the pre-Union Parliament of Scotland provided for the award of damages "For preventing wrongous Imprisonments and against undue delayes in tryals".[39] But while

---

32 J Blackie, "The history of personality rights in Scots law", in Whitty and Zimmermann, *Rights of Personality* (forthcoming, n 6).

33 *Inst* 1.9.4.

34 *Inst* 1.10. 21-26.

35 See Sir George Mackenzie of Rosehaugh, *Laws and Customs of Scotland, in Matters Criminal* (1678) 1.30 ("Of Injuries, Personal, and Real; and of infamous Libels"); Blackie, "History of personality rights" (n 32).

36 Jury Trials (Scotland) Act 1815.

37 Court of Session Act 1825, s 28.

38 Stair, *Inst* 1.9.4; Bankton, *Inst* 1.2.69, and, in much greater detail, Bell, *Prin* §§ 2034-2042, (on contexts ranging from prisons to lunatic asylums, and analysis as to relevance of malice).

39 1701, APS, vol 10, 272-5 (c 6) (directed at some of the procedural grievances set out in the Claim of Right Act of 1689).

the Institutional writers had a general sense of what would now be called proportionality,[40] the case law[41] has provided the medium for development of specific rules on when public interest should prevail over private right – on when malice is required, or when arrest which is *prima facie* unlawful is nevertheless justified.[42]

As in Louisiana, however, the proliferation of "delicticles" has not entirely obscured the Civilian general principle. Unlike English law, the law in Scotland is not burdened with the legacy of the forms of action, and in principle the categories of intentional delicts may, exceptionally, be capable of further development if there are cogent reasons why a particular interest should be recognised.[43] Thus imposition of secondary obligations may in appropriate cases follow from recognition of the primary rights. As Lord Dunedin put it, in a well-known passage:[44]

> Of course, different actions have different names, but the question in Scotland was never as to the remedy – it was always as to the right. You ask for what you want in your summons ... You may not get what you want, but that will be because you failed to show that you had the right to get it.

Nevertheless, there is plainly a practical difference between application of the general clause of the Louisiana Civil Code and application of uncodified general principle based upon the Civilian concept of *iniuria*. This contrast may be illustrated in relation to the tort of battery/delict of assault.

In the Scots delict of assault[45] it is possible to discern, even today,[46] the Civil Law legacy of the *actio iniuriarum* as a general organising principle,

---

40 "Though liberty be a most precious right, yet it is not absolute" (Stair, *Inst* 1.2.5).
41 The impact of English law has been fairly slight by comparison with Scotland's own common law in this particular area – perhaps because of the relative quantity of the latter, and perhaps because of the important of local factors such as the rules of criminal procedure on validity of arrest without warrant.
42 For the most concise modern statement see commentary by Sheriff Principal Cox in *McKinney v Chief Constable Strathclyde Police* 1998 SLT (Sh Ct) 80 at 82.
43 See K McK Norrie, "History and functions of delict", SME, vol 15, (1996) para 213: "Scots law has never accepted the English approach of extending the law only by analogy with previous precedents; rather, it is the civilian approach of looking for general principles that motivates legal development"; see also *Micosta SA v Shetland Islands Council* 1986 SLT 193 per Lord Ross at 198.
44 "The divergencies and convergencies of English and Scottish law" (fifth lecture on the David Murray Foundation in the University of Glasgow, 21 May 1935). See also J Guthrie Smith, *The Law of Damages: A Treatise on the Reparation of Injuries*, 2nd edn (1889) 40.
45 In modern usage "assault" is used for both actual and threatened violence. The terms were distinguished in earlier times, e.g. Bankton, *Inst* 1.10.22. Bell, in his *Principles*, headed § 2032 "Assault and Battery", but this was changed to "Reparation for Assault" by Shaw, the editor of the 5th edn, in 1860.
46 On the modern nomenclature of assault see D M Walker, *The Law of Delict in Scotland*, 2nd edn (1981), 490-492.

in that the notion of affront, the "gist"[47] of the *actio iniuriarum*, seems to be combined with the element of physical aggression. The Institutional writers maintained that a blow, actual or threatened, was reparable as much because of the "disgrace" suffered by the victim – the blow to dignity – as because of the physical harm.[48] Admittedly, there have been few modern cases where insult could be regarded as predominating over physical injury, [49] but such an action remains competent in principle.[50] At the same time, uncodified Civilian authority appears to offer an insecure basis for development of the law to meet new circumstances.

The judicial response to citation of Civilian authority can be illustrated by comparing *Ward v Scotrail*,[51] a Scottish case decided in 1998 with the 1995 decision in the Louisiana case of *Martin v Bigner*.[52] Both involved claims of damages against an employer for emotional distress caused by harassment. In the Louisiana case, the scope of the general clause was admittedly considered in the light of common law authority,[53] but liability was based upon article 2315; an employer or operator of premises had a duty not to expose employees to unreasonable risk of harm, and was in principle at fault if it failed to intervene to avert harm. There was therefore a *prima facie* cause of action against the employer. *Ward*, on the other hand, indicates that the Scots courts have more restricted navigational tools for extending liability into uncharted areas. In the absence of authority directly in point, the court

---

47 R W Lee, *An Introduction to Roman-Dutch Law*, 5th edn (1953) at 335.

48 Bankton, *Inst* 1.10.22. Bell qualified his treatment of assault at § 2032 in the 4th edition of his *Principles* (1839) by adding that "the civil claim of damage is not merely for damage sustained, but in solatium for affront and insult" (under reference to *Cruickshanks v Forsyth* (1747) Mor 4034). See, e.g., *Ewing v Earl of Mar* (1851) 14 D 314, in which damages were awarded against a nobleman for the "gross and opprobrious insult" committed by spitting at the local butcher and riding his horse at him (Lord President Boyle at 315).

49 Walker's examples in this category (n 46, at 490-492) are largely either foreign or pre-twentieth-century. Cf *Rutherford v Chief Constable for Strathclyde Police* 1981 SLT (Notes) 119, in which £3,000 in damages was awarded following an assault by a police officer, but the court rejected the pursuer's additional claim for solatium on the ground of affront or insult: "This is an element which on the older authorities may be allowed in cases of civil claims for assault (Bell's Principles ...) ... In the whole circumstances of this case ... I do not think it appropriate to make any award for this element" (Lord Maxwell at 120).

50 E.g., *McKie v Chief Constable of Strathclyde* 2002 Rep LR 137, affd 2003 SC 317, in which a former police officer, alleged that she was assaulted by being arrested and strip-searched by colleagues in humiliating circumstances. Her claim failed because she could not prove malice on the part of police officers, but there was no indication that limited but hostile physical contact of this nature could not, in principle, constitute an assault.

51 1999 SC 255.

52 665 So 2d 709 (La App 2 Cir 12/06/95).

53 In particular the court noted common law authority to the effect that an employer's inaction in the face of employee complaints about colleague harassment may give rise to a claim for intentional infliction of emotional distress (*Ford v Revlon Inc* 153 Ariz 38, 734 P 2d 580 (1987)).

in *Ward* appeared to concede that an intentional affront *could* be action-able, but it rejected arguments developing the general Civilian concept of *iniuria* because there were no specific pleadings of deliberate intention or malice. Instead proof was allowed with regard to pleadings in negligence; but since duty of care is significantly restricted in relation to non-physical harm, the distressed employee would be required to establish that specific psychi-atric illness had been caused by the employer's conduct. In other words, the ultimate outcome of the case was to turn on a narrow Common Law analysis as to the scope of duty in relation to this particular type of harm. Insofar as it was recognised, the Civilian legacy was regarded as the source of a specific, clearly circumscribed "delicticle", rather that as providing a general organising principle from which liability might be deduced in a new set of circumstances.[54]

A further contrast in the handling of Civil Law authority is observed with regard to the so-called "aggressor doctrine" – or provocation – in relation to assault. In *Landry v Bellanger*,[55] decided in 2003, the Supreme Court of Louisiana was called upon to consider the interplay between this doctrine and the doctrine of self-defence and comparative fault. Before this decision, the aggressor doctrine was regarded not simply as reducing any damages award but as precluding recovery altogether in cases of provocation by the plaintiff unless the retaliatory force was excessive. Justice Victory opened his judgment by referring to the "broad Civilian concept of 'fault'".[56] Noting that the "purpose of the aggressor doctrine, which condemns actions by barring recovery, is adequately served by the Civilian concepts of comparative fault, duty/risk, and privileges",[57] he felt able to eliminate the aggressor doctrine, and along with it the "inequities inherent in the 'all or nothing' recovery rules".[58]

The reasoning in *Landry*, with extensive commentary on the Code and reference to Planiol, presents a very different picture as compared with the most recent Scottish case, *Ross v Bryce*.[59] Although the result was much

---

54 Although for a more extended discussion of the *actio iniuriarum* see *Stevens v Yorkhill* [2006] CSOH 143 where proof was allowed as to whether the pursuer might recover on this basis for injury to feelings consequent upon removal of organs from her child at post mortem (further commentary at N R Whitty, "Rights of personality, property rights and the human body in Scots law" (2005) 9(2) EdinLR 194).

55 851 So 2d 943 (La 2003).

56 At 950.

57 At 953.

58 Ibid. In the event, however, it was held that the defendant had been acting in self-defence and a complete defence was therefore available to him.

59 1972 SLT (Sh Ct) 76. Obiter remarks by Lord Maxwell in *Rutherford v Chief Constable for Strathclyde Police* 1981 SLT (Notes) 119 at 120 similarly lacked focus: "there is a problem which

the same – that provocation might mitigate the award of damages rather than barring it completely – Sheriff Principal Kidd based her decision on a brief survey of Scots decisions, adding that: "The fact that the underlying principle of Scots law in actions of reparation for intentional wrong is based upon culpa is the reason why a pursuer in such an action must come into court with clean hands."[60] Beyond this no Civil Law authority was adduced nor was there any discussion as to how that general principle affected the question whether the award of damages should merely be reduced or eliminated altogether.

Thus there is no doubting the historical importance of the Civil Law legacy in the protection of personality rights in Scotland therefore, but in the absence of a Civil Code the historically-minded lawyer struggles to relate that legacy to the modern law.

D. THE "GRAVITATIONAL PULL" OF THE COMMON LAW

In a seminal article in the 1970s Justice Barham argued that the pull towards custom and the Common Law did not undermine the Civilian identity of Louisiana jurisprudence. It is in the Civilian tradition that "the source of law second only to legislative will is custom" and "our courts will of necessity resort to appraisals of customs without our state boundaries ... because we are a part of a larger community of common customs in many areas of law".[61] In Professor Palmer's estimation, however, the Common Law has not only brought detail and structure to the generality of the tort provisions in the Code[62] but has also moulded patterns of reasoning. It has been difficult to resist "the gravitational pull of the restrictive common law categories of tort" as the "mixed-jurisdiction mind instinctively seeks to narrow and reduce broad civilian tort principle into smaller focused liability categories".[63]

---

will one day have to be resolved as to the test to be applied in determining whether provocation by physical violence amounts to a complete defence to a civil claim for damages for assault or merely mitigates damages. It may be, as suggested in Bell's Principles, that the test is the same as is applied in considering the defence of self-defence in a criminal charge. It may be that some less stringent test applies."

60 At 78.

61 M E Barham, "A renaissance of the civilian tradition in Louisiana" (1973) 33 La LR 357 at 372.

62 E.g., *Caudle v Betts* 512 So 2d 389 (La 1987) (distinguishing intentional and negligent harm since the former was not within the scope of insurance cover) the Supreme Court of Louisiana used the Restatement §§ 13 onwards on battery as harmful contact and Prosser and Keeton's commentary thereon (*Torts* (n 9 above) §§ 8-12) as its starting point alongside Stone's account in the *Civil Law Treatise*: "a court must apply the legal precepts of general tort law related to the particular intentional tort alleged" (per Justice Dennis at 391).

63 Palmer, "Collapse of the general clause" (n 20) at 197.

Comparable "gravitational" forces have made themselves felt in Scotland. Given that the framework of liability drawn by the Institutional writers is relatively rudimentary and fragmented, and also rooted in a very different social and economic context, those pleading in the courts have naturally tended to structure their arguments drawing upon detail produced by the case law. Walker's *The Law of Delict in Scotland*, for example, uses Bankton and Bell's definitions as the starting point for the analysis of assault, but focuses primarily upon Scots cases, supplemented by reference to English authority.[64] Similarly in the courts, native resources are the starting point, but where there is no direct Scots authority, and new areas of potential liability present themselves, English case law[65] is the most obvious resource.

The law of confidentiality provides a striking illustration. In early sources the principle that certain information should be kept secret manifested itself mainly in discussion as to the categories of witness who should be privileged against giving evidence;[66] there was little analysis of liability for unauthorised disclosure beyond the courtroom. In the nineteenth century, cases began to appear in which a remedy was claimed for what is today termed "breach of confidence", but they were few in number and mainly concerned breach of their employer's trade secrets by former employees. The English authorities, by contrast, were more plentiful and more diverse. Unsurprisingly, when protection came to be claimed for secrets in new contexts, the Scottish courts readily drew upon English sources, notwithstanding that protection for confidentiality south of the border rested mainly upon the law of equity.[67]

---

64 2nd edn (1981), at 488 ff, citing, *inter alia*, Bankton, *Inst* 1.10.22, and Bell, *Prin* § 2032; a scattering of Canadian and South African cases, Prosser on *Torts*, e.g. at 490 note 21; and the *Restatement (Second) of Torts*, § 18, e.g., at 491 n 43, 492 n 79. Glegg, author of an earlier text on *The Law of Reparation* first published in 1892 (4th edn, by J L Duncan, 1955), cited English authority more or less interchangeably with Scots.

65 E.g., *Henderson v Chief Constable, Fife Police* 1988 SLT 361, in which the requirement that a woman detainee in police custody should remove her bra was an actionable "infringement of liberty"; see Lord Jauncey at 367: "I see no reason why the law should not protect the individual from this infringement just as it does from other infringements and indeed as the law of England did in very similar circumstances in *Lindley v Rutter*" ([1981] 1 QB 128). Of course such English authority may itself be "mixed": see, e.g., *Watkins v Secretary of State for the Home Department* [2006] 2 AC 395, per Lord Walker at para 68 on the continuing significance of affront in trespass to the person; also the classic case of *Wilkinson v Downton* [1897] 2 QB 57, on the intentional infliction of emotional distress, per Wright J at 59.

66 Stair, *Inst* 4.43.9; Bankton, *Inst* 4.3.27 (2, 491), 4.4.10 (2, 495); Erskine, *Inst* 4.2.25; Sir George Mackenzie of Rosehaugh, *Observations upon the XVIII. Act of Parliament XXIII. K. James VI. against dispositions made in defraud of creditors* (1699), 58-60 (commentary on statute of 1621 concerning unlawful dispositions and alienations by bankrupts).

67 Which has no formal status as a source of law in Scotland. For detailed discussion of jurisdictional sources for breach of confidence in English law see F Gurry, *Breach of Confidence* (1984) 25-57.

In the early twentieth-century case of *M'Cosh v Crow*,[68] for example, inter-dict was granted against the unauthorised use of photographs of the pursuer's daughters. The principles applied derived from recent English case law,[69] under explanation that "the law of England is to the same effect as our own. Indeed the laws could not well be different."[70] Similar *dicta* occur in more recent case-law.[71] As a result, delictual protection for secrets has been not been established by reference to the general Civilian concept of *iniuria*[72] or relevant (foreign-language) authority from Civil Law systems (except insofar as now available in English in the judgments of the European Court of Human Rights). Pleaders in the Scottish courts have yielded to the more powerful "pull" of the principles drawn from the English equitable wrong.

F. DIFFERENT COMMON LAW TRADITIONS?

At one time interest in the Common Law seems readily to have extended beyond the immediate Common Law neighbour. Vernon Palmer has documented the continual "temptation" for Louisiana judges in the early part of the nineteenth century to translate and re-order the Civil Law by reference to Anglo-American cases and treatises, filtering Gaius and Pothier through Coke and Blackstone.[73] On the other side of the Atlantic certain Scots lawyers were attentively following developments in American law. As documented elsewhere in this volume,[74] there were scholarly exchanges in the early part of the nineteenth century between George Joseph Bell in Scotland and James Kent and Joseph Story in the United States,[75] and there are intriguing

68 (1903) 5 F 670.

69 *Pollard v Photographic Co* (1889) LR 40 Ch D 345.

70 *Morton & Co v Muir Brothers & Co* 1907 SC 1211 per Lord McLaren at 1224.

71 See, e.g., the leading Scots case of *Lord Advocate v Scotsman Publications Ltd* 1989 SC (HL) 122 (where breach of confidentiality derived from publication by a third party of the memoirs of a former employee of the government security services) in which it was similarly accepted that "the substance of the law in [Scotland and England] is the same" (per Lord Keith at 164).

72 See, e.g., *Hardey v Russel and Aitken* 2003 GWD 2-50 (confidentiality of medical records in hands of third party) in which Lord Johnston made little comment on the pursuer's reference to the *actio iniuriarum*, but based his decision on the assumption that the principles applicable to English and Scots law were the same.

73 Palmer, "Collapse of the general clause" (n 20) at 198-199; also R B Fischer, "The Louisiana Supreme Court, 1812-1846: Strangers in a strange land" (1973) 1(4) Tul Civ L F 1. See, e.g., *Stachlin v Destrehan* 2 La Ann 1019, 1847 WL 3298 (La 1847), an assault case citing Blackstone (3 Blac Com 121) on the scope of the defence of protecting property (and see also extensive discussion of English authorities including Blackstone in *Hubgh v New Orleans & CR Co* 6 La Ann 495, 1851 WL 3649 (La 1851) (allegedly wrongful death of plaintiff's husband in workplace)).

74 See ch 1 at 2-3.

75 On Bell's reading of Kent and correspondence with Story see D M Walker, *The Scottish Jurists* (1985) 349-351. Kent's *Commentaries on American Law* make numerous references to Bell's

parallels between the treatment of the "Rights of Persons" in part IV of Bell's *Principles* (first edition, 1829) and in part IV of Kent's *Commentaries on American Law*, volume 2 of the first edition of which appeared in 1827.[76] Bell's successor as Professor of Scots Law at the University of Edinburgh, John More, drew his students' attention to the writings of Story and Kent, and specifically commended to them the reading of American case law.[77] Against this background, it is not surprising that some references to American cases appear in the late nineteenth-century Scots reports.[78]

An example is *Reid v Mitchell*,[79] a leading case still on the meaning of intention in intentional assault. A farm worker engaged in friendly horseplay gave an intentional push to a colleague, resulting in (unintended) serious injury. In finding liability, Lord Young prefaced his Court of Session judgment with the words: "I think that the principle which governs this case is quite an obvious one, and that we do not require to borrow from the law of England or any other source in order to settle it",[80] but in the lower court, the decision of Sheriff Guthrie Smith had made reference to the 1872 Massachusetts case of *Fitzgerald v Cavin* that "if the defendant intended to do the act done by him, and that act was unlawful and unjustifiable, and the act caused bodily harm, the plaintiff could recover".[81] It is perhaps unsurprising, therefore, to find parallels in the analysis of intention as between the modern Scots and Louisiana cases, both focusing on the intention to make offensive contact rather than the intention to cause injury.[82]

Commentaries on the Law of Scotland, and, in later editions, the *Principles*, although more frequently in relation to property law rather than tort.

76 Compare Bell, *Prin* § 2027: "The rights which belong to persons in their individual capacity, may be distinguished as absolute or relative; the former having reference to the condition of the person in respect of safety, freedom and reputation; the latter having reference to the relation in which they stand with other individuals"; and the opening of Kent's Lecture XXIV: "The rights of persons in private life are either absolute, being such as belong to individuals in a single unconnected state; or relative, being those which arise from the civil and domestic relations."

77 There are several references, but see *Lectures on the Law of Scotland* (1864, ed J McLaren), vol 1, 5: "The works of Kent, and of Story, and of Greenleaf, are well known and justly appreciated; but it is in the Reports of some of the American Courts, in the elaborate arguments of the Bar, and the admirable judgments delivered from the Bench, that the true glory of the American Jurisprudence is to be found."

78 And notably also (although admittedly by English judges) in the leading twentieth-century Scots negligence cases of *Donoghue v Stevenson* 1932 SC (HL) 31 (see Lord Atkin at 56) and *Bourhill v Young* 1942 SC (HL) 78.

79 (1885) 12 R 1129.

80 At 1132.

81 110 Mass 153 (Mass 1872), per Putnam J at 153. (Guthrie Smith had found the citation in *Underhill on Torts*). This case is one of the illustrative examples in the Reporter's Note accompanying § 892A of the *Restatement (Second) Torts* (on the defence of consent).

82 In Louisiana cases involving practical jokes between colleagues that misfired, the requisite level of intention is found in "an intent to bring about a result which will invade the interests of another

Today transatlantic cross-referencing is rare. American authorities are seldom encountered in modern Scots cases, at least in this area of law, and in Louisiana, similarly, leading English texts are cited only occasionally and Scottish texts never or almost never.[83] Moreover, significant divergence between the English and American Common Law traditions has pulled Scots and Louisiana law in different directions. The law of privacy can be taken as an example.

At one time the common resource found in Anglo-American law led to obvious parallels. In Louisiana the landmark decision is *Denis v Leclerc* in 1811, while in Scotland a very similar case, *Cadell and Davies v Stewart*,[84] was heard in 1804. Both involved the publication of letters without the permission of the original author (or in the Scots case, of his executors), and both rested primarily on the authority of an English case, *Pope v Curl*,[85] to the effect that sending a letter transferred the paper upon which it was written but not "the liberty and profit" of publishing its contents.[86] It seems worth adding that the English and the Scottish cases both concerned significant literary figures, respectively Alexander Pope and Robert Burns. While, however, *Denis v Leclerc* seems generally regarded as the starting point for privacy protection in Louisiana,[87] no such development followed on in Scotland from the pursuer's success in *Cadell*,[88] and the laws soon began to diverge. For this the explanation probably lies in the very different courses followed by the respective Common Law neighbours. American law has come close to codifying

---

in a way that the law forbids"(*Caudle v Betts* 512 So 2d 389, 391 (La 1987), per Justice Dennis at 392). See also *Villa v Derouen* 614 So 2d 714 (La App 3rd Cir 1993) per Judge Saunders at 717: "the harmful or offensive contact and not the resulting injury is the physical result which must be intended"; and *Baugh v Redmond* 565 So 2d 953 (La App 2nd Cir 1990) per Judge Jones at 958: "The intention of the defendant need not be malicious nor need it be an intention to inflict actual damage. It is sufficient if the actor intends to inflict either a harmful or physical contact without the other's consent."

83 E.g., *Mashburn v Collin* 355 So 2d 879 (La 1977) refers to the then current edition of the leading English text, *Gatley on Libel and Slander*, 7th edn of 1974, in determining the scope of the defence of fair comment in defamation; *Fricke v Owens-Corning Fiberglas Corp* 571 So 2d 130 (La 1990) refers to R Dias and B Markesinis, *Tort Law*, 1st edn (1984) in analysing the meaning of consent in relation to assault.

84 (1804) Mor App Literary Property No 4.

85 (1741) 2 Atk 342.

86 On this point see also Bell, *Comm* vol 1, 111-112,

87 E.g., by Stone, "Tort doctrine" (n 7) § 192. See also D E Bennett, "Injunctive protection of personal interests – a factual approach" (1939) 1 Tulane LR 665 at 680; Note by RHD, (1946) 21 Tulane LR 289 at 29.

88 But followed, e.g., in *Caird v Syme* (1887) 14 R (HL) 37 in which students of the pursuer, the Professor of Moral Philosophy at Glasgow University, were prevented from publishing pamphlets containing their transcripts of his lecture notes – another case in which significant American authority was cited to the court by the pursuer.

privacy in the Restatement (Second) of Torts § 652. As noted above, English law, by contrast, has failed to develop a general tort of breach of privacy, preferring to "shoehorn"[89] privacy into other torts and breach of confidence, and, so far at least, the position has not been changed by the incorporation of the European Convention on Human Rights into UK domestic law by the Human Rights Act 1998.

Following the example of England, Scots law protects privacy only insofar as incidental to interests already recognised as protected by delict, such as breach of confidence,[90] defamation,[91] and, in earlier times, verbal injury.[92] There are faint signs of change. In one modern case it was said that:[93]

> [I]t does not follow that, because a specific right to privacy has not so far been recognised, such a right does not fall within existing principles of the law. Significantly my attention was not drawn to any case in which it was said in terms that there is no right to privacy.

In that case the pursuer claimed damages in respect of over-intrusive surveillance of his home by a private investigator. There was debate between counsel as to the applicability of the Roman Law *actio iniuriarum* to deal with this type of invasion of privacy, with reference to the *Digest*[94] and to Zimmermann's *The Law of Obligations*.[95] Notwithstanding such reference to

---

89 This metaphor seems to have been used first in this context in H Beale and N Pittam, "The Impact of the Human Rights Act 1988", in D Friedmann and D Barak-Erez (eds), *Human Rights in Private Law* (2001) 131 at 140. The term is taken up by Lord Phillips in *Douglas v Hello* [2006] QB 125 at para 53.

90 *McCosh v Crow* (1903) 5 F 670. Reference was also made to the English case of *Pollard v Photographic Co* (1888) 40 Ch D 345, in which use of photographs was enjoined in similar circumstances on the ground that there was an implied contract not to use the negative for such purposes, and also on the ground that such use in breach of confidence was an equitable wrong. See also *X v BBC* 2005 SLT 796 (interdict imposed on BBC from using embarrassing images of pursuer in television broadcast, primarily on basis of breach of confidence).

91 See, e.g., *Robertson v Keith* 1936 SC 29 (unsuccessful action for defamation following heavy-handed police surveillance); also *Adamson v Martin* 1916 SC 319, in which, a decade after *Itzkovitch* (n 102 below) in Louisiana, a suspect in a Scots case, against whom charges were dropped, succeeded in compelling the local constabulary to delete his photograph and fingerprints from its "Thieves' Gallery". The court referred to the general principle that what was done was not authorised by any enactment. However, he was unsuccessful in obtaining damages under the head of defamation.

92 See, e.g. Hume, *Lectures*, vol 3, 139: "Redress may be had for the imputation even of mere defects and misfortunes, such as are attended with no manner of blame, if they are such as expose the person to ridicule, or derision, and thus tend to exclude the individual from society, or to depreciate and degrade him there (examples were revelations of cancer, scrophula, "or other loathsome disease", insanity, castration, impotence, incurable disease).

93 Per Lord Bonomy in the Outer House case of *Martin v McGuiness* 2003 SLT 1424 at para 28.

94 Noted in Lord Bonomy's judgment at para 29 as "*Digest of Justinian*, Mommsen (ed), at para 21.7 and 21.18", although it is not clear which passages are indicated by this reference.

95 R Zimmermann (the author's name is misspelt in the report), *The Law of Obligations: Roman Foundations of the Civilian Tradition* (1990), 1053-1059 (on "The different forms of iniuria").

Civilian authority, however, the court was not prepared to be drawn as to the status of any freestanding privacy right.[96] No reference was made to the broad conceptual structure of the law of delict in Scotland or to Civilian jurisdictions elsewhere in Europe. Since the case for damages was in any event held irrelevant and the point did not require to be decided, Lord Bonomy merely noted the arguments in the briefest of terms. He did, however, conjectured that "[i]t may ... be only a short step from an assault on personality of the nature of an insult to the dignity, honour or reputation of a person, causing hurt to his feelings, to deliberate conduct involving unwarranted intrusion into the personal or family life of which the natural consequence is distress"[97] (which might accordingly meet the criteria for the *actio iniuriarum*).

An important recent development in England has been the expansion of breach of confidence to provide a broad level of protection for informational privacy. Indeed, in the personal context, the equitable wrong of breach of confidence has been reconceptualised as a new tort of misuse of private information[98] which dispenses with the need for a pre-existing confidential relationship between the parties.[99] Given the readiness to adopt English authority on breach of confidence in Scotland, it seems probable that the law of confidentiality will progress along similar lines there too. An important limitation is that the new tort addresses only informational privacy and not the equally deserving territorial[100] and personal/corporeal[101] zones of privacy. In those domains, therefore, the scope of protection in Scots law is likely to remain uncertain.

96 Although in another recent case, *Response Handling Ltd v BBC* 2008 SLT 51 (concerning a media exposé of the pursuer's working practices), the court appeared to accept as axiomatic, and the defenders did not dispute, that a corporate right to privacy of possessions existed, on the authority of art 1 of the First Protocol to the ECHR, and European jurisprudence.

97 Para 29.

98 *Campbell v Mirror Group Newspapers* [2004] 2 AC 457 per Lord Nicholls at para 14; *McKennitt v Ash* [2008] QB 73 per Buxton LJ at para. 8; *Murray v Express Newspapers plc* [2008] EMLR 12. The main catalyst for this development was the need to give appropriate recognition to Art 8 ECHR, protecting private and family life, home and correspondence. It is now recognised that in England as in Scotland, Arts 8 and 10 (freedom of expression) ECHR are no longer "merely of persuasive or parallel effect" but have become "the very content" of the common law (*McKennitt v Ash* [2008] QB 73 per Buxton LJ at para 11, citing Lord Woolf CJ in *A v B plc* [2003] QB 195 at para 4).

99 On the demands of "conscience" placed by Equity upon the parties in a prior relationship of confidence and the shift in attention to the private nature of the information itself: see *Campbell v Mirror Group Newspapers Ltd* [2004] 2 AC 457 per Lord Hoffmann at para 44.

100 As threatened, e.g., by over-intrusive surveillance of the individual's home: see *Martin v McGuiness* 2003 SLT 1424.

101 See, e.g., *Wainwright v Home Office* [2004] 2 AC 406 per Lord Hoffmann at para 35 (refusing recognition of a general tort of privacy offering a remedy in respect of an inappropriate strip-search by public officials); see also *Wainwright v UK* (2007) 44 EHRR 40.

By contrast, the levels of protection for privacy are considerably more developed in Louisiana, primarily because of the very different course followed by American Common Law. While protection of privacy may be grounded in the general clause of the Civil Code, this area of law demonstrates not only the flexibility of that clause but also its vulnerability. It seems clear that, as in other states of the US, the "right to be left alone" was taken not from the Civil Law but from the American Common Law, in the wake of publication of the famous Warren and Brandeis article in 1890.[102] Since the 1960s, Prosser's four-part analysis of the right of privacy,[103] which is mirrored in the Restatement (Second) of Torts,[104] has also been important in shaping the development of the doctrine in the Louisiana courts.[105] It is thus uncontroversial in Louisiana that damages may be claimed where appropriation of name, image or personal details for unauthorised use has caused distress to the individual concerned.[106] And although earlier case law suggested that no damages would be awarded where no such emotional impact had been caused by publication,[107] there are signs that a more expansive approach may now be adopted. In the 2004 case of *Capdeboscq v Francis*, for example, the plaintiffs found that immodest Mardi Gras images of themselves had been appropriated by the defendants for the cover of a video. The court said that "if the Plaintiffs prove that Defendants misappropriated their likeness, they would be entitled to emotional damages, *as well as* the reasonable market value of the use of the Plaintiffs' identity or persona in the commercial setting in which Defendants have used it",[108] although in the event the plaintiffs adduced insufficient evidence of market value on which to quantify such a claim. The authorities which were central

---

102   See *Itzkovitch v Whitaker* 115 La 479, 39 So 499 (1905), in which the plaintiff successfully compelled the removal of his photograph from a "rogues' gallery" put together by the local police; also *Schulman v Whitaker* 115 La 628, 39 So 737 (1905).

103   (1960) 48 *California Law Review* 383, later substantially reproduced in ch 20 of *Torts* (n 9 above).

104   § 652A-I.

105   E.g., in cases such as *Jaubert v Crowley Post-Signal Inc* 375 So 2d 1386 (La 1979).

106   *Jaubert v Crowley Post-Signal Inc.* Earlier cases include *McAndrews v Roy* 131 So 2d 256 (La App 1961) (health studio publishing "before and after" pictures of client's physique without his consent); *Lambert v Dow Chemical Co* 215 So 2d 673 (La App 1st Cir 1968) (employer using pictures of an employee's injury as a warning).

107   *Slocum v Sears Roebuck and Co* 542 So 2d 777(La App 3d Cir 1989). See comments in P N Broyles, "Intercontinental identity: The right to the [sic] identity in the Louisiana Civil Code" (2005) 65 La LR 823 at 851 ff.

108   2004 WL 1418392 per Mcnamara J (emphasis added). See also *Prudhomme v Proctor and Gamble* 800 F Supp 390 (E D La 1992) in which a celebrity chef sued two coffee companies because their advertisements used an actor who resembled him. It was held that although the Louisiana courts had not yet explicitly recognised that a right of publicity could be protected by invoking the general clause, neither had they excluded it and the chef should not be prevented from presenting an argument on that ground (as well as on various others).

to the court's deliberations were the Restatement (Second) of Torts § 652, as well as Common Law texts such as David Elder's *Privacy Torts* and Thomas McCarthy's *The Rights of Publicity and Privacy*.

F. PUBLICITY RIGHTS: SURVIVAL OF CIVILIAN ANALYSIS?

In both jurisdictions it remains to be seen whether recognition of the commercial value of "image" or "publicity" rights, as discussed in the previous section, leads to a reappraisal of their character – in particular to an acceptance that some types of personality right may be proprietorial (proprietary) in nature. For the time being, however, it seems that such Common Law notions have not been decisive in moulding analysis.

It comes as no surprise, of course, that Louisiana has been influenced by writing from other parts of the United States on the "reification" of personality.[109] But Professor Yiannopoulos has drawn attention to the continuing relevance of Civilian doctrine in asserting the extra-patrimonial nature of personality rights:[110]

> [T]he incidents of human personality are not things susceptible of appropriation. Thus, one's name, likeness, liberty, personal integrity, and honor are not objects of property, but are incidents of a comprehensive "right of personality" that is accorded an almost absolute protection without regard to rules of property law.

In Scotland these issues have been little explored. In respect of English law the House of Lords has declined to recognise a proprietorial interest in personal information, although accepting that Equity provides remedies when information is misused.[111] North of the border, there is no authority directly in point,[112] but in principle there remains a clear distinction between

---

109 See G M Armstrong, "The reification of celebrity: Persons as property" (1991) 51 La LR 443; E H Reiter, "Personality and patrimony: Comparative perspectives on the right to one's image" (2002) 76 Tulane LR 673; M Jacoby and D L Zimmerman, "Foreclosing on fame: Exploring the uncharted boundaries of the right of publicity" (2002) 77 N Y U L Rev 1322.

110 "Property" (n 7) at § 17. See also Broyles, "Intercontinental identity" (n 107). For further exposition of the Civilian model see, e.g., J Neethling, J M Potgieter and P J Visser, *Neethling's Law of Personality*, 2nd edn (2005), 11-14, para 3.2.1; P Kayser, "Les droits de la personnalité: Aspects théoriques et pratiques" (1971) *Revue trimestrielle de droit civil* 445; C Schmidt-König, *Introduction à la langue juridique française*, 2nd edn (2006), 185 and 203.

111 *Douglas v Hello* [2008] 1 AC 1 per Lord Hoffmann at para 124; Lord Walker at para 293, but cf *Irvine v Talksport* [2002] EMLR 32 in which a passing-off action was used to protect the "goodwill" attached to the image of a celebrity. For discussion see H Carty, "The common law and the quest for the IP effect", 2007 *Intellectual Property Quarterly* 237.

112 There is authority to support the grant of interdict *McCosh v Crow* (1903) 5 F 670; *X v BBC* 2005 SLT 796, but there has been no case in which damages have been obtained for false appropriation of name or image per se – apart from actions for defamation or breach of confidence.

personality rights on the one hand, and the right to defend or control those rights by means of the law of contract or delict on the other. The former – the "être" rights – remain extra-patrimonial, while the latter – the "avoir" rights which derive from them – are patrimonial.[113] Thus while an individual may contract with another with regard to the use of his or her image, and the benefits of such a contract might, in turn, be assigned elsewhere, no mechanism has been asserted by which one individual might assign image, name or honour to another, nor are these rights that creditors claim in the event of bankruptcy.

In this area the framework, in both jurisdictions, rests upon established Civilian principles of property law. It may therefore prove easier to resist any "pull" by the Common Law towards recognition of a new hybrid form of property right than it has been to withstand Common Law influence in structuring and giving content to the law of tort/delict.

G. DIFFERENT "CONSTITUTIONAL MOMENTS"

A further point of divergence for the law of personality rights in Louisiana and Scotland derives from the contrasting "constitutional moments"[114] which have inspired the constitutionalisation of private law in the neighbouring Common Law systems. Hannes Rösler has described the background to the adoption of the First Amendment as one in which "the protection of political speech and the abolition of censorship [was seen] as 'the essential difference between the British government and the American constitutions'".[115] He contrasts the circumstances surrounding the development of European human rights law in the years following the Second World War, which had "a strong negative reference point: a past order to overcome by means of constitutionalism".[116] Generally speaking, primacy is given to freedom of speech in the US marketplace of ideas, whereas in the European context the starting point is the protection of dignity:[117]

---

113 See, e.g., *Milne v Gaulds Trs* (1841) 3 D 345 in which a claim of damages for wrongful imprisonment was held to be an "assignable claim" of a pecuniary nature (per Lord Meadowbank at 350).

114 H Rösler, "Harmonizing the German Civil Code of the nineteenth century with a modern constitution – the Lüth Revolution 50 years ago in comparative perspective" (2008) 23 Tul Eur & Civ L F 1 at 3.

115 Ibid at 7, citing Madison's *Report on the Virginia Resolutions* (1800).

116 Ibid at 7.

117 *R (on the application of A) v East Sussex County* [2003] EWHC 167 (Admin) per Munby J at para 86. Protection of dignity is similarly ranked above other rights in being placed in art 1 of the German Constitution: see R J Krotoszynski, "A comparative perspective on the first amendment: Free speech, militant democracy, and the primacy of dignity as a preferred constitutional value in Germany" (2004) 78 Tulane LR 1549.

[T]he phrase [human dignity] is not used in the Convention but it is surely immanent in article 8, indeed in almost every one of the Convention's provisions. The recognition and protection of human dignity is one of the core values – in truth *the* core value – of our society and, indeed, of all the societies which are part of the European family of nations and which have embraced the principles of the Convention.

This broad distinction has important practical implications for the protection of personality rights, in particular where there are conflicting civil liberties concerns. The law of defamation illustrates.

The interplay of Civilian and Common Law traditions is apparent in the development of the law of defamation in both Louisiana and Scotland. In Louisiana, liability is rooted in articles 2315 and 2316 of the Civil Code, requiring fault – which encompasses negligence or intention.[118] But the courts have made use of Common Law terminology in drawing the boundaries of the delict, in particular in distinguishing statements which are defamatory and defamatory *per se*, falsity and malice being presumed in relation to the latter but not the former.[119] In Scotland liability was originally premised upon the Civilian concept of *iniuria*,[120] but by the early nineteenth century, perhaps partly as a result of the expansion of newspapers, Scots law followed English law[121] in "slipping into strict liability".[122] The presumption of *animus iniurandi* became irrebuttable, but *veritas*, which in earlier times had not always exculpated, became a complete defence, as in English law.[123] English authority is readily cited in modern Scots cases,[124] although Scotland has not adopted the Common Law distinction between libel and slander – and does not therefore deem the former to be actionable *"per se"* and the latter to require "special" damage.

In both jurisdictions, constitutional concerns have been mediated primarily through reception of the law of the Common Law neighbour. This means that a significantly different approach is adopted in prioritising freedom of speech, particularly political speech.

---

118 *Costello v Hardy* 864 So 2d 129 (La 2004).
119 *Madison v Bolton* 234 La 997 102 So 2d 433 (La 1958); *Kennedy v Sheriff of East Baton Rouge* 935 So 2d 669 (La 2006).
120 And to this day, unlike in English law, there is no requirement that the defamatory remarks should have been published to a third party, since solatium may be claimed for "injury to feelings", "distress of mind" or "disturbance of peace": Hume, *Lectures*, vol 3, 155; *Mackay v McCankie* (1883) 10 R 537 per Lord President Inglis at 539; *Ramsay v Maclay and Co* (1890) 18 R 130 per Lord President Inglis at 133.
121 See P Mitchell, *The Making of the Modern Law of Defamation* (2005) ch 5.
122 As analysed by J Blackie, "Defamation", in Reid and Zimmermann, *History*, vol 2, 633 at 662.
123 Ibid 671.
124 For an example of a modern case see *Adams v Guardian Newspapers* 2003 SC 425 in which by far the majority of the authorities discussed were English or Commonwealth.

The landmark US Supreme Court decision in *New York Times Co v Sullivan*[125] limited liability for defamation of public officials by requiring the plaintiff to establish with "convincing clarity" that the offending remarks were published with "actual malice".[126] Subsequent decisions have extended this requirement to alleged defamation of public figures (not only public officials),[127] and a sequence of further US Supreme Court cases have addressed the question as to how far First Amendment concerns should affect defamation cases brought by private individuals.[128] This jurisprudence is at the heart of the reasoning of the Louisiana courts, as illustrated in the decision of the Louisiana Supreme Court in *Kennedy v Sheriff of East Baton Rouge*,[129] a case involving a matter of public concern but brought by a private plaintiff against a private defendant. The judgment of Justice Weimer recognised the *New York Times* decision as "seminal", and although it claimed flexibility in setting standards of liability in relation to private individuals, it acknowledged that "the protections afforded by the First Amendment supercede the common law presumptions of fault, falsity, and damages with respect to speech involving matters of public concern, at least insofar as media defendants are concerned".[130]

By contrast, the path followed by the Scottish courts is markedly different in that it follows developments in the English law of defamation. A series of English cases in the late 1990s reviewed the mechanisms for balancing protection for free speech against protection of reputation. In particular, scrutiny was applied to the defence of qualified privilege as applied to media reports on matters of public interest. The leading English case of this period was *Reynolds v Times Newspapers Ltd*,[131] in which a leading Irish politician sued following newspaper allegations of misconduct in public duties. At the time when *Reynolds* was decided, the Human Rights Act 1998 had not yet come into force, but Lord Steyn's speech described the Act as the "new landscape" which provided the "taxonomy" of privilege, and in which the "starting point"

---

125 *New York Times Co v Sullivan* 376 US 254 (1964).
126 At 285-286 and 280.
127 *Curtis Publishing Co v Butts* 388 US 130 (1967). It was accepted in *Kennedy v Sheriff of East Baton Rouge* 935 So 2d 669 (La 2006) that a public figure was a "non-public official who is intimately involved in the resolution of important public questions or who, by reason of his or her fame, shapes events in areas of concern to society at large".
128 *Rosenbloom v Metromedia Inc* 403 US 29 (1971) which was generally considered to have gone too far in this regard; *Gertz v Robert Welch Inc* 418 US 323 (1974); *Philadelphia Newspapers v Hepps* 475 US 767 (1986).
129 935 So 2d 669 (La 2006) (although it was the defendant rather than the plaintiff who was a public servant in that case).
130 At 677.
131 [2001] 2 AC 127.

was the right of freedom of expression.[132] Nonetheless, the court declined to recognise a wide category of qualified privilege attaching to "political infor- mation" to counteract the "chilling"[133] effect of the threat of libel actions on freedom of expression. Reference was made to the forms of generic privi- lege recognised for political comment in other jurisdictions, and in particular there was discussion of *New York Times Co v Sullivan*.[134] However, counsel did not press upon the court "the full amplitude of the doctrine" laid down in *New York Times*,[135] and the court acceded to the recommendations of the Faulks[136] and Neill[137] committees that adoption of a similar category in England would tilt the balance of the law of defamation too far against the defamed plaintiff – even in relation to the publication of political informa- tion.[138] Instead, the existing category of qualified privilege was re-appraised and a more detailed focus given to the established criteria.[139] In a subse- quent Scottish case, *Adams v Guardian Newspapers Ltd*, it was accepted that *Reynolds*, and the English jurisprudence which flowed from it, provided "authoritative guidance" as to the defence of qualified privilege.[140]

H. CONCLUSION

In Louisiana and Scotland, the Civil Law basis for the delictual protection of personality rights is both obvious and uncontested. Nevertheless, the contrast between codified and uncodified traditions is very apparent. In Louisiana, despite a powerful draw towards the "torticles" of the Common Law, the Code remains the centre of gravity. By contrast, Scots lawyers have struggled to build on the Civilian tradition set out, admittedly in undeveloped form, in the writings of the "Institutional" period. In dealing with new situations it has often proved easier and more fruitful to borrow structures from English

132 At 208.
133 Discussed notably in E M *Barendt, Libel and the Media: The Chilling Effect* (1997).
134 For detailed comparison between US and English/Commonwealth defamation law, see A T Kenyon, *Defamation: Comparative Law and Practice* (2005) 240-253; S Deakin, A Johnston, and B Markesinis, *Markesinis and Deakin's Tort Law*, 6th edn (2008), 865-869.
135 Per Lord Bingham (Court of Appeal) at 161.
136 Committee on Defamation, Cmnd 5909 (1975), paras 603-617.
137 Report on Practice and Procedure in Defamation (1991) 164.
138 Lord Nicholls at 198.
139 In the leading speech, at 205, Lord Nicholls identified ten factors which assisted in determining whether there was a public duty to publish political information, and whether the public had a corresponding interest in receiving it. These factors were further glossed and particular atten- tion given to the importance of "responsible journalism" in *Jameel v Wall Street Journal Europe* [2007] 1 AC 359.
140 2003 SC 425 per Lord Reed at para 52.

law. Less explicably, where such structures have been lacking, as in the case of protection for privacy, there has been reluctance to pursue an independent Scottish line. Moreover, the "gravitational pull" of the Common Law has not only been exerted at unequal levels of force but it has also, in modern times, pulled Scotland and Louisiana in rather different directions, as demonstrated in relation to recognition, or failure to recognise, the tort of privacy. In particular, the jurisprudence of each Common Law neighbour reflects different priorities in weighing personality rights against other constitutional rights. In summary, therefore, while interesting parallels may be drawn in the interplay between Civil Law and Common Law traditions in nineteenth-century Louisiana and Scotland, comparative analysis of the modern law is, for the most part, a study in difference.

Index

The index is arranged in word by word order. References to Civil Code entries are to principal extracts. References to authors are those discussed in the text.

accessory rights
  consequences of doctrinal choice,
    13–16
  doctrinal basis, 11–13
  implied grant, 13
  implied terms, 13, 14
  intention of parties, 14–16
  Louisiana Civil Code, 12–13
  parking, 8, 10–11
  prescriptive servitudes, 15
acquiescence, 21
acquisitive prescription, 4, 99
actio in de rem verso, 325, 327, 329, 338
actio iniuriarum, 219, 229, 394–5, 402, 403
actus merae facultatis, 78
adoption
  degrees of affinity, 183, 187, 189
adult domestic relationships
  20th century, 148–56
  21st century, 156–70
  cohabitation, 156–60
  comparisons, 171–2
  covenant marriage, 167–70
  divorce, 153–4
  financial consequences of divorce, 155–6
  generally, 146–8, 170–2
  marriage, 148
  personal consequences of marriage, 149–50
  property consequences of marriage, 150–2
  same-sex relationships, 160–7
  succession rights of spouses, 152–3
  unregistered relationships, 156–60

affirmative business obligations, 32
affirmative land obligations, 34n
affirmative servitude, Louisiana, 68
altius non tollendi, 83
asbestos litigation
  asymptomatic exposure, 381
  Compensation Act 2006, 378, 380
  concurrent exposure, 379
  indivisible injuries, 379, 390
  joint and several liability, 378
  liability *in solidum*, 377, 378
  Louisiana, 378, 379, 383–4, 385, 390
  pleural plaques, 381–4, 386
  pursuer to demonstrate materiality, S, 379, 380
  Scotland, 377, 378, 379, 380
  solidary liability, 377, 378
  substantial factor criterion, 378, 379
  use of jury trials in Louisiana, 383–4, 385
  see also causation
assythment, 218, 219
Aynès, L, 233

Balfour, *Practicks*, 250
Barham, M E, 397
Bell, G J, *Principles*
  communication with US, 2–4, 400
  consideration, 274
  French influences, 5–7, 25
  Louisiana Civil Code and, 2–4
  ownership of trust property, 140
  personality rights, 393
  prudent purchaser, 8
  recompense, 337–8

benefited property, 68n
Birks, P, 323
Black, R, 219
Blackie, J, 294

cas fortuit, 249, 252
causa pro qua debenture, 261
causation
    analytical differences, 358–60
    asbestos-related injuries, 376–81
    "but for" test, 363, 364, 365, 376
    causa causans, 373, 374, 375
    cause-in-fact, 359, 360, 363–9
    competing theories of negligence,
        358–60
    differences, 356–8, 385–6
    duty/risk analysis, 356, 361, 370, 371
    ease of association, 371–2, 375
    fault and, 253–5
    future illness or injury, 381–2
    generally, 355–6
    Housley presumption, 366
    indeterminate, 363, 365, 368
    interminate, 375–6
    jurisprudence constante, 356, 357
    liability, scope of, 369–75
    material contribution, 366, 367, 369
    negligence, 357–8
    NESS test, 365, 385
    NESS test, meaning, 365n
    over-determined, 363, 364
    parallels between Louisiana and Scot-
        land, 385
    pleural plaques, 381–4
    procedural differences, 356–8
    proximate cause terminology, 370–1,
        373, 374, 385
    remoteness of injury, 360
    scope of liability, 369–75
    sine qua non test, 363, 364, 368
    stare decisis, 356, 357
    substantial factor test, 364, 367–9, 385
    terminology, 360–3, 385
    use of jury trials in Louisiana, 357,
        383–4, 385
    supervening cause, 362, 373–4, 375
cause
    definition, 290
    error and, 264–5, 269–70
    failure, 262, 264

Louisiana, 247, 261–5
    Scots law, 261
    see also contract
cause-in-fact, 359, 360, 363–9
Celtic Church, 185
civil marriage, South Africa, 170
civil partnership, 115, 128, 162–3, 190,
    204
Civil Union marriage, South Africa, 170
Code Noir, 191, 192, 194
cohabitation
    common law of Scotland, 156–7
    criminalisation, 159n
    domestic violence, 158–9
    Family Law (Scotland) Act 2006, 158
    financial settlement on separation, S,
        158
    "illegitimate" recognition, 159
    legal treatment in other US states,
        159n
    Louisiana, 158–60
    Scotland, 156–8
    status, 158
    succession rights, 158
    surviving cohabitant title to sue, 157
    withholding of benefits, 159
community property
    composition, 151
    consequences of marriage, 150–1
    effect, 151
    effect of divorce, 155
    fruits of the paraphernal property, 138
    generally, 119–20, 125, 129
    protection, 121
    surviving spouse, 111, 125, 129
    termination, 151, 152
    usufruct, 111, 125, 129
concubinage, meaning, 167n
condictio causa data causa non secuta,
    250, 347, 348, 349, 353
condictio indebiti, 325, 329, 337, 338, 339
condictio ob causam finitam, 347, 348,
    349
condictio ob turpem causam, 346
connubium, 176
consensus, 176
consideration, 285, 287–9; *see also* prom-
    issory estoppel
contract
    analysis, 246

assumption of risk: Louisiana law, 255–9, 260; Scots law, 259–60
awareness of purpose, 269–70
breach preceding unexpected event, 254–5
cas fortuit, 249, 252
cause: generally, 247; Louisiana law, 247, 261–5; Scots law, 261
comparison between Scots law and Louisiana law, 269–72
condictio causa data causa non secuta, 250, 273–4
consideration, 274
coronation cases, 266, 271
delectus personae, 268
dissolution, 334–6
Draft Common Frame of Reference, 248, 260, 276–7, 280, 297
drafting, 269–70
economic frustration cases, 257–8
enrichment and contract, 345–50; *see also* unjustified enrichment
error and cause, relationship, 264–5, 269–70
European Union law, 248
extraordinary event, 256
failure of cause, 262, 264
fault, 246–7
fault and causation, 253–5
force majeure, 249, 273
foreseeability, 252
fortuitous event, 252
frustration, 250, 251, 255, 260, 273–5
frustration of purpose, 266–9, 271, 278
generally, 245
good faith, 247–8
illegal, 346
impossibility, 249, 250, 260
impossibility of performance, 264
imprévision, 249
negotiation, 346
over-performance, 333, 347
pacta sunt servanda, 249
partial impossibility, 272
pre-contract, 345–6
rebus sic stantibus, 248, 249
rei interitus, 250
retention, 276
structural differences, 246–8
superior force, 252n

supervening event, definition, 253
supervening impossibility, 250–1
suspensive condition, subject to, 347
unexpected circumstances: consequences, 272–7; Louisiana, 272–3; use of term, 246
United States influence, 277
unjustified enrichment, 273, 274; *see also* unjustified enrichment
void, 332
voidable, 347–8
contracts of intellectual gratification
aircraft noise, 225
development of exception in *Diesen*, 224–6
distress claims, 212
dommage moral, 222, 234
France, comparison, 213–14
generally, 242–3
immaterial damages, 210
justification for non-pecuniary damages, 222
meaning, 208–10
mental upset or distress, 224
mere vexation, 212
moral damages, 210, 212–13, 242
non-pecuniary damages award, 211
physical inconvenience, 223, 225
promise of marriage, 233–5
Quebec, comparison, 213–14
reduced enjoyment, 224
remoteness, 226, 227–8
similarities in development, 233–8
solatium, 226
solatium *ex contractu*, 210, 211
sole purpose, 222
South Africa, comparison, 213
specific implementation, 210
specific performance, 210–11
stigma damage, 225n
uncertainty, 211
verbal insults, 214
very object of a contract, 223
contracts of intellectual gratification – Louisiana
breach of promise of marriage, 233, 234–5
category broadened, 229
Code revision 1985, 240
codification regarding *nonpecundam*,

228–30
contemplation test, 229
intentional aggrievement, 229
interpretations, 230–2: after 1985,
240–2
Meador interpretation, 238–40
mistaken translations, 230–2
object and cause, communication on,
237–8
non-delivery of wedding trousseau
dresses, 236–7
railway case, 237–8
undelivered telegram, 235–6
contracts of intellectual gratification –
Scotland
Addis case, 219–21
assythment, 218, 219
breach of promise of marriage, 233,
235
Erskine, 217
holidaymakers' cases, 221–2
Hume, 217–18
influence of *Diesen*, 221–2
pain and suffering, 214–15
recovery of immaterial loss, 218
solatium, 215, 217, 218
Stair, 216–17
Cooper, Lord, 259, 274, 278
coronation cases, 266, 271
Council of Trent, 191
covenant marriage
Declaration of Intent, 168
explicit obligations, 167–8
grounds for divorce, 168
introduction, 167
premarital counselling, 168
Crawford, W, 362
culpa in contrahendo, 303, 319
customary marriage, South Africa, 170

Dagan, H, 36–7, 50
David, R, 124
DCFR *see* Draft Common Frame of
Reference
Defence of Marriage Act, US, 116n
delectus personae, 268
delicticles, 390, 393, 394
Denson Smith, J, 262
Destination du père de famille doctrine, 7,
17–18, 20, 25–8

Devine, T, 49
Diocletian, 164n
divorce
availability, 153
financial consequences, 155–6
financial settlement, 154
grounds, 168
no-fault, 153, 169
non-cohabitation period, 154, 169
welfare of child, 154
divorce – Louisiana
adultery, 154
community property, 155
conviction of a felony, 154
imprisonment at hard labour, 154
periodic support award, 155
sentence to death, 154
violation of marital obligations, 153
divorce – Scotland
adultery, 153
clean break, 155–6
desertion, 153
matrimonial property, 155
domestic partner registration scheme, 128
domestic violence
cohabitants, 158–9
same-sex couples, 158n, 166, 172
dominant estate, Louisiana, 68
dominant tenement, Scotland, 68
dommage moral, 222, 234
donatio non praesumitur, 295n
donation, 295n
Draft Common Frame of Reference
(DCFR)
assumption of risk, 260
generally, 248, 280
promise, 297
variation in contract, 276–7
Du Plessis, J, 279

economic frustration cases, 257–8
equitable estoppel, 304
Erskine, *Institute*
consideration, 274
damages, 217
liferent, 129
promise, 319
res merae facultatis, 78, 82
servitude by prior use, 17
servitudes, 100

estoppel letters, 310
European Convention on Human Rights
  respect for private life, 389
Evans-Jones, R, 347
existing marriage, 177–8, 186

fidei commissa, 133
fiduciary fee, 140
force majeure, 249, 273
forced heirship, 106
fortuitous event, definition, 252
France
  contracts of intellectual gratification,
    213–14
  enrichment, 323, 324–6, 353
  general clause, 388
  influence on Bell, 5–7
  inheritance laws, 110
  moral damage, 213–14
  performance, 249
  privacy, 389–90
  unexpected circumstances, 278
  unity of harm, 214n
  unjustified enrichment, 324–6, 353
frustration
  assumption of risk, 259–60
  definition, 251, 255
  development, 250–1
  effect of, 273–5
frustration of purpose, 266–9, 271, 278
Fuller, L, 317

Gaius, 102, 399
Gale, C J, 25, 26
Galligan, Prof, 362–3
gay liberation, 147
gay pride, 147
gender equality, 149n
general clause *see* Louisiana Civil Codes
Germany
  enrichment, 323
  rebus sic stantibus, 249
Gloag & Henderson, *The Law of Scot-
    land*, 347
Gloag, W M, 260, 346
good faith, 247–8
Gretton, G, 144

Hale, Baroness, 166
Hansmann, H, 35–6

Hogg, M, 310, 344
Holmes, O W, 164–5
homologation, meaning, 291
homophobia, 165, 202n
Hope, *Practicks*, 299, 301
household goods, 152
Hume, *Lectures*, 217–18
Hurricane Katrina, 125n, 245, 258, 259

impediments to marriage
  absolute, 175, 176–8, 180–2
  decline in number, 197–8
  difference of race, 197
  differences, 202–4
  generally, 175
  identity of sex, 175
  impotence, 175, 177, 181
  impuberty, 175, 176–7, 180–1
  projections, 204–7
  relationship, 175, 178–9, 182–3, 205
  relative, 178–80, 182–4
  relaxation of, 198
  religious identification, 200–1
  same-sex marriage, 175
  secularisation, 198–202
  similarities, 198–202
implied servitude, 23, 24, 25
impossibilitatis coeundi, 181
impossibility, 249, 250, 260, 264, 272
impotence
  Louisiana, 193
  Roman law, 177, 181
  Scots Law, 185–6, 187–8
  see also impediments to marriage
imprévision, 249
impuberty
  Louisiana, 193, 195
  Roman law, 176–7, 180–1
  Scots law, 186–7, 187
  see also impediments to marriage
in faciendo principle, 7, 53, 56, 57, 60, 63,
    65, 66
incest taboo, 178–9
inheritance laws – surviving spouse
  aliment right, 122–3, 125
  civil partnerships, 115, 128
  cohabitants, 114
  community property, 111, 119–20,
    121, 125–6, 128–9, 153
  courtesy, 112, 113

development of rights, 109–13
differences, 124–31
domestic partner registration scheme,
    128
forced heirship, 106
France, 110
jus relictae, 112, 122
jus relicti, 112, 122
legal families, 124
legal rights, 121–2
Louisiana: development of rights,
    109–11; same-sex marriage, 115–16
marital fourth, 123
marital portion, 123–4, 125
mournings, right to, 123n
personal and heritable property dis-
    tinction, 111–12
preference, 106, 114–20
presumed will, 106
prior rights, 113, 118–19, 126
protection, 106, 121–4
public attitudes in Scotland, 119
public attitudes in US, 105n, 120
purpose, 105–6
same-sex marriage in Louisiana,
    115–16
same-sex partner, 117–18
Scotland: development of rights,
    111–13; public attitudes, 119
second families, 126–7
second spouse, 152
separate property, 153
similarities, 107–9
step-parents, 126–7, 152, 153
terce, 112, 113
Uniform Probate Code, 130
usufruct, 111, 125, 129, 153
who is surviving spouse, 114–18
widow's homestead, 124n
with children, 108–9
without children, 107–8, 153
iniuria, 394, 399, 407
institutional writers, 140, 393, 394
intentional torts, 391
ius commune, 299, 302

Jackson, B, 222
jus relictae, 112, 122
jus relicti, 112, 122

Kent, J, 3, 399, 400
Kraakman, R, 35–6

Lands Tribunal of Scotland
    establishment, 9
    positive servitude, dual aspect, 98
    praedial servitudes, 9
    rejection of compensation claims, 49
    title conditions in restraint of trade,
        50–1, 52
    variation and discharge of title condi-
        tions, 62, 63, 66, 77
lease exclusives, 32
Lee, R W, 137
legal causation, 360, 361–2
letters of intent, 308
Lewinson-Zamir, D, 36
LGBT community, 147
liability
    causa causans, 373, 374, 375
    duty/risk analysis, 356, 361, 370, 371
    ease of association, 371–2, 375
    Louisiana, 370–2
    novus actus interveniens, 362, 373–4,
        375
    proximate cause terminology, 370–1,
        373, 374, 385
    rather than legal causation, 369–70
    Scotland, 372–5
    see also causation
liferent, 129
Lindon, R, 390
Lislet, M, 6, 7
Litvinoff, S
    cause, 261–2, 262–3, 269, 270
    consideration, 287
    dissolution of contract, 272
    fault, 254
Louisiana Civil Code 1808, 3
Louisiana Civil Code 1825, 3
Louisiana Civil Code 1870, 3–4
Louisiana Civil Code
    art 4, fairness or equity, 248
    art 1873, impossibility, 249–50, 251–2,
        263–4, 278, 279
    art 1873, exceptions, 253–9, 260,
        263–4, 277
    art 1876, dissolution, 262, 272
    art 1877, partial impossibility, 272, 273,
        275, 276

art 1928, contracts of intellectual gratification, 209
art 1967, defining cause, 262, 290, 307,
308, 311, 314
art 2018, effects of dissolution, 334
art 2033, absolute nullity, 333
art 2298, enrichment without cause:
compensation, 328
art 2299, payment of a thing not owed,
331, 332
art 2315, general clause, 391–2
accessory rights, 12–13
consideration, 287–9
prerequisites to marriage, 195–7
Louisiana *Code Noir*, 191, 192, 194
Louisiana Digest of 1808
unexpected circumstances, 249
Louisiana State Law Institute
promissory estoppel, 283, 289–90, 302
Lovett, J, 10
Lubbe, G, 261

McBryde, W W, 221, 259, 266, 301
MacCormack, G, 274
Mackenzie, G, 78
Mackenzie Stuart, A, 132
MacQueen, H L, 296, 301, 308, 310, 314
Malaurie, P, 233
marriage
age of party, 148
choice of residence, 150
community property, 150–1
definitions, 148
divorce, 153–6
duress, 148
free consent, 148
gender equality, 149n
household goods, 152
incurable impotency, 163
inter-racial ban, 164
married woman's surname, 150
nullity, 163
parental authority over children, 150
permission, 148
personal consequences, 149–50
position of women, 149
property consequences, 150–2
property rights in Scotland, 151–2
reset, 150
separate property, 151

social and personal obligations, Scotland, 169
South Africa, 170
wife under age of majority, 149–50
see also adult domestic relationships
marriage – Christian adaptations
absolute impediments, 180–2
adoptive relatives, 183
existing marriage, 181–2
identity of sex, 184
impotence, 181
impuberty, 180–1
indissolubility of marriage, 182
relationship, 182–3
relative impediments, 182–4
spiritual relatives, 183
status, 183–4
marriage – Louisiana
absolute impediments, 193, 195
adoptive relations, 195
age requirement, 193
American period part 1, 193–5
American period part 2, 195–7
Code Noir, 191, 192, 194
Council of Trent, 191
existing marriage, 193, 195
French period (first), 190–2
French period (second), 193
homophobia, 202n
identity of sex, 195, 196–7, 203–4
impediments, 191
impotence, 193, 195
impuberty, 193, 195, 203
relationship, 194, 195–6, 203, 206–7
relative impediments, 194–5, 195–7
relatively null, 188n
same-sex couples, 196, 202n, 206–7
slave law, 192
Spanish period, 192
spiritual relatives, 191, 194
status, 194, 196
marriage – Roman law
absolute impediments, 176–8
Christian adaptations, 180–4
existing marriage, 177–8
identity of sex, 179–80
impotence, 177
impuberty, 176–7
incest taboo, 178–9
relationship, 178–9

relative impediments, 178–80
status, 179
marriage – Scots Law
absolute impediments, 185–6, 187–8
adoptive relatives, 187, 189
age requirement, 186
Celtic Church, 185
civil partnership, 190
existing marriage, 185–6, 188
from late twentieth century, 187–90
identity of sex, 187, 189–90, 203–4
impotence, 185–6, 187–8, 202
impuberty, 185–6, 187
nonage, 185
Reformation, 185
relationship, 186–7, 188–9, 203
relative impediments, 186–7, 188–90
status, 187, 189
voidable, 188
Married Women's Emancipation
legislation, 149
Married Women's Property (Scotland)
Acts, 149
matrimonial agreement, 151
Melville Monument liability, 292–4
Merrill, T, 34–5, 44, 51n
Miller, S, 348

naturalis aequitas, 248
negative prescription, 68, 100–1
negative servitudes
abolition in Scotland, 9, 68
use in Louisiana, 9, 68
see also real burden
negotiorum gestio, 325, 328, 337
nemo dat quod non habet, 143
nemo plus juris ad alium transferre potest
quam ipse haberet, 142, 143
NESS test
generally, 365, 385
meaning, 365n
see also causation
Nicholas, B, 323, 327, 331
nonage, 185, 198
non-marital cohabitation, 156–60
novus actus interveniens, 362, 373–4, 375
nudum pactum rules, 299
numerus clausus
account, 33–7
consolidation of expectations, 37

content of real rights, 34
difference between content and types,
34
economic efficiency, 36, 48
enforceability, 35–6
information costs, 34–5
meaning, 33
native assessment, 37–8
property types, 34
standardisation, 34–5

omne verbus de ore fideli cadit in debitum, 319

pacta sunt servanda, 249
Paisley, R, 38
Palmer, V V, 391, 397, 399
Pardessus, J-M, 6, 18–19, 25
parking servitude, 8, 10–11
Pascal, R A, 133–4
personal bar
donative intent, 295
homologation, 291, 292
Melville Monument liability, 292–4
presumption against donations, 295n
presumption of legal knowledge, 295
rationalisation of doctrine, 294
rei interventus rule, 291, 292
scope, 290
statutory form, 295–6
personality interests
liability for infringement, 391–2
personality rights
actio iniuriarum, 394–5, 402, 403
aggressor doctrine, 396
appropriation of name, image or
personal details, 404
assault, 394–5, 398, 400
breach of confidence, 403
common law, 397–405
concept, 387–8
confidentiality, 398
defamation, 407, 409
delicticles, 393, 394, 396
differences between Lousiana and
Scotland, 409–10
dommage, 389
ECHR article 8, 389
emotional damages, 404
emotional distress, 395

faute, 389, 391
freedom of speech, 406, 407–8
generally, 387–91
harassment, 395
iniuria, 394, 399, 407
insult, 395
intentional assault, 400
Louisiana general clause, 391–2
political speech, 406–9
privacy: Louisiana, 404–5; Scotland, 401–3
protection of dignity, 406–7
provocation, 396, 397
publication of letters without permission, 401
publicity rights, 405–6
qualified privilege, 408–9
Quebec Civil Code article 3 definition, 388
Scotland, 393–7, 401–3
surveillance, 402–3
use of English case law, 398–9
wrongful deprivation of liberty, 391–2, 393–4
pleural plaques, 381–4, 386
polygamous marriage, 206, 207
pomponius, 90, 91
positive prescription, 99
positive servitude, Scotland, 68
pothier, 215, 234, 324, 325, 338, 399
praedial servitudes *see* servitudes
predial servitudes
use of term, 1n, 68, 99
see also servitudes
Prescription and Limitation (Scotland) Act 1973, 72, 83, 100
prescription by non-use, 68, 101–3
prescription of liberty, 68
pretium affectionis, 216, 217, 219n
Principles of European Contract Law, 297
Principles, Definitions and Model Rules of European Private Law see Draft Common Frame of Reference
promise
Carbolic Smoke Ball case, 300, 301
detrimental reliance, 292
generally, 290–1
limitation, 293
option, meaning, 300n

proof, 300
reward cases, 300
Stair's *Institutions*, 297–300
unaccepted, 298
written resolution compared with, 298, 315–16
promissory estoppel
advertising, 308
article 1967, 307, 308, 311
at-will employment cases, 314–15
bankers' letters of credits, 308–9
bankruptcy remoteness, 309–10
cases, 306–16
cause, definition, 290
cause and consideration, Louisiana law, 287–9, 302
characteristics, 282–4
codification in Louisiana, 302–4
commercial transactions, 308
completed bargain cases, 307, 308
completed contract, 306–7, 312
consideration, 285, 287–9
construction contracts, 308
contract and, 305–6
credit agreements, 305
culpa in contrahendo, 303, 319
"cusp of contract" cases, 311–12
detrimental reliance, 317
England, 286, 300–1
estoppel letters, 310
evidentiary function, 317–19
family promises and gifts, 307, 313
formalitites, 317–19
historical introduction in Louisiana law, 287–90
irrevocable offers and options, 308
lack of acceptance, 313n
lending, 309
letters of intent, 308
liability, 316–17
loan cases, 305
Louisiana, in, 289–90, 302–4
mixing of Common and Civil Law, Louisiana, 302–4
moral implications, 282–3
omne verbum de ore fideli cadit in debitum, 319
option cases, 311
options, 305
personal bar, Scots law, 291–7

precontractual liability, 305
promise, Scots law, 290–1
promise supported by cause, 303
proof of promise, 312–13
public authorities, 313
reliance to be clear and reasonable, 314, 317
requirements contracts, 308
Requirements of Writing (Scotland) Act 1995, 295–6
Restatement (Second) of Contracts, 284–6, 296, 302–4, 319
statutory form in Scots law, 295–6
United States, 284–6, 296, 297
value requirement, 288
venire contra factum proprium, 304, 319
writing or authentic act, 318
writing requirement, 307
written resolution compared with promise, 298. 315–16
reward cases, 308
Proposition 8 debate, 165n
prosser, 404
Provosty, O, 52–8
proximate cause, 370–1, 373, 374, 385
pubertas, 176
puberty, 176–7, 180–1

Quebec
moral damage, 213–14
personality rights, 388
unexpected circumstances, effect on contracts, 279
Quebec Civil Code article 3, 388

racially restrictive covenant, 55–7
Rankine, J, *Landownership*, 27, 48, 49, 50
real burden
content, 44n
duration, 46
enforcement, 40
generally, 9
land development obligations, 61–3
legislation, 9, 39, 52
modern development, 49
negative limitations, 43
negative servitude and, 9, 96n
as real right, 61
requirements, 42–3

restricted use, 43–5
utilitas, 39
see also title conditions in restraint of trade
real rights, *numerous clausus* of, 33–8
rebus ipsis et factis doctrine, 18, 21, 22. 23
rebus sic stantibus, 248, 249
reformation, 185
Register of Sasines, 8
rei interitus, 250
rei interventus rule, 291, 292
Reid, E C, 294, 314
remoteness, 226, 227–8, 309–10, 360
répétition de l'indu, 325
Requirements of Writing (Scotland) Act 1995, 295–6
res merae facultatis
adjacent servient land, 86
aspects, 81–7
civil law, 90–1
class of permitted purposes, 84–5
common law, 89–90
exercise of servitude, 81–2
generally, 72, 74, 77, 95–6
length of initial period, 87–9
meaning, 78
negative servitudes, 83–4
property right, 79–80
retention, 81
right to be exercised at future date, 85–7
servitude, 80–7
suspensively conditional servitude, 91–5, 96
reset, 150
Restatement (Second) of Contracts, promissory estoppel, 284–6, 296, 302–4, 319
restitutio in integrum, 348
Rösler, H, 406
Rudden, B, 33–4, 36

same-sex couples
civil partnership, 190
Louisiana, 196, 202n, 206
same-sex marriage
impediment, 175
opposition to, 206–7
same-sex relationships

civil partnership, 162–3
domestic violence, 158n, 166, 172
ECHR compatibility, 161n
Louisiana, 160, 163–7
marriage bar, 160
non-discrimination principle, 161
religious beliefs, 161–2
threat to marriage, 163–4
Schlesinger, R B, 283
Schwartzmann, 392
scope of liability, 369–75; see also causation
Scottish Law Commission
Attitudes Towards Succession Law,
119, 127, 130, 152
existing marriage, 188
impotency, 187–8
Nature and the Constitution of Trusts,
145
preferences on property distribution at
death, 119
Remedies for Breach of Contract, 227
requirements of writing, 318
Scottish Social Attitudes Survey 2004,
114n
Sedgwick, T, 214–15, 219
separate property
claim by surviving spouse, 153
composition, 151
matrimonial agreement, 151
meaning, 151
servitude
Bell's definition, 4
Louisiana Civil Code 1870 (as
amended) definition, 4
servitude by prior use
comfortable enjoyment of property,
22, 23
comparisons, 23–4
continuous and apparent, 6, 17, 26
control factors, 23
destination du père de famille doctrine,
17–18, 20, 25–8
destination, 17–18, 20, 25–8
disallowed by the Netherlands, 17n
divided land, 16–17
doctrinal differences, 23–4
doctrine of acquiescence, 21
entailed estate, 20–1
French influence on Louisiana, 17–20

grant by implication, 21
implied terms, 23, 24, 26
intention, 23–4
intention at severance, 19
owner's intention through action, 19
Scottish cases, 20–3
servitudes
absence of positive activity, 100–1
accessory rights, 10–16, 74–5
acquisitive prescription, 4, 99
affirmative, 68, 96
airspace, 70
altius non tollendi, 83
ancillary rights, 75–6
benefited property, 68n
classifications, 4
compensation provision, 10
contractual freedom, 7–8
created by prior use, 16–28
creation, 4
definitions, 4
discharge, 9
dominant estate, 68
dominant tenement, 68
drafting suspensive, 95
engineering works, 74
exceptions to negative prescription,
77–8
extinction, 4, 72–6, 68–9, 100–1
extinction by non-use, 68, 101–3
French influences, generally, 5–7, 28,
29
future development sites, 70–1
general differences between Louisiana
and Scotland, 28–9
indivisibility, 102
known, 7, 23, 24
landlocked property, 69–70
legal relief, 71–2
minerals extraction, 76–7
natural, 68
negative, 68, 98
negative aspect of positive servitude,
97–9
negative prescription, 68, 100–1
obligation to refrain from certain
acivities, 97–8
parking, 8, 10–11
period of time to extinguish, 72–4
policy of extinction, 68–9

positive and negative aspects, 96–9,
    101–3
positive prescription, 99
postitive, 68, 96
predial, 1n, 68, 99
"prudent purchaser" protection, 8
publicity principle, 8, 23
real burden and, 9
rebus ipsis et factis, 18, 21, 22, 23
reconstitution, 69
registration, 8
res merae facultatis, 72, 74, 77, 78–87
right of access to public road, Scotland,
    71
right of forced passage, Louisiana, 71
*servitus in faciendo consistere non
    potest*, 97
similarities between Bell and Louisi-
    ana Civil Code, 4–5
suspension, 76–7
suspensively conditional, 91–5, 96
time restrictions, 101–3
utilitas requirement, 39–41
variation, 9
servitus in faciendo consistere non potest,
    97
Shaw, P, 338
Smith, H, 34–5, 44, 51n
Smith, L, 330
Smith, T B, 271, 297, 300–1, 308
solatium
    disappointed expectations, 226
    ex contractu, 219–28
    Hume, 217, 218
    in delict, 214–19
    injured feelings, 224
    mental upset, 224
    remoteness, 226, 227–8
    restricted to social contracts, 226
    South Africa, 213
    see also contracts of intellectual gratifi-
        cation
South Africa
    adult domestic relationships, 148, 170
    contracts of intellectual gratification,
        213
    forms of marriage, 170
    promissory estoppel, 301
    same–sex relationships, 162, 166
    solatium, 213

Spaht, K, 167, 168, 171
Stair, *Institutions*
    damages, 216–17
    personality rights, 393
    promise, 297–300, 319
    promissory estoppel, 316, 317
    servitude by prior use, 17
    servitudes, 98
    unjustified enrichment, 337
stare decisis, 356, 357
Story, J, 3, 399, 400
supervening event, 253
supervening impossibility, 250–1
succession rights of spouses
    balance between surviving spouse and
        children, 152–3
    claim over separate property, 153
    no surviving issue, 153
    second spouse, 152
    step-parents, 126–7, 152, 153
    usufruct over community property, 153
    see also inheritance laws – surviving
        spouse

Tate, A, 331
Thomson, J, 296
Tiends, meaning, 250n
title conditions
    generally, 30–2
title conditions in restraint of trade
    in faciendo principle, 7, 53, 56, 57, 60,
        63, 65, 66
    affirmative obligations, 61–5
    comparative conclusions, 65–6
    meaning, 32
    tying stipulations & affirmative bus
        obligs, 60–5
    utilitas, 39–41
title conditions in restraint of trade –
        Louisiana
    1907–1915, 52–8
    1988–2006, 58–60
    anti-competitive covenant, 58–9
    building restrictions, 41, 63–5, 66
    information-measurement costs, 53, 59
    limitation on permissible rights, 53–5
    negative restrictions, 53–4, 58–60
    Provosty triumvirate, 52–8
    racially restrictive covenant, 55–7
    real right customisation, 57–8

restricted affirmative obligations, 63–5
stipulation pour autrui, 56
title conditions in restraint of trade –
      Scotland
   1760–1840, 41–3
   1880–1920, 43–52
   Aberdeen Varieties, 46–8, 50
   affirmative obligations, 44–5, 61–3
   ambiguity to rationalisation, 41–3
   amenity, 50–1
   commoditisation, 48–50
   Co-operative Wholesale Society, 50–1
   duration, 46, 49
   information-measurement costs, 48
   legislation, 51, 52
   negative limitations, 43
   proximity, 47–8, 50
   uncertainty, 52
   value and amenity, 44
Title Conditions (Scotland) Act 2003, 9,
      39, 52, 68, 96n, 98
torticles, 388, 393, 409
Trahan, R, 167
Treitel, G, 222
trust
   definitions, 132–3
   compared with contract, 134–5
   necessity for, 134–5
trust property
   bankruptcy of trustee, 135
   class trusts, 143
   community property, 138
   distinguishing between real rights,
      144
   dual patrimony theory, 133, 145
   fiduciary fee, 140
   fruits of paraphernal property, 138–9
   insolvency, 135–6
   Louisiana, 135–9
   ownership: generally, 133; Louisiana,
      137–9; Scotland, 140–1
   ownership subject to trust, 144
   personal bar doctrine, 143–4
   Scotland, 140–1
   title, 144
   trustee or beneficiary as owner, 141–4
tying stipulations, generally, 32, 45
typenfixierung, 34, 56
typenzwang, 34, 56

Uniform Commercial Code, 297, 309
Uniform Probate Code, 130
unjustified enrichment
   comparison, 350–4
   contract, 273, 274
   French tradition, 324–36, 353
   generally, 322–4
   indirect enrichment, 352–3
   similarities, 350
   subsidiarity, 350–2
unjustified enrichment – Louisisana
   absence of any other remedy, 326,
      327–8
   absolute nullity, 333
   actio in de rem verso, 325, 327, 329
   conditional obligations, 334
   development of general action, 326–9
   directory clause, 326
   dissolution of contract, 334–6
   enrichment and contract, 328, 331–6
   French background, 324–6, 353
   nullity of obligations, 332–3
   obligations subject to a term, 334
   over-payment, 333
   over-performance, 333
   payment of a thing not owed, 331, 332
   payor's error, 334
   prerequisites, 327
   subsidiarity, 329–31
   suspensive agreement failure, 332
   void contract, 332
   without cause, 328, 331
unjustified enrichment – Scotland
   condictio causa data causa non secuta,
      347, 348, 349, 353
   alternative remedy, 340
   condictio ob causam finitam, 347, 348,
      349
   condictio indebiti, 337, 338, 339
   contract subject to suspensive condi-
      tion, 347
   development, 337–9
   enrichment and contract, 345–50
   frustration by supervening events, 348
   illegal contract, 346
   incidental enrichments, 342
   indirect enrichment, 345, 349–50
   interference with innocent party's
      rights, 349
   justification by legal ground, 342

material breach of contract, 348, 349
multi-party enrichment, 345, 349–50
negotiation of contract, 346
over-performance of contract, 347
pre-contract, 345–6
reasons for reversal, 342–5
recompense, 337–8
remedies, 342–5
restitution, 337, 338
reversal of enrichments, 343
subsidiarity of recompense, 339–41,
    343–4
subsidiary in contractual context,
    344–5
undue performance, 347
unresolved questions, 348–9
voidable contract, 347–8
unmarried wives, 157n

unregistered relationships, 156–60
usufruct, 111, 125, 129, 153
utilitas requirement, 39–41

venire contra factum proprium, 304, 319
Visser, D, 351–3
Von Bar, C, 387

Washburn, E, 26–7
Watson, A, 131
Whitty, N, 343–4, 351
Wolbrette, 231, 237
written resolution, promise compared
    with, 298, 315–16
wrongful deprivation of liberty, 391–2,
    393–4

Yiannopolous, A N, 16, 37–8, 144, 405

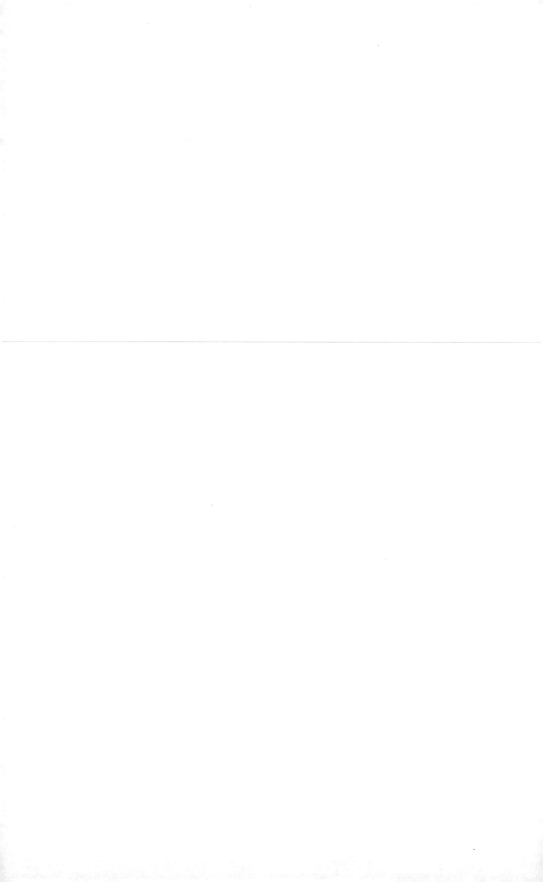